# Principles of Irish Contract Law

# Principles of Irish Contract Law

By
## Máiréad Enright

BCL (NUI), MA (Lond.) BL (King's Inns)

*Published by*
Clarus Press Ltd,
Griffith Campus,
South Circular Road,
Dublin 8.

*Typeset by*
Datapage International Limited,
18 Docklands Innovation Park,
East Wall Road,
Dublin 3.

Printed in Ireland by Colourbooks, Dublin

*Front Cover Illustration*
Fabrice Robin | fabrice@encoredesign.eu

*ISBN*
13 digit: 978-1-905536-10-8
10 digit: 1-905536-10-0

Reprinted 2009

A CIP catalogue record for this book is available from the British Library.

Disclaimer
Whilst every effort has been made to ensure that the contents of this book are accurate, neither the publisher nor author can accept responsibility for any errors or omissions or loss occasioned to any person acting or refraining from acting as result of any material in this publication.

For Mam, Dad, Tricia and James.

# PREFACE

While it is hoped that this book will be of general benefit to anyone studying Irish contract law, it is written with the needs of the undergraduate law student in mind. This does not pretend to be a comprehensive blackletter text. The Irish market is already well served with fine books of this kind. I have concentrated on those areas of law which best exemplify the key themes in Irish contract law. For the time being, students should know that this book aims simply to provide an accessible introduction to the key principles which form the backbone of most undergraduate contract law courses. In addition, it aims to introduce students to the foundational ideology of contract law and to some of the more well-known critical perspectives on that ideology. Novel features of the book include the discussion of contract theory in Chapter 1, the discussion of the commodification of private life in Chapter 20, and the focus on e-commerce in Chapters 5, 11 and 14. I have included substantial excerpts from important judgments. I hope that students will not shy away from these, but rather will use them as stepping stones to further reading of the case law. Readers should also note that the terms "plaintiff" and "defendant" are used throughout rather than the English "claimant" and "defendant". I have attempted to state the law on the basis of the materials available to me as at April 15, 2007, although some later developments are also included. I wish those students who read this book every success in their studies.

Máiréad Enright, BCL (Cork) MA (London) Barrister-at-Law
Lecturer in Law, Manchester Metropolitan University

# ACKNOWLEDGEMENTS

A number of reviewers made helpful comments and offered support during the writing of this book. Thanks in this regard go to my great friends Lisa Kinsella, Claire Murray, Yvonne Daly, Kate Egan BL, Cian Murphy, Roberta Guiry, Patrick O'Callaghan and Tracy Lyne. The chapters on mistake and frustration are sounder for Dr Clíona Kelly's thorough and incisive review. Kieran Walsh BL, Aoife O'Donoghue and Fiona de Londras went far beyond the call of any friend's duty and I hope one day to be able to repay them the past year's favours many times over. I am grateful to my students, who have borne the brunt of my struggles and experiments with contract law, and to my long-suffering colleagues. Damian Mather and Catherine Russell in particular provided much needed distraction as the date for completion loomed while Daniel Collins and Linda Delany very kindly reviewed some of the knottier chapters. Finally, warm thanks are due to David McCartney at Clarus Press who let deadlines come and go with his customary grace and patience. All errors and omissions are mine.

# CONTENTS

# Contents

# TABLE OF LEGISLATION

**Secondary Irish Legislation**

# TABLE OF CASES

# Table of Cases

# Table of Cases

# Table of Cases

# Table of Cases

# CHAPTER 1
# Important Themes in the Law of Contract

*Contract is an instrument of peace in society. It reconciles freedom with order.*[1]

## I. Introduction: A Critical Approach to Contract Law

The study of contract is the study of legally binding agreements. Contract law is concerned with the types of agreement that will be upheld by the courts, with the parties who have entitlements under them, with the rules for their formation and with the remedies for their breach. Contract is one of the great caselaw subjects of the common law. It is therefore tempting to adopt what is known as a Formalist view of the operation of the law of contract: that contract law is a bundle of set and certain rules, which are to be applied mechanically to the facts of any case without reference to moral or political concerns. Formalist contract law deals only in generalities and abstractions. Suppose John and Mary embark on the process of contracting with one another. The law understands them not as individuals but as "disembodied spirits",[2] versions of established categories of market relation—offeror and offeree, vendor and purchaser, promisor and promisee. As Friedman has written[3]:  **[1–01]**

> "Pure contract doctrine is blind to details of subject matter and person. It does not ask who buys and sells, and what is bought and sold ... Contract law is an abstraction – what is left when all particularities of person and subject matter are removed."

To some extent, this traditional approach is related to a conservative view of the proper scope of State power; one which says that the law draws its legitimacy from "tradition and routine observance", from objectivity, neutrality and impartial application.[4] However, it is also a misleading approach:  **[1–02]**

> "The law of contract creates a master image of the well-ordered society; a society in which law appears as a 'haven of justice', divorced from the dirtiness

---

[1] Kessler, Gilmore and Kronman, *Contract: Cases and Materials* (3rd ed, Little Brown, 1986) p 5.
[2] *Davis Contractors v Fareham UDC* [1956] AC 696.
[3] Friedman, *Contract Law in America* (University of Wisconsin Press, 1965) p 20.
[4] Collins, *The Law of Contract* (4th ed, LexisNexis, 2003) p 7.

of business, politics, power and the conflict of interests and values; a society which rises above the uncertainty and incoherences of political and moral argument."[5]

**[1–03]** Most modern theorists (and indeed many modern judges) have espoused a Realist philosophy of contract law that is immersed in politics and ethics.[6] This view of the nature of contract law focuses less on the literal substance of the rules of contract law and more on the result of their application. Judges have expressed themselves to be quite willing to subvert the contract rule book in order to achieve a just result in a given case. For instance, Lord Devlin once wrote that: "the true spirit of the common law is to override theoretical distinctions when they stand in the way of doing practical justice".[7]

**[1–04]** Even if the courts did not adopt an overtly Realist approach to contract law adjudication, the process of judicial reasoning could never be considered wholly objective, neutral or impartial. This is because adjudication necessarily involves the exercise of discretion. Judges have discretion to select, and indeed to create, the rules of contract law that they will apply to the situation before them. As regards selection, Critical Legal Studies,[8] an American movement in legal theory from the 1970s, reminds us that, in contract law, as in physics, for every action there is an equal but opposite reaction. For every principle of contract law there is a counter-principle. For example, it is a fundamental rule that a contract will not be enforced without consideration (see Chapter 8) *unless* the doctrine of promissory estoppel applies (see Chapter 9). As the judgments of Lord Denning in particular demonstrate, judges also have discretion to select the facts of the case before them and present them in a particular way. What is more, the result that will come from the application of a general rule of contract law to a new and unique fact pattern is never pre-ordained. HLA Hart, in his influential work *The Concept of Law*, wrote that while there is a core of certainty to each legal rule, there is also a "penumbra of doubt" such that in "hard cases" the application of the rule to the facts does not yield any concrete result and questions of pure policy must come into play.[9] In addition, contract law draws not merely on rules, but on broader standards, such as that of the "reasonable man", which are intensely vulnerable to conscious or unconscious judicial manipulation (see para 2–10).

**[1–05]** All of this is not to say that contract law is unpredictable but that the reasons for its predictability are not to be found in the substance of the black letter law. There are patterns to contract law but the Critical Legal Scholars maintain that those patterns reflect, reinforce and perpetuate the existing hierarchies of power in the wider polity. Perhaps that is to be expected when we consider the traditional make-up of the judiciary and their position at the apex of power in society. For example, the law on intention to create legal relations in domestic agreements is long established and its application is easily predicted. The rule is that agreements between spouses are

---

[5] Thompson, "The Law of Contract" in *The Critical Lawyer's Handbook*.
[6] Adams and Brownsword, "The Ideologies of Contract Law" (1987) 7 *Legal Studies* 205.
[7] *Ingram v Little* [1961] 1 QB 31.
[8] See Dalton, "An Essay in the Deconstruction of Contract Law Doctrine" (1985) 94 Yale LJ 1010; Feinman, "Critical Approaches to Contract Law" [1983] *UCLA Law Review* 829.
[9] Hart, *The Concept of Law* (Clarendon Press, 1961) p 119.

presumed not to have contractual effect because they are concluded in the context of an intimate domestic relationship. This reflects one arrangement of power in society: that between women and men.[10] The work that women do in the home is not recognised as having economic value. By the same token, contract law deprives the sphere where women have traditionally done most of their work, the marital home, of the legitimating stamp of contract law (see Chapter 7).

Contract law, ultimately, is a political concept and it can only be properly    **[1–06]**
understood by examining the policies that animate it. The aim of this chapter is provide a basic whistle-stop tour of the key ideological tensions that are traditionally understood to drive the modern law of contract. This book will revisit each of them in somewhat greater detail in the substantive chapters that follow.

## II. Contract Law and the Market

*If we all do exactly as we please, no doubt everything will work out for the best.*

Friedman

The paradigmatic model of contract law is that which was at its height from    **[1–07]**
1770 to 1870. The "classical" contract law was very much a creature of its time.[11] The development of classical contract theory was inextricably linked with the growth of capitalism. The dominant economic theory in the nineteenth century, which drew on the theories of Adam Smith, favoured the private ordering of market transactions. Laissez-faire economics held that when market actors were left to their own devices, with minimal interference from the State, they would tend to act rationally in their own self-interest and would therefore engage in mutually beneficial transactions. For example, suppose A voluntarily contracts to sell B his horse for €2,000. A enters into the contract in order to acquire something that he desires: the €2,000. B enters into the contract in order to acquire the horse that he desires. At the end of this transaction, both parties have achieved their aim and each is better off than he was before. In the broadest sense, each is wealthier than before. What is more, the wealth of society was understood in terms of the total wealth of individuals. Thus, because a policy of non-interference increased individual wealth, it also improved the overall wealth of society. The role of contract law was understood to be the facilitation of these wealth-generating transactions through the adoption of a non-interventionist stance. The main purpose of the law was to lay down the bare minimum of rules necessary to remove the main disincentives to entering into these beneficial transactions. First, the prospect that contracts could be broken with impunity would discourage some potential dealers from entering the market. During the heyday of classical contract law, contracts between strangers, operating at a distance from one another with no ties of community to bind them, became more common so that social deterrents to unjustified breach were of limited significance. The law filled the resulting gap by providing for the payment of remedies such as damages (see Chapter 25) in the event that contracts were

---

[10]  Wiegers "Economic Analysis of Law and 'Private Ordering': A Feminist Critique" (1992) 42 U Toronto LJ 170.
[11]  See Horowitz, *The Transformation of American Law: 1760 to 1860* (Harvard, 1997) Ch 6.

broken.[12] Secondly, the law developed bright line rules such as those on agreement (see Chapters 3 to 5), which aimed to reduce the uncertainty around market transactions and increase confidence in the mechanism of contract. Thirdly, the law generally followed and supported existing commercial practice (see, for example, para 13–49). Under classical theory, the rule of the market was the rule of law.

### Modern Economic Analysis

[1–08] Laissez-faire economic policy is, therefore, the bedrock of our modern contract law. In more recent years, theorists have embarked once again on an economic analysis of the role of contract law which largely justifies the classical conception of contract. Richard Posner argues that the rules of contract law have developed in such a way that, on the whole, they tend to promote economic efficiency. Efficiency refers to the state in which the market maximises the overall wealth in society because resources tend to gravitate towards the most valuable uses. Posner says that economic efficiency will be assured where the law facilitates voluntary exchanges. The role of contract law then is to correct defects in the market which tend to undermine or prevent voluntary exchange.[13] So, for example, contract law intervenes where one party abuses the size of his market share to impose terms on another which a truly competitive market would not permit. An example of this intervention is seen in the law on standard form contracts (see para 14–03). It also regulates the extent to which one party can exploit his superior information about a transaction to impede the other's ability to evaluate the transaction in a meaningful manner. The doctrines of reasonable notice in the incorporation of terms (see para 14–03), mistake (see para 17–06), disclosure (see para 16–01) and misrepresentation (see para 15–02) are concerned with the acceptable use of power over information.

## III. Freedom of Contract

[1–09] The law's policy of minimal intervention in the market finds its expression in the doctrine of freedom of contract. Sir George Jessel MR explained the doctrine in a famous *dictum* in *Printing and Numerical Registering Co v Sampson*[14]:

> "[I]f there is one thing which more than another public policy requires it is that men of full age and competent understanding shall have the utmost liberty of contracting, and that their contracts when entered into freely and voluntarily

---

[12] But see Wightman, *Contract: A Critical Commentary* (Pluto, 1996) pp 71–72 arguing that, in practice, social disincentives to breach were more important than contract law in ensuring that nineteenth century businessmen kept to their bargains.

[13] "[T]hat a market is less than perfectly competitive does set the stage for transactions in which the bargain principle loses much or all of its force, because it is supported by neither fairness or efficiency. For example, a market that involves a monopoly sets the stage for exploitation of distress; a market in which transactions are complex and differentiated rather than simple and homogenous sets the stage for exploitation of transactional incapacity; a market in which actors do not simply take a price established by a general market and are susceptible to transient economic irrationality sets the stage for unfair persuasion; a market that involves imperfect price-information sets the stage for the exploitation of price ignorance." Eisenberg "The Bargain Principle and Its Limits" (1982) 95 Harv L Rev 741.

[14] (1875) LR 19 Eq 462.

shall be held sacred and shall be enforced by Courts of justice. Therefore, you have this paramount public policy to consider – that you are not lightly to interfere with the freedom of contract."

Freedom of contract has three key aspects: freedom *to* contract, freedom *of* contract and freedom *from* contract. Freedom to contract entails the liberty to enter into contracts. The capacity to enter into contracts is withheld only from a limited sector of society (see Chapter 26).

[1–10]

Freedom of contract involves the liberty to decide on and negotiate one's contractual obligations. In general, contractual obligations are self-imposed. The circumstances in which the court may impose them are rare (see Chapter 13). This element of contractual freedom is secured by the notion of the sanctity of contract encapsulated in the maxim *pacta sunt servanda*: agreements freely chosen will be upheld. Parties will, in addition, be held to agreements freely made regardless of what comes after, regardless of the sympathy the court may have for the parties' plight. The excuses for non-performance of a contract are therefore rigidly circumscribed (see Chapters 15–22) as are the grounds for termination of a contract (see Chapter 24).

[1–11]

Freedom from contract entails that a party shall not be bound to any contractual obligation that he has not chosen. Insofar as the contract was understood to draw its legitimacy from individual choice, the ideas of consent, agreement and intention are crucially important to the classical contract law. Because classical theory placed so much store by intention (see Chapters 6 and 13) it is often referred to as the "will theory" of contract. Freedom from contract also grounds the doctrine of privity, which holds that the parties to a contract are liable only to one another and will not incur obligations to other persons unconnected to their bargain (see Chapter 10). Perhaps most importantly, the notion of freedom from contract is concerned to preserve spheres of purely private life which contract law cannot reach (see Chapter 7).

[1–12]

There are non-market-based justifications for the law's concern with freedom of contract. The most important is rooted in autonomy: the right of every competent individual, consistent with his human dignity, to make choices for himself. This dignity is what the theorist Patricia Williams refers to when she writes that contract law constituted her, a black woman whose ancestors were things to be bargained for, as "a bargainer of separate worth and power".[15] Indeed, the law's reluctance to remake badly drafted contracts (see Chapter 13) or to strike down bargains purely because they are ill-advised (see Chapter 18) demonstrates the law's concern not to interfere in a man's life for paternalistic reasons. Kessler and Sharp explain[16]:

[1–13]

"Courts have only to interpret contracts made by the parties; they do not make them. This attitude is in keeping with liberal social and moral philosophy, according to which it pertains to the dignity of man to lead his own life as a reasonable person and to accept responsibility for his own mistakes."

---

[15] Williams, "Alchemical Notes: Reconstructing Ideals from Deconstructed Rights" (1987) 22 Harv CR-CLL Rev 401.

[16] Kessler and Sharp, *Contracts: Cases and Materials* (1953) p 36.

**[1–14]**     The Victorian theorists felt that the classical contract law was a tool of social progress. Sir Henry Summer Maine wrote famously of the progress of modern societies "from status to contract". Because contract law did not restrict contractual capacity to those in a position of power within society, it introduced "equality in place of social hierarchy".[17] Because it would only enforce bargains supported by consideration (see Chapter 8), it valued "reciprocity instead of exploitation".[18]

## IV. Fairness and Contract Law

**[1–15]**     Freedom of contract is not an absolute rule. In *John Lee and Son (Grantham) Ltd and Others v Railway Executive*[19] Lord Denning wrote that: ". . . there is a vigilance of the common law which, while allowing freedom of contract, watches to see that it is not being abused". The key debate at the heart of the contract theory concerns the extent to which the courts may legitimately interfere with freedom of contract on the grounds of fairness. In *Hart v O'Connor*[20] Lord Brightman explains that, traditionally, there are two ways in which a contract may be deemed to be unfair:

> "It may be unfair by reason of the unfair manner in which it was brought into existence; a contract induced by undue influence will be unfair in this sense. It will be called 'procedural unfairness'. It may also, in some contexts, be described (accurately or inaccurately) as 'unfair' by reason of the fact that the terms of the contract are more favourable to one party than to the other. In order to distinguish this unfairness from procedural unfairness, it will be convenient to call it 'contractual imbalance'."

**[1–16]**     Procedural fairness is concerned with the means by which a party enters into a contract. It sets limits to the tactics that a party can use in pursuit of his self-interest. It is consent-focused. A contract will not be upheld where one party has abused his power so as to rob the other's consent to the contract of its validity. The doctrines of reasonable notice in the incorporation of terms (see para 14–03), mistake (see para 17–06), disclosure (see para 16–01) and misrepresentation (15–02) are concerned with the acceptable use of power over information. They govern the extent to which one party may use his superior knowledge to his advantage by concealing information from the other or presenting it in a particular way. To some degree also, the objective test of intention (see Chapter 2) prevents one party from manipulating his presentation of information to defeat the other's reasonable expectations. The doctrines of duress (18–03) and undue influence (18–35) are concerned with the voluntariness of the parties' consent. They deal with situations where one party abuses his power to pressure the other into contracting with him.

---

[17] "Instead of a structure of rank and privilege fixing entitlements to wealth and power, the distributive mechanism of the market allocates resources to those persons both able and willing to pay the highest price for them. Thus anyone with sufficient money may purchase a Rolls Royce, or employ someone as a servant, or set himself or herself up in a country seat. The market order avows blindness to claims of privilege or force, so it recognizes no claims of an inherent right to govern or to possess superior wealth." Collins, *The Law of Contract* (4th ed., LexisNexis, 2003) 12.

[18] Collins, *The Law of Contract* (4th ed., LexisNexis, 2003) 22.

[19] [1949] 2 All ER 581.

[20] [1985] 3 WLR 214.

It should be noted that the courts' interference in the mechanisms of contract formation is generally limited to those situations where the consent of one party is in question. There is no general duty to behave fairly in contract negotiations (see para 12–14). Neither will one party be deprived of a bargain purely because he has procured it from someone weaker than he, unless he has engaged in some radically unconscionable conduct (18–66). Kennedy explains the link between this position and the laissez-faire philosophy[21]: **[1–17]**

> "The Court's function in all this is to ensure procedural fair play: the Court is the umpire to be appealed to when a foul is alleged, but the Court has no substantive function beyond this. It is not the Court's business to ensure that the bargain is fair, or to see that one party does not take undue advantage of another, or impose unreasonable terms by virtue of a superior bargaining position. Any superiority in bargaining power is itself a matter for the market to rectify. If there is free competition in the market, mere size or skill should not in any case confer an undue advantage, since the forces of competition will ensure fairness in terms and prices."

The courts have been even less ready to inquire into the substantive fairness of contracts. The courts, for example, will, in theory at least, uphold a contract in spite of a grossly unfair price (see para 8–07). Their efforts to limit the negative side effects of standard form contracts (see para 14–07) and other aspects of the law on exemption clauses (Chapter 14) are important here but these have waned in importance as consumer law has gained the upper hand. The situations in which a court will void a contract for illegality or public policy are limited and here the courts are arguably concerned less with fairness and more with the presence of wrongdoing on the part of one or more of the parties (see Chapters 19–21). Generally, however, the work of redressing unfairness in the content of contracts has been done by the legislature (see for example paras 13–62, 14–88 and 14–98). Kessler and Sharp explain the position[22]: **[1–18]**

> "True, fraud and force must be ruled out by the courts in the exercise of their function of making sure that the 'rules of the game' will be adhered to. But this qualification was thought to be of no great moment, owing to the policing force of the competitive market. Except for according protection against force and fraud, it is not the function of the courts to make contracts for the parties or to strike down or tamper with improvident bargains."

This non-interventionist market-based philosophy is inconsistent with any conception of social justice. Economic efficiency is often measured using a test called the Kaldor/Hicks criterion. This holds that a transaction is efficient even if it is not mutually beneficial as long as one party gains more than the other loses. In theory, economically efficient theft is possible. Greed is a virtue. Economic efficiency is not **[1–19]**

---

[21] Kennedy, "Form and Substance in Private Law Adjudication" (1976) 19 Harvard LR 1685.
[22] Kessler and Sharp, *Contracts: Cases and Materials* (1953) p 36.

concerned to aid the perennial losers of the market.[23] If economic efficiency is the sole goal of contract law, then it will tend to channel resources into the hands of those who are already wealthy. Does contract law have any role in redistributing the wealth in society so that traditionally weaker market players get a larger slice of the pie? The traditional, laissez-faire philosophy is that it does not.

[1–20]     Lord Devlin once remarked that, for the classical contract lawyers, "free dealing was fair dealing".[24] However, there is a limit to the extent to which the law should privilege voluntariness over other values. Contract law is a sorely impoverished subject if the economic efficiency at the core of the doctrine of freedom of contract is its only goal. Gilmore, in his influential book *The Death of Contract*, wrote[25]:

> "As we look back on the nineteenth century theories, we are struck most of all, I think, by the narrow scope of social duty which they implicitly assumed. No man is his brother's keeper; the race is to the swift; Let the devil take the hindmost ... [A] system in which everyone is invited to do his own thing, at whatever cost to his neighbour, must work ultimately to the benefit of the rich and powerful."

---

[23] Cohen "The Basis of Contract" (1933) 44 Harv L Rev 533, 563: "[A]s happiness consisted in a maximum of pleasure, and that as each man knows best what will please him most, a contract in which two persons freely express what they prefer is the best way of achieving the greatest good of the greatest number. The argument blandly ignores the fact that though men may be legally free to make whatever contract they please, they are not actually or economically free. The mere fact of litigation, of appeal to the courts for enforcement, proves that the parties do not achieve real agreement or that their compact has not been found to serve the interests of the parties. Men in fact do not always know what will turn out to their advantage, and some of them have a talent for exploiting the ignorance or the dire need of their neighbours to make the latter agree to almost anything."

[24] Devlin, *The Enforcement of Morals* (Oxford, 1965) p 47.

[25] Gilmore, *The Death of Contract*, (Ohio State Press, 1973) p 95. Pettit, "Private Advantage and Public Power" (1987) 38 Hastings LJ 317 "The rhetoric of promise-keeping and personal autonomy comes easily to those who seek to enforce the promises of others. Those with the power to negotiate favourable contracts naturally support rules that enforce those contracts to the fullest extent."

# CHAPTER 2
# The Objective Test of Intention

> *"[T]he 'objective theory of contract' . . . the great metaphysical solvent — the critical test for distinguishing between the false and the true."*
>
> Grant Gilmore

> *"A contract has, strictly speaking, nothing to do with the personal, or individual intent of the parties . . . [If] it were proved by twenty bishops that either party, when he used the words, intended something else than the usual meaning which the law imposes upon them, he would still be held."*
>
> Learned Hand J

## I. Introduction

This chapter is about an important preliminary matter — what are the courts doing when they say that they are trying to determine the "intention" of the parties? Intention has been fundamental to contract law since the "consensus" or "will" theory was first proposed. In 1806, William David Evans explained the "will" theory of contract as follows:      **[2–01]**

> "As every contract derives its effects from the intention of the parties, that intention, as expressed, or inferred, must be the ground of every decision respecting its operation and extent, and the grand object of consideration in every question with regard to its construction."[1]

The importance of intention is consistent with what we have said so far about the ideology of contract law. If someone is contractually bound, it is because he has chosen to be bound. The concept of legal obligations stemming from personal choice ties in perfectly with the philosophy and rhetoric of freedom of contract. For example, when a court analyses the existence and scope of the agreement between the parties, it is said to be looking for *consensus ad idem* — a meeting of the parties' minds. Surprisingly, however, the actual state of mind of a party to an alleged contract is of no      **[2–02]**

---

[1] In Appendix V to his edition of Pothier's *A Treatise on the Law of Obligations, or Contracts* at p 35 quoted in Simpson, "Historical Introduction" in Furmston, *Cheshire, Fifoot and Furmston's Law of Contract* (14th ed., Butterworths Lexis Nexis 2001), p 13.

interest to the court. In everyday terms, an "intention" connotes a real choice consciously made in one's own "innermost mind". This might be called a "subjective intention", but the test for intention in contract law is not subjective. The American Supreme Court Justice Oliver Wendell Holmes explained:

> "... the making of a contract depends not on the agreement of two minds in one intention but on the agreement of two sets of external signs – not on the parties having *meant* the same thing but on their having *said* the same thing."[2]

[2–03]       That is to say that whenever a court is concerned with intention in contract law, be that intention to agree, to create legal relations, to have a particular term signify a particular thing or so on, the court takes an objective stance.[3] It looks at external evidence, at what the parties said and wrote and did and omitted to do. Usually, it looks at those things in the overall context of their transaction.[4] Then it asks what the reasonable man, looking at that evidence, would conclude their intent to be.

## II. What Evidence is Relevant to the Objective Test?

[2–04]       Only outward factors are relevant to the objective test for intention: words, actions and context.[5] Arguments about what a party "really" thought or "really" meant are of no consequence. To fully grasp this idea, in the American case of *Phillip v Gallant*[6] the idea of objective intention was explained as follows:

> "The law imputes to a person an intention corresponding to the reasonable meaning of his words and acts. It judges his intention by his outward expression and excludes all questions in relation to his unexpressed intention. If his words or acts, judged by a reasonable standard, manifest an intention to agree in regard to the matter in question, that agreement is established, and it is immaterial what may be the real, but unexpressed state of his mind on the subject."

---

[2] O.W. Holmes, "The Path of the Law" in *Collected Legal Papers* (1920), pp 167, 178.

[3] "Agreement ... is not a mental state but an act, and as an act, is a matter of inference from conduct. The parties are to be judged, not by what is in their minds, but by what they have said or written or done." Furmston, *Cheshire, Fifoot and Furmston's Law of Contract* (14th ed., Butterworths Lexis Nexis 2001), p 32. See also *Solle v Butcher* [1950] 1 KB 671 at 691 *per* Lord Denning: "[O]nce a contract has been made, that is to say, once the parties, whatever their inmost states of mind, have to all outward appearances agreed with sufficient certainty in the same terms on the same subject matter, then the contract is good ...".

[4] *Investors Compensation Scheme Ltd. v West Bromwich Building Society* [1998] 1 WLR 896; *Cf L'Estrange v Graucob* [1934] 2 KB 394; *Butler Tool Machine Co v Ex-Cell-O-Corp* [1979] 1 WLR 401.

[5] "Subjective intention or understanding, unaccompanied by some overt objectively ascertainable expression of that intention or understanding, is not relevant." *Ove Arup v Mirant Asia Pacific Construction* [2004] BLR 49 *per* May LJ.

[6] 62 NY 256.

Lord Denning summarised the concept with his usual simplicity when he said in *Storer v Manchester City Council*[7]:

[2–05]

> "In contracts you do not look into the actual intent in a man's mind. You look at what he said and did. A contract is formed when there is, to all outward appearances, a contract. A man cannot get out of a contract by saying: 'I did not intend to contract', if by his words he has done so."[8]

## III. What Perspective Does a Judge Adopt in Applying the Objective Test?

The objective test means that the court looks at the facts, not from the personal perspective of either party, but from the point of view of an impartial third party or "reasonable man".[9] There are two issues in relation to the formation of the contract: first, did the parties intend to agree at all (did the offeror intend to make an offer and did the offeree intend to accept it); and, second, did each party intend to create legal relations by his agreement? In answering these questions, the court applies a "promisee objectivity"[10] test. Under this test, words (and actions) are interpreted as they would be understood by the reasonable hearer, not the speaker.[11] For example, in *Moran v University of Salford*,[12] the university wrote to Mr Moran offering him a place on one of its courses. Mr Moran accepted the place. Later, the university attempted to withdraw the offer claiming that it had not meant to offer it in the first place. The offer had been the result of a clerical error. How was the court, in this case, to determine if there was an agreement between Mr Moran and the university under which the university was compelled to admit him to the course? The reasonable man receiving the university's letter would think that it was an offer of a place. Since the university's apparent intent was to offer that place, it was bound to honour the letter. A famous judicial statement of that doctrine is found in *Smith v Hughes*,[13] where Lord Blackburn said:

[2–06]

---

[7] [1974] 1 WLR 1403 at 1408.

[8] See also *Skycom Corp v Telstar Corp* 813 F 2d 810 (7th Cir 817): "[I]ntent does not invite a tour through [a party's] cranium with [that party] as the guide ... Secret hopes and wishes count for nothing. The status of ... a contract depends on what the parties express to each other and the world, not on what they keep to themselves".

[9] "The reasonable man goes round in bogey because he plays the orthodox shots, is never in trouble and is not called on to do the unexpected". *Blaikie & Others v British Transport Commission* [1961] SLT 190 *per* Thomson LJ. He is "the man who takes the magazines at home and in the evenings pushes the lawn mower in his shirt sleeves". *Hall v Brooklands Auto-Racing* [1933] 1 KB at 224 *per* Greer LJ.

[10] Howarth, "The Meaning of Objectivity in Contract" (1984) 100 LQR 265.

[11] "[T]he judicial task is not to discover the actual intentions of each party; it is to decide what each was reasonably entitled to conclude from the attitude of the other". *Gloag on Contract*, (2nd ed., 1929), p 7, approved by Reid LJ in *McCutcheon v David MacBrayne Ltd* [1964] 1 WLR 125 at 128.

[12] *The Times*, 27 October 1993.

[13] [1871] LQR 6 QB 597. See also *Centrovincial Estates plc v Merchant Investors Assurance Co Ltd*. [1983] *Comm LR* 158 *per* Slade LJ: "[It is a] well-established principle of the English Law of contract that an offer falls to be interpreted not subjectively by reference to what has actually passed through the mind of the offeror, but objectively, by reference to the interpretation which a reasonable man ... would place on the offer".

"If, whatever a man's real intention may be, he so conducts himself that a reasonable man would believe that he was assenting to the terms proposed by the other party, and that other party upon that belief enters into the contract with him, the other man thus conducting himself would be equally bound as if he had intended to agree to the other party's terms."

[2–07]     A particularly dramatic example of the operation of this rule is the American case of *Lucy v Zehmer.*[14] WO Lucy and AH Zehmer had known each other for 15 or 20 years. The case concerned a piece of land called the Ferguson farm, which was owned by Zehmer. The two men met in a restaurant at around 8.00pm on the night of 20 December 1952. According to Zehmer, Lucy had "got some good liquor" and was already "pretty high". Zehmer testified that he himself had taken several drinks in the course of the day and was "as high as a Georgia pine". Neither one, however, was too drunk to make a contract. The two men discussed the farm and Lucy eventually said to Zehmer: "I bet you wouldn't take $50,000 for it". A debate ensued between the pair as to whether Lucy possessed $50,000 in cash. At that point, at Lucy's suggestion, Zehmer wrote the following on a piece of paper: "We hereby agree to sell to W Lucy the Ferguson farm complete for $50,000, title satisfactory to buyer". He signed it and got his wife to sign it, whispering to her that the whole matter was a joke, that he was "just needling" Lucy "and it didn't mean a thing in the world". However, he did not expressly say to Lucy that he was joking with him until after Lucy gave him $5 to seal the bargain. In his testimony, Zehmer insisted that the transaction "was just a bunch of two doggoned drunks bluffing to see who could talk the biggest and say the most". Unfortunately, Lucy did not see the joke. He took Zehmer's offer of sale quite seriously, accepted it, hired a lawyer to investigate the title to the land and insisted on the performance of his contract. The Supreme Court of Appeals of Virginia agreed with Lucy stating that:

"the mental assent of the parties is not requisite for the formation of a contract ... So a person cannot set up that he was merely jesting when his conduct and words would warrant a reasonable person in believing that he intended a real agreement."

[2–08]     Objectively, Zehmer had discussed the terms of the sale with Lucy for a long time and did not indicate to him that the matter was a joke until after Lucy had demonstrated his agreement. The reasonable man would interpret Zehmer's actions as an offer to sell the land, and so they were construed accordingly.[15]

---

[14] 196 Va 493, 84 SE 2d 516, 518 at 520 (1954). See also *Barnes*, 549 P 2d at 1155: "[I]f the jest is not apparent and a reasonable hearer would believe that an offer was being made, then the speaker risks the formation of a contract which was not intended."

[15] See also *Berry v Gulf Coast Wings Inc* (No 01-2642) Div J (Fla 14th Cir Ct) in which a waitress at Hooter's sued her manager. Ms Berry alleged that her manager, Mr Blair, had promised a Toyota to whichever waitress at the restaurant sold the most beer. Ms Berry won the contest and was awarded, not a car, but a doll of a Star Wars character—a toy Yoda. More such cases are detailed in Rowley, "You Asked For It, You Got It: Practical Jokes, Prizes and Contract Law" (2003) 3 *Nevada Law Journal* at 256.

## IV. Why an Objective Test?

One reason for adopting an objective test is that it would be difficult for a court to discern the presence of subjective intention in any useful manner. After all, it is impossible to read what is really in a person's mind at any given moment. As Brian CJ famously observed, the "Devil himself knows not the intent of man".[16] Perhaps the court could simply ask each party what was really going on in his mind at the time of contracting, but a moment's thought reveals the huge risk that such a test would allow. Usually a person's inner or subjective intention will correspond with his outer expression of that intention. However, there is always the possibility that one party will secretly harbour an intention inconsistent with his words or actions. A purely subjective test might allow a party to deliberately distort his intention, promising one thing at the time of bargaining but claiming another when the matter comes to court. Certainty and security are essential to the market. More importantly, co-operation and trust are integral to the proper functioning of the bargaining process. Thus, the law must make sure that parties can rely on one another's statements[17] in planning their business affairs.[18] In *Bowerman v ABTA*,[19] Hobhouse LJ said simply that "[a] party cannot escape contractual liability by saying he had his fingers crossed behind his back". Of course, the application of the objective test means that, in some cases, a man will be bound to his mistake because he has not expressed his intention accurately. This may seem unfair, but the courts think it more unfair that the other party, unaware of the mistake, should have his agreement torn asunder when he has relied on that man's statement honestly and reasonably. The objective test provides a strong incentive for parties to communicate clearly and accurately. Finally, while contract law is about autonomy, autonomy implies taking responsibility for one's own choice. This is the human side of contract—effective engagement with another person is privileged over selfish self-realisation. In many ways then, as Chen-Wishart notes, the objective test shows that contract is more about "communication of choice"—about conveying and receiving meaning—than it is about choice itself.[20]

[2–09]

## V. Criticisms of the Objective Test

It is very difficult to reconcile the objective test with the idea that consent is the foundation of contract law. Collins notes that "although in most instances no doubt the entry into a contract coincides with the intention to make a contract, such an intention is not required".[21] All that is required is the appearance of such an intention. Collins asks, therefore, whether the objective test is really a test of intention at all. Since

[2–10]

---

[16] *Anon*, (1478) YB 17 Edw 4, Pash fo 1, pl 2. See also O Holmes, "The Theory of Legal Interpretation" 12 *Harvard Law Review* 417 at 420: "I do not suppose that you could prove ... that the parties to a contract orally agreed that when they wrote five hundred feet it should mean one hundred inches, or that Bunker Hill Monument should signify the Old South Church".

[17] Steyn, "Contract Law: Fulfilling the Reasonable Expectations of Honest Men" (1997) 113 LQR 433. *Trentham Ltd. v Archital Luxfer Ltd.* [1993] 1 Lloyd's Rep 25 at 27 *per* Steyn LJ.

[18] "[T]he objective test of agreement ... will prevent a party to negotiations from denying the reasonable expectations he has excited in another". Halson, *Contract Law* (Longman, 2001), p 21.

[19] [1996] CLC 451 [CA].

[20] Chen-Wishart, *Contract Law* (Oxford University Press, 2005), p 55.

[21] Collins, *The Law of Contract* (4th ed., Butterworths Lexis Nexis, 2003), p 123.

the test of "intention" is based on whether a reasonable man would rely on a party's statement and conduct, perhaps the test should be expressed as one of reliance? In that case, it seems that a contract is less to do with what is chosen but is more, as Learned Hand J suggested, "an obligation *attached by the mere force of the law to certain acts of the parties*, usually words, which ordinarily represent and accompany a known intent."[22] A further criticism is grounded in the very idea of the reasonable man. The reasonable man is, of course, a fiction. Arguably, judges simply apply their own personal standard of reasonableness, or, indeed, a standard of reasonableness common to the social background from which judges typically come.[23] Bias may thereby find its way, even subconsciously, into a supposedly impartial standard.

---

[22] *Hotchkiss v National City Bank of New York* 200 F 287 at 293 (SDNY 1911) *aff'd* 201 F 664 (2d Cir 1912) 231 US 50 (1913). Emphasis added.

[23] Cahn, "The Looseness of Legal Language: The Reasonable Woman Standard in Theory and in Practice" (1992) 77 Cornell L Rev 1398.

# Chapter 3
# Agreement: The Law of Offer

## I. Introduction to Agreement

In essence, all contracts consist of an agreement made with the intention to create legal **[3–01]** (Chapter 7) relations and supported by consideration  (Chapter 9). Why is agreement an essential element of the contract? You know that contractual obligations are different from any other legal obligation. For example, in the private realm the law of tort imposes duties on us. The criminal law imposes a code of behaviour on us at public law. By contrast, we choose our contractual obligations. The principle of contractual autonomy, in the sense of freedom from contract, is crucial here. Contractual liability can only ever arise where we have voluntarily assumed it. Suppose that A sues B claiming that B has not lived up to a contractual obligation to pay him €1,000. The court's first step in resolving the matter consistent with the fundamental principle of freedom from contract must be to satisfy itself that B actually chose the obligation to pay €1,000. It must analyse all of A's dealings with B and find a moment when B voluntarily assumed the contractual obligation which A is seeking to enforce. Traditionally, the courts have looked for a moment of *agreement*—a moment when B chose to take on certain responsibilities in relation to A and vice versa. As a matter of convention, the cases express this moment of agreement in terms of offer and acceptance. A makes a proposal to B in certain terms and B accepts the terms of that proposal; this is the agreement, the cornerstone of the contract.

In all cases, the parties to a purported contract will have gone through a period of **[3–02]** negotiation (however short) before reaching the crucial moment of agreement. They may have made any number of communications to one another before getting down to the business of finalising their bargain. During the negotiation of a contract for the supply of goods, for example, letters may be written, e-mails sent, gestures made, goods shown and examined, voice mails left, text messages sent, conversations had, advertisements seen, presentations made and so on. But only two of these elements, the offer and the acceptance, are relevant to the question of contractual liability. The others might be mere statements of fact or statements of intention, statements intended to get the bargaining process going (invitations to treat) or statements seeking clarification. The essence of this chapter explores the process by which the courts winnow the offer from the mass of communication that may have gone on between the parties.

## II. Offer

[3–03] An offer is a definite statement of the offeror's willingness to be bound should certain conditions be met. There are four important elements to this definition.

### Statement

[3–04] "Statement" is shorthand for both words and actions. Perhaps "manifestation" would be a more accurate word in some senses. As illustrated by the cases, an offer can be made in by word or by deed. The use of the word "statement" also refers to another requirement of an effective offer. Naturally, because the test for the existence of an offer is objective, it is not enough for the offeror to have formed an intention to make an offer—he must communicate that intention to the offeree by word or by action.[1] The statement does not have to be made to any offeree in particular. It can be made to the readership of a newspaper,[2] to everyone who sees a website or to the whole world.

[3–05] That much is clear from the seminal case of *Carlill v Carbolic Smokeball Co*[3] where Bowen J observed in regard to an offer made in a newspaper advertisement:

> "It is said that the contract is made with the whole world – that is, with everybody; and that you cannot contract with everybody. It is not a contract made with all the world. There is the fallacy of the argument. It is an *offer* made to all the world; and why should not an offer be made to all the world which is to ripen into a contract with anybody who comes forward and performs the condition."

### Willingness to be Bound

[3–06] The phrase "willingness to be bound", or intention to be bound, refers to the purpose behind the offer. An offer is a statement which, viewed objectively, suggests that the party making it intended to confer on the offeree the power to bind him in a contract. If it seems that the person's purpose in making a certain statement was something else (for example, to seek out further information or to stimulate further bargaining), or if he seems merely to be feeling his way towards agreement, the courts will not characterise that statement as an offer. It is for this reason that quotations and estimates are not offers. Contrast *Boyers & Co v Duke*[4] with *Dooley v Egan.*[5] In *Boyers* a statement of the lowest price at which canvas would be sold was not an offer; it was a quotation merely intended to stimulate bargaining. But in *Dooley*, a quote for a medical cabinet issued for "immediate acceptance only" was an offer. This phrase; "for

---

[1] *Gibson v Manchester City Council* [1979] 1 WLR 294.
[2] *Kennedy v London Express Newspapers* [1931] IR 532.
[3] [1893] 1 QB 256.
[4] [1905] 2 IR 617.
[5] (1938) 72 ILTR 155.

immediate acceptance only" made the difference. It introduced an element of finality. Objectively, the offeror appeared willing to be bound if the offeree accepted.

## Should Certain Conditions be Met

The phrase "should certain conditions be met" refers to the fact that an offer is not binding as and of itself. The offeror (the person making the offer) is not bound until the moment when the offeree (the person to whom the offer is made) accepts it. He may make any number of offers, but until an offer is accepted, no contractual consequences arise.

[3–07]

## Definite

The word "definite" refers to one of the most important parts of the test for an offer. When someone intends to make an offer by his statement, that intention will be reflected in the manner in which he makes it, in the words which he uses (if any), and so on. His intention will be objectively clear from the manner of his statement. His intention in making the statement is to lay out his deal in clear terms so that all that remains for the offeree to do is accept. His statement, therefore, will have a finality about it. It will not contemplate any further negotiations, and it is likely to be clear and unambiguous in its terms. If a statement is vague, the court will feel that its maker's intention was unsettled, and it will be classed as a mere statement or an invitation to treat. So, for example, the certain statement, "Tom, I will sell you 500 choc-ices for €250, delivery on Friday" would probably be considered an offer, while the vague query, "Anyone for the last few choc-ices?" falls into the lesser category of invitation to treat. Offers must be certain as to their essential terms. In *Central Meats v Carney*,[6] the Directors of Dublin Boned Meat Ltd agreed to supply as many cattle as possible to the plaintiffs and guaranteed "on no account to supply meat to any other Dublin or provincial canner without the consent of Central Meat Products and Irish Meat Suppliers". The court found that as the statement contained no specifics as to essentials, such as the number of cattle, the price or the quality of meat, it could not be regarded as a final offer.

[3–08]

It is worth observing at this stage that the strictness with which this certainty requirement is applied will vary according to the subject of the contract. The courts will require greater certainty, indicative of a clear intent, in a contract for the sale of land, for example, than in a contract for the sale of less valuable goods.[7] In *Clifton v Palumbo*,[8] Lord Greene wrote:

[3–09]

> "There is nothing in the world to prevent an owner of an estate ... contracting to sell it to a purchaser, who is prepared to spend so large a sum of money, on terms written out on a half sheet of note paper of the most informal description ... But I think it legitimate, in approaching the construction of a

---

[6] (1944) 10 Jur Rep 34.

[7] See for example *Harvey v Facey* [1893] AC 592 where, in response to the plaintiff's enquiry as to whether the defendants would sell them a particular plot of land, the defendants telegraphed that the lowest price for which they would sell it was £900. This was held to be a mere statement of fact and not an offer.

[8] [1944] 2 All ER 497.

document of this kind ... to bear in mind that possibility of parties entering into so large a transaction, and finally binding themselves to a contract of this description couched in such terms, is remote."

[3–10]         *Gibson v Manchester City Council*[9] shows how the courts' reasoning around certainty operates. Mr Gibson alleged that the following statement made by the Council to him in a letter was an offer by them to sell him his council house:

> "The Corporation may be prepared to sell the house to you at the purchase price of £2,275 less 20% =£2,180 (freehold) ... If you would like to make a formal application to buy your council house, please complete the enclosed application form ...".

[3–11]         The House of Lords did not find for Mr Gibson. Their lordships looked at the Council's statement objectively, searching for the element of definiteness that would reveal an intention by the Council to offer the house to Mr Gibson for sale. However, that element was not present. Looking objectively at the language first, we can see that the elements of finality and definiteness were missing there, particularly in what Lord Diplock called the "fatal" words "*may* be prepared to sell".[10] This language is more characteristic of an invitation to treat, intended to open the matter up to negotiation. Even though the price for the house was specified, the language was not certain enough overall to show the requisite intention. Objectively, the Council still intended for other matters to be settled before they would be bound. Secondly, the circumstances around the statement were not consistent with an offer. For example, the letter makes clear that Mr Gibson was only making "a formal application to buy". Objectively, it appears that the Council intended Mr Gibson's reply to their letter to be an early step in a process of negotiations rather than an acceptance creating a binding agreement. They did not intend to offer him anything at that time.

[3–12]         The point can be driven home by an examination of *Storer v Manchester City Council.*[11] Storer argued that the Council had offered to sell him a house. He was armed with the following statement of the Council: "If you will sign the Agreement and return it to me, I will send you the Agreement signed on behalf of the [Council] in exchange". The Court of Appeal held that this statement amounted to an offer. First, there was no element of doubt in the language here as there was in *Gibson*. There is more commitment in "will" than in "may be prepared". Furthermore, the circumstances, in particular the exchange of formal documents, were also consistent with an intention to finalise an agreement—to make an offer that only remained to be accepted by a simple signature. From the standpoint of the reasonable reader then, this was an offer.

### III. Traditional Categories of Case

[3–13]         Is there any cast-iron type of statement or formula of words that will always amount to an offer? The only answer is that no one factor is determinative. Even if a

---

[9] Above, n 1.

[10] The same reasoning applied in *Clifton v Palumbo* [1944] 2 All ER 497 where the Court held that the statement "I am prepared to offer you my estate for £600,000" was not an offer.

[11] [1974] 3 All ER 824.

communication is expressed to be "an offer", it may turn out not to be an offer at all.[12] Likewise, certain types of statement are generally categorised as invitations to treat. In examining these categories further, it is important to recognise that these categories are not the whole story. To summarise the focus you ought to adopt as we explore them, consider the definition of an offer provided by the Supreme Court of Minnesota in *Lefkowitz v Greater Minneapolis Surplus Stores*[13]: an offer is "clear, definite and explicit and [leaves] nothing open to negotiation". Offers are clear; offers have an element of finality about them.

### Advertisements

*Partridge v Crittenden*[14] is authority for the statement that advertisements are generally categorised as invitations to treat. Price lists, menus and catalogues are treated similarly.[15] Consider, for example, *Guildford v Lockyer*,[16] a criminal law case where a man was charged with theft. He had gone to a Chinese restaurant and had selected one dish from the restaurant's menu. However, he was served a different dish. He tried it, found that he did not like it and left the restaurant without paying. The court found that the menu was an invitation to treat. The customer's order was an offer. That offer could have been accepted by providing him with the meal he had ordered, but because a different meal was provided, no contract was formed which would oblige him to buy the meal in question.

[3–14]

    The reasoning here is simple: ordinarily, the seller who has finite quantities of a good will not intend to bind himself to supply it to each person from among the general public who might act on his advertisement, thereby "accepting" his "offer".[17] Usually, a man's intention in advertising his goods is merely to drum up interest among prospective purchasers. That sort of intention is associated with an invitation to treat rather than an offer. It could also be said that the principle of freedom from contract means that the advertiser should retain the right to hold off on agreement until a late stage in the bargaining. If an advertisement is an offer, then, depending on the terms of that offer, the reader of the advertisement could accept it and bind the advertiser into a contract simply by writing to the advertiser or sending money. If this rule applied, the advertiser would, by advertising his goods, be ceding a good deal of control over the bargaining process. It could be said that the principle that advertisements are generally invitations to treat protects advertisers' contractual autonomy by leaving a further element of control in their hands. In *Boyers & Co v Duke*,[18] Madden J explained in a more pragmatic fashion why advertising in the form of distribution of a catalogue to customers ought not to be considered an offer:

[3–15]

---

[12] *Clifton v Palumbo* [1944] 2 All ER 497; *Spencer v Harding* (1870) LR 5 CP 561; *iSoft Group plc v Misys Holdings Ltd.* [2003] EWCA Civ 229; *Harvela Investments Ltd. v Royal Trust Co of Canada* [1986] AC 207; *Bigg v Boyd Gibbons Ltd.* [1971] 2 All ER 183 *obiter*.

[13] (1957) 86 NW 2d 689.

[14] [1968] 2 All ER 421. An advertisement that the defendant had placed in the classifieds section of a magazine which stated "Bramblefinch cocks and hens, 25s each" was an invitation to treat. See also *Rooke v Dawson* [1895] 1 Ch 480.

[15] *Grainger & Son v Gough* [1896] AC 325.

[16] [1975] Crim LR 235.

[17] See *Grainger*, above, n 15.

[18] Above n 4.

"Business could not be carried on if each recipient of a priced catalogue offering a desirable article – say a rare book – at an attractive price, were in a position to create a contract of sale by writing that he would buy at the price mentioned. The catalogue has probably reached many collectors. The order of one only may be honoured. Has each of the others who write for the book a right of action?"

[3–16]      As would be expected, however, no sweeping generalisation is possible. Consider what is perhaps the most famous contract case of all: *Carlill v Carbolic Smokeball Co*[19] The defendants advertised their medicinal product, the carbolic smokeball, in various newspapers. The advertisement stated that the company would pay £100 as a reward to anyone who contracted influenza after having used the ball three times daily for two weeks as according to the instructions supplied with it. The advertisement went on to say that, "shewing our sincerity in this matter", the company had deposited £1,000 with the Alliance Bank on Regent Street. Ms Carlill bought a ball and used it as required by the advertisement but still contracted influenza. She sued for payment of the £100 arguing that the advertisement was an offer of reward, which she had accepted by her purchase and appropriate use of the ball. Counsel for the company argued that this advertisement was a mere puff. Bowen LJ punctured this argument, focusing on the matter of the bank deposit and saying:

"The advertisement says that £1000 is lodged with the bank for the purpose [of paying the reward]. Therefore, it cannot be said that the statement that £100 would be paid was intended to be a mere puff. I think it was intended to be understood by the public as an offer which was to be acted upon".

[3–17]      Since a reasonable person reading the advertisement would conclude that the Carbolic Smokeball Co intended to be bound by the promise contained therein, the advertisement was an offer.[20] The deposit would be a tipping point for the reasonable reader, as would the advertisement's reference to the offeror's "sincerity" in offering the reward. *Lefkowitz v Great Minneapolis Surplus Store*[21] is an American case that similarly demonstrates how an element of certainty can turn what is normally an invitation to treat into an offer. The advertisement in this case read: "Saturday 9 a.m ... 1 Black Lapin Stole ... worth $139.50 ... $1.00; First Come, First Served". Mr Lefkowitz argued that this amounted to an offer to sell him the stole for $1 when he presented as the first customer on that Saturday at 9am. Here the tipping point was "First Come, First Served"—an element that operated to narrow a vague invitation to treat down to a clear offer.

[3–18]      Contract law is not entirely humourless when it comes to advertising. An amusing example of the application of the objective test for an offer is the US case of

---

[19] Above, n 3. For an entertaining account of the background to the case, see Simpson, "Quackery and Contract Law: the Case of the Carbolic Smokeball" (1985) 14 *Journal of Legal Studies* 345.

[20] See also *O'Brien v MGN Ltd.* [2001] EWCA Civ 1279.

[21] Above, n 13.

*Leonard v PepsiCo.*[22] In that case, John Leonard argued that PepsiCo, in its "Pepsi Stuff" television advertisement, offered a Harrier Jet in exchange for 7,000,000 points, available to collect with containers of Pepsi. The advertisement displayed a number of items available as part of the Pepsi promotion, together with the number of points needed to claim each one. The dramatic finale featured a teenager landing a jet in his school carpark accompanied by the tagline "Harrier Jet 7,000,000 points". The plaintiff was, according to his memorandum, "typical of the 'Pepsi Generation' ... young, [with] an adventurous spirit, and the notion of obtaining a Harrier Jet appealed to him enormously". Accordingly, he set out to collect 7,000,000 Pepsi Points by consuming Pepsi products. When he discovered that it was possible to buy Pepsi points, he raised about $700,000 through acquaintances. He sent PepsiCo the cheque, along with their official order form, on which he duly ordered one Harrier Jet. The Court found that the reasonable man would understand the advertisement as mere humorous puffery rather than an offer to sell a military fighter jet with offensive and defensive capabilities. It therefore held that no offer was present.

## Display of Goods

Like advertisements, displays of goods on a shop shelf or in a shop window are generally characterised as invitations to treat.[23] The same reasoning, based in general assumptions about intention and freedom from contract,[24] holds here as in the advertising cases. In *Pharmaceutical Society of Great Britain v Boots*,[25] the Court of Appeal explained the process of contracting beginning with a display of goods as follows: the display of items on the shelf is an invitation to treat, the customer makes an offer to buy by putting certain items into his basket and the shopkeeper accepts that offer at the cash desk.[26] The agreement, therefore, is completed at the point of payment and not out on the shop floor. Lord Goddard explained his reasoning as follows:

[3–19]

> "[A person] might go into a shop where books are displayed. In most book-shops customers are invited to go in and pick up books and look at them even if they do not actually buy them. There is no contract by the shopkeeper to sell until the customer has taken the book to the shopkeeper or his assistant and said "I want to buy this book" and the shopkeeper says "Yes". That would not prevent the shopkeeper, seeing the book picked up, saying: "I am sorry I cannot let you have that book; it is the only copy I have got and I have already promised it to another customer."

---

[22] 210 F 3d 88 (2nd Cir 2000) discussed in Graw, "Puff, Pepsi and 'That Plane' – The John Leonard Saga" (2000) 15 JCL 281.

[23] *Fisher v Bell* [1961] 1 QB 394 at 400; *Minister for Industry and Commerce v Pimm Bros Ltd.* [1966] IR 154.

[24] Winfield "Some Aspects of Offer and Acceptance" (1939) 55 LQR 499, noting that a shop is not a place for "compulsory sales".

[25] [1952] 2 QB 795.

[26] Poole, citing *Re Charge Card Services* [1988] 3 All ER 702, notes that the same reasoning would not apply at a self-service petrol station, since, once the customer fills his tank with petrol, it is difficult for the seller to refuse him the goods. Poole, *Textbook on Contract Law* (7th ed, Oxford, 2004), p 43.

[3–20]     The perhaps surprising consequence is that the shopkeeper is entitled to refuse to sell an item to his customer at the price marked or, indeed, to sell it to him at all. It is possible, in exceptional cases, for a display of goods to be converted into an offer. For example, in *R v Warwickshire CC ex p Johnson*,[27] a notice in a shop window that "We will beat any TV ... price by £20 on the spot" was construed as an offer.

## Auctions

[3–21]     *Harris v Nickerson*[28] is authority for the proposition that the advertisement of an auction, like any other advertisement, will usually be an invitation to treat. If it were ordinarily held to be an offer, it might be accepted by people turning up to bid, and the auctioneer would not be free to cancel the auction in the event of poor attendance. In an auction the auctioneer is the conduit for the seller's communications with potential buyers. So, first of all, the auctioneer's call for bids on a lot is the seller's invitation to treat. Again, it is easy to understand the reasoning here. The auctioneer's intent in calling for bids is to kick-start the bargaining process on behalf of the seller by encouraging others to make offers. Each bid is a separate offer. Each offer lapses or is terminated (Chapter 4) on the making of a new bid. The auctioneer accepts one buyer's offer by the fall of the hammer or equivalent signal.[29] Under this analysis, too, the auctioneer is free to withdraw a lot that does not reach its reserve price, if there is one.

[3–22]     A special problem, however, arises in the case of auctions expressed to be "without reserve".[30] An auction is "without reserve" if the seller has not specified a minimum price at which the lot must be sold. In this case bidders can reasonably expect that it is the auctioneer's intent that the auction will go ahead and that the lot will be knocked down to the highest bidder, however low the price. Therefore, the auctioneer is held to make an offer to sell the lot to the highest bidder.

[3–23]     An auction "without reserve" may give rise to two contracts: the main contract for sale between seller and buyer and an ancillary contract between the auctioneer and the highest bidder.[31] This much was established as a matter of English law in

---

[27] [1993] AC 583 at 588.

[28] (1873) LR 8 QB 286. Blackburn J said that the converse would be "a startling proposition and would be excessively inconvenient if carried out. It amounts to saying that anyone who advertises a sale by publishing an advertisement becomes responsible to everybody who attends the sale for his cab hire or travelling expenses".

[29] *Payne v Cave* (1789) 3 Term Rep 148; *British Car Auctions v Wright* [1972] 3 All ER 462. See also Sale of Goods Act 1893, s 58(2).

[30] See Slade, "Auction Sales of Goods without Reserve" (1952) 68 LQR 238; Gower "Auction Sales of Goods without Reserve" (1952) 68 LQR 456; Slade "Auction Sales of Goods without Reserve" (1953) 69 LQR 21; Cox, "Auctions without Reserve – A Schematic Approach" (1982) 132 NLJ 719.

[31] A Scottish court has used a one-agreement analysis—the statement that the auction will be "without reserve" converts what is usually an invitation to treat (the advertisement of the auction) into an offer. *Fenwick v Macdonald, Fraser & Co* [1904] 6 F (Ct of Sess) 850.

*Warlow v Harrison*[32] and again in *Barry v Davies t/a Heathcote Ball.*[33] The auctioneer, by advertising that the auction is "without reserve" offers to accept the highest bid. The highest bidder, by making the highest bid, accepts that offer. If the auctioneer does not knock the lot down to the highest bidder, no contract of sale arises between the buyer and the seller because the auctioneer has not made any acceptance on the seller's behalf. However, as is set out in *Tully v Irish Land Commission*,[34] by failing to knock the lot down as he promised, the auctioneer was in breach of his own contract with the highest bidder.

## Tenders

An invitation to tender for the supply of goods or services is usually an invitation to treat, a "mere proclamation that the [invitors] are ready to chaffer for the sale of the goods, and to receive offers for the purchase of them".[35] It follows that the person who submits a tender in response is making an offer, which the person seeking tenders may choose to accept or reject, however good the tender.[36] Thus, in *Spencer v Harding*,[37] the defendant had invited tenders for the purchase of stock. The highest bidder claimed that he had accepted an offer to sell the stock by sending the highest bid. The Court rejected his claim—the tender is an offer and not an acceptance. The person seeking a tender may choose to cement this conclusion by including a privilege clause in the invitation to the effect that they reserve the right not to accept any particular tender.[38] In *Howberry Lane Ltd v Telecom Éireann*,[39] Morris J found to be effective a clause in an invitation to tender which stated that the party inviting tenders reserved the right "to accept or reject any offer made irrespective of whether it is the highest offer". **[3–24]**

A similar conundrum arises in tender cases as in the "without reserve" problem in auctions. Suppose that a person inviting tenders states that he will accept the highest bid or the lowest bid. In *Smart Telecom v RTE*,[40] Kelly J held that such an invitation to tender will simply be an offer. **[3–25]**

Alternatively, we can adopt a two-contract analysis. Under this analysis, the invitation to tender is an invitation to treat. The tender itself is an offer which may be accepted or rejected. If this offer is accepted, it generates the first contract. Next, we turn to the second contract. By stating that they will award the tender to the highest **[3–26]**

---

[32] (1859) 1 E&E 309; *cf Johnston v Boyes* [1899] 2 Ch 73 at 77. See also Meisel, "What Price Auctions Without Reserve" (2001) 64(3) MLR 465.
[33] [2000] 1 WLR 1962.
[34] (1961) 97 ILTR 174.
[35] *Spencer v Harding* (1870) LR 5 CP 561.
[36] See also *Smart Telecom v RTE* [2006] IEHC 176.
[37] (1870) LR 5 CP 561.
[38] *Meudell v Mayo etc of Bendigo* (1900) 26 VLR 158; *Gregory v Rangitikei District Council* [1995] 2 NZLR 208.
[39] [1999] 2 ILRM 232.
[40] [2006] IEHC 176.

bidder, the party inviting the tender has made an offer, which is accepted by the bidder in supplying the highest bid, forming the agreement. The party inviting the tender is free to reject the offer in the tender if he pleases, but if the tender is the highest bid, by rejecting it he breaches this second agreement. This analysis has been adopted in Canadian Law.[41] However, in *Howberry Lane v Telecom Éireann,*[42] Morris P rejected it as part of Irish law.

---

[41] *MJB Enterprises v Defence Construction Ltd.* [1999] 1 SCR 619.
[42] [1999] 2 ILRM 232.

# CHAPTER 4

# Agreement: Termination of an Offer

## I. Introduction

An offeree cannot accept an offer that is no longer available for acceptance. An offer **[4–01]** may be terminated where the offeree rejects it. The offeror may change his mind and revoke the offer. The offer may lapse on the death of one of the parties, or it may expire after a certain time. This chapter will examine each of these ways in which an offer can be terminatcd.

## II. Rejection and Counter-Offer

An offer will die if the offeree rejects it—an offeree is not obliged to accept any offer.[1] **[4–02]** Rejection may be expressed or it may be inferred from an offeree's actions. Rejection might also be implicit in the fact that the offeree has responded to the offer with a new proposal, or counter-offer, of his own. Suppose A offers to sell B his car for €1,000 and B responds by saying: "I will give you €750 for it." This is not an acceptance of A's offer. A requirement of acceptance is that the acceptance matches the offer in all its key terms. This requirement is often called the "mirror image" rule. B's reply is a counter-offer; it is a new offer of his own, which may be accepted in its own right and which also has the effect of terminating A's original offer. In *Tansey v College of Occupational Therapists*,[2] Murphy J explained the concept of a counter-offer as follows:

> "Ordinarily a communication in the course of negotiations leading to a contract which contains conditions not previously agreed by the party to whom

---

[1] This freedom is subject to the Equal Status Acts 2000–2004, which prevent the rejection of an offer on grounds of race or religion. Article 82 EC and the Competition Acts 1991–2002 prevent a supplier who has a monopoly over a particular commodity from refusing to supply that commodity without good reason.
[2] [1995] 2 ILRM 601.

the communication is addressed will be treated as a new or counter-offer rather than an acceptance."

[4–03]     A key case which illustrates this point is *Hyde v Wrench*.[3] The defendant offered to sell land to the plaintiff for £1,000. The plaintiff replied that he would purchase the land for £950. The defendant rejected this proposal whereupon the plaintiff purported to accept the original offer to sell for £1,000.

[4–04]     The plaintiff's reply to the defendant's original offer was at variance with the offer. Therefore, it amounted to a counter-offer rather than an acceptance, and it terminated the original offer to sell the land at £1,000. The offer of £1,000 was no longer in existence when the plaintiff finally tried to accept it. The plaintiff's change of mind was without effect. All that can be said of the plaintiff's statement that he was willing to buy the land for £1,000 was that it was a new offer, which the defendant was free to accept or reject as he chose. Had the plaintiff's first response to the defendant's original offer been a proposal to buy the land for £1,000, this would have amounted to an acceptance and the land would have been his.

[4–05]     Along the same lines is the Irish case of *Swan v Miller*.[4] The contract was for the sale of the leasehold interest in a house. The plaintiffs telegraphed the defendants offering £4,750 for the premises. The defendants replied that they would accept £4,750, plus £50 ground rent. This reply constituted a counter-offer rather than an acceptance because it did not match the offer.

[4–06]     An offer will not be terminated by an enquiry that is "merely exploratory".[5] A counter-offer does something more than this—it seeks to vary the material terms of the offer or to introduce new material terms. Any term as to price, payment mechanism, delivery, liability or any dispute mechanism is likely to be considered material.[6] The idea of an exploratory enquiry is illustrated by *Stevenson, Jacques & Co v McLean*.[7] The parties in this case were negotiating the sale of some iron. McLean offered to sell the iron for "40s net cash", and Stevenson responded with a telegraph reading: "Please wire whether you would accept forty for delivery over two months, or if not, longest limit you would give". Now, this response was plainly not an acceptance. Should it be construed as a counter-offer, which would terminate McLean's offer, or could Stevenson still accept McLean's original offer in spite of his initial response?

[4–07]     Lush J found that the telegraph contained "nothing specific by way of offer or rejection, but a mere inquiry, which should have been answered and not treated as a rejection". Accordingly, McLean's offer remained open to acceptance.[8]

---

[3] [1840] 3 Beav 334.

[4] [1919] IR 151.

[5] *Gibson v Manchester City Council* [1979] 1 All ER 972 at 978.

[6] Poole, *Textbook on Contract Law* (7th ed., OUP, 2004), p 53.

[7] (1880) 5 QBD 346. See also *Culton v Gilchrist* 92 Iowa 718, 61 NW 384 (1894).

[8] See also *The Society of Lloyds v Twinn* (2000) 97 (15) LSG 40 *per* Scott V-C: "An acceptance which seeks an indulgence will be effective if it is [objectively] clear that the offeree was unconditionally accepting the offer."

The distinction between a counter-offer and a simple request for further **[4–08]** information is not an easy one. *Butler v Ex-Cell-O Corp*[9] demonstrates the extent to which the courts may be willing to bend the concepts of "counter-offer" and "mere statement" in order to find agreement.[10] This is a classic "battle of the forms" case. The parties dealt with the sale of a machine via the exchange of standard documents. The plaintiffs offered to sell the machine to the defendants on the basis of the plaintiffs' standard terms, which contained a price escalation clause. The defendants responded by ordering the machine using their own standard order form, based on their own standard terms, which did not contain any such clause. The form included a detachable slip, which read: "We accept your order on the terms and conditions stated thereon". The plaintiffs signed, completed and detached the slip, and returned it to the defendants with a letter that referred back to their own original offer. In the Court of Appeal, the majority found that an agreement had been made for the sale of the machine, governed by the defendants' standard terms. Their reasoning was as follows. The plaintiffs had made an offer to sell on their terms. The defendants had not accepted that offer on the proposed terms, attempting instead to accept on their own terms. They had therefore made a counter-offer. By returning the tear-off slip, the plaintiffs accepted that counter-offer.

On this analysis, the letter the plaintiffs included with the tear-off slip is **[4–09]** irrelevant. The majority felt that the letter was included merely to enable the defendants to locate the original correspondence in their files.

However, an alternative analysis was available to the Court, had it been willing **[4–10]** to take account of the letter. The letter's reference back to the original offer could be interpreted as demonstrating the plaintiffs' intent to contract on their own terms rather than on the defendants' terms. The plaintiffs' reply to the defendants' counter-offer, could, therefore, have been treated as a counter-offer of their own. If the Court had reached this decision, of course, no agreement could have been found. Two counter-offers do not make a contract. It might be said that, by ignoring the letter, the Court bent the facts of the case to fit the rule, allowing agreement to be found.

## III. Revocation

Revocation refers to an offeror's power to withdraw an offer. An offeror does not give **[4–11]** up his freedom from contract the minute he makes an offer. The offeror is master of his offer. An offer may be withdrawn expressly or by implication. Implicit revocation might take place when an offeror acts inconsistently with the existence of the offer, such as by selling the thing offered to someone other than the offeree, or by making a substantially different offer in relation to the same thing.[11] An offer does not generate any legal obligations until it is accepted. Logically then, and in line with the doctrine of freedom of contract, an offer can generally be withdrawn or revoked at any time prior

---

[9] [1979] 1 WLR 401.

[10] For international solutions, see The Vienna Convention on Contracts for the International Sale of Goods, Art 19; the Unidroit Principles for International Commercial Contracts, Art 2.11; the Statement of Principles of European Contract Law, Art 2.209; and the Uniform Commercial Code, s 2-207.

[11] *Pickfords Ltd v Celestica Ltd* [2003] EWCA 1741.

to acceptance. That point may be made clearer by contrasting two key cases: *Dickinson v Dodds*[12] and *Byrne v Van Tienhoven*.[13] *Dickinson v Dodds* concerned Dodds' offer to sell his house to Dickinson. Dickinson revoked the offer on a Thursday and Dodds attempted to accept it on the following Friday.

[4–12]    Clearly, Dickinson's revocation came before the acceptance,[14] so the Court found that the revocation was valid and, accordingly, the attempted acceptance was meaningless.

[4–13]    In *Byrne*, by contrast, an offer was made and accepted on 11 October. The offeror attempted to revoke the offer on 20 October. The revocation was ineffective because it came after acceptance when the offeror was already bound.

[4–14]    The power to revoke is not limited by requirements of justice or good faith. In *The Guardians of the Navan Union v McLoughlin*,[15] the defendant responded to an invitation to tender by the guardians of the town's poor which sought certain articles. The invitation to tender was an invitation to treat, and the defendant's tender was an offer. The Union intended to accept the tender, but before they did so, the defendant learned that they were in debt and were unlikely to be able to pay him. He therefore revoked the offer. The Court held that he was entitled to do so, notwithstanding the injustice of his decision.

### Revocation Must be Communicated

[4–15]    It is a key limitation on the offeror's freedom to revoke, consistent with the objective test, that revocation will not take effect until it has been communicated to the offeree. Bacon V-C observed in *Dickinson v Dodds*[16] that:

> "... in order to be withdrawn from, information of that fact must be conveyed to the mind of the person who is to be affected by it. It will not do for the Defendant to say, 'I made up my mind that I would withdraw but I did not tell the Plaintiff'".

[4–16]    Although Bacon V-C speaks of "conveying revocation to the mind" of the offeree, the communication requirement is looser than that. The offeror does not have to ensure that each individual offeree has read or heard his revocation. Suppose, for example, that the offer to be revoked was made by newspaper advertisement or by some other sort of mass communication. The American case of *Shuey v US*[17] concerned Henry Saint-Marie who claimed a reward of $25,000 offered by the US Government for the "discovery and apprehension" of John Surratt, a man wanted in

---

[12] (1876) 2 Ch D 463.

[13] (1880) 5 CPD 344. See also *GNR v Witham* (1873) LR 9 CP 16; *Percival v LCC Asylums* (1918) 97 LJKB 677.

[14] Cf *Livingston v Evans* [1925] 4 DLR 769.

[15] (1855) 4 ICLR.

[16] Above, n 12. See also Holmes J in *Brauer v Shaw*, 168 Mass 198 at 200, 46 NE 617 at 618 (1897): "It would be monstrous to allow an inconsistent act of the offeror, not known or brought to the notice of the offeree, to affect the making of the contract".

[17] (1875) 92 US 73. cf *Carr v Mahaska County Bankers Assn*, 222 Iowa 411 at 289 NW 494 (1936).

connection with the assassination of President Lincoln. Mr Saint-Marie had provided information about Surratt's whereabouts. Unbeknownst to him, however, the offer of the reward had been revoked five months before he provided that information. The Court held that this did not matter; it was enough for an offeror to communicate his revocation of that offer that he published his retraction by a medium which gives "the same notoriety" to the revocation as was given to the offer. He does not have to go to extreme lengths to contact everyone who saw the original advert.

Along the same lines, suppose A has made B an offer and A communicates his revocation to B by e-mail. When will the revocation take effect? Will A have to wait for B to read the e-mail? It appears that the revocation will take effect when it ought to have been read. In *The Brimnes*[18] a revocation was sent by telex. It arrived on the offeree's telex machine between 17.30 and 18.00 but was not read until the next day. The Court of Appeal held that, even though it was not read until the next day, it took effect when it arrived on the machine. This was because it had arrived during office hours.[19] So an e-mail communication of revocation sent to an office on a Sunday will not take effect until the following Monday because it is unreasonable to expect that e-mails will be accessed outside of office hours. It could be said, further, that the offeror does not even have to communicate his revocation himself. As long as the offeree learns of the revocation, whether from the offeror or indirectly, the revocation is effective. This principle comes from *Dickinson v Dodds*.[20] The defendant offered to sell his house to the plaintiff, but the following day, and before the plaintiff had accepted his offer, the defendant sold the house to another person. The plaintiff learned of the sale that evening from a fourth person. The Court found that it was immaterial that the defendant had not informed the plaintiff of the revocation himself as Dickinson "knew that Dodds was no longer minded to sell the property to him as plainly and clearly as if Dodds had told him in so many words".

[4–17]

## Time Limits and "Firm Offers"

A common issue that arises under the heading of revocation is whether an offeror who sets a closing date for an offer is prevented from revoking before that closing date.[21] The promise to keep the offer open until a particular date is called a "firm" offer. In the case of *Scammell v Dicker*,[22] the offeror made an offer which she promised would remain open for 21 days. However, before the time was up and before the offer had been accepted, she revoked the offer, communicating her revocation to the offeree. The Court found that the revocation was valid, regardless of the time limit.

[4–18]

To similar effect is *Routledge v Grant*,[23] in which an offeror successfully revoked an offer after three weeks, even though he had promised to keep it open for six weeks. *Mountford v Scott*[24] was decided quite differently. The offer here was of an option to

[4–19]

---

[18] [1975] QB 929.

[19] See also *Eaglehill Ltd v J Needham* [1973] AC 992 at 1011.

[20] See also *Cartwright v Hoogstoel* (1911) 105 LT 628.

[21] One of the oldest cases on this question is *Cooke v Oxley* (1790) 3 TR 653. See also *Offord v Davies* (1862) 12 CBNS 748; *Lloyd's v Harper* (1880) 16 Ch D 290.

[22] [2001] 1 WLR 631. See also *Pitchmastic plc v Birse Construction Ltd, The Times*, 21 June 2000.

[23] (1828) 4 Bing 653.

[24] [1975] 2 WLR 114.

purchase a house for £10,000. The time limit for the option was six months. The option was granted on payment of £1. This offer could not be validly revoked before the end of the six-month period. The difference between *Mountford* and *Scammell* lies in that £1. The offers made in each case can be split into two parts. Both offerors made two promises: the main offer itself and the promise to keep the offer open. In *Mountford* the promise to keep the offer open was accepted by the offeree and was supported by consideration of £1 (see Chapter 8 for more on consideration). The promise to keep the offer open was, therefore, binding on the offeror. The equivalent promise in *Scammell* was not binding for want of consideration. If the offeree in *Scammell* had given something to the offeror to bind his promise, the offeror would not have been entitled to revoke as he did. Without consideration, a promise to keep an offer open is worthless. This rule has been criticised on the basis that it leads to uncertainty. It conflicts with our instinctive sense that "firm" offers ought to be binding on their maker.[25]

### Protecting the Offeree: The Irrevocability of Unilateral Offers

[4–20] At this point, it is important to explain the distinction between a unilateral and a bilateral offer. A bilateral offer asks for acceptance by promise as when, for example, A offers to sell B his car for €1,000 and B accepts his offer by promising to pay him €1,000 for it. After a bilateral contract is formed, the remaining obligations are, as expected, two-sided: both parties have obligations left to perform. In the example cited, A must perform by supplying B with his car, and B must perform by paying A €1,000. A unilateral offer asks for acceptance by performance. The classic example of a unilateral offer is the offer of a reward to anyone who finds a lost dog and returns him to his owner. That offer is accepted by the performance of an act-the discovery and return of the dog to his owner. After a unilateral contract is formed, only one party has any obligations left to perform. Acceptance of a unilateral offer is also performance of the offeree's obligations under the contract. In the example, the person who returns the dog has performed his part of the contract. It still remains for the dog's owner to play his part by paying the reward.

[4–21] The problem of the revocability of unilateral offers is an old one. Wormser, in a 1916 article, proposes the following hypothetical:

> "Suppose A says to B, 'I will give you $100 if you walk across the Brooklyn Bridge.' ... B starts to walk across the Brooklyn Bridge and has gone about one-half of the way across. At that moment A overtakes B and says to him, 'I withdraw my offer.' Has B then any rights against A? Again, let us suppose that after A has said, 'I withdraw my offer,' B continues to walk across the Brooklyn Bridge and completes the act of crossing. Under those circumstances, has B any rights against A."[26]

---

[25] Sharp, "Promissory Liability" (1939) 7 U Chi L Rev 10.

[26] Wormser, "The True Conception of Unilateral Contracts" (1916) 26 Yale LJ 136 at 136-137. See the equivalent UK hypothetical of offering 100 to a person if he will walk to York. *Rogers v Snow* (1573) Dalison 94; *GNR v Witham* (1873) LR 9 CP 16.

Wormser applies the traditional principles of revocation to the problem. An [4–22] offeror can revoke at any time up until acceptance:

"What A wanted from B, what A asked for, was the act of walking across the bridge. Until that was done, B had not given to A what A had requested. The acceptance by B of A's offer could be nothing but the act on B's part of crossing the bridge. It is elementary that an offeror may withdraw his offer until it has been accepted. It follows logically that A is perfectly within his rights in withdrawing his offer before B has accepted it by walking across the bridge – the act contemplated by the offeror and the offeree as the acceptance of the offer."[27]

If an offer requests an act, nothing but that act will amount to an acceptance. It [4–23] is not difficult to see, however, that the unyielding application of that rule will often lead to injustice. The law may provide a solution to this problem by preventing an offeror from revoking a unilateral offer once the offeree has entered into performance of the act of acceptance.[28] In *Errington v Errington*,[29] a father took out a mortgage on a house and promised his son and daughter-in-law that the house would be theirs if they made the mortgage repayments. They duly began to make the payments, but before the final payment had been made, the father died and his personal representatives attempted to recover possession of the house. Lord Denning found that the father's offer was a unilateral one: he had promised to transfer the house into the young couple's ownership in exchange for their act of repaying the mortgage. On Lord Denning's analysis, the father had made two offers: an express offer to transfer the ownership of the house and an implied offer not to revoke the express offer if the young couple would continue to pay the mortgage instalments. The couple had accepted the latter offer by making the payments, rendering it binding on the father and, accordingly, on his personal representatives. Lord Denning's approach was endorsed *obiter* by Lord Goff in *Daulia v Four Milbank Nominees*[30]:

"Whilst I think the true view of a unilateral contract must in general be that the offeror is entitled to require full performance of the condition which he has imposed and short of that he is not bound, that must be subject to one important qualification, which stems from the fact that there must be an implied obligation on the part of the offeror not to prevent the condition becoming satisfied, which obligation it seems to me must arise as soon as the offeree starts to perform."[31]

---

[27] Wormser, "The True Conception of Unilateral Contracts" (1916) 26 Yale LJ 136 at 136–137. Wormser recanted at (1950) *3* J Leg Educ at 146.

[28] In Australia, see *Abbott v Lance* (1860) *Legge's New South Wales Reports* 1238.

[29] [1952] 1 KB 290. *cf Peterson v Pattberg* 248 NY 86, 161 NE 428 (1928).

[30] [1978] Ch 231. *cf Luxor (Eastbourne) Ltd. v Cooper* [1941] AC 108, which suggests that the promise not to revoke the main offer will only be implied where necessary to give commercial efficacy to the contract.

[31] *ibid.* at 239.

## IV. Time Limits

[4 24] Where an offer is expressed to be subject to a time limit, the offer lapses when the deadline passes.[32] If no explicit time limit is set out, one may be implied from the method used to communicate the offer. So, in *Quenerduaine v Cole*,[33] the Court held that it was implicit in the fact that the offer was made by telegram that a quick response was required. Similarly, in *Dooley v Egan*,[34] an offer expressed to be "for immediate acceptance only" was held to lapse soon after it was made. If no time limit is expressed or implied, the offer will be held to last for a reasonable amount of time. In *Ramsgate Victoria Hotel v Montefiore*,[35] an offer for the sale of shares was held to have already expired when the offeree tried to accept it five months after it was first made. In the American case of *Loring v City of Boston*,[36] an offer of a reward for the apprehension and conviction of certain people was held to have lapsed after four years, even though it was never expressly revoked because "the exigency under which it was made having passed, it must be presumed to have been forgotten by most of the officers and citizens of the community".[37] The lifespan of the offer will depend on the shelf life of the item offered. So an offer to sell fresh milk will not last as long as an offer to sell tins of baked beans. In the same way, a long time limit might reasonably apply to an offer to sell something which does not undergo rapid changes in price, as is often the case with land. Later communications made after the initial offer may serve to prove that the offer still stands. In *Lynch v St Vincent's Hospital*,[38] a consultant was offered a new contract with a hospital in February and again in September. He did not accept the offer until December. However, the Court found that the offer had not lapsed by that stage, notably because the hospital had forwarded the doctor a Department of Health circular reminding consultants of the final date for entering such contracts. Similarly, in the Canadian case of *Earn v Kohut*,[39] an offer to settle a civil claim lasted two and a half years, reinforced by the fact that the defendant's lawyer had telephoned the plaintiff's lawyer to confirm that the defendant remained eager to settle the claim.

## V. Death of the Offeror or Offeree

[4–25] *Dickinson v Dodds*[40] is authority for the proposition that an offer dies with the offeror. However, the better view is probably that this rule only applies to offers of personal service, such as an offer to paint a picture or give a performance. Where a good has been offered, that good can always be supplied out of the offeror's estate. In such a case, *Coulthart v Clementson*[41] suggests that, unless it is terminated by the offeror's personal representatives, an offer will survive and can be accepted until such time as the offeree learns of the offeror's death. There is also some authority in the shape of

---

[32] *Parkgrange Investments v Shandon Park Mill*, unreported, High Court, 2 May 1991; *Commane v Walsh*, unreported, High Court, 3 May 1983.
[33] (1883) 32 WR 185.
[34] (1938) ILTR 155.
[35] (1866) LR Exch. 109.
[36] (1884) 7 Metcalf 409.
[37] *ibid.* at 414.
[38] Unreported, High Court, 31 July 1987.
[39] [2002] MBQB at 84.
[40] Above, n 12 at 475.
[41] (1879) 5 QBD 42 at 46.

*Bradbury v Morgan*[42] to the effect that where an offeree accepts an offer without notice of the offeror's death, the offeror's estate will be bound.

It can be argued that where an offer is made to a specific offeree, his death will **[4–26]** undermine the offeror's intention to contract. This is particularly true of personal contracts. In *Reynolds v Atherton*,[43] Warrington LJ said *obiter* that:

"... the offer having been made to a living person who ceases to be a living person before the offer is accepted, there is no longer an offer at all. The offer is not intended to be made to a dead person or his executors, and the offer ceases to be an offer capable of acceptance".

---

[42] (1862) 1 H&C 249 at 255 *per* Bramwell B *obiter*.
[43] (1921) 125 LT 690 at 695–696.

# CHAPTER 5
# Agreement: The Law of Acceptance

## I. Introduction

An offer is a statement of willingness to enter into a contract, conditional on the **[5–01]** offeree's acceptance. An acceptance, then, is a statement of willingness to enter into the contract as offered. Acceptance is the act which creates the contract—at the moment of acceptance, the parties to the contract are bound. An acceptance cannot be revoked.[1] The law on acceptance comes in two main parts: first, an acceptance must match the offer in its material terms—this requirement is often called the "mirror image rule". In addition, and as one might expect under the objective test of intention, the acceptance must be communicated to the offeror.

## II. The Mirror Image Rule

As a result of the doctrine of freedom of contract, the offeror must be master of his **[5–02]** offer. It is he who defines the terms upon which he will be bound. He creates the offer and he decides its scope. So he decides both the content of the acceptance and the manner in which that acceptance will be performed. For example, an offeree whose acceptance does not match the offer in content makes a counter-offer (4-02) which, instead of creating an agreement, terminates the original offer. So an acceptance must be unconditional—it must fit the offer without varying or adding to it. In addition, an offeree who attempts to communicate his acceptance to the offeror by a method other than that requested may fall foul of the mirror image rule and fail to form a contract.

---

[1] There is, however, some suggestion in Scottish law that a posted acceptance can be recalled before it reaches the offeror: *Dunmore v Alexander* 1830 9 Sh (Ct of Sess) 190.

### Battle of the Forms

[5–03]  Very often, large firms will employ "canned" forms containing their own standard terms when contracting. When two parties attempt to contract on the basis of conflicting standard forms, a "battle of the forms" occurs. The mirror image analysis applied to such a situation may not produce any contract at all. The offer is made on one set of standard terms, which is met by a different set producing a counter-offer, which is met by a conflicting set producing another counter-offer, and so on *ad infinitum*. The problem is illustrated by *Butler Machine Tool Co Ltd v Ex-Cell-O Corporation Ltd*[2] (4–08). As noted in the previous chapter, it is possible to analyse the facts of this case as a set of counter-offers leading to a dead end. However, one technique which the courts use to turn a set of facts like this into an agreement is called the "last shot" doctrine. This technique involves analysing the last exchange in the series as a counter-offer and acceptance. The majority of the Court of Appeal in *Butler* did this. The sellers had expressly accepted the buyers' last shot (their order form) by completing the tear-off slip. The letter that accompanied the tear-off slip was treated as irrelevant and drafted purely for filing purposes. The minor inconsistency involved in the letter could be ignored.

### Mode of Acceptance Stipulated

[5–04]  Under the mirror image rule, if an offeror instructs an offeree to "reply in writing" and the offeree replies by telephone, it could argued that no acceptance has taken place.[3] An offeror has the right to demand an exclusive mode of acceptance from the offeree. In theory, he can specify any mode of acceptance he likes, and if that method is not complied with, there is no acceptance. An example of this rule in operation is *Walker v Glass*.[4] On 27 February, the defendant had offered to sell property for £400,000. He specified that acceptance was to be by means of a form annexed to the offer, and further specified that the form had to be delivered to his solicitors together with a deposit of £40,000 before 5pm on 13 March. The plaintiff signed the acceptance and telephoned the defendant's solicitors on 2 March to inform them of it. Later that same day the defendant withdrew his offer. It was not until 12 March that the plaintiff gave the signed acceptance form and the deposit to the defendant's solicitors.

[5–05]  The plaintiff argued that the revocation of 2 March was invalid because it came after his purported acceptance by telephone. However, this acceptance did not take the form requested and, accordingly, it was ineffective. Because there was no effective acceptance, the offeror was perfectly entitled to revoke his offer on 2 March, thereby killing off any possibility of a binding agreement.

[5–06]  Generally speaking, however, it is important that the offeror has made it clear that a particular method of acceptance, *and that method only*, will suffice. If he does not do so, he may find that another method of acceptance can be substituted for the one he mentions. Because the courts are keen to find agreement, they will interpret the words

---

[2] [1979] 1 WLR 401.
[3] *Financings Ltd. v Stimson* [1962] 1 WLR 1184 at 1186.
[4] [1979] NI 129.

that the offeror uses to specify his chosen type of acceptance flexibly. Only an express and unequivocal formula will guarantee that a particular method of acceptance *must* be used. In *Manchester Diocesan Council for Education v Commercial and General Investments Ltd*,[5] the Court stated that "[i]f an offeror intends that he shall be bound only if his offer is accepted in some particular manner it must be for him to make this clear". So in *Tinn v Hoffmann*,[6] the offeror had stipulated that acceptance be "by return of post", yet the Court interpreted the phrase to mean "you may reply ... by any means not later than a letter ... by return of post would reach us". To similar effect is *Yates Building Co Ltd. v Pulleyn & Sons (York) Ltd.*,[7] where the defendants had requested that acceptance of their offer be "by notice in writing ... to be sent by registered or recorded delivery post" to the defendants or their solicitors. The plaintiffs accepted by ordinary post and the defendants argued that it was, therefore, not a valid acceptance. The Court found that the words used were not clear enough to make registered or recorded delivery post the mandatory method of acceptance. Where no mandatory mode of acceptance has been clearly stipulated, *Manchester Diocesan Council for Education v Commercial and General Investments Ltd.*[8] is authority for the proposition that it is enough that the different mode of acceptance used is in every way as beneficial to the offeror as the mode of acceptance suggested.[9] Thus, if A sends B an offer by e-mail without stipulating a mandatory method of acceptance and B replies by fax, it is likely that B's method of acceptance will suffice because both methods of communication are equally quick, and both produce a written record.

## III. Communication of Acceptance

It is not enough that an acceptance fits the mirror image rule in content and method— it must also be communicated. A secret acceptance is no acceptance at all. Theisger LJ said in *Household Fire and Carriage* that:   [5–07]

> "an acceptance which remains in the breast of the acceptor without being actually and by legal implication communicated to the offeror, is no binding acceptance".[10]

This principle was applied in *Parkgrange Investments v Shandon Park Mills*.[11] The defendant had signed a formal contract of sale signifying his acceptance of the plaintiff's offer for sale. However, he never returned the document to the plaintiff. Since the acceptance was not communicated to the plaintiff, it did not take effect.   [5–08]

---

[5] [1970] 1 WLR 241.

[6] (1873) 29 LT 271 at 278.

[7] [1975] 237 EG 183.

[8] [1970] 1 WLR 241.

[9] *Manchester Diocesan Council for Education v Commercial and General Investments Ltd* [1970] 1 WLR 241.

[10] (1879) 4 Exch Div 216. In *Guardians of Navan Union v McLoughlin* (1855) 4 ICLR, Monahan CJ held that "it is not enough for one [party] to accept the other's proposal in his own mind or in his own office, but he must by some act, binding on himself, communicate his acceptance to the other party".

[11] Unreported, High Court, 2 May 1991.

## When Acceptance is Not Explicitly Communicated

### Acceptance by Silence and Waiver

[5–09]     In *The Santa Clara*,[12] Lord Steyn memorably stated that: "in the practical world of businessmen an omission to act may be as pregnant with meaning as a positive declaration". Nevertheless, as far as bilateral offers go, silence will only exceptionally amount to acceptance.[13] Under the principle of freedom from contract, an offeree's inertia cannot be exploited to force a contract on him. He has no duty to expressly reject an offer in order to avoid acceptance. As is set out in the US case of *More v Insurance Co*[14]:

> "A person is under no obligation to do or say anything concerning a proposition which he does not choose to accept. There must be actual acceptance or there is no contract."

[5–10]     Moreover, a holding that silence with nothing more amounts to acceptance is inconsistent with the objective test. Silence is ambiguous and there is no good reason why an objective third party should consider that silence signified acceptance. Indeed, Llewellyn argued that an argument to the contrary "in a systematic centering on overt manifestations is, one may suggest, almost lewd".[15]

[5–11]     It is open to an offeror to expressly waive the communication requirement. Yet, as is demonstrated in the case of *Felthouse v Bindley*,[16] while such a waiver relieves the offeree of the need to communicate his acceptance, it cannot be used to force acceptance on him. In that case, Paul Felthouse and his nephew John were negotiating for the sale of a horse. The plaintiff wrote to the nephew offering to buy the horse for 30l 15s, adding that "[i]f I hear no more about him, I consider the horse is mine [at that price]". Willes J found that it was:

> "clear that the uncle had no right to impose upon the nephew a sale of his horse for 30 1. 15s. unless he chose to comply with the condition of writing to repudiate the offer. The nephew might, no doubt, have bound his uncle to the bargain by writing to him".

[5–12]     An Irish statement of the same principle is found in *Russell & Baird v Hoban*.[17] The plaintiff had posted a sale note to the defendant offering to supply goods, indicating in correspondence that if there was no reply within three days, acceptance

---

[12] *Vitol SA v Norelf Ltd.* [1996] 3 WLR 105 at 114.
[13] But see *Rust v Abbey Life Assurance Co Ltd.* [1979] 2 Lloyd's Rep 334 (silence of seven months amounted to acceptance where there was a prior course of dealing between the parties); *Minories Finance Ltd. v Afribank Nigeria Ltd.* [1995] 1 Lloyd's Rep 134; *Weatherby v Banhan* (1832) C and P 228.
[14] 130 NY 537 at 547.
[15] Llewelyn, "Our Case-Law of Contract: Offer and Acceptance. Pt. 2" (1939) 48 *Yale Law Journal* 779 at 801, n 35.
[16] (1862) 11 CB (NS) 869.
[17] [1922] 2 IR 159.

would take place. The Court held that silence does not signify acceptance. There was no contract.

So just as freedom from contract requires that the offeror is master of the offer, **[5–13]** so too it requires that the offeree is master of the acceptance and cannot have acceptance forced on him by his silence unless he agrees to it. Now, *Felthouse* might have been decided in favour of the uncle if John had said to him: "if you hear no more about him by next Friday you can consider the horse yours at that price". This is because in such a case, the offeree would have been acting as master. He would have taken on himself the responsibility to expressly communicate his rejection of his uncle's offer. In *Re Selectmove*[18] Peter Gibson LJ suggested that by giving such an undertaking to speak his rejection, an offeree undertakes to be bound to acceptance by his silence:

> "Where the offeree himself indicates that an offer is to be taken as accepted if he does not indicate to the contrary by an ascertainable time, he is undertaking to speak if he does not want an agreement to be concluded. I see no reason in principle why that should not be an exceptional circumstance such that the offer can be accepted by silence."

The requirement of communication can also be waived implicitly. *Carlill v* **[5–14]** *Carbolic Smokeball Co*[19] (3-16) is authority for the proposition that all unilateral offers (4-20) contain an implied waiver of the communication requirement. So Mrs Carlill was not obliged to write to the smokeball company and tell them that she intended to accept their offer by using their product. Bowen LJ vividly explained his reasoning:

> "If I advertise to the world that my dog is lost, and that anybody who brings the dog to a particular place will be paid some money, are all the police or other persons whose business it is to find lost dogs expected to sit down and write me a note saying that they have accepted my proposal? ... The essence of the transaction is that the dog should be found, and it is not necessary under such circumstances, as it seems to me, that in order to make the contract binding there should be any notification of acceptance."

## Acceptance Inferred from Conduct—Words not Required

Even though an offeree is silent, there may be something in his conduct which allows **[5–15]** the court to infer that he has accepted the offer put to him. It must, however, be clear from the offeree's conduct that he did the action with the intention, objectively viewed of course, of accepting the offer.[20] An example is *Billings v Arnott*,[21] a case in which an employer had offered his workers half pay if they would join the army. The plaintiff employee joined the army without informing his employers that he was doing so. His conduct in joining up was enough to constitute acceptance. A key case, *Brogden v Metropolitan Railway Co*,[22] concerned a contract for the supply of coal. Brogden had

---

[18] [1995] 1 WLR 474 at 478.
[19] [1893] 1 QB 256.
[20] *Day Morris Associates v Voyce* [2003] All ER 368.
[21] (1945) 80 ILTR 50.
[22] (1877) 2 AC 666.

been supplying the railway company with coal for four years. Brogden then suggested to the railway company that they enter into a formal contract for the coal. In response, the railway company supplied Brogden with draft terms of an agreement. Brogden added the name of an arbitrator to the document, signed it, marked it "approved" and returned it to the railway company. The railway company manager put the document in his desk and did not reply to it.

[5–16]     Even though the railway company did not reply to the amended document supplied by Brogden, they ordered and received coal on the strength of the terms set out in it. The question for the Court was whether the railway company had accepted Brogden's counter-offer. Certainly, the mere private act of keeping the document could not be an acceptance. But could the railway company's conduct in acting on the basis of the amended document amount to an acceptance? The House felt that they could. Lord Cairns' judgment in particular is instructive. He says that "there may be a *consensus* between the parties far short of a complete mode of expressing it". Although no formal acceptance had been expressed, the only reasonable account to be given of the parties' conduct subsequent to the return of the amended draft was that the railway company had accepted those terms. Accordingly, a contract came into existence between the parties from the moment the railway company ordered the first load of coal from Brogden upon the new terms.[23]

### When is Communication Effective?

[5–17]     It has been established that an un-communicated mental determination to accept is not an acceptance. But when does communication of acceptance take place? The old law drew a distinction between agreements *inter praesentes* (agreements made by parties in each other's company) and agreements *inter absentes* (agreements made by parties not in each other's company, usually made by post). It is easy to determine when communication of acceptance takes place in an agreement *inter praesentes* — an acceptance takes place when the offeree's words of acceptance "strike the ear"[24] of the offeror. The current law recognises that new methods of communication allow parties to negotiate as effectively as if they were in one another's company. So the law on agreements *inter absentes* now distinguishes non-instantaneous from instantaneous methods of communication. Post is a non-instantaneous method governed by the postal rule set out below. Telex, fax and telephone are instantaneous methods because, even though the communication is not completely instantaneous, the methods are so quick that parties ought to be treated as if they were in each other's presence.[25] These methods of communication are governed by the receipt rule: acceptance by these methods is effective when it is received.

### *The Receipt Rule*

[5–18]     When communication of acceptance is performed by an instantaneous method, it takes effect when the offeror reads or hears it. In *Mondial Shipping and Chartering BV v*

---

[23] See also *Western Electric v Welsh Development Agency* [1983] QB 796.

[24] *Caldwell v Cline* 109 W Va 553 at 156 SE 55 (1930).

[25] See *Entores Ltd v Miles Far East Corp* [1955] 2 QB 327 *per* Parker LJ. On faxes see *JSC Zestafoni G Nicoladze Ferralloy Plant v Ronly Holdings* [2004] 2 Lloyd's Rep 335.

*Astarte Shipping Ltd.,*[26] Gatehouse J said that, as regards instantaneous methods of communication, "[w]hat matters is not when the notice is given/sent/despatched/issued by the owners but when its content reaches the mind of the [offeror]". What should happen if there has been a failure of communication as in a case where the offeror does not hear the offeree's acceptance? In *Entores v Miles Far East Corporation*,[27] Lord Denning set out an answer as follows:

> "Suppose, for instance, that I shout an offer to a man across a river or a courtyard but I do not hear his reply because it is drowned out by an aircraft flying overheard. There is no contract at that moment. If he wishes to make a contract, he must wait till the aircraft is gone and then shout back his acceptance so that I can hear what he says. Not until I have his answer am I bound ... Suppose, for instance, that I make an offer to a man by telephone and, in the middle of his reply, the line goes 'dead' so that I do not hear his words of acceptance. There is no contract at that moment ... Suppose next, that the line does not go dead, but it is nevertheless so indistinct that I do not catch what he says and I ask him to repeat it. He then repeats it and I hear his acceptance. The contract is made, not on the first time when I do not hear, but only on the second time when I do hear."

Spoken acceptances fit Lord Denning's reasoning easily, but technology can be **[5–19]** temperamental and the possibilities for failure of communication by machine are myriad. Should the courts always insist on acceptance having been communicated to the mind of the offeror? What if the offeror does not read an acceptance communicated by an instantaneous method? Lord Wilberforce, writing *obiter* in *Brinkibon Ltd v Stahag Stahl GmbH*[28] aptly notes that:

> "[n]o universal rule can cover all such cases, they must be resolved by reference to the intentions of the parties, by sound business practice and in some cases by judgment where the risks should lie".

In *Entores*, Lord Denning goes some way to suggesting where risks should lie. **[5–20]** He adopts a fault-based analysis. Lord Denning says that where the offeree is aware that his acceptance has not been heard, it falls to him to repeat it if he wants a contract to be formed. However, he goes on to say that where the offeree is not so aware and where it is the *offeror's* fault that the acceptance has not been received, "he will be estopped [or prevented] from saying that he did not receive the message of acceptance" and an agreement is formed. Suppose an acceptance is sent by fax and the ink in the fax machine runs out half way through. There may be no full communication of the acceptance, but the offeror, by reading the half-communicated fax, is aware of that. It is his fault that the acceptance has not been communicated properly, and so if he fails to seek further clarification, Lord Denning argues that he must take the acceptance as is.

---

[26] [1995] CLC 1011.

[27] [1955] 2 QB 327.

[28] [1983] 2 AC 34. See also *Apple Corps v Apple Computer Inc* [2004] EWHC 768.

**[5–21]**     Along the same lines it can be said that if an acceptance is sent to a business by some means of instantaneous communication during office hours, it takes effect at the time it has been received, even if it is not actually read until some time later. In such circumstances it is the offeror's fault if he does not read the acceptance. So Megaw LJ says in *The Brimnes*[29] that:

> "if a notice arrives at the address of the person to be notified, at such a time and by such means of communication that it would in the normal course of business come to the attention of that person on its arrival, that person cannot rely on some failure of himself or his servants to act in a normal businesslike manner in respect of taking cognisance of the communication so as to postpone the effective time [of acceptance]".

**[5–22]**     On the other hand, *Mondial Shipping and Chartering BV v Astarte Shipping Ltd*[30] establishes that if an offeree chooses to send his acceptance to a business by an instantaneous method of communication outside of office hours, that acceptance will not take effect until the beginning of the next working day. This is because the offeree cannot reasonably expect that the offeror would be available to read the acceptance outside of normal business hours. In this instance, it is the offeree's fault that his acceptance may not take effect for several days because he has chosen to communicate it at an inopportune time.

### The Postal Rule

**[5–23]**     When an acceptance is communicated by post,[31] it takes effect the moment the letter of acceptance is posted.[32] The key case here is *Adams v Lindsell*.[33] The defendants wrote to the plaintiffs offering to sell them wool on 2 September. The plaintiffs received this letter on 5 September. They posted their acceptance on the same day but it was not received until 9 September. However, the defendants had sold the wool to someone else on 8 September. The Court, formulating and applying the postal rule, found that the plaintiffs' acceptance took effect on 5 September. There was a contract for the wool on that date, and accordingly, the defendants breached that contract when they sold the wool to a third party.

**[5–24]**     Special note should be taken of the fact that the postal rule only applies to acceptance. It does not apply to offers or to rejections or revocations. Offers, rejections and revocations sent by post are not effective until they are received.

**[5–25]**     The postal rule is of particular importance in determining where a contract was formed. A contract is formed wherever acceptance takes place. *Sanderson v Cunningham*[34] concerned an insurance contract between a Dublin insured and a London

---

[29] [1975] QB 929.

[30] [1995] CLC 1011.

[31] Or telegram. See *Cowan v O'Connor* (1888) 20 QBD 640.

[32] Coote argues that the postal rule should also apply to answering machines. Coote "The Instantaneous Transmission of Acceptances" (1971) 4 NZULR 331.

[33] (1818) 1 B & Ald 681.

[34] [1919] 2 IR 234.

insurer. The acceptance was posted in London and, therefore, the Court held that the contract was concluded in London. Along the same lines is *Kelly v Cruise Catering*.[35] Kelly was an Irish employee working on a ship sailing from Mexico to Texas. His contract of employment had been drafted in Oslo. He had signed it and posted it in Dublin. Acceptance took place in Dublin when the completed contract of employment was posted.

In *Adams v Lindsell* the letter of acceptance arrived late. Does the postal rule **[5–26]** apply even if the letter never arrives at all? *Household Fire and Carriage v Grant*[36] was a case involving a letter which never arrived. The Court found that its non-arrival was irrelevant; the acceptance took effect the instant it was posted. In *Byrne v Van Tienhoven*,[37] Lindley J says clearly:

> "It may be taken as now settled that, where an offer is made and accepted by letters sent through the post, the contract is completed the moment the letter accepting the offer is posted, even though it never reaches its destination."

How can the postal rule be justified? Thesiger LJ in *Household Fire and* **[5–27]** *Carriage v Grant* suggested that the postal service was the agent of both the offeror and the offeree, so that by posting his acceptance:

> "the contract is made as complete and final and absolutely binding as if the acceptor had put his letter into the hands of a messenger sent by the offeror himself as his agent to deliver the offer and receive the acceptance".

Two other justifications are available which focus on the proper allocation of **[5–28]** the risk of a letter of acceptance going astray. The postal rule places that risk on the offeror. First, this is because an offeror who consents to the negotiation of a contract through the post clearly accepts the risk inherent in that method of communication.[38] Secondly, the offeror may protect himself from that risk by ousting the postal rule so that it does not apply to any acceptances sent to him by post, and they do not take effect unless and until they are received.

The operation of the postal rule may not be as harsh as all that.[39] First of all, **[5–29]** it is always open to the offeror to oust the postal rule by express words. So Bramwell LJ says in *Household Fire and Carriage Accident Insurance Co v Grant* that the postal rule could be "rendered nugatory by every prudent man saying 'Your answer by post is only to bind if it reaches me'". The plaintiff in *Nunin Holdings v Tullamarine Estates*[40] successfully ousted the postal rule by stating that a contract would not form until acceptance by post was actually received. Accordingly, the plaintiff was entitled to revoke the offer even after acceptance had been posted. *Holwell Securities*

---

[35] [1994] 2 ILRM 394.

[36] (1879) 4 Ex D 216.

[37] (1880) 5 CPD 344.

[38] *Butler v Foley* 211 Mich 668 at 179 NW 34 (1920).

[39] For criticisms of the rule, see Gardner, "Trashing with Trollope: A Deconstruction of the Postal Rules in Contract" (1992) 12 OJLS 170.

[40] [1994] 1 VR 74.

*Ltd v Hughes*[41] is another case in point. The defendant asked for acceptance to be communicated "by notice in writing to [the defendant]". The plaintiffs communicated their acceptance by posting a letter, but the letter never arrived. The question for the Court was whether the postal rule applied in this instance. If it did then, of course, there was a contract between plaintiff and defendant—acceptance had taken place the instant the letter of acceptance was posted. Russell LJ found that the postal rule had been displaced in this case; that the words "notice . . . to":

> "should be taken expressly to assert the ordinary situation in law that acceptance requires to be communicated or notified to the offeror, and is inconsistent with the theory that acceptance can be constituted by the act of posting".

[5–30]    Another possible exception to the postal rule can be constructed by recalling the Courts' reasoning for imposing the risk of the letter of acceptance never arriving on the offeror. It has been noted that the offeror, by expressly requesting acceptance by post or by impliedly indicating that he consents to acceptance by post, takes the risk of ineffectiveness of communication. There may be circumstances where the use of the postal service falls outside the scope of this consent by the offer. For example, it is not right to imply that the offeror has consented to accept the risk of non-arrival of the letter of acceptance in circumstances where the offeree has not stamped and addressed the letter properly.[42]

## IV. E-commerce and the Offer & Acceptance Framework

[5–31]    The rules of offer and acceptance are applicable even to the relatively new scenario of electronic contracts.[43] The Electronic Commerce Act 2000 confirms that in principle, electronic communications[44] are no less valid than those conducted on paper. Section 9 sets out that "[i]nformation . . . shall not be denied legal effect, validity or enforceability, solely on the grounds that it is wholly or partly in electronic form, whether as an electronic communication or otherwise." The Act evidences a market driven *laissez-faire* approach to the regulation of electronic contracts. Its contribution to the law of offer and acceptance is minimal; it aims to bring certainty to a novel area by firmly deferring to the traditional rules of offer and acceptance, allowing parties to circumvent those rules by their own agreement if they choose. However, the boundaries of offer and acceptance in electronic contracting are far from clear.

---

[41] [1974] 1 WLR 155.

[42] See *Re London and Northern Bank ex p Jones* [1900]1 Ch 220. In the US, see *Busher v Insurance Co* 72 NH 551 at 552, 58 A 41 (1904). See also *British & American Telegraph Co v Colson* (1871) LR 6 Exch 108, which argues that the postal rule should not apply where it would lead to "manifest inconvenience or absurdity".

[43] For a good guide to the principles, see New Zealand Law Commission, *Electronic Commerce Part One: A guide for the legal and business community* (1998) Report 50.

[44] Electronic communications are defined in s 1 of the Act as "information communicated or intended to be communicated to a person or public body, other than its originator, that is generated, communicated, processed, sent, received, recorded, stored or displayed by electronic means or in electronic form, but does not include information communicated in the form of speech unless the speech is processed at its destination by an automatic voice recognition system".

## E-mail: Postal Rule or Receipt Rule?

The Electronic Commerce Act sets out when electronic communications are deemed to have been sent and received. In this respect, it follows the UNCITRAL Model Law on Electronic Commerce, which was adopted on 12 June 1996. As regards sending, the Act provides at s 21(1) that, unless otherwise agreed, an e-mail is deemed to have been sent when it enters the first information system outside the control of the sender.[45] If the offeror has designated a particular system for receiving electronic communications, the e-mailed acceptance is received when it arrives in that system. If no system has been designated, the e-mail is received "when it comes to the attention of the addressee".[46]

[5–32]

But there is no legislation or decision that tells us whether an acceptance takes effect when it is sent or when it is received.[47] The Electronic Commerce Act defers to the traditional principles of common law. In one sense, the receipt rule ought to apply to e-mail. E-mail is a near-instantaneous method of communication, akin to telex, and the same rules should apply.[48] On the other hand, an analogy may be drawn between e-mail and post. E-mail is not an entirely instantaneous method of communication. As with ordinary mail, there is a time lag between sending and receiving an e-mail. Like a posted letter, an e-mail leaves the control of the sender as soon as it is sent over the Internet. As a letter passes into the control of the third party postal service, so too an e-mail passes into the control of a third party server.

[5–33]

As always, however, the key question is this: who should bear the risk that the e-mailed acceptance will not arrive? If the offeror should bear that risk, then the postal rule should apply. If the offeree should bear the risk, a receipt rule should apply. On the one hand, the risk should lie with the offeror because by consenting to contract by e-mail, he accepts the risks of technical faults and server crashes that go along with it. The contrary argument is also persuasive. The offeree should take the risk of failure of communication, not least because he will usually be able to tell almost instantly by means of error messages if his e-mail has not been sent. Many e-mail programmes also enable the offeree to request automatic confirmation that an e-mail has reached its intended recipient. Applying Lord Denning's reasoning in *Entores*, where the offeree is aware that his communication has been unsuccessful, he should bear the consequences. It could be argued, however, that the lack of a settled legal position on this matter is not hugely significant as many electronic contracts now specify when and where contract formation will take place.

[5–34]

## Websites

How does the offer and acceptance framework apply to a purchase from a website such as Amazon? This point awaits a definitive decision, and the development of a general

[5–35]

---

[45] However, s 20 allows the sender to avoid this provision because it states that where an electronic communication is sent which requires an acknowledgement, and no acknowledgement is received, the communication will be treated as if it had never been sent.

[46] This provision overcomes the ambiguity in Art 11 of the Directive which said that the e-mail was received when the recipient was "able to access" it.

[47] See Hedley, *The Law of Electronic Commerce and the Internet in the UK and Ireland* (Cavendish, 2005), p 246.

[48] See *Chwee King Keong v Digiland* [2004] SGHC 71.

rule covering all the permutations of online trading is unlikely.[49] However, it is likely that a website such as Amazon, which displays details of the goods available to purchase together with their price, will be treated as analogous to an advertisement. Logically, if one thinks of websites as just another means of communication, the advertisement of an item for sale on a website should amount to an invitation to treat. An offer will then be made when a customer indicates his intention to buy one of the products on the site by submitting an order. This intention will usually be indicated by a series of deliberate actions[50]: the offeror will typically type in his details and credit card number and click on a "send" or "checkout" button to confirm his order. Often a facility will be available which enables him to cancel his order before it is accepted, allowing revocation. As always, at this point, the seller will still be free to accept or reject that offer.

[5–36]     It is not impossible, however, to conceive of circumstances where details of a product such as a website could be considered to amount to an offer. Imagine a *Lefkowitz*-type scenario (3-17) where the website makes clear that a particular product is only available to the first three purchasers so that the usual argument about binding sellers to provide an indeterminate quantity of stock (3–15) does not apply. In that instance, the site could reasonably be treated as an offer. A music vendor like iTunes, or a website which supplies software that can be downloaded from the site immediately on purchase, might, in principle, be said to be offering particular MP3 files for sale rather than merely inviting offers to buy them. The limited stock argument does not apply here[51] because, ordinarily, the stock of programmes or tunes never runs out.

[5–37]     In the website scenario, a further problem arises in terms of the seller's acceptance. On many websites, if A orders merchandise online and that merchandise is in stock, A will receive an automatic confirmation of his order[52] and/or an automatic confirmation that his item has been dispatched for delivery to him. The response that A receives will be generated by software without any human intervention. Suppose that his order is characterised as an offer. Also assume that circumstances justify treating

---

[49] Under Art 10 of the E-Commerce Directive (Directive 2003/31 EC), a website must provide information on the different technical steps that a consumer must follow to conclude a contract. This information must be provided clearly, comprehensibly and unambiguously and prior to the order being placed by the recipient of the service.

[50] "The situation is a little less clear where the computer makes an error, and does not do what the human being who programmed it intends. It is likely that the human being will be bound unless the computer acted in such a way that the other party could not reasonably have thought that it was operating correctly." Arden, "Electronic Commerce" (1999) 149 NJL at 1685.

[51] Jones argues that copyright legislation may operate to restrict the stock available for download: Jones, "Trading on the Internet: Contracting in Cyberspace", (1997) PLC 41.

[52] Under Art 14 of the Electronic Commerce Directive (Directive 2003/31 EC) where the recipient of services places an order through electronic means, the service provider must acknowledge receipt of the order without undue delay and by electronic means. "Order" and "acknowledgement" do not appear to be synonyms for "offer" and "acceptance". The idea behind this provision is that the consumer is protected against accidental contracting. The original proposal required an acknowledgement of the receipt of the acknowledgement in order for a contract to be formed.

the confirmation of the order as an acceptance. When does communication take place? Arguably, a receipt rule should apply in this instance.[53] The argument is not based on time but on responsibility. Unlike acceptance by post, if A is accepting an offer on a website by clicking a checkout button, he will generally know immediately if his acceptance has been successful. If the website fails, A will receive an immediate error message. Similarly, if a website is accepting his offer, the software will generally be programmed to automatically detect failure in its communication of acceptance.

If acceptance has been communicated, where is the fact of acceptance? Where is    [5–38]
the intention to accept? Does a valid contract not require objective evidence of a deliberate, human expression of intention? The courts have dealt with the lack of direct intention before. Take *Thorton v Shoe Lane Parking*,[54] where Lord Denning was concerned with a customer's insertion of a card into an automatic ticket machine[55] at the entrance to a car park. As with an automatically programmed website, the ticket machine was designed to react automatically to the customer's action without any human intervention. Lord Denning translated this transaction easily into the language of offer and acceptance:

> "The customer pays his money and gets a ticket. He cannot refuse it ... he was committed at the very moment when he put his money into the machine. It can be translated into offer and acceptance in this way: the offer is made when the proprietor of the machine holds it out as being ready to receive the money. The acceptance takes place when the customer puts his money into the slot."

It may be argued that there is a problem here because one cannot say that a    [5–39]
complex computer programme, designed by a third party, will always reflect the autonomous decision of the vendor. The counter-argument must come down, as always, to the allocation of risk and responsibility. If a vendor chooses to use a website which generates automated confirmations, he must assume the attendant risk of liability.[56]

## V. Offer and Acceptance: Critical Analysis

It is not so controversial to say that the "offer and acceptance" framework is somewhat    [5–40]
artificial. In *The Eurymedon*, Lord Wilberforce emphasises the strong formalism that has characterised reasoning in this area of law:

> "English law, having committed itself to a rather technical and schematic doctrine of contract, in application takes a practical approach, often at the cost

---

[53] See Glatt, "Comparative Issues In The Formation Of Electronic Contracts" (1998) 6 IJL&IT 34.
[54] [1971] 2 QB 163.
[55] On more sophisticated types of agent software involved in e-transactions, see Thurlow, "Varying Approaches to the Elimination of Paper and Pen" (2001) 5.3 *Electronic Journal of Comparative Law*.
[56] See Glatt, "Comparative Issues In The Formation Of Electronic Contracts" (1998) 6 IJL&IT 34.

of forcing the facts to fit uneasily into the marked slots of offer [and] acceptance."[57]

**[5–41]**     Despite their acknowledged artificiality, these rules have such a strong footing in contract law that it is easy to forget that they are invented rules of law, probably no older than *Adams v Lindsell*.[58] Yet the rules on offer and acceptance have no particular justification beyond a judicial concern with certainty; the rules of offer and acceptance are such that it is always clear whether or not the parties are in a transaction. As the battle of the forms cases show in particular, they bear little relation to what is supposed to be the focus of contract law—the intention of the parties. Intention is subordinated to certainty and tradition. Lord Selbourne in *Hussey v Horne-Payne*[59] noted:

> "The observation has often been made that a contract established by letters may sometimes bind parties who, when they wrote those letters, did not imagine that they were finally settling the terms of the agreement by which they were to be bound."

**[5–42]**     The rules are also criticised for their failure to reflect the reality of agreement in everyday life. The offer and acceptance model is adversarial. It suggests an exchange of discrete communications between polarised parties, culminating in an abrupt transition from no liability to liability. The leading American academic Farnsworth explains that this model is grossly at odds with the practice in high-powered commercial contracts:

> "The terms are reached by negotiations, usually face-to-face over a consider-able period of time and often involving corporate officers, bankers, engineers, accountants, lawyers and others. The negotiations are a far cry from the simple bargaining envisioned by the classic rules of offer and acceptance, which evoke an image of single-issue, adversarial, zero-sum bargaining as opposed to multi-issue, problem-solving, gain-maximizing negotiation."[60]

**[5–43]**     Despite these flaws, the rules on offer and acceptance have often been enforced with a rigour worthy of a better cause. Lord Denning made an attempt in *Butler Machine Co v Ex-Cell-O Corporation (England) Ltd*[61] and *Gibson v Manchester City Council*[62] to strike a blow for realism against this formalist tradition and set aside the offer and acceptance test in favour of a holistic fact-based analysis. In *Gibson* he said: "To my mind it is a mistake to think that all contracts can be analysed into the form of offer and acceptance. I know in some textbooks it has been the custom to do so; but, as I understand the law, there is no need to look for a strict offer and acceptance". Lord Denning argued that the courts should look at the totality of the parties' documents and conduct in order to find agreement. The question of whether their relationship

---

[57] *New Zealand Shipping Co Ltd. v AM Satterthwaite & Co Ltd., The Eurymedon* [1975] AC 154 at 167 *per* Wilberforce LJ.
[58] (1818) 1 B & Ald 681.
[59] (1879) 4 App Cas 311 at 323.
[60] Farnsworth, *Contracts* (2nd ed., Little, Brown & Co, 1990), pp 117–118.
[61] [1979] 1 WLR 401.
[62] [1978] 1 WLR 520.

could be labelled in terms of "offer" and "acceptance" was irrelevant. Lord Denning further argued in the battle of the forms case of *Butler* that:

"The better way is to look at the communications passing between the parties and glean from them, or from the conduct of the parties whether they have reached agreement on all material points, even though there may be differences between the forms and conditions printed on the back of them ... If [the] differences are irreconcilable, so that they are mutually contradictory, then the conflicting terms may have to be scrapped and replaced by a reasonable implication".[63]

His break with tradition, however, was firmly put down by Lord Diplock in the House of Lords decision in *Gibson*.[64] Karl Llewellyn explains wonderfully why the rules on offer and acceptance continue to have such a firm hold on the legal imagination:  **[5–44]**

"The rules of Offer and Acceptance have been worked over; they have been written over; they have been shaped and rubbed smooth with pumice, they wear the rich deep polish of a thousand class rooms; they have a grip on the vision and indeed on the affections held by no other rule "of law," real or pseudo. For it was Offer and Acceptance which first led each of us out of laydom into The Law. Puzzled, befogged, adrift in the strange words and technique of cases, with only our sane feeling of what was decent for a compass, we felt the warm sun suddenly, we knew that we were arriving, we knew we too could "think like a lawyer"; That was when we learned to down sea-sickness as A revoked when B was almost up the flag-pole. Within the first October, we had achieved a technical glee in justifying judgment then for A; and succulent memory lingers, of the way our dumber brethren were pilloried as Laymen still. This is therefore no area of "rules" to be disturbed. It is an area where we *want* no disturbance, and will brook none. It is the Rabbit-Hole down which we fell into the Law, and to him who has gone down it, no queer phenomenon is strange; he has been magicked; the logic of Wonderland we then entered makes mere discrepant decision negligible. And it is not only hard, it is obnoxious, for any of us who have gone through that experience to even conceive of Offer and Acceptance as perhaps in need of re-examination."[65]

---

[63] [1979] 1 WLR 401.

[64] Diplock L did, however, admit that certain exceptional types of contract might not be required to fit the "offer and acceptance" template. For example, in *Trentham Ltd. v Archital Luxfer Ltd* [1993] 1 Lloyd's Rep 25, Steyn LJ suggested that, often, contracts that have come into existence as a result of performance will not have to fit that mould. Poole suggests that this decision is consistent with a policy of recognising executed agreements as contracts wherever possible. Poole, *Textbook on Contract Law* (7th ed, Oxford, 2004), p 37.

[65] Llewellyn, "Our Case-Law of Contract: Offer and Acceptance" (1938) 48 *Yale Law Journal* 1.

# CHAPTER 6
# Certainty and Completeness

## 1. Introduction

If an agreement is to be enforced as a contract, it must be sufficiently certain and complete. The parties may have exchanged a valid offer and acceptance but that is not enough. Where an agreement is vague, or essential terms have not been settled, the court will not be able to find the *consensus ad idem* which is fundamental to an enforceable contract. Of course, uncertainty and incompleteness may be said to be the natural by-products of all but the most meticulously conducted negotiations. The following extract from Macaulay's famous study of non-contractual relations in business[1] hints at some of the reasons for parties' failure to express their intention comprehensively and clearly: **[6–01]**

> "Businessmen often prefer to rely on a 'man's word' in a brief letter, a handshake or 'common honesty and decency'—even when the transaction involves exposure to serious risks. [Lawyers interviewed] complained that businessmen desire to 'keep it simple and avoid red tape' even where large amounts of money and significant risks are involved. One stated that he was 'sick of being told "We can trust Old Max" when the problem is not one of honesty but one of reaching an agreement that both sides understand.' Another said that businessmen when bargaining often talk only in pleasant generalities, think they have a contract, but fail to reach agreement on any of the hard, unpleasant questions until forced to do so by a lawyer."

The reluctance to enter into a comprehensive agreement is also well known in Ireland. In *McCarron v McCarron*,[2] Murphy J expressed his sympathy for: **[6–02]**

> "that natural courtesy (which John Millington Synge associated with the west of Ireland) which often results in unwillingness to pursue discussion to a logical

---

[1] Macaulay "Non-contractual Relations in Business" (1963) 28 Am Soc Rev 55. See also Staughton LJ in *Corson v Rhuddlan Borough Council* [1989] 59 P & CR 185: "If one party is a company with an in-house legal adviser, he may whisper words of caution; but the managing director will tell him that it is the task of lawyers to solve problems, not to create them."
[2] Unreported, Supreme Court, 13 February 1997.

and perhaps harshly expressed commercial conclusion ... [I]n some particularly rural areas, a meeting of minds can be achieved without as detailed a discussion as might be necessary elsewhere."

[6–03]    In *Brown v Gould*,[3] Megarry J held that a court should not refuse to enforce a contract for want of certainty or completeness unless it was "driven to it". The courts are not blind to the realities of commercial practice and so the cases reflect their general willingness to give parties the benefit of the doubt. So it is said that it "is in the interest of commercial convenience that, in general, apparent contracts should be enforced."[4] In the key case of *Hillas v Arcos*,[5] Lord Wright explained the courts' tolerance for imperfect expression of contractual intention:

> "The document of the 21st May 1930 cannot be regarded as other than inartistic, and may appear repellent to the trained sense of an equity draftsman. But it is clear that the parties both intended to make a contract and thought they had done so. Businessmen often record the most important agreements in crude and summary fashion; modes of expression sufficient and clear to them in the course of their business may appear to those unfamiliar with the business far from complete or precise. It is accordingly the duty of the court to construe such documents fairly and broadly, without being too astute or subtle in finding defects, but, on the contrary, the court should seek to apply the old maxim of English law *verba ita sunt intelligenda ut res magis valeat quam pereat* [words are to be understood that the object may be carried out and not fail]."

[6–04]    That said, Lord Wright recognises that the court's duty is to divine the intention of the parties and uphold their contract accordingly, not to make a contract for them where they have failed to demonstrate any clear contractual intention at all. The parties cannot abdicate their responsibility to complete their contract to the courts:

> "That maxim, however, does not mean that the Court is to make a contract for the parties, or to go outside the words they have used, except insofar as there are appropriate implications of law ..."

## II. Agreements Void for Uncertainty

[6–05]    In *Scammell v Ouston*,[6] Viscount Maugham stated the key principle which operates in uncertainty cases:

> "In order to constitute a valid contract, the parties must so express themselves that their meaning can be determined with a reasonable degree of certainty. It is plain that unless this can be done it would be impossible to hold that the contracting parties had the same intention; in other words the *consensus ad idem* would be a matter of mere conjecture."

---

[3] (1972) Ch 53.
[4] *Fitzsimons v O'Hanlon* [1999] 2 ILRM 551 *per* Budd J.
[5] (1932) 147 LT 503.
[6] *Scammell v Ouston* [1941] AC 251.

There are two major types of uncertain term: ambiguous terms and illusory terms. Both can be fatal to the existence of a contract. Before we examine these areas, it is important to remind ourselves that the courts will make every effort to find that a contract is certain enough to be enforced.[7] Certainty means certainty as to the contract's essential terms. Uncertainty as to the peripheral terms will not normally prevent a contract from being upheld.

**[6–06]**

## Ambiguity

An ambiguous term is one which can be interpreted in at least two ways. In *Scammell v Ouston*,[8] a term that referred to "hire purchase terms" was ambiguous because the Court held that it could be interpreted in five different ways. Lord Russell observed:

**[6–07]**

> "An alleged contract which appeals for its meaning to so many skilled minds in so many different ways is undoubtedly open to suspicion. For myself I feel no doubt that no contract between the parties existed at all; notwithstanding that they may have thought otherwise."

The leading Irish case is *ESB v Newman*,[9] which was about a contract between Dublin Corporation and the defendant. The defendant agreed to discharge "the accounts for electricity supplied to [Mrs. Waddington]". Electricity was supplied to Mrs Waddington at four different premises. Therefore, the phrase "the accounts" was ambiguous; it was unclear whether that phrase referred to some or all of Mrs Waddington's accounts. In this sort of case, the court will try to *divine* the intention of the parties in order to choose between the competing interpretations of the ambiguous term. Davitt J upheld the contract. From the surrounding circumstances, he divined that the defendant had not intended a contract that would cover the supply of electricity to Mrs Waddington at all four of her premises. The contract was interpreted accordingly. We know, however, that the court's job is to discover the contract, not to write it.[10] If there is such a degree of ambiguity surrounding the contract that the court cannot determine which was intended to be the definitive version, the contract must fall. The courts cannot patch together a replacement contract. This much is clear from *Mackey v Wilde*.[11] In this case, the plaintiff and the defendant agreed that 25 annual fishing permits and "a few" day tickets would be issued. Obviously, the phrase "a few" is vague and ambiguous; so vague, in fact, that the Court was unable to choose between the many meanings. Barron J noted that the "learned trial judge has held that ten day tickets would be reasonable. But equally any number between two and ten would have been said also to have been reasonable." The Court could not determine what, if anything, the parties had intended to agree and, therefore, the purported contract between them could not be upheld.

**[6–08]**

---

[7] In *Greater London Council v Connolly* [1941] AC 251 Lord Denning stated that "[t]he courts are always loath to hold a contract bad for uncertainty. They will give it a reasonable interpretation whenever possible".

[8] *Scammell v Ouston* [1941] AC 251.

[9] (1993) 67 ILTR 124.

[10] *Fitzsimons v O'Hanlon* [1999] 2 ILRM 551 *per* Budd J.

[11] [1998] 2 IR 578.

**[6–09]**     We have said that the court's first concern is to discover the intention of the parties and to interpret the contract accordingly. It is worth exploring the techniques that the court employs in its hunt for the elusive intention of the parties. The court adopts an objective standpoint. The types of evidence to which the court will have regard have also been shown: words, documents, surrounding circumstances, any past course of dealing and so on. This process can be seen in operation in *Hillas v Arcos*.[12] The contract was for the sale of timber. The disputed phrase was "100,000 standards". In order to determine what that phrase meant with certainty, the Court looked at a contract from the previous year which involved "22,000 standards of fair specification". The Court also heard expert evidence on what was considered "fair specification" within the trade. Having regard to all of these matters, Lord Tomlin held that "standards of fair specification" meant goods distributed over kinds and qualities and sizes in fair proportions having regard to the output of the season. Lord Thankerton set out the Court's thinking:

> "The question ... is whether the words 'of fair specification', on their proper construction, will enable the subject to be identified by the Court. In other words, do they provide a standard by which the Court is enabled to ascertain the subject-matter of the contract, or do they involve an adjustment between the conflicting interests of the parties, which the parties have left unsettled and on which the Court is not entitled to adjudicate."

**[6–10]**     Sometimes, the context of the contract will not provide much of a basis on which the courts can proceed. For example, in *Nicolene v Simmonds*[13] a contract was too uncertain to be enforced which stated that "the usual conditions of acceptance apply". There were no usual conditions of acceptance as between the parties and so the clause was so uncertain as to be meaningless.

**[6–11]**     One of the most important areas in the case law on certainty concerns the agreement of the contract price. The cases state that the parties do not have to agree upon an exact price at the time of contracting. In *Black Country Housing Association v Shand*,[14] the Court of Appeal held that an agreement is sufficiently certain where the parties agree to sell at a fair and reasonable price. Chadwick LJ drew a distinction between agreements where the parties intended to set *a* price in the future, which are not binding, and agreements to sell at a fair and reasonable price, which are binding. Why the difference? Chadwick LJ explains that where the parties have agreed merely that they will agree a price in the future, the court has no indication of what that price may be. The agreement is too uncertain as it stands. If, however, the parties agree that a fair and reasonable price will apply, the court can, "if necessary, direct an inquiry in order to ascertain what the fair and reasonable price is ...". The parties, by agreeing to charge a "fair and reasonable" price, give the court an objective point to steer by thereby remedying any uncertainty in their agreement.

---

[12]  Above, n 5.

[13]  [1953] 1 All ER 822.

[14]  Unreported, Court of Appeal, 22 May 1998.

The key point here is that an element of finality must be present. It is not enough that the parties have agreed to negotiate a price. They must actually have agreed that an *ascertainable price* will be paid. Unless some final, albeit flexible, decision has been reached about pricing, the contract will not be upheld.[15] So, for example, in the leading case of *May and Butcher v R*,[16] a contract was not upheld which provided that "[t]he price ... to be paid, and the date or dates on which payment is to be made to the purchasers ... shall be agreed upon from time to time between the Commission and the purchasers ...". The contract in *Loftus v Roberts*[17] was held void for uncertainty on this same basis. Roberts, a theatre owner, had agreed to pay Loftus, an actress, a salary "to be mutually agreed between us". This phrase indicated that the parties had not yet finalised a price with any degree of certainty and so the contract could not be upheld. Similarly, in *King's Motors (Oxford) Ltd v Lax*,[18] a lease that contained an option for the tenant to accept a further lease "at such rental as may be agreed upon between the parties" was unenforceable for want of certainty. In any of these cases, if the parties had specified some objective mechanism by reference to which the price would eventually be agreed, the contract could have been upheld.

[6–12]

On the same point, the phrase "fair and reasonable price" is not a magic one. If the parties have agreed to charge a "fair and reasonable price" but there is no objective means of determining what a fair and reasonable price would be in the circumstances, the contract must fall. So in *Baird v Marks and Spencer*,[19] a term in a contract between the supermarket chain and Baird stated that Marks and Spencer would acquire garments from Baird "in quantities and at prices which in all the circumstances were reasonable". The Court of Appeal found that there was no objective means of assessing what quantities and prices were reasonable. Any attempt to do so would amount to imposing terms on the parties and so the contract was void for uncertainty. As a final point, it appears that the parties do not even have to expressly agree that they will sell at a fair and reasonable price. In an appropriate case, the courts will imply an intention to sell at a fair and reasonable price.[20]

[6–13]

The idea of a "fair and reasonable" price can be one objective guideline by which the courts may determine the price to be paid under a contract. However, the parties may themselves expressly agree on an alternative method of determining the price. For example, they may provide in the contract that the price to be paid should be a function of a given price index or that it should be determined by an independent third party valuer.[21] A reasonable mechanism of this nature will generally be accepted by the courts as establishing the price with the required degree of certainty. An example of an acceptable valuation mechanism comes from the case of *Shell v Lostock Garage*

[6–14]

---

[15] *Courtney & Fairbairn v Toulani Bros* [1975] 1 WLR 297.
[16] [1934] 2 KB 17.
[17] (1902) 18 TLR 532.
[18] [1970] 1 WLR 426.
[19] [2001] EWCA 274.
[20] See *Beer v Bowden* [1981] 1 WLR 522; *Corson v Rhuddlan Borough Council* [1989] 59 P&CR 185.
[21] *Sudbrook Trading Estates Ltd v Eggleton* [1983] 1 AC 44. See McLaughlan "Rethinking Agreements to Agree" (1998) 18 NZULR 77.

*Ltd*[22] where the parties agreed that the buyer would pay for petrol "at a price which shall be the wholesale price ruling at [the] date and place of delivery". The inclusion of an arbitration clause in the written contract may also help the court to justify enforcing an uncertain contract on the basis that the parties have already provided a means of resolving any problems caused by the incomplete agreement.[23] If the valuation mechanism provided for by the parties is not essential and if that mechanism breaks down, the court will substitute a mechanism of its own. In *Sudbrook Trading Estate v Eggleton*,[24] a lease contained an option to purchase certain land. The price was to be agreed by two valuers, one to be nominated by each party. The lessors later refused to appoint a valuer. The valuation mechanism had broken down. The House of Lords found that the contract did not fall. The valuation mechanism here was not essential. Lord Fraser held that the general intention in all contracts for the sale of land was to sell at a fair and reasonable price.[25] The two valuers, had they been appointed, would also have set a fair and reasonable price. There was no meaningful distinction between what parties ordinarily intend in such cases and what the actual parties intended in the instant case. Therefore, the Court was entitled to intervene and to decide a fair and reasonable price for the land. As against that, it is clear from *Gillatt v Sky Television*[26] that the Court will not substitute a valuation process of its own for that agreed by the parties where it is clear that the parties regarded it as essential that valuation be carried out by the specified mechanism and the parties have not attempted to use that mechanism.

[6–15]      Finally, it is important to note that if some performance of the purported contract has already taken place, the court will be reluctant to find that no contract exists. This is because, by performing the contract, the parties have indicated that they perceived a broad agreement existed between them. Lord Steyn explained in *G. Percy Trentham v Archital Luxfer*[27] that "the fact that the transaction is executed makes it easier to imply a term resolving any uncertainty, or alternatively, it may make it possible to treat a matter not finalised in negotiations as inessential". The old maxim *certum est quod certum reddi potest*[28] applies.

### Illusory Terms

[6–16]      An illusory term amounts to an empty promise. Suppose A contracts with B to supply apples to him, but the contract exempts A from all liability if he changes his mind and chooses not to supply any apples at all. The promise to supply apples is illusory: A has given with one hand and taken away with the other. A good example of this type of illusory term occurred in the Australian case of *MacRobertson Miller Airline Services v Commissioner of State Taxation*.[29] The High Court there considered a contract under

---

[22] [1977] 1 All ER 481.

[23] *Foley v Classique Coaches Ltd* [1934] 2 KB 1.

[24] Above, n 21.

[25] Lord Russell very much disputed that this was the case: "Why should it be thought that potential vendor and purchaser intended the price to be 'fair'? The former would intend the price to be high, even though 'unfairly' so. And the latter vice versa. Vendors and purchasers are normally greedy."

[26] [2000] 1 All ER 461.

[27] [1993] 1 Lloyd's Rep 25. See also *Foley v Classique Coaches Ltd* [1934] 2 KB 1.

[28] If something is capable of being made certain, it should be treated as certain.

[29] (1975) 133 CLR 125.

which an airline company promised to fly a passenger from one location to another. However, the airline reserved to itself the power to cancel any flight or ticket or booking. The Court held that the promise to fly the passenger was illusory because, although the airline seemed to be making a promise to the passenger, that promise was empty:

> "[T]he issuing airline operator does not by the terms of the ticket assume or offer to assume any obligation to carry the intending passenger ... The exemption of the ticket in this case fully occupies the whole area of possible obligation, leaving no room for the existence of a contract of carriage."

A promise will also be illusory where the promisor retains total discretion as to whether or not he will fulfil it. For instance, in *Provincial Bank of Ireland v Donnell*,[30] a contract taking security for loans was void for uncertainty because the bank retained absolute discretion as to whether the loans would be advanced at all. However, it appears that only a very wide discretion indeed will produce enough uncertainty to render the promise illusory and rob the contract of all effect. For example, in *O'Mullane v Riordan*,[31] a purchaser of land agreed to pay £1,500 per acre or such larger price as the purchaser later stipulated. The contract was upheld, because even though the purchaser retained a great deal of discretion a minimum degree of certainty was present: the purchaser would definitely pay at least £1,500 per acre. There was no suggestion that he retained discretion as to whether he would pay at all. Remember that the point here is not discretion itself. The point is the level of uncertainty that the discretion breeds. In *Donnell*, the guarantor could not be certain as to whether loans would ever be advanced, but in *O'Mullane*, the vendors knew that they would receive a minimum price. The parties, in the exercise of their contractual autonomy, are entitled to build flexibility into their agreement. They must be careful, however, to express their intentions in this regard plainly so that the court can be satisfied that an agreement is in fact present. *Lombard v Paton*[32] is illustrative of this point. This case concerned a credit agreement. It was an express term of the agreement that the credit supplier had absolute discretion to vary the interest payable provided he gave due notice to the buyer. The term built flexibility into the agreement but it did not drive the agreement over the line into uncertainty. For one thing, the power of variation was an express term of the agreement, so that the Court could see that the parties had agreed on it. Secondly, this discretion could be justified by reference to the context of the contract. Staughton LJ held that it was "part of the background, matrix or surrounding circumstances that market rates of interest are known to vary from time to time and that some variation was very likely to occur during the lifetime of this agreement".

[6–17]

## Remedies

If a term is so uncertain that it cannot be enforced, there are two main solutions available. The first is applicable where one party has already performed his half of the bargain. In this event, what has happened is that the other party is arguing that there was no contract to begin with; that any agreement was too uncertain to be enforced;

[6–18]

---

[30] (1932) 67 ILTR 142.
[31] Unreported, High Court, 20 April 1978.
[32] [1989] 1 All ER 918.

and, that, accordingly, he is not bound to do anything in return. In this event restitution[33] will be available to prevent unjust enrichment. So if A has painted B's house in exchange for the promise that B "might pay €100", A will be entitled to recover the €100. The second solution is severance. Severance means that the illusory or ambiguous term can be cut out of the contract, leaving the rest of the contract to be enforced.

## III. Incomplete Agreements

[6–19] Even if the parties have set out an agreement which is certain in all its terms, the agreement may fail to be enforced because it omits one or more essential terms altogether. As Corbin eloquently explained:[34]

"Communications that include mutual expressions of agreement may fail to consummate a contract for the reason that they are not complete, some essential terms not having been included. Frequently, agreements are arrived at piecemeal, different terms and items being discussed and agreed upon separately. As long as the parties know that there is an essential term not yet agreed on, *there is no contract;* the preliminary agreements on specific items are mere preliminary negotiations building up the terms of the final offer that may or may not be made."

[6–20] *Central Meats v Carney*[35] demonstrates the effect of failure to agree on essential terms. The agreement was for the sale of cattle. However, the fundamental matters of the number, price and quality of the cattle were not agreed upon. Therefore, the agreement was incomplete and could not be enforced as a contract. In *Dore v Stephenson*,[36] an agreement for the sale of a café was held incomplete because it did not make any provision as to the parties' rights regarding access to the premises or ownership of the foyer at the entrance to the premises. The café was on the first floor of the building and so the nature of the premises was such that agreement about access and ownership of the foyer was essential. *McGill Construction Ltd v McKeon and others*[37] is a more recent case in point. The plaintiff alleged that it had concluded an agreement to purchase the entire issued share capital of Whitefield Construction Ltd. The share capital was held by six of the defendants. Hugh McGill, a director of the plaintiff company, and Gerry Tierney, a representative of the defendants, had

---

[33] See *British Steel Corporation v Cleveland Bridge and Engineering Co* [1984] 1 All ER 504; *Folens v Minister for Education* [1984] ILRM 265.
[34] Corbin, *Corbin on Contracts* (1st ed., 1950) p.66. Emphasis added. See also *North Down Hotels v Province-Wide Filling Station* [1993] NI 261 *per* Carswell J: "Although the courts wherever possible seek to uphold rather than destroy bargains freely made, where major questions such as the ascertainment of the purchase price or the settlement of essential conditions have been left for future decision the contract is unenforceable. It is not a complete agreement capable of enforcement by the court, but merely a contract to make a contract." See also *May and Butcher v R* [1934] 2 KB 17 *per* Lord Buckmaster: "It has long been a well recognised principle of contract law than an agreement between two parties to enter into an agreement in which some critical part of the contract matter is left undetermined is no contract at all".
[35] (1944) 10 Ir Jur Rep 34.
[36] Unreported, High Court, 24 April 1980.
[37] [2004] IEHC 88.

conducted a meeting and exchanged telephone conversations about the sale. Mr McGill subsequently made a telephone offer to buy at 3.6 million euro. He contended that a binding agreement for the purchase of the share capital was concluded at that price. Finnegan P found that there was no concluded agreement, especially as the agreement involved the sale of a company that has traded. Such a sale will normally be attended by a great deal of formality and complexity: in particular, a detailed formal contract. Finnegan P explained:

> "There were many other matters yet to be agreed and resolved before a concluded agreement could exist. Both parties I am satisfied envisaged a formal agreement of the nature normally involved in the sale of the issued share capital in a company which has traded with warranties and indemnities tailored to meet the circumstances of the particular company. There was no discussion or agreement with regard to a deposit. There had been no consideration given as to how the taxation liabilities of Whitefield Construction Limited in respect of the development which it had carried out would be dealt with ... No closing date was agreed. There was no agreement in relation to the show apartment. All these matters suggest to me that there was no concluded agreement"

As might be expected, where the terms that remain to be agreed are not essential, the courts are likely to uphold the contract. In *Pagnan Sp A v Feed Products Ltd*,[38] a contract was upheld where parties, price, identity and quality of goods and terms of shipment had been agreed, even though the loading rate, demurrage and dispatch charges had not been agreed. *Parkgrange Investments v Shandon Park Mills*[39] concerned a contract for the sale of property. All of the main terms of the contract had been agreed upon but the parties had not agreed on the transfer of an insurance policy to the purchaser. The Court held that this was a peripheral matter. The contract was complete in substance and could be enforced. Whether a term is essential will normally depend on the circumstances of the individual contract. For example, in *Boyle v Lee*[40] Finlay CJ held that agreement about a deposit was essential to a contract for the sale of land because "it was too important a part of a contract for the sale of land in the large sum of £90,000". By contrast, in *Supermac's Ireland v Kateson*,[41] Hardiman J found that a deposit was not an essential term in a franchise contract that involved the sale of assets other than real property. Price is always an essential term of a contract. In *Kirwan v Price*,[42] a contract for the sale of horse fell because no price had been agreed at all. As seen above, the parties retain some power to retain flexibility as to price, provided that they make some reasonably certain provision for it. In sale of goods cases, if the parties have not agreed a price and if they have not agreed to negotiate a price at a future date, s 8(2) of the Sale of Goods Act requires the payment of a reasonable price.

[6–21]

---

[38] [1987] 2 Lloyd's Rep 601. See *De Jongh Weill v Mean Fiddler Holdings* [2003] EWCA Civ 1058.
[39] Unreported, High Court, 2 May 1991.
[40] [1992] 1 IR 555.
[41] [2001] 1 ILRM 401.
[42] [1958] Ir Jur Rep 56.

[6–22]     It appears from the Supreme Court's decision in *Supermac's Ireland v Kateson*[43] that *express* agreement on all of the essential terms of the contract is not necessary. The test as to whether there is a concluded agreement is whether "everything intended to be covered by the agreement has been either expressly or impliedly agreed". For example, a contract will generally be upheld despite the fact that the parties have failed to expressly agree on a completion date. Egan J explained in *Boyle v Lee*[44] that "where no time for performance is agreed the law implies an undertaking by each party to perform his part of the contract within a time which is reasonable having regard to the circumstances of the case." Similarly, in *Supermac's Ireland v Kateson*,[45] the Court held that where no completion date is agreed the Court may be able to imply "a term that the agreement will be completed within a reasonable time". This liberal approach is indicative of the courts' policy of finding and enforcing a contract wherever possible. Implication of terms will be dealt with in more detail in Chapter 13.[46]

## IV. Certainty and the Pre-Contractual Stage

[6–23]     An agreement to agree or an agreement to negotiate[47] is unenforceable for want of certainty and completeness. An example of an agreement to agree was that in *Little v Courage Ltd*.[48] There were suggestions in the case of implied terms that the parties would "take all reasonable steps to reach agreement" and "use their best endeavours to reach agreement" about the renewal of a business agreement between the tenant of a public house and his landlords. The Court of Appeal held that this agreement could not be enforced. In *The Scapetrade*,[49] Lloyd J said of an agreement to agree or an agreement to negotiate[50]: "It is a thing writ in water. It confers no rights or obligations of any kind." The position of such agreements in Ireland is somewhat unclear. Support for their enforcement might be taken from *Guardians of Kells Union v Smith*.[51] In that case, the plaintiff Guardians of a poor law district invited tenders for the supply of meat. The advertisement provided that a formal contract would be signed on a fixed day. The defendant supplied the winning tender. However, he refused to sign the formal contract. The Court held that the defendant had thereby broken a contract to contract, or a contract to enter into the formal contract. The plaintiffs were awarded nominal damages. On the other hand, in *Cadbury Ireland v Kerry Co-Op Creameries*,[52] Barrington J observed that a clause in an agreement was not binding because it was merely "a commitment to enter into honest negotiations". To similar effect is the

---

[43] Above, n 41.

[44] Above, n 40.

[45] Above, n 41.

[46] *Hillas v Arcos* (1932) Com Cas 23 *per* Lord Wright "[T]he court is [not] to make a contract for the parties ... except in so far as there are appropriate implications of law, as for instance, the implication of what is just and reasonable to be ascertained by the court as a matter of machinery where the contractual intention is clear but the contract is silent on some detail."

[47] Also called a "lock-in" agreement.

[48] (1995) 70 P and CR 469.

[49] [1981] 2 Lloyd's Rep 425.

[50] O'Sullivan & Hilliard, *The Law of Contract*, (OUP, 2006) 74 argue that agreements to agree are not analogous to agreements to negotiate.

[51] (1917) 52 ILTR 65.

[52] [1982] ILRM 77.

observation of Barron J in *R McD v McD*[53] that "agreements to agree subsequently" were not binding. *Bula v Tara Mines*[54] concerned the enforceability of agreements to agree in some detail. The courts considered Clause (f) of a mining lease which provided that the lessee would co-operate with the lessor to make sure that the ore would be exploited efficiently. The lessee also agreed to act reasonably in all relevant negotiations. Lynch J in the High Court stated in regard to Clause (f) that:

> "the problem of enforcing an undertaking to co-operate and to act reasonably in all the negotiations remains and might just as likely be regarded as no more than agreement to agree which is a nullity."

The major reason for not enforcing such agreements is that is difficult to predict precisely what the outcome would be if an agreement to negotiate was fulfilled. It is therefore very difficult to determine what the damages should be when such an agreement is not fulfilled. Lord Denning in *Courtney v Tolaini*[55] said that a contract to negotiate "is too uncertain to have any binding force. No court could estimate the damages because no one can tell whether the negotiations would be successful or would fall through; or if successful, what the result would be." By contrast, in *Hillas v Arcos*[56] Lord Wright contemplated that in some circumstances, damages could be calculated for breach of such agreements: **[6–24]**

> "There is then no bargain except to negotiate, and negotiations may be fruitless and end without any contract ensuing; yet even then, in strict theory, there is a contract (if there is good consideration) to negotiate, though in the event of repudiation by one party the damages may be nominal, unless a jury think that the opportunity to negotiate was of some appreciable value to the injured party."

In the discussion of certainty as to price (6–11), it was noted that a contract will not be enforced where the parties have simply agreed to agree in the future *a* price for goods to be sold. However, the contract will be enforced if the parties if the parties agree to enter into a contract to sell goods where the price, though not fixed at the date of contracting, can later be determined with sufficient certainty. The same principle applies to agreements generally: an agreement to negotiate is not enforceable, but an agreement to achieve a reasonably certain goal is. This is why so-called lock-out agreements are enforceable. "Lock-out" agreements can be contrasted with lock-in agreements. Under a "lock-in agreement" or an "agreement to negotiate" (see para 6–28) the parties agree that they will only negotiate with each other. They are "locked in" to the negotiations. Under a "lock-out" agreement, the parties agree that they will not negotiate with any third party. Third parties are "locked out" of the negotiations. Where a "lock out" agreement is time limited it amounts to an agreement to achieve a definite goal and will be enforced. For example, *Pitt v PHH Asset Management Ltd*[57] concerned an oral agreement between the parties that the vendors would not consider **[6–25]**

---

[53] [1993] ILRM 717.

[54] [1987] IR 95.

[55] [1975] 1 All ER 716.

[56] [1932] All ER 494.

[57] [1993] 4 All ER 961.

any offers from third parties if the purchasers exchanged contracts within two weeks of receiving a draft. The time limit rendered the agreement sufficiently certain to be enforced. By contrast, in *Walford v Miles*[58] the parties also entered into a lock-out agreement of unspecified duration. This agreement could not be enforced for want of certainty.

[6–26]    Similarly, the law appears to be that the courts will enforce an obligation to make reasonable efforts to achieve a definite result. In *Lambert v HTV Cymru*,[59] Morritt LJ held that the assignee of copyright in cartoon characters was bound to his agreement to use reasonable endeavours to obtain future book rights for the assignor in any subsequent dealings regarding the characters:

> "In this case, where the obligation is to use all reasonable endeavours, it is clear and sufficiently certain what it is that the contracting party is to do. The aim at which the contracting party is to direct those efforts is likewise sufficiently certain, and nonetheless so because there is a range of possible goals at which those efforts are to be directed."

[6–27]    An Irish case to the same effect is *Rooney v Byrne*,[60] in which a purchaser agreed to buy a house "subject to me getting an advance on the property". This was interpreted as creating a binding agreement under which the purchaser was bound to make reasonable efforts to secure the advance. Similarly, in *Obagi v Stanborough Developments Ltd*,[61] an agreement to use best efforts to secure planning permission was upheld as binding.

### Good Faith Obligations

[6–28]    It should be clear by now that parties negotiating at the pre-contractual stage are often quite vulnerable. In the stages before the complete acceptance of a certain offer, neither party appears to have any significant rights against the other. Mechanisms for creating such rights, such as agreements to negotiate, have been rejected by the courts. An unscrupulous party may abuse this relative freedom, for example by pulling out of negotiations for what might be considered unfair reasons. Would it be possible to impose a duty on negotiating parties to deal with one another fairly and in good faith? In *Walford v Miles*,[62] the House of Lords dealt with a lock-out agreement which lacked sufficient certainty to be enforced because it was not time-limited. The parties were negotiating the sale of a photography business. They had entered into a lock-out agreement which provided that the sellers would not negotiate with any third parties about the sale of this business. However, negotiations broke down and the sellers sold the business to someone else. Counsel argued that the agreement could be made sufficiently certain by implying a duty to negotiate in good faith as part of the contract. Lord Ackner rejected the idea of a duty to negotiate in good faith on two main grounds. The first was that any such obligation was intrinsically uncertain because it

---

[58]  [1992] 1 All ER 453.
[59]  [1998] EMLR 629.
[60]  [1933] IR 609.
[61]  [1995] 69 P and CR 573.
[62]  [1992] 2 AC 128.

would be too difficult to determine the circumstances in which the negotiating party would be entitled to call off the negotiations without falling foul of the duty to negotiate in good faith. The second ground was concerned with freedom of contract. A person is entitled to act as he pleases until he binds himself under a contract. The imposition on a party of any separate duty in the pre-contract stage runs contrary to this key principle of contract law. Lord Ackner remarked:

> "[T]he concept of a duty to carry on negotiations in good faith is inherently repugnant to the adversarial position of the parties when involved in negotiations ... How is the court to police such an agreement? A duty to negotiate in good faith is as unworkable in practice as it is inherently inconsistent with the position of the negotiating party."

However, Cumberbatch[63] provides an effective rebuttal to this argument:      [6–29]

> "At first blush it may seem odious, and a flagrant infringement of [freedom of contract] to force one party to negotiate with another. However, once it is accepted that the source of such an obligation is the serious promise of that same party, freely given in a commercial context and for good consideration, much of that objection is removed."

In the recent case of *Triatic Limited v Cork County Council*,[64] Laffoy J      [6–30] considered the possibility of the imposition of a duty to negotiate in good faith in Irish law. The plaintiffs were in negotiations with the Council. The objective of these negotiations was to achieve an agreement on terms for the development, subject to planning permission, and the acquisition by the plaintiff of a historic site called Fort Camden. If an agreement was reached, its terms would be submitted for consideration to the elected representatives of the Council. The plaintiffs argued that they had an agreement with the defendants that negotiations would continue until they would come to fruition in the form of a formal contract. Laffoy J refused to enforce this agreement for lack of certainty because *inter alia* the ultimate contract involved was such a complex one that the Court could not be expected to determine when negotiations, even on the price, had come to fruition. The plaintiffs then argued that the defendant was under a duty not to disengage from negotiations except for a good faith reason. Laffoy J rejected this argument. She expressed general approval of the reasoning of Lord Ackner in *Walford v Miles*. She then applied his first reason for refusing to adopt a duty of good faith in negotiation to the facts before her, focusing in particular on the issue of price:

> "The breach alleged is that the defendant was not entitled to disengage other than for *bona fide* and valid reasons and none such existed. But, if ... negotiations had continued, and if the parties were unable to reach consensus on the acquisition price, how could it be said that one or other party could not withdraw? If the defendant persisted in an asking price of £500,000, and the plaintiff considered that the property was worth only half that price, would

---

[63] Cumberbatch, "In Freedom's Cause: The Contract to Negotiate" (1992) 12 OJLS 586, 589.
[64] [2006] IEHC 111.

the plaintiff not have been entitled to withdraw? If there was to be a contract on the lines suggested by the plaintiff, both contracting parties would have to be locked into it. If either party withdrew because it considered the acquisition price proposed by the other to be unsatisfactory, to adopt the terminology of Lord Ackner, how could a court be expected to decide whether a proper reason existed for termination?"

[6–31]    None of this means to say that there are no circumstances in which a duty to negotiate in good faith will be binding. In the recent case of *Petromec Inc v Petroleo Brasileiro SA Petrobas*,[65] the Court held that, while such a duty will not be implied, an expressly agreed duty to negotiate in good faith will be upheld, where that express duty is sufficiently certain to overcome the vagueness objections in *Walford v Miles*. Mance LJ stated:

> "It is not irrelevant that [the good faith obligation] is an express obligation which is part of a complex agreement drafted by City of London solicitors … It would be a strong thing to declare unenforceable a clause into which the parties have deliberately and expressly entered. I have already observed that it is of comparatively narrow scope. To decide that it has 'no legal content' to use Lord Ackner's phrase would be for the law deliberately to defeat the reasonable expectations of honest men …"

[6–32]    It was important in this case that the circumstances in which the party bound by the duty was entitled to withdraw from the contract were clear, and that the cost to the innocent party of breach of this duty could be assessed with some certainty.

[6–33]    In addition, certain specific good faith obligations apply to the tendering process. English law, in the public sector at least, is that a party who invites tenders impliedly agrees to consider all the tenders fairly.[66] If he has published criteria for tenders, he must adhere to those criteria.[67] The leading case in this area is *Blackpool & Fylde Aero Club Ltd v Blackpool Borough Council*.[68] The Council owned and managed an airport. They invited seven parties, including the plaintiffs, to tender for the concession for operating pleasure flights from the airport. A number of criteria applied to the tenders. They had to be submitted in a provided, unmarked envelope which was to be submitted by 12 noon on 17 March 1983. The plaintiff adhered to all of these criteria. However, the Tender Committee ignored the plaintiff's tender. The post-box at the Town Hall had been cleared late so that the Committee assumed that the plaintiff had not delivered his tender on time. The Court of Appeal found that the Council, by imposing such complex criteria on the tenders, had implicitly promised to consider all tenders which met those criteria. Due to the negligence of their own servants they had not done so. Accordingly, the plaintiffs were entitled to damages.

---

[65] [2005] EWCA Civ 891.

[66] *Harmon CFEM Facades (UK) Ltd v Corporate Officer of the House of Commons* (1999) 67 Con LR 1.

[67] *Hughes Aircraft Systems International v Airservices Australia* (1997) 146 ALR 1.

[68] [1990] 1 WLR 1195.

# CHAPTER 7
# Intention to Create Legal Relations

## I. Introduction

> *"If people make arrangements to go for a walk or to read a book together, there is no agreement in a legal sense. Why not? Because their intention is not directed to legal consequences, but merely to extra-legal ones; no rights or duties are to be created."*[1]

Should all reciprocal agreements be enforceable as contracts? Suppose A and B **[7–01]** agree to go to the cinema together on a Saturday night. A says that he will buy the tickets if B buys him a pint afterwards. B agrees but on Saturday night he does not come to the cinema, preferring instead to stay in and watch football on the television. A and B have made an agreement. Should A be entitled to sue on foot of his agreement with his friend, B? Most of us would agree that he should not. The requirement of intention to create legal relations is a final doorkeeper in contract. It determines which agreements supported by consideration shall be covered by contract law and which shall merely be morally binding. This requirement was expressly stated for the first time in *Heilbut, Symons & Co v Buckleton*,[2] where Lord Moulton stated: "Not only the terms of such contracts but the existence of an *animus contrahendi* on the part of all parties to them must be clearly shown."[3]

This area of law has as much to do with public policy as with intention.[4] Collins **[7–02]** explains the requirement of intention to create legal relations as designed to "delineate the boundaries between the public and private spheres".[5] It is designed to keep contract out of private and domestic agreements and confine it to the commercial

---

[1] Pollock, *Principles of Contract* (1st ed, London, 1876) at p 2. Atkin LJ uses a similar example in *Balfour v Balfour* [1919] 2 KB 571.
[2] [1913] AC 30.
[3] *ibid.* at 47.
[4] McKendrick, *Contract Law: Text, Cases and Materials* (2nd ed, OUP, 2003), p 304.
[5] Collins, *The Law of Contract* (LexisNexis Butterworths, 2003), p 67.

world where it belongs. There is also a feeling that the imprimatur of contract should be reserved for only the most serious agreements. Contracts "must not be the sports of an idle hour, mere matters of pleasantry and badinage, never intended by the parties to have any serious effects whatever".[6]

## II. Intention and Presumptions

[7–03]     As always, the test for intention here is objective. Thus, the courts impute intention to the parties on the basis of external factors rather than on the workings of the parties' innermost minds. Lord Cross made this clear in *Albert v Motor Insurer's Bureau*[7]:

> "It is not necessary in order that a legally binding contract should arise that the parties should direct their minds to the question and decide in favour of a legally binding relationship. If I get a taxi and ask the driver to take me to Victoria Station it is extremely unlikely that either of us directs his mind to the question whether we are entering into a contract."

[7–04]     It is important to understand that, at this stage of proceedings, some external evidence of intent carries special weight with the law. In particular, the relationship between the parties is significant. As noted, the courts are keen to enforce agreements between commercial partners as contracts while they are reluctant to enforce agreements between friends or family members. In determining whether the parties' contract was made with intention to create legal relations, the court will weight their relationship using a device from the law of evidence—the presumption. There are two chief presumptions to be understood[8]: first, there is a presumption that commercial agreements are made with intention to create legal relations. On the other hand, agreements between friends and family members are presumed to be made without intention to create legal relations.

[7–05]     A presumption is not an absolute rule. A commercial agreement might turn out to have been made without the requisite intention. A domestic agreement might turn out to have been intended to be legally binding. The presumptions are simply the law's way of expressing that these things are not always the case. Presumptions can be "rebutted" or displaced by actual and convincing evidence showing that the instant contract is, in fact, unusual—that it is intended to be binding where ordinarily contracts of that type are not, and vice versa.

## III. Social and Domestic Agreements

[7–06]     A close family or social relationship raises a presumption of lack of intention to create legal relations. Before delving into the cases on this presumption, one must first

---

[6]  *Darymple v Darymple* (1811) 2 Hag Con 54.
[7]  [1971] 2 All ER 1345. *cf Coward v Motor Insurer's Bureau* [1963] 1 QB 259.
[8]  For evidence of a contextual approach, see *Edmonds v Lawson* [2000] QB 501. See also *Sadler v Reynolds* [2005] EWHC, which suggests that there is scope for the recognition of intermediate categories. This case concerned an agreement which was neither definitively commercial nor definitively social. The court held that the presumption of lack of intention to create legal relations applied, but it was not as heavy as the presumption applying to purely social agreements.

consider why it is employed. If the rule were that social and domestic agreements were always legally binding, the courts might be flooded with petty disputes and "the small Courts of this country would have to be multiplied one hundredfold".[9] The second, more important, reason is rooted in a libertarian idea of autonomy. It is felt that people should have the freedom to make certain types of private, personal agreements without drawing the interference of the law into their lives. The theory is that, especially where intimate relationships are concerned, we all ought to enjoy a sphere of personal liberty that should remain free from commodification by the law of contract unless there is good reason to the contrary. In *Balfour v Balfour*,[10] Atkin LJ famously wrote of agreements between husband and wife:

> "Agreements such as these are outside the realm of contracts altogether. The common law does not regulate the form of agreements between spouses. Their promises are not sealed with seals and sealing wax. The consideration that really obtains for them is the natural love and affection which counts for so little in these cold courts ... In respect of these promises, each house is a domain into which the King's writ does not seek to run, and to which his officers do not seek to be admitted."

Smith explains the *Balfour* doctrine in a way quite significantly removed from thoughts of autonomy. He says that, unlike the archetypal arms-length transaction, the family agreement is made to protect *"shared* interests".[11] It is not about self-interest but rather promotes and strengthens the core of an interdependent relationship.[12] As Atkin LJ seemed to understand in *Balfour*, in some sense, this special aspect of domestic agreements would be diminished or tainted by the encroachment of the law. To underline this point, contrast the archetypal family relationship with Macneil's description[13] of the ideal arms-length contractual encounter envisaged by the classical theory of contract law: **[7–07]**

> "These are contracts of short duration, with limited personal interactions ... They are transactions requiring a minimum of future co-operative behaviour between the parties and not requiring a sharing of benefits or burdens ... The parties view such transactions as deals free of entangling strings and they certainly expect no altruism ... The epitome of [this ideal type of contract]: two strangers coming into town from opposite directions, one walking and one riding a horse. The walker offers to buy the horse, and after a brief dickering a deal is struck in which delivery of the horse is to be made at sundown upon the handing over of $10. The two strangers expect to have nothing to do with each other between now and sundown, they expect never to see each other again thereafter, and each has as much feeling for the other as has a Viking trading with a Saxon."

---

[9] *Balfour v Balfour* [1919] 2 KB 579 *per* Atkin LJ.

[10] [1919] 2 KB 571.

[11] Smith, *Contract Theory* (OUP, 2004), p 214.

[12] *ibid.*

[13] Macneil, "Restatement (Second) of Contracts and Presentation" (1976) 60 Virginia LR 589.

[7–08]     *Balfour* demonstrates how the presumption operates. This case was about a husband and wife. Mr Balfour was leaving England to return to his employment in Ceylon. His wife was to remain at home on doctor's orders. He promised her a monthly allowance of £30. The Court refused to enforce the promise for want of intention to create legal relations. The parties were in a family relationship and, thus, lack of intention to create legal relations was automatically presumed. The wife could not show any evidence of actual intention to create legal relations which might rebut the presumption, and so it stood. *Rogers v Smith*[14] shows that the same principle can be applied to other family relationships, such as that between parent and child. *MacKey v Jones*[15] applies it to uncle and nephew. The closer the blood relationship the more readily the presumption will be raised. In fact, the High Court has said in *Leahy v Rawson*[16] that the presumption only applies to "the closest family kinships, such as parent and child and spouses". Thus, a contract between a woman and her non-marital partner's brother did not attract the presumption.

[7–09]     The courts have also applied the same principle to social agreements[17] and friendships.[18] For example, in *Hadley v Kemp*,[19] the Court raised a presumption that an agreement as to the sharing of a songwriter's royalties with the other members of his band (Spandau Ballet) was not intended to create legal relations. The decision was explained as follows:

> "The members of the band had known each other since their schooldays. They have all stressed how at the time they were a close-knit group of friends who were in company with each other constantly. They had formed themselves into a band not just for the business purpose of making money (though they had certainly wanted to do that, and rightly so) but also because they loved what they were doing."

[7–10]     It would appear that a degree of intimacy is required as between the parties in order to raise the presumption. The issue is not one of status but of closeness. So McKendrick suggests that *Balfour* probably applies to co-habiting partners as well as to married couples.[20] The situation of an estranged couple, by contrast, is much closer to that of arms-length commercial transactors and, accordingly, they are treated as such. Therefore, a contract between separated partners will not attract the presumption. So we can contrast *Balfour* with *Merritt v Merritt*.[21] As in *Balfour*, the parties were husband and wife and the agreement concerned an allowance, yet, in *Merritt*, the Court chose to enforce the agreement. *Merritt* is distinguished, however, on the grounds that the husband and wife therein were separated—they were not in a close relationship any longer and so the presumption of lack of intention to create legal

---

[14] Unreported, Supreme Court, 16 July 1970.

[15] (1959) 93 ILTR 177.

[16] Unreported, High Court, 14 January 2003.

[17] See *Lens v Devonshire Club*, *The Times*, 4 December 1914; *Simpkin v Pays* [1955] 3 All ER 10.

[18] See *Peck v Lateu* (1973) 117 SJ 185 where the court found intention to create legal relations between two women who agreed to share bingo winnings.

[19] [1999] EMLR 589.

[20] McKendrick, *Contract Law: Text, Cases and Materials* (2nd ed, OUP, 2003), p 301.

[21] [1970] 2 All ER 760.

relations could not be raised. It simply would not be sensible. As Lord Denning observed:

> "It is altogether different when the parties are not living together in amity but are separated or about to separate. They then bargain keenly. They do not rely on honourable understandings. They want everything cut and dried. It may safely be presumed that they intend to create legal relations."[22]

For the same reason, and as appears from *Courtney v Courtney*,[23] a separation agreement will not attract the presumption of lack of intention to create legal relations. **[7–11]**

It is the parties' relationship at the time of contracting which matters. That is clear from the mother-daughter case of *Jones v Padavatton*.[24] Violet Jones had agreed to maintain her daughter, Ruby, in London if she left Washington and came to England to read for the Bar. Subsequently, they varied their agreement so that Violet bought a house for Ruby, the rent from which Ruby used to maintain herself. Some time later the relationship between the two women broke down. However, the presumption of lack of intention to create legal relations stood. Fenton Atkinson LJ said: **[7–12]**

> *"At the time when the first arrangement was made*, mother and daughter were, and always had been, to use the daughter's own words, 'very close'. I am satisfied that neither party *at that time* intended to enter into a legally binding contract, either then or later when the house was bought. The daughter was prepared to trust her mother to honour her promise of support, just as the mother no doubt trusted her daughter to study for the Bar with diligence, and to get through the examinations as early as she could."

### Rebutting the Presumption

The party alleging that a family agreement was intended to be legally binding bears the onus of rebutting the presumption that it was not so intended. There is no set list of means by which the presumption of intention to remain free of legal obligations can be rebutted. However, a number of factors will be influential. It is significant that a family agreement was made in a business context. So, for example, an agreement made in connection with a family business, such as that between brothers, directors of the company in *Snelling v John G Snelling Ltd*,[25] is unlikely to fall foul of the presumption of lack of intention to create legal relations. The words used by the parties in setting out their agreement and, in particular, the level of certainty attaching to the agreement are also important. The fact that the parties have taken the time to set out their agreement with formality and precision is a factor tending to suggest that they **[7–13]**

---

[22] *ibid.* at 1213.

[23] (1923) 57 ILTR 42.

[24] [1969] 1 WLR 328.

[25] [1973] 1 QB 87. See also *Hynes v Hynes*, unreported, High Court, 21 December 1984.

intended to be legally bound.[26] On the other hand, where the agreement is expressed in vague terms, it tends to suggest that the parties did not intend to create a legally binding agreement. That much is clear from *Vaughan v Vaughan*.[27] This case concerned a couple who were no longer living in amity. They had agreed that the wife could stay in the matrimonial home. However, they had not decided how long she could stay for, or on what terms. Accordingly, their agreement was so vague in its essentials that the Court could not infer intention to create legal intentions from it.

[7–14]     There is some authority to the effect that the courts are more likely to find that the presumption of lack of intention to create legal relations has been rebutted where one party has relied on the agreement. *Parker v Clark*[28] involved two couples who were also good friends. Herbert and Jane Clark were the elder couple by some 20 years. They and Dudley and Madeline Parker agreed that if the Parkers sold their cottage, "The Thimble", and moved in with the Clarks, Herbert would leave some of his considerable estate to the Parkers on his death. Some time after the move the couples fell out and the Parkers were forced to leave the Clarks' home. They sued the Clarks for breach of contract. Could they show that the agreement was made with intention to create legal relations? Because the parties had a close social relationship at the time of contracting, the presumption was that it was not. However, the Court found that the Parkers' detrimental reliance on the agreement in leaving their home was a factor strong enough to rebut the presumption, and intention to create legal relations was thereby found.

## IV. Commercial Agreements

[7–15]     A business relationship raises a presumption that intention to create legal relations is present. Provided that there is some express agreement before the court, the party seeking to prove the existence of a contract between himself and another commercial partner has a light burden. The court presumes intention to create legal relations.[29] The burden of proof is on the party seeking to deny it and that burden, according to *Edwards v Skyways*,[30] is a heavy one.

### *Rebutting the Presumption*

[7–16]     It is, of course, possible to rebut the presumption. Again, there are a number of factors that will influence a court towards a finding that business partners did not, in fact, intend to be bound by their agreement. Certainty and formality are key factors again. A little informality will not be enough to rebut the presumption. So, in *J Evans & Son (Portsmouth) Ltd. v Andrea Merzario Ltd*,[31] a contract initiated during a "courtesy call" between long-established business partners raised the presumption of legally

---

[26] See the Canadian case of *Beaudoin v Waters* (1998) 203 AR 1 at 10 *per* Fruman J "Human emotions being somewhat predictable, people who are closely connected should take extra care to properly document their business arrangements in contemplation of the day that the romance dies, and with it, the willingness to pay."

[27] [1953] 1 QB 762 at 765. See also *Rogers v Smith*, unreported, Supreme Court, 16 July 1970.

[28] [1960] 1 WLR 286.

[29] *The Commodity Broking Co Ltd v Meehan* [1985] IR 12 at 148.

[30] [1964] 1 WLR 349 at 355.

[31] [1976] 2 All ER 930.

binding intent. However, vagueness on the essential terms of the contract tends to suggest an absence of intention to create legal relations. For example, the courts will rarely be able to find intention to create legal relations in so-called sales puffs. Thus, in *Lambert v Lewis*,[32] no contract arose from a manufacturer's statement that his product was "foolproof" and "required no maintenance" because his statements were "not intended to be, nor were they, acted on as being express warranties".[33] The classic exception, of course, is *Carlill v Carbolic Smokeball*[34] where the Smokeball company's deposit of £1000 was proof of their intention to be bound. As a matter of policy, the courts find it "undesirable to allow a commercial promoter to claim that what he has done is a mere puff, not intended to create legal relations" where he has gained commercial advantage by his actions.[35]

*Cadbury Ireland Ltd v Kerry Co-op*[36] shows how a number of such factors can operate to rebut the presumption of intention to create legal relations. The agreement was for the supply of milk from the defendant to the plaintiff. The presumption of intention to create legal relations applied because this was a commercial agreement. The presumption was bolstered by the solemnity with which the relevant part of the agreement was drafted. However, a number of other factors combined to rebut the presumption. First, the clause itself was not set out in very specific terms. Secondly, and crucially, the parties had not relied on the agreement, choosing instead to negotiate new contracts for the supply of milk. Accordingly, the presumption was rebutted. There was no intention present to create legal relations and the contract was, therefore, not binding on the parties.  [7–17]

## Contracting Out of the Presumption

If parties in a business relationship are eager that their agreement should not have contractual effect, they can, in line with the principle of freedom of contract, contract out of the presumption. It is possible for parties to a commercial agreement to exclude the presumption of intention to create legal relations. However, they must do so expressly and in the clearest possible terms. To this end, in *Rose and Frank Co v Crompton & Bros Ltd*,[37] Scrutton LJ stated that he could see:  [7–18]

> "no reason why, even in business matters, the parties should not intend to rely on each other's good faith and honour, and to exclude all idea of settling disputes by any outside intervention, with the accompanying necessity of expressing themselves so precisely that outsiders may have no difficulty in understanding what they mean".[38]

The Court found wording precise enough to rebut the presumption in *Jones v Vernon's Pools Ltd.*,[39] where a football pools coupon stated that any agreement or  [7–19]

---

[32] [1982] AC 225.
[33] [1982] AC 225 at 262.
[34] [1893] 2 QB 256.
[35] *Esso Petroleum Ltd. v Commissioners of Customs and Excise* [1976] 1 WLR 1.
[36] [1982] ILRM 77.
[37] [1923] 2 KB 261.
[38] [1923] 2 KB 261 at 288.
[39] [1938] 2 All ER 626.

transaction in respect of the pools "shall not be attended by or give rise to any legal relationship, rights, duties or consequences whatsoever or be legally enforceable or the subject of litigation". *Edwards v Skyways Ltd*[40] confirms the great strength of the presumption; where wording of such a clause is ambiguous, the courts will favour the interpretation that tends to suggest that the agreement was made with intention to create legal relations.

## V. Collective Agreements

[7–20]   Suppose a trade union negotiates an agreement with an employer on behalf of its members. Should that agreement attract a presumption that intention to create legal relations is present? In the English case of *Ford Motor Co Ltd v Amalgamated Union of Engineering and Foundry Workers*,[41] it was said that the presumption in relation to collective agreements is that they are not made with the intention to create legal relations because of the following characteristics considered typical of collective agreements:

> "Agreements such as these, composed largely of optimistic aspirations, presenting grave practical problems of enforcement and reached against a background of opinion adverse to enforceability, are in my judgment not contracts in the legal sense and are not enforceable at law. Without clear and express provisions making them amenable to legal action, they remain in the realm of undertakings binding in honour."

[7–21]   Nevertheless, Irish law takes the contrary view, tending to favour the enforcement of collective agreements via contract. So in *Ardmore Studios v Lynch*,[42] McLoughlin J suggested *obiter* that a collective agreement which is set out in a clear and specific manner will have legal effect. The Supreme Court took up this thread in *Goulding Chemicals v Bolger*.[43] Although the statements made therein are also *obiter*, they are important on two points. First, Kenny J stated that *Ford* is not binding law in Ireland. Second, the Supreme Court applied the test in *Edwards v Skyways*,[44] to the agreement. This test provides that "when an apparent agreement in relation to business relations is entered into, the onus on the party who asserts that it was not intended to have legal effect is a heavy one". For the purposes of Irish law, it seems safe to say that collective agreements can be enforced in the same manner as any other commercial agreement and attract the presumption that the intention to create legal relations is present. In *O'Rourke v Talbot Ireland*,[45] Barrington J treated a collective agreement as a commercial agreement. Similarly, in *King v Aer Lingus*[46] the Supreme Court took the view that some (though not all) of the commitments given by Aer Lingus to its employees as part of a collective agreement were binding. A problem that continues to afflict collective agreements, however, is their characteristically vague language—the majority of collective agreements will be void for uncertainty (see Chapter 6).

---

[40] [1964] 1 All ER 494.
[41] [1969] 2 All ER 481.
[42] [1965] IR 1.
[43] [1977] IR 211.
[44] [1964] 1 WLR 349.
[45] [1984] ILRM 587.
[46] Unreported, Supreme Court, 20 December 2005.

## VI. Letters of Comfort

A letter of comfort is a document designed to reassure the person to whom it is [7–22] provided about certain matters while stopping short of making any binding promise. Such a letter, by definition, is made without intention to create legal relations. Whether a particular letter amounts to a comfort letter or a contract depends on the intention of the parties rather than on some presumption as to the legal effects of the letter of comfort. *Kleinwort Benson Ltd v Malaysia Mining Corporation*[47] provides a solid example. Kleinwort Benson had agreed to lend £10 million to a subsidiary company of Malaysia Mining. Malaysia Mining refused to guarantee the loan but wrote to Kleinwort Benson on behalf of its subsidiary that "it is our policy that [our subsidiary] is at all times in a position to meet its liabilities to you under the above arrangement". This letter was taken to be nothing more than a statement of policy rather than a contractually binding undertaking. It is not clear why the Court of Appeal chose not to apply the presumption of the presence of intention to create legal relations to comfort letters given their commercial nature. In the Australian case of *Banque Brussels Lambert v Australian National Industries Limited*,[48] Rogers CJ criticised the legal position as follows:

> "There should be no room in the proper flow of commerce for some purgatory where statements made by a businessman, after hard bargaining and made to induce another business person to enter into a business transaction would, without any express statement to that effect, reside in a twilight zone of merely honourable engagement. The whole thrust of the law today is to attempt to give proper effect to commercial transactions."

---

[47] [1989] 1 All ER 785.
[48] (1989) 21 NSWLR 502.

# CHAPTER 8
# Consideration

*"Consideration is to contract law as Elvis is to rock-and-roll: the King"*[1]

## I. What is Consideration?

Compare the following two scenarios:                                    [8–01]

1.  A agrees to give B his leather coat. A does not give B the coat.
2.  A agrees to sell B his leather coat for €50. A does not give B the coat.

   In which of these scenarios is B entitled to sue A to recover the coat? An   [8–02]
agreement is present in both cases. However, a contract is more than an agreement.
One might feel that A has behaved badly in the first scenario. Arguably, he is morally
obliged to give the coat to B as agreed. However, his promise does not give rise to
any binding contractual obligations. He is said to have made a "gratuitous" or bare
promise. In the second scenario, A's promise of the coat is no longer gratuitous.
It is supported by something of value, tendered in exchange for A's promise—
B's promise of €50. A's promise is therefore legally binding. The principle of law
which says that a promise is legally enforceable where it is supported by a reciprocal

_____

[1] Gordon, "A Dialogue About the Doctrine of Consideration" (1990) 75 *Cornell Law Review* 987.

promise of something of value is called the doctrine of consideration. In *Dunlop v Selfridge*[2] Lord Dunedin adopted Pollack's metaphor of purchase and sale to explain consideration. He called consideration "the price for which the promise of the other is bought".[3]

## II. Why does the Doctrine of Consideration Exist?

[8–03] Stevens says that the requirement of consideration exists because, intuitively, the law feels that someone who has provided consideration for a promise is more deserving of relief than one who has not.[4] For example, if A has provided €250 to B in exchange for B's promise to supply him with apples and B breaks that promise, then a number of things occur. First, B has been unjustly enriched; he has been given €250 and he has provided nothing in exchange. Second, A has lost his €250. Finally, from the point of view of the wider economy, B's promise to supply apples is of a type which ought to be binding because "contracts involving an exchange of values tend to promote an increase in the public wealth".[5] Law and economics theorists argue that by promoting mutually advantageous exchange transactions such as that between A and B here, the law helps to ensure that goods and services are allocated to the use in which they are most valuable, thereby maximising the wealth in society.[6]

[8–04] There are deeper points to be made about consideration based on the interaction between the doctrine and fundamental human values. MacNeil[7] eloquently explains consideration as a mechanism for striking a balance between the selfish and altruistic aspects of human nature:

> "Man is both an entirely selfish and an entirely social creature, in that man puts the interests of his fellows ahead of his own interests at the same time that he puts the interests of his fellows ahead of his own interests at the same time that he puts his own interests first ... Two principles of behaviour are essential to the survival of such a creature: solidarity and reciprocity. Getting something back for something given neatly releases, or at least reduces, the tension in a creature desiring to be both selfish and social at the same time;

---

[2] [1915] AC 847.

[3] *ibid.* at 855. The concept of consideration began with an idea drawn from the Roman notion of a "causa", meaning the reason for a promise—what the promisor was thinking about or considering when he made the promise.

[4] Stevens, "The Contracts (Rights of Third Parties) Act 1999" (2004) 120 LQR 292 at 322.

[5] Eisenberg, "Donative Promises" (1979) 47 U Chi L Rev 1 at 3.

[6] Posner, "Gratuitous Promises in Economics and Law" (1977) 6 J Leg St 411.

[7] MacNeil, "Relational Contract Theory as Sociology" (1983) Northwestern U LR 340 at 348. MacNeil's observation mirrors that of Hobbes that "the bonds of words are too weak to bridle men's ambition, avarice, anger and other Passions": Hobbes *Leviathan* (Oxford, 1955), pp 89–90. Adam Smith's writings are also apposite here: "Whoever offers to another a bargain of any kind proposes to do this: Give me that which I want and you shall have this which you want, is the meaning of every such offer; and it is in this manner that we obtain from one another the far greater part of those good offices which we stand in need of. It is not from the benevolence of the butcher, the brewer, or the baker, that we expect our dinner, but from their regard to their own interest. We address ourselves, not to their humanity but to their self-love ...". Smith, *The Wealth of Nations* (London, 1789).

and solidarity – a belief in being able to depend on another – permits the projection of reciprocity through time."

## III. What Forms Does Consideration Take?

If A promises to give B his coat for free and later changes his mind, B does not have any recourse to the law because B has not given A something of value in the eyes of the law in exchange for A's coat. The something of value required in order to enforce a promise will often be money. For example, suppose A promises B that he will give him his dog. B gives A €100 in exchange. The €100 is consideration for A's promise of the dog. Consideration may also take the form of an act. For instance, in the last example, A *gave* his dog in consideration for B's promise of €100. Similarly, if A promises B that he will give him €200 if B paints his house, B's action in painting the house forms the consideration for A's promise and vice versa.[8] Consideration may also be provided for a promise by forbearing from doing something in return for that promise. The classic example of forbearance as consideration is the American case of *Hamer v Sidway.*[9] When William E Story was 15 years old, his uncle promised to pay him $5,000 if he would "refrain from drinking liquor, using tobacco, swearing and playing cards and billiards for money until he should become 21 years of age". The Court found that young Willie's forbearance from indulging in these vices at his uncle's request was good consideration for his uncle's promise of money. The promisee's forbearance is consideration if the promisor expressly requests it.

      Finally, consideration may take the form of a promise. For example, A promises to work for B in exchange for which B promises to pay A a regular salary. B's promise to pay A a salary is consideration for A's promise to work for B and vice versa. Such future-oriented consideration is commonly called executory consideration.

[8-05]

[8-06]

---

[8] See the American case of *Schumm v Berg* 37 Cal 2d 174, 231 P 2d 39 where a promise by a child's mother to name her unborn child after its father (Wallace if it was a boy, Wally if it was a girl) was consideration for the father's promise to support the child.

[9] 124 NY 538, 27 NE 256 (1891). Uncle Story had worked incredibly hard to raise this $5,000. The following is excerpted from a letter reprinted in the report of the case: "The first five thousand dollars that I got together cost me a heap of hard work. You would hardly believe me when I tell you that to obtain this I shoved a jack-plane many a day, butchered three or four years, then came to this city, and, after three months' perseverance, I obtained a situation in a grocery store. I opened the store early, closed late, slept in the fourth story of the building in a room 30 by 40 feet and not a human being in the building but myself. All this I done to live as cheap as I could to save something. I don't want you to take up with this kind of fare. I was here in the cholera season of '49 and '52 and the deaths averaged 80 to 125 daily, and plenty of smallpox. I wanted to go home, but Mr. Fisk, the gentleman I was working for, told me, if I left them, after it got healthy he probably would not want me. I stayed. All the money I have saved I know just how I got it. It did not come to me in any mysterious way and the reason I speak of this is that money got in this way stops longer with a fellow that gets it with hard knocks than it does when he finds it. Willie, you are twenty-one and you have many a thing to learn yet. This money you have earned much easier than I did, besides acquiring good habits at the same time, and you are quite welcome to the money. Hope you will make good use of it. I was ten long years getting this together after your age." See also *Sharon v Sharon* 68 Cal 29, 8 P 614 (1885) where a woman's desisting from "making unwelcome visits and annoying and disturbing" a man in his rooms and making "demands" on him was sufficient consideration for his promise to pay her $250 a month for a year.

## IV. Consideration need not be Adequate but it must be Sufficient

[8–07] This doctrine means that courts will not inquire into the economic value of the consideration given provided that it is of some value in the eyes of the law.[10] The value of the consideration given can be negligible or inadequate compared to the economic value of the promise for which it is given. Thus, in *Thomas v Thomas*,[11] a widow's promise to pay £1 per year was sufficient consideration for a promise that she could continue to live in a house for the rest of her life. This was the case even though, economically, that amount was vastly out of proportion with the value to the widow of occupying the house. Similarly, in *Chappell v Nestlé*,[12] the House of Lords found that a music fan's supply of 1s 6d and three chocolate bar wrappers formed sufficient consideration for Nestlé's promise to give him a copy of a "smash hit" album called "Rockin' Shoes", even though the wrappers were of negligible value to Nestlé. In *O' Keeffe v Ryanair Holdings*,[13] a woman's surrender of her anonymity and privacy together with her participation in the generation of publicity around a Ryanair promotion were good consideration for a promise to grant her unlimited travel on Ryanair routes for the rest of her life. This aspect of the doctrine of consideration is sometimes called the "peppercorn theory" since even a peppercorn can be good consideration for something far more valuable.[14] A boot or a pea or a hairpin, "be it ever so small"[15] can be consideration even for a plot of land if the parties so choose, even though it is not a reasonable price for something so valuable.

[8–08] This "hands-off" approach refers back to the notion of freedom of contract; the parties must be free to set their own price. The courts have observed that "businessmen know their own business best even when they appear to grant an indulgence".[16] However, although a contract can exist on the basis of a very small consideration, the inadequacy of that consideration may alert the court to other

---

[10] *Bolton v Madden* (1873) LR 9 QB 55 *per* Blackburn J See also *Grogan v Cooke* (1812) 7 Ball & B 234 *per* Manners LC: "If there be a fair and *bona fide* consideration the Court will not enter minutely into it and see that it is full and ample". It is salutary to note that natural love and affection are not of value in the eyes of the law in this sense. *Bret v JS* (1600) Cro Eliz 756.

[11] (1842) 2 QB 851.

[12] [1960] AC 87. "A peppercorn does not cease to be good consideration if it is established that the promisee does not like pepper and will throw away the corn", *per* Lord Somervell.

[13] [2002] 3 IR 228.

[14] W Blackstone, *Commentaries on the Laws of England* p 440 (1766): "in the case of leases, always reserving a rent, though it be but a peppercorn: and of which consideration will, in the eye of the law, convert the gift ... if not executed, into a contract"; *E Coke on Littleton* 222 (1628): "and yet if the rent were by one graine of wheat, or one seed of comyn, or one pepper corne".

[15] *Sturlyn v Albany* (1587) Cro Eliz 67.

[16] *Woodhouse AC Israel Cocoa Ltd. SA v Nigerian Produce Marketing Co Ltd.* [1972] AC 741 *per* Lord Hailsham LC "The value of a thing is what it will produce, and admits of no precise standard. It must be in its nature fluctuating, and will depend upon a thousand circumstances. One man in the disposal of his property may sell it for less than another would; he may sell it under pressure of circumstances which may induce him to sell it at a particular time." *Griffith v Spratley* (1787) 2 Cox Eq Cas 383 *per* Eyre CB; Hobbes *Leviathan* Ch 15: "The value of all things contracted for, is measured by the Appetite of the Contractors: and therefore the just value is that which they be contented to give."

factors which might suggest that the contract should not be enforced. Slight consideration often suggests some wrongdoing. For example, if the parties are of unequal bargaining power and the weaker party has received very little from the stronger in exchange for something very valuable, the contract might be considered an unconscionable bargain (see para 18–85).[17] So for instance, in *Noonan v O'Connell*,[18] valuable land was sold for fifty pence. The fifty pence was sufficient consideration for the land but its inadequacy alerted the Court to the possibility of other problems with the transaction. It turned out that the purchaser had exploited the fact that the vendor suffered from senile dementia, and accordingly, the transaction was set aside as unconscionable.

The courts, therefore, retain some power to come to the aid of a person trapped [8–09] in an unjust transaction. But that power does not come at the stage of formation of the contract. Some commentators have argued that the rule that consideration need not be adequate has had the effect of divorcing consideration from ideas of morality and justice.[19] Consideration is a mere technicality "as much a form as a seal".[20] Forms have a peculiar draw. Llewellyn complained that the technical idea of consideration blinds judges to more important factors at the heart of cases: "And the Law said, 'Let there be Promise for a Promise *or* Promise for an Act.' And that binds eyes as ancient China did a little lady's feet".[21] Forms can also conceal other factors at play in a judgment. In *Lipkin Gorman v Karpnale*,[22] for example, a solicitor stole £150,000 from his firm's account and gambled it at the Playboy club. The firm sued the club to recover the money. The club argued that it had a contract with the solicitor. It could not argue that it had a gambling contract since such were void under statute. So it argued that the gaming chips provided to the solicitor were consideration for the £150,000. A reading of *Chappell v Nestlé* (8–11) might persuade one that this argument should have held. But the Court disagreed on the basis that the chips had no value to either party. The same could have been said of the wrappers in Nestlé. So why the difference? Chen-Wishart suggests that the difference can be explained by the House of Lords' objective in *Lipkin*. Their Lordships wanted to avoid finding a contract so that the club would not be entitled to keep the money.[23] Many commentators have complained that the doctrine is easily eroded and manipulated in this way. To this end, Treitel has famously argued that the courts have a wide discretion to "invent consideration" where it is necessary to do so in the perceived interests of justice. Furmston is equally critical, calling a finding that consideration is present "an *ex post facto* rationalisation of an *a priori* decision based on considerations of the perceived morality, justice or commercial

---

[17] "If a man who meets his purchaser on equal terms, negligently sells his estate at an under value, he has no title to relief in equity. But a Court of Equity will inquire whether the parties really did meet on equal terms; and if it be found that the vendor was in distressed circumstances and that advantage was taken of that distress, it will avoid the contract.", 3 Maddock's Chan 216 *per* Leach V-C.
[18] Unreported, High Court, 10 April 1987.
[19] Compare the current doctrine with that set out by Lord Mansfield in *Hawkes v Saunders* (1782) 1 Cowp 289.
[20] *Krell v Codman*, 154 Mass 454, 456, 28 NE 578 (1891).
[21] Llewellyn, "Our Case-Law of Contract: Offer and Acceptance" (1938) 48 *Yale Law Journal* 1.
[22] [1991] 2 AC 548.
[23] Chen-Wishart, *Contract Law* (OUP, 2005), p 137.

convenience of a particular case".[24] Lord Steyn[25] confirms this as the judicial attitude to consideration. He has argued that "in recent times the courts have shown a readiness to hold that the rigidity of the doctrine of consideration must yield to practical justice and the needs of modern commerce."

## V. Consideration must not be Past

[8–10]   It is said that past consideration is no consideration.[26] *Roscorla v Thomas*[27] is the key case here. This case concerned the sale of a horse. After the contract of sale was completed, the defendant promised the plaintiff that the horse was sound and free from vice. This turned out not to be true and the plaintiff sued the defendant on the strength of his promise. Could the plaintiff succeed? What consideration had the plaintiff provided for the promise that the horse was sound? One might answer that the plaintiff had paid for the horse. However, that consideration had already been given when the promise at issue was made. It was past consideration. Therefore, the promise that the horse was sound was not binding.

[8–11]   In *Re McArdle*,[28] a woman was suing on foot of a promise made by her husband's brothers and sisters that they would repay her for certain improvements that she had made to her mother-in-law's house. The trouble was that the promise to pay had been made some time after the improvements had been carried out. Thus the improvements could not be consideration for the promise to pay; they were past consideration. Whether the sister-in-law was to be paid was a matter for "the tribunal of conscience".[29] Similarly, in *Morgan v Rainsford*,[30] improvements to a property made before a contract for reward was entered into was insufficient consideration to support that contract. As a matter of common sense, a promise to pay for something that has already been done is "a promise to pay something for nothing".[31]

[8–12]   The most important Irish case on this point is *Provincial Bank of Ireland v Donnell*.[32] The bank in this case had sued the defendant on a deed in which she had agreed to provide security for her husband's overdraft in consideration of "advances heretofore made or that might hereafter be made". The "advances heretofore made" could not be consideration for the wife's promise of security as they amounted to past consideration.

### The Exception in *Lampleigh v Brathwait*

[8–13]   The exception to the rule against past consideration is that past consideration is good where that consideration was given at the promisor's request, and it was understood

---

[24] Furmston, *Law of Contract* (14th ed, OUP, 2005), p 105.
[25] Steyn, "Contract Law: Fulfilling the Reaosnable Explanations of Honest Men" (1997) 113 LQR 433 at 437.
[26] *Hunt v Bate*, 2 Dyer 272a, 73 Eng Rep 605 (1568).
[27] (1842) 3 QB 234.
[28] [1951] Ch 669.
[29] *Mills v Wyman* 20 Mass (3 Pick) at 209–210.
[30] (1845) 8 Ir ER 299.
[31] *ibid.*
[32] (1932) 67 ILTR 142.

that payment would be forthcoming in return.[33] This much was restated in *Pao On v Lau Yiu Long*[34] as follows:

"An act done before the giving of a promise to make a payment or to confer some other benefit can sometimes be consideration for the promise. The act must have been done at the promisor's request, the parties must have understood that the act was to be remunerated either by a payment or the conferment of some other benefit, and payment, or the conferment of a benefit, must have been legally enforceable had it been promised in advance."

This exception applies in many day-to-day situations. For example, when a person goes to his GP for an appointment, they probably do not talk about payment until after the GP has completed his consultation, but the GP examines that person and diagnoses that person's difficulty at his request and there is an unspoken understanding between them that the person will pay the GP for his services. Therefore, it seems eminently reasonable that the person should be bound to pay him. How the doctrine of consideration operates here can be explained by saying that, while the person has not expressly promised to pay the doctor for his services, the promise still exists. The exception here is derived from the case of *Lampleigh v Brathwait*.[35] Anthony Lampleigh had ridden and journeyed to and from London and Newmarket at his own expense to secure a pardon for Thomas Brathwait, who had been convicted of killing a man. Brathwait had asked Lampleigh to try to secure the pardon for him. He made no mention of a reward for doing so. However, when Lampleigh succeeded, Brathwait promised him £100. When Brathwait did not deliver on his promise, Lampleigh sued. His argument was that his securing the pardon was consideration for Brathwait's promise of payment. Of course, at first glance he fell foul of the rule against past consideration—securing the pardon was to be the consideration for the promise of payment, and the pardon had already been secured before the promise of payment was ever made. However, the Court held that Brathwait's request that Lampleigh obtain the pardon carried with it an unspoken promise that his services would be paid for eventually, and Lampleigh's actions were consideration for this unspoken promise. As the Court summarised: "the promise [of payment] though it follows, yet it is not naked".[36] Obviously, if Brathwait had made clear to Lampleigh at the beginning that he would not be paying him for his trouble, or that he considered Lampleigh's act of generosity to be a friendly favour, the Court could not have found any unspoken promise. His express words would have trumped any implied pledge.

**[8–14]**

The exception in *Lampleigh v Brathwait* was applied in *Bradford v Roulston*,[37] a case in which Roulston was employed by Bradford to find a purchaser for Bradford's boat. Roulston found a purchaser for Bradford's boat, but the purchaser did not have the full purchase price. Roulston nevertheless asked Bradford to sign the bill of sale. After

**[8–15]**

---

[33] In the US see "the officious intermeddler doctrine", *Tipper v Great Lakes Chemical Co* 281 So 2d 10 (Fla 1973).

[34] [1980] AC 614.

[35] (1615) Hib 105. See also *Re Casey's Patents, Stewart v Casey* [1892] 1 Ch 104; *Kennedy v Brown* (1863) 13 CBNS 677.

[36] (1615) Hib 105.

[37] (1858) 8 IRCL 468.

Bradford had signed it, Roulston promised that he would ensure payment of the balance of the purchase price the following day. The question was whether Bradford had provided consideration for this promise by Roulston so that Roulston was contractually bound to ensure payment of the balance. Bradford argued that his signature of the bill of sale was consideration, but his signature had taken place before Roulston made his promise to ensure payment. Bradford's consideration was clearly past, and past consideration is no consideration. The next question was whether the exception in *Lampleigh v Brathwait* applied so that the signature could amount to consideration, notwithstanding that it was past. Pigot CB found that it did. Bradford had signed the bill of sale at Roulston's request, and the parties clearly intended that payment would be forthcoming at a later date. So Roulston was bound after all.

## VI. Performance of an Existing Duty

[8–16]  Pollock wrote that "Neither the promise to do a thing nor the actual doing of it will be a good consideration if it is a thing which the party is already bound to do either by the general law or by a subsisting contract with the other party."[38]

[8–17]     Is A obliged to pay a policeman who protects his business from thieves if the policeman is already bound to do as much under statute? If A promises his employee a bonus for carrying out the ordinary work for which he already receives a salary, must A keep his promise?

### Public Duties

[8–18]  Performance of a duty owed under law is not good consideration for a promise of payment. So in *Collins v Godefroy*,[39] the giving of evidence, which the plaintiff was bound by law to give in any case, was not sufficient consideration for a promise of money. The exception to this rule is that going over and above the call of a duty owed under law can be good consideration. This exception was outlined in *Glasbrook Bros v Glamorgan*[40] Here, the owners of a mine promised the police £2,200 to maintain a full-time guard at their mine during a strike. The police accepted that they had a duty to protect the mine, but it was found that this duty only extended to regular checks by a police patrol. Accordingly, by maintaining a full-time guard at the mine, they had gone over and above the call of their existing legal duty, and they had given Glasbrook Bros more than they were already entitled to under law. Therefore, they had provided good consideration for Glasbrook Bros' promise of £2,200.

[8–19]     Defining the scope of the duty is the key issue in these cases, as demonstrated by *Harris v Sheffield United FC*.[41] Here again, the football club argued that the police's provision of officers at their ground for matches was part of a pre-existing legal duty, and accordingly, could not form good consideration for a promise of payment. However, the Court found that the defendants had voluntarily scheduled their matches

---

[38] Pollock, *Principles of Contract* (9th ed, 1921), p 196.
[39] (1893) 1 B & Ad 950.
[40] [1925] AC 270.
[41] [1988] QB 77.

for Saturday afternoons when the risk of disorder was higher, and when policemen would have to be assigned to work on their rest day and, consequently, have to be paid overtime. Therefore, the provision of a police guard at these football games went beyond the scope of the police's existing duty and amounted to consideration for the promise of payment. An interesting case, also along these lines, is *Ward v Byham*.[42] Mr Byham had promised his estranged partner, Ms Ward, £1 per week maintenance if she would ensure that their daughter, who had gone to live with her, was "well looked after and happy". After some years, Byham ceased the payments and Ward sued. What consideration had Ward provided for Byham's promise? Byham argued that, under statute, Ward was already under a duty to maintain the child. It followed that she had provided no consideration for his promise of maintenance. The court found, however, that Ms Ward had promised, not only to maintain the child, but to keep her happy. Statute did not require that she keep the child happy. Thus, she had promised to go beyond her bare statutory duty, and therefore, she had provided good consideration for Byham's promise of money. The only Irish case of this type appears to be *McKerring v Minister for Agriculture*.[43] In this case, the plaintiff was a farmer who argued that he was contractually entitled to certain grant payments from the Department of Agriculture. He argued that the consideration he had provided for the promise of the grant was his compliance with regulations under the Tuberculosis and Brucellosis Eradication Scheme. The farmer was obliged to comply with some of these regulations as a matter of legal duty, and accordingly, the Department argued that his compliance could not be good consideration for the promise of money. However, compliance with others of the regulations was not a matter of legal obligation and O'Hanlon J found that, by his compliance with *these*, the farmer had provided good consideration.

## Contractual Duties Owed to the Promisor

Two main types of contract must be considered under this heading: the increasing pact [8–20] and the decreasing pact. The cases in this section are best understood in terms of two separate contracts. The typical increasing pact scenario involves an original contract followed by the increasing pact itself. Under the original contract, A owes B a certain contractual duty in exchange for which he receives a certain reward. Under the increasing pact, B promises A a greater reward than he is entitled to under the original contract if A will perform the same or a slightly modified version of the contractual duty which he is already bound to carry out under that original contract.

In a decreasing pact scenario, there are also two contracts. Usually, under the [8–21] original contract, A owes B a certain duty. For example, he may owe B a sum of money which he is bound to pay back in full. Under the decreasing pact, B promises A that he will accept a lesser performance than he is entitled to under the original contract. A is not bound to perform his end of the bargain in full anymore. For example, A may be allowed to pay back only half of the debt that he owes. The question is whether increasing and decreasing pacts are binding. What consideration is involved?

---

[42] [1956] 2 All ER 318.
[43] [1989] ILRM 82.

## Increasing Pacts: Consideration for Promises of More Money

### The Old Position

[8–22]    Until quite recently the rule was that the performance of an existing contractual duty owed to the promisor could not be good consideration for a promise of extra money. The classic case here is *Stilk v Myrick*.[44] In this case, a captain of a ship, faced with the desertion of two of his crew, promised the remaining nine sailors extra wages if they would continue to work on the ship. The promise of extra money was a variation of the sailors' contracts of employment and, therefore, required fresh consideration. The sailors were already "bound by the terms of their original contract to exert themselves to the utmost to bring the ship home", and that was what they continued to do after their two shipmates left. Accordingly, the Court held that since they had only done for their employer what he was already entitled to expect under the original contract of employment, they had not provided consideration for the promise of extra money.

[8–23]    There is a very narrow exception to the rule in *Stilk v Myrick*. *Hartley v Ponsonby*[45] suggests that the rule as to pre-existing contractual duties is susceptible to the same type of exception as the rule on pre-existing public duties. The facts in *Hartley* are very similar to those in *Stilk*. Here again, the captain of a ship had promised extra wages to his crew if they continued to work on board despite the desertion of some of their fellows. Here again, the question was whether these sailors, by remaining on board and continuing to work, had provided the fresh consideration necessary to a promise of extra money. But in *Hartley*, the Court found that the men had provided good consideration. The main distinction was that, while the crew in *Stilk* had only been two men down, the crew in *Hartley* were 17 men short so that sailing the ship post-desertion was a very different and more dangerous task than what they had contracted to do in the first place. They had done more than their employer was already entitled to under their contract of employment. They had given him extra consideration in exchange for his promise of extra payment.

### A New Exception

[8–24]    The comparatively recent case of *Williams v Roffey Bros*[46] seems to create a new exception to the rule in *Stilk v Myrick*. Williams owed Roffey Bros certain duties under a contract for carpentry work. They were hired by Roffey Bros to carry out

---

[44] (1809) 2 Camp 317.

[45] (1857) 7 E&B 872.

[46] [1991] 1 QB 1. By the 1950's, Lord Denning had begun to challenge the rule in *Stilk v Myrick*. In *Ward v Byham* [1988] QB 77, he said: "I have always thought that a promise to perform an existing duty, or the performance of it, should be regarded as good consideration". He made the same point in *Williams v Williams* [1957] 1 All ER 305, saying that the performance of an existing duty could be good consideration unless there were solid public policy reasons to the contrary. However, the rule in *Stilk v Myrick* was still hale and hearty by the judgment of Macotta J in *North Ocean Shipping Co Ltd. v Hyundai Construction Co Ltd.* [1979] QB 705.

carpentry work as part of the refurbishment of a block of flats by a certain date. Before the work was completed, it became clear that Williams would not be able to finish the work on time. Roffey Bros needed the job to be completed on time. If it were not, the owners of the block of flats would penalise them. Therefore, they offered Williams £10,300 extra if they would finish the carpentry on time. They also agreed that Williams would work on the flats one by one, allowing other tradesmen to begin work on the flats earlier than would have been the case if they had worked on a number of them at once. The work was finished on time but Roffey Bros did not pay up. The question before the Court of Appeal was whether Williams were entitled to the £10,300—whether they had provided the fresh consideration necessary to ground the promise of extra money. Applying *Stilk v Myrick*, their prospects were grim. After all, they had done nothing more than what they had originally contracted to do in finishing the job on time. Or had they? The Court of Appeal found that Williams *had* given something extra for Roffey Bros' promise of extra money. By finishing the job on time and following the new working arrangements, they had given Roffey Bros benefits as follows: Roffey Bros avoided the financial penalties which would otherwise have been imposed on them, they further avoided the inconvenience of obtaining a new carpenter to complete the job and they were able to manage their project more efficiently as a result of the new working arrangements. In addition, Williams did not exercise their entitlement to breach the existing contract which, while securing Roffey Bros a remedy in the long run, would have necessitated an expensive and inconvenient lawsuit.

Glidewell J established a principle for the future as follows:  **[8–25]**

1.  If A has entered into a contract with B to do work for or supply goods or services to B in return for payment by B, and
2.  at some stage before A has completely performed his obligation under the contract B has reason to doubt whether A will, or will be able to, complete his side of the bargain, and
3.  B thereupon promises A an additional payment in return for A's promise to perform his contractual obligations on time, and
4.  as a result of giving his promise B obtains in practice a benefit, or obviates a disbenefit, and
5.  B's promise is not given as a result of economic duress or fraud on the part of A, then
6.  the benefit to B is capable of being consideration for B's promise, so that the promise is legally binding.[47]

Furmston[48] suggests that this relaxation of the rule in *Stilk v Myrick* is an acceptance that the original rule had less to do with the doctrine of consideration and more to do with the principle that sailors ought not to be in a position to  **[8–26]**

---

[47] *ibid.* at p 15–16.
[48] Furmston, *Cheshire, Fifoot and Furmston's Law of Contract* (14th ed, Butterworths LexisNexis, 2001) at p 101.

abuse the vulnerability of their captains to procure better conditions.[49] In *Harris v Watson*,[50] a case striking in its factual similarity to *Stilk v Myrick*, Lord Kenyon noted:

> "If this action was to be supported, it would materially affect the navigation of this kingdom ... [The] rule [of maritime law] was founded on a principle of policy, for if sailors were in all events to have their wages, and in times of danger were entitled to insist on an extra charge on such a promise as this, they would in many cases suffer a ship to sink, unless the captain would pay any extravagant demand they might think proper to make."

[8–27]     However, a doctrine of economic duress in contract see para (18–15) has since been developed to cover such situations and so it no longer falls to consideration to prevent the procurement of contracts by threat.[51] Another rationalisation of the approach in *Williams v Roffey Bros* is that the courts have at last privileged fairness, justice and good business sense[52] over hard doctrine in the operation of the doctrine of consideration. By requiring entirely fresh consideration for each variation on an agreement, the courts treated each variation as a new contract rather than what it is— a readjustment of a going deal. The *Williams v Roffey Bros* tactic restores to businessmen the freedom to manage their own long-term agreements according to their own designs. It may even be argued that the law prior to *Williams v Roffey Bros* pushed consideration beyond its proper scope, so that the doctrine took a role in the regulation of contracts as well as in their formation.[53] There is, however, a more critical view. McKendrick argues[54] that the Court in *Williams v Roffey Bros* has preferred businessman's pragmatism to the important public interest in seeing that contracts are adhered to as originally negotiated.

---

[49] Our knowledge of *Stilk v Myrick* comes from two law reporters: Campbell, later the Lord Chancellor, who locates the *ratio* in the doctrine of consideration, and the less reliable Espinasse, the junior counsel in *Stilk* (Isaacs J is once reputed to have said that he did not care for Espinasse or any other ass), who says that it is a case about policy, the rule in which is aimed to prevent sailors on the high seas from extorting undeserved sums from their masters. See Luther, "Campbell, Espinasse and the Sailors: Text and Context in the Common Law" (1999) 19 *Legal Studies* 526.

[50] 170 Eng Rep 94.

[51] "Now that there is a properly developed doctrine of the avoidance of contracts on the grounds of economic duress, there is no warrant for the court to fail to recognize the existence of some consideration even though it may be insignificant": *Vantage Navigation Cpn v Suhail and Saud Bahwan Materials Ltd. (The Alev)* [1989] Lloyd's Rep 138 *per* Hobhouse J.

[52] Adams & Brownsword, "Contract, Consideration and the Critical Path" (1990) 53 MLR 536.

[53] "... the law will seek to give effect to freely accepted reciprocal undertakings. The importance of consideration is as a valuable signal that the parties intend to be bound by their agreement, rather than an end in itself". *Antons Trawling Co Ltd. v Smith* [2003] 2 NZLR 23 *per* Baragwanath J.

[54] McKendrick, *Contract Law* (6th ed., Palgrave, 2005), p 99. See also Colman J in *South Carribean Trading v Trafigura Beheer* [2004] EWHC 267.

## Decreasing Pacts: Consideration for Promises to Accept Less Money

Suppose A has made a loan of €2,000 to B. Some time into the term of the loan B [8–28] comes back to A and says that he will not be able to repay A the full sum. B says that he can pay A only €1,500 and asks for A's promise that he will accept this amount and not sue for the remaining €500. If A does so, is he bound to that promise, or can he change his mind later on and sue for the €500 that B has not repaid? Under the rule in the very old case of *Pinnel*[55] as adopted by the House of Lords in *Foakes v Beer*,[56] A is not so bound. Payment of a lesser sum on the day in satisfaction of a greater sum cannot be any satisfaction for the whole. B's promise to pay A €1,500 instead of €2,000 cannot be fresh consideration for A's promise not to sue for the €500. B already owes A the €1,500 under their original loan contract; B is not giving A anything extra by paying him money to which he is already entitled.

An Irish application of the rule in *Pinnel's Case* is found in *The Mayor,* [8–29] *Aldermen and Burgesses of the Borough of Drogheda v Rev Edward Fairclough*.[57] In that case the plaintiffs agreed to accept an annual payment of £5 6s in full satisfaction of the sum of £11 9s 8d due as rent for the lease of property by the plaintiffs to the defendants. Lefroy CJ, in finding that the plaintiffs were not bound by the new agreement, reiterated "the principle of the common law, which is, that payment merely of a lesser sum ... cannot, by the common law, be deemed to be any satisfaction whatsoever of a greater liquidated sum." Lefroy CJ, however, went on to note that: "the law will allow the payment of smaller sum to be satisfaction of a greater liquidated sum, if there be, along with the payment of the smaller sum, any collateral advantage, however small, attending the transactions".

The rule in *Pinnel's Case* can thus be circumvented if B gives A something else, [8–30] however small, along with his €1,500. For example, if in addition to the money B gives A some other item, "a hawk, a horse or a robe", B has conferred some extra benefit on A to which A was not already entitled. This will suffice to provide fresh consideration for A's promise not to sue, and A will be bound by that promise.[58] Similarly, if B pays his €1,500 early, or by a more convenient method of payment, B will have given A an extra benefit sufficient to ground A's promise not to sue.[59]

---

[55] (1602) 5 Co. Rep 117a.
[56] (1884) 9 App Cas 605.
[57] (1858) 8 ICLR 98.
[58] *Anon* (1495) YB 10 HY 7, fo 4, pl 4. "The action is brought for £20, and the concord is that he shall pay only £10, which appears to be no satisfaction for the £20; for the payment of £10 cannot be payment of £20. But if it was of a horse which was to be paid according to the concord, this would be good satisfaction, for it does not appear that the horse be worth more or less than the sum in demand." *per* Brian CJ.
[59] "So if I am bound in £20 to pay you £10 at Westminster, and you request me to pay you £5 at the day at York, and you will accept it in full satisfaction of the whole £10, it is a good satisfaction for the whole: for the expenses to pay it at York is sufficient satisfaction." *Pinnels' Case*, above, n 55.

[8–31]     Is there scope for a *Williams v Roffey Bros* "practical benefit" exception to the rule in *Pinnel's Case*? In *Foakes v Beer* Lord Blackburn observed that business people "do every day recognise and act on the ground that prompt payment of a part of their demand may be more beneficial to them than it would be to insist on their rights".[60] As the saying goes, "a bird in the hand is worth two in the bush".[61] Even Jessel MR has seen the absurdity of the rule, famously noting that

> "a creditor may accept anything in satisfaction of his debt except a less amount of money. He might take a horse, a canary or a tomtit if he chose, and that was accord and satisfaction; but, by a most extraordinary peculiarity of the English Common Law, he could not take 19s 6d in the pound".[62]

[8–32]     Yet in *Re Selectmove*,[63] the suggestion that a "practical benefit" exception might apply in a *Pinnel* scenario was brushed aside by the House of Lords.[64] In that case, the Revenue agreed that a company that owed a significant amount of income tax could pay its existing debts by instalments and pay future taxes as they fell due. Subsequently, the Revenue reneged on this agreement. The House of Lords found that they were entitled to do so since they were not bound by the agreement for want of consideration. Counsel for the company submitted that while, ostensibly, the company had done no more than promise to pay what it already owed, it had conferred additional practical benefits on the Revenue in that the Revenue was likely to recover more money under the new arrangement than if they had enforced their debt against the company. The House, loyal to the principle of *stare decisis*, rejected this argument. Furmston provides a vivid critique of the position as follows:

> "It is tempting to think of a creditor as like a villain in a Victorian melodrama, twiddling his wax moustache at the thought of foreclosing the mortgage on the heroine's ancestral home. This vision tends to obscure the fact that in real life, it is often the debtor who behaves badly, fobbing off the creditor with excuses and using every device to avoid repayment so that in the end the creditor is driven to accept less than is due. The real criticism of [the rule] is perhaps that it provides no means by which such cases can be treated differently from genuine bargains."[65]

---

[60] Above, n 56 at 622.

[61] In Canada, the New Brunswick Court of Appeal has adopted this point into law. In *Robichaud v. Casse Populaire* (1990) 69 DLR (4th) 589, Angers JA held that "it cannot be denied that a financial institution, of its own accord and knowing all the consequences of its action, entered into an agreement by which it agreed to waive the priority of a judgment in its favour in return for part payment of the debt due to it. The consideration for the Caisse Populaire was the immediate receipt of payment and the saving of time, effort and expense".

[62] *Couldery v Bartrum* (1881) 19 Ch D 394 at 399.

[63] [1995] 1 WLR 474. See also *Re C (a debtor) The Times*, 11 May 1994.

[64] By contrast, the Supreme Court of New South Wales in *Musumeci v Winadell Pty Ltd.* [1995] ALMD 1670 has been happy to hold that *Williams v Roffey Bros* applies to *Pinnel*-type cases. See also *Anangel Atlas Compania Naviera SA v Ishikawajima-Harima Heavy Industries Co Ltd. (No 2)* [1990] 2 Lloyd's Rep 526.

[65] Furmston, *op. cit.*, p 102.

Nevertheless, the inconsistency between *Pinnel* and *Williams v Roffey Bros* is clear. In both cases, something less than full performance of the contract is tendered as full performance.[66] Yet in each case, a different rule applies. **[8–33]**

For the moment, there are two further important exceptions to the rule in *Pinnel* that ought to be noted briefly. The first covers compositions with creditors. A composition occurs when a debtor faces bankruptcy. He does not have enough money to pay all of his creditors, and there is a danger that they may not be able to pay them anything at all. It is in the creditors' interest that each takes less than he is owed so that each can be sure of getting something. In this circumstance, the creditor is bound to accept a smaller sum in satisfaction of the greater sum owed to him. Thus, in *Morans v Armstrong*,[67] as part of a compromise agreement, a partner in a creditor firm was bound to his promise to accept 6s 8d in the pound on sums owed to his firm. **[8–34]**

The second exception occurs where a creditor allows a third party to pay a debtor's debts. Strictly speaking, in this circumstance, the debtor has not provided any consideration for the creditor's promise to accept a third party's payment in satisfaction of his debt. Nevertheless, the creditor's promise to accept payment from a third party is binding. In *Hirachand Punamchand v Temple*,[68] a father paid part of a debt owed by his son, intending his payment to be accepted in full satisfaction of the whole. The creditors, nevertheless, sued his son for the balance. The Court, in finding against the creditors, adopted the dictum of Willes J in *Cooke v Lister*[69] that "[i]f a stranger pays part of the debt in discharge of the whole, the debt is gone, because it would be a fraud on the stranger to proceed". **[8–35]**

## Contractual Duties Owed to a Third Party

Can A's performance of a contractual duty which he owes to B be good consideration for a promise made to him by C? This was the issue in *Shadwell v Shadwell*[70] where the *dramatis personae* were Charles Shadwell, his nephew Lancey and Lancey's wife Ellen, née Nicholl. At the time of *Shadwell*, an engagement was considered a contract to be married. So once Lancey was engaged to Ellen, he was contractually bound to marry her.[71] His uncle Charles, on hearing of the engagement, wrote to Lancey and promised to pay him £150 annually for as long as the uncle was alive or until Lancey, a new barrister, was earning 600 guineas a year. The Court held that by marrying Ellen Nicholl, even though he was already bound to do so, Lancey had provided consideration for his uncle's generous promise. Lancey's marriage was an "object of interest" to his uncle and so (perhaps unflatteringly for poor Ms Nicholl) by not leaving his fiancée at the altar, he had paid a sufficient price for his uncle's promise of an allowance. **[8–36]**

---

[66] *Musumeci v Winadell Pty Ltd.* (1994) 34 NSWLR 723.

[67] (1840) Arm Mac Og 25.

[68] [1911] 2 KB 330. See also *Lawder v Peyton* (1877) 11 IRCL 41.

[69] (1863) 13 CBNS 543 at 594, 595. See also *Welby v Drake* (1825) 1 C & P 557.

[70] (1860) 9 CBNS 159. See also *Saunders v Cramer* (1842) 5 Ir Eq R 12.

[71] Poole observes that although *Shadwell* is commonly used in support of this proposition, in fact none of the majority judgments expressly refer to Lancey's contractual obligation to his fiancée. Perhaps this case is better explained on the basis of Lancey's reliance on his uncle's promise. Poole, *Casebook on Contract Law* (7th ed., OUP, 2005), p 130.

[8–37]     *Scotson v Pegg*[72] works along the same lines. The contract at issue was that between the plaintiff and the defendant. The plaintiff had promised to deliver a cargo of coal to the defendant in consideration for the defendant's promise to unload that coal at a stated rate. However, the plaintiffs were already bound to deliver the coal to the defendant under an earlier contract with a third party, X. The Court held that the defendants benefited by the plaintiffs' adherence to their contract with X. After all, they could have chosen to breach their contract with X and pay damages rather than performing their obligations, leaving the defendant in the lurch. In not exercising the option of doing so, they paid a price for the defendant's promise to unload the coal.

[8–38]     In *Pao On v Lau Yiu Long*,[73] the Court went so far as to say that the mere promise of performing a contractual duty owed to a third party would be good consideration for a promise by a new promisor. This flexibility is remarkable when contrasting the law on pre-existing contractual duties owed to third parties with the more cautious law on pre-existing contractual duties owed to the promisor. O'Sullivan and Hilliard suggest that this difference is more easily explained in terms of policy than by reference to doctrine. In particular, the scope for duress is less in third party cases; the promisor is less likely to be influenced by a threat to breach a contract with a third party than by one to breach the contract with him.[74]

## VII. Consideration Must Move from the Plaintiff

[8–39]     In *Thomas v Thomas*,[75] Patteson J defined consideration as "something which is of some value in the eyes of the law, moving from the plaintiff".[76] The essential rule is that you cannot rely on a contract unless you have provided some consideration to support it, even if that contract was made for your benefit. An example of the rule in action is *Price v Easton*.[77] The defendant in this case had made a promise to X that he would pay certain money to the plaintiff. In consideration for that promise, X did certain work for the defendant. However, the defendant never paid the money to the plaintiff. The plaintiff, eager to get his money, attempted to sue the defendant. However, the Court rejected his claim for want of consideration.

[8–40]     Consideration was provided for the defendant's promise, but it was provided by X and not the plaintiff. So even though there was consideration, it had not moved from the plaintiff as required by the rule set out in *Thomas v Thomas*. Of course if X had wanted to sue the defendant, this problem would not have arisen. To similar effect is *McCoubray v Thompson*.[78] In that case, A had agreed to donate land to B if B would, in exchange, pay C an amount of money. When B did not pay, C could not sue him on his promise. He had not provided any consideration for that promise himself. In *Tweddle v Atkinson*,[79] Wrightman J summarised the position by noting that "no

---

[72] (1861) 6 H & N 295. See also *The Eurymedon* [1975] AC 154.

[73] Above, n 34.

[74] O'Sullivan and Hilliard, *The Law of Contract* (OUP, 2004), p 152.

[75] (1842) 2 QB 851.

[76] *ibid.* at 859.

[77] (1883) 4 B & Ad 433.

[78] (1868) 2 IRCL 226.

[79] (1861) B & S 393.

stranger to the consideration can take advantage of a contract, though made for his benefit". *Barry v Barry*[80] is an Irish case that puts an interesting spin on the *McCoubray v Thompson* scenario. In *Barry,* a farmer had two sons. The farmer, in his will, bequeathed the whole farm to one son. In exchange, that son was obliged to pay certain sums to other family members. So far, the scenario looks like *McCoubray v Thompson*, and it could be said that when the heir did not pay, his relatives could not sue as they had provided no consideration for his promise to pay them money. However, the Court reached a different conclusion. The other relatives had a legal right to challenge the will. By not challenging it, the Court found that they had provided consideration for the heir's promise to pay them money.

---

[80] (1891) 28 LR (Ir) 45.

# CHAPTER 9
# Promissory Estoppel

*Nemo potest mutare consilium suum in alterius injuriam*[1]

## I. Introduction

In the previous chapter we discussed the rules on consideration. It was said that, in    **[9–01]**
general, an agreement will not be upheld as a contract in the absence of sufficient
consideration. However, there is an important equitable[2] limitation to this rule—the
doctrine of promissory estoppel. In *Crabb v Arun District Council*,[3] Lord Denning
explained it as follows:

> "What then, are the dealings which will preclude [a man] from insisting on his
> strict legal rights? If he makes a binding contract that he will not insist on the
> strict legal position, a court of equity will hold him to his contract. Short of a
> binding contract, if he makes a promise that he will not insist upon his strict

---

[1] A maxim of Roman law that means: No one may change his plan of action to the injury of
another.

[2] The distinction between common law and equity is "historical labelling, going back to the
division in the courts, before the Supreme Court of Judicature Acts 1873–5, between the common
law courts and the Court of Chancery. To describe a rule or principle as common law was to say
that it had its historical roots in the law administered in the common law courts prior to 1873. To
describe a rule or principle as equitable was to say that it had its historical roots in the law
administered in the Court of Chancery prior to 1873. The effect of the Supreme Court of
Judicature Acts 1873–5 was to merge the common law courts and the Court of Chancery into one
Supreme Court administering both common law and equity." Burrows, "We Do This At
Common Law But This At Equity" (2002) 22(1) OJLS.

[3] [1976] Ch 179.

legal rights – then, even though that promise may be unenforceable in point of law for want of consideration or want of writing – then, *if he makes the promise knowing or intending that the other will act upon it, and he does act upon it, then again a court of equity will not allow him to go back on that promise.*"[4]

## II. The Doctrine Illustrated

[9–02] Imagine A has agreed to lend B €1,000. This is a contract supported by consideration; B's promise to pay back the €1,000 is consideration for A's promise to lend it and vice versa. Some weeks later, B comes to A and says that he can only afford to pay A €500. As demonstrated in the previous chapter, this is a pre-existing contractual duty scenario: B is trying to modify a contractual duty he already owes to A—the duty to pay A €1,000. As noted from *Pinnel* and *Foakes v Beer* (see para 8–28), even if A agrees to accept €500, he may still come back to B at a later date to claim the remaining €500. This is because A's promise to accept €500 in full satisfaction of B's larger debt is unsupported by consideration.

[9–03] Suppose now that A agrees to accept €500 from B in full satisfaction of that debt of €1,000. Some time later he changes his mind, so he sues B to recover the other €500 owed to him. B still cannot afford to pay the €500. At common law, A is perfectly entitled to sue. However, there is an equitable defence available to B under the doctrine of promissory estoppel. This doctrine operates in very limited circumstances. Before discussing it in detail, below is a list of the set of criteria for the operation of the doctrine of promissory estoppel.

| If .... | Applied to A & B |
| --- | --- |
| 1. The parties have a contract supported by consideration *and* | A and B have a contract under which A agrees to lend €1,000 to B. |
| 2. They make a new agreement to modify or discharge a duty under the pre-existing contract *and* | A agrees to accept €500 from B to discharge B's pre-existing contractual duty to pay €1,000. |
| 3. This new agreement is not supported by consideration *and* | Under *Pinnel* and *Foakes v Beer*, B has not provided any fresh consideration for this new agreement. |
| 4. This new agreement is clear and unequivocal *and* | ✓ |
| 5. The promisor intended this new agreement to be binding *and* | ✓ |
| 6. The promisor intended the promisee to rely upon it *and* | ✓ |
| 7. The promisee in fact relied upon it *and* | ✓ |

---

[4] Emphasis added.

(*Continued*)

| If .... | Applied to A & B |
|---|---|
| 8. The promisor has now attempted to act inconsistently with the agreement *and* | A is claiming the remaining €500 from B even though he promised that he would not. |
| 9. It would be inequitable to allow the promisor to act inconsistently with the agreement. <br> ....*then the promisor will not be permitted to renege on his agreement*. | B has relied on A's promise that he would not reclaim the remaining €500. <br> All nine criteria are fulfilled so A will not be permitted to recover the €500. A is estopped from claiming that B has breached his contractual obligation to pay €1,000. |

As seen from the above example, a person is estopped[5] when he is prevented from denying something. In our example, A was prevented from denying and going back on his promise to B. In law, an estoppel is a bar to a right of action—A was prevented from suing B to enforce their original contract of debt. There are many types of estoppel but a detailed consideration of all of these is properly the focus of a course in equity. This chapter concentrates solely on the fundamentals of promissory estoppel.

[9-04]

## III. Important Characteristics of Promissory Estoppel

### The Promise must be Clear and Unequivocal

The promise upon which promissory estoppel is founded must be clear and unequivocal. So, in *Folens v Minister for Education*,[6] McWilliam J said that "a definite commitment or representation" was required. The promise must clearly demonstrate two things: that the promisor intended his promise to affect the legal rights as between the parties; and that the promisor was giving up his strict legal rights against the promisee. The test here is an objective one.[7] Crucially, it is not enough that the promisor has merely failed to insist on his strict contractual rights. In *Woodhouse AC Israel Cocoa SA v Nigerian Produce Marketing*,[8] Lord Hailsham wrote:

[9-05]

---

[5] Birks explains the word "estoppel" as follows: "The word 'stop' in the middle gives a clue. The French original means 'bung' or 'stopper'. It was when it came to bottling wines that estoppels had their natural home. The law makes liberal use of binding and being bound. It is in 'obligation' and in 'liable', more obviously in 'bond'. 'Estoppel' is another version of the same metaphor. As a wine bottle is corked, so one is restricted or shut up. In short, one is bound." Birks, "Equity in the Modern Law: An Exercise in Taxonomy" (1996) *26 University of Western Australia Law Review* 1 at 21–22.

[6] [1984] ILRM 265. See also *Keegan & Roberts v Comhairle Chontae Átha Cliath*, unreported, High Court, 8 March 1981.

[7] *Bremner Handelsgesellschaft mbH v Vanden Avenne-Izegem PVBA* [1978] 2 Lloyd's Rep 99.

[8] [1972] AC 741 at 757. This requirement was confirmed by the Court of appeal in *Northstar Land Ltd v Maitland Brooks* [2006] EWCA Civ 67.

"Counsel for the appellants was asked whether he knew of any case in which an ambiguous statement had ever formed the basis of a purely promissory estoppel ... He candidly replied that he did not. I do not find this surprising, since it would really be an astonishing thing if, in the case of a genuine misunderstanding as to the meaning of an offer, the offeree could obtain by means of the doctrine of promissory estoppel something that he must fail to obtain under the conventional law of contract."

[9–06]        This requirement was applied in the recent Irish case of *Bennett Construction v Greene*.[9] The plaintiff had purchased a site from the defendants with the benefit of outline planning permission. The planning permission was based on a site layout plan which showed a drain for the disposal of sewage from the house running across a portion of land retained by the defendants. Subsequent to the completion of the sale, one of the defendants informed the plaintiff that he was not prepared to allow the drain for the disposal of the sewage to cross his land as shown on the site layout plan. The plaintiff claimed that the defendant had made a clear and unambiguous representation that the drain would cross his land and was estopped from reneging on that promise. Keane CJ found that the plaintiff had failed to establish the existence of "a clear and unambiguous promise or assurance":

"Both the attendance of the defendants' solicitor recording the first named defendant's insistence that the sewage should not be disposed of in that manner and the subsequent seeking by the plaintiff of an assurance from the first named defendant that he would be permitted so to dispose of the sewage are entirely inconsistent with any such unambiguous promise or assurance having been given by the defendants to the plaintiff before or at the time the contract was executed by the parties."

Accordingly, the defendant was not estopped.

### The Necessity of a Pre-Existing Contractual Obligation

[9–07]        Promissory estoppel cannot replace the requirement of consideration in all contractual situations. In *Combe v Combe*,[10] Lord Denning said that consideration "still remains a cardinal necessity of the formation of a contract, though not of its modification or discharge." So if C promises to give D €1,000 on Monday, and on Tuesday C changes his mind, D cannot use promissory estoppel to enforce Monday's promise. Promissory estoppel cannot substitute for consideration as one of the essential ingredients in the formation of a contract. Promissory estoppel comes into play when one party promises not to insist on the strict contractual obligations already owed to him by the other.[11]

[9–08]        This requirement goes hand in hand with the next—that promissory estoppel can only be used as a defence to an action and cannot ground an action in itself. This principle is part of Irish law under *Chartered Trust Ireland Ltd. v Thomas Healey*.[12]

---

[9] Unreported, Supreme Court, 25 February 2004.
[10] [1951] 2 KB 215.
[11] See Mee, "Lost in the Big House: Where Stands Irish Law on Equitable Estoppel?" (1998) 33 Ir Jur 187.
[12] Unreported, High Court, 10 December 1985.

However, there are indications that the Irish approach to this requirement is more relaxed than that imposed in England and Wales. The scope of promissory estoppel was expanded in Ireland when Kenny J held in *Revenue Commrs v Moroney*[13] that it would be enough if it were intended that a contract would come into existence between the parties in the future. Kenny J said:

> "In my view there is no reason in principle why the doctrine of promissory estoppel should be confined to cases where the representation related to existing contractual rights. It includes cases where there is a representation by one person to another that rights which will come into existence under a contract to be entered into will not be enforced."

It is said, therefore, that promissory estoppel raises a defensive equity to vary an existing obligation. **[9–09]**

## A Shield, Not a Sword

It is often said that promissory estoppel is best understood as "a shield and not a sword". This means that promissory estoppel can only be used as a defence, and not to create an independent cause of action where none existed apart from the estoppel.[14] In the A and B scenario above, B used promissory estoppel as a shield when A sued him on his original contractual obligation to pay €1,000. He was able to defend himself against the enforcement of that contractual obligation by reference to his new agreement with A, even though that new agreement was not supported by consideration. However, promissory estoppel cannot be used as a replacement for consideration. Indeed, in *Brikom Investments v Carr*,[15] Lord Roskill emphasised that "it would be wrong to extend the doctrine of promissory estoppel . . . to the extent of abolishing in this back-handed way the doctrine of consideration". Suppose A promised to give B a gift of a horse one morning, and by evening he had changed his mind. Would B be able to sue A to recover the horse? The answer must be "no". A's promise to B is gratuitous—it is unsupported by consideration. Furthermore, promissory estoppel is of no use to B here. He cannot sue A on the basis of promissory estoppel; to do so would be to treat the doctrine as an independent cause of action—as a sword instead of as a shield. Lord Denning explained in *Combe v Combe*[16]: **[9–10]**

> "Seeing that the principle never stands alone as giving a cause of action in itself, it can never do away with the necessity of consideration when it is an essential part of a cause of action. The doctrine is too firmly fixed to be overthrown by a side wind . . ."

---

[13] [1972] IR 372.

[14] For a more detailed consideration of this issue see McKendrick, *Contract Law* (6th ed, Palgrave, 2005), pp 113–115; and Halson, "The Offensive Limits of Promissory Estoppel" [1999] *Lloyd's Maritime and Commercial Law Quarterly* 257.

[15] [1979] QB 467.

[16] [1951] 2 KB 215.

**[9–11]**    This position remains in force in England as confirmed in the case of *Baird Textile Holdings v Marks and Spencer*.[17] The defensive approach to promissory estoppel is not followed in either Australia[18] or the United States.[19] The judgment in *In re JR*[20] (9–24) provides some limited authority for the idea that promissory estoppel may ground a cause of action in Irish law.[21] Mee has also argued that the famous Supreme Court decision in *Webb v Ireland*[22] is another example of the use of promissory estoppel as a sword.[23] However, in *Association of General Practitioners v Minister for Health*,[24] O'Hanlon J affirmed that the traditional position is also the Irish position, stating that "the doctrine of promissory estoppel cannot create any new cause of action where none existed before".

### It Must Be Inequitable to Allow Promisor to Renege on his Promise

**[9–12]**    In *Truck and Machinery Sales v Marubeni*,[25] Keane J said that a person would not be able to enforce his strict legal rights where "it would be inequitable having regard to the dealings which have taken place between the parties". For example, it may be inequitable to allow a promisor to resile from his promise where a great deal of time has passed since the promise was first made. This requirement, as seen below, is strongly related to the requirement of reliance. Ordinarily, if the promisee can demonstrate that he has changed his position in reliance on the promisor's promise, the court will find that it is inequitable or unjust to allow the promisor to renege on it. It is important to remember that the requirement of equitable conduct works both ways. It is said that "he who comes to equity must come with clean hands". So, in *D & C Builders v Rees*,[26] the defendants argued that the plaintiffs were estopped from reneging on a promise to accept a smaller sum in full satisfaction of a larger debt. The Court refused to find an estoppel because the defendants had threatened the plaintiff that, if he did not accept the reduced payment, they would not pay him at all. The defendants' own inequitable conduct destroyed their case in promissory estoppel.

## IV. The Origins of Promissory Estoppel

**[9–13]**    The seeds of promissory estoppel were sown in *Hughes v Metropolitan Railway Co.*[27] In that case, a landlord gave his tenant six months' notice requiring him to carry out certain repairs. The tenant then asked the landlord whether he would be interested in purchasing the tenant's interest in the property for £3,000. It was agreed that the six-month period would be suspended while the negotiations were carried out and would

---

[17] [2001] EWCA Civ 274.

[18] *Walton Stores v Maher* (1988) 164 CLR 387; *Commonwealth of Australia v Verwayen* (1990) 170 CLR 394; *Giumelli v Giumelli* (1999) 196 CLR 101.

[19] Restatement of Contracts (2d) s 90.

[20] [1993] ILRM 657.

[21] However, McDermott points out that the promisee was primarily relying on estoppel as a defence. McDermott, *Contract Law*, (LexisNexis, 2000), p 145.

[22] [1988] IR 353.

[23] Above, n 11 at 215.

[24] [1995] 2 ILRM 481.

[25] [1996] 1 IR 12.

[26] [1965] 3 All ER 837.

[27] (1877) 2 App Cas 439.

not start to run again until the negotiations were over. However, negotiations broke down. The landlord ignored the agreement regarding the suspension of time period for the carrying out of the repairs. When the original six months' notice had expired, he sought to forfeit the lease because the tenants had not carried out the repairs in the time initially agreed. The House of Lords held that the tenant was entitled to equitable relief against forfeiture of the lease; the agreement regarding suspension of time was upheld, notwithstanding the absence of consideration. Lord Cairns LC set out:

> "[I]f parties who have entered into definite and distinct terms involving certain legal results ... afterwards by their own act or with their own consent enter upon a course of action which has the effect of leading one of the parties to suppose that the strict rights arising under the contract will not be enforced, or will be kept in suspense, or held in abeyance, the person who otherwise might have enforced those rights will not be allowed to enforce them where it would be inequitable having regard to the dealings which have thus taken place between the parties."

The doctrine of promissory estoppel established in *Hughes* languished in **[9–14]** obscurity until it was resurrected in the judgment of Lord Denning in *Central London Property Trust v High Trees House*.[28] In this case, a landlord had leased out flats in London for £2,500 a year. The flats were sub-let by the tenants. During World War II, the tenant found it difficult to sub-let the flats. The landlord, therefore, agreed to accept £1,250 per year in full satisfaction of the tenant's obligation to pay £2,500 a year. Lord Denning considered whether, at the end of the War, the landlord could go back on his promise to accept £1,250 per year and claim the full contract price of £2,500 per year in respect of the war years. Recall that under *Pinnel* and *Foakes v Beer* the landlord would be entitled to do so—because a promise to pay a lesser sum can never amount to full satisfaction of a larger debt.

Lord Denning stated *obiter* that he would apply Lord Cairns' principle in **[9–15]** *Hughes* to the landlord's promise to reduce the rent during the War. He set out his understanding of the principle as follows: "a promise intended to be binding, intended to be acted on, and in fact acted on, is binding so far as its terms properly apply". In *Kenny v Kelly*,[29] Barron J confirmed that the principle in *High Trees* is part of Irish law. The successful applicant in this case argued that she was entitled to a place as a student at University College Dublin. The University had assured her that she had the right to defer her place at UCD until the following year. The promise was intended to be binding and intended to be acted upon. The promisee acted on it by making partial payment of her fees. Accordingly, an equity was raised in her favour and the University was estopped from going back on its promise.

---

[28] [1947] KB 130. Although this is now considered one of the great contract cases, Treitel notes that the editors of the *All England Reports* did not think it worth mentioning until 10 years after it was decided. Treitel, *Some Landmarks of Twentieth Century Contract Law* (OUP, 2002), p 30. Megarry called the decision "scarcely reportable much less epoch making" [1947] 68 LQR 278. The decision is also remarkable for being heard and decided in one day. Treitel notes that "if there was any time for reflection, it could at most have been the luncheon recess".
[29] [1988] IR 457.

**Lord Denning and Judicial Reasoning**

[9-16]    It is important to look more closely at how Lord Denning created promissory estoppel. His judgment has become a classic study in activist judicial technique. There are three key steps to his reasoning: Lord Denning's first step deals with *Jorden v Money*,[30] an established case which emphatically stated that estoppel could only apply to statements of fact and never to promises such as that in *High Trees*. In *Jorden*, the promisor had promised that he would not seek to recover a debt from the promisee. The promisee, accordingly, took on new family obligations. The Court nevertheless held that the promisor was entitled to recover the debt because a promise had to be embodied as a contract or it was nothing. *Jorden* was the cornerstone of the common law understanding of estoppel. Lord Denning, from the beginning, sets his face against received wisdom. Lord Denning deals with *Jorden* as follows: he acknowledges that his estoppel is different from that governed by *Jorden* but maintains that his estoppel has firm roots in the common law.

[9-17]    Lord Denning's second step says that those who think that estoppel begins and ends with *Jorden* are wrong. In the 50 years since *Jorden*, the courts have recognised another, broader type of estoppel at common law:

> "in which a promise was made which was intended to create legal relations and which, to the knowledge of the person making the promise, was going to be acted on by the person to whom it was made and which was in fact so acted on".[31]

[9-18]    Finally, having distinguished *Jorden* safely into the margins and mustered some support at common law for his new doctrine, Lord Denning turns to Equity. He says that *Hughes* and other cases[32] demonstrate that a promisor will not be entitled to renege on a promise intended to be binding, intended to be acted upon and, in fact, acted upon. Lord Denning now has indications of support for his doctrine from both law and equity. He then creates promissory estoppel out of these two lines of cases. He justifies this conclusion as the "natural result" of what he perceives as the substantive fusion of Law and Equity: "At this time of day ... when law and equity have been joined together for over seventy years, principles must be reconsidered in the light of their combined effect".

[9-19]    The judgment in *High Trees* reflects competition between the desire to do equity and the draw of established precedent. It is possible to level a formalist critique at Lord Denning's creative manoeuvres in *High Trees*. The formalist view involves a narrow construction of the judicial role and holds that the judicial role is declaratory rather than creative: the judge states what the law is, he does not create new law. According to formalism, the judge's job is to adhere strictly to precedent. A more flexible approach may be criticised on the basis that it breeds uncertainty and tempts judges to tailor the

---

[30] (1854) 5 HLC 185. The same principle is part of Irish law under *Munster & Leinster Bank v Croker* [1940] IR 185.

[31] However, it is important to note that Lord Denning marshals a number of little-known authorities in support of this distinction: *Fenner v Blake* [1900] 1 QB 436; *In re Wickham* (1917) 34 TLR 158; *Re William Porter & Co.* [1937] 2 All ER 361; *Buttery v Pickard* [1946] WN 25.

[32] *Birmingham and District Co v London & North Western Rly Co* (1888) 40 Ch D 268 at 286; *Salisbury v Gilmore* [1942] 2 KB 38 at 51.

law to their own personal preferences. Lord Denning in *High Trees* essentially creates a novel and controversial doctrine while attempting to stay within the boundaries of precedent. Arguably, he fails to do so. His attempt to distinguish *Jorden* has been described as tenuous.[33] More damningly, even though he clearly contemplates that *High Trees* creates an exception to the decreasing pact rule in *Foakes v Beer*, saying that "the logical consequence" of the doctrine is that "a promise to accept a smaller sum in discharge of a larger sum, if acted upon, is binding, notwithstanding the absence of consideration", he gives that case only a passing mention. He simply says, probably as an afterthought, "this aspect was not considered in *Foakes v Beer*". Lord Denning's failure to engage more fully with *Foakes* is especially surprising, considering *Foakes* was decided after *Hughes* so that there may be some doubt as to whether *Hughes* was still a "live" precedent by the time *High Trees* fell to be decided.[34] Finally, Lord Denning plays "fast and loose" with a fundamental legal distinction—that between Law and Equity. Lord Denning's assumption that the fusion of Law and Equity brought about by the Judicature Act mandates "the creation ... of a new body of law containing elements of law and equity but in character quite different from its components",[35] and his technique of reasoning from common law to equity and back again, have been criticised as breeding "some new jurisprudence conceived by accident, born by misadventure and nourished by sour but high-minded wet nurses".[36]

No one would ever mistake Lord Denning for a formalist. He famously wrote: [9–20]

"I never say I regret having to come to this conclusion but I have no option. There is always a way round. There is always an option—in my philosophy—by which justice can be done."[37]

As with many of his creations, the doctrine of promissory estoppel has the aim [9–21] of mitigating the rigours and rigidity of the common law. Promissory estoppel stretches the category of agreements, which the courts will uphold beyond those based on bargains to those grounded in good faith reliance. In his book, *The Discipline of Law*, Lord Denning made the relationship between promissory estoppel and his search for justice in contract law clear:

"[Estoppel] is a principle of justice and of equity. It comes to this: When a man, by his words or conduct, has led another to believe that he may safely act on the faith of them – and that other does act on them – he will not be allowed to go back on what he has said or done when it would be unjust or inequitable for him to do so."

Certainly, there are occasions where a strict application of the doctrine of [9–22] consideration leads to injustice. For example, in the discussion of consideration (8–31) it was noted that the rule in *Pinnel* is frequently criticised for producing unfair results and defeating reasonable commercial expectations. Perhaps, then, promissory estoppel is to be welcomed for lightening the burden on trusting promisees.

---

[33] Koffmann and McDonald, *The Law of Contract* (OUP, 2005), p 85.
[34] See Treitel's discussion of this point in Treitel, *Some Landmarks of Twentieth Century Contract Law op. cit.*, p 32.
[35] Meagher, Gummow and Lehane, *Equity, Doctrines and Remedies* (3rd ed, 1992), para 221.
[36] *ibid.*, para 225.
[37] Denning, *The Discipline of the Law* (Butterworths, 1979), p 208.

## V. Unresolved Questions about Promissory Estoppel

[9–23] Despite the clarity with which Lord Denning set out his new principle, it remains the subject of much academic debate. In some ways, the formalists have been proven right—uncertainty has followed in the wake of Lord Denning's solo run. In *Woodhouse AC Israel Coca SA v Nigerian Produce Marketing Co*,[38] Lord Hailsham observed:

> "The time may soon come when the whole sequence of cases based on promissory estoppel since the war, beginning with [*High Trees*] may need to be reviewed and reduced to a coherent body of doctrine by the courts. I do not mean to say that any are to be regarded with suspicion. But as is common with an expanding doctrine, they do raise problems of coherent exposition which have never been systematically explored."

### Must the Promisee Rely on the Promise to his Detriment?

[9–24] There are some English *dicta* to suggest that the promisee must have relied to his detriment on the promisor's so that he will be harmed if the promise is revoked.[39] Arguably, in *Hughes v Metropolitan Railway*, the tenants relied on the landlord's promise to their detriment because, in reliance on that promise, they lost time that they could have spent in repairing the property. In Ireland, detriment will also seem to be required under the decision in *Re JR*.[40] This was a case in which the promisor had asked the promisee to come live with him, assuring her that she would be looked after and would have a home for the rest of her life. The promisee proved detrimental reliance on the promisor's assurance that she would be sure of a house for the rest of her life because she left her own home and moved in with him. Arguably, the Supreme Court has settled the point in more recent years. In *Daly v Minister for the Marine*,[41] Fennelly J set out that, as Kenny J observed in *Doran v Thompson*,[42] Irish law requires the promisee to show not merely reliance, but detrimental reliance. Fennelly J rejected a more flexible approach to the detriment requirement and stressed, in particular, the need to keep promissory estoppel within its proper boundaries:

> "It is the fact that it would be unconscionable for one party to be permitted to depart from a position, statement or representation upon which the other party has acted to his detriment that justifies the courts in intervening to restrain him from doing so. If the recipient of a promise or representation is to be dispensed from any obligation to demonstrate reliance, the doctrine would be more than exceptionally generous. It would be a virtually ungovernable force ...".

[9–25] However, the more correct view, and indeed the view which Lord Denning himself took in *Alan v El Nasr*[43] and again in *Brikom Investments v Carr*,[44] seems to be that the promise need only have altered his position in reliance on the promise, whether

---

[38] [1972] AC 741 at 757.
[39] See *The Scapetrade* [1983] 1 All ER 301; *Lowe v Lombank* [1960] 1 WLR 196 *per* Carswell J.
[40] [1993] ILRM 657; See also *Industrial Yarns Ltd. v Greene* [1948] ILRM 15.
[41] [2001] 3 IR 513.
[42] [1978] IR 223.
[43] [1972] 2 QB 189.
[44] [1979] QB 467.

to his benefit or to his detriment. In *High Trees*, for example, the elements of promissory estoppel were made out because the tenants had changed their position in that they paid less rent. However, they could not reasonably be said to have suffered any detriment.[45] In *The Post Chaser*,[46] Robert Goff J explained the nature of the reliance required in terms of the requirement of inequitable consequences.[47] The promisee may have incurred a detriment or received a benefit, yet it may be inequitable to allow the promisor to renege on his promise:

> "The fundamental principle is ... that the representor will not be allowed to enforce his rights 'where it would be inequitable having regard to the dealings which have thus taken place between the parties'. To establish such inequity, it is not necessary to show detriment; indeed, the representee may have benefited from the representation, and yet it may be inequitable, at least without reasonable notice, for the representor to enforce his legal rights."

## What is the Effect of Promissory Estoppel?

Does promissory estoppel have extinctive or merely suspensive effect? Does it render a [9–26] promise irrevocable or does it merely temporarily prevent the promisor from revoking his promise, for example until he has given the promisee adequate notice of his intention to revoke? It is interesting to note that in *Hughes*, the landlord was entitled to reactivate the six-month repair period once he had given his tenants adequate notice. In *Tool Metal Manufacturing v Tungsten Electric Co Ltd*,[48] the respondents were contractually bound to pay royalties to the appellants. They were also bound to pay compensation if they manufactured more material than was permitted under the contract. The appellants agreed to suspend their right to compensation. They then revoked this agreement. The Court held that they were estopped from doing so unless they gave adequate notice to the respondent. In *Emmanual Ayodeji v RT Briscoe*,[49] Lord Hodson stated that a promise is never set in stone as long as the promisee can resume his original position. A similar position was adopted in the High Court in *Association of General Practitioners v Minister for Health*.[50] O'Hanlon J said that as long as it was possible for the promisee to resume his original position, then the promisor may revoke his promise, provided he allows the promisee a reasonable amount of time to resume that position.

---

[45] Thompson, "Estoppel and Change of Position" (2000) Conv and Prop Law 548.

[46] [1982] 1 All ER 19 at 26–27. See similarly Mee's observation that if "one interprets acting to one's 'detriment' to mean conduct which would make it unconscionable for the representor to withdraw the representation, then this difference seems to disappear"; Mee, *op. cit.* at 201.

[47] To similar effect is *Gillet v Holt* [2000] 2 All ER 289: "The detriment need not consist of the expenditure of money or other quantifiable financial detriment, so long as it is something substantial. The requirement must be approached as part of a broad inquiry as to whether repudiation of an assurance is or is not unconscionable in all the circumstances."

[48] [1955] 1 WLR 761.

[49] [1964] 3 All ER 556.

[50] [1995] 2 ILRM 481.

# CHAPTER 10
# Privity of Contract

## I. Introduction

The doctrine of privity of contract governs who may sue and who may be sued on **[10–01]** the basis of a contract. Just as the law on remoteness of damages prescribes the range of harms for which a breaching party may be held liable, so the doctrine of privity prescribes to whom he may be held liable. *Price v Easton*,[1] a classic case on privity of contract, concerned an agreement between Easton and X. In Chapter 8 on consideration, the ruling in this case was explained on the basis of the rule that consideration must move from the plaintiff (8–40). Here are the facts again. X promised to do certain work for Easton, who in return promised to pay Price £19. X did the work but Easton never paid Price. Price then sued Easton for the £19, and lost. This was because, amongst other things, his case fell foul of the doctrine of privity of contract. As Price was a mere third party to the contract, he had no right to sue on it.

We can explain the doctrine of privity by saying that a contract is "private" **[10–02]** to its parties. Collins says that: "all contracts resemble a marriage in so far as no third party can claim the right to share the intimate relations established between the spouses".[2] A contract only affects its parties; only those privy to the contract can sue on it, and only they are bound by it. A third party, or "stranger", to the contract cannot enforce it, and neither can he find it enforced against him. So Monahan CJ in *Murphy v Bower*[3] says that: "where the foundation of the right of action is rested upon contract, no one can maintain an action who is not a party to the contract."

---

[1] [1883] 110 ER 518.
[2] Collins, *The Law of Contract* (LexisNexis, 2003) 314.
[3] (1868) 2 IRCL 506.

**[10–03]**     In *McCoubray v Thompson*[4], A had agreed to donate land to B if B would, in exchange, pay C an amount of money. The contract was between A and B. As C was not privy to the contract he could not sue upon it. A famous English case along the same lines, *Tweddle v Atkinson*,[5] concerned an agreement between William Tweddle's father John and his prospective father-in-law, Mr Guy. In view of the upcoming marriage, father and father-in-law had a contract that they would pay William £100 and £200 respectively. The marriage took place as planned, but Mr Guy died before paying his £200. William accordingly sued Atkinson, the executor of Mr Guy's will, for that £200. Naturally, he lost for want of privity; he was attempting to sue on foot of a contract to which only the father and the father-in-law were parties. He himself was a stranger to the contract.[6] *Clitheroe v Simpson*[7] is a similar Irish case which concerned a contract between a father and his son. They agreed that the father would transfer property to the son and that the son in return would pay his sister a sum of money. The sister's estate was not entitled to sue on that contract, as the sister was a stranger to the contract, notwithstanding that she stood to gain from it.

**[10–04]**     The doctrine finds its modern statement in the complex case of *Dunlop v Selfridge*.[8] There were three main actors and two contracts in this case.

Dunlop, a middle-man distributor, and Selfridges were the actors. The first contract (C1) was a contract for the sale of tyres between Dunlop and the distributor. There were two important promises in C1. First, the distributor agreed that he would not resell the tyres at undervalue. Secondly, he agreed that if he sold them to a trade buyer, he would impose that same price clause on the buyer. The second contract (C2) was a contract for the sale of the tyres between the distributor and Selfridges, a trade buyer. The distributor sold the tyres at an appropriate price. By way of fulfilling his second promise in C1, the distributor imposed an important condition in C2: that Selfridges would pay Dunlop a £5 penalty for every tyre sold at undervalue. Now, Selfridges repeatedly sold tyres at inappropriately low prices and, as a result, Dunlop eventually sued Selfridges. Why would Dunlop's action fail? Obviously, C1 and C2 both contained clauses preventing the resale of the tyres at undervalue. But neither C1 nor C2 could ground an action between Dunlop and Selfridge. There was no contractual nexus between Dunlop and Selfridge. Selfridge could not be sued on C1 for want of privity; they were not a party to it. And since Dunlop was not a party to C2 they could not sue on it. Selfridges had slipped through the cracks of privity. Viscount Haldine LC famously said:

---

[4] (1868) 2 IRCL 226.

[5] (1861) 1 B & S 393.

[6] "Here my hearty,/ We find you're not the proper party;/ Your father made the pact, 'Dog on it'/ And he's the one to sue upon it./To this agreement you're a stranger,/A puppy dog locked in a manger/ Although it benefited you,/John Tweddle, he alone can sue". Russell, "Tweddle vs. Atkinson" in Fletcher & Russell, *Crustula Juris*, (Carswell) 49.

[7] (1879) 4 LR (Ir) 59.

[8] *Dunlop Pneumatic Tyre Co. Ltd v Selfridge & Co. Ltd* [1915] AC 847.

"My Lords, in the law of England certain principles are fundamental. One is that only a person who is party to a contract can sue on it. Our law knows nothing of a *jus quesitum tertio* arising by way of contract."

A key Irish case on privity is *Murphy v Bower*.[9] Again, there were two contracts here. The first was between the plaintiff railway contractors and a railway company: this was a construction contract. The second was a contract between the railway company and its employee, Bower, under which Bower was employed as an engineer to supervise and certify the railway contractor's work. There was no contract between Bower and the railway contractors. When Bower refused to issue certificates, the railway contractors sued Bower. The action failed for want of privity. There was no contract between Bower and the railway contractors. *MacKey v Jones*[10] is also an important Irish case on privity. The plaintiff was a boy of 14. The boy's uncle had promised his mother that if the boy came to live with him and work on his farm he would leave the farm to the boy in his will. The boy was unable to enforce the contract for want of privity: the contract to be enforced was between his uncle and his mother.

[10–05]

## II. Why the Doctrine of Privity?

The first and most basic justification for the doctrine of privity is a "floodgates" argument. If there were no privity rule at all, then anybody could potentially enforce any contract, regardless of whether they had a legitimate interest in doing so. Indeterminate liability, it is argued, would generate an unwieldy mass of litigation. The second justification for the doctrine is rooted in contractual autonomy: it would be unjust to bind a person into a contract without their consent, and equally, it would be wrong to render them contractually liable to strangers, perhaps an infinite pool of strangers, against their wishes. Thus in *Choate, Hall & Stewart v SCA Services Inc*,[11] an American court called the privity rule a reflection of "simple neighbourly society" under which reasonable people would not want to involve another party to their contract in litigation with a stranger. In addition, parties to a contract should be free to modify and vary that contract if they choose, without seeking leave from any third party. As against this point, in the important Australian case of *Trident General Insurance Co Ltd v McNiece Proprietary Ltd*,[12] Mason CJ suggested that it is possible to balance this concern for contractual freedom with the rights of third parties. His reasoning is worth quoting at length:

[10–06]

"The recognition of an unqualified entitlement in a third party to sue on the contract would severely circumscribe the freedom of action of the parties,

---

[9] Above, n 3.
[10] (1958) 93 ILTR 177.
[11] (1979) 378 Mass 535, 543.
[12] (1988) 165 CLR 107.

particularly the promisee. He may rescind or modify the contract with the assent of the promisor, arrive at a compromise or assign his contractual rights. He may even modify the contract so that he diverts to himself the benefit initially intended for the third party. Professor Corbin suggested that any entitlement in the third party to enforce the provision in his favour would necessarily exist at the expense of the rights, privileges and liberties that the contracting parties enjoy under the common law rules ... But this does not entirely follow. The entitlement of the third party to enforce the provision in his favour can be subordinated to the right of the contracting party to rescind or modify the contract, in which event the third party would lose his rights except in so far as he relied on the promise to his detriment."

[10–07]  In other words, a system of hierarchy of rights is preferable to total non-recognition of third party rights. Thirdly, there is also what might be called an equitable justification for the rule. It might be asked why a person who has contributed nothing to the contract should have the privilege of enforcing it. There has been no exchange, no bargain. As the doctrine of consideration shows, the law will not enforce gratuitous contracts. In addition, the doctrine of privity prevents an imbalance of contractual rights as between parties and a third party: why should a third party be permitted the benefit of suing on a contract when he cannot in turn be sued? In *Tweddle* Crompton J observed that:

> "It would be a monstrous proposition to say that a person was a party to the contract for the purposes of suing upon it for his own advantage, and not a party to it for the purpose of being sued."

## III. Problems with Privity

[10–08]  The doctrine of privity has been described judicially as "a blot on our law and most unjust"[13] and as "an anachronistic shortcoming".[14] The trouble with the doctrine of privity is that it does not cater for the everyday reality of commercial transactions. Parties frequently need to make contracts for the benefit of others. It is abundantly clear, however, that if the contract is breached, the third party beneficiary will take no benefit and cannot sue successfully by himself. He will have to seek the assistance of the non-breaching party to the contract. The third party cannot obtain an order compelling the non-breaching party to sue the breaching party. He must rely on the non-breaching party's sense of altruism. The rule thus produces inefficient and unnecessary chains of contract claims. Even if the non-breaching party is willing to sue, practical problems arise. First, he can only sue for the, usually minimal, loss which he has himself suffered by the breach, not for the benefit which the third party stood to gain. There are only two important exceptions to this principle, developed, as Lord Steyn observes, "to provide a remedy where no other would be available to a person sustaining loss which under a rational legal system ought to be compensated by the person who has caused it".[15]

---

[13] *Forster v Silvermere Golf and Equestrian Centre* (1981) 125 Sol Jo 397.
[14] *Swain v Law Society* [1983] 1 AC 598.
[15] *Darlington Borough Council v Wiltshire Northern Ltd* [1995] 1 WLR 68.

The first applies where a person contracts for a "family holiday" (or some similar contract such as booking a table for a party or a taxi for a group).[16] This category of contracts might be referred to as "quasi-agency" categories in domestic or social settings. The party to the contract is not recovering for his family member's individual distress and upset but for his "loss of amenity". He recovers damages for *his* loss of satisfaction, enjoyment and peace of mind arising from the breaching party's failure to confer the agreed benefit (the enjoyable holiday) on the third parties (his family). It would appear that if the party recovers damages for *his* loss, then the damages are *his*. However, there is some authority to the effect that the party holds those damages as money "had and received for the use of the third party". The third party can recover that money from him by legal action if he declines to hand it over.[17]

[10–09]

The second exception applies to contracts for the sale of goods or property where it is in the contemplation of the parties that the buyer will not be the end user of the property, but will, in turn, sell it to a third party. These are cases in which it could be foreseen at the time of contracting[18] that the damage caused by any breach would be suffered not by the original contracting party, but by the end user. If the buyer resells the property before it is discovered that the seller has been guilty of breach of contract (for example, by supplying defective goods) the buyer is still entitled to recover damages from the seller.[19] The buyer has suffered no loss because, for example, he has sold on the defective goods. The person who has suffered the loss is the third party, who is left, for example, with worthless goods on his hands. In this instance, the buyer holds the damages on trust on behalf of the subsequent third party purchaser.[20] However, it is important to note that this exception only applies where there is no other direct remedy available to the third party.[21]

[10–10]

As an alternative to damages, the third party may be able to persuade the non-breaching party to sue for specific performance—an order compelling the breaching party to carry out his side of the bargain. A case in point is *Beswick v Beswick*,[22] which concerned a widow who wished to sue on a contract between her deceased husband and his nephew. The Court held that, under the doctrine of privity of contract, if she sued her nephew in her personal capacity she would lose. Luckily, she was in a position such that the non-breaching party could sue her nephew for specific performance of his contractual obligation. By suing as administratrix of her late husband's estate, in *his* personal capacity, she was able to sue to have the contract carried out. Counsel for the

[10–11]

---

[16] *Jackson v Horizon Holidays Ltd* [1975] 1 WLR 1468, approved in *Woodar Investments Ltd v Wimpey* [1980] 1 WLR 277. Contrast the alternative view of Lord Denning in *Jackson*: "I consider it to be an established rule of law that where a contract is made with A for the benefit of B, A cannot sue on the contract for the benefit of B, and recover all that B could have recovered if the contract had been made with B himself".

[17] *Jackson v Horizon Holidays* [1975] WLR 1468.

[18] *Rolls-Royce Power Engineering plc v Ricardo Consulting Engineers Ltd* [2003] EWHC 2871.

[19] *Linden Garden Trust v Lenesta Sludge Disposals* [1994] AC 85; *Darlington Borough Council v Wiltshire Northern Ltd*, above, n 15.

[20] *Darlington Borough Council v Wiltshire Northern Ltd*, above, n 15.

[21] *Alfred McAlpine Construction Ltd v Panatown Ltd* [2001] 1 AC 518. For further analysis of this exception see Poole, *Textbook on Contract Law* (Oxford University Press, 2006) 459–463.

[22] [1968] AC 58. See also *Crow v Rogers* (1724) 1 Str 592, *Mackey v Jones* (1959) 93 ILTR 177.

nephew argued that the widow should not be able to proceed in this manner as the estate had suffered no loss by his breach of the contract. However, Lord Reid responded thus:

> "Why should the estate be barred from exercising its full contractual rights merely because in doing so it secures justice for the widow who, by a mechanical defect of our law, is unable to assert her own rights? Such a principle would be repugnant to justice and fulfil no other object than that of aiding the wrongdoer. I can find no ground on which such a principle should exist."

[10–12]     That said, the remedy of specific performance is an equitable one and is only awarded at the judge's discretion. The complexity of performance involved in a three party scenario may persuade a judge to exercise his discretion against granting the order. This is also the case where the contract sought to be performed is a contract of personal service: the courts view orders compelling a party to provide a personal service to another as akin to contracts of slavery. Moreover, specific performance is useful where the breaching party refuses to perform at all but is of little use where the third party requires compensation for defective performance.

[10–13]     The overall effect is that, as *Price v Easton* and *Dunlop v Selfridge* demonstrate, the doctrine of privity can facilitate a party in flouting the terms of a contract unpunished, even where the other party has performed his side of the bargain in good faith. Privity also creates a black hole into which the rights of third parties to a remedy disappear. In *Dunlop* itself, Lord Dunedin noted that the doctrine of privity makes it "possible for a person to snap his fingers at a bargain deliberately made, a bargain not in itself unfair, and which the person seeking to enforce it has a legitimate interest to enforce". Unjust enrichment may occur where the defaulting party takes the benefit of the other's performance, and then does not perform his own obligations in return. It is important to remember, also, that the third party may know of the existence of the contract and may have justifiably incurred expenditure in reliance on it so that he suffers, not only disappointment when the contract is not performed, but finds himself out of pocket.

[10–14]     A further point is that parties' attempts to negotiate the doctrine of privity have bred complexity in the law and this has, in turn, made the process of contracting a lengthy and costly one. The construction industry is a case in point. The construction industry in Ireland is no longer characterised by large companies that handle the whole building process from beginning to end. Instead, contract managers, who divide the project between a large team of sub-contractors, are the norm.[23] As a result of the privity rule, none of these sub-contractors are bound to each other, or to the subsequent owners and tenants of the building. The construction industry has developed an armoury of complex standard form agreements to cope with this problem. The complexity of these manoeuvres means that it is often difficult to outline the rights of interested parties in a clear fashion. In addition, the transaction costs associated with drafting a comprehensive network of documents are high.

---

[23] LRC CP 40-2006, 21–24.

Finally, and most importantly, *Tweddle* shows that the doctrine can sometimes frustrate a party's intentions; for example, Tweddle's father-in-law wanted him to have the money promised but this was not possible. Indeed, privity can allow the defaulting party to unilaterally alter the effect of the contract by ignoring his contractual obligations to the third party. This final point seems to answer the argument made in favour of the doctrine of privity that it safeguards the parties' autonomy. Why should the parties' autonomy not be respected when they expressly agree to extend their contractual liability to cover a third party? Certainly, the parties may take advantage of the exceptions to the doctrine of privity but these are complex and often counter-intuitive: it is unlikely that they serve the layman's need to give life to his contractual intention.

[10–15]

The judiciary are not ignorant of these arguments. In *Darlington Borough Council v Wiltshire Northern*,[24] Lord Steyn wrote forcefully:

[10–16]

> "The case for recognising a contract for the benefit of a third party is simple and straightforward. The autonomy of the will of the parties should be respected. The law of contract should give effect to the reasonable expectations of contracting parties. Principle certainly requires that a burden should not be imposed on a third party without his consent. But there is no doctrinal, logical or policy reason why the law should deny effectiveness to a contract for the benefit of a third party where that is the expressed intention of the parties. Moreover, often the parties, and particularly third parties, organise their affairs on the faith of the contract. It is therefore unjust to deny effectiveness to such a contract."

However, although aware of the doctrine's shortcomings, the judiciary are also cognisant of what is perceived as a great weight of precedent in its favour, so significant that "[w]e must uphold it until it is altered".[25] The trouble with the doctrine of privity, however, is that it appears to have a far less illustrious precedential pedigree than is often claimed for it. Lord Reid wrote in *Tomlinson v Hepburn*[26]:

[10–17]

> "No doubt the principle preventing *jus quesitum tertio* has been firmly established for at least half a century. But it does not appear to me to be a primeval or necessary principle of the law of England."

Flannigan supports this conclusion in a leading article[27] in which he observes that privity's precedential roots are not as deep as traditionally asserted. Lord Steyn has described the doctrine as having a "suspect" genesis.[28] Some of the older decisions, in particular *Bourne v Mason*,[29] accepted the proposition that a stranger to the consideration could take advantage of a contract made for his benefit. Little wonder then that Toohey J in the Australian case *Trident General Insurance Co Ltd v McNiece*

[10–18]

---

[24] Above, n 15.
[25] *Tomlinson (A) (Hauliers) Ltd v Hepburn* [1966] AC 451.
[26] *ibid.*
[27] Flannigan, "Privity: The End of an Era (Error)" (1987) 103 LQR 564.
[28] *Darlington Borough Council v Wiltshire Northern Ltd*, above, n 15.
[29] 1 Ventr 6.

*Bros Proprietary Ltd*[30] expressed the view that there should be no objection to judicial law reform:

> "[W]hen a rule of the common law harks back no further than the middle of the last century, when it has been the subject of constant criticism and where, in its widest form, it lacks a sound foundation in jurisprudence and logic and further, when that rule has been so affected by exceptions or qualifications."

**[10–19]**     It is worthwhile to explore some of the more important exceptions and qualifications to the privity doctrine. These carefully developed loopholes are of doubtful virtue. In *Swain v Law Society*[31] Lord Diplock described them as "juristic subterfuges ... to mitigate the effect of the lacuna resulting from the non-recognition of jus quaesitum tertio".

## IV. Tort of Negligence

**[10–20]**     The duty of care in negligence is a long-established device for side-stepping the privity doctrine. Suppose a solicitor draws up a will for a client. The contract for the drawing up of that will is between the solicitor and that client. Those who stand to benefit under the will cannot sue on that contract for want of privity. However, the solicitor owes a professional duty of care to the beneficiaries of the will. So in *Wall v Hegarty*[32] the High Court found that a person who stood to benefit under a will which turned out to be invalid could sue the solicitor who negligently drew up the will.[33] Along similar lines, in *Ward v McMaster*[34] the High Court found that a negligent builder was liable to owners of the house subsequent to the original purchaser.

## V. Assignment

**[10–21]**     A party to the contract can assign his contractual rights to a third party. Suppose A enters into a contract with B for the benefit of C. If B does not perform his contractual obligations, C will be injured, yet C will not be able to sue to enforce those contractual obligations. However, A can give his rights under the contract to C, allowing C to sue as if he were A. C, the assignee, assumes A, the assignor's contractual rights as against the other party to the contract. B's consent is not required. The rules of assignment are complex and will not be discussed in any great detail here.[35] However, it is worth noting that it is not possible to assign contracts of a personal nature or to assign a contract which is expressed to be non-assignable.

## VI. Constructive Trusts

**[10–22]**     A trust is an equitable obligation to hold money or property or a chose in action on behalf of another party. So, one party can hold his rights under a contract on trust for a third party. The party who holds his rights under the contract on trust for the third

---

[30] Above, n 12.
[31] Above, n 14.
[32] [1989] ILRM 124.
[33] See also *White v Jones* [1995] 2 AC 207.
[34] [1985] IR 29.
[35] See McDermott, *Contract Law* (LexisNexis Butterworths, 2000) pp 965–974.

party is called the trustee. The third party for whose benefit those rights are held is called the beneficiary. Rights under a contract can become the subject of a trust where the trustee so provides in the main contract. Suppose, for example, that X promises to pay A £10 if A will give B a book. Imagine now that A takes the £10 but does not give the book to B. Under the doctrine of privity, B cannot compel A to give him the book, even though the contract between X and A was for B's benefit. However, as Lush LJ set out in *Lloyd's v Harper*[36]:

> "I consider it an established rule of law that where a contract is made with A for the benefit of B, A can sue on the contract for the benefit of B and recover all that B could have recovered if the contract had been made with B himself."

Because the contract in our example was made for B's benefit, a trust is constructed with B as beneficiary: A holds his own rights under the contract on trust for B. B as beneficiary can secure his rights under the trust either indirectly or directly. He can enforce the contract directly in equity. In *Gandy v Gandy*[37] Cotton LJ stated that:  **[10–23]**

> "[I]f the contract, although in form it is with A, is intended to secure a benefit to B, so that B is entitled to say that he has a beneficial right ... under that contract; then B would, in a Court of Equity, be allowed to insist upon and enforce that contract."

There is also an indirect enforcement mechanism open to the beneficiary. A trustee will owe certain duties to a beneficiary. The beneficiary can sue the trustee to enforce those duties: the court will essentially compel the trustee to execute his trust, thereby providing a means whereby the beneficiary may force the breaching party to perform.[38]  **[10–24]**

*Tomlinson v Gill*[39] shows how the court will create a trust in favour of the beneficiary. Gill had contracted with a widow that if she would appoint him as administrator of her late husband's estate, he would use his own funds to meet any debts that the estate could not discharge. One of the late husband's creditors sought to sue on this contract. Obviously, he was barred by the doctrine of privity: the contract was between Gill and the widow. However, the Court held that this case fell within one of the exceptions to the doctrine of privity. Lord Chancellor Hardwicke reasoned: "the plaintiff ... could not maintain an action at law, for the promise was made to the widow; but he is proper here, for the promise was for the benefit of the creditors and the widow is a trustee for them". Accordingly, the creditor could rely on the contract regardless of the lack of privity. *Drimmie v Davies*[40] is an Irish case in which the trust exception was used to circumvent the doctrine of privity. A father and son contracted to establish a dental practice. As part of this contract the son agreed to pay allowances to his siblings in the event that his father pre-deceased him. When the father died, the siblings sued to enforce this aspect of the contract. Obviously, they were barred from  **[10–25]**

---

[36] (1880) 16 Ch D 290.
[37] 30 Ch D 57.
[38] *Drimmie v Davies* [1899] IR 176.
[39] (1756) Amb 330.
[40] Above, n 38.

doing so by the doctrine of privity. However, the contract had been made for their benefit and so Chatterton V-C held that a trust was raised in their favour at equity:

> "The equitable rule was that the party to whose use or for whose benefit the contract has been entered into has a remedy in equity against the person with whom it was expressed to be made. The Court deems the latter a trustee for the former, and would compel him to execute his trust according to the apparent intention of the contracting parties."

**[10–26]**     The key thing to remember about this type of trust is that the trustees in these cases have not demonstrated an express intention to create a trust. That intention is constructed by the courts from the surrounding circumstances. The trust is a fiction, used by judges to work practical justice in favour of the third party. In more recent cases, the courts have become more reluctant to use this tactic without a very clear mandate from the parties. So Furmston has written that:

> "At one time it looked as if the trust concept might provide a convenient equitable means to circumvent the common law rule. Over the last fifty years, however, without locking the door the courts have consistently failed to open it."[41]

**[10–27]**     Furmston's comment is based on the courts' increasing insistence that the parties demonstrate not merely an intention to *benefit* the third party, as was required in *Tomlinson*, but also an intention to *create a trust* in his favour. For a long time, although the courts required both elements, they tended to infer the existence of the latter from the presence of the former. The first significant move in a new direction was the dissenting judgment of Walker LJ in *Kenney v Employer's Liability Insurance Corporation*.[42] His lordship would have required both evidence of an intention to confer a beneficial right on the beneficiary and evidence of intention on the part of the trustee to hold his contractual rights on trust for the beneficiary. Despite this strong dissent, the House of Lords reaffirmed the traditional position in *Les Affréteurs Réunis SA v Leopold Walford Ltd*.[43] However, the position in England and Wales now appears to be that the courts are unlikely to find an intention to create a contractual trust in the absence of express words to that effect. In *Re Schebsman*,[44] Du Parcq LJ stated:

> "It is true that, by the use possibly of unguarded language, a person may create a trust as Monsieur Jordain talked prose, without knowing it, but unless an intention to create a trust is clearly to be collected from the language used and the circumstances of the case, I think that the court ought not to be astute to discover indications of such an intention."

**[10–28]**     The same principle appears from the more recent case of *Swain v The Law Society*[45] in which the UK Law Society had arranged an insurance scheme for all

---

[41] Furmston, *Law of Contract* (Oxford University Press, 2006) 580.
[42] [1901] IR 301.
[43] [1919] AC 801.
[44] [1944] Ch 83.
[45] Above, n 14.

practising solicitors, participation in which was compulsory. The agreement was expressed to be made by the society "on behalf" of the solicitors. The question was whether a trust arose in the solicitors' favour, so that the Law Society would be accountable to an individual solicitor in respect of the commission charged on his premium. The House of Lords held that the words "on behalf" did not demonstrate an intention to create a trust. Lord Brightman explained:

> "I find myself unable to accept the proposition that The Law Society should have imputed to it the intention to constitute itself a trustee of the master policy contract. The words "on behalf of" clearly do not *express* a trust, and they do not necessarily *imply* a trust. There are numerous authorities to that effect, to which it is unnecessary to refer. It would, indeed, be surprising if a society of lawyers, who above all might be expected to make their intention clear in a document they compose, should have failed to express the existence of a trust if that was what they intended to create."

*Cadbury (Ireland) v Kerry Co-Op Creameries Ltd and Dairy Disposal Co. Ltd*[46] **[10–29]** demonstrates a similar attitude to contractual trusts in Irish law. In that case, Cadbury sought to enforce a term in a contract of sale between Kerry Co-Op and Dairy Disposal Ltd. This term was for Cadbury's benefit: it concerned an undertaking by Kerry Co-Op to supply Cadbury with milk. Cadbury argued that a contractual trust arose in its favour on foot of this undertaking. Barrington J, however, could not find the necessary intention to create a trust. In particular, this was because the language of the undertaking was vague: it amounted to little more than a "commitment to enter into honest negotiations".

## VII. Agency

An agent is a person who enters into a contract, not on his own behalf, but on behalf of **[10–30]** another person, called a principal. Even though the contract is "private" to the agent and the other party, the principal has rights and obligations under that contract as if he had made the contract himself. The agent can sue on foot of the contract and he can recover damages on the principal's behalf. Alternatively, the principal can sue for himself. Agency is one of the most common means of defeating the doctrine of privity. Suppose, for example, that a consumer buys a hammer at a branch of a hardware chain. Although, on the face of it, the transaction takes place between the consumer and the sales assistant, the sales assistant is acting as an agent for a principal: the hardware company. Therefore, the true parties to the contract are not the customer and the assistant but the customer and the hardware company. The sales assistant is not a party to the contract at all. By recognising an agency exception to the doctrine of privity, the courts have adopted an approach firmly grounded in commercial realism.

A relationship of agency will enable a third party to avoid the doctrine of **[10–31]** privity where it satisfies the four-part test established in *The Eurymedon*[47] and drawn from *Midland Silicones Ltd v Scruttons Ltd.*[48] In *The Eurymedon*, a drilling machine

---

[46] [1982] ILRM 77.
[47] [1975] AC 154.
[48] [1962] AC 446.

was to be transported by ship from Liverpool to Wellington. The defendants were stevedores, who were hired by the shippers to unload the drilling machine at Wellington. The shippers were also a subsidiary of the defendants. The contract at issue was between the consignors and the shippers. It included a clause which limited the liability of the shippers and a so-called "Himalaya clause" which extended that immunity to their employees, agents and independent contractors. The defendants were negligent in unloading drilling machine. The question for the Court was whether the defendants could escape liability for their negligence by relying on the clause in the consignor-shipper contract. They could do so if they could show that the shippers had entered into the contract with the consignors as the defendants' agents. The Court held that the defendants could take the benefit of this clause as principals if they satisfied all four elements of the test. First, the contract must have made it clear that the benefit of the clause extends to the principal. Second, the agent must have contracted in two capacities: in his personal capacity and as agent for the principal. Third, the agent must either have been authorised to act as agent at the time of contracting or his actions must have been ratified later by the principal. Note that the contract does not have to expressly name the agent: it is enough that it is clear from the contract taken as a whole that the agent was so authorised.[49] Finally, the principal must have provided good consideration for the agent's promise to allow him to take the benefit of the main contract. Each of these elements can be understood as meeting the key objections to any relaxation of the doctrine of privity. The first three elements address the contractual freedom of the main parties and the third party by examining whether they objectively consented to relinquish the protection of the privity doctrine. The final consideration element addresses the mutuality justification for the doctrine of privity: the principal is not merely invading a private contract but has bargained for the benefit he seeks. You should note as well that the rules in *Midland Silicone* allow for an undisclosed principal: it was not necessary that the consignors should have been aware that the shippers were contracting as agents for the defendants. The table below shows how the Court applied these principles to find a relationship of agency between the shippers and the defendant stevedores.

| *Midland Silicone* principles | Applied to *Eurymedon* facts |
| --- | --- |
| 1. The contract must have made it clear that the benefit of the clause extends to the principal. | The exemption clause was very widely drafted so that it described all parties who might be involved in transporting the machinery.<br>The first element of the test was satisfied. |
| 2. The agent must have contracted in two capacities: in his personal capacity and as agent for the principal. | As the shippers were a subsidiary of the defendants, the Court inferred that the shippers were contracting on the defendants' behalf.<br>The second element of the test was satisfied. |

---

[49] See more recently *The Romina G* [2003] 2 Lloyd's Rep 520.

*(Continued)*

| Midland Silicone principles | Applied to Eurymedon facts |
|---|---|
| 3. The agent must either have been authorised to act as agent at the time of contracting or his actions must have been ratified later by the principal. | Again, as the shippers were a subsidiary of the defendants, the Court inferred that the shippers were contracting on the defendants' behalf.<br>The third element of the test was satisfied. |
| 4. The principal must have provided good consideration for the agent's promise to allow him to take the benefit of the main contract. | The defendants' performance of the service of unloading the drilling machinery was consideration for the shippers' agreement to allow them to take the benefit of the exemption clause.<br>The final element of the test was satisfied. |

An Irish case in which agency was used to circumvent the doctrine of privity was *Hearn and Matchroom Boxing v Collins*.[50] Barry Hearn successfully relied on a contract between the boxer Steve Collins and Matchroom Boxing. Even though Hearn was not a party to the contract, he successfully argued that Matchroom Boxing had contracted with Collins as Hearn's agent under the principles in *Midland Silicone*. Accordingly, Hearn was able to avoid the doctrine of privity and enforce a contract to which he was a stranger. [10–32]

## VIII. Collateral Contracts

Sometimes, a court may analyse a privity scenario in terms of two contracts: the main contract between the original parties, and a separate contract between one of the parties and the third party beneficiary. This second, collateral contract will contain that clause in the main contract upon which the third party seeks to rely. In *Shanklin Pier v Detel*,[51] the plaintiffs had a contract with a contractor for the repair and painting of their pier. The contractor had a contract with the defendant for the supply of paint. The defendants had assured the plaintiffs that their paint would last seven years on the pier. On the basis of that promise, the plaintiffs, as part of their agreement with the contractor, required them to use the defendants' paint. Now, the paint in fact only lasted three months, and the plaintiffs went to considerable expense in remedying the problem. The plaintiffs sued the defendants. At first glance, the case seems to fall foul of the privity doctrine since there is no clear contractual nexus between Shanklin and Dettel. However, the Court found that a collateral contract existed between them. Dettel had promised its paint would last seven years, and by way of consideration for that promise, Shankin had compelled its contractor to use Dettel's paint. *Shanklin Pier* was followed in this jurisdiction in *McCullough Sales Ltd v Chetham Timber Co. Ltd.*[52] [10–33]

The collateral contract analysis might also be used where a third party seeks to take the benefit of an exemption clause in the main contract. An exemption clause is a [10–34]

---

[50] Unreported, High Court, 3 February 1998.
[51] *Shanklin Pier Ltd v Detel Products Ltd.* [1951] 2 KB 854.
[52] Unreported, High Court, 1 February 1983.

clause that aims to exclude or limit a party's liability in the event that he breaches the contract or commits a tort. The doctrine of privity of contract affects such clauses where a party to a contract attempts to extend the protection of such a clause to a third party (his employee, sub-contractor or agent). *The Eurymedon*[53] demonstrates the use of the collateral contract analysis to circumvent the doctrine of privity in such cases. The main contract in this case, you will remember, was between the consignor of a machine and the shipper. The contract contained an exemption clause, conferring immunity from liability for loss or damage on the shippers and a Himalaya clause extending that immunity to the shipper's servants, agents and so on. The defendant stevedores sought to take the benefit of this contract. We have already examined the agency analysis of this scenario. However, the Privy Council also analysed the scenario in terms of two contracts: the main contract between consignor and shipper and a second, collateral contract between the consignor and the defendant stevedores. The Privy Council argued that the combined effect of the limitation clause and the Himalaya clause was that the consignor was making a unilateral offer to enter into a contract with anyone who unloaded the goods. The content of that offer was "if you unload the goods, the consignor promises that you will be covered by the limitation clause in the main contract". The defendant stevedores accepted this offer by the act of unloading the goods, forming a collateral contract and so they were covered by the limitation clause.[54] The Privy Council's approach here sacrifices elegance to pragmatism and has been criticised as excessively technical.[55] It was in this case, after all, that Lord Wilberforce famously remarked on the courts' tendency towards "forcing the facts to fit uneasily into the marked slots of offer, acceptance and consideration". Lord Bingham was more complimentary about the decision in his decision in *The Starsin*,[56] remarking that it was "a deft and commercially inspired response to technical English rules of contract, particularly those governing privity and consideration". However, in *Southern Water Authority v Carey*,[57] Judge Smout QC refused to stretch the facts of the case to fit the unilateral collateral contract analysis, declaring "it strikes me as uncomfortably artificial".

## IX. Statutory Exceptions

[10–35] The Oireachtas has created a number of *ad hoc* statutory exceptions to the doctrine of privity in such areas as insurance,[58] consumer protection,[59] company law[60] and employment.[61] Section 7 of the Married Women's Status Act 1957 gives the widow and children of a deceased man the right to sue upon a life insurance or endowment policy

---

[53] Above, n 47.
[54] But see *Raymond Burke Motors v Mersey Docks and Harbour* [1986] 1 Lloyd's Rep 155 where stevedores could not take the benefit of a similar limitation clause where they damaged the goods before unloading, i.e. before the act of acceptance which lead to the collateral contract.
[55] See *The Mahkutai* [1996] AC 650.
[56] [2003] UKHL 12.
[57] [1985] 2 All ER 1077.
[58] Section 62 Civil Liability Act 1961; s 76(1) Road Traffic Act 1961.
[59] Section 13(2) Sale of Goods and Supply of Services Act 1980; s 80 Consumer Credit Act 1995 (especially important in relation to defects in motor vehicles).
[60] Section 25 Companies Act 1963.
[61] See, for example, Directive 2001/23/EC Transfer of Undertakings and theSafeguarding of Employees' Rights, implemented by the European Communities(Protection of Employees on Transfer of Undertakings) Regulations 2003 (SI No 131of 2003).

which he has taken out in their favour. The old position at common law was that the insurance policy was a contract between the insurance company and the insured such that no third party could claim on it.[62] Section 8 of the same statute provides that any contract entered into by a married person with the aim of benefiting their spouse or their children shall be enforceable by that child or spouse. The benefit must be expressly conferred on the child or spouse; an implied intention to confer that benefit is insufficient. That much is clear from *Burke (a minor) v Dublin Corporation*.[63] The minor plaintiff sued on foot of the lease between his parents and Dublin Corporation for damages to compensate the exacerbation of his asthma by unfit living conditions. He argued that he could avoid the doctrine by reliance on s 8 of the Act; because the local authority differential rents were based on the number of children resident in the home, the lease was a contract entered into by a married person with the aim of benefiting their child. However, Finlay CJ found that this implied reference to children was not enough to bring the case within s 8. The reference had to be express.

## X. Suggestions for Reform

In November 2006, the Law Reform Commission published a consultation paper[64] **[10–36]** which suggests that the privity rule be reformed by legislation so that, in certain circumstances, third parties would be able to enforce rights under contracts made for their benefit. Legislation to this effect already exists in England and Wales, in the shape of the Contracts (Rights of Third Parties) Act 1999.[65] Similar reforms have taken place in Canada, New Zealand, Australia and Singapore. More importantly, the legal systems of most European countries recognise the rights of third parties to enforce contracts.[66] Space is too short here to discuss all of the features of the paper and students are encouraged to read it for its in-depth discussion of the law of privity in other jurisdictions.

The Commission accepted that legislative reform of this area of law is needed **[10–37]** because judicial reform is too slow a process. Judges' ability to remake common law rules is hampered by the doctrine of precedent. In particular, judges must wait for a case to present itself which raises the appropriate issues before they can commence to reform an area. There are also other stock debates about the proper role of judicial law reform. In the Canadian case of *Fraser River Pile and Dredge Ltd v Can Dive Services Ltd*,[67] Iacobucci J set out in detail the traditional argument against leaving "big picture" reform of the privity doctrine up to the judges:

"Privity of contract is an established rule of contract law, and should not be lightly discarded through the process of judicial decree. Wholesale abolition of

---

[62] *Cleaver v Mutual Reserve Fund Life Assoc* [1892] 1 QB 147.
[63] [1991] 1 IR 341.
[64] LRC CP 40-2006. For a comment on this consultation paper see Kelly, "Reform of Privity of Contract and Third Party Rights" (2007) 1 *Commercial Law Practitioner*, 8.
[65] See Andrews, "Strangers to Justice No Longer: The Reversal of the Privity Rule under the Contracts (Rights of Third Parties) Act 1999" [2001] CLJ 353.
[66] See e.g. Principles of European Contract Law, Art 6.110; French Code Civil, Art 1121; German Burgerliches Gesetzbuch, Art 328.
[67] [1999] 3 SCR 108.

the rule would result in complex repercussions that exceed the ability of the courts to anticipate and redress. It is by now a well-established principle that courts will not undertake judicial reform of this magnitude, recognizing instead that the legislature is better placed to appreciate and accommodate the economic and policy issues involved in introducing sweeping legal reforms.

That being said, the corollary principle is equally compelling which is that in appropriate circumstances, courts should not abdicate their judicial duty to decide on incremental changes to the common law necessary to address emerging needs and values in society."

Thus, judicial reform of the law tends to creep along slowly over the years: the courts tend to be unwilling to effect change on a larger scale. The Commission's paper therefore considers the various options for legislative reform.

[10–38]     A simple abolition of the rule is rejected as inappropriate, for the very reason highlighted in Iacobucci J's *dictum*. While it would have the advantage of simplicity, such reform would not achieve the key aim of reform in this area: restoring clarity and certainty to the law. A more detailed legislative provision is necessary to remedy the Byzantine complexity of the current law of privity and to give judges adequate guidance to ensure that clarity becomes and remains a hallmark of the reformed law. However, the Commission also rejects the opposite approach: reformation of the doctrine of privity by creating new statutory exceptions to the doctrine. While we know that the legislature has provided for certain specific exceptions to meet particular sites of injustice, the Commission takes the view that piecemeal legislation does nothing to reduce the confusion and complexity surrounding the privity doctrine.

[10–39]     The Commission has suggested a test of enforceability based on the intentions of the parties to the contract. The third party would be able to enforce a contract if he satisfies two requirements. First, the parties to the contract must have intended that he was to receive the benefit of the contract or of one of its terms. The Commission has argued that this intent will be evident if the beneficiary has been identified by name or by description. Second, the parties must have intended that the beneficial contract or term was to be enforceable by him in his own name. There are a number of important features of this proposal. The type of intention required is important. This is a dual test of intention: the third party will not have any rights if he was merely intended to benefit from the contract. It must also have been intended that he would be able to sue on it. This test for this intention is as stringent as, and similar in nature to, the usual test of intention to create legal relations as applied to direct parties to a contract. As you would expect, the test of intention is objective. Third, this is an opt-in scheme: in effect, the privity rule would apply unless the parties specifically contracted otherwise. This aspect of the scheme ties in with a fourth important observation: the focus on the intent of the parties as the trigger for third party rights. Under the proposed scheme it would not be enough that the third party has relied on a contract, even where his reliance is reasonable and justifiable. The parties' freedom of contract is protected by the focus on intention; their contract will remain private to them and unassailable by the State or by third parties unless they expressly decide to relinquish the shield of the privity doctrine. The only important concession to the third party's reasonable expectations is the Commission's provisional recommendation that once the first element of the dual intention test is satisfied, it will be presumed that the second element has been satisfied. If it is established that the third party was intended to take the benefit of the contract or one of its terms, it will be presumed that it was intended that the third party would be entitled to enforce the contract in his own name. This presumption would be rebuttable and generally speaking, parties who do not wish to confer a right of enforcement on a third party should state so clearly in their contractual document.

The Commission has not come to a final decision on what should be done with the existing statutory and common law exceptions to the doctrine of privity. Certainly the new legislation must make some reference to them: if the statute remains silent as to the established exceptions, the potential for confusion is significant. Should the new legislation set out all of these exceptions expressly or should it simply provide that the existing exceptions will continue to exist alongside the new legislation? On the one hand, the Commission has accepted that by listing the exceptions and setting out their place in the law with precision, codification would introduce new certainty and clarity to the law. However, the legislation required to do this would necessarily be very long and detailed; the accessibility sought might be lost in the maze of sections. Therefore, the Commission has provisionally recommended that the legislation should include a general section preserving the existing exceptions to the doctrine of privity and their associated remedies. The existing law would be supplemented rather than supplanted. However, the Commission observes that there are significant dangers in allowing the new regime to co-exist with the old common law and statutory exceptions to the doctrine of privity. For example, if a third party finds that his action is covered both by the new statute and by one of the original exceptions can he choose the most advantageous action? Such "shopping around" might only add to the complexity of litigation in this area. **[10–40]**

# CHAPTER 11
# The Statute of Frauds

**Harry Field:** *"A verbal agreement . . ."*
**Fannie Field:** *". . . is not worth the paper it's written on."*

From *Be Yourself* (1930)

## I. Introduction

Suppose A has an oral contract with B for the sale of B's farm, Blackacre. Soon after   **[11–01]**
the agreement is made, B changes his mind and refuses to part with the farm. He
breaches his contract with A. A then sues for specific performance: an order
compelling B to carry out the contract as agreed. How would A be required to prove
that he has a contract with B? Would his word be enough? What if B denied that there
was ever a contract? Would A require written evidence? Would a formal contract
document be required or would a letter or a receipt do?

Generally speaking, contracts do not need to be *made* in writing. A contract   **[11–02]**
can exist without any formal written document, and it is possible to enforce a purely
oral contract even where the subject matter is very valuable indeed. For example, in
*Pernod Ricard v FII Fyffes plc*,[1] a sale of shares valued at several million pounds was
conducted on the basis of an oral contract. However, under s 2 of the Statute of Frauds

---

[1] Unreported, High Court, 21 October 1985.

(Ireland) Act 1695, the following types of contract will not be enforced[2] unless evidenced in writing[3]:

1.  Contracts to pay for the default or miscarriage of another;
2.  Agreements made in consideration of marriage;
3.  Contracts for the sale of land or an interest therein;
4.  Contracts for the sale of goods in excess of £10;
5.  Contracts not intended to be performed within one year.

[11–03]     Why does the statute exist?[4] It goes further than formality for formality's sake. Although businessmen may prefer to contract on the basis of handshakes or gentlemen's honour,[5] Karl Llewellyn observes that the phrase, "'His word is as good as his bond' contains a biting innuendo preaching caution."[6]

[11–04]     By denying the promisee the right to establish the contract by parol evidence, the statute discourages fraud. The statute is the Irish version of the 1677 Act for the Prevention of Fraud and Perjuries, which was enacted in England in the aftermath of Oliver Cromwell's rule. At the time, fraud was rife and was being used in the courts by a litigious population as a means of undermining property rights; "the confusion attending the rapid succession of Civil War, Cromwellian dictatorship and Restoration had encouraged unscrupulous litigants to pursue false or groundless claims with the help of manufactured evidence".[8] Court procedure and the rules of evidence were underdeveloped at the time and were incapable of coping with this new problem. It was decided, therefore, that in order to enforce a contract, "mere words of mouth should not be sufficient but ... something besides should be necessary for that purpose".[9] By requiring written evidence of contracts, the Statute, as Fuller observed of other formalities, "furnishes a simple and external test of enforceability [which] Ihering described as 'the facilitation of judicial diagnosis'".[10] Ihering eloquently explained this function:

> "Form is for a legal transaction what the stamp is for a coin. Just as the stamp of the coin relieves us from the necessity of testing the metallic content and weight – in short, the value of the coin (a test which we could not avoid if

---

[2] A contract which does not comply with the statute is unenforceable but it is not void; *Thomas v Brown.* (1876) 1 QBD 714; *Re a Debtor, The Times,* 25 November 1991.

[3] The Oireachtas has also imposed similar requirements in relation to hire purchase contracts, (s 58 of the Consumer Credit Act 1995) arbitration clauses (The Arbitration Acts 1954–1998) and assignment of copyright (s 120(3) of the Copyright and Related Rights Act 2000).

[4] For an excellent critical analysis see Ní Shúilleabháin, "Formalities of Contracting: A Cost-Benefit Analysis of Requirements that Contracts be Evidenced in Writing" (2005) 12(1) DULJ 113.

[5] Macaulay, "Non-contractual Relations in Business: A Preliminary Study" (1963) 28 Am Soc Rev 55 at 58; Bernstein, "Opting Out of the Legal System: Extralegal Contractual Relations in the Diamond Industry" (1992) *21 Journal of Legal Studies* 115.

[6] Llewellyn, "What Price Contract? – An Essay in Perspective" 40 Yale LJ 704 at 707.

[8] Cheshire, Fifoot and Furmston, *Law of Contract* (11th ed, OUP, 1986), p 94.

[9] *Norton v Davison* [1899] QB 401 *per* Earl of Halsbury LC.

[10] Fuller, "Consideration and Form" (1941) 41 Colum L Rev 799.

uncoined metal were offered to us in payment), in the same way legal formalities relieve the judge of an inquiry *whether* a legal transaction were intended."

In addition to its evidentiary function, the statute performs what Lon Fuller called a "cautionary" function.[11] Where contracts are concluded informally, there is a danger that they will be concluded quickly and with a minimum of thought. McCarthy J observed in *Boyle v Lee*[12]:

[11–05]

> "It is a feature of property transactions in Ireland that they are often made with a minimum of formality, the circumstances, including the venue, of such bargains not being always conducive to the 'dusty purlieus of the law'."

Thus, the statute is "a paternalistic device designed to protect people from the consequences of hasty or ill-considered contracts" which are likely to result from negotiation conducted in these kinds of contexts.[13] The idea is that, by requiring the parties to record their contract in writing, the statute stimulates reflection and consideration of the contract.[14] This function is aided by the layman's perception that a written contract has special significance—that he is "really" bound once a document is in place.[15] However, the usefulness of written records for this purpose may be doubted, particularly where the written memorandum of the contract takes the shape of a standard form drafted by the more powerful party to protect his own interests.

[11–06]

Despite its advantages, the statute is open to criticism on a number of grounds. First, it actually directs the court to ignore reliable oral evidence about the agreement's existence. Jeremy Bentham noted that writing requirements of this type could frustrate genuine claims which were not in writing.[16] An unscrupulous party may exploit the fact that a contract is not in writing to escape his proper obligations and defeat the other party's commercial expectations.[17] The statute was repealed in the UK in 1954 except for the provisions dealing with suretyship and contracts for the sale of land because, *inter alia*, it was felt that the statute promoted more frauds than it prevented.[18] Since the earliest years of the statute, the courts have interpreted it in a flexible (or perhaps strained) manner, making particular use of equity, to temper this unwanted side-effect. Wilmot J observed that had it "been always carried into execution according to the letter, it would have done ten times more mischief than it has done good, by protecting

[11–07]

---

[11] *ibid.*

[12] [1992] ILRM 65.

[13] Smith, *Atiyah's Introduction to the Law of Contract* (6th ed, OUP, 2005), p 94.

[14] "Persons are so likely to be led into such promises inconsiderately, that the law has wisely required them to be manifested by writing". *Warden v Jones* [1857] 2 De Gex & J 76.

[15] Collins, *The Law of Contract* (4th ed, LexisNexis, 2003), p 17.

[16] Cited in Smith, *Atiyah's Introduction to the Law of Contract* (6th ed, OUP, 2005), p 94. McCarthy J makes a similar observation in *Boyle v Lee*: "genuine bargains could not be enforced because of the absence of the note or memorandum or some inadequacy".

[17] See e.g. *Russell and Baird v Hoban* [1922] 2 IR 159; *Hopton v McCarthy* (1882) 10 LR (Ir) 266; *Lee v Griffin* (1861) 1 B & S 272.

[18] Lord Campbell observed as much in *Marvin v Wallis* (1856) 6 El & Bl 726 at 736.

rather than by preventing, frauds".[19] That said, over-eagerness in developing fresh interpretations of the statute breeds a difficulty of its own: "the burgeoning of actions based on subtleties and niceties to get around the clear wording of the statute".[20]

[11–08]     Arguably, however, the importance of the statute lies not in the courts but in its impact on the day-to-day practice of contractors. Void wrote in 1931[21]:

> "[T]he cases that justify the statute are not primarily the litigated cases themselves, where it often looks as if a tricky defendant slides out of an honest bargain on the mere technicality of the lack of the statutory writing. The cases that justify the statute are the thousands of uncontested current transactions where misunderstanding and controversy are avoided by the presence of a writing which the statute at least indirectly aided to procure."

[11–09]     It might be said that reform of this "rogue's charter", instead of bringing justice, might only succeed in increasing uncertainty, misunderstanding and controversy, and breed litigation as barristers grapple with a change from more than 300 years of legal tradition.[22] Arguably, if any significant reform is attempted, the statute should be, to borrow Hugh Collins' phrase, "stirred but not shaken".

## II. The Scope of the Statute

[11–10]     It is sometimes suggested that the statute applies to particularly important categories of contract. However, there are some especially lucrative types of contract that are not required to be evidenced in writing at all. All in all, the statute applies to a somewhat arbitrary set of contract types.

### Contracts to Pay for the Default or Miscarriage of Another

[11–11]     The cautionary function of the statute is especially important here. The pause for thought afforded by a requirement of writing encourages the promisor to take time to consider the risk that he is taking and to assess the debtor's solvency. This is especially important in domestic contexts as where a parent may feel under pressure to become a guarantor for a child's burdensome loan. The statute applies to contracts of guarantee[23] but not to contracts of indemnity. A contract of guarantee involves a promise to pay a creditor if his debtor defaults. Both the debtor and the promisor are liable for the debt. The original debtor is called the principal debtor and the promisor is called the secondary debtor or the guarantor. A contract of indemnity is an

---

[19] *Simon v Metivier* (1766) 1 Black W 599 at 601 *per* Wilmot J.

[20] Above, n 11 *per* O'Flaherty J.

[21] Void, "The Application of the Statute of Frauds under the Uniform Sales Act" (1931) 15 Minn L Rev 391 at 393–394.

[22] See LRC 59-1999, 3.21.

[23] However, the statute does not apply to the following types of guarantee: contracts where the defendant provides the guarantee in his capacity as a *del credere* agent (an agent who gets a higher commission for making sure that the principal is paid by the other party); contracts where a guarantee is given by the guarantor to free his property from some liability to the creditor; and contracts where liability rests on an implied promise or on an account stated. See McDermott, *Contract Law* (LexisNexis, 2000), p 193–195.

agreement to pay in any event—it involves a promise to pay a creditor regardless of whether anyone is in default. Only the promisor is liable for the debt. The distinction here is a difficult one to draw and, for this reason, it is often criticised. It has been called "a disgrace to the law and a trap for the unwary".[24] It is also difficult to see the justification for this distinction. Surely the risk of fraud and the need for caution are as great with contracts of indemnity as with contracts of guarantee?

As well as contracts for debt, the statute covers contracts to answer for the "miscarriage" of another. For example, in *Kirkham v Marter*[25] the defendant had made an oral promise to compensate the plaintiff for the loss he had suffered as a result of the defendant's son's negligence. Because this contract was covered by the statute and was not evidenced in writing, it could not be enforced.    [11–12]

## Agreements Made in Consideration of Marriage

Marriage contracts are no longer enforced. This category is most important now in relation to transfers of money or land to an engaged couple.    [11–13]

## Contracts for the Sale of Land or An Interest Therein

The protective effect of the statute is felt particularly keenly in relation to the sale of land. This is especially so because the purchase or sale of land is such an important and substantial financial transaction to both the individual and to the market economy in general. The statute clearly applies to contracts for the sale of all interests in land, and contracts of assignment, leases, incorporeal hereditaments and the sale of things sufficiently attached to land must also be evidenced in writing if they are to be enforced. Contracts which are about land, but which do not grant an interest in land, fall outside the scope of the statute. So a mere license does not have to be evidenced in writing.    [11–14]

A difficulty arises in relation to crops or other plants growing on the land. Are they part of the land so that their sale must be evidenced in writing, or are they "goods"? At common law, a distinction was drawn between *fructus naturales* and *fructus industriales*. *Fructus naturales* were plants such as grass or trees that did not involve much cultivation except for the initial planting. These would sometimes form part of the land. *Fructus industriales* were plants that required much more labour before they could be enjoyed such as wheat, potatoes and other annual crops. These never formed part of the land. Section 62 of the Sale of Goods Act 1893 helps to show where the modern line is drawn. It says that goods include "industrial growing crops and things attached to or forming part of the land which are agreed to be severed before sale or under the contract of sale". So any plant or crop attached to the land is a good and falls outside the statute, provided it is to be severed from the land before sale. For example, in *Scully v Carboy*,[26] an agreement to let the meadowing of a field was held to be a sale of a good and not a sale of an interest in land. The sale of such an item will not have to be evidenced in writing unless its value is greater than £10.    [11–15]

---

[24] The Law Reform Commission of Australia, 34th Report (1975).
[25] (1819) 2 B & Ald 613.
[26] [1950] IR 140.

### Contracts for the Sale of Goods in Excess of £10

[11–16]    A contract for the sale of goods valued in excess of £10 (now €12) must be evidenced in writing. The most striking thing about this category is the small value of contracts involved. The equivalent provision in the US Uniform Commercial Code refers to goods in excess of $500. Because this category covers such a wide range of contracts, the three exceptions to this category are exceptionally important. Written evidence can be dispensed with if the buyer accepts and receives part of the goods, if he has given something in earnest to bind the bargain or if the buyer has made full or part payment.

### *Acceptance and Receipt of Goods by the Buyer*

[11–17]    If the buyer receives and accepts goods valued in excess of £10, the contract for the sale of those goods can be enforced without written evidence.

[11–18]    Acceptance of part of the goods will be enough. In *Tradax v Irish Grain Board* the purchaser's acceptance of 1,800 tonnes out of a 12,000 order of grain was enough to do away with the need for written evidence of the contract. The goods must be accepted by the buyer, not by a third party. In *Hopton v McCarthy*,[27] a coach-builder in Tipperary ordered materials from the plaintiffs in England. The seller sent the materials by rail. The materials were held in the carrier's warehouse awaiting collection by the defendant. The coach-builder did not collect them. He had decided not to proceed with the purchase because business was slow. Could the sellers enforce the contract? There was no written evidence of the contract. The sellers argued that the goods had been accepted and received by the buyer, so no writing was required. The Court found that acceptance into the custody of the carrier, a third party, was not enough to satisfy the statute. In addition, the intent of the buyer is important. If the goods have been delivered to his premises without his consent, this will not count as acceptance. Similarly, it is not acceptance for the buyer to take custody of the goods simply to protect them from deterioration or destruction.

### *Seller Accepts Something in Earnest Given by the Buyer to Bind the Bargain*

[11–19]    This exception is a puzzling one. It is not clear what is meant by "something in earnest". In *Farr, Smith & Co v Messers Ltd*, Wright J said:

> "... it is somewhat difficult to give a precise definition of the word 'earnest'. Certain characteristics, however, seem to be clear. An earnest must be a tangible thing, in which definition it may be that a deposit is included, but in the old cases it was always some tangible thing. That thing must be given at the moment at which the contract is concluded, because it is something given to bind the contract, and, therefore, it must come into existence at the making or conclusion of the contract. The thing given in that way must be given by the contracting party who gives it, as an earnest or token of good faith, and as a guarantee that he will fulfil his contract, and subject to the terms that if, owing to his default the contract goes off, it will be forfeited".

---

27  (1882) 10 LR (Ir) 266 (Exch)

McDermott suggests that giving a credit card number over the phone or the [11–20] Internet might suffice.[28] The seller must accept the thing given in earnest if the exception is to apply.[29]

### Seller Accepts Payment for the Goods, in Full or in Part

No memorandum is required where full or part payment has been made for the goods. [11–21] It is not enough that payment is offered. So posting a cheque will not do unless the cheque is cashed. In *Kirwan v Price*,[30] the purchaser's offer of payment for a horse was refused by the seller. A written memorandum was still required in order to enforce this contract.

### Contracts Not Intended to be Performed within One Year

The idea behind the inclusion of this category in the statute is to guard against failing [11–22] memory. The idea is that if more than one year passes between bargain and lawsuit, the parties are unlikely to have a clear and reliable memory of the terms of the contract. If a contract is not intended to be performed within one year of being agreed, written evidence will be required if it is to be enforced. In *Tierney v Marshall*,[31] a contract intended to run for 12 years was not enforced for want of written evidence. Similarly, in *Naughton v Limestone Land Co Ltd*,[32] the Court refused to enforce an oral contract of employment that was to run for four years because there was no written record of it. If a contract is intended to run its course within the year, it can be enforced without written evidence. In *Hynes v Hynes*,[33] therefore, a verbal contract for the transfer of a business from one brother to another was enforced despite the lack of sufficient written evidence. This was because at the time of entering into the contract, the parties intended that it would be implemented immediately.

The key point here is that the statute only applies to contracts that are not [11–23] *intended* to be performed within one year. The courts examine the parties' intention at the time of making the contract. Hindsight is not used, so the date of actual performance is immaterial. In *Farrington v Donohoe*,[34] Monahan CJ draws a distinction between the date of performance contemplated by the parties and the date on which the contract was actually determined or performed. The contract was a promise to maintain a five-year-old child until she was able to "do for herself". It was argued that no memorandum was required because the child might have died within one year. However, the possible date of performance was unimportant:

> "So here the agreement to maintain the child til able to maintain itself clearly contemplated an event not to be performed within a year, though, of course, the agreement would have been determined by the collateral event – the death of the child – which might have happened within the year."

---

[28] McDermott, *op. cit.*, p 203.
[29] *Kirwan v Price* [1958] Ir. Jur. 56.
[30] [1958] Ir Jur 56.
[31] (1857) 7 ICLR 308.
[32] [1952] Ir Jur 19.
[33] Unreported, High Court, 21 December 1984.
[34] (1866) IR 1 CL 675.

[11–24]     Suppose in January 2007, A hires B to build him a house. They intend the house to be completed by January 2009. However, owing to B's extraordinary efficiency, the house is completed in November 2007. The contract has taken less than one year to perform. Suppose A refuses to pay and B wants to enforce the contract. The statute applies and B will require written evidence of the contract because it was intended that the contract would take more than one year to perform. Imagine on the other hand that in January 2007, A hired C to build him a shed, intending it to be completed by June 2007. Because C is incredibly incompetent, the shed is not completed even by January 2010. C refuses to do any more work on the shed and A sues for specific performance. A will not be required to produce written evidence of the contract because it was intended to be performed within one year. This comparison undermines the justification for the limitations on this category of contract as part of the statute. Is it really more likely that A and B's memories in the first scenario are less reliable than those of A and C in the second scenario?

[11–25]     In the absence of a memorandum to establish a contract not intended to be performed within one year, the courts will not sever the contract. So in *Naughton v Limestone Land Co*, it was argued that the final three years of the employment contract should be severed from the first year and the first year should be treated as a separate contract. This would not require written evidence and could be enforced. However, the Court refused to do this.

### III. Compliance with the Statute

[11–26]     The statute requires that contracts that fall within its scope are evidenced in writing. The requirements are flexibly interpreted, in keeping with the courts' reluctance to lose a genuine bargain to an insistence on the literal import of the statute. The statute does not require that the contract must have been made in writing—written evidence of an oral contract is sufficient. This written evidence is called a note or a memorandum. The statute further requires that the memorandum is signed by the person against whom the contract is sought to be enforced, or his agent. So if A wants to sue B for specific performance of a contract agreed between them for the sale of land, A must provide a written memorandum of its key terms signed by B or his lawfully authorised agent. The idea is that by signing the memorandum, you have evidenced your intention to adopt its contents. Generally speaking, any mark, even a rubber stamp or an X, will count as a signature if it was placed on the memorandum as a mark of intention to adopt the contents rather than merely for informational purposes. The distinction is clear from a comparison of *Casey v Intercontinental Bank*[35] and *Kelly v Ross and Ross*.[36] In *Casey*, a solicitor's letterhead counted as a signature for the purposes of the statute because it was intended as a mark of authenticity. By contrast, in *Kelly*, a solicitor's initials on a document were held not to be a signature because he had only initialled the document for reference purposes.

[11–27]     The memorandum is not a special document; it does not have to take any particular form. In *Doherty v Gallagher*,[37] details of a contract written on the bottom

---

[35] *Casey v Irish Intercontinental Bank* [1979] IR 364.
[36] *Kelly v Ross and Ross,* unreported, High Court, 29 April 1980.
[37] Unreported, High Court, 9 June 1975.

of a cheque were sufficient. In *Tradax v Irish Grain Board*,[38] a note of a contract for the sale of grain contained in part of a letter from the defendant was a memorandum. As explained in the next chapter, it is because a letter can amount to a memorandum proving the existence of a contract that parties and their solicitors commonly head their correspondence "subject to contract" to deny the existence of any contract until a formal document is prepared. There is no requirement that the parties intended the document used to serve as a memorandum. *In re Hoyle*,[39] the Court held that it was not "in quest of the intention of the parties, but only of evidence under the hand of one of the parties to it that he has entered into it."

The memorandum does not have to detail all of the contract's terms, but it must contain the essentials. Thus, in contracts for the sale of land, the so-called 3 P's must be present: it must be possible to use the memorandum to identify the parties to the contract,[40] the price[41] and the property.[42] In *Godley v Power*,[43] Maguire CJ said that: **[11–28]**

"A memorandum must contain all essential terms. The parties, the property and the consideration must always be ascertainable from it, but it need not contain any terms which the general law would imply ...".

There are two important points in that *dictum*. First, a term that would be implied into the contract by law (13-82) does not need to be expressed in the memorandum.[44] Secondly, it is enough that the essentials are in ascertainable form. So the parties need not be named precisely. Kenny J in *Bacon v Kavanagh*[45] said that: **[11–29]**

"it is not necessary that the actual names of the parties should appear in the memorandum, but if the parties are sufficiently described or indicated or referred to, so that there is no real doubt as to their identity, the statute is satisfied".

External evidence may be used to prove the meaning behind a vague label. In *Rossiter v Miller*,[46] parol evidence was admissible to prove the identity of a party identified in the memorandum only as "the owner". In *Bacon v Kavanagh*, the words "you" and "your employment" were enough to identify one party. In *Law v Roberts*,[47] the Court said that it was enough that the parties were identifiable from the correspondence and oral evidence of the surrounding circumstances even though they were not precisely named. The same was said of property in *Guardian Builders v* **[11–30]**

---

[38] [1984] IR 1.

[39] [1893] 1 Ch 84.

[40] *Law v Roberts* [1964] IR 292.

[41] *ibid*.

[42] *Viscount Massereene v Finlay* (1850) 13 Ir LR 496.

[43] (1961) 95 ILTR 135 at 145.

[44] See also *Supermac's Ireland Ltd. v Kateson* [2001] 1 ILRM 401.

[45] (1908) 42 ILTR 120.

[46] (1878) 3 App. Cas. 1124.

[47] [1964] IR 292.

*Patrick Kelly and Park Avenue Ltd*.[48] To the same effect, *McQuaid v Lynam*[49] sets out that the price need not be stated precisely, provided that some method of ascertaining the price is mentioned.

[11–31]    The test for essential terms is a subjective one. If there are other terms that the parties considered essential to the contract, the memorandum must contain these too. In *Stinson v Owens*,[50] McDermott LCJ said:

> "that a memorandum may satisfy the requirements of the statute without mentioning every term that has been agreed between the parties, but that to be good it must mention all the terms which are essential or material. And I am further of the opinion for the purposes of this requirement what is material or essential must be considered, at any rate primarily, from the point of view of the parties themselves".

[11–32]    The memorandum need not be contained in just one document. Several documents can be read together to constitute a memorandum. In *McQuaid v Lynam and Lynam*,[51] a receipt for payment and an application for a loan were laid alongside one another to form a memorandum of an agreement to rent premises. In *Tradax v Irish Grain Board*,[52] a letter and a telex were read together to form a memorandum of an agreement for the sale of barley. This process is called "joinder of documents". In *McQuaid v Lynam*[53] Kenny J explained:

> "The many cases on the issue whether a number of documents read together can constitute such a memorandum or note in writing show a progressively liberal approach by the courts to this question. I think that the modern cases ... establish that a number of documents may come together to constitute a note or memorandum in writing if they have come into existence in connection with the same transaction or if they contain internal references which connect them with each other."

[11–33]    It is clear from that dictum that joinder is impossible unless the documents refer to each other either expressly or impliedly. In *Kelly v Ross*,[54] nine documents could not be read together to form a memorandum for want of internal references. In addition, the signed document must have been signed after all the others were created. "[I]t would be absurd to hold that a person who signed the document could be regarded as having signed another document which was not in existence when he signed the first."[55]

---

[48]  Unreported, High Court, 31 March 1981.
[49]  [1965] IR 564.
[50]  107 ILTSJ 239.
[51]  [1965] IR 564.
[52]  [1984] IR 1.
[53]  [1965] IR 564.
[54]  Unreported, High Court, 29 April 1980.
[55]  Above, n 52.

## IV. Problems with E-commerce, Signatures and the Statute

Under s 13(1) of the Electronic Commerce Act 2000, the E-Sign Directive[56] is **[11–34]** implemented so that "electronic signatures may be used wherever a signature is required by law or otherwise". Section 22 further provides that "electronic evidence is admissible in legal proceedings and will be afforded the same evidential value as traditional forms of paper evidence". So, it appears that an e-mail will suffice as a memorandum for the purposes of the statute and that an electronically signed document will meet statutory requirements.

Electronic signature is a generic technology-neutral term defined in the statute **[11–35]** as "data in electronic form attached to, incorporated in or logically associated with other electronic data and which serves as a method of authenticating the purported originator". For the purposes of the statute, electronic signatures have equal legal status with handwritten signatures. This provision is very much in accordance with the legislative policy of promoting e-commerce. The statute does not address the issue of the genuineness of an electronic signature. If a question of the authenticity of an electronic signature arises, it appears that the facts surrounding the signature will be assessed on their own merits—electronic signatures do not attract any special presumption of validity. Likewise, the question of whether an electronic signature demonstrates the necessary intent will be left to the courts.

However, it is important to realise that these questions of intent and **[11–36]** genuineness will be key to the development of the law in this area. After all, there are many types of mark or word or symbol which could conceivably fall within the scope of s 13. The definition is broad enough to include a name or initials typed at the end of an e-mail[57] or a scanned image of a handwritten signature on an e-mail[58] as well as so-called "advanced electronic signatures". The Act defines advanced electronic signatures as electronic signatures which are uniquely linked to the signatory, are capable of identifying the signatory, are created using means that the signatory can maintain under his sole control and are linked to the electronic data to which they relate in such a manner that any subsequent change of the data is detectable. The most familiar type of advanced electronic signature is commonly known as digital signature, or PKI (public key infrastructure). Well-known brand names include VeriSign, Activcard and Cybertrust.[59] In order to send digitally signed messages, A must obtain

---

[56] Directive 1999/93/EC.

[57] See Brennan "Trouble Down the Line" (2001) *Law Society Gazette* 18.

[58] Scanned images will satisfy the more stringent definition of an electronic signature under s 7 of the English Electronic Communications Act 2000: Reed, "What is a Signature?" (2000) 3 *Journal of Information, Law and Technology* at 1.2; Law Commission (2001) *Electronic Commerce: Formal Requirements in Commercial Transactions*; Mason "Electronic Signatures Are Here To Stay" (2004) Ad Bus 2.10(7).

[59] In 1998, US President Bill Clinton and Taoiseach Bertie Ahern signed a joint communiqué using specially provided smart cards and entering secret personal numbers into separate laptops. For a guide to the basics, see Froomkin, "The Essential Role of Trusted Third Parties in Electronic Commerce" (1996) 75 Oregon L Rev 49.

"keys" from a body known as a certification service provider.[60] Alternatively, these keys may be generated by secure signature creation software. Each key has a unique digital identity. A receives a public key, which is available to anyone who should have it, and a private key. If B wants to send a digitally signed message to A, he must type it and encrypt it with A's public key. Because A's public key is certified, B can be sure that it belongs to A. He can then sign the message with his own private key and send it. When A opens the message, his software will check B's message. If it works properly, the software will verify that that the message was digitally signed using B's private key and that the message has not been tampered with since B sent it.[61] A less common form of advanced electronic signature involves "signature dynamics". Sign-it and PenOp are well-known brands. An electronic drawing tablet and stylus are used to record the direction, speed and coordinates of a handwritten signature. The signature dynamics and data are encrypted and attached to the document sent. Other biometric methods use encrypted voice recordings, retinal scans and fingerprints in much the same way. This method of advanced electronic signature is very secure because it links the signature to the signer and not to the document. No third party is needed to verify the signature. It is open to question whether these signatures should be mandatory where an electronic message is tendered as a valid memorandum for the purposes of the statute.

[11–37]     On the one hand, there is the argument that there is no justification for discriminating between one type of electronic signature and another. What matters is not the form that the signature takes but the intention with which it was applied. In *Re A Debtor*,[62] Laddie J noted:

> "Once it is accepted that the close physical linkage of hand, pen and paper is not necessary for the form to be signed, it is difficult to see why some forms of non-human agency for impressing the mark on the paper should be acceptable while others are not."

[11–38]     In addition, the Act espouses technology neutrality as one of its key aims; Article 5(2) of the original Directive sets out that for most purposes it is undesirable to treat advanced electronic signatures more favourably than electronic signatures *simpliciter*. However, the security risks involved in allowing a scanned signature, a name or an automated signature footer (arguably the equivalent of the solicitor's

---

[60] For more on the regulation of certification service providers, see McDonagh and White, "Electronic signatures: the legal framework and the market reality in Ireland" (2003) 10(8) CLP 228.
[61] See Keenan & Brady, "Signed, Sealed, Delivered" (2003) 97 (2) LSG 27.
[62] [1996] 2 All ER 345, 351 See also *Howley v Whipple*, 48 NH 487 (1869): "It makes no difference whether that operator writes the offer or the acceptance . . . with a steel pen an inch long attached to an ordinary penholder, or whether his pen be a copper wire a thousand miles long. In either case the thought is communicated to the paper by use of the finger resting upon the pen; nor does it make any difference that in one case common record ink is used, while in the other case a more subtle fluid, known as electricity, performs the same office". But see the dissenting judgment of Denning LJ in *Goodman v J Eban Ltd.* [1954] 1 QB 550, arguing that a rubber stamp could not be a signature: "This is such common knowledge that a 'rubber stamp' is contemptuously used to denote the thoughtless impress of an automation in contrast to the reasoned attention of a sensible person."

letterhead in *Casey*) on an unencrypted e-mail to establish a contract are myriad. The Internet is an open network. E-mails can be manipulated and altered by third parties without detection. In addition, it is difficult to identify the source of an ordinary e-mail: who's to say that someone sent an e-mail simply because it came from his account? An ordinary e-mail is arguably not even as secure as a traditional ink signature on paper. It lacks the "semi-permanence of ink embedded in paper, unique attributes of some printing processes, watermarks, the distinctiveness of individual signatures, and the limited ability to erase, interlineate, or otherwise modify words on paper".[63] While legislation in the area of e-commerce must recognise the need for flexibility in trading, it is also important that the law demands an equivalent level of security in online transactions as is available from traditional paper contracting.[64] Reliability has never been a condition of the prima facie validity of a signature, but as advanced electronic signatures become more common and the technology becomes more widely available, the case for requiring advanced electronic signatures becomes stronger.

That said, the recent English High Court decision *Nilesh Metha v J Pereira Fernandes SA*[65] suggests that the courts will apply the requirements of the Statute of Frauds to electronic communications with some rigour. The Manchester District Registry refused to enforce a personal guarantee given by e-mail on the grounds that the e-mail had not been signed. The Court held that the guarantor's e-mail address could not constitute a signature because a person's e-mail address is inserted automatically on the e-mails they send out. Like the solicitor's initials in *Kelly*, it was merely incidental to the document. It was not "intended for signature", nor did it indicate an "authenticating intention". Judge Pelling likened an e-mail address to a fax number. He said:

[11–39]

> "It is well known that the recipient of a fax will usually receive a copy that has the name and/or number of the sender automatically printed at the top together with a transmission time. Can it sensibly be suggested that the automatically generated name and fax number of the sender of a fax on a faxed document that is otherwise a [document covered by the Statute] would constitute a signature for these purposes?"

## V. Solutions When a Contract does not Comply with the Statute

The courts have devised many means of circumventing the potentially draconian effect of the statute, and they are applied liberally. There are ways in which defects in a memorandum can be remedied or ignored. There are means by which a contract that has not been properly evidenced can be enforced, and, alternatively, ways in which remedies can be provided to a party who is disadvantaged by the non-enforcement of a contract for lack of compliance with a statute.

[11–40]

---

[63] Robertson, "Electronic Commerce on the Internet and the Statute of Frauds" (1998) 49 SC L Rev 787 at 796.
[64] See New Zealand Law Commission, *Electronic Commerce Part One: A guide for the legal and business community* (1998) Report 50 108–118.
[65] (2006) EWHC 813.

### Rectification

[11–41]     Rectification is an equitable remedy (17–65). It allows a document to be revised if there has been a mistake in recording an oral agreement in writing so that it fails to reflect the intentions of the parties to that contract. A deficient memorandum can be revised so that it is adequate for the purposes of the statute. In *Whiting v Dover Plumbing and Heating*,[66] Tipping J explained that "if rectification is granted the instrument is deemed to have been in its rectified form from the start".

### Estoppel

[11–42]     *Black v Grealy*[67] provides another option. If rectification is not possible, but the defendant has at some point noticed the mistake in the memorandum and has expressly agreed to accept it, mistake and all, as a true record of the oral agreement, he cannot later say that it is inadequate. He may be estopped from doing so.

### Waiver

[11–43]     Suppose a memorandum is defective because some essential term has been left out. If that term is solely for the plaintiff's benefit, he is entitled to waive performance of that term and insist on completion of the rest of the contract. This idea is best explained by example. In *Anom Engineering Ltd. v Thompson*,[68] the defendants had entered into an oral agreement to sell property to the plaintiffs. The agreement was evidenced in a draft contract and documents of title prepared by the defendants' solicitors. However, these documents made no reference to the right to connect at agreed points on the defendants' land to obtain a supply of power and water. The defendants refused to complete. The plaintiffs sued for specific performance. In principle, the contract could not be enforced because the draft contract and documents of title did not form a sufficient memorandum for the purposes of the statute because they did not mention what were considered to be the essential matters of power and water. This was where waiver came in. Because the terms as to power and water were entirely for the plaintiff's benefit, he was entitled to waive them and insist on specific performance of the rest of the contract. Where the omitted term is for the benefit of both parties or for the benefit of the defendant alone, waiver will not be available.

### The Statute Cannot be Used as an Engine of Fraud

[11–44]     It would be ironic if a statute that was devised to prevent fraud could be used to perpetrate fraud. The courts may enforce a contract notwithstanding the lack of a sufficient memorandum for the purposes of the statute if it appears that the defendant is relying on the technicalities of the statute to protect his own sharp practice. *O'Mullane v Riordan*[69] concerned a written agreement for the sale of land. The purchaser subsequently agreed to allow the seller to connect water and sewage to the rest of his lands. A further agreement to this effect was written but the vendor never

---

[66] [1992] 1 NZLR 560.
[67] *Black v Grealy*, unreported, High Court, 10 November 1977.
[68] Unreported, High Court, 1 February 1984.
[69] Unreported, High Court, 20 April 1976. See also *McGillicuddy v Joy* [1959] IR 189; *Doherty v Gallagher*, unreported, High Court, 9 June 1975.

signed it. The vendor then refused to perform and the purchaser sued for specific performance. The vendor argued that there was no sufficient memorandum for the Statute of Frauds because there was no signed document that referred to the essential matter of the wayleave. McWilliam J held that "it would be an abuse of this statute if I were compelled to hold that the entire agreement were unenforceable because this extra term was not signed by the defendant although it was signed in his presence, at his request and for his benefit and was witnessed by his wife".

## Part Performance

In some circumstances, a plaintiff who has partly performed a contract is entitled to specific performance of that contract, notwithstanding that there is no sufficient memorandum of the contract for the purposes of the statute. Note that while the requirement of a signed memorandum refers to the defendant, this alternative refers to the plaintiff. Acts of the defendant can never amount to part performance. The doctrine of part performance stems from the maxim just considered: "that the court will not allow a Statute which was passed to prevent fraud to be made itself an instrument of fraud".[70] The doctrine of part performance is an equitable one. Its functions are a mixture of evidence and estoppel. First, part performance is said to be probative of the contract—the plaintiff has done certain things in the aftermath of the agreement which are consistent with the contract and this is evidence that it exists.[71] So part performance may be said to replace one type of evidence with another—acts of part performance are a type of *res gestae*. In addition, there is an idea based on unconscionability. This idea is that, where the plaintiff has partly performed the contract—for example, by spending money in reliance on it—an equity arises in his favour "which is so affixed upon the conscience of the defendant that it would amount to fraud on his part to take advantage of the fact that the contract is not in writing." [72] The defendant is "breaking faith"[73] with the plaintiff by taking the benefit from the plaintiff's performance and then denying the existence of the contract when his own turn for performance comes.

[11–45]

The best example of the doctrine of part performance in action is *Lowry v Reid*.[74] The plaintiff, William Lowry, and his mother, Mary, contracted orally that she would leave her property to him if he transferred his farm, Ballykeigle, together with £200, to his brother, Andrew. William carried out the transfer and went to live with his mother. However, Mary did not leave her property to William as agreed and he only received a life interest in it. There was no sufficient memorandum of the

[11–46]

---

[70] *Lowry v Reid* [1927] NI 142 *per* Andrews LJ.

[71] See *Actionstrength Ltd. v International Glass Engineering* [2003] 2 WLR 1060.

[72] Above, n 69. See also *Hope v Lord Cloncurry* (1874) IR 8 Eq 555 *per* Chatterton V-C: "The principle upon which the rule in cases of part performance was engrafted on the Statute of Frauds is, that it would be a fraud on the part of the person who had entered into an agreement by parol for a lease or sale, and had allowed expenditure to be made upon the faith of it, afterwards to turn around and say that it did not legally exist."; *Bond v Hopkins* 1 Sch & L 413 at 433 *per* Lord Redesdale: The court will grant a remedy: "where the party seeking relief has been put into a situation which makes it against the conscience of the other party to insist on the want of writing so signed, as a bar to his relief".

[73] See *Mackey v Wilde,* unreported, Supreme Court, 17 December 1997 *per* Barron J.

[74] [1927] NI 142.

contract for the purposes of the Statute of Frauds. The question was whether the plaintiff could obtain specific performance of his contract with his mother. William's part performance was that he had given up his own property to his own detriment. Moore LCJ held that William was therefore entitled to specific performance of the contract.

[11–47]     Every case in which part performance is alleged will be considered on its own particular facts.[75] In *Mackey v Wilde*,[76] the Supreme Court said that four conditions must be satisfied before specific performance will be granted on the basis of part performance. The plaintiff must prove these conditions on the balance of probabilities:

1.  There is a concluded oral agreement;
2.  The plaintiff acted in such a way as to show an intention to perform the contract;
3.  The defendant induced these acts or stood by while they were being performed;
4.  It would be unconscionable and a breach of good faith to allow the defendant to rely upon the terms of the Statute of Frauds to prevent performance of the contract.

### Concluded Oral Agreement

[11–48]     In *JC v WC*,[77] the defendant claimed that he had worked extensively on the family farm for very little money from the age of 13. He had been withdrawn from school permanently at 15 to work the farm. From that time until 1999, he believed that the farm would be his home and his living throughout his life, and that he would inherit the farm on his father's death. However, the plaintiff could not prove that any oral agreement had ever existed regarding the property and so any claim of part performance was irrelevant.

### Intention to Perform

[11–49]     The first and third parts of the test in *Mackey v Wilde* will ordinarily be satisfied. Parts two and four require further exploration. The second part of the test is the most complex. First, there is an evidentiary question to consider. There has been some debate as to the type of act that will demonstrate intention by the plaintiff to perform the contract. The plaintiff's acts must be shown to relate to the contract. The older cases required that these acts were "uniquely referable" to the contract alleged to exist and no other. In *Maddison v Alderson*,[78] the Earl of Selborne said that "[a]ll the

---

[75] *McCarron v McCarron*, unreported, Supreme Court, 13 February 1997.

[76] Above, n 72.

[77] [2004] 2 IR 314.

[78] 8 AC 457 at 479. See also Lord O'Hagan in the same case: an act of part performance "must be sufficient of itself and without any other information or evidence, to satisfy a court, from the circumstances it has created and the relations it has formed, that they are only consistent with the assumption of the existence of a contract".

authorities show that the acts relied upon as part performance must be unequivocally and in their own nature referable to some such agreement as that alleged". This approach emphasised the evidentiary function of the doctrine of part performance—the act had to relate to the alleged contract and no other. That requirement was so difficult to satisfy that it limited the doctrine almost out of all existence. It has since been relaxed as the courts shift their emphasis to the element of unconscionability at the core of part performance. What seem to be required now under *Mackey v Wilde* [79] are acts which are consistent with the existence of *some* contract and consistent with the existence of *the* contract alleged to a reasonably clear extent. [80] An example of this part of the test in action is *McCarron v McCarron*. [81] The plaintiff alleged that he had formed an oral contract with the deceased Mr McKenna who had agreed to leave his property to the plaintiff in remuneration for his work on the farm. There was no memorandum of the contract and, indeed, the oral contract was based on a number of very vague and limited conversations in which, *inter alia*, Mr McKenna had promised the plaintiff: "You will be a rich man after my day." The plaintiff's 16 years of work for the deceased were enough to show an intention to perform. There was no other significant explanation for the fact that the plaintiff had worked for the deceased without remuneration bar a contract and his actions were consistent with a contract along the lines of that which the plaintiff alleged. Murphy J elaborated:

> "This was never a case in which it might have been suggested that work was done or humanitarian services provided on a purely neighbourly or charitable basis for some person in need. Nor does it seem to me that the help and assistance provided by the plaintiff was undertaken and continued in the vague hope that [the deceased] might at his discretion remember his kindness when he came to make a will."

Other examples of acts indicating the intention to perform include a purchaser entering into possession of land with the vendor's agreement, [82] a purchaser's entry onto land and demolition of property on it [83] and draining and planting of agricultural land. [84] **[11–50]**

Does the payment of money demonstrate the type of intention required by the second element of the test? Traditionally, payment of money did not satisfy the second part of the test. However, this position was altered by the ruling of the House of Lords in *Steadman v Steadman*. [85] Their lordships indicated that the plaintiff's payment of money could constitute an act demonstrating the required intention where it was referable to a contract for the disposition of an interest in land and where the defendant had accepted the money. This principle was followed in *Howlin v Power* [86]: the defendant and the plaintiff had an oral agreement concerning a lease. There was no **[11–51]**

---

[79] [1998] 2 IR 578.

[80] See also *Lowry v Reid*, above, n 73.

[81] Unreported, Supreme Court, 13 February 1997.

[82] *Kennedy v Kennedy*, unreported, High Court, 12 January 1984.

[83] *Starling Securities v Woods*, unreported, High Court, 24 May 1977.

[84] *Howe v Hall* (1870) 4 I Rep Eq 242.

[85] [1976] AC 536. See also *Re Gonin* [1977] 2 All ER 720.

[86] Unreported, High Court, 5 May 1978.

memorandum sufficient for the purposes of the statute. The plaintiff paid £200 of the purchase price. The defendant refused to complete the sale and offered to repay the £200. McWilliam J found that the payment of £200 was an act which showed an intention to perform the contract.

### Unconscionability

[11–52]    The fourth requirement is that of unconscionability. This requirement contemplates that the plaintiff has suffered some detriment by his act of part performance so that it would be a fraud for the defendant to deny the existence of the contract. For example, in *Howlin*, above, the plaintiff eventually failed to establish part performance. This was because there was no unconscionability present because the defendant had tendered repayment of the £200. This is one of the reasons why a refundable booking deposit does not amount to part performance of a contract for the sale of land. A vendor is entitled to withdraw from an agreement to sell a house notwithstanding such a deposit.[87] The point of this part of the test is that the performing party has taken such significant steps that it would be inequitable not to enforce the oral contract which he alleges exists. In *Howlin*, the Court said that the plaintiff must take:

> "some conclusive or irrevocable or prejudicial step in pursuance of the contract, such as conveying land to a third party, entering into occupation of premises agreed to be let or sold to him, ejecting tenants at the request of the other party or commencing to carry on a business in partnership in pursuance of an agreement to do so".

[11–53]    It is for this reason that preparatory acts, such as raising a loan, consulting an estate agent or carrying out a survey, cannot amount to acts of part performance; these acts are neither conclusive, nor irrevocable, nor prejudicial.

### Restitution

[11–54]    If part performance is unavailable, a party who has performed his part of a bargain which cannot be enforced for want of a sufficient memorandum may have a restitutionary claim in *quantum meruit*. *Quantum meruit* is a remedy under which a party who has provided a benefit and who cannot obtain payment under the contract can recover reasonable compensation for the benefit he has provided. In *Savage v Canning*,[88] the plaintiff had carried out work and labour on foot of a contract that could not be enforced because of non-compliance with the Statute of Frauds. The plaintiff recovered £500 because he had performed his part of the contract. The Court held:

> "It would be a very extraordinary state of things if in such a case the law enabled the Defendant to say: 'It is impossible for you, the Plaintiff, to prove the contract I entered into, and it is in fact no contract at all. I therefore cannot be made to pay for the work and labour I have taken the benefit of."

---

[87] But see the controversial Circuit Court decision of Buckley J in *Prendville v Gable* (1998) ILT 125.
[88] (1867) IR 1 CL 674.

# CHAPTER 12
# Agreements Subject to Contract

## I. Introduction

The phrase "subject to contract" is a delaying mechanism. In essence, the use of the **[12–01]** rubric "subject to contract" engages with the principle of intention to create legal relations.[1] Parties use it to indicate that, while they are acknowledging the terms of their contract in writing, they do not intend the agreement to bind them until a more formal contractual document has been executed. Lord Denning in *Tiverton Estates v Wearwell*[2] sets out that "the effect of the words 'subject to contract' is that the matter remains in negotiation until the formal contract is executed". This principle has been a part of Irish law since the judgment of Molony CJ in *Thompson v The King*.[3]

The phrase "subject to contract" itself need not necessarily be used, though it is **[12–02]** probably wiser to do so. Where alternative words are used, the courts will attempt to divine the parties' intent from the words used in the overall context of the agreement.

---

[1] Smith, *Atiyah's Introduction to the Law of Contract* (6th ed., OUP, 2005), p 102. The doctrine is also explained in terms of conditions precedent. See *Rossiter v Miller* (1878) 3 App Cas 1124 at 1139 *per* Lord Cairns LC:

> "[I]f you find, not an unqualified acceptance of a contract, but an acceptance subject to condition that an agreement is to be prepared and acted upon between the parties, and until that condition is fulfilled no contract is to arise, then undoubtedly you cannot, upon a correspondence of that kind, find a concluded contract."

[2] [1975] Ch 146. In *Winn v Bull* (1877) 7 Ch D 29, Jessel MR explains: "Where you have a proposal or agreement made in writing expressed to be subject to a formal contract being prepared, it means what it says, it is subject to and is dependant upon a formal contract being prepared." See also *Irish Mainport Holdings v Crosshaven Sailing Centre Ltd.*, unreported, High Court, 16 May 1980 *per* Keane J.: The words "subject to contract" "have, in law, a precise significance and, save in exceptional circumstances, are construed as postponing the incidence of liability until a formal contract has been executed".

[3] [1920] 2 IR 365. McDermott *Contract Law* (LexisNexis, 2000), p 82 suggests that under *Thompson v The King*, "subject to contract" has a second meaning: that the parties acknowledge a concluded oral agreement which will be implemented by a formal agreement in the future. Gibson J held at 386 that:

For example, in *Silver Wraith v Siúcra Éireann*,[4] "subject to full lease being agreed" was recognised as akin to "subject to contract" in a context where the parties using the phrase were laymen.

**[12–03]**        When used properly, the phrase "subject to contract" affords breathing space. Parties do not have to worry about being bound by stray pieces of correspondence. An agreement can be settled and put on ice until the parties are ready to take the final steps. If difficulties arise in the meantime, either party can withdraw or seek to re-negotiate, knowing that he will not be liable for breach of contract.

## II. Suspending the Contract

**[12–04]**        If the phrase "subject to contract" is to be effective, it must be used before the agreement is concluded.[5] So an offer made subject to contract does not result in a binding contract even if it is accepted.[6] "Subject to contract" is effective where used during negotiations before the contract is concluded—for example, in the letters that pass between the parties during bargaining. If the phrase is first used after the agreement has been concluded, it is probably ineffective. This proposition was established by McWilliam J in *O'Flaherty v Arvan Property*.[7] In that case, the purchasers of property were handed a receipt for a deposit. The receipt contained all the material terms of the contract of sale. It was expressed to be "subject to contract". The phrase "subject to contract" had not been used at any stage during negotiations. It appeared for the first time in this receipt, after the agreement had been concluded. Therefore, the phrase was ineffective and the Court ordered completion of the sale. Similarly, in *Casey v Irish Intercontinental Bank*,[8] Kenny J found that a contract came into existence despite the use of the words "subject to contract". This was because the phrase was not introduced into the transaction until 2nd February when an oral contract for sale had already been completed. This approach was confirmed by Hardiman J in the Supreme Court in *Supermac's Ireland v Kateson*.[9] In that case, he said: "In my view it is plainly arguable that this rubric ... does not preclude the existence of a 'done deal' between the parties themselves".

---

"Where an offer and acceptance are made subject to a subsequent formal contract, if such a contract is a condition or term which until performed keeps the agreement in suspense, the offer and acceptance have no contractual force. On the other hand, if all the terms are agreed on, and a formal contract is only contemplated as putting all the terms in legal shape, the agreement is effectual before and irrespective of such formal contract".

In these circumstances, a court may order specific performance where there is a valid memorandum for the purposes of the Statute of Frauds or sufficient part performance.

[4] Unreported, High Court, 8 June 1989.

[5] The phrase will also be ineffective where it is used by mistake as in *Michael Richards Properties v Corporation of Wardens of Saint Saviours Southwark* [1975] 3 All ER 416, or where its use is wholly inconsistent with the rest of the contract as in *Alpenstowe v Regalian Properties Ltd.* [1985] 1 WLR 721.

[6] *Thompson*, above, n 3.

[7] Unreported, High Court, 3 November 1976.

[8] [1979] IR 364.

[9] [2001] 1 ILRM 401.

## III. Subject to Contract and the Statute of Frauds

"Subject to contract" has a particular relevance to contracts for the sale of land. As
noted, such contracts must pass two tests before they are enforced: an enforceable
contract for sale must be concluded and it must be appropriately evidenced in writing.
As noted before, if "subject to contract" is used for the first time in a document made
after the conclusion of a contract, it does not affect the contract itself; the phrase has
been used too late. The contract remains binding on the parties. However, a party may
grasp a second chance to stall the contract if a document including the phrase "subject
to contract" is submitted as a memorandum for the purposes of s 2 of the Statute of
Frauds. Then evidentiary issues arise. A memorandum is prepared as proof of
agreement; the parties are declaring "we have a binding contract for the sale of this
land". But if the memorandum is headed by the phrase "subject to contract", the
parties are stating exactly the opposite—they are saying "there is no binding contract
between us yet and there will not be until we have executed a final contractual
document". Thus, in Ireland, *Boyle v Lee*[10] confirms that a memorandum headed with
the phrase "subject to contract" is insufficient for the purposes of the Statute, and
ordinarily, no contract thus memorialised will be enforced. For a time, however, two
High Court decisions seemed to strip "subject to contract" of its effect in this context.
Both *Kelly v Park Hall School*[11] and *Casey v Irish Intercontinental Bank*[12] held that the
phrase was meaningless where all the other terms of the contract had been agreed.

[12–05]

Hence, a document headed "subject to contract" could still be a valid
memorandum. These cases probably have less to do with "subject to contract" itself
and more to do with the perceived injustice caused by the memorandum requirement
of the Statute of Frauds in preventing genuine bargains. Naturally, these cases were
controversial because "subject to contract" had been viewed for so long as an
automatic denial of a contract.

[12–06]

In *Mulhall v Haren*,[13] Keane J appeared to restore the traditional position on
subject to contract. He held that, in the vast majority of circumstances, a memorial
containing the words "subject to contract" was not a sufficient memorandum for the
purposes of the Statute of Frauds. The memorandum must acknowledge the contract's
existence. In *Mulhall*, the plaintiff and defendant had concluded an oral agreement.
After the agreement had concluded, the plaintiff's solicitor wrote to the defendant's
auctioneers requesting a formal contract "as the sale is subject to contract". The
defendant refused to complete the sale and the plaintiff sued for specific performance.
The case turned on the effect of the phrase "subject to contract". Keane J held that:

[12–07]

"the wording of s.2 of the Statute of 1695 plainly envisages a writing which is
evidence of a contract entered into by the party sought to be charged and that
this is not met by a writing which uses language inconsistent with the existence
of a concluded contract...[T]he use of the words 'subject to contract' is

---

[10] [1992] 1 IR 555.
[11] [1979] IR 340.
[12] [1979] IR 364.
[13] *Mulhall v Haren* [1981] IR 364.

inconsistent with the existence of a concluded agreement, save in the most exceptional cases".

[12–08]     In *Boyle v Lee*,[14] the Supreme Court also took the view that the use of the phrase "subject to contract" denies the existence of a concluded oral contract. In this case, the plaintiff bought an investment property. He claimed that an agreement had been reached with the seller to sell the property for £90,000. The defendant's solicitor had written to him accepting his offer to buy for £90,000 but subject to contract. Finlay CJ and Hederman and McCarthy JJ held that the letter could never be a sufficient memorandum for the purposes of the Statute because the phrase "subject to contract" had been used. O'Flaherty and Egan JJ accepted that there might be exceptional cases in which the phrase was ineffective. *Boyle* is a difficult authority because four of the five judges held that no oral agreement had been completed in the case. Therefore, they spoke *obiter* on the issue of the status of the phrase "subject to contract". It is clear, however, that the general thrust of *Boyle* is that a document headed "subject to contract" will not be a sufficient memorandum for the purposes of the Statute. A contract evidenced in this way cannot be enforced unless there is another document not containing the words "subject to contract", which is a valid memorandum for the purposes of the Statute, or there are acts of part performance. This approach was further endorsed in *Jodifern Ltd. v Fitzgerald*.[15]

[12–09]     One chink of uncertainty remaining in this area of law is that opened by the Supreme Court in *Jodifern Ltd. v Fitzgerald*.[16] There the Court, while confirming that "subject to contract" at the head of a document had its traditional effect, suggested that using the phrase in the document's body had somewhat less certain consequences: "it is a matter of construction of the writing as a whole whether it is intended to deny the existence of a complete agreement".

[12–10]     The shift from the position in *Kelly* to that in *Boyle* can be explained in terms of policy. "Subject to contract" was a phrase which had taken on a very precise meaning universally understood by solicitors. There is a tremendous risk involved in changing such a familiar principle. As Templeman LJ observes in *Sherbrooke v Dipple*[17]: "Once one gets away from principle, then all is difficulty, and reliance on odd conversations and letters produces uncertainty in law". Finlay CJ made a similar point in *Boyle v Lee*:

"[A]ll one's experience of the massive losses and inconvenience which can be suffered by prospective purchasers or vendors of land from non-completion of

---

[14] [1992] IR 555.
[15] [2000] 4 IR 273. This approach follows that adopted by Lord Denning in *Tiverton Estates v Wearwell* [1975] Ch 146 at 153.

"I cannot myself see any difference between a writing which (i) denies there has been a contract, (ii) does not admit there was any contract (iii) says the parties are in negotiation or (iv) says that there was an agreement 'subject to contract' for it comes to the same thing. The reason why none of these writings satisfies the statute is because none of them contains any recognition or admission of the existence of a contract."

[16] [2000] 4 IR 273.
[17] 41 P & CR 173.

what they believe to be a contract, and the subsequent delays and difficulties arising from complicated litigation concerning it, indicates that the requirements of justice are that the law applicable to the formation of contracts for the purchase of land should be as certain as it is possible to make it. In modern times, probably the most important legal transaction a great number of people make in their lifetime is the purchase or sale of their house. The avoidance of doubt and, therefore, the avoidance of litigation concerning such a transaction must be a worthwhile social objective ... To that end, certainty in the question of what is or is not a sufficient note or memorandum is a desirable aim. In my view the...principle that no...note or memorandum which contains any term or expression such as "subject to contract" can be sufficient ... achieves that certainty."

McCarthy J recognised that *Kelly* and *Casey* had their hearts in the right place:    [12–11]

"[Section 2 of the Statute of Frauds] came to be construed as liberally as possible—seeking to "find" the necessary evidence once the bargain was proved until, as appears to me to be the case, a note or memorandum which necessarily denied the existence of a bargain became itself evidence to support its enforcement. ... It may well be thought that [not allowing a memorandum using the words "subject to contract" to satisfy the statute] will result in genuine bargains not being enforced and that a court should, as I believe it has in the past 'to do a great right, do a little wrong' ... Portia's rule of construction is the preferred alternative."

## IV. Gazumping and the Good Faith in Bargaining

"Subject to contract" is most controversially used to facilitate "gazumping"[18] in    [12–12] property sales. Suppose a vendor feels that he has found a suitable purchaser for his house but wishes to have one last go at negotiating with others for a better price. Entering into an agreement "subject to contract" with his purchaser allows him to do so. It is perfectly legal for V to approach P and seek a higher sum at any stage before a formal contract document is signed. If P refuses, V may "gazump" him by entering into a new contract for the sale of the property with another buyer. P has no cause of action. This may seem unfair but it makes perfect sense at law. The bare "agreement subject to contract" between V and P is, quite literally, not worth the paper it is written on. This is because no formal document has been produced, leaving the intended conditions of the agreement's effectiveness unfulfilled. V's new binding contract with his competitor naturally trumps it. In his turn, V, in coming to P asking for a higher price, has done nothing more than make a new offer, which P refused to accept. P may

---

[18] In *Tevanan v Norman Brett*, Brightman J said that the word gazumping was an unattractive one, "no doubt reflecting the unattractive qualities of such behaviour". See *Report on Gazumping* (LRC 59-1999).

have given a refundable booking deposit, but that does not give him any viable interest in the property.[19] So Sachs J astutely speaks in *Goding v Fraser*[20] of:

> "this hybrid type of 'subject to contract' transaction which is so often referred to as a gentleman's agreement but which experience shows is only too often a transaction in which each side hopes the other will act like a gentleman and neither intends to so act if it is against his material interests".

[12–13]    Notwithstanding the injustice it can cause, "subject to contract" is more than a "get out of jail free" card. It allows those dealing with private property an optimal measure of autonomy in their transactions. In addition, "subject to contract" can equally be exploited by the purchaser. He may abandon the agreement if he finds a better deal or if he is unable to raise a mortgage.

[12–14]    Practices like gazumping are an inevitable side effect of a common law system that refuses to acknowledge a pre-contractual duty to bargain in good faith.[21] Clarke has observed, as illustrated below, that the "foundations of a general rule of good faith can be discerned in the common law dust".[22] Indeed, at one time, the great Lord Mansfield[23] championed such an idea as part of the common law. More recently, Lord Steyn said that a good faith principle, which he describes as the protection of "the reasonable expectations of honest men … has been and still is the principal moulding force of our law of contract".[24] The orthodox position, however, is that there is no room for a doctrine of good faith at the stage of negotiations. Brownsword[25] summarises the reasons why adversarial dealing remains "the only game in town" as follows:

> "To sum up, the case against the adoption of a general principle of good faith is that English contract law is premised on adversarial self-interested dealing (rather than other-regarded good faith dealing); that good faith is a vague idea, threatening to import an uncertain discretion into [the] law; that the implementation of a good faith doctrine would call for difficult inquiries into contracting parties' reasons in particular cases; that good faith represents a challenge to the autonomy of contracting parties; and, that a general doctrine cannot be appropriate when contracting contexts vary so much."

[12–15]    The alternative to the imposition of a good faith doctrine at the procedural stage of contracting seems to be an ad hoc development of solutions in those cases where the device of "subject to contract" is used mala fides. The exceptional situations

---

[19] *Re Barrett* [1985] IR 350; *Embourg v Tyler* [1996] 3 IR 480; *Butler v Greenhills Construction Ltd.*, *Irish Times*, 22 October 1998.
[20] [1967] 1 WLR 286 at 293.
[21] For a comprehensive rejection of this duty, see the judgment of the Supreme Court of Canada in *Martel Building Ltd v Canada* (2000) 193 DLR (4th) 1.
[22] Clarke, "The Common Law of Contract in 1993: Is There a General Doctrine of Good Faith" (1993) 23 HKLJ 318 at 319.
[23] *Carter v Boehm* (1766) 3 Burr 1905.
[24] *First Energy (UK) Ltd. v Hungarian International Bank Ltd.* [1993] 2 Lloyd's Rep 194 at 196.
[25] Brownsword, *Contract Law: Themes for the Twenty-First Century* (2000), [5.9].

mentioned by O'Flaherty and Egan JJ contemplate such potential solutions. It is not immediately clear that such a piecemeal approach is a better solution than a coherent duty to bargain in good faith. In 1956,[26] Powell argued that a good faith doctrine would be a more powerful tool than the "contortions" and "subterfuges" to which judges are otherwise forced to resort in their quest for justice. Brownsword elaborates on this argument.[27] He says that a direct and open judicial approach to the pursuit of fairness in contractual dealings is preferable to one which is covert and indirect. A coherent doctrine of good faith would encourage judges at all levels to deal with bad faith negotiation in a more effective manner.[28] Rather than defeating the objective of certainty in contract law, a duty of good faith is likely to promote it. As far as autonomy is concerned, a duty of good faith would arguably enhance the promotion of the parties' contractual intent by giving effect to their reasonable expectations.[29] Brownsword suggests that a reluctance to view contract negotiations through any other lens than that of adversarial "tough dealing" makes a nonsense of any argument that the parties will reasonably expect good faith dealing of one another. However, particularly in the context of the purchase of a home, the parties will reasonably expect co-operation from one another. In any case, the argument against a duty to bargain in good faith tends to ignore the fact that, as Collins has argued, the courts treat contractual autonomy less as a right and more as a privilege, the exercise of which can be restricted in the interests of the other party.[30] Finally, Brownsword argues that by adopting a doctrine of good faith, the courts could contribute to a culture of trust and co-operation. Certainly, such an approach should be encouraged given the admitted importance of property transactions and the acknowledged vulnerability of would-be homeowners for whom the purchase of a house may be a once-in-a-lifetime event. There is a danger, however, that such attempts at contractual engineering will meet with judicial distaste. While the common law seems unlikely to breed a duty of good faith bargaining, EC consumer law has begun to provide some tools to fill this void. The Consumer Protection Act 2007 gives effect to the Unfair Commercial Practices Directive 2007. The Act prohibits bad faith, unfair commercial practices which would impair the ability of the average consumer to make an informed decision as to whether to enter into a contract.

---

[26] Powell, "Good Faith in Contracts" (1956) 9 CLP 16 at 26.

[27] Brownsword, *op. cit.*, 5.15.

[28] See Mason, "Contract, Good Faith and Equitable Standards in Fair Dealing" (2000) 116 LQR 66.

[29] See also Steyn, "Contract Law: Fulfilling the Reasonable Expectations of Honest Men" (1997) 113 LQR 433 at 439.

[30] Collins, *The Law of Contract* (4th ed, LexisNexis, 2003), p 219.

# CHAPTER 13
# The Terms of the Contract

## I. The Primacy of Intention

Every contract consists of terms. Terms are the individual obligations that the parties **[13–01]** have assumed under the contract. One of the court's main functions in any contract case, then, will be to identify the terms which the parties have mutually chosen. However, it will not always clear be what these terms are. It is worth examining first the difficulties relating to express terms: the written and oral terms of the contract. One party may produce a contractual document, but the other may argue that the document does not contain all of the contract. He may say that the contract is spread out over more than one document, in which case the court must look to the canons of incorporation (14–07). Or he may say that oral promises were also made which ought to be treated as legally binding. The court will use the parol evidence rule to decide whether to hear evidence of matters outside the four corners of the contractual document (13–07). In addition, A may allege that B made promises during contractual negotiations which were assimilated into the main contract, while B insists that these were mere statements which he did not intend to be contractually binding. The court will have to decide whether the statements at issue were mere representations or warranties of the contract (13–16). What is more, terms may come from sources outside the contractual document. The court may consider whether terms must be implied into the contract (13–26) to give effect to the unspoken intention of the parties or to give effect to judicial or legislative policy about the minimum content of certain types of contract.

While the law of terms covers a number of disparate areas, there is a thematic **[13–02]** thread which connects them all: the principle, inherent in the concept of freedom of contract, that the parties are not to be bound by any contractual obligation unless they intended to be so bound. The flip side of this fundamental idea in classical contract law is obviously that if, from an objective standpoint, it appears that a party intended to be bound by a particular term, he must be held to it. With contractual autonomy also comes contractual responsibility. The courts will hold a party to his apparently intended bargain even where he has made an unwise or unreasonable bargain. The

149

courts will not interfere because the parties are considered to be the best judges of their own self-interest. McCarthy J was evidently a member of this school of thought. In *Tradax Ireland v Irish Grain Board*[1] he wrote that:

> "[i]t is not the function of a court to write a contract for parties who have not met upon commercially equal terms; if such parties want to enter into unreasonable, unfair or even disastrous contracts, that is their business, not the business of the Court."

**[13–03]**     Traditionally, the courts' function is to discover the bargain the parties agreed to and hold them to it; it is only if some shadow is cast over the reality of the parties' agreement, as where the contract is tainted by mistake (Chapter 17) or misrepresentation (Chapter 15) duress or undue influence (Chapter 18), that the court has jurisdiction to intervene. The courts will uphold a contract that is formed according to certain minimal procedural standards, but will not engage with the substance of the parties' agreement. This philosophy of the judicial role is evident in a number of areas in this chapter. The courts created the parol evidence rule (13–07) which said that, where the parties intended to reduce their contract to one document, they should be bound by that document. The court would not hear any arguments about other terms not contained in the final printed contract, no matter what injustice might result. Similarly, we see that where terms are implied in fact, (13–28) the stated function of the court is to discover the intention of the parties and provide terms which give effect to that intention. However, the court must exercise this power cautiously so that it is not tempted to write a different, perhaps fairer, contract for the parties.

**[13–04]**     This narrow classical portrayal of the judicial role does not tell the whole story of the law of contract terms. The pairing of pure contractual autonomy and absolute contractual responsibility is not enough to ground a satisfactory system of contract law. Increasingly, the courts understand their role as correcting those imbalances in the bargaining process which tend to lead to substantively unfair contracts. For example, the courts have substantially relaxed the parol evidence rule so that one party is not allowed to rely on a printed document to avoid his obligations to the other (13–11). In the law of warranties and representations, a statement is more likely to be treated as a warranty, and therefore as contractually binding, if the party making the statement ought to have greater knowledge of the matter (13–24). In this way, the law allocates responsibility for the truth of statements in line with disparities in knowledge. The law of terms implied in fact shows that the courts are increasingly willing to annex extra obligations to the parties' contract, which are not clearly mandated by the parties' intention, in order to bring about a fairer bargain (13–28). Terms are implied, or rather imposed, at common law (13–52), at statute (13–62) and under the Constitution (13–61), not in order to give effect to the parties' intention, but on the basis of pure policy. For example, certain mandatory terms are implied into consumer contracts in order to redress the traditional imbalances of information and bargaining power as between consumer and seller (13–62).

---

[1] [1984] IR 1.

When reading this chapter, therefore, it is important to consciously chart the law's navigation between the Scylla of fidelity to the parties' intention and the Charybdis of distributive justice. **[13–05]**

## II. Finding the Express Terms

The express terms of a contract are those terms which have been written down or spoken by the parties. **[13–06]**

### The Document as Exclusive Evidence of the Contract

One of the court's first tasks will be to determine what the parties said or wrote. If the contract is entirely oral, the judge will make a precise finding of fact as to what the parties said. Where the contract is intended to be entirely written, the old rule is that the court is confined to the four corners of the final contractual document. Neither party can adduce extrinsic evidence (called "parol evidence") to show that the document is not an accurate record of his contractual intention. Corbin gives the best statement of the parol evidence rule[2]: **[13–07]**

> "When two parties have made a contract and have expressed it in a writing to which they have both assented as the complete and accurate integration of that contract, evidence ... of antecedent understandings and negotiations will not be admitted for the purpose of varying or contradicting the writing."

The purpose of this rule is to promote certainty. Neither party should be able to usurp the contract by (perhaps fraudulently) alleging the existence of new terms which were not included in the final document. This reason for the rule was set out in the *Countess of Rutland's* case,[3] where Chief Justice Popham declared that it would be "inconvenient": **[13–08]**

> "... that matters in writing made by advice and on consideration, and which finally import the certain truth of the agreement of the parties should be controlled by averment of the parties to be proved by the uncertain testimony of slippery memory."

A more dramatic exposition of this justification is found in the US case of *Cargill Commn Co v Swartwood*[4]: **[13–09]**

> "Were it otherwise, written contracts would be enforced not according to the plain effect of their language, but pursuant to the story of their negotiations as told by the litigant having at the time being the greater power of persuading the trier of fact. So far as contracts are concerned, the rule of law would give way to the mere notions of man as to who should win law suits. [Without the parol evidence rule] there would be no assurance of the enforceability of a written contract. If such assurance were removed today from our law, general disaster would result because of the consequent destruction of confidence, for the

---

[2]  Corbin, *Corbin on Contracts* (Yale, 1960) § 573.
[3]  5 Co 26a (1604) 77 Eng Rep 89.
[4]  159 Minn 1, 198 NW 636 (1924).

tremendous but closely adjusted machinery of modern business cannot function at all without confidence in the enforceability of contracts."

[13–10]     In addition, by limiting the parties to the four corners of the contractual document, the rule limits the number of issues which can arise in a given case, thereby acting as a control on litigation. However, the rule can also work injustice, as Frank J explains in the American case of *Zell v American Seating Co*[5]:

> "The rule, then, does relatively little to deserve its much advertised virtue of reducing the dangers of successful fraudulent recoveries and defenses brought about through perjury. The rule is too small a hook to catch such a leviathan. Moreover, if at times it does prevent a person from winning, by lying witnesses, a lawsuit which he should lose, it also, at times, by shutting out the true facts, unjustly aids other persons to win lawsuits they should and would lose, were the suppressed evidence known to the courts."

[13–11]     For this reason, in practice, the rule is subject to a number of exceptions. Some of them will be looked at more closely here. The first, and most important, exception is that the rule does not apply where the document was not intended to be the whole of the contract[6]: where there were other oral terms which were intended to bind the parties. For example, in *J Evans & Son (Portsmouth) Ltd v Andrea Merzario Ltd*[7] the parties had a written contract that governed the transport of the plaintiffs' goods with the defendant on board ship. The written contract gave the defendant complete freedom to store the goods on ship as he pleased. However, the defendants had assured the plaintiffs orally that the goods would be stored below deck. The contract here was therefore part written and part oral and the Court was not confined to the contract document but was entitled to "look at all the evidence from start to finish to see what the bargain was that was struck between the parties". Similarly, in *Clayton Love v B & I*[8] the Supreme Court permitted oral evidence of a phone call to be adduced in order to prove certain terms of the contract not included in the final contractual document. The successful introduction of evidence under this exception involves rebutting the presumption "that a document which *looks* like a contract is to be treated as the *whole* contract."[9] The presumption is not especially difficult to displace. In *Gillespie Bros & Co v Cheney, Eggar & Co*[10] Lord Russell CJ wrote:

> "[A]lthough when the parties arrive at a definite written contract the implication or presumption is very strong that such a contract is intended to contain all the terms of their bargain, it is a presumption only, and it is open to either of the parties to allege that there was, in addition to what appears in the written agreement, an antecedent express stipulation not intended by the parties to be excluded, but intended to continue in force with the express written agreement."

---

[5]  138 F 2d 641 (2d Cir 1943).
[6]  *Allen v Pink* (1838) 4 M & W 140.
[7]  [1976] 1 WLR 1078. See also *Couchman v Hill* [1947] KB 554.
[8]  (1970) 104 ILTR 157.
[9]  *Gillespie Bros v Cheney, Eggar & Co* [1896] 2 QB 59.
[10]  *ibid.*

Secondly, parol evidence is admissible to prove terms that must be implied into the agreement[11] or to prove a custom that must be implied into it.[12] For example, in *Wilson Strain v Pinkerton*[13] parol evidence was introduced to show that it was the practice in Belfast on the retirement of a bread delivery man for his employer to take on any outstanding debts. Thirdly, parol evidence is admissible to show that the contract is invalid on the grounds of mistake, (see Chapter 17), fraud or *non est factum*[14] (17–77). Fourthly, parol evidence is admitted to show that there is a mistake in the document itself which should be rectified (17–65). Fifthly, parol evidence may be adduced to prove that the contract has not yet come into operation or has ceased to operate.[15]

[13–12]

Next, parol evidence on the context of the contract is admissible to clear up ambiguity or uncertainty surrounding the agreement. In *Revenue Commissioners v Moroney*[16] parol evidence was admitted to show that what appeared to be a written contract for the sale of land was actually a gift. In *Chambers v Kelly*[17] parol evidence was admitted to show that a written contract which, on the face of it, accorded felling rights in respect of trees on certain lands was in fact intended to apply to some of those trees only. In *Ulster Bank v Synott*[18] parol evidence was used to prove that the phrase "acceptances made" was intended to refer to future as well as past acceptances made on the defendant's account. In *Electricity Supply Board v Newman*[19] oral evidence was admitted to show the meaning of the ambiguous phrase "accounts". *Black v Grealy*[20] establishes that where the amount of consideration is unclear or is not set out in the written contract, parol evidence is admissible to prove it. This principle has an opposite number. If the agreement is unambiguous as it stands, the court will be reluctant to admit parol evidence which will taint it with uncertainty.[21]

[13–13]

Most importantly, parol evidence may be admitted to show that the parties concluded a separate agreement which runs alongside the main contract.[22] A so-called collateral contract (10-33) may contradict the terms of the main contract. For example, in *Harling v Eddy*[23] a heifer was sold at auction. The written standard terms stated that the heifer was sold without warranty. However, parol evidence was admitted of the seller's oral assurance that he would guarantee the heifer in every respect. The purchaser could sue on this assurance when the heifer proved tubercular. In *City and*

[13–14]

---

[11] *ibid.*

[12] *Hutton v Warren* (1836) 1 M & W 466.

[13] (1897) 3 ILTR 86.

[14] *Campbell Discount Co v Gall* [1961] 1 QB 431.

[15] *Pym v Campbell* (1856) 6 E & B 370; *Godley v Power* [1961] 95 ILTR 135.

[16] [1972] IR 372.

[17] (1873) 7 IRCL 231.

[18] (1875) 5 IR Eq 595. See also *Provincial Bank of Ireland v Donnell* (1932) 67 ILTR 142.

[19] (1933) 67 ILTR 124.

[20] Unreported, High Court, 10 December 1977.

[21] *Kinlen v Ennis UDC* [1916] 2 IR 299; *Marathon Petroleum v Bord Gais Éireann*, unreported, Supreme Court, 31 July 1972.

[22] *Mann v Nunn* (1874) 30 LT 526.

[23] [1951] 2 KB 739.

*Westminster Properties v Mudd*[24] the parties concluded a lease that contained a covenant prohibiting the tenant from living on the premises. The tenant was allowed to adduce parol evidence of an oral agreement, collateral to the main contract under which he was allowed to use the building for residential purposes. A similar case is *Brikom Investments v Carr*.[25] The lease in this case required the tenants to contribute to the cost of external repairs. The Court admitted parol evidence to show that the landlord had given an oral assurance that he would repair the roof at his own expense. This exception was applied in Ireland in *Godley v Power*.[26] The case concerned a contract for the sale of a pub. The parties had orally agreed that the stock in trade at the time of the sale would pass to the buyer on purchase of the pub. However, there was nothing in the memorandum of sale to this effect. The Court held that there were two contracts in this case: the main contract of sale for the pub and a collateral contract of sale for the stock in trade. Parol evidence was admissible to prove the collateral contract. In *Mendelssohn v Normand*[27] Phillimore LJ explained the effect of a collateral agreement:

> "There are many cases in the books when a man has made, by word of mouth, a promise or a representation of fact, on which the other party acts by entering into the contract. In all such cases the man is not allowed to repudiate his representation by reference to a printed condition ... nor is he allowed to go back on his promise by reliance on a written clause ... The reason is because the oral promise or representation has decisive influence on the transaction—it is the very thing which induces the other to contract—and it would be most unjust to allow the maker to go back on it. The printed condition is rejected because it is repugnant to the express oral promise or representation ... Whether you regard that promise as ... a collateral term of the contract, or whether you regard the contract as being partly oral and partly in writing ... it seems to me it can make no real difference."

[13–15]     In *Cotter v Minister for Agriculture*[28] Murphy J suggested that the principles relating to collateral contracts do not really constitute an exception to the parol evidence rule. Using parol evidence to prove the existence of a collateral contract does not amount to varying or adding to the original agreement because the collateral contract is an entirely separate agreement from the main contract.

### Representations and Warranties

[13–16]     Warranty is a technical phrase that simply means a "term" of the contract. A warranty is a part of the contract between the parties. A representation is a statement which is made around about the time of contracting but which does not actually constitute a term of the contract. The remedies available for breach of a term and those for a false representation are different. Suppose A sells a cow to B. At the time of contracting, A states that the cow is in calf. The cow turns out not to be pregnant at all. If the fact that

---

[24] [1959] Ch 129.

[25] [1979] QB 467.

[26] (1961) 95 ILTR 135.

[27] [1970] 1 QB 177.

[28] Unreported, High Court, 15 November 1991.

the cow is in calf is a warranty of the contract, then this warranty has been breached. B's remedies are in breach of contract (Chapter 23). The standard remedy for breach of contract is damages (Chapter 25). If the statement that the cow is in calf is a mere representation, however, the remedies are in misrepresentation (Chapter 15). The standard remedy for misrepresentation is rescission, (15–42) an equitable remedy which involves unravelling the contract so that the parties are put in the same position as if they had never entered into the contract.

## The Test

The test of whether a statement amounts to a warranty or to a mere representation is a "reasonable man" test (Lord Denning called him "the intelligent bystander"[29]), which depends on the intention of the parties. Essentially, a warranty is a *promise* that the facts contained in a statement are true. In *Oscar Chess v Williams*[30] Lord Denning wrote that "[e]veryone knows what a man means when he says 'I guarantee it' or 'I warrant it' or 'I give you my word on it'. He means that he binds himself to it". The question for the court then is whether, objectively, it is reasonable to conclude that the parties intended the impugned statement to be contractually binding upon its maker; whether he was promising that it was true. Atiyah[31] provides a reminder here that the courts' search is not for the subjective intention of the parties, but for the idealised and technical notion of objective intention:

[13–17]

> "In the first place, it is highly unlikely that the parties had any intention at all on the matter, for such an intention would virtually require an appreciation of the legal distinction between a term of the contract and a mere representation. In the second place, it is almost certain that the parties will claim that they had different intentions, for if they did not, the case would probably not be in court at all."

What factors will a court take into account in determining whether a statement was reasonably intended to be a warranty of the contract?[32] There are a number of these factors but it is important to remember that none is determinative. In *Heilbut Symons & Co v Buckleton*[33] Moulton LJ gave the following warning:

[13–18]

> "[These factors] cannot be said to furnish decisive tests, because it cannot be said as a matter of law that the presence or absence of those features is conclusive of the intention of the parties. The intention of the parties can only be deduced from the totality of the evidence and no secondary principles of such a kind can be universally true."

The first factor of importance is whether the party making the statement has indicated by his words or actions that he intends to take responsibility for its truth. For

[13–19]

---

[29] [1957] 1 WLR 370.

[30] *ibid.*

[31] Smith, *Atiyah's Introduction to the Law of Contract* (6th ed, Oxford University Press, 2005) p 134.

[32] See *Ecay v Godefry* (1947) Lloyd's Law Rep 286 *per* Lord Goddard CJ.

[33] [1913] AC 30.

example, in *Schawel v Reade*[34] the contract was for the sale of a horse. The plaintiff was examining the horse in the defendant's stables. The defendant interrupted him and said: "You need not look for anything; the horse is perfectly sound". The plaintiff stopped his examination. The question was whether the statement that the horse was sound was a term of the contract or not. Lord Moulton held that it was. He explained:

> "It would be impossible, in my mind, to have a clearer example of an express warranty where the word 'warranty' was not used. The essence of such a warranty becomes plain by the words and action of the parties that it is intended that in the purchase the responsibility of the soundness shall rest upon the vendor; and how in the world could a vendor more clearly indicate that he is prepared to and intended to take upon himself the responsibility of the soundness than by saying 'You need not look at the horse because he is perfectly sound', and sees that the purchaser thereupon desists from his immediate independent examination."

[13–20]     On the other hand, the party making the statement may expressly indicate that he does not take responsibility for the statement's truth and that he is casting that responsibility onto the hearer. For example, in *Ecay v Godfrey*,[35] Ecay agreed to purchase a boat from Godfrey, who stated that the boat was "sea-going and capable of going overseas, in excellent condition and with a sound hull". In fact, as Lord Goddard observed, the boat was "on its last legs" and "in a pretty dicky condition". Ecay could not sue for breach of contract because the statement about the boat's condition was not a warranty. This was because, before the sale, Godfrey recommended that Ecay have the boat surveyed. If Godfrey had intended to warrant the truth of his statement about the boat, he would not have recommended the survey at all: there would not have been any need for it.

[13–21]     Secondly, the more important the statement to the hearer's decision to enter the contract, the more reasonable it is to find that the statement was a warranty. In *Bannerman v White*,[36] White asked Bannerman if the hops that he was selling had been treated with sulphur. He said that if they had been treated in this manner, he would not purchase them. Bannerman said that they had not been treated with sulphur. It turned out that 5 out of the 300 acres had been. The stipulation that the hops were not treated with sulphur was a warranty. Erie CJ explained that it was clearly a warranty because the statement was so important that if it had not been made, White would not have entered into the contract at all. Similarly, in *Couchman v Hill*,[37] the Court considered whether a statement that a heifer was "unserved" was a warranty of the contract for her sale. The buyer had specifically asked both the seller and the auctioneer whether the heifer was served. The Court found that, because this matter was clearly of great importance to the buyer, it was reasonable to conclude that it was intended as a warranty. An Irish case along these lines is *Carey v Independent Newspapers*.[38] In this case, a journalist was told by her prospective employer that she could work from home

---

[34] [1913] 2 IR 81.

[35] Above, n 32.

[36] (1861) 10 CB(NS) 844.

[37] [1947] KB 554.

[38] [2003] IEHC 67.

for part of the working day. This statement was a warranty of her contract of employment because the matter was so important to her that, were it not for this assurance, she would not have entered into the contract at all.

Thirdly, the courts feel that the closer in time the making of the statement is to the conclusion of the contract, the more likely it is that it was intended as a contractual term. For example, *Routledge v McKay*[39] concerned the sale of a motorcycle. A written contract of sale was concluded on 30 October. A week earlier, the defendant had told the plaintiff that the cycle was a 1942 model. The Court held that the distinct time gap between the statement and the contract's conclusion meant that this statement was a mere representation.  [13–22]

Fourthly, the courts set great store by the reduction of a contract to writing as evidence of the parties' intention. If a statement made during contractual negotiations was not included in the final contract document, it is reasonable to conclude that it was not intended to be part of the contract, i.e. that it is not a warranty. It is not necessary that the word "warranty" should have been used.[40] A document will carry less weight where it was a standard form contract (14–03) rather than an individualised document that is the product of actual negotiations between the parties.[41]  [13–23]

Finally, it is more reasonable to interpret a statement of fact as a promise of the truth of those facts where the person making the statement is in a position to know whether they are true or not. In *Oscar Chess Ltd v Williams*,[42] Williams sold a car to the car dealers Oscar Chess Ltd. Williams said that the car was a 1948 model. This was what his registration book said. In fact the car was a 1939 model and was therefore worth much less. Lord Denning held that the statement that the car was a 1948 model was a representation, not a warranty. This was because Williams was not in a position to know whether this statement was true or not. He was not in possession of any extra information: he was relying on the misleading registration book as much as the dealer. Furthermore, the dealer could have taken relatively simple steps to determine the correct age of the car. *Dick Bentley Productions v Harold Smith*[43] shows what will happen when the roles are reversed. In this case, car dealers sold a car to Dick Bentley Productions. The dealers incorrectly stated that the car had done 20,000 miles. This was the figure stated on the mileage recorder. Nevertheless, the Court held that the statement of mileage was a term of the contract. This was because the Court felt that a dealer should know whether the statement of mileage is true. If he does not know, he can find out the truth by contacting the manufacturers.  [13–24]

An examination of *Oscar Chess* and *Dick Bentley* indicates that the decisions in these cases have less to do with the parties' actual knowledge and more to do with their relative positions. The courts are more concerned with who should, as a matter of  [13–25]

---

[39] [1954] 1 All ER 855.
[40] *Scales v Scanlan* (1843) 6 IRCL 432.
[41] *Evans J & Son v Andrea Merzario Ltd* [1976] 1 WLR 1078.
[42] Above, n 29.
[43] [1965] 1 WLR 623.

policy, bear the risk of a statement turning out to be untrue than they are with who has actually agreed to bear that risk.[44] If an expert makes a statement about matters which ought to be within his knowledge, he will be held accountable for the truth of that statement. In addition, while the courts focus on intention in determining whether a statement is a term or a representation, they cannot fail to be influenced by the results of labelling the statement as one or the other. This was especially true of the old cases decided when the remedies for misrepresentation were limited. In particular, *Oscar Chess* and *Dick Bentley* predate the English Misrepresentation Act 1967 so that, if the cases had been decided differently, the weaker parties would have had access only to a narrow range of remedies. Even today, the measure of damages for breach is generally more generous for breach of contract than for misrepresentation. In some ways, these cases suggest that the courts are content to manipulate the malleable notion of intention in order to do justice as between the parties.

### III. Finding the Implied Terms

[13–26] The law on implied terms governs the situations in which a term of a contract may be "found" which has not actually been expressed by the parties. The idea is that some term may form part of a contract but the parties did not give voice to it, for example, because of pressures of time or because the term was so obviously a part of the contract that there was no need to say so formally. For example, if I offer to sell you my car for €7,000 and you accept, our contract is not complete. It is likely that our contract has all sorts of other terms to it that have not been mentioned. Parties rely on informal understandings to ground their dealings more often than might be expected. In their well-known empirical study of contracting in the Bristol engineering manufacturing industry, Beale and Dugdale[45] found that there were a number of reasons for parties' failure to plan their contract in any great detail. First, the parties rely on the customs or "unwritten laws" of their particular trade to flesh out the gaps in the contracts between them. Second, where the parties had a long contractual relationship marked by regular dealings, they tended not to insist on detailed contract provisions. This was because parties who are familiar with one another tend to make assumptions about what will happen, for example, in the event of breach, and do not feel the need to agree on these. There may also be a feeling between them that an insistence on detailed negotiation might sour a relationship based on informality and trust. Third, detailed contractual planning is expensive. Small firms with limited resources tend to be content simply to agree on the main obligations under the contract, especially where the financial risk associated with the contract is limited.

[13–27] It is worth examining the precise relationship between express and implied terms. Lord Diplock explained it in *Photo Productions v Securicor*[46] as follows:

> "A basic principle of the common law of contract ... is that parties to a contract are free to determine for themselves what primary obligations they will

---

[44] Smith, *Atiyah's Introduction to the Law of Contract* (6th ed, Oxford University Press, 2005) p 146.
[45] Beale and Dugdale, "Contracts Between Businessmen" (1975) 2 Brit J Law & Soc 45.
[46] [1980] AC 827.

accept. They may state these in express words in the contract itself, and, where they do, the statement is determinative; but in practice a commercial contract never states all the primary obligations of the parties in full; many are left to be incorporated by implication of law from the legal nature of the contract into which the parties are entering. But if the parties wish to reject or modify primary obligations which would otherwise be so incorporated they are fully at liberty to do so by express words."

## Terms Implied in Fact

A term is implied in fact on the basis that both parties would have agreed that the term was a necessary part of their contract if, at the time of contracting, they had applied their mind to the question now before the court. The courts are not writing a new term for the parties, they are simply filling a gap in the contract's express terms by finding a term that was there all along. In *Tradax Ireland v Irish Grain Board*[47] O'Higgins CJ described the court's role here as "repair[ing] an intrinsic failure of expression". O'Higgins CJ here touches on the great debate which animates the law on terms implied in fact. Traditionally, it has been understood that a term will not be implied in fact into a contract unless it is necessary to give effect to the true intention of the parties or is otherwise required by law. A court may not, for example, imply a term into a contract because that term would be reasonable, desirable or commercially sensible. As O'Higgins CJ warned in *Tradax Ireland*,[48] the courts have:

[13–28]

> "... no role in acting as contract makers, or as counsellors, to advise or direct what agreement ought to have been made by two people, whether businessmen or not, who chose to enter into contractual relations with each other ...".

Sir Thomas Bingham MR in *Philips Electronique Grand Public SA v British Sky Broadcasting*[49] put the point more fully:

[13–29]

> "The implication of contract terms involves ... the interpolation of terms to deal with matters for which *ex hypothesi* the parties have made no provisions. It is because the implication of terms is so potentially intrusive that the law imposes strict constraints on the exercise of this extraordinary power ... [In addition] the issue of whether a term should be implied, and if so what, almost inevitably arises after a crisis has been reached in the performance of the contract. So the court comes to the task of implication with the benefit of the hindsight, and is tempting for the court then to fashion a term which will reflect the merits of the situation as they then appear. Tempting but wrong."

The courts' careful approach to the power to imply terms in fact is reflected in a number of initial restrictions on its use. First, a term will not be implied if it is too vague. The courts will not use their power of implication if it only serves to muddy the contractual waters further. This was one of the reasons why, in *Walford v Miles*,[50] the

[13–30]

---

[47] Above, n 1.
[48] *ibid.*
[49] [1995] EMLR 472.
[50] [1992] 2 AC 128.

Court refused to imply an indeterminate duty to negotiate in good faith into a contract for the sale of a business (6–28). Second, under *Ashmore v Corporation of Lloyd's*[51] a term will not be implied if it is very complex. The implication of a very detailed term looks too much like rewriting the contract for the parties. Finally, the courts will generally defer to the expressed intention of the parties. This means that a term will not be implied which is inconsistent with the express terms of the contract. Along the same lines, the Court in *Shell v Lostock Garage*[52] noted that the more detailed the existing written contract, the less likely the Court is to imply a term in fact. This is because a detailed written agreement suggests that the parties have already agreed the totality of their contract and did not intend it to be supplemented by other terms.

[13–31]    Terms are implied in fact under three tests: the officious bystander test, the business efficacy test, and the custom and practice test. Each will be considered in turn.

### The Officious Bystander Test

[13–32]    The courts have used a fictitious third party, called the "officious bystander", as a device for determining the intention of the parties to a contract. The key statement of this approach is that of MacKinnon LJ in *Shirlaw v Southern Foundries*.[53] Mr Shirlaw was appointed the manager of Southern Foundries for ten years. Subsequently, Federal Foundries became the beneficial owners of Southern Foundries. Three years into Shirlaw's contract, they changed the articles of association of Southern Foundries so that they could remove him as Director. The Court implied a term into Shirlaw's contract with Southern Foundries that he would not be removed from his post in this manner before the ten-year term had run out. This was done on the basis of the officious bystander test. MacKinnon LJ wrote:

> "*Prima facie* that which in any contract is left to be implied and need not be expressed is something so obvious that it goes without saying; so that if while the parties were making their bargain, an officious bystander were to suggest some express provision for it in the agreement, they would testily suppress him with a common 'Oh of course!'"

[13–33]    In *Ward v Spivack*[54] Davitt P set out the test in evocative language:

> "Imagine the parties at the moment they have agreed on the expressed terms of their contract. Then envisage one of them saying, with regard to the term sought to be implied: 'Of course such and such is understood?' If it is quite certain that the other would say, 'Of course!' then the term may be implied. If it is quite certain that he would say 'Absolutely not, I will agree to nothing of the kind' then clearly the term cannot be implied no matter how desirable or reasonable it may seem, as the court cannot make a contract for the parties, it can only determine what they agreed on, either expressly or impliedly."

---

51  *Times Law Reports*, 7 July 1992.
52  [1976] 1 WLR 1187.
53  [1939] 2 KB 206.
54  [1957] IR 40.

It is clear from these statements of the test that the officious bystander is not **[13–34]**
the reasonable man. The focus in this test is on the parties' assumed answer to his
standard question, not on his conclusion. The question for the court is not whether the
reasonable man would have thought that the term sought to be implied formed part of
the contract at issue.

The officious bystander test was applied in *Gardner v Coutts & Co.*[55] The **[13–35]**
plaintiff had inherited some property from A. The defendants were the executors of B,
who had sold the property to A originally. At the time of sale, A and B agreed that, if at
any time during his life B wished to sell the adjoining property, A or her successors
would have first refusal. B gave that property to his sister as a gift without giving the
plaintiff the option of purchase. The plaintiff accordingly sued the defendants for B's
breach of contract. The written contract provided that the option to purchase arose if
B sold the property. It said nothing about a gift. However, Cross J employed the
*Moorcock* test to imply a term that the option also arose in the event of B making a gift
of the property. He reasoned as follows:

> "I am confident that at the time, whatever views [B] may have formed later, if
> somebody had said to him, 'You have not expressly catered for the possibility of
> your wanting to give away the property', he would have said, as undoubtedly
> [A] would have said, 'Oh, of course that is implied. What goes for a
> contemplated sale must go for a contemplated gift'."

The test was successfully applied in Ireland in *Kavanagh v Gilbert*[56]; a case in **[13–36]**
which an auctioneer refused to sign a memorandum of agreement after the sale of land.
Of course, this meant that the contract of sale would not be enforced having regard to
the Statute of Frauds. The question for the Court was whether it was an implied term
of the auctioneer's contract that he would take such steps as were necessary to enable
any sale to be enforced. The test applied in order to answer this question was the
officious bystander test; if a hypothetical bystander was present at the time of making
the contract and asked the parties whether that obligation was part of the contract,
would he receive an affirmative answer? The Court held that he would. Accordingly,
the term was implied.

By contrast, the officious bystander test did not yield an implied term in *Spring* **[13–37]**
*v National Amalgamated Stevedores and Dockers Society*.[57] The defendants and a
union agreed at the Trade Union Congress at Bridlington in 1939 that certain standard
rules would apply whenever a union member transferred to a new union. This was
called the "Bridlington Agreement". In 1955, the defendants admitted the plaintiff to
their Society in breach of the Bridlington Agreement. The agreement was not included
in the defendants' rules and the plaintiff knew nothing about it. The question was
whether a term could be implied into the contract between the defendants and the

---

[55] [1967] 3 All ER 1064.
[56] (1875) IR 9 CL 136.
[57] [1956] 2 All ER 221. See more recently *National Bank of Greece SA v Pinios Shipping Co* [1989]
1 All ER 213.

plaintiff that they would comply with the Bridlington Agreement. The Court, applying the *Moorcock* test, refused to imply the term sought:

> "If that test were to be applied to the facts of this case and the bystander had asked the plaintiff, at the time when the plaintiff paid his 5s and signed the acceptance form, 'Won't you put into it some reference to the Bridlington Agreement?' I think (indeed I have no doubt) that the plaintiff would have answered, 'What's that?'"

[13–38]    *Spring* underlines the fact that the officious bystander test is only fulfilled where *both* parties would have answered the bystander's hypothetical question in the affirmative. The courts are looking for the shared intention of the parties. We can draw the same conclusion from *Carna Foods Ltd v Eagle Star Insurance*.[58] The defendants were an insurance company who cancelled the plaintiff's policy without giving any reasons. The plaintiff claimed that because this lack of reasons would make it difficult for it to get insurance with any other company, it must have been an implied term of the contract of insurance that reasons would be given in the event of declinature or cancellation. Lynch J found that the term could not be implied and set out his decision as follows:

> "If the officious bystander had interrupted ... and had asked the defendant 'If you do cancel, will you give your reasons for cancelling?' the defendant's answer would have been an emphatic 'No' whereas to imply such a term into the policies the answer would have to be by both parties 'Yes, of course' expressed rather testily to discourage the officious bystander from further interrupting."

[13–39]    Therefore, even though the plaintiff would have been keen on the inclusion of this term, the term could not be implied. An especially interesting case on this point is *MR v TR*.[59] The case concerned a separated couple who had created and frozen some embryos together. The wife wished the embryos to be implanted in her uterus. The husband did not want this to happen. The wife argued that a term should be implied in fact, based on the presumed intention of the parties, that the embryos would be implanted in her womb in the circumstances which had arisen. McGovern J, applying the test in *Shirlaw*, found that there was no such shared intention and, accordingly, the term could not be implied.

### The Business Efficacy Test

[13–40]    The law presumes that contracting parties intend to create a workable, effective contract. Therefore, a court is entitled to imply such unexpressed terms into a contract as are necessary to make the contract work.[60] Collins says, for example, that a court could imply into a contract for the sale of a lock a term that the seller would also supply a key. This is because without a key, the purchaser's purpose in buying the lock

---

[58] [1997] 2 ILRM 499.

[59] Unreported, High Court, 18 July 2006.

[60] The converse of this principle appears to be that a term will not be implied which would defeat the purpose of the contract; *Karim Aga Khan v Firestone* [1992] ILRM 31.

would be defeated.[61] In *Karim Aga Khan v Firestone*[62] Morris J explained that this test allows a term to be implied where "through mischance, such a term as is sought to be implied has been omitted from the contract and is necessary in order to give the contract efficacy and to prevent the failure of the contract". The test comes from the judgment of Bowen LJ in *The Moorcock*[63]:

> "I believe if one were to take all the cases, and there are many, of implied warranties or covenants in law, it will be found that in all of them the law is raising an implication from the presumed intention of the parties, with the object of giving the transaction such efficacy as both parties must have intended that in all effects it should have."

The plaintiff and the defendants agreed that the plaintiff's steamship, *The Moorcock*, would be discharged and loaded at the defendants' wharf and that it would be moored alongside the jetty so that it would be aground at low tide. The steamship was moored at the jetty. It went aground at low tide and it suffered damage caused by a ridge of hard ground on the riverbed. The Court of Appeal implied a term into the contract that the defendants were under a duty to see that the bottom of the river was fit for the plaintiff's purpose, or that, if it was not fit for that purpose, that the defendants would inform the plaintiff of this. This term was necessary in order to give business efficacy to the contract because it was impossible for a vessel like *The Moorcock* to be moored at the jetty without going aground at low tide. The Irish case *Butler v McAlpine*[64] is the mirror image of *The Moorcock*. In this case a barge was damaged when it struck a concrete block near a wharf which its owners had leased. The Court used the business efficacy test to imply a term into the lease that the wharf would be safe for use. **[13–41]**

It should be noted that there is some suggestion in both England and Ireland that the business efficacy and officious bystander tests are simply different ways of saying the same thing.[65] Scrutton LJ in *Reigate v Union Manufacturing Co.*[66] conflates the tests: **[13–42]**

> "A term can ... be implied if it is necessary in the business sense to give efficacy to the contract, i.e. if it is such a term that it can confidently be said that if at the time the contract was being negotiated someone had said to the parties: 'What will happen in such a case?' they would both have replied 'Of course so and so will happen; we did not trouble to say that; it is too clear'."

In the Irish case of *Sweeney v Duggan*[67] Murphy J treats the tests as equivalent. **[13–43]**

---

[61] Collins, *The Law of Contract* (4th ed, LexisNexis, 2003) p 240.

[62] [1992] ILRM 31.

[63] (1889) 14 PD 64.

[64] [1904] 2 IR 445.

[65] *Ultraframe v Tailored Roofing Systems Ltd* [2004] EWCA Civ 585.

[66] [1918] 1 KB 592.

[67] [1997] ILRM 211.

### The Necessity Threshold

[13–44]    The burden of proof for the implication of a term into a contract under both the business efficacy and the officious bystander tests is necessity. In *Hughes v Greenwich LBC*[68] Lord Lowry said that a term will not be implied under the officious bystander test unless there is "a compelling reason for deeming that term to form part of the contract." Lord Pearson made the same point in more detail in *Trollope and Colls Ltd v North West Metropolitan Regional Hospital Board*[69]:

> "An unexpressed term can be implied if and only if the court finds that the parties must have intended that term to form part of their contract: it is not enough for the court to find that such a term would have been adopted by the parties as reasonable men if it had been suggested to them: it must have been a term that went without saying, a term *necessary* to give business efficacy to the contract, a term which, although tacit, formed part of the contract which the parties made for themselves."

[13–45]    Lord Lowry in *JM Reilly v Belfast Corpn*[70] emphasised the distinction between necessity and reasonableness. If they were to imply terms on the basis that they would improve the parties' contract, the courts would fall foul of the rule that they must not remake the parties' bargain:

> "It is not enough for the court to conclude ... that such a term would have made the contract more reasonable; terms will be implied not in order to make for the parties a contract which the court considers fair, but only to make effective the contract which the parties have made for themselves."

[13–46]    A number of Irish cases have applied the necessity threshold for the implication of terms. In *O'Toole v Palmer*[71] Gavan Duffy J refused to imply a term on the basis that the term was not necessary; the contract would work perfectly well without it. In *Sweeney v Duggan*,[72] the plaintiff was employed by a quarrying company. He was injured while he was operating a drill, sued the company and was awarded damages. At the time of the award, the company was in voluntary liquidation. It had no employer's liability insurance and was unable to pay its debts. The plaintiff argued

---

[68] [1994] 1 AC 170.

[69] [1973] 2 All ER 260. See also *Hamlyn & Co v Wood & Co* [1891] 2 QB 488 *per* Esher MR: " ... the court has no right to imply in a written contact any such stipulation, unless, on considering the terms of the contract in a reasonable and business manner, an implication necessarily arises that the parties must have intended that the suggested stipulation should exist. It is not enough to say that it would be a reasonable thing to make such an implication. It must be a necessary implication in the sense that I have mentioned"; *Liverpool City Council v Irwin* [1977] AC 239 *per* Lord Cross: "What the court is being in effect asked to do is to rectify a particular – often a very detailed – contract by inserting in it a term which the parties have not expressed. Here it is not enough for the court to say that the suggested term is a reasonable one the presence of which would make the contract a better or fairer one; it must be able to say that the insertion of the term is necessary".

[70] [1994] 1 AC 170.

[71] [1945] Ir Jur Rep 59.

[72] Above, n 67.

that the company was obliged to pay his award because it was a term of his contract of employment that the managing director of the company had a personal duty to procure employer's liability insurance or to warn the plaintiff that no such insurance had been procured. There were no express terms in the contract to this effect. The question was whether such terms could be implied. Murphy J found that an application of the business efficacy test did not require the implication of either term as the contract operated perfectly well without them. They were not necessary and accordingly would not be implied. To similar effect is *Murphy Buckley & Keogh v Pye*.[73] The plaintiffs in this case were hired to sell factory premises. They were hired on a "sole agency" basis. This means that the defendants agreed not to retain any other agents to sell the premises and that a commission would be payable to the plaintiffs if they managed to secure a sale. However, the defendants found a purchaser by themselves, without the plaintiffs' help. The plaintiffs claimed that they were still entitled to their commission either because it was an implied term of the contract that the defendants would not sell the premises by themselves or because it was an implied term that commission would still be payable in those circumstances. However, the contract expressly and comprehensively set out the circumstances under which commission would be payable. The Supreme Court held that the suggested terms would not be implied because they were not necessary in order to make the contract work. The test was necessity-based and so it was irrelevant that the suggested terms were common in contracts of this type, that they were commercially sensible or that they were prudent. In *Wildgust v Carrickowen Ltd*[74] the plaintiff made an arrangement with the Bank of Ireland that he would pay life insurance premiums for himself and his wife by direct debit. Due to a breakdown in the system, a direct debit payment due on 1 March 1992 was not paid. As a result, the life insurance policy lapsed. The plaintiff's wife died in 1993 and, due to the lapse, the insurance company refused to make any payments on the strength of the policy. The plaintiff argued that it was an implied term of his contract of insurance that the insurance company would inform him if a breakdown in the direct debit system occurred such that his monthly premium was unpaid. He argued that the officious bystander test required the implication of this term because the term was "one so normal and natural and obvious that it would go without saying that it was included." Morris J did not agree that this argument from convenience was enough to satisfy the officious bystander test. The term was unnecessary and therefore could not be implied. The recent Supreme Court decision *Dakota Packaging Limited v AHP Manufacturing BV*[75] appears to put paid, albeit *obiter*, to the idea of the implication of terms into contracts on the grounds of reasonableness. The Court held that: "In particular, the courts do not have 'a broad discretion' to imply terms. It is not enough that a term to be implied is 'fair and reasonable'."

[13–47] In England, however there is some authority to suggest that the test for the implication of terms in fact is closer to reasonableness than to necessity. Lord Steyn in *Equitable Life Assurance Society v Hyman*[76] said that the test for implication of terms

---

[73] [1971] IR 57.

[74] [2001] ILRM 24.

[75] [2004] IESC 102.

[76] [2000] 3 WLR 529.

was satisfied where the term was necessary "to give effect to the reasonable expectations of the parties". Furthermore, in *Paragon Finance v Nash*[77] Dyson LJ implied a term on the basis that it was "necessary in order to give effect to the reasonable expectations of the parties". Bryan and Ellinghaus[78] have written about a move from the "officious bystander" to the "reasonable bystander". They explain the difference thus:

> "Substituting the 'reasonable bystander' for the 'officious bystander' involves a reversal of the roles of bystander and the parties. The bystander's role is no longer that of an interrogator who elicits from the parties whether they would have instantaneously agreed on the term sought to be implied by one of them. Rather the bystander replaces the parties as the source of any implied term. The bystander does not ask for a response from the parties but rather decides what, if anything, reasonable parties would have agreed on in the circumstances."

**[13–48]**     An announcement of an English move from officious to reasonable bystander may be somewhat premature. It is important to remember that the terms implied in both *Hyman* and *Paragon* were also justifiable under the usual business efficacy/ officious bystander test. In *Hyman* the implied term restricted directors' exercise of a discretion as to the distribution of bonuses amongst with profits pension holders who made different elections. Arguably, this term was necessary to give business efficacy to the contract. In *Paragon* the Court of Appeal implied a term that a lender's discretion to vary interest rates would not be exercised "dishonestly, for an improper purpose, capriciously or arbitrarily". The Court expressly said that this term was in keeping with the officious bystander test as well as according with the parties' reasonable expectations. These decisions, then, may be taken simply to express the status quo in a new way, with "reasonable expectation" as a cipher for the "intention" of the parties.

### The Custom and Practice Test

**[13–49]**     Terms can be implied into a contract concluded in a particular industry in order to give effect to the custom and practice of that industry. In *Hutton v Warren*[79] Baron Parke explained the rationale here:

> "It has long been settled that in commercial transactions extrinsic evidence of custom and usage is admissible to annex incidents to written contracts, in matters with respect to which they are silent. The same rule has also been applied to contracts in other transactions of life, in which known usages have been established and prevailed; and this had been done upon the principle of presumption that, in such transactions, the parties did not mean to express in writing the whole of the contract by which they intended to be bound but to contract with reference to these known usages."

---

[77] [2002] 1 WLR 685.
[78] [2000] 22 Syd LR 636.
[79] Above, n 12.

For example, in *O'Connail v The Gaelic Echo*[80] a term was implied into a    **[13–50]**
Dublin journalist's contract of employment that he would receive holiday pay. This
term was implied on the basis of evidence that holiday pay for journalists was the
custom in Dublin. It is not enough, however, for a party to produce evidence of some
custom or other. The custom must be well known so that an outsider making
reasonable inquiries could not fail to discover it.[81] Maguire P in *O'Reilly v Irish Press*[82]
said that it must be "notorious" and "so generally known that anyone concerned
should have known of it, or could easily have become aware of it." In addition,
Maguire P required that the custom should have been "acquiesced in [so] that in the
absence of agreement in writing it is to be taken as one of the terms of the contract
between the parties …". It is not enough that the custom is frequently repeated. It
must be clear that people in the particular industry regard it as contractually binding.
Slade LJ made this point in *General Reinsurance Corp v Forsakringsaktiebolaget*[83]:

> "There is, however, the world of difference between a course of conduct that
> is frequently, or even habitually, followed in a particular commercial commu-
> nity as a matter of grace and a course which is habitually followed because
> it is considered that the parties concerned have a legally binding right to
> demand it."

Express terms displace terms sought to be implied in fact. This rule was applied    **[13–51]**
in *Les Affréteurs Réunis Société Anonyme v Walford*. In that case, Walford, a broker,
had negotiated a contract for the hire of a ship between the owners of the ship and a
fuel oil company. The ship was requisitioned by the French Government before the
ship could be hired. It was a custom of the trade that commission was only payable to
the broker when the hire had actually been earned. However, a term to this effect could
not be implied into the contract because it was an express term of the contract that
commission was payable on signing the contract. A term could not be implied in the
face of this express provision. Lord Birkinhead explained that:

> "[A] custom [may not] be given effect to in commercial matters which is entirely
> inconsistent with the plain words of an agreement into which commercial men,
> clearly acquainted with so well-known a custom have nevertheless thought
> proper to enter."

---

[80] (1958) 92 ILTR 156.
[81] *Kum v Wah Tah Bank* [1971] 1 Lloyd's Rep 439.
[82] (1937)71 ILTR 194. See also the judgment of Ungoed-Thomas J in *Cunliffe-Owen v Teather &
Greenwood* [1967] 1 WLR 1421: "'Usage' as a practice which the court will recognise is a mixed
question of fact and law. For the practice to amount to such a recognised usage, it must be certain,
in the sense that the practice is clearly established; it must be notorious, in the sense that it is so
well known in the market in which it is alleged to exist, that those who conduct business in that
market contract with the usage as an implied term; and it must be reasonable … What is
necessary is that for a practice to be a recognised usage it should be established as a practice
having binding effect."
[83] [1983] QB 856.

**Terms Implied in Law**

[13–52] There are certain types of contract which are routine and commonplace and which feature sets of contractual duties and rights which are usual in that type of contract to the extent of being standard. Examples include leases, contracts for the sale of goods and contracts of employment. Where a contract falls into such a recognised pattern of contractual relationship, the court will readily imply certain terms which are seen as usual incidents of that class of contract. For example, it is an implied term of every lease of a furnished house that the house shall be reasonably fit for human habitation,[84] and it is an implied term of every contract of employment that the employee will serve his employer faithfully.[85] This method of implication draws on long years of judicial experience and accepted legal practice.

[13–53] The implication of terms in law has nothing to do with the parties' intention. Terms are imposed on the parties for reasons of pure policy. In *Shell v Lostock Garages*[86] Lord Denning MR explained:

"In such relationships the problem is not solved by asking: what did the parties intend? Or, would they have unhesitatingly agreed to it if asked? It is to be solved by asking: has the law already defined the obligation or the extent of it? If so, let it be followed. If not, look to see what would be reasonable in the general run of such cases ... and then see what the obligation shall be."

[13–54] Because this power of implication constitutes a clear interference with the parties' own bargain, the courts have traditionally been cautious in its use. Along these lines, there are a number of initial points before we look in detail at the test for implication itself. These are similar to those we made about the implication of terms in fact. The first point is that the intention of the parties is paramount and it must be respected where it has been expressly set out. Thus, the more detailed the contract, and thus the more precise the parties have been in setting out their intention, the less scope there will be for the implication of terms.[87] By the same token, no term will be implied which flatly contradicts the express language of the bargain. So, in *Lynch v Thorne*[88] the defendant contracted to sell a plot of land to the plaintiff. There was a partially completed building on the land and, as part of the contract, the defendant was bound to finish constructing it. The contract expressly provided that the walls were to be of brick and built nine inches thick. The defendant built the walls as specified but they were too thin to keep out the rain and as a result the house was unfit for human habitation. Now, for hundreds of years a term was implied at common law into all contracts for house building that the house should be fit for human habitation. The Court found, however, that the term was not implied into this contract, because the express language of the contract provided otherwise. It is important to note, however, that the courts arguably have more latitude here as regards the parties' intention than they do when they imply terms in fact. This means that the court may be willing in an

---

84 *Siney v Dublin Corporation* [1980] IR 400; *Burke v Dublin Corporation* [1991] IR 341.
85 *Lister v Romford Ice & Cold Storage* [1957] AC 555.
86 Above, n 52.
87 *ibid.*
88 [1956] 1 All ER 744.

appropriate case to read the express terms of the contract in a narrow fashion so as to eliminate any contradiction between those terms and the term sought to be implied.[89]

Second, the more gaps there are in a contract, the more reluctant the court will be to imply a term in law. Implication of terms in this sort of situation comes too close to writing the contract for the parties.[90] Third, the court will not imply a vague term. If the term sought to be implied cannot be expressed with precision,[91] it will not be implied at all. The power to imply terms is designed to remedy uncertainty and this cannot be achieved by reading vague terms into the contract.[92] Fourth, terms will only be implied in law if the contract is of a recognised type.[93] If the contractual relationship before the court is a unique one, the court will have to rely on the tests for implication of terms in fact. Finally, the courts will not imply in law a term which is tailored to the precise facts of the contract at issue. The terms implied will be generic terms which are found in *all* contracts of that particular type.[94] Whereas the power to imply terms in fact requires the court to devise a one-off term, peculiar to the situation at hand, the power to imply terms in law involves the imposition of standardised terms.

[13–55]

The key case on the implication of terms in law is *Liverpool City Council v Irwin.*[95] The tenants of a notorious 15-storey block of flats had refused to pay their rent in protest at the fact that the flats were constantly vandalised. As a result, the lifts, stair lighting and rubbish chute hardly ever worked. The Council sought to evict the tenants. The tenants argued that the Council was in breach of implied terms of the contract. The written tenancy agreement listed only the obligations of the tenants. It did not mention the obligations of the Council. The Court found that it was an implied term of all leases of this type that the landlord owed a duty to take all reasonable care to ensure that the common parts of the premises were useable and were in reasonable repair. This term could not be implied under the business efficacy test: while it was essential that the premises be kept in good repair in order for the purpose of the lease to be achieved, it was not essential that the landlord be the one to do it. Neither would this term have passed the officious bystander test. Lord Roskill wrote in the Court of Appeal:

[13–56]

> "I find it absolutely impossible to believe that the Liverpool City Council, if asked whether it was their intention as well as that of their tenants of these flats that [this term] should be written into the contract, would have given an affirmative answer. Their answers would clearly have been 'No'."

These observations emphasise the gap between this type of implied term and any notion of the intention of the parties. Instead, the term was implied on the basis that, in leases for buildings of multiple occupations, the duty to maintain the building in reasonable repair should fall on the landlord.

[13–57]

---

[89] *Johnstone v Bloomsbury Health Authority* [1992] QB 333.

[90] *Hillas v Arcos* (1932) 147 LT 503.

[91] *R(M) v R(T)*, above, n 59.

[92] Above, n 52.

[93] *ibid.*

[94] *Reid v Rush & Tompkins plc* [1989] 3 All ER 228.

[95] [1977] AC 239.

**[13–58]**     What is the minimum threshold for the implication of a term in law? It has been shown that it is lower than the threshold for implication of a term in fact but how much lower is it? The Irish position seems to be that of Murphy J in *Sweeney v Duggan*[96]: if a term is to be implied into a contract in law "it must be not merely reasonable but also necessary". The position in England is somewhat more complex. Lord Denning in the Court of Appeal held in *Liverpool City Council* that a term could be implied whenever it was reasonable to do so. He wrote of the cases on terms implied in law:

> "[I]n none of them did the court ask: what did both parties intend? If asked, each party would have said he never gave it a thought: or the one would have intended something different from the other. Nor did the court ask: Is it necessary to give business efficacy to the transaction? If asked, the answer would have been: 'It is reasonable, but it is not necessary'. The judgments in all those cases show that the courts implied a term according to whether or not is was reasonable in all the circumstances to do so ... This is to be decided as a matter of law, not as a matter of fact."

**[13–59]**     The House of Lords imposed a higher threshold. The term could only be implied if it was strictly necessary to do so. However, even though they applied different tests, both the Court of Appeal and the House implied the same landlord's duty. It appears, therefore, that the test applied by the House was not one of strict necessity. It was not absolutely necessary to live in the block of flats that the lifts would be kept in adequate repair. The test must therefore be close to one of "reasonable necessity". The same conclusion can be drawn on the basis of the House of Lords decision in *Scally v Southern Health and Social Services.*[97] The House implied a term into a doctor's contract of employment that his employers would notify him of complex statutory regulations governing his pension entitlements. Their Lordships applied the necessity test in *Liverpool CC v Irwin*. However, it is clear that the test applied is not one of incontrovertible necessity. The plaintiff could have found out about his pension entitlements by other means. Furthermore, in *Scally*,[98] Lord Bridge noted that the test of necessity here is not the same as the strict test of necessity employed under the business efficacy test:

> "[There is] a clear distinction between the search for an implied term necessary to give business efficacy to a particular contract and the search, based on wider considerations, for a term which the law will imply as a necessary incident of a definable category of contractual relationship."

**[13–60]**     This liberal approach to the notion of necessity is exemplified in the recent case of *Crossley v Faithful & Gould Holdings Ltd*.[99] The question for the Court of Appeal in this case was whether a term that "an employer will take reasonable care for the economic well-being of his employee" should be a standard implied term in all contracts of employment. The Court held that it should not. This was because, *inter*

---

[96]  Above, n 67.
[97]  [1992] 1 AC 294.
[98]  *ibid.*
[99]  [2004] EWCA Civ 293.

*alia*, such a term would "impose an unfair and unreasonable burden on employers" and there were "no obvious policy reasons to impose on an employer the general duty to protect his employee's economic well-being". Dyson LJ argued that the Court ought not to focus on the "protean" concept of necessity but instead should "recognise that, to some extent at least, the existence and scope of standardised implied terms raises questions of reasonableness, fairness and the balancing of competing policy considerations".

## Terms Implied by the Constitution

The Constitution and the rights arising under it take priority over all rights at common law. This means that terms will automatically be implied into relevant contracts in order to give effect to a party's fundamental personal rights under the Constitution. For example, *Glover v BLN*[100] is authority for the principle that it is an implied term of an employee's contract of employment that he will obtain a fair hearing before being dismissed from employment. He is entitled, at a minimum, to be informed of the charge against him, to be given the opportunity to answer it and to make submissions.[101] This term is implied under the constitutional principle of natural justice, arising under Art 40.3, which sets out that, in respect of decisions which impact seriously on a person, that person has the right to hear and challenge the case against him before an impartial body. This principle has been reaffirmed in *Bolger v Osborne*.[102] Perhaps surprisingly, it appears that the parties will be able to override the implication of constitutional rights by the express words of their contract. It may be possible for a party to contract out of certain constitutional rights, provided that he is in a position to freely negotiate that contract and that he understands the contract.[103]

[13–61]

## Terms Implied by Statute and Consumer Law

The Sale of Goods Act 1893 and the Sale of Goods and Supply of Services Act 1980 import a number of terms into contracts for the sale[104] of goods and supply of services. The Acts do not apply to gifts and they do not apply to the sale of land. The old rule with regard to the sale of goods was that the courts would not imply any term which had not been expressly inserted into the contract. The maxim *caveat emptor* applied.[105] The purchaser was supposed to use his own judgment when buying goods. This meant that, provided the goods were open to inspection and in the absence of fraud, the purchaser could not complain of any defects in the article he had bought. If the purchaser wanted any extra protection, he could achieve it by expressly agreeing suitable contractual terms with the seller. The assumption underlying this old position was that both buyer and seller are equal in a contract of sale. However, with the passage of time, it became clear that this assumption was unrealistic and that standard terms should be implied into contracts of sale as a matter of policy, in order to

[13–62]

---

[100] [1973] IR 388.

[101] *Dooley v Great Southern Hotels Ltd* [2001] ELR 340.

[102] [2000]1 ILRM 250.

[103] *Murphy v Stewart* [1975] IR 97.

[104] In *Flynn v Mackin* [1974] IR 101 the Acts were applied when a car was traded in against the purchase price of a new car.

[105] "No man can be cheated except be it with his own consent, and we commonly say caveat emptor." Child, *A New Discourse on Trade*, p 111. See *Chandelor v Lopus* (1603) Cro Jac 4.

introduce substantive equality into this arena and to protect the reasonable expectations of consumers. Collins explains:

> "Although an ordinary consumer and a large business such as a retail chain store enjoy the formal equality to own property and enter bargains, it is clear that a business can often call upon much greater technical knowledge and legal expertise in order to secure favourable transactions. These disparities become particularly noticeable in complex transactions, as where the consumer requires a credit arrangement or loan in order to complete the purchase, or when the item purchased involves complex technology as in the case of a car or electrical goods. But disparities appear in even a simple purchase of a can of beans at the supermarket, where the business is likely to have a much better understanding of the contents of the tin, which may include, besides the beans, various sources, preservatives, colourings and so forth. The modern law recognises these differentials in knowledge and expertise by introducing measures of consumer protection, and in so doing drops the presumption that citizens may enter the market on equal terms."[106]

[13–63]    The key terms implied into consumer contracts by the sale of goods and supply of services legislation will be examined in turn.[107] Space permits only a brief discussion. The exemption of liability for breach of these terms is considered separately (14–88).

### Section 39—Supply of Services

[13–64]    Section 39 of the 1980 Act provides for the implication of four terms into all contracts for the supply of services where the seller is acting in the course of business. The seller must have the necessary skill to provide the service. He must supply the service with due skill, care and diligence.[108] If he uses materials in providing the service, they must be sound and reasonably fit for the purpose for which they are required.[109] If goods are supplied under the contract of service, they must be of merchantable quality (13–67).

### Section 12—Good Title

[13–65]    This section implies three main terms into contracts for the sale of goods: a condition that the seller has the right to sell the goods[110]; a warranty that the goods are not subject to any overriding claim by a third party; and a warranty that the buyer will have the right to use the goods without interference. As the first term is a condition (24–14) the contract may be terminated in the event of breach. This means that the buyer is entitled to reject the goods and claim the purchase price back if the seller turns out not to have the right to sell them; for example because the goods are stolen. Only damages are available for breach of the other two terms because they are mere warranties

---

[106] Collins, *The Law of Contract* (4th ed, LexisNexis, 2003) p 31.

[107] For more detail see Ellis, *Modern Irish Commercial and Consumer Law*, (Jordan's, 2004); Clark, *Contract Law in Ireland* (Round Hall, 2004) Ch 8.

[108] *O'Flynn v Balkan Tours*, unreported, Supreme Court, 7 April 1997; *McKenna v Best Travel Ltd*, unreported, High Court, 17 December 1996.

[109] *Irish Telephone Rentals Ltd v Irish Civil Service Building Society Ltd* [1991] ILRM 880.

[110] See *Mallett and Son (Antiques) Limited v Rory Rogers* [2005] IEHC 131.

(24–14). Section 12(2) of the Act deals with the situation in which a vendor agrees with the purchaser that he will not transfer the full title in the goods sold, but only such limited title as he possesses. Such transactions are subject to an implied warranty that the vendor has disclosed all overriding claims on the goods at the time of making the contract and that the vendor will not disturb the buyer's quiet possession of the goods. The same sub-section governs cases where the vendor transfers a third party's title in the goods. Such contracts of sale are subject to an implied warranty that the third party will not disturb the buyer's quiet possession of his purchase.

### Section 13—Sale by Description

Where goods are sold, whether in the course of business or between private parties, on the basis of a written or oral account of their features, a condition is implied that the goods as sold will correspond to that account.[111] The description will include any reference to the goods on packaging, labels or other descriptive matter accompanying the goods.[112] In *O'Connor v Donnelly*[113] the Court held that the condition can be implied even where the goods are shown to the buyer. No liability attaches where the purchaser has not relied on the description.[114] **[13–66]**

### Section 14—Quality of Goods

This section is notable in that it does not apply to transactions between private parties. It only applies where the vendor is selling in the course of business. In such circumstances, the vendor is obliged to ensure that the goods sold are of "merchantable quality"[115]; that they are "as fit for the purpose for which goods of that kind are commonly bought and as durable as it is reasonable to expect having regard to any description applied to them, the price (if relevant) and all other relevant circumstances." The law under this section is in many ways easier stated than applied. As a guideline, Lord Denning suggested in *The Hansa Nord*[116] that, as breach of any of these conditions entitles the buyer to reject the goods, a fair way of testing merchantability is to ask whether, in a commercial sense, the breach is serious enough to justify rejection. **[13–67]**

The section states that goods must be "as durable as it is reasonable to expect" having regard to certain listed factors. As the section suggests, "merchantable quality" will mean something different in every case. A second-hand product will not be expected to meet the same standards as its new equivalent. Thus, in *Bernstein v Palmer Motors*[117] and *Bartlett v Sidney Marcus*[118] it was set out that a second-hand car, **[13–68]**

---

[111] See *Jones v Just* (1868) LR 3 QB 197 for the common law origins of this condition. See also s 15 on sale by sample.

[112] *Re Moore & Co v Landauer & Co* [1921] 2 KB 519.

[113] [1944] Ir Jur Rep 1.

[114] *Beale v Taylor* [1967] 1 WLR 1193.

[115] See *Jones v Bright* (1829) 5 Bing 533 for the common law origins of this condition.

[116] [1976] QB 44, 62.

[117] [1987] 2 All ER 220.

[118] [1965] 2 All ER 753.

although not in prime condition, would be of merchantable quality provided only that it could be driven safely. Lord Denning explained with typical pragmatism:

> "A buyer should realise that, when he buys a second hand car, defects may appear sooner or later; and, in the absence of an express warranty, he has no redress. Even when he buys from a dealer the most that he can require is that it should be reasonably fit for the purpose of being driven along the road."

[13–69]     In *Lutton v Saville Tractors*[119] Carswell J suggested that the test was more sophisticated than a simple distinction between old and new. He observed:

> "At one end of the scale is the purchase of a seven year old family car with a high mileage at a low price. A buyer of such a car would not ordinarily expect that vehicle to be free of potentially troublesome defects, and if some developed during the first weeks after his purchase he would unlikely be able to return the car. At the other end is a transaction concerning a luxury car, a few months old and with a small mileage, for which the price is correspondingly high. The development of defects in such a car on a scale which the buyer would have to tolerate in the case of the elderly model might well be sufficient cause for [termination] of the sale, because the parties contemplated that the car would give high performance and trouble-free motoring, and these characteristics were necessary to make it of merchantable quality in the circumstances of that transaction. In between these extremes it is a matter of fact and degree on which side of the line the case falls …".

[13–70]     The section also stipulates, at s 14(4), that goods sold in the course of business must be fit for the purpose for which they are commonly bought. This implied condition was breached in *Egan v McSweeney*,[120] in which a bag of coal contained a copper detonator. It is important to note that there is no exception in the case where the vendor does not realise or could not have known that the goods are not fit for purpose. Liability here is strict. Take *Wallis v Russell*[121] in which a lady bought two crabs from a fishmonger for a meal. The fishmonger sold her boiled crabs, which, unknown to him, were defective. The condition was breached. It was enough that the fishmonger knew by implication that the crabs were to be eaten, because crabs are usually eaten, and the crabs were not fit for that purpose. It was reasonable to impute to the fishmonger the knowledge that the crabs would be eaten because crabs are ordinarily only used for that purpose.[122]

[13–71]     Sometimes, it is not reasonable to say that the vendor knows by implication the purpose to which a good bought will be put. Take *Stokes and McKiernan v Lixnaw Co-op*,[123] in which the contract was for the sale of alcohol. Alcohol is usually for drinking. But the purchasers in this case, unknown to the vendor, bought the alcohol to use in testing milk. This is an unorthodox use for alcohol. Accordingly, we cannot say that

---

[119] [1986] NI 327.
[120] (1955) 90 ILTR 40.
[121] [1902] 2 IR 585.
[122] *Grant v Australian Knitting Mills* [1936] AC 84, *per* Lord Wright.
[123] (1937) 7 ILTR 70.

the vendor knew by implication the purpose to which it would be put. In this case, where a good is bought for an unusual purpose, it is incumbent upon the purchaser to expressly inform the vendor of the purpose he has in mind. Otherwise, the vendor will not be liable if the good turns out not to be fit for its special purpose. In *Stokes*, because the vendor knew that the alcohol was being sold to a co-op and that the alcohol would be used to test milk, the vendor was liable when the alcohol turned out to be unsuitable.

The idea in this section, as throughout this body of legislation, is that the **[13–72]** vendor has superior knowledge about the goods, or at least that he is in a better position to obtain that knowledge. In some circumstances, however, part of that imbalance is removed. If the purchaser has some expertise as to the goods he is purchasing and fails to detect that they are unfit for his purpose, it seems proper that the s 14 condition should not be breached. Section 14(4) states that the seller will not be liable where "the circumstances show that the buyer does not rely, or that it is unreasonable for him to rely, on the seller's skill or judgement". In *Draper v Rubenstein*,[124] for example, an experienced butcher purchased cattle which were not fit to eat. The Court held that the butcher, as a man of some skill in the purchase of cattle, had relied on his own judgment and not that of the seller, and so the seller was not liable. If the buyer has relied even partially on the seller's judgment, the seller will be liable.[125] Along the same lines is s 14(3), which provides that the condition as to merchantability is not implied in relation to defects which are specifically drawn to the buyer's attention before the contract. Where the goods have been examined before contracting, the condition is not implied in relation to defects which ought to have been revealed by the examination.

## Section 15

This section governs the sale of goods by sample. If goods supplied have been sold by **[13–73]** sample, there is a condition implied that they will correspond with the sample. If the goods correspond exactly with the sample, but both the sample and the goods are of unmerchantable quality, the seller is not liable unless the defect would have been apparent on reasonable examination of the sample. The buyer must have been given a reasonable opportunity to inspect the sample.

## Implied Terms and Justice

It has been demonstrated that the intent-based justification for implied terms does not **[13–74]** always hold water. In many instances, terms are imposed on parties rather than implied into their contracts. How then can implied terms be justified if not by reference to the intention of the parties? Law and economics theorists justify the implication of terms on the basis of economic efficiency. Collins says that the practice of implying terms "enhances the utility and efficiency of contracts as an economic mechanism, for it saves the parties from having to spend time discussing and agreeing the details of the transaction".[126] Implied terms function as "default rules": terms that will automatically form part of a particular contract unless the parties expressly contract out of

---

[124] (1925) 59 ILTR 119.
[125] *Ashton Piggeries v Christopher Hill Ltd* [1972] AC 441; *Jewsons Ltd v Boykan* [2004] BLR 31.
[126] Collins, *The Law of Contract* (4th ed, LexisNexis, 2003) 242.

them. They eliminate important transaction costs which would otherwise be borne by the parties. The parties do not have to spend time, money and expertise on negotiating every last detail of their contract because they know that they can leave certain gaps to be filled by the courts.

[13–75]     The more likely explanation is that, by implying terms, the courts are allocating the risks of breach in the fairest possible way. This is, in some ways, a redistributive exercise. The courts impose obligations on the stronger party, or on classes of stereotypically stronger parties, in order to shift contractual control[127] to the weaker, or presumptively weaker, party. This distributive function is a controversial one, usually reserved to the Oireachtas. However, it is doubtful whether the implication of terms does much to level the playing field as between weak and strong. First, the stronger party can often use his resources to escape or limit the effects of implication. For example, he may be able to use exemption clauses (Chapter 14) so that he is not liable in the event that he breaches an implied term. Or he may simply charge higher prices to pay for the cost of insuring against the consequences of breach.[128] Kronman traces this argument in a discussion of the implication of terms in consumer contracts[129]:

> "Where there is a striking imbalance in the bargaining power of the parties to a contract, so that one is able to dictate terms to the other – to insist that the exchange be on his terms or not at all – the contract is said to be one of adhesion. Consumer contracts are often characterised as adhesive, since the consumer has little or no control over the terms of the agreement. In recent years, courts and legislatures have intervened in the exchange process, with increasing frequency, to correct the imbalance of bargaining power that contracts of this sort appear to involve. Typically, the first step has been the judicial or statutory implication of warranty terms that increase the consumer's rights under the contract, giving him what he wants but has no power to demand. But so long as the party with the greater bargaining power can force the other to waive whatever liability these implied terms create, he can easily restore the original imbalance the warranty is meant to correct. At this point, a court or legislature determined to achieve greater equality in bargaining power may be tempted to make the implied warranty nondisclaimable."

---

[127] Kronman, "Paternalism and the Law of Contract" (1983) 92 Yale LJ 772.
[128] See Smith, *Atiyah's Introduction to the Law of Contract* (6th ed, Oxford University Press, 2005) 163.
[129] Kronman, *op. cit.* at 770.

# CHAPTER 14
# Exemption Clauses

## I. Introduction

Exemption clauses are of two main types. The first is the exclusion clause, which seeks   **[14–01]**
to absolve one party of all liability in the event that he breaches the contract or
commits a tort. The second is the limitation clause,[1] which simply restricts the remedies
available to one party in the event that the other breaches or commits a tort, for
example by limiting damages to a particular sum of money or by providing that the
non-breaching party must fulfil certain conditions, such as complying with a time-
limit, before he can claim any remedy. This chapter explores the regulation of
exemption clauses at common law and under statute.

---

[1] For example: "providing always that our total liability for loss, damage or injury shall not
exceed the total value of the contract" *Harbutt's Plasticine Ltd v Wayne Tank and Pump* [1970] 1
QB 447; "Whatever the difference of the shipment may be in value from the grade, type or
description specified ... such question shall not ... entitle the buyers to reject the delivery or any
part thereof" *J Aron & Co. Inc. v Comptoir Wegimont* [1921] 3 KB 435; "The goods delivered shall
be deemed to be in all respects in accordance with the contract ... unless the sellers shall within
14 days after the arrival of the goods ... receive notice" *Beck & Co. v Szymanowski* [1924] AC 43.
For an especially detailed and analytical discussion of exemption clauses in England see
Koffmann & MacDonald, *The Law of Contract* (5th ed, Oxford University Press, 2004) pp
165–306.

## II. Common Law: The Judicial Attitude to Exemption Clauses

[14–02] Exemption clauses are a very useful tool. As terms of a contract, they allow the parties to allocate responsibility for certain contractual risks or for insuring against them. If the contract says "A shall not be liable in the event of X", then B will often insure against the risk of X. It may well be cheaper for B to insure against this risk. In addition, A avoids the expense of taking out this insurance; he does not have to add the cost of insurance to his goods and he may sell them to B at a lower price. Exemption clauses are, nevertheless, at the outer margins of acceptable behaviour in the creation of contracts. The party who relies on the clause often has had the benefit of time and expert advice in preparing it while the party affected by such a clause may have neither. The party affected may not have time even to read and digest the exemption clause, and may be discouraged by devices such as small print and difficult language from reading it at all. Therefore, when breach occurs, he may be unfairly surprised at what he turns out to have agreed to. More importantly, there is a feeling that exemption clauses are liable to be deliberately exploited by the party with superior bargaining power, to the detriment of the weaker party. Now, it has been said many times that freedom of contract is a key principle of contract law. In line with that principle it might be said that a party is entitled to have such terms in his contract as he pleases. In particular, he is entitled to protect himself against future risks where he can, and he is entitled to use his resources and skill to carve out the most favourable bargain for himself. What is more, if the weaker party fails to protect himself from a bad bargain the courts ought not to come to his aid. Contract law requires rugged individualism. However, the courts do not seem to see things this way. As shall be demonstrated, concern for the little man motivates a certain judicial hostility towards exemption clauses.

## III. The Issue of Standard Form Contracts

[14–03] This hostility is especially evident in cases involving standard form contracts. A company will often use the same "canned" terms whenever it enters into a contract. By using a standard form contract a company can save time and resources that would otherwise be spent on negotiating complex individual agreements. The advantages of this tool are such that, as Karl Llewellyn memorably wrote in his book *The Common Law Tradition*, that "it would be a heart-warming scene ... if only all businessmen and all their lawyers would be reasonable."[2] But businessmen and lawyers are frequently unreasonable. Standard form contracts are often used to narrow the obligations of the party who drafts the contract and to unreasonably enhance those of the affected party. Often this is done in a way that flouts the moral requirement of good faith. In *George Mitchell (Chesterhall) Ltd v Finney Lock Seeds*[3] Lord Denning explained the trouble with exemption clauses in his inimitable style:

> "None of you nowadays will remember the trouble we had – when I was called to the Bar – with exemption clauses. They were printed in small print on the back of tickets and order forms and invoices. They were contained in catalogues

---

[2] Quoted in Fuller and Eisenberg, *Basic Contract Law* (6th ed, West Publishing Co, 1996) p 650.
[3] [1983] QB 284.

178

or timetables. They were held to be binding on any person who took them without objection. No one ever did object. He never read them or knew what was in them. No matter how unreasonable they were, he was bound. All this was done in the name of 'freedom of contract'. But the freedom was all on the side of the big concern which had the use of the printing press. No freedom for the little man who took the ticket or order form or invoice ... The big concern could and did exempt itself from liability in its own interest without regard to the little man. It got away with it time after time."[4]

The possibilities for the abuse of the weaker party's good faith are myriad and, in many ways, a person dealing on the basis of a company's standard form contract trusts himself to that company's mercy. Llewellyn in *The Common Law Tradition* goes on to say: **[14–04]**

"[P]ower, like greed, if it does not always corrupt, goes easily to the head. So that the form-agreements tend either at once or over the years, and often by whole lines of trade, into a massive and almost terrifying jug-handled character; the one party lays his head into the mouth of a lion – either, and mostly, without reading the fine print, or occasionally in hope and expectation (not infrequently solid) that it will be a sweet and gentle lion."[5]

Even if a company does not abuse the tool of standard form contracts deliberately so that the contract is substantively unfair, the courts tend to feel that all standard form contracts are subject to certain inherent flaws going to the parties' consent. Where standard form contracts are used, the individual terms are not up for negotiation and so there is no bargain in the traditional sense. Often, terms will be standard across an entire industry, or the party offering the standard terms will have a monopoly on a particular commodity, so that the party who needs a particular good or service has no alternative but to accept them.[6] Some judges, such as Lord Denning above, have felt that freedom of contract ought not to be a primary consideration in dealing with these cases because the weaker party has not really entered the contract with a sufficient degree of freedom. As Kessler has observed, such a party's contractual intention is "but a subjection, more or less voluntary, to the terms **[14–05]**

---

[4] *ibid.* at 296.

[5] Quoted in Fuller and Eisenberg, *op. cit.*

[6] In *Schroeder Music Publishing v Macauley* [1974] 3 All ER 616 Lord Diplock contrasts standard form contracts of ancient origin such as bills of lading and charterparties which are "widely used by parties whose bargaining powers are fairly matched" with standard form contracts of comparatively modern origin. "[These are] the result of the concentration of particular kinds of business in relatively few hands ... The terms of this kind of standard form of contract have not been the subject of negotiation between the parties to it, or approved by any organisation representing the interests of the weaker party. They have been dictated by that party whose bargaining power, either exercised alone or in conjunction with another providing similar goods or serviced, enables him to say: 'If you want these goods or services at all, these are the only terms on which they are available".

dictated by the stronger party".[7] In *McCord v ESB*[8] Henchy J seemed receptive to this argument:

> "[The weaker party] is compelled, from a position of weakness and necessity ... to enter into what falls into the classification of a contract and which, as such, according to the theory of contract law which was evolved in the *laissez-faire* atmosphere of the nineteenth century, is to be treated by the courts as if it had emerged by choice from the force of the market place at the behest of parties who were at arm's length and had freedom of choice. The real facts show that such an approach is largely based on legal fiction ... such an instrument has less affinity with a freely negotiated interpersonal contract than with a set of bye-laws or with any other form of autonomic legislation."

**[14-06]** This attitude is evidenced throughout the common law on exemption clauses. First of all, the courts take a strict line on the issue of whether an exemption clause has been successfully incorporated into the contract. Thus, exemption clauses will frequently be found not to be part of the contract at issue. Second, even if the clause is found to have been incorporated effectively, the court may hold, whether as a matter of interpretation or as a matter of law, that it does not cover the breach of contract which occurs. Third, the court will not allow a party to exempt himself from liability for fundamental breach.

## IV. Incorporation

> *Grandpa Joe: Mister Wonka?*
> *Willy Wonka: I am extraordinarily busy, sir.*
> *Grandpa Joe: I was just wondering about the chocolate. The lifetime supply of chocolate? For Charlie? When does he get it?*
> *Willy Wonka: He doesn't.*
> *Grandpa Joe: Why not?*
> *Willy Wonka: Because he broke the rules.*
> *Grandpa Joe: What rules? We didn't see any rules, did we, Charlie?*
> *Willy Wonka: Wrong, sir. Wrong. Under section 37B of the contract signed by him, it states quite clearly that all offers shall become null and void if—and you can read it for yourself in this photostatic copy—"I, the undersigned, shall forfeit all rights, privileges, and licenses herein and herein contained," et cetera, et*

---

[7] Kessler, "The Contract of Adhesion" (1943) Col L Rev 629. See also Rakoff, "Contracts of Adhesion: An Essay in Reconstruction", (1983) 96 Harv L Rev 1174: "[O]nce it is recognized that contracts of adhesion arise from the matrix of organizational hierarchy, the argument for enforcement of form terms as a recognition of 'freedom of contract' in its usual sense is unsupportable."

[8] [1980] ILRM 153. It is important to be aware of the very different approach which the courts will take to commercial cases where the parties are of equal bargaining power. In *Grimstead & Son v McGarrigan* [1999] CA Transcript 1733, Gloster J discussed an acknowledgment of non-reliance in a commercial contract between parties of equal bargaining power, both of whom were professionally advised. He argued that in such circumstances, the commercial desirability of certainty and of equal parties measuring and allocating risk between them justified upholding the clause. See also *Six Continents Hotels Inc v Event Hotels GmbH* [2006] EWHC 2317.

*cetera ... "Fax mentis incendium gloria cultum," et cetera, et cetera ..."Memo
bis punitor delicatum." It's all there, black and white, clear as crystal ... You lose.
Good day sir.*

From: *Willie Wonka and the Chocolate Factory* (1971)

It is possible that an oral contract or written contractual document may not [14–07]
contain the parties' entire agreement. There may be other documents that contain the
rest of the contract's terms. We have already suggested that exemption clauses are
rarely brought to the attention of the contracting party in any effective sense. Often,
they are hidden in the small print of the contract document. Or they may be in another
document entirely, with only the merest reference to their existence in the main
contract document. The courts seem to consider these practices a form of foul play and
have tried to counter them in the rules on the incorporation of terms. Collins[9] provides
an economic perspective on this area of law. He says that the courts' aim in the
exemption clause cases goes beyond mere expression of disapproval at sharp market
practices. Their aim is transformative. They seek to correct a market failure; "to
challenge uncompetitive markets in an attempt to force traders to offer different and
competing terms". For example, one of the reasons for the sluggish market in
exemption clauses is that customers are ignorant of all but the key terms of contracts.
Because customers tend to be aware of key terms such as price, there is an incentive for
suppliers to compete with one another to offer the best prices. The rules on
incorporation require traders to bring these clauses expressly to consumers' attention,
increasing the chance that consumers will demand more favourable clauses.

The cases on incorporation may be split into two categories: the cases on signed [14–08]
contracts and the cases on unsigned contracts. If I sign a contractual document which
embodies certain terms, I am bound by those terms. If, on the other hand, I have not
signed any contractual document, I am only bound by terms if the party seeking to rely
on them has taken such steps as are reasonable in all the circumstances to give me
notice of those terms.

## Signed Contracts

It is an important rule of contract law that a person who signs a contractual document [14–09]
is bound by its contents, no matter whether he has read them or understands them. As
Lord Denning has noted in *Curtis v Chemical Cleaning and Dyeing Co. Ltd*,[10] a party's
signature is "irrefragable evidence of his assent to the whole contract, including the
exempting clauses". It may be that, in truth, the special rule as to signature has nothing
to do with the objective test. It may be, as Atiyah has claimed, that the law on
signatures simply reflects the popular perception that a signature is and ought to be a
definitive and final contractual formality.[11] The effect of this signature rule is that the
party seeking to rely on an exemption clause does not have to make any effort to give

---

[9] Collins, *The Law of Contract* (4th ed, LexisNexis, 2003) pp 260–261.
[10] [1951] 1 KB 805.
[11] Atiyah, "Form and Substance in Contract Law" in *Essays on Contract* (Oxford University
Press, 1986) p 109.

the signer reasonable notice of the contents of the document that he is signing.[12] In *L'Estrange v Graucob*,[13] the proprietor of a café signed but did not read a contract concerning the purchase of a cigarette vending machine. Soon after its purchase, it became clear that the machine was not fit for the purpose for which it had been purchased. However, the contract signed contained an exemption clause, which provided for exclusion of the warranty as to fitness for purpose. The clause was contained in a part of the contract that might easily have escaped notice and was typed in "regrettably small print" on poor quality brown paper. Maugham LJ repeatedly expressed his displeasure at the small type in which the exemption clause was printed. However, he agreed with Scrutton LJ and held that the contract had to take effect according to its terms because:

> "[w]hen a document containing contractual terms is signed, then, in the absence of fraud, or, I will add, misrepresentation, the party signing it is bound, and it is wholly immaterial whether he has read the document or not."

[14–10]   The leading Irish application of this rule is *Duff v Great Northern Railway Co*.[14] The plaintiff had signed a contract for the shipment of his cattle. Contained in the contract was an exemption clause to the effect that a drover could accompany the cattle for free but did so at his own risk. The plaintiff himself chose to travel with the cattle and was injured. The Court did not inquire into the question of whether adequate steps were taken to incorporate the exemption clause into the contract. Because the plaintiff had signed, his consent to the exemption clause could not be interrogated.

[14–11]   It is immaterial whether the signer can or did read the document he has signed. The law's failure to make special provision for those who do not read what they sign has been justified in terms of certainty:

> "This is rather thin ice on which to skate to the shores of non-liability ... The whole business structure of America would become a shambles if signers in serious transactions were to be allowed to repudiate their obligations on the basis that they did not know what they were signing. The ever-constant possibility of such a disavowal would turn into water the bricks of every contractual wall; such an accepted possibility would wreck every business dealing at the slightest touch of the repudiator."[15]

[14–12]   The case of *Barclay's Bank v Schwartz*[16] shows that it may not even matter whether the person signing can read or understand what he is signing. In that case a Romanian man claimed that he was not bound when he signed a contract written in

---

[12]   *L'Estrange v Graucob* [1934] 2 KB 394, 403 *per* Scrutton LJ: "In cases in which the contract is contained in a railway ticket or unsigned document, it is necessary to prove that an alleged party was aware, or ought to have been aware, of its terms and conditions. These cases have no application when the document has been signed."
[13]   *ibid.*
[14]   (1878) 4 LR 178.
[15]   *General Refrigerator and Store Fixture Co. v Fry* 141 A 2d 836 at 838 (1958) *per* Musmanno J. See also *Peninsula Business Services v Sweeney* [2004] IRLR 49.
[16]   *The Times*, 2 August 1995.

English, because he did not speak the language well. Nevertheless, he was bound to the contract, purely on the strength of his signature. To similar effect is *The Luna*[17] in which the Dutch master of a fishing vessel, *The Luna*, signed an agreement with the tugboat *Kingston* to tow *The Luna* from the mouth of the Humber into Hull at a price of 15 shillings. The document contained conditions, including an indemnity clause which provided that the owners of *The Luna* would be liable in respect of any damage that might be caused during the towage. The *Kingston* towed *The Luna* into another ship; *The Frances and Jane*. The owners were held liable because the master had signed the contract. This was so even though he spoke little English and could not read it well. That said, under the doctrine of *non est factum*, where an illiterate person signs a contractual document the contents of which have been misrepresented to him, he is not bound by his signature (17-77). This is set out in the old case known as *Thouroughgood's Case*.[18]

It appears from the English cases that there are only two circumstances in which the rule in *L'Estrange* does not apply. In *Curtis v Chemical Cleaning and Dyeing Co.*[19] the Court of Appeal held that dry cleaners could not rely on the following clause to exempt them from liability for negligent damage to the fabric of the plaintiff's wedding dress: "This article ... is accepted on condition that the company is not liable for any damage however arising". This was because the dry cleaners' assistant had misrepresented to the plaintiff that the clause only applied to damage to beads and sequins. The second circumstance in which the rule does not have any application is when the document signed is not a contractual document. In *Grogan v Robin Meredith Plant Hire*[20] a signature on a time sheet had no effect on the incorporation of terms into the parties' contract. This was because a reasonable man, looking at the nature of the document and the circumstances of its use between the parties, would not conclude that it purported to have contractual effect; it was a purely administrative document. **[14–13]**

The approach in *L'Estrange v Graucob* has been roundly criticised.[21] In *McCutcheon v David MacBrayne Ltd*[22] Lord Devlin disputed the application of *L'Estrange* to standard form contracts. **[14–14]**

> "If it were possible for your Lordships to escape from the world of make-believe which the law has created into the real world in which transactions of this sort are actually done, the answer would be short and simple. [Signature] should make no difference whatever. This sort of document is not meant to be read, still less to be understood. Its signature is in truth about as significant as a handshake that marks the formal conclusion of the bargain."

However, the decision in *L'Estrange* is considered justified on the basis of the objective test: Miss L'Estrange signed the document so that any reasonable observer would have concluded that she was assenting to the terms of the contract. However, **[14–15]**

---

[17] [1920] P 22.

[18] (1584) 2 Co Rep 9a.

[19] Above, n 10.

[20] [1996] 53 Con LR 87.

[21] See e.g. Spencer, "Signature, Consent and the Rule in *L'Estrange v Graucob*" [1973] CLJ 104.

[22] [1964] 1 WLR 125.

we might argue that Miss L'Estrange's case comes within an exception contemplated by the doctrine of mistake (Chapter 17). We might argue that it was or ought to have been clear to Graucob's representative that Miss L'Estrange did not intend to sign up to the exemption clause. In the Canadian case of *Tilden Rent-A-Car Co. v Clendinning*,[23] the Court of Appeal of Ontario applied that principle to a case analogous to Miss L'Estrange's case. The contract was for a rental car and contained an exemption clause that had the effect of imposing liability for any damage to the car on the defendant who was renting it. The defendant had signed the contract without reading it. It was apparent to the rental company's clerk that he had not read it. The Court rejected the notion of an automatic signature exception to the relying party's duty to take reasonable steps to bring an exemption clause to the affected party's attention. It is worth reviewing the Court's reasoning at some length:

> "In ordinary commercial practice where there is frequently a sense of formality in the transaction, and where there is a full opportunity for the parties to consider the terms of the proposed contract submitted for signature, it might well be safe to assume that the party who attached his signature to the contract intends by so doing to acknowledge his acquaintance to its terms, and that the other party entered into the contract upon that belief."

[14–16]    The Court then contrasted that ideal scenario with that in Mr Clendinning's case, where the clerk knew that he had not considered or read the contract and indeed where the important provisions were concealed on the reverse of the contract in very small type. In those circumstances, the rental company was not reasonably entitled to claim that it believed Mr Clendinning's signature to indicate his assent to their exemption clause. The Canadian view has not yet found favour on this side of the Atlantic. In England, there was some suggestion in the shape of *Ocean Chemical Transport Inc. v Exnor Craggs Ltd*[24] that an especially onerous or unusual term will not automatically be incorporated by signature unless the clause has been expressly brought to the signer's attention. However, the great weight of case law favours the traditional position. In *Peekay Intermark Ltd v Australia and New Zealand Banking Group*[25] Moore-Bick LJ said that the approach in L'Estrange's case "underpins the whole of commercial life; any erosion of it would have serious repercussions far beyond the business community".

### Signature and Websites

[14–17]    Is a click a signature? Electronic and paper signatures are equivalent for the purposes of the Electronic Commerce Act (11-34) and it seems clear that a digital signature, a scanned signature or a deliberately typed name at the end of an e-mail could be a signature for the purposes of the rule in *L'Estrange*. The position on clicking an icon

---

[23] (1973) 83 DLR (3d) 400. See also *Crocker v Sundance Northwest Resorts Ltd* (1988) 51 DLR (4th) 321.

[24] [2000] 1 Lloyd's Rep 446, 454 *per* Evans LJ, suggesting that this principle would apply only in limited circumstances where signature was obtained under significant pressure of time or circumstances. But see *Jonathan Wren & Co. Ltd v Microdec plc* (1999) 65 Con LR 157; *Bankway Properties Ltd v Penfold-Dursford* [2001] EWCA Civ 528; *HIH Casualty v New Hampshire Insurance* [20001] EWCA Civ 735.

[25] [2006] 2 Lloyd's Rep 511.

requires further exploration. In 2001, the English Law Commission[26] argued that clicking on a website button might be treated as an electronic signature for the purpose of s 7[27] of the English Electronic Communications Act 2000. Arguably, the definition of electronic signature under this Act is more rigorous than its Irish equivalent. The Commission sets out that clicking on a button to confirm an order placed on a website could be treated as a concluding signature because what matters is the function of the click and not its form. The Commission argues that clicking on a website button demonstrates the intention to enter into a contract. The click is analogous to a rubber stamp or a manuscript X. A click's position as a signature is strengthened when the click is performed in combination with the user's details or password. Now, if the concluding click of the "confirm order" or "checkout" button is equivalent to a signature on a written contract then, arguably, the rule in *L'Estrange v Graucob* applies and standard terms which are referred to in the website at some point before clicking are incorporated into the contract between the purchaser and the online vendor.[28] The effect of this rule could be mitigated by arguments to the effect that the web-pages encountered by the clicking party would not reasonably be perceived as having contractual effect. Arguments about accidental clicking and website malfunction going to the intention to sign might also be fruitful. Again it is arguable that the mere act of clicking on a web button does not indicate intention to be legally bound in the same way that a signature does. Lay parties may not associate legal status with such a simple act. One is reminded of the dissenting judgment of Denning LJ in *Goodman v J Eban Ltd*[29] where he argued that a rubber stamp could not be a signature: "This is such common knowledge that a 'rubber stamp' is contemptuously used to denote the thoughtless impress of an automaton in contrast to the reasoned attention of a sensible person." It is therefore desirable that if clicking a "checkout" button on a website is to be treated as a signature that websites bear a suitably conspicuous notice advising would-be purchasers of the obligations that may spring from a press of their mouse button.

## Unsigned Contracts

If the parties' contract is not embodied in a single document, the exemption clause will [14–18] only be incorporated if reasonable steps have been taken to bring it to the affected party's notice. Obviously, if the party affected by the clause has actually read it, the courts will find that adequate notice is present; actual notice is always adequate notice.[30] If the relying party actually points the content of the clause out to the other

---

[26] Law Commission, *Electronic Contracts: Formal Requirements in Electronic Transactions* (2001), pp 15–16.

[27] An electronic signature is defined as "so much of anything in electronic form as–

(a) is incorporated into or otherwise associated with any electronic communication or electronic data; and

(b) purports to be so incorporated or associated for the purpose of being used in establishing the authenticity of the communication or data, or both."

[28] Koffmann & McDonald, *The Law of Contract* (5th ed, Oxford University Press, 2004) p 173; Poole *Contract Law* (8th ed, Oxford University Press, 2006) p 214.

[29] [1954] 1 QB 550.

[30] *Leo Laboratories Limited v Crompton B.V (formerly Witco B.V)* [2005] IESC 31.

party he will have done enough. So, in *Sweeney v Mulcahy* [31] the standard terms of the Royal Institute of Architects of Ireland were incorporated into a contract between the plaintiff and the defendant because the defendant had specifically written to the plaintiff saying that these conditions would apply. It is clear, however, that parties are rarely so obliging and, indeed, they are not required to be. There is a temptation to bury references to exemption clauses in masses of small type, or to detail them in an inaccessible document, while only making the barest reference to them at the time of contracting. An American judge has spoken of these practices in disparaging terms, comparing them to the acts of the Roman tyrant Caligula, who had the laws "inscribed upon pillars so high that the people could not read them".[32] Notice is so important because it can enable a party who might be disadvantaged by a clause to "vote with his feet" and decline to enter into a Draconian contract. For example, Judge Davitt in *Shea v Great Southern Railways* [33] observes that a passenger on public transport can read the terms presented to him and if he "is not prepared to accept the conditions he is at liberty to get off the bus". For this reason, it is important that the rules on notice are reasonably strict in favour of the affected party.

### What is Notice?

[14–19] The key case on notice is *Parker v South Eastern Railway*.[34] Parker had deposited luggage at a railway station cloakroom. He received a paper ticket. On the front of the ticket was a number, a date, the opening times of the office and the words "see back". On the back of the ticket were a number of terms including one which said that the company would not be responsible for any package exceeding £10 in value. Parker did not read these. Parker's luggage was lost and the question was whether the terms on the back of the ticket formed part of his contract with the railway. Since this was not a signed contract the key question was whether he had received adequate notice of the terms. The Court held that he had, because, as Lord Bramwell opined, Parker should have known from the ticket that terms existed in the contract between him and the railway that affected the nature of their obligations to him:

> "The plaintiffs, having notice of the printing, were in the same situation as though the porter had said 'Read that, it concerns the matter in hand'; that if the plaintiffs did not read it, they were as much bound as if they had read it and had not objected."

[14–20] The first point to take from *Parker* is that a clause can be incorporated into the parties' contract notwithstanding the affected party has not read it. As a matter of policy it is unreasonable to expect that a party will always have the opportunity to point out an exclusion clause to each individual with whom he contracts. For example, a railway company will form many hundreds of contracts a day. It cannot be expected to take the time to apprise each customer of the details of the terms and conditions on

---

[31] [1993] ILRM 289.
[32] *Cutler Corp. v Latshaw* 374 Pa 1,6, 97 A 2d 234, 237 (1953).
[33] (1944) Ir Jur Rep 26.
[34] (1877) 2 CPD 416.

which the contract is based, and few busy commuters would want it to do so. In *Shea v Great Southern Railway*[35] Judge Davitt wrote that:

> "[I]f it were legally necessary to ensure that every condition were specifically brought to the notice of each passenger, then a ridiculous state of affairs would result, involving many delays and tending seriously to hold up transport."

Neither is it unreasonable to expect customers to take some responsibility for their own contractual fate. The courts have traditionally had little patience with those who enter into contracts without reading the fine print.[36] In *Parker v South Eastern Railway*[37] Bramwell LJ spoke forcefully about this kind of recklessness. Clearly, Bramwell LJ would not have agreed with Lord Denning's pragmatic observation in *Thornton v Shoe Lane Parking*[38] that: "[n]o customer in a thousand ever read the conditions. If he had stopped to do so, he would have missed the train or the bus": **[14–21]**

> "Now they claim to charge the company, and to have the benefit of their own indifference. Is this just? Is it reasonable? Is it the way in which any other business is allowed to be conducted? Is it even allowed to a man to 'think', 'judge', 'guess', 'chance' a matter, without informing himself when he can, and then when his 'thought', 'judgment', 'guess' or 'chance' turns out wrong or unsuccessful, claim to impose a burthen or duty on another which he could not have done had he informed himself as he might?"

It is also important to note that, as with unsigned contracts, the fact that the affected party is unable to read the terms and conditions at issue is irrelevant.[39] The test is objective; it focuses on reasonableness so that the reader's subjective characteristics are written out of the equation. Mellish LJ explained the reasoning behind this position in *Parker*: **[14–22]**

> "The railway company, as it seems to me, must be entitled to make some assumptions respecting the person who deposits luggage with them: I think they are entitled to assume that he can read, and that he understands the English language, and that he pays such attention to what he is about as may be reasonably expected from a person in such a transaction as that of depositing luggage in a cloak-room ... I think that a particular plaintiff ought not to be in a better position than other persons on account of his exceptional ignorance or stupidity or carelessness."

---

[35] Above, n 32.

[36] In *Hood v Anchor Line* [1918] AC 837 Viscount Haldane set out that "the real question was not whether they read it, but whether they can be heard to say that they did not read it".

[37] Above, n 33.

[38] [1971] 2 QB 163.

[39] See *Thompson v London, Midland and Scottish Railway* [1930] 1 KB 41. However, if the party relying on the clause is aware that the other party will have difficulty in understanding it, as where he has poor English, his duty to bring the nature of the clause home may be higher; *Geier v Kujawa, Weston and Warne Bros.* [1970] 1 Lloyd's Rep 364.

**[14–23]**     The cases since *Parker* have gone further. So it does not seem to matter that, even if the plaintiff wanted to read the terms, they are squirreled away in an inaccessible document. In *Shea v Great Southern Railway*[40] Judge Davitt held that a plaintiff who knows that terms exist is bound by them "even whether he can conveniently read them or not". An example of this principle in operation is *Early v Great Southern Rly Co*.[41] In that case, the plaintiff purchased a cut-price railway ticket. There was a poster in the station which stated that reduced price tickets were issued subject to conditions contained in the railway company's timetables. There was also a notice on the back of the ticket which said that it was issued "subject to the conditions and regulations in the company's timetables, books, bills and notices". No copies of the timetable, books, bills or notices were available for inspection at the stop where the plaintiff boarded. Nevertheless, the Supreme Court held that those terms were incorporated.

**[14–24]**     The key point is that the affected party must have known that terms *existed*. It does not matter that he did not know what they *were*. In *Parker*[42] Baggally LJ held that adequate steps will have been taken to bring a clause to the affected party's notice if he merely "had good reason to believe that there were upon the [document] statements intended to affect the relative rights of himself and the company". In *Carroll v An Post*[43] Costello P held that, since the plaintiff knew that there were rules printed on the back of the payslip he had been given, he was bound by them, regardless of whether he knew what those rules contained. This is because once a party is on notice as to the existence of terms he is put on inquiry as to their content: as we have already noted, it is his job to read them if he chooses. But regardless of whether the affected party can or does read the *terms* the *statement which alerts him to the existence* of those terms must itself be legible. If there is no statement at all to alert him to their existence, as where a ticket has terms on the back but there is no statement on the front to alert the purchaser to their presence, the term is unlikely to stand.[44] If it is so badly set out that the affected party could not discover the terms' existence without special inquiry, he will not be bound by them.[45] Treitel observes that adequate notice is not present:

> "... if there are no words on the face of the document drawing attention to [the clause], or if, though there are such words, the back of the document is blank ... or if the words are made illegible by a date stamp, or if the exemption clause is buried in a mass of advertisements."

**[14–25]**     In sum, the courts will look more favourably on a case if there has been "an express acknowledgement in the contractual documents that the terms and conditions in the contract were incorporated."[46]

---

[40] Above, n 32. See also *O'Brien v MGN Ltd* [2001] EWCA Civ 1279.
[41] [1940] IR 409.
[42] Above, n 33.
[43] [1996] IR 443.
[44] *Henderson v Stevenson* (1875) LR 2 HL Sc App 470.
[45] *Ryan v Great Southern and Western Rly Co.* (1898) 12 ILTR 108.
[46] *Ocean Chemical Transport Inc. v Exnor Craggs Ltd* [2000] 1 Lloyd's Rep 446, 454.

## When Will Reasonable Steps Have Been Taken to Give Notice?

It is difficult to say with any precision whether there is a cast-iron way of incorporating    **[14–26]**
an exemption clause into a contract by notice. Generally speaking, the case law since
*Parker* has developed a four-fold framework. First, the steps taken to give notice must
come in good time, before the conclusion of the agreement. Second, if notice of the
clause is given in a document, that document must be contractual in nature. Third, the
more onerous or unusual a clause, the greater the effort that must be made to bring it
to the other party's attention. Finally, an exemption clause may be incorporated
automatically where it is familiar to both parties, whether from a past course of dealing
or because it is common in the parties' industry. Remember that in analysing each of
these elements, the courts' focus is on what the party relying on the clause has done,
not on how the party affected by the clause has reacted. To some extent, the rules in
*Parker* are mitigated by the principles that come next. These principles are:

1.  Notice of the clause must be given in good time.
2.  Notice of the clause must be given in a contractual document.
3.  More will be required to give notice of an unusual or onerous term.
4.  A clause can be incorporated by a course of dealing between the parties.
5.  A clause can be automatically incorporated into the parties' contract because it
    is common in their industry.

## Time of Notice

A clause will only be incorporated into an unsigned contract if the affected party was    **[14–27]**
actually aware of its existence or ought to have been aware of its existence before the
contract was concluded. An exemption clause cannot be unilaterally introduced at some
time subsequent to the contract's conclusion so that the affected party could not possibly
have known that it existed at the time of entering into the contract. A well-known case
here is *Olley v Marlborough Court*.[47] The contract here was for the rental of a hotel
room. The contract was concluded at the hotel reception desk. Now, there was a notice
in the hotel room itself, which contained a clause limiting the hotel's liability in the event
of theft. While the hotel porter was cleaning a bust of the Duke of Marlborough at the
foot of the staircase, a thief entered the hotel, stole a key and broke into the Olleys' room.
Mrs Olley's furs and jewellery were stolen from the hotel. The question for the Court was
whether the exemption clause in the hotel room notice protected the hotel from liability
for this event. Because the notice did not make an appearance until after the contract
was concluded, the exemption clause contained therein was no part of the contract and
accordingly was ineffective to protect the hotel. Similarly, in *Sproule v Triumph Cycle
Co.*,[48] a limitation clause was contained in a document given to the purchaser of a
motorcycle after the contract for sale had been completed. Of course, the clause was
ineffective because it was introduced too late to form part of the contract. Perhaps the
most famous case on this point is *Thornton v Shoe Lane Parking Ltd*.[49] The contract here
was for parking one's car in a multi-storey automatic car park. Entry to the car park was
via an automatic gate, where the customer received a ticket. The ticket stated that the

---

[47] [1949] 1 KB 532.
[48] [1927] NI 83.
[49] [1971] 2 QB 163.

contract was subject to terms. The exemption clause, purporting to exclude liability for personal injury, was contained in these terms. However, the terms were displayed inside the car park and could not be seen from the automatic gate. Denning MR held that the contract was completed at the time of entry into the car park. Since the exemption clause did not, therefore, come on the scene until after the contract had been completed, it formed no part of the contract and was entirely ineffective.

### Contractual Documents

[14–28]  It is not possible to give the affected party notice of an exemption clause simply by referring to it on some piece of paper. It has been said already that the affected party will be bound by terms if he knows that the document used to give him notice contains contractual terms of some sort. It will not be reasonable to impute knowledge of such terms to him if the document which he has been given would not be expected to have contractual effect. So if it is sought to give notice of a clause in a document, that document must be one intended to have contractual effect.[50] So, in *Chapelton v Barry UDC*,[51] an attempt to incorporate an exemption clause by reference on a receipt, which was intended merely as a memorial of a contract for the hire of a deckchair, was a failure. The test of whether the document was intended to have contractual effect is objective: would the reasonable man have thought that this was a contractual document?

### Onerous or Unexpected Clauses

[14–29]  A party will have to make an extra effort to give adequate notice of exemption clauses that are unusual or onerous in the ordinary course of things.[52] In *Parker*[53] Bramwell LJ stated that: "there is an implied understanding that there is no condition unreasonable to the knowledge of the party tendering the document and not insisting on its being read".[54] In *Carroll v An Post*[55] Carroll J confirmed that the same principle is part of Irish law and is of particular application where the incorporating document is one which it is generally known are not read by those to whom they are given: examples would be tickets and invoices. Accordingly, where an unreasonable condition is present it falls to the party seeking to rely on that condition to do more than simply present the incorporating document to the affected party, leaving to his discretion whether to read the document or not. For example, Lord Denning found that the exemption clause in *Thornton v Shoe Lane Parking*[56] was "so wide and destructive of rights that the court should not hold any man bound by it unless it is drawn to his attention in the most explicit way."[57] The steps to be taken will depend on the nature

---

[50]  See *Grogan v Meredith Plant Hire* (1996) 15 Tr L R 371; *Burnett v Westminster Bank Ltd* [1966] 1 QB 742.

[51]  [1940] 1 KB 532.

[52]  *Hood v Anchor Line (Henderson Bros.) Ltd* [1918] AC 837, 846–847 *per* Dunedin LJ: "Accordingly it is in each case a question of circumstances whether the sort of restriction that is expressed in any writing (which, of course, includes printed matter) is a thing that is usual, and whether, being usual, it has been fairly brought before the notice of the accepting party."

[53]  Above, n 33.

[54]  *ibid.* at 428.

[55]  Above, n 42.

[56]  Above, n 48.

[57]  *ibid.* at 170.

of the exemption clause. What might be adequate notice of one clause might not be adequate notice of another. As Lord Denning memorably remarked in *J Spurling Ltd v Bradshaw*[58]: "Some clauses I have seen would need to be printed in red ink on the face of a document with a red hand pointing to it before the notice could be held to be sufficient."[59]

*Interfoto Picture Library v Stiletto Visual Programmes*,[60] although not an **[14–30]** exemption clause case, illustrates the extent of the relying party's duty. Stiletto and Interfoto had not dealt with one another before. Stiletto telephoned Interfoto to obtain photographic transparencies. The transparencies were dispatched to Stiletto in a bag which also contained a notice bearing nine conditions. Condition 2 stated that a £5 charge per transparency per day applied to any transparency kept beyond 14 days. Stiletto did not return the transparencies on time. Interfoto sought to claim £3,500 in late delivery charges. The question for the Court was whether Condition 2 had been incorporated successfully into the contract between the parties. The Court of Appeal held that it had not. Bingham LJ based his decision on the onerous and unusual nature of Condition 2. He explained:

> "The defendants are not to be relieved of liability because they did not read the condition, although doubtless they did not; but in my judgment they are to be relieved because the plaintiffs did not do what was necessary to draw this unreasonable and extortionate clause fairly to their attention."[61]

*AEG (UK) Ltd v Logic Resources Ltd*[62] is to similar effect. In that case the **[14–31]** plaintiff sold goods to the defendants, who sub-sold them to buyers in Iran. The goods turned out to be defective and they were shipped back to the plaintiffs' factory in the UK at a cost of £4,230. The plaintiffs sought to rely on a clause in the contract which stated that "the purchaser shall return the defective parts at his own expense." The Court found that this term was onerous and unusual within the meaning of *Interfoto*, particularly because the contract did not provide the defendants with any other options (Hirst LJ said that they had been "confronted with Hobson's choice in their contractual terms")[63] in the event that the goods turned out to be defective. The plaintiffs were under a stringent duty to bring this clause to the defendants' attention. They did not do so and, thus, the clause was no part of the contract.

---

[58] [1956] 1 WLR 461.

[59] *ibid.*

[60] [1989] QB 433.

[61] *ibid.*

[62] [1995] CCH CLR 265. See, however, the important dissenting judgment of Hobhouse LJ: "It is desirable as a matter of principle to keep what is said in the *Interfoto* case within its proper bounds. A wide range of clauses are commonly incorporated into contracts by general words. If it is to be the policy of English law that in every case those clauses are to be gone through with a fine toothcomb to see whether they were entirely usually and entirely desirable in the particular contract, then one is completely distorting the contractual relationship between the parties and the ordinary mechanisms of making contracts. It will introduce uncertainty into the law of contract ...".

[63] *ibid.*

**[14–32]**     The onerousness of a clause is a matter to be judged in the overall context of the contract. This point comes from *Western Meats Ltd v National Ice and Cold Storage*,[64] a case involving a contract for the storage of goods. The storage company mislabelled goods belonging to the plaintiff and as a result some of them could not be found and others were damaged. The company sought to rely on an exemption clause contained in their standard terms to avoid liability for the plaintiff's loss. However, Barrington J found that such a clause was onerous, given that one would ordinarily expect a specialist storage firm to accept liability in those circumstances. He said: "[A] businessman, offering a specialist service, but accepting the responsibility for it, must bring home clearly to the party dealing with him that he accepts no such responsibility". Accordingly, extra steps were required to give adequate notice of the exemption clause to any customer.

**[14–33]**     *Carroll v An Post*[65] is also instructive. The plaintiff claimed that he had lost a lottery prize because the lottery agent had negligently failed to enter his chosen numbers into the lottery draw. A blue arrow and the words "See instructions on reverse" were printed on the front of the Lotto payslip in red block letters. Extracts from the lottery rules were printed on the back of the payslip together with the statement that a summary of the rules could be inspected at the player's local Lotto agent. These rules contained an exemption clause which limited the defendant's vicarious liability for the negligence of its agents. Costello J held that the exemption clause was not onerous in the circumstances. He noted that every exemption clause will impose a detriment on the affected party; this did not in itself make the clause onerous. The clause was not onerous because first, the threat sought to be protected against, that of fraudulent claims, was huge and it was reasonable to use an exemption clause to guard against it. Second, it was important that the clause was a limitation of liability and not an absolute exclusion of liability.

**[14–34]**     Finally, *McCarthy v JWT*[66] falls for consideration. In this case, a package holiday agreement contained a standard arbitration clause which compelled the customer to submit any dispute to arbitration before the Irish Travel Agents Association. The arbitration clause amounted to a limitation clause because the maximum award to be made in arbitration was £5,000. In addition, the clause excluded liability for personal injury. Carroll J held that because the clause was so onerous, it had to be specifically drawn to the customer's attention. It was not enough that the clause had been mentioned in general terms in the box for signature in the booking form.

### The Effect of a Course of Dealing

**[14–35]**     In *McCutcheon v David MacBrayne Ltd*[67] Lord Reid explains the effect of a course of dealing as follows:

> "If two parties have made a series of similar contracts each containing certain conditions, and then they make another without expressly referring to those

---

[64] [1982] ILRM 101.

[65] Above, n 42.

[66] [1991] ILRM 813.

[67] Above, n 22. See also *Petrotrade Inc v Texaco* [2000] CLC 1341, 1349 *per* Clarke LJ: "Given the course of dealing ... both parties will have made the oral agreement on the basis that the contract would be subject to the same terms as before."

conditions it may be that those conditions ought to be implied. If the officious bystander had asked them whether they had intended to leave out the conditions this time, both must, as honest men, have said 'of course not'."

This rule accommodates commercial practice: once the parties have established   **[14–36]** a firm and consistent business relationship the law will automatically fill the gaps that they leave in their negotiations. The courts understand that "a contract is not made in a vacuum, but against a background of present and past facts."[68]

*Spurling v Bradshaw*[69] is a good example of the rule in action. The defendant   **[14–37]** had stored eight barrels of orange juice at the plaintiff's warehouse. The orange juice was lost and the plaintiff sought to rely on an exemption clause which exempted him from liability in case of "loss or damage occasioned by negligence or wrongful act or default". The defendant did not receive the document containing this clause until after the contract for the storage of the orange juice was complete. Had the exemption clause been incorporated into the contract? The Court found that it had, but not by the document, which, of course, came too late. The clause was incorporated because the parties had conducted a long course of previous similar dealings on the basis of a similar exemption clause. So the exemption clause was automatically part of the contract by virtue of the course of dealings, without any need to include it expressly. *Miley v McKechnie*[70] is an Irish case along the same lines. The plaintiff had a long course of dealings with the defendant's laundry. The plaintiff was always given a receipt on depositing clothes with the laundry. The receipt always contained an exemption clause exempting the laundry from liability for damage to the plaintiff's clothes. That exemption clause was incorporated into the parties' contract by that long and consistent course of dealing. A course of dealing of the type in *Spurling* or *Miley* will serve to incorporate terms automatically in all future dealings unless one party expressly states that they are not to apply.

How long must the course of dealing be? *Hollier v Rambler Motors (AMC)*   **[14–38]** *Ltd*[71] held that three dealings in five years was insufficient to establish a "course of dealing". The same terms had not been used so often that the parties as reasonable people would consider them an automatic part of any future contract. A course of dealing would appear to be something closer to the regular three or four transactions per month over three years which occurred in *Henry Kendall & Sons (A Firm) v William Lillico & Sons.*[72] In *Circle Freight International v Medeast Gulf Exports Ltd*[73] eleven previous instances of dealing amounted to a sufficient course of dealing.

---

[68] *SIAT di del Ferro v Trades Overseas SA* [1978] 2 Lloyd's Rep 470, 490 *per* Donaldson J.
[69] Above, n 57.
[70] (1949) 84 ILTR 89
[71] [1972] 2 QB 71.
[72] [1969] 2 AC 31. Note that in this case the standard terms were always delivered after acceptance. Therefore, if the case had concerned the first time the parties had contracted, the terms would not have been incorporated by a course of dealing. However, the cumulative effect of the delivery of the terms, albeit late on each occasion was such that both parties could reasonably expect that the terms would always form part of contracts of that type between them, unless otherwise stated.
[73] [1988] 2 Lloyd's Rep 427

**[14–39]**     It is also important that the course of dealing take substantially the same form each time so that it is consistent. In *McCutcheon v David MacBrayne Ltd*[74] a man called McSporran arranged for MacBrayne to ship McCutcheon's car from the Hebrides to the mainland. McSporran and MacBrayne had dealt with one another three or four times in the past. McSporran had signed a risk note on only two of these occasions. On this occasion McSporran did not sign it. The risk note contained an exemption clause. The ship sank and McSporran sought to rely on that clause. Obviously, the clause had not been incorporated by signature on this occasion so the question was whether it could be incorporated by a past course of dealing. The House of Lords held that it could not because the course of dealing between McSporran and MacBrayne lacked the necessary consistency. Because the exemption clause was sometimes a feature of the parties' dealings and sometimes not, it was impossible to say that the parties, as reasonable persons, expected that all of their dealings would be covered by the exemption clause unless otherwise stated.

**[14–40]**     There is another way to explain *McCutcheon* which emphasises the importance of careful attention to the facts in the course of dealings cases. In the later case of *Circle Freight International v Medeast Gulf Exports Ltd*[75] Taylor LJ explained the *McCutcheon* decision thus:

> "[W]hereas some of the previous dealings in that case had involved a contractual document, on the occasion of the sinking the contract was purely oral. It was the departure from the ordinary course of business which excluded the condition."

**[14–41]**     This dictum warns us that we should not be too ready to fill in the gaps by reference to a course of dealing. It may be that, by failing to incorporate a clause on a given occasion, the parties are expressing an intention to abandon their usual exemption clause.

**[14–42]**     Just as the exemption clause may be incorporated by a regular course of dealing, so too a course of dealing may suggest that a clause has not been incorporated into the parties' contract. In *Western Meats Ltd v National Ice and Cold Storage Co. Ltd*[76] the defendants, operators of a meat storage warehouse, attempted to rely on an exclusion clause to exclude their liability for their loss of the plaintiff's meat. The clause had never been brought expressly to the plaintiff's attention and he was not aware of it. The parties had dealt together over many years. However, Barrington J noted that the parties' relationship was informal and never made reference to the standard conditions. This tended to suggest that the exclusion clause was not incorporated into the contract.

### Common in the Industry

**[14–43]**     Exemption clauses which are standard within are particular industry are likely to be automatically incorporated into contracts concluded within that industry. The

---

[74] Above, n 22; *Mendelssohn v Normand Ltd* [1970]1 QB 177.
[75] Above, n 72.
[76] Above, n 63 at 433.

leading case is *British Crane Hire v Ipswich Plant Hire*,[77] where Lord Denning MR set out that:

> "[W]here parties to a contract of hire were both in the trade and of equal bargaining power the conditions habitually imposed in such contracts would be incorporated into the contract on the basis of the common understanding of the parties that the usual conditions would apply."

In *British Crane Hire*, Ipswich hired a crane from British Crane. The companies had dealt with one another only twice before. The contract was concluded over the phone. After the contract had been concluded, British Crane sent Ipswich a printed form setting out its standard terms and conditions. These standard terms resembled those used throughout the trade; in fact, Ipswich themselves used a similar set of standard terms. The question was whether these standard terms were part of the contract between British Crane and Ipswich. The document provided fell foul of the rule in *Olley* because it came after acceptance. An argument from past course of dealing could not succeed because the parties had contracted together only twice before. However, because the parties were of equal bargaining power and had a common trade background and because the terms involved were standard in their trade, the Court of Appeal found that they were automatically incorporated into the instant contract. The reasoning behind this category is the same as that behind incorporation by past course of dealings; the parties as reasonable persons would have expected the terms which were standard in the industry to govern their transactions because they would have encountered those terms many times before. This understanding is reflected in the judgment of Morris P in *Lynch Roofing Systems Ltd v Bennett & Son Ltd*.[78] He said that the question for a court applying *British Crane Hire* was:  **[14–44]**

> "Did the parties habitually trade under contracts which incorporated [clauses of this type] so that a court would be forced to conclude that the parties expected and knew that this clause would govern their contract?"

In *McCrory Scaffolding v McInerney Construction*[79] the defendant sent the plaintiff a letter of appointment stating that it intended to enter into a signed contract with it incorporating the GDLA 82 conditions of contract. No formal written agreement was ever actually signed by the parties, but the plaintiff commenced performance of the contract as agreed. The question was whether the GDLA 82 conditions had been successfully incorporated into the contract between the parties. Peart J applied the test in *British Crane Hire*. He held that there was no issue of inequality of bargaining power because even though the defendant company was much larger than the plaintiff company and had superior financial resources, both were significant commercial entities. Secondly, both had considerable experience in the trade so that, objectively, they must have expected and known that the GLDA 82 governed  **[14–45]**

---

[77] [1975] Q.B. 303
[78] [1999] 2 IR 450.
[79] [2004] IEHC 346.

their contract. Accordingly, the terms of the GLDA 82 were successfully incorporated under the test in *British Crane Hire v Ipswich Plant Hire*.

### Websites and Adequate Notice

[14–46] Suppose that contracts concluded online come within the category of unsigned contracts. One would imagine that such issues as the requirements in relation to onerous terms, the effects of repeat contracting with an online provider and the prevalence of particular standard terms within a given industry will be as important online as they have been in the traditional cases. However, it is worth examining more generally the typical methods by which websites attempt to give their users notice of exemption clauses. Website providers commonly use two types of notice to impose standard terms and conditions for the online sale of goods and services. A "click-wrap" notice provides notice of terms and conditions on a webpage or in a pop up textbox. Users must indicate their agreement to the terms and conditions by clicking on an icon. If they do not click on the icon, they cannot access the good or service they wish to purchase. Websites that use "browse-wrap" notices provide notice of terms and conditions by placing a hyperlink on a webpage that reads, for example, "Terms of Use." The user does not have to click on the hyperlink to continue with his transaction. The idea is that by continuing with his transaction he consents to the terms and conditions contained elsewhere in the website.

[14–47] Suppose I buy a laptop computer online. The application of offer and acceptance to websites was examined earlier (5-35). I have offered to buy the computer by filling in my details and credit card number on an order form on the site and by clicking an icon which says "checkout". When I click "checkout" a pop-up window appears which describes the standard terms and conditions of my future contract with the computer retailer. If I scrolled all the way down this window I could read all of these terms and conditions in some detail. I am asked to select either a button reading "I Agree" or a button reading "I Don't Agree" at the bottom of this pop-up window. I select the former without reading the contents of the pop-up window. An automatic confirmation of my order appears on the screen. This is the acceptance. Have the terms and conditions that were mentioned in that pop-up box been incorporated into my contract for the purchase of the programme? In particular, have I been given adequate notice of these terms?

[14–48] In America, the click-wrap means of giving notice of terms has been repeatedly upheld as adequate.[80] The adequacy of the click-wrap method as a means of giving notice has two bases. First, the terms and conditions are quite forcefully placed before the party affected by them; he cannot proceed with the transaction without encountering them. Secondly, he must indicate his assent to those terms by the

---

[80] *Caspi v Microsoft Network LLC* 732 A 2d 528 (NJ Super AD 1999); *In re RealNetworks, Inc., Privacy Litig.*, No. 00-C-1366, 2000 WL 631341 (ND Ill 8 May 2001). For more information on the US cases see Condon, "Electronic Assent to online contracts" (2004) 16 RULR 433. For criticism see Nimmer, "International Information Transactions: An Essay on Law in an Information Society", (2000) 26 Brook J Int'l L 5; Harrison, "Note, Just Click Here: Article 2B's Failure to Guarantee Adequate Manifestation of Assent in Click-Wrap Contracts" (1998) 8 Fordham Intell Prop Media & Ent LJ 907.

deliberate act of clicking an icon. It should be noted, however, that commentators have doubted whether clicking an icon indicates assent to anything. So Gautrais[81] writes that:

> "It is also important to take into account the idea that it is part of the very nature of the internet to proceed with speed thereby skipping over some steps. It may therefore be necessary to deliberately slow down the process in order to give consumers time to absorb contractual clauses fully. It is essential that the consumer become aware that an effortless 'click' has legal significance, and that the importance of the action of 'clicking' be internalized by the consumer."

Contrast the click-wrap scenario with this one. I can order a book from Amazon.com by filling in information on successive web pages linked by a "continue" icon and then clicking on an icon stating "Place your order." I can then review my shipping information, my payment method and the title and price of my books. At no time am I asked to signify that I accept any other contract terms. Those contract terms can be found at the bottom of the page, behind a link entitled "Conditions of Use." If I were to click the link, I would discover clauses on the risk of my books being lost in transit and so on. This is a browse-wrap agreement. **[14–49]**

Browse-wrap notices have been treated rather more firmly by the US courts. In the case of *Ticketmaster Corp. v Tickets.com, Inc*[82] a Court held without any significant explanation that a browse-wrap agreement lacked "sufficient proof of agreement by defendant to be taken seriously." The hyperlinks that are fundamental to browse-wrap notices tend to embody the worst forms of abuse of the doctrine of incorporation. In *Specht v Netscape Communications Corp.*,[83] Netscape provided free copies of the software program SmartDownload on its website. Users clicked on a box in order to download the software. They did not have to click an "I accept" button or otherwise indicate their acceptance to Netscape's standard terms before they were able to download the SmartDownload software. The only reference to Netscape's standard terms appeared in the text of a link which read: "Please review and agree to the terms of the Netscape Smart-Download software license agreement." This link was only viewable if the user scrolled down to the bottom of webpage. The Court held that Netscape's standard terms were not incorporated into their contracts with the users of SmartDownload. In *Pollstar v Gigmania*,[84] the only notice given of the vendor's standard terms consisted of the words "subject to the license agreement" which were printed in small grey letters on a grey background. They were not underlined. The Court found that this browse-wrap notice was inadequate. By contrast, in *Register.com v Verio Inc*,[85] the District Court enforced a browse-wrap notice because the software vendor automatically presented its standard terms in clear view where online users would easily notice them. A paragraph next to the order button on the website read: "by submitting this query, you agree to abide by these terms." Generally speaking, browse-wrap notices are of dubious worth. A click-wrap contract does as much as was **[14–50]**

---

[81] Gautrais "The Colour of E-consent" (2003) 1 UOLTJ 189.
[82] No. CV99-7654-HLH (BQRx), 2000 US Dist LEXIS 12987 (CD Cal 10 August 2000).
[83] 306 F3d 17, 25 (2d Cir 2002).
[84] 170 F Supp 2d 974 (ED Cal 2000).
[85] 126 F Supp 2d 238 (SDNY 2000).

done in the old ticket cases; it makes words of warning immediately accessible to the affected party so that he may choose to explore his contractual obligations further. A browse-wrap contract of the type in *Register.com* places the onus on the affected party, not simply to explore the content of any exclusion clause by which he may be bound, but to discover whether he is bound by *any* clauses beyond those of which he has actual notice. Website contracting does not generally allow scope for negotiation. Standard terms are unilaterally imposed by the vendor. In these circumstances, where the bargaining power of the purchaser is limited, it is important that the consumer is facilitated in informing himself of the content of his potential contractual obligations and so a browse-wrap agreement should not stand. If nothing else, a public perception that it is possible to be bound by clauses lurking unobtrusively in dark corners of websites with disastrous consequences is unlikely to stimulate confidence in online trading.

[14–51]     There is, however, a body of European consumer protection law that limits the potential dangers inherent in click-wrap and browse-wrap agreements by ensuring that consumers are given more full notice of the terms of the agreement into which they are entering. The Electronic Commerce Directive[86] has been transposed by way of the Electronic Commerce Act 2000 and by SI No 68 of 2003. Article 10(3) of the Directive requires that online contract terms and general conditions are made available in a way that allows the consumer to store and reproduce them. A click-wrap or browse-wrap agreement that displays terms in a separate window from which they cannot be downloaded or printed will arguably fall foul of this requirement. The contractual terms should appear on the screen before making any purchase. The Distance Selling Directive[87] as transposed into Irish law by the European Communities (Protection of Consumers in Respect of Contracts Made by Means of Distance Communication) Regulations 2001 provides for a power by the consumer to revoke the contract within seven days of the supply of goods. This "cooling-off" period allows the consumer ample time to examine the goods which he has purchased as well as the "fine print" of his contract with the supplier and make a reasoned decision as to whether or not he should withdraw from the contract. The Directive also obliges the supplier to inform consumers of that right of withdrawal on its website, before or in the course of the ordering process. This information, together with information on the key terms of the contract, must be provided to the consumer in a clear and comprehensible manner. It must be provided in a durable form in order to facilitate further examination and reflection. However, empirical research conducted by Donnelly and White[88] casts doubt on the effectiveness of this tool in the consumer's armoury. Their study demonstrates that the level of compliance with the duty to inform among online suppliers is low. Over 30 per cent of the suppliers surveyed failed to inform consumers of their right to withdraw from the contract. In addition, the "cooling off" period has limited clout because, according to Donnelly and White, consumers are unlikely to avail of it because they are not aware of it. Seventy-eight per cent of the consumers surveyed were not aware of any laws which protect consumers when buying online.

---

[86]  Directive 2000/31/EC.
[87]  97/7/EC [1997] OJ L144/19.
[88]  Donnelly & White, "Regulation and Consumer Protection: A Study of the Online Market" (2006) 13(1) DULJ 27.

Absent wider efforts to publicise it, this counter-intuitive legal right to withdraw is likely to go largely unused. In addition, if consumers do not insist on the right, suppliers are unlikely to abide by it. This is borne out by the findings of the same study that online suppliers indulged in dissuasive tactics such as charging consumers to return goods, requiring reasons for withdrawal from the contract, insisting that the goods be returned in a certain condition or insisting on a shorter "cooling off" period than the legal minimum. This happens even though, in principle, non-compliant suppliers run the risk of criminal prosecution.

## V. Interpretation of Exemption Clauses

Even if an exemption clause is successfully incorporated into the contract between the parties, it may not be effective because it does not cover the breach which has taken place. Before looking at at the rules of construction proper, there is some authority for the proposition that the rules of construction ought to be applied more flexibly to limitation clauses than to exclusion clauses. In *Ailsa Craig Fishing Co. v Malvern Fishing Co.*[89] Lord Wilberforce held that:     [14–52]

> "Clauses of limitation are not regarded by the courts with the same hostility as clauses of exclusion; this is because they must be related to other contract terms, in particular to the risks to which the defending party may be exposed, the remuneration which he receives and possibly also the opportunity of the other party to insure."

It is worth noting that the very same points might be made about exclusion clauses. In addition, a wide-ranging limitation clause might have near enough the same effect as an exclusion clause. It should be questioned, therefore, whether there is any legitimacy in drawing a distinction between limitation and exemption clauses in this manner.     [14–53]

Four further important policy-based rules of interpretation have been devised which seek to limit the effectiveness of exemption clauses:     [14–54]

1. An exemption clause must not be construed inconsistently with an oral promise made before or at the time of contracting.
2. An exemption clause must be construed to ensure that it does not defeat the main purpose of the contract.
3. If the meaning of an exemption clause is ambiguous, the court will construe it against the person seeking to rely on it.
4. It is especially difficult to exclude liability for negligence.

### Oral Promises

The English cases set out that an exemption clause will be overridden which is inconsistent with an oral promise made at or before the contract was concluded. So in     [14–55]

---

[89] [1983] 1 WLR 964. See also *George Mitchell (Chesterhall) Ltd v Finney Lock Seeds Ltd* [1983] 2 AC 803; *EE Caledonia v Orbit Valve plc* [1994] 1 WLR 1515; *BHP Petroleum v British Steel* [2000] 2 All ER 133; but cf *Darlington Futures Ltd v Delco Australia Pty Ltd* (1987) 61 AJLR 76.

*J Evans & Son v Andrea Merzario*[90] an oral undertaking that goods would be stored below deck cancelled out an inconsistent clause. Similarly, in *Mendelssohn v Normand*[91] a car park attendant's express promise that he would look after a car after parking it was construed as an implied promise that the car would be safe. This promise overrode an inconsistent printed exemption clause.

### The Main Purpose Rule

[14–56] The English cases also set out that an exemption clause should always be interpreted so that it does not defeat the main purpose of the contract. It will not be possible, therefore, to exclude total non-performance of the contract. This is often called the "repugnancy" rule. In *Glynn v Margetson*[92] Lord Halsbury said that:

> "[O]ne must look in the first instance at the whole of the instrument and not at one part of it only. Looking at the whole instrument, and seeing what one must regard ... as its main purpose, one must reject words, indeed whole provisions, if they are inconsistent with what one assumes to be the main purpose of the contract."

[14–57] The rule was applied in *Sze Hai Tong Bank Ltd v Rambler Cycle Co. Ltd*.[93] This was a case involving a carrier of goods. The main object of the contract included an obligation on the carrier's part to deliver the goods only to someone entitled to delivery. In breach of this obligation, the carrier delivered the goods to a consignee. The carrier sought to rely on an exclusion clause to protect itself from liability for the breach. Lord Denning held that the exclusion clause was ineffective as follows:

> "If such an extreme width were given to the exemption clause, it would run counter to the main object and basis of the contract. For the contract ... has, as one of its main objects, the proper delivery of the goods by the shipping company ... It would defeat this object entirely if the shipping company was at liberty, at its own will and pleasure, to deliver the goods to somebody else, to someone not entitled at all, without being liable for the consequences. The clause must therefore be limited and modified to the extent necessary to enable effect to be given to the main object and intent of the contract."

[14–58] Similarly, in *Tor Line v Alltrans Group*[94] the House of Lords refused to construe the word "damage" in an exclusion clause in a shipping charterparty so that it would cover economic loss suffered by the charterers. To do so would be contrary to the main purpose rule and would render the charterparty "a statement of intent by the owners, in return for which the charterers are obliged to pay large sums by way of hire".

---

[90] [1983] 1 WLR 964.
[91] [1970] 1 QB 177.
[92] [1893] AC 351.
[93] [1959] AC 576.
[94] [1984] 1 All ER 103.

## The Contra Proferentem Rule

The *contra proferentem* rule states that where a contract term is ambiguous[95] it must be **[14–59]** construed strictly against the *proferens*: the person seeking to rely on it. The Supreme Court decision in *Analog Devices v Zurich*[96] confirms that the *contra proferentem* rule remains a part of Irish law. Note that this rule does not apply to all exemption clauses, but only to those capable of two or more meanings. The rule incentivises plain drafting. In *re Sweeney and Kennedy's Arbitration*[97] Kingsmill Moore J justified the application of the *contra proferentem* rule to a contract of insurance as follows:

"But, even if I am wrong in my conclusion that the interpretation is reasonably free from doubt, the case must be decided against the underwriters if the words are ambiguous ... They were at liberty to adopt any phraseology which they desired ... If, then, they choose to adopt ambiguous words it seems to me good sense, as well as established law, that those words should be interpreted in the sense which is adverse to the persons who chose and introduced them."

The *contra proferentem* rule also protects parties affected by exemption clauses **[14–60]** by ensuring that they are set out in clear terms and by guaranteeing that, where they are not, they will be interpreted in the manner most favourable to the affected party. Take, for example, *Houghton v Trafalgar Insurance Co. Ltd*,[98] where a car insurance policy excluded liability for damage "caused or arising whilst the car is conveying any load in excess of that for which the car was constructed". The Court found that this clause was ambiguous; Romer LJ stated that he had "not the least idea" what the clause meant in relation to a private car. The clause was held not to exclude liability when the car crashed with an excess of passengers inside. A similar case is *Webster v Higgins*[99] in which a clause that provided that "no warranty, condition or description or representation is given" was held not to apply to undertakings which had been previously given. In *Andrews v Singer*[100] an exclusion clause purported to exclude "all conditions, warranties and liabilities implied by common law, statute or otherwise".

---

[95] *Tan Wing Chen v Bank of Credit and Commerce Hong Kong Ltd* [1996] 2 BCLC 69, 77.

[96] [2005] 2 IR 282.

[97] [1950] IR 85, 98–99 See also *Woolfall & Rimmer Ltd v Moyle* [1942] 1 KB 66, 73 *per* Lord Greene MR: "... if underwriters wish to limit by some qualification a risk which, *prima facie*, they are undertaking in plain terms, they should make it perfectly clear what that qualification is. They should, with the aid of competent advice, make up their minds as to the qualifications they wish to impose and should express their intention in language appropriate for achieving the result desired. There is no justification for underwriters, who are carrying on a widespread business and making use of printed forms either failing to make up their minds what they mean, or, if they have made up their minds what they mean, failing to express it in suitable language. Any competent draughtsman could carry out the intention which [counsel] imputes to this document, and, if that was really intended, it ought to have been done."; *McNally v Lancs & York Rly* (1880) 8 LR (Ir) 81 *per* Lord O'Hagan: "There can be no hardship imposed by requiring companies to be clear and explicit in the frame of conditions designed for their own security. The humble and ignorant dealers who enter into transactions with them are at a disadvantage, and at least they should be held strictly to the terms of the contracts deliberately prepared by their skilled advisers".

[98] [1954] 1 QB 247.

[99] [1948] 2 All ER 127.

[100] [1934] 1 KB 17.

The exclusion clause did not protect the defendants against breach of an express term because the clause was ambiguous and an express term is not "implied". In *Beck & Co v Szymanowski*[101] a contract included a limitation clause, which provided that goods delivered were deemed satisfactory unless returned within 14 days. The Court held that this clause did not apply to goods which were not delivered at all. To the same effect is *Walls, Son & Wells v Pratt and Haynes*,[102] in which a clause that excluded liability for breach of warranty was held not to cover liability for breach of condition.

[14–61]    It might be thought that the courts went too far in these cases by inventing ambiguity where there was none. Lord Denning in *Gillespie Bros. v Roy Bowles Ltd*[103] summarises the position:

> "[J]udges have ... time after time, sanctioned a departure from the ordinary meaning. They have done it under the guise of 'construing' the clause. *They assume that the party cannot have intended anything so unreasonable*. So they construe the clause 'strictly'. They cut down the ordinary meaning of the words and reduce them to reasonable proportions. They use all their skill and art to that end."

[14–62]    It should be clear, however, that the decisions discussed so far are much more easily justified in terms of protectionist policy than of intention. Lord Hoffmann wryly observed in *Bank of Credit and Commerce International SA v Ali*[104] that: "[w]hen judges say that 'in the absence of clear words' they would be unwilling to construe a document to mean something, they generally mean ... that the effect of the document is unfair." We can return to Lord Denning in *George Mitchell (Chesterhall) Ltd v Finney Lock Seeds*[105] for an elaboration on the courts' real intention:

> "When the courts said to the big concern 'You must put it in clear words', the big concern had no hesitation in doing so. It knew well that the little man would never read the exemption clauses or understand them ...
>
> Faced with this abuse of power – by the strong against the weak – by the use of the small print of the conditions – the judges did what they could to put a curb upon it. They still had before them the idol, 'freedom of contract'. They still knelt down and worshipped it, but they concealed under their cloak a secret weapon. This weapon was called 'the true construction of the contract.' They used it with great skill and ingenuity. They used it so as to depart from the natural meaning of the words of the exemption clause and to put upon them a strained and unnatural construction. In case after case, they said that the words were not strong enough to give the big concern exemption from liability; or in the circumstances the big concern was not entitled to rely on the exemption clause."

---

[101] [1924] AC 43.

[102] [1911] AC 394.

[103] [1973] 1 QB 400, 415.

[104] [1999] 4 All ER 83.

[105] Above, n 3.

However, it is widely agreed that the fire has gone out of the *contra proferentem* **[14–63]** rule in recent years as consumer protection legislation fulfils the interventionist role formerly assumed by the courts. In *George Mitchell v Finney Lock Seeds Ltd*[106] Lord Diplock noted that the passing of the Unfair Contract Terms Act in England and Wales has "removed from judges the temptation to resort to the device of ascribing to the words appearing in exemption clauses a tortured meaning so as to avoid giving effect to an exclusion or limitation of liability when a judge thought that in the circumstances to do so would be unfair". By *BCCI v Ali*[107] Lord Hoffmann was able to speak of the old style of use of *contra proferentem* rule as "judicial creativity, bordering on judicial legislation . . . a desperate remedy, to be invoked only if it is necessary to remedy a widespread injustice." The courts today, while favouring a strict interpretation of exemption clauses, will not go so far as to strain them. In short, it is accepted that:

> "[a]scertaining the intention of the parties remains the paramount concern, and that intention in many cases can best be achieved by focussing less on asserted ambiguities in the exclusion clause and more on the meaning of the contract as a whole."[108]

In particular, the courts will hesitate to use the *contra proferentem* rule where **[14–64]** the parties are of equal bargaining power. In *Photo Productions v Securicor*[109] Lord Diplock warned:

> "[I]n commercial contracts negotiated between businessmen capable of looking after their own interests . . . it is, in my view, wrong to place a strained construction on words in an exemption clause which are clearly and fairly susceptible of one meaning only."

It is worth noting, in addition, that the *contra proferentem* rule is part of Irish **[14–65]** legislation under reg 5(1) of the Unfair Terms in Consumer Contract Regulations (UTCCR). These Regulations are considered later in the chapter. However, for now it is important to note that the UTCCR imposes a general duty on anyone who is selling goods or supplying services to a consumer in the course of business to ensure that any written terms provided to the consumer are in plain and intelligible language. Regulation 5(2) of the UTCCR provides that "where there is doubt about the meaning of a term, the interpretation most favourable to the consumer shall prevail".

## Liability for Negligence

The cases on exemption of liability for negligence are marked by "the law's **[14–66]** disinclination to let people contract out of the consequences of their own neglect."[110] Fullagar J in *Wilson v Darling Island Stevedoring and Lighterage Co Ltd*[111] referred

---

[106] *ibid.* at 810.
[107] [2001] UKHL 8.
[108] *Livingstone v Roskilly* [1992] 3 NZLR 230, 239.
[109] [1980] 2 WLR 283.
[110] *Casson v Ostley P.J. Ltd* [2003] BLR 147.
[111] [1956] 1 Lloyd's Rep 346.

disapprovingly to "a curious, and seemingly irresistible, anxiety to save grossly negligent people from the normal consequences of their negligence". Negligence in this instance means negligent performance of the contract or the tort of negligence and refers to the negligence both of the *proferens* and of his servants. An exemption clause will only be exempt from liability for negligence where it passes the test in *Canada Steamships Co. v The King*.[112] The test is set out in the following diagram:

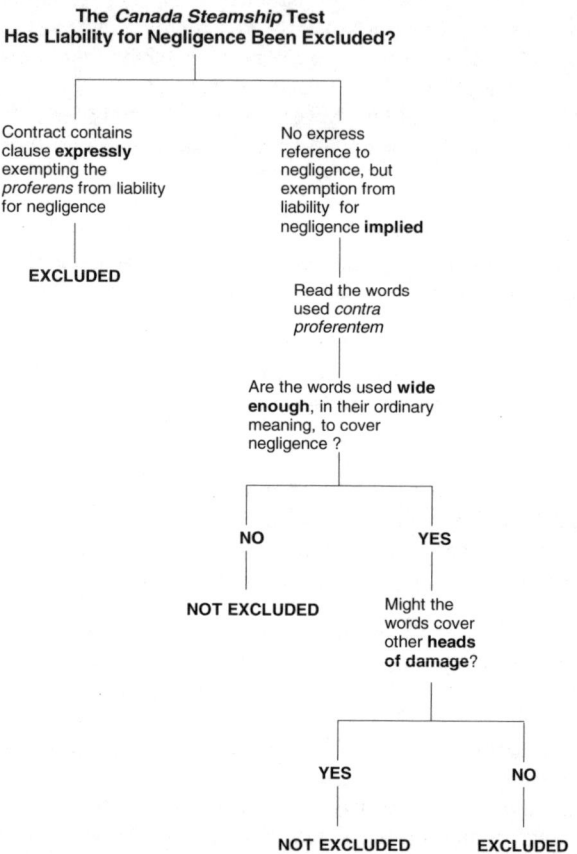

The *Canada Steamship* Test
Has Liability for Negligence Been Excluded?

Contract contains clause **expressly** exempting the *proferens* from liability for negligence

**EXCLUDED**

No express reference to negligence, but exemption from liability for negligence **implied**

Read the words used *contra proferentem*

Are the words used **wide enough**, in their ordinary meaning, to cover negligence?

NO — **NOT EXCLUDED**

YES — Might the words cover other **heads of damage**?

YES — **NOT EXCLUDED**

NO — **EXCLUDED**

**[14–67]**     As you can see, there are three stages to the test. The first stage of the test states that if the clause expressly and clearly exempts the *proferens* from liability from his negligence and he is sued for negligence, he can rely on the clause successfully to deny the injured party a remedy. The word negligence or some synonym such as "default" or "neglect" must be used.[113] If there is no such express exemption of liability for negligence, the court moves to the second stage of the test: the clause may impliedly exempt liability for negligence.

---

[112] [1952] AC 192; *Shell Chemicals Ltd v P&O Roadtanks Ltd* [1995] 1 Lloyd's Rep 297; *Smith v UMB Chrysler (Scotland) Ltd* 1978 SC 1.

[113] *Monarch Airlines Ltd v London Luton Airport Ltd* [1997] CLC 698; *Smith v South Wales Switchgear Co. Ltd* [1978] 1 WLR 165.

The second stage requires the court to do two things. First, the words of the clause must be read *contra proferentem*. By definition, they are ambiguous: it is not immediately clear that they protect the *proferens* from liability for his negligence. Second, the court asks whether the words used are wide enough to cover liability for negligence. Phrases such as "any loss howsoever caused",[114] "loss whatsoever or howsoever occasioned",[115] "lost or damaged by fire or any other cause"[116] or "liability at common law"[117] will generally be wide enough for this purpose. If they are not wide enough, then the exemption clause does not work and the injured party will be able to recover a remedy for the *proferens'* negligence.

[14–68]

If the words are wide enough to cover negligence the court proceeds to the third stage of the test: are the words wide enough to cover some other head of damage arising in the case (for example strict liability in contract) as well as negligence? If they are, then the clause will only work to exempt the *proferens* from liability for the other head of damage and he will still be liable for his negligence. If they are not wide enough to cover any other relevant head of damage besides negligence, then the *proferens* is protected from liability for his negligence. The alternative source of liability must not be "fanciful or remote".[118] It must be a sufficiently realistic source to allow the courts to conclude that the parties intended the clause to apply to it.

[14–69]

The law essentially says: You cannot have your cake and eat it. You must draft your clauses clearly if you want to protect yourself from liability in negligence. You will not be allowed to "shelter behind language which might lull the customer into a false sense of security",[119] or get away with vague, wide-ranging clauses designed to capture every possible head of liability. In *Gillespie Bros & Co v Roy Bowles Transport Ltd*[120] Buckley LJ set out the rationale behind the courts' insistence on clarity:

[14–70]

"[I]t is inherently improbable that one party to the contract should intend to absolve the person in whose favour it is made from the consequences of the latter's own negligence. The intention to do so must therefore be perfectly clear."

The test can be applied to two cases. The first is *White v Warwick*.[121] The plaintiff in that case hired a tradesman's tricycle and was injured when the saddle slipped. The contract of hire contained an exemption clause which stated that the defendant was not liable "for any personal injuries to the riders of the machines hired." The question was whether this phrase could exclude liability for the negligence to which the plaintiff's injury was attributable. Under the first stage of the test in *Canada Steamship*, the words used obviously did not expressly exclude liability for negligence. The second stage of the test asks whether the words used impliedly excluded liability

[14–71]

---

[114]  *Bishop v Bonham* [1988] 1 WLR 742.
[115]  *Shell Chemicals UK Ltd v P&O Roadtanks Ltd* [1995] 1 Lloyd's Rep 297.
[116]  *Stent Foundations Ltd v Gleeson plc* [2001] BLR 134.
[117]  *Ailsa Craig Fishing Ltd v Malvern Fishing Ltd*, above, n 88.
[118]  *The Raphael* [1982] 2 Lloyd's Rep 42.
[119]  *Hollier v Rambler Motors*, above, n 70 *per* Salmon LJ.
[120]  Above, n 102.
[121]  [1953] 1 WLR 1285.

for negligence. Remember to read the words *contra proferentem* so that the interpretation which favours the plaintiff is adopted. The court asked whether the words used, read *contra proferentem*, were wide enough in their ordinary meaning to exclude liability for negligence. These words covered "any" personal injuries. Therefore, they were wide enough to exclude liability for negligence. The court then moved to the third stage of the test. The question here was whether the words were also wide enough to cover other heads of damage. The Court held that as well as being wide enough to cover negligence, the words at issue were wide enough to cover strict liability in contract for supplying a defective cycle. Lord Denning explained:

> "In the present case there are two possible heads of liability on the defendants, one for negligence, the other for breach of contract. The liability for breach of contract is more strict than the liability for negligence. The defendants may be liable in contract for supplying a defective machine even though they were not negligent ...".

[14–72]     Because another head of damage was covered by the clause, liability for negligence was not excluded. The plaintiff could not recover for the injuries that he sustained which were attributable to the defendant's breach of his strict contractual obligations but he could recover for those injuries attributable to the defendant's negligence.

[14–73]     In *Alderslade v Hendon Laundry Ltd*[122] the Court reached a different conclusion. The plaintiff left 10 large Irish linen handkerchiefs with the defendant to be washed. The contract was subject to a limitation clause which stated that: "the maximum amount allowed for lost or damaged articles is 20 times the charge made for laundering". This amounted to 11 shillings five and a half pence. The handkerchiefs were lost and the plaintiff sued for damages of two pounds, one shilling and five pence. The question was whether the limitation clause could cover the negligent loss of the handkerchiefs. Starting with the first stage of the *Canada Steamship* test it will be noted that the exclusion clause did not expressly exempt liability for negligence. But, looking at the second stage of the test, the words, read *contra proferentem*, were wide enough to cover negligence. So Lord Greene MR's judgment turned on the third stage; whether other heads of damage were available to the plaintiff. Lord Greene found that the laundry could not be strictly liable for the loss of goods given to them for washing. The same duty was imposed in contract as in tort: the duty to exercise reasonable care. Because no other head of damages was available, the exemption clause protected the *proferens* from liability in negligence. The application of *Canada Steamship* brought about a similar result in *Hughes v JJ Power Ltd*,[123] a case in which the *proferens* was engaged to service the plaintiff's tractor engine. A clause was incorporated into the parties' contract which said that the work was at the plaintiff's risk. Did this clause protect the *proferens* from liability for his negligence? When Blayney J came to the heads of liability stage—he held that the clause worked to exclude liability for damage caused by the *proferens'* negligence. This was because the same duty was imposed on the *proferens* in contract as in tort: the duty to exercise reasonable skill and care.

---

[122] [1945] 1 KB 189.
[123] Unreported, High Court, 11 May 1988.

The *Canada Steamship* test is often criticised for its complexity. In particular, **[14–74]**
the test is troublesome because, in order to exclude liability for negligence without
doing so expressly (and doing so expressly will often be a turn off for customers),[124] a
drafter must draft a clause which is at once wide enough to cover negligence but
narrow enough so that it does not apply to other heads of liability.[125] Commercial
parties, of course, can employ professionals who can get around complex rules.
In *EE Caledonia v Orbit Valve plc*[126] Hobhouse J made this point:

> "[C]ommercial contracts are drafted by parties with access to legal advice . . . The
> parties are always able by the choice of appropriate language to draft their
> contract so as to produce a different legal effect. The choice is theirs."

However, the same may not be true of parties with lesser resources, and as **[14–75]**
McGarvie J notes in the Australian case of *Schenker & Co. v Malpas Equipment and
Services*: "[t]he law serves the community best if citizens understand it and are able to
resolve their disputes themselves without resorting to lawyers or courts."[127] A further
point is that the parties may well intend to exclude liability both for negligence and for
other heads of liability, but, under the third part of the *Canada Steamship* test, this will
frequently prove impossible. Despite these criticisms, the courts have repeatedly
endorsed the *Canada Steamship* test.[128] It is worth noting, however, that the recent
House of Lords decision in *HIH Casualty and General Insurance Ltd v Chase
Manhattan Bank*[129] has tempered the test somewhat. The House provided a timely
reminder that the intent of the parties is paramount, so that the *Canada Steamship*
guidelines should not be applied so strictly that they frustrate the parties' clear
intention. In other words, the courts emphasise that *Canada Steamship* provides a set
of guidelines for the courts rather than a bundle of insurmountable rules. There is some
evidence of the adoption of this approach in *National Westminster Bank plc v Utrecht-
America Finance Company*[130] in which it was held that there was "no room" for the
application of *Canada Steamship* where the parties were large banks of equal
bargaining power, advised by commercial lawyers: the assumption was that such
parties are capable of expressing their intentions competently so that if they exclude
liability for negligence, they mean it.

## Fundamental Breach

Suppose an exemption clause is properly incorporated into the parties' contract and **[14–76]**
that, construed properly, it covers the breach which has occurred. Suppose now that
the breach is a particularly serious one; so serious, in fact, that it is almost impossible

---

[124] See *EE Caledonia v Orbit Valve* [1994] 1 WLR 1515 *per* Lord Steyn.
[125] For a clause which failed this test see *Dorset County Council v Southern Felt Roofing Co Ltd*
(1989) 48 Build LR 96.
[126] [1993] 4 All ER 165, 173.
[127] [1990] VR 834, 846.
[128] *EE Calendonia Ltd v Orbit Valve plc*, above, n 123; *The Fiona* [1994] 2 Lloyd's Rep 506; *Shell
Chemicals UK Ltd v P&O Roadtanks Ltd* [1995] 1 Lloyd's Rep 297, 301.
[129] [2003] 2 Lloyd's Rep 161. See also *Investors Compensation Scheme v West Bromwich Building
Society* [1998] 1 WLR 896.
[130] [2001] 3 All ER 733.

to contemplate that the parties could have agreed to exclude liability for it. Should the exemption clause work in respect of that breach or should the court strike it down? During the 1950s and 1960s, the English courts developed a rule that it was impossible to contract out of liability for fundamental breach. What is a fundamental breach? Davitt P said in *Clayton Love v B. & I. Transport*[131] that it involves one of two things. A fundamental breach is one where the party "is guilty of a breach which goes to the root of [the contract]" *or* one where the party "has committed a breach of a fundamental term of the contract". In the Supreme Court Ó Dálaigh CJ cited this definition with evident approval. What is a fundamental term of the contract? Under *Smeaton, Hanscomb & Co. v Sassoon I Setty, Son & Co*[132] a fundamental term is "something which underlies the whole contract so that, if it is not complied with, the performance becomes something different from that which the contract contemplates". Classic examples of fundamental breach include supplying peas where the contract was for beans[133] or supplying a stylish silk hat where the contract was for a cloth cap.[134]

[14–77]    The rule that it is never possible to exempt a *proferens* from liability for fundamental breach was first stated by Lord Denning in *Karsales v Wallis*.[135] Lord Denning said that: "exempting clauses ... no matter how widely they are expressed only avail the party when he is carrying out his contract in its essential respects". In that case, the *proferens* had sold a car to the plaintiff on hire purchase. When the car was delivered it was very different to the car the plaintiff had seen when he made the decision to purchase. Only the body and registration number were the same: the car's new tyres had been swapped for old, its engine was so badly damaged that the car could not be driven and the car's radio had been removed. There was clearly a fundamental breach of contract at issue here. The *proferens'* multitude of breaches went to the very root of his contract with the defendant. Nevertheless, the *proferens* sought to exempt himself from liability for this breach by relying on a clause in his contract with the defendant which stated that "no condition or warranty that the vehicle is roadworthy, or as to its age, condition or fitness for any purpose is given by the owner or implied herein." Lord Denning held that he was not entitled to do so:

> "[The *proferens*] is not allowed to use [exempting clauses] as a cover for misconduct or indifference or to enable him to turn a blind eye to his obligations. They do not avail him when he is guilty of a breach which goes to the root of the contract. The thing to do is to look at the contract apart from the exempting clauses and see what are the terms, express or implied, which impose an obligation on the party. If he has been guilty of a breach of those obligations in a respect which goes to the very root of the contract, he cannot rely on the exempting clauses."

---

[131] (1970) 104 ILTR 157.
[132] [1953] 1 WLR 1468.
[133] *Chanter v Hopkins* (1838) 4 M & W 399.
[134] *Fogarty v Dickson* (1913) 47 ILTR 281.
[135] [1956] 1 WLR 936.

In *Clayton Love v B. & I. Transport*[136] Ó Dálaigh CJ in the Supreme Court **[14–78]**
imported the same rule into Irish law. He said that:

"[A] party, who ... has been held to be in breach of a fundamental obligation
cannot rely on a time bar in the contract to defeat a claim for damages. Equally
with other exempting provisions such as a time clause cannot be prayed in aid."

The defendants had contracted to carry frozen scampi from Dublin to **[14–79]**
Liverpool. The scampi was not loaded at the proper temperature, with the result
that it decayed so badly that it was condemned on arrival at Liverpool. The defendants
sought to rely on two exemption clauses to protect them from liability for the ensuing
loss to the plaintiffs. The clauses were useless because the breach that had occurred was
a fundamental breach. As Davitt P had noted in the High Court: "[t]he service which
the plaintiffs got under their contract was ... something radically different from the
service for which they had contracted".

Despite its unquestioning adoption of Lord Denning's approach, the Supreme **[14–80]**
Court decision in *Clayton Love* is on shaky ground. The English approach is now that
"it is no longer permissible at common law to reject or circumvent the clause by
treating it as inapplicable to a 'fundamental breach'."[137] In *U Finance Ltd v National
Mortgage Bank of Greece*[138] an English court opined that the doctrine of fundamental
breach was:

"... not an independent rule imposed by the court on the parties willy-nilly in
disregard of their contractual intention. On the contrary it is a rule of
construction based on the intention of the contracting parties."

Before *Clayton Love* was decided, in *Suisse Atlantique v NV Rodderdamsche*[139] **[14–81]**
the House of Lords rejected Lord Denning's version of the doctrine of fundamental
breach as part of the law of England and Wales. The position in England now is that it
is possible to exempt liability for fundamental breach; however, especially clear words
are required to do it successfully. The trouble with the doctrine of fundamental breach
is that it involves a sweeping bar to the use of exemption clauses in a particular
situation which pays no regard whatever to the intention of the parties. In *Suisse
Atlantique v NV Rotterdamsche*[140] Viscount Dilhorne *obiter* observed that the doctrine
of fundamental breach conflicts with ideas of freedom of contract:

"In my view it is not right to say that the law prohibits and nullifies a clause
exempting or limiting liability for a fundamental breach or breach of a
fundamental term. Such a rule of law would involve a restriction on freedom of
contract and in the older cases I can find no trace of it."

---

[136] Above, n 130.
[137] *Edmund Murray Ltd v BSP International Foundations Ltd* (1993) 33 Con LR 1.
[138] [1964] 1 Lloyd's Rep. 446, 450.
[139] [1967] 1 AC 361.
[140] *ibid.* at 392.

[14–82]     Lord Denning's unsophisticated approach rests on the assumption that all cases of exemption of liability for fundamental breach are equally dangerous and equally worthy of condemnation. It is true that some such cases are repugnant because they involve the unilateral imposition of an illusory contract on a weak party by a strong party. Others, however, involve the considered, intentional allocation of risk of non-performance as between parties of equal bargaining power.[141] In the latter type of case, the court should give effect to the parties' reasonable expectations by deferring to the intent of the parties and upholding the contract they have chosen. Lord Reid wrote:

> "[Lord Denning's] rule appears to treat all cases alike. There is no indication in recent cases that the courts are to consider whether the exemption is fair in all the circumstances or is harsh and unconscionable or whether it was freely agreed by the customer. And it does not seem to me to be satisfactory that the decision must always go one way if, [for example] defects in a car or other goods are just sufficient to make the breach of contract a fundamental breach, but must always go the other way if the defects fall just short of that."

[14–83]     It was a while before Lord Reid's position was fully accepted. In *Harbutt's Plasticine v Wayne Tank Corp*[142] Lord Denning managed to conclude that the House of Lords had affirmed, rather than rejected, his rule in *Karsales*. However, in *Photo Production Ltd v Securicor Transport Ltd*[143] the House of Lords finally exorcised the ghost of fundamental breach. The defendant security company provided security for the plaintiff's factory. A security guard employed by the defendants was on duty at the factory. He deliberately set some crates on fire. The fire raged out of control, destroying a large part of the factory. This was clearly a fundamental breach of the contract between the parties: the breach went to the root of the contract. Burning down a factory is a pretty radical departure from the core contractual promise to keep it secure. The defendant *proferens* sought to rely on an exemption clause in their contract with the plaintiffs which said: "Under no circumstances shall the company be responsible for any injuries, act or default by any employee". You will know that under *Karsales*, under *Harbutt* and, indeed, under the decision of Ó Dálaigh CJ decision in *Clayton Love* this clause would be useless to the defendant. *Suisse Atlantique*, on the other hand, suggested that there was some scope to exempt liability for fundamental breach. The House of Lord in *Securicor* came down firmly on the side of Lord Reid in *Suisse Atlantique*. Lord Wilberforce set out that the proper approach to cases of fundamental breach was to decide them "straightforwardly on what the parties have bargained for". He held it was possible to exclude liability for fundamental breach, provided clear enough words were used:

> "[T]he question whether, and to what extent, an exclusion clause is to be applied to fundamental breach, or a breach of a fundamental term, or indeed to any breach of contract, is a matter of construction of the contract."

---

[141]  See *DHL International (NZ) v Richmond Ltd* [1993] 3 NZLR 10.

[142]  [1970] 1 QB 447.

[143]  Above, n 108.

Because Securicor's exemption clause was drafted so plainly, they were entitled to rely on it to protect themselves from liability for fundamental breach. Lord Wilberforce's view was clearly that, while a protective approach to the doctrine of fundamental breach was justified in many instances, a blanket ban on the exemption of liability for fundamental breach was a disproportionate judicial intervention: **[14–84]**

> "Many difficult questions arise and will continue to arise in the infinitely varied situations in which contracts come to be breached ... But there are ample resources in the normal rules of contract law for dealing with these without the superimposition of a judicially invented rule of law."

It is worth noting that Davitt P had adopted a similar approach at High Court level in *Clayton Love*: **[14–85]**

> "[T]he primary consideration must always be the words which the parties themselves have selected to express their agreement in making their contract. In the absence of any statutory prohibition to that effect, and I know of none, there is nothing to prevent parties who wish to do so from entering into a contract containing exception clauses which will exempt one or other or both from liability even in the case of a breach of a fundamental term. If that is done clearly and unequivocally I see no reason why such a provision should not be effective."

In more recent years, the Irish courts have come to accept that, where the parties voluntarily agree to exclude liability for fundamental breach, the court ought to respect that decision. *Photo Production* was cited with approval in *Western Meats Ltd v National Ice and Cold Storage*.[144] Barrington J suggested that such exemption was perfectly acceptable where the parties were of equal bargaining power. **[14–86]**

## VI. Exemption Clauses and Legislation

Exemption clauses are affected by two important pieces of statute law: the Sale of Goods and Supply of Services Act 1980 and the Unfair Terms in Consumer Contract Regulations (UTCCR). These comparatively recent pieces of legislation are important for two reasons. The first is that they have provided judges with a new means of controlling exemption clauses. The second, more subtle reason is that they have had the effect of limiting judges' reliance on the common law rules on incorporation and interpretation as a means of protecting consumers. As we have already noted in the context of our discussion of the *contra proferentem* rule, because the courts can deal directly with exemption clauses under this legislation, they have less need to manipulate the common law tests as a means of doing justice. **[14–87]**

### Unfair Contract Terms

The Unfair Contract Terms Directive[145] is an important piece of EC consumer protection law which became part of Irish law by virtue of the Unfair Terms in **[14–88]**

---

144 Above, n 63.
145 (1993) OJ L095/29.

Consumer Contracts Regulations 1995.[146] The UTCCR has important implications for the law on exemption clauses. Certain terms will have to pass a "fairness" test under the UTCCR or they will not be binding on the consumer. They will be held ineffective notwithstanding that they have passed the tests for incorporation, interpretation, fundamental breach and so on as discussed above.

[14–89]     The Regulations have limited scope. First, they only apply to contracts for the sale of goods or the supply of services.[147] Second, they only apply to contracts in which the purchaser is a consumer and the seller deals in the course of business. There is some scope for criticism here as, while the Regulations are obviously aimed at redressing the imbalance of power as between consumer and businessman, they could go further in achieving this purpose. The gulf between business and consumer contracts is not absolute; issues of inequality of bargaining arise where two businesses deal on the basis of one business's set of standard terms or where a small business deals with a large firm.[148] Third, the Regulations apply to any contract term that has not been individually negotiated. It is immediately noticeable that these Regulations aim to tackle the problems around standard form contracts and so they have special relevance to exemption clauses. If a term has been pre-formulated or drafted in advance of the contractual negotiations so that the consumer has not been able to influence its content, the term falls to be considered under the test for unfairness.

[14–90]     For the purposes at hand, there are three important categories of term under the UTCCR. These are core obligations, grey-listed terms, and all other terms to which the UTCCR are applicable. A different sequence of tests applies to each under the Regulations.

### Core Terms

[14–91]  Core terms of consumer contracts for the sale of goods or supply of services do not have to pass the fairness test, provided that they are written in plain and intelligible language. This element of the UTCCR should remind you of the *contra proferentem* rule: the Regulations demonstrate the same policy of encouraging the seller to set out his stall in clear terms so that the purchaser can enter the contract with his eyes open. The core terms of a contract are terms which define the subject matter of the contract or which set out the price of the thing being sold. If a core term is not drafted in a way that would be plain and intelligible to the ordinary consumer, it must pass the fairness test just like any ordinary term. In *Director General of Fair Trading v First National Bank*[149] Lord Steyn held that the idea of a "core term" should be interpreted restrictively so that the purpose of the Regulations is not "frustrated by endless formalistic arguments as to whether a provision is a definitional or an exclusionary provision". The same point was made by Gross J in *Bairstow Eves London Central Ltd v*

---

[146] SI No 1995 of 27.

[147] But see *London Borough of Newham v Khatun* [2004] EWCA Civ 55 where the Court of Appeal, referring to the background to the Directive and to the use of the phrase "vendeur de biens" in the French text, concluded that the Directives could apply to land.

[148] See Law Commission, *Report, Unfair Terms in Contracts*, Law Com No 292, Cm 6464, February 2005.

[149] [2001] UKHL 52.

*Smith*,[150] who felt that the contrary approach would allow a "coach and horses" to be driven through the Regulations. Note that the Regulations do not inquire into the fairness of the price charged. In this regard, they are in step with the common law rule that consideration need not be adequate.

### Grey-Listed Terms

Schedule 3 to the UTCCR 1995 sets out a "grey list" of terms. These are 17 examples **[14–92]** of terms which may be unfair. The examples that are relevant to the discussion of exemption clauses include terms which have the object or effect of:

    a.   excluding or limiting the legal liability of a seller or supplier in event of the death of a consumer or personal injury to the latter resulting from an act or omission of the seller or supplier (thus the clause in *Duff v Great Northern Railway Co*.[151] would be grey-listed).

    b.   inappropriately excluding or limiting the legal rights of the consumer vis-à-vis the seller or supplier or another party in the event of total or partial non-performance or inadequate performance by the seller or supplier of any of the contractual obligations, including the option of offsetting a debt owed to the seller or supplier against any claim which the consumer may have against him.[152]

### The Fairness Test

Regulation 3(2) of the UTCCR says that: **[14–93]**

> "[A] contract term shall be regarded as unfair if, contrary to the requirement of good faith, it causes a significant imbalance in the parties' rights and obligations under the contract to the detriment of the consumer, taking into account the nature of the goods or services for which the contract was concluded and the circumstances attending the conclusion of the contract and all other terms of the contract or of another contract on which it is dependent."

To recap, core terms that have not been written in plain and intelligible **[14–94]** language must pass this fairness test. Grey-listed terms must also pass it. Finally, all other terms falling within the scope of the UTCCR must pass the test. It is up to the *proferens* to show that the term on which he seeks to rely has been individually negotiated; and that the consumer has been able to have an influence on the content of the term (whether he chose to exercise that opportunity is quite another matter) and therefore escapes the need to be checked for fairness. The clause must not have been imposed on the consumer. The time at which fairness is measured is the moment of entering into the contract. The test has two main parts: the good faith requirement and the element of significant imbalance as between the parties' contractual rights and obligations. As appears from reg 3(2), fairness is to be measured in the overall context of the contract.

---

[150] [2004] EWHC 263.
[151] Above, n 14.
[152] See *Stewart Gill v Horatio Myer & Co Ltd* [1992] 1 QB 600.

**[14–95]**  The Regulations incorporate two alternative grounds for a finding of unfairness: lack of good faith and the presence of any significant imbalance in the parties' rights and obligations which would prejudice the consumer. Although the grounds were intended as alternative bases for a finding of unfairness, the practice in England so far has been to require evidence of both an imbalance and of a lack of good faith. There has been some indication of support for this approach in Irish law.[153] Good faith, as previously discussed, is an unfamiliar concept to the common law. In *Director General of Fair Trading v First National Bank plc*[154] the House of Lords emphasised the connection between good faith and fair dealing: "good standards of commercial morality and practice". As Lord Bingham set out, good faith, for their Lordships, is concerned with the avoidance of unfair surprise and the promotion of real choice in contracting:

> "The requirement of good faith in this context is one of fair and open dealing. Openness requires that the terms should be expressed fully, clearly and legibly, containing no concealed pitfalls or traps. Appropriate prominence should be given to terms which might operate disadvantageously to the consumer."

**[14–96]**  Peter Gibson LJ elaborated further:

> "A term to which the consumer's attention is not specifically drawn but which may operate in a way which the consumer might reasonably not expect and to his disadvantage may offend the requirement of good faith. Terms must be reasonably transparent and should not operate to defeat the reasonable expectations of the consumer. The consumer in choosing whether to enter into a contract should be in a position where he can make an informed choice."

**[14–97]**  Significant imbalance, on the other hand, is concerned with the substantive fairness or unfairness of the contract. Lord Bingham described significant imbalance as follows:

> "The requirement of significant imbalance is met if a term is so weighted in favour of the supplier as to tilt the parties' rights and obligations significantly in his favour. This may be by the granting to the supplier of a beneficial option or discretion or power; or by imposing on the consumer of a disadvantageous burden or risk or duty ..."

### Exempting Liability for Breach of the Obligations Implied under the Sale of Goods and Supply of Services Act 1980

**[14–98]**  The terms and contractual obligations which are automatically implied into all contracts for the sale of goods and supply of services under ss 12–15 of the 1980 Act were examined in the discussion of implied terms (see para 13–62). Section 55 of the Act deals with the enforceability of clauses which seek to exempt the seller from liability for breach of those obligations. In some cases, regardless of whether a clause has been properly incorporated and notwithstanding that it is expressed so as to cover the breach which occurs, it will be

---

[153] *Director General of Fair Trading v First National Bank plc*, above, n 148; *Bryen & Langley v Boston* [2005] EWCA 973. In Ireland see the somewhat vague judgment of Murphy J in *Marshall v Capitol Holdings* [2006] IEHC 271, citing *Bryen* with apparent approval.
[154] *ibid.*

void under the 1980 Act. First, where the buyer is a consumer,[155] it is impossible for the seller to be exempted from liability in the event that goods sold by sample or by description do not correspond to the sample or description provided (ss 13 and 15) or that they are not merchantable or fit for purpose (s 14). Secondly, it is impossible to exempt liability for breach of s 12 of the 1893 Act—the implied term that the seller of goods has title to those goods, regardless of whether the buyer is a consumer or not.

However, where the buyer buys in the course of his own business, it is possible **[14–99]** for a seller to use an exemption clause to protect himself from liability for breach of the implied obligations under ss 13, 14 and 15, provided that his exemption clause is "fair and reasonable". So, for example, a meat wholesaler may use a fair and reasonable exclusion clause to avoid paying damages where the beef he supplies to a butcher does not correspond to the sample provided. However, a butcher would not be able to take similar steps in relation to his contract for the sale of meat to an ordinary customer. Finally, there are no absolute restrictions on the use of exemption clauses in relation to contracts for the supply of services. It is possible to enforce an exemption clause which seeks to protect the supplier of services from the consequences of his breach of the terms implied into a service contract by s 39 of the 1980 Act, whether the purchaser is a consumer or not. However, if the purchaser is a consumer, the clause must be "fair and reasonable". If the purchaser is not a consumer, the clause can be enforced regardless of whether it is fair and reasonable within the meaning of the 1980 Act.

### The "Fair and Reasonable" Test

|  | Term | Impossible to Exempt Liability. | Possible to Exempt Liability Provided Clause is "Fair and Reasonable." | Possible to Exempt Liability Whether Clause is "Fair and Reasonable" or not. |
|---|---|---|---|---|
| Consumer | s.12 | ✓ | | |
| Contract | s.13 | ✓ | | |
|  | s.14 | ✓ | | |
|  | s.15 | ✓ | | |
|  | s.39 | ✓ | | |
| Non-consumer | s.12 | ✓ | | |
| Contract | s.13 | | ✓ | |
|  | s.14 | | ✓ | |
|  | s.15 | | ✓ | |
|  | s.39 | | | ✓ |

---

[155] A consumer contract is defined in s 3 of the Act as one where one of the parties:

(a)  ... neither makes the contract in the course of a business nor holds himself out as doing so, and

(b)  the other party does make the contract in the course of a business, and

(c)  the goods or services supplied under or in pursuance of the contract are of a type ordinarily supplied for private use or consumption.

See *O'Callaghan v Hamilton Leasing* [1984] ILRM 146; *Cunningham v Woodchester*, unreported, High Court, 16 November 1984.

**[14–100]** As can be seen from the above table, this test determines the enforceability of clauses exempting liability for breach of ss 13–15 of the 1980 Act in business contracts and clauses exempting liability for breach of s 39 of the 1980 Act in consumer contracts. The test mirrors that under the English Unfair Contract Terms Act 1977. The *proferens* bears the burden of showing that his exemption clause is "fair and reasonable". Lord Bridge, applying the equivalent English test in *George Mitchell v Finney Lock Seeds Ltd*,[156] said that in applying the test the Court "must entertain a whole range of considerations, put them in the scales on the one side or the other, and decide at the end of the day on which side the balance comes down." Under the Schedule to the Act, regard must be had to each of a number of factors in assessing the fairness and reasonableness of the clause. These will be considered in turn. Remember that no one factor is decisive; what matters is the balance between them. In addition, it is important to emphasise that, because the application of the test in a given case depends so much on context, each case tends to turn on its own facts, so that the established precedents are of limited value.[157]

*Relative Bargaining Power*

**[14–101]** The first factor is the relative bargaining power of the parties. Equality of bargaining power is not a determinative factor, but it can cover a multitude of sins. For example, in *Stag Line Ltd v Tyne Shiprepair Group*[158] clauses were held reasonable which were "in such small print that one can barely read them" and written so badly that "one almost needs an LL.B to understand them" in a commercial context where the parties were of equal bargaining power. Naturally, the courts are less protective in non-consumer contracts than in consumer contracts because the same issues of power are perceived not to arise. Tucker LJ has said[159] that the courts should be "less enthusiastic about … intrusion into contracts between commercial parties of equal bargaining strength, who should generally be considered capable of being able to make contracts of their choosing and expect to be bound by their terms." In *Watford Electronics Ltd v Sanderson CFL Ltd*[160] Chadwick LJ elaborated on this policy:

> "Where experienced businessmen representing substantial companies of equal bargaining power negotiate an agreement, they may be taken to have had regard to the matters known to them. They should, in my view be taken to be the best judge of the commercial fairness of the agreement which they have made; including the fairness of each of the terms in that agreement. They should be taken to be the best judge on the question whether the terms of the agreement are reasonable. The court should not assume that either is likely to commit his company to an agreement which he thinks is unfair, or which he thinks includes unreasonable terms. Unless satisfied that one party has, in effect, taken unfair advantage of the other – or that a term is so unreasonable

---

[156] Above, n 3.

[157] *Phillips Products v Hyland* [1987] 1 WLR 659.

[158] [1984] 2 Lloyd's Rep 48.

[159] *Granville Oil & Chemicals Ltd v Davies Turner & Co Ltd* [2003] 1 All ER 819.

[160] [2001] All ER 290. See also *Sonicare International Ltd v East Anglia Freight Terminal Ltd* [1997] 2 Lloyd's Rep 48; *cf Britvic Soft Drinks Ltd v Messer UK Ltd* [2002] 1 Lloyd's Rep 20.

that it cannot properly have been understood or considered – the court should not interfere."

However, there is some suggestion in the form of *George Mitchell v Finney Lock Seas*[161] that a non-consumer contract will be subject to greater scrutiny where it is a contract between a small businessman and a larger enterprise.

[14–102]

*Alternative Sources*

The second point to be considered is whether the affected party could have acquired his goods or service elsewhere on more favourable terms.[162] This factor is directed against effective cartels. So in *George Mitchell v Finney Lock Seeds*[163] the Court, in finding a limitation clause in a contract for the sale of seeds unreasonable, highlighted the fact that: "a similar limitation of liability was universally embodied in the terms of trade between seedsmen and farmers and had been for many years". Similarly, in *Waldron-Kelly v British Railways*[164] a clause that limited the liability of a railway in respect of a lost suitcase was unreasonable because, *inter alia*, similar if not identical exemption clauses were used throughout the trade. In both these cases, the prevelance of the offending clauses in the trade meant that the affected party had no real choice but to accept the exemption. The *proferens* can guard against a finding of unreasonableness under this heading by providing a greater range of options to the consumer: for example, by providing a more expensive alternative service with a less restrictive limitation of liability or by directing the consumer's attention to such services provided by competitors.[165]

[14–103]

*Inducement*

The third factor is whether there was an inducement to enter into the contract. For example, if the affected party received some advantage or bonus for accepting the exemption clause, the clause will be more likely to be considered reasonable. Thus, in *Green v Cade Bros*[166] a limitation clause in relation to uncertified seed potatoes that would otherwise have been unreasonable was upheld, in part because the purchaser bought them at a reduced price. The inducement must, however, be considered in the context of the alternatives open to the affected party. Consider *Woodman v Photo Trade Processing*.[167] The plaintiff recovered 13 photographs from a 36 exposure film. The pictures were of a friend's wedding. A clause in the developing contract limited liability to the value of a replacement film. The clause was held to be unreasonable because there was a Code of Practice in the business which said that a two-tier pricing system ought to be offered to consumers so that it would be possible to pay more for a more secure service. This was not offered. If, on the other hand, the plaintiff had been offered the more expensive service but had deliberately chosen the cheaper service it

[14–104]

---

[161] Above, n 3.
[162] *Overseas Medical Supplies v Orient Transport* [1999] CLC 1243.
[163] Above, n 3.
[164] [1981] CLY 303.
[165] (1981) 131 NLJ. 933.
[166] [1978] 1 Lloyd's Rep. 602.
[167] Above n 164.

would be likely that the clause would be held reasonable because the consumer could genuinely be said to have accepted the risk of loss.

*Knowledge*

[14–105] The fourth factor is whether the purchaser knew or ought to have known about the existence or extent of the clause. Particular attention is paid in this regard to industry custom and to the existence of a course of dealing between the parties. To some extent this requirement mirrors the common law reasonable notice requirement. However, while the common law test for incorporation requires merely that the affected party is aware of the existence of the clause, the fairness and reasonableness test is to some degree concerned with the extent to which he had notice of its *content*. The best way to demonstrate that the affected party had sufficient knowledge of the content of a clause is to show that the clause was negotiated.[168] This will be an especially powerful point if the affected party had legal advice on the terms.[169]

[14–106] In addition, it appears that widely drafted exclusion clauses are likely to meet with disapproval, especially where they conflict with the express promises made under the contract.[170] In *Danka Rentals Ltd v Xi Software Ltd*[171] the Court considered a clause that attempted to exclude absolutely all liability. The Court held that the clause was so wide as to be "offensive to reason". Thus the clause was unenforceable.

[14–107] Another important point as regards knowledge turns on clauses which are expressly part of the parties' contract but which habitually go unenforced. If a clause is never enforced, it is reasonable to conclude that the affected party was not fully aware of it. For example, in *Western Meats v National Ice and Cold Storage*[172] it was significant to the court's refusal to enforce the clause at issue that the parties ordinarily resolved any disputes informally without recourse to the courts. That is not to say that the fact that the *proferens* has not habitually relied on the clause automatically means that the clause must fall. Thus, in *Schenkers Ltd v Overland Shoes*[173] the Court of Appeal found that a clause was reasonable which was not habitually enforced as between the parties because the clause was in common use and there was no significant inequality of bargaining power as between the parties. The case for a clause is even stronger where it is the result of negotiations between representative bodies within the industry. So, in *Green v Cade*[174] a clause in a seed contract was held reasonable because it had been "in use for many years with the approval of the negotiating bodies acting on behalf of both seed merchants and farmers". The position is different where industry-wide practice is not to enforce a particular standard clause. This has less to do with issues of law, however, than with the sense that if most people in a given industry

---

[168] *Britvic Soft Drinks Ltd v Messer UK Ltd* [2002] Lloyd's Rep 20.

[169] *Walker v Boyle* [1982] 1 All ER 634; *McCullough v Lane Fox and Partners Ltd*, *The Times* December 22, 1995.

[170] *Lease Management Services Ltd v Purnell Secretarial Services* [1994] Tr LR 337.

[171] (1998) 17 TLR 74.

[172] Above, n 63.

[173] [1998] 1 Lloyd's Rep 498. See also *Monarch Airlines v London Luton Airport* [1997] CLC 698.

[174] [1978] 1 Lloyd's Rep 602.

are unwilling to enforce a particular clause, it suggests a widespread recognition that the clause is unreasonable.[175]

### Compliance with Obligations Practicable

The fifth factor is whether compliance with any obligation placed on the purchaser was   **[14–108]** practicable. This refers to situations where liability is conditional on compliance with a condition. An example would be where liability is conditional on a written complaint being placed within seven days of purchase. In *Green v Cade*,[176] such an obligation was held to be unreasonable in the context of a contract for seed potatoes because it would be impossible to detect defects with seeds within that short space of time.

### Special Order

The sixth factor is whether any goods were made, processed or adapted to the   **[14–109]** purchaser's special order. In this circumstance, it is perfectly reasonable for the manufacturer to exclude liability for breach of all obligations except conformity with the specification.

### Further Factors

The English law also specifies that the court should have regard to the resources   **[14–110]** available to the *proferens* and, in particular, his capacity to insure against the loss in respect of which he seeks to exempt himself from liability. It will be unreasonable for one party to impose a Draconian exemption clause on the other when he could very easily have protected himself from the consequences of liability by taking out insurance. So, in *Smith v Eric S Bush*[177] the House of Lords held that a disclaimer in a mortgage valuation was unreasonable given that the valuer could easily protect himself from loss by taking out professional indemnity insurance while the purchaser of the house would find it very difficult to acquire or even afford insurance sufficient to cover the massive loss they would sustain in the event of negligent valuation.[178] These cases involve a normative judgment as to which party should be obliged to bear the risk of loss arising from breach of the contract. The contract in *George Mitchell v Finney Lock Seeds*[179] concerned the sale of cabbage seed between a supplier and a farmer and included a limitation clause that limited recovery in damages to the cost of the seeds. The seeds cost £200. The seeds did not grow properly and the farmer suffered loss to the tune of £61,000. Kerr LJ found that the clause was unreasonable because *inter alia*:

> "Farmers do not, and cannot be expected to insure against this kind of disaster;
> but suppliers of seeds can ... I am not persuaded that liability for rare events of

---

[175] *George Mitchell v Finney Lock Seeds Ltd*, above, n 3.

[176] Above, n 173.

[177] [1990] 1 AC 831.

[178] Note that what is important is the *proferens'* opportunity to take out insurance at the time the contract was concluded which is important and not his actual insurance position at the time of breach: *The Flamar Pride* [1990] 1 Lloyd's Rep 434. See also *Moores v Yakeley Assoc Ltd* (1999) 62 Con LR 76.

[179] Above, n 3.

this kind cannot be adequately insured against. Nor am I persuaded that the cost of such cover would add significantly to the cost of seed ... To limit the supplier's liability to the price of seed in all cases, as against the magnitude of the losses which farmers can incur in rare disasters of this kind, appears to me to be a grossly disproportionate and unreasonable allocation of the respective risks."

[14–111]     This *dictum* leads on to a related point: the *proferens* will often be expected to demonstrate that the level of protection he has contracted for is in proportion both to his financial resources and to the financial risk sought to be protected against. For example, in *St Albans City and District Council v International Computers Ltd*[180] a clause in a computer contract which limited liability to £100,000 was held to be unreasonable. It might be expected that a limitation clause is more likely to be held reasonable than a blanket exclusion clause. That is as may be. However, the *proferens* could not provide an objective justification for the figure, especially considering that the *proferens* was insured and, more importantly, as the parties who stood to make a profit from the transaction, in a better position to bear the financial risk associated with breach.

[14–112]     The clause is more likely to be unreasonable where the financial risk is slight. In *Smith v Eric S Bush*[181] it was significant that the valuer's task was not an onerous one: he was safe from the consequences of breach provided only that he reached that degree of reasonable care and skill which the law in general demands of valuers.

---

[180] [1996] 4 All ER 481.
[181] Above, n 176.

# CHAPTER 15
# Misrepresentation

## I. Introduction

The law on misrepresentation exists to provide a remedy to a party who has suffered **[15–01]** loss because he relied on a misleading statement in entering into a contract. Suppose A contracts with B for the sale of a painting. Before entering into the contract, A tells B that the painting is the work of Jack Yeats. B accordingly pays €3.5 million for the painting. Some years later, B has the painting valued and it transpires that it is not by Jack Yeats at all. What remedy does B have against A? The first point to note is that B's remedy depends on whether the statement that the painting is by Jack Yeats constitutes a term of the contract or merely a representation. If it is a term of the contract, the contract is breached when the painting turns out not to be by Jack Yeats. If it is simply a representation, B has an action in misrepresentation and may have access to one of the range of special remedies discussed in this chapter. Misrepresentation may also act as a defence to an action for breach of contract. For example, a party may respond to a suit for specific performance with the argument that the contract should not be enforced because it was tainted from its inception by misrepresentation.

We have noted already that classical contract law is more concerned with **[15–02]** procedural justice (issues surrounding the making of the contract) than it is with substantive justice (issues surrounding the content of the contract). The regulation of misrepresentation ties in with this concern for procedural justice. Misrepresentation is a vitiating factor—a defect in the formation of the contract going to the agreement. The defect is that one of the parties did not give full and informed consent to the making of the contract. Even though misrepresentation can be explained as a creature of traditional contract law, Atiyah[1] notes that the development of a concept of misrepresentation represents a move away from a tradition of pure individualism:

> "In the shadow of nineteenth century individualism, lawyers still pay lip service (and sometimes more) to the fundamental belief that a man should rely on himself, and not on others. But in practice, in actual decisions, and in actual legislation, it is evident that this individualism no longer represents the values underlying the law ... The Courts began to insist on the duty of a party not to mislead the other party by extravagant and unjustified assertions."

## II. The Elements of Misrepresentation

[15–03]  The definition of misrepresentation in Irish law comes from *Colthurst v La Touche Colthurst*.[2] In that case, McCracken J said that a misrepresentation is an untrue representation of fact, which induced the plaintiff to enter into the contract. Each of these elements will be discussed in full. In testing a fact pattern for misrepresentation, one must first identify a representation. One must then establish that the representation was false. Next one must demonstrate that the representation was one of fact. Finally, one must generally show that the representation induced the person to whom it was made to enter the contract.

### A Representation is Made

[15–04]  What will count as a representation? The first point is that things other than written and oral statements can amount to representations. It is possible to make a representation by conduct. For example, in *Ridge v Crowley*[3] the act of concealing defects in the foundations of a house amounted to a representation by conduct. In *Spice Girls v Aprilia*,[4] five members of a pop group took part in a commercial photo shoot for the advertisement of a scooter. Alas, Ginger Spice left the group some time after the shoot with the result that the scooter company could not benefit from the photo shoot. The Court held that the members' participation in the shoot amounted to a representation that none of the Spice Girls had a declared intention to leave the group at that date.

[15–05]  The question of whether silence can amount to a misrepresentation is a more difficult one. Generally speaking, there is no duty to disclose material facts in contract law (16-04).[5] However, an exception arises where one party's silence distorts a representation that has already been made. In other words, a half truth is still an untruth. In *Doolan v Murray*[6] Keane J stated that "... if a person elects to make a partial disclosure, instead of remaining silent, he may, depending on the circumstances, render himself ... liable to an action based on misrepresentation". An interesting

---

[1]  Atiyah, "The Resurgence of Reliance-Based Liabilities," *The Rise and Fall of Freedom of Contract* (Oxford University Press, 1985), pp 771–772.
[2]  Unreported, High Court, 9 February 2000.
[3]  (1958) 172 EG 637; see also *Clincare v Orchard Homes* [2004] EWHC 1694.
[4]  [2000] EMLR 478.
[5]  *O'Donnell v Truck & Machinery Sales* [1998] 4 IR 191.
[6]  Unreported, High Court, 21 December 1993.

example comes from the case of *Gill v McDowell*.[7] This case concerned the interaction of a representation by conduct and silence. The representation by conduct was the owner's action of bringing the animal to a fair where bullocks and heifers were sold. The purchaser bought the animal, thinking he was buying a bullock or a heifer, when in fact the animal was hermaphrodite. The owner remained silent and did not disclose the animal's true nature. Lord O'Brien CJ found that this silence constituted a false representation because the seller's failure to disclose the animal's nature distorted his original representation by conduct.

## The Representation is Untrue

The essence of misrepresentation is that the statement made is a false one. It must be false at the time of entering into the contract.[8] A statement is treated as true if it is true in all material aspects: minor inaccuracies will not give rise to a remedy.[9] On the other hand, a half truth will be treated as an untruth. If the representor makes a statement that is literally true but nonetheless misleading, he will be liable in misrepresentation. For example, in *Dimmock v Hallett*[10] a farm was described as let to a certain tenant at £290 a year. This was literally true. However, the description was treated as a misrepresentation because the full truth was very different: the tenant had given notice to quit and no replacement tenant had been found.  **[15–06]**

What is the law if a statement is true at the time it is made but subsequently becomes untrue? Is the representor bound to notify the representee of the change in circumstances? The rule in *With v O'Flanagan*[11] applies here. The seller of a medical practice began negotiations with a prospective purchaser in January. He represented that the practice was worth £22,000. Shortly afterwards he became ill so that by the time the practice was sold in May, it had suffered a significant drop in value. The Court held that the vendor should have informed the buyer of the change in circumstances.  **[15–07]**

A similar duty applies where the representor believes the statement he is making is true at the time he makes it but subsequently discovers it is untrue. In *Davies v London & Provincial Marine Ins Co*,[12] Fry J stated:  **[15–08]**

> "[I]f one of the negotiating parties has made a statement which is false in fact, but which he believes to be true and which is material to the contract, and

---

[7] [1903] 2 IR 463.

[8] *Briess v Woolley* [1954] AC 333.

[9] *Dawsons Ltd v Bonin* [1922] 2 AC 413.

[10] (1866) 2 Ch App 21.

[11] [1936] Ch 575.

[12] (1878) 8 Ch D 469. See also *Sargent v Irish Multiwheel Ltd* (1955) 21–22 Ir Jur Rep 42. This duty was also recognised by Lord Blackburn in the older case of *Brownlie v Campbell* (1880) 5 App Cas 925: "I further agree in this: that when a statement or representation has been made in the bona fide belief that it is true, and the party who has made it afterwards comes to find that it is untrue, and discovers what he should have said, he can no longer honestly keep up that silence on the subject after that has come to his knowledge, thereby allowing the other party to go on, and still more, inducing him to go on, upon a statement which was honestly made at the time when it was made ..."

during the course of negotiations he discovers the falsity of that statement, he is under an obligation to correct his erroneous statement ...".

[15–09]   The law imposes an exacting duty on the representor who aims to correct an earlier misstatement. He must show that the truth was plainly brought to the attention of the representee at the time of contracting.[13]

### It is a Representation of Fact

[15–10]   The representation must be a representation of past or existing fact. Generally speaking, statements of intention, statements of opinion and sales puffs are not treated as statements of fact.

### *Statements of Intention*

[15–11]   Ordinarily, a statement of intention is not a statement of fact. Statements of intention are statements as to the future and, unlike a statement of fact, a statement as to the future can neither be true nor false at the time it is made-it only becomes true or false later on. Thus, a representee has no remedy in misrepresentation where the representor states that he intends to do a particular thing in the future and subsequently changes his mind. For instance, in *The Seaflower*[14] the owners of a ship stated that they "would obtain" the approval of an oil company within 60 days. This was a statement of intention honestly held. There was no misrepresentation when they did not obtain the approval after all. Similarly, in *Wales v Wadham*[15] a separated wife told her husband that she had no intention of remarrying and, consequently, he entered into an agreement with her that she would receive £13,000 from the sale of their former home. When it became clear that she did intend to remarry, the husband had no claim in misrepresentation. Tudor Evans J held that "a statement of intention is not a representation of existing fact, unless the person making it does not honestly hold the intention he is expressing".

[15–12]   If, however, as Tudor Evans J observed, a person dishonestly states that he holds an intention which he does not in fact hold, the person to whom that statement is made may have a case in misrepresentation. This is because the representor is making a false statement about the state of his mind, and the state of his mind is an existing fact. In *Edgington v Fitzmaurice*[16] Bowen LJ famously said:

> "[T]he state of a man's mind is as much a statement of fact as his digestion. It is true that it is very difficult to prove what the state of a man's mind at a particular time is, but if it can be ascertained it is as much a fact as anything else. A misrepresentation as to the state of a man's mind is, therefore, a statement of fact."

[15–13]   In *Edginton* the representors were directors of a company. They issued a prospectus inviting submissions for debentures. This prospectus stated that they

---

[13]   *Buxton v The Birches Time Share Resort Ltd* [1991] 2 NZLR 641.
[14]   [2000] 2 All ER (Comm) 169.
[15]   [1977] 1 WLR 199.
[16]   (1885) 8 App Cas. 467 at 483.

intended to use the money raised to complete alterations to the company's buildings and to buy horses and vans. In fact, it was proven that they really intended to use the money to pay off certain liabilities. They had, therefore, misrepresented the state of their minds—they had made a statement of fact.

An interesting question is whether the famous dictum in *Edgington* mandates that the state of a man's mind be treated in the same way as any other state of affairs touching on the contract. If it is, the judgment in *Wales v Wadham*[17] is out of kilter with that in *With v O'Flanagan*.[18] In *With v O'Flanagan*, when the representor became aware that the statement of fact he had made regarding his business was now untrue, he was obliged to rectify it. In *Wales v Wadham*[19] the wife changed her mind about marriage. She became aware that the statement of fact she had made regarding the state of her mind was now untrue. Why was she not under a duty to alert her husband to this change before entering into the contract with him?[20] **[15–14]**

## Statements of Opinion

A statement of opinion is not a statement of fact. The courts, in distinguishing between statements of fact and statements of opinion, focus not so much on whether the statement *was* one of fact or one of opinion, but on whether the representee has reasonably relied on it as fact so that the court *ought to treat it as such*. The courts will thus concentrate on any special characteristics of the representor, which would have justified the representee in concluding that his opinion had a basis in existing fact. To this end, an opinion will be treated as a statement of fact where it draws on some special expertise or knowledge. **[15–15]**

In *Esso Petroleum v Mardon*[21] an agent of Esso told a prospective tenant that, in his opinion, a petrol station would sell 200,000 gallons per annum by its third year in business. This did not happen. The question was whether the statement of opinion in this case could be treated as a statement of fact and thus as a misrepresentation. The agent had 40 years of experience in the business. The tenant was, therefore, entitled to conclude that the agent had exercised reasonable skill and care in making the statement. Accordingly, the statement of opinion was held to be a statement of fact. Similarly, in *Smith v Land and House Property Corp*[22] the vendor of a house described the sitting tenant as "most desirable". Bowen LJ explained that this statement of opinion was treated as a statement of fact because[23]: **[15–16]**

> "Now a landlord knows the relations between himself and his tenant, other persons either do not know them at all or do not know them equally well, and if the landlord says that he considers that the relations between himself and his

---

[17] Above, n 15.
[18] Above, n 11.
[19] Above, n 15.
[20] Halson, *Contract Law* (Longman, 2001), pp 32–33.
[21] [1976] QB 801.
[22] (1884) 28 Ch D 7.
[23] *ibid. per* Bowen LJ: "But if the facts are not equally well known to both sides, then a statement of opinion by one who knows the facts best involves very often a statement of material fact, for he impliedly states that he knows facts which justify his opinion".

tenant are satisfactory, he really avers that facts peculiarly within his own knowledge are such as to render that opinion reasonable."

[15–17]     By contrast, in *Bisset v Wilkinson*[24] the vendor of a holding in New Zealand told a prospective purchaser that, in his opinion, the land could carry 2,000 sheep. The land had never been grazed by sheep before so, to the purchaser's knowledge, the vendor had no special knowledge about its capacity. In addition, both parties were farmers and, therefore, in an equal position as judges of the land. Therefore, the statement of opinion was treated as just that and not as a statement of the actual capacity of the land.

[15–18]     It is possible for the representor, by choosing his words with appropriate care, to avoid his statement of opinion being treated as a statement of fact. In *Hummingbird Motors v Hobbs*[25] the defendant sold a car to the plaintiff. He signed a document stating that, to the best of his knowledge and belief, the reading on the mile-o-meter was correct. In fact, the reading was incorrect to the tune of more than 40,000 miles. However, the defendant could not be bound to his opinion because, by qualifying his opinion to the effect that it was true to the best of his knowledge and belief, he had moved the goal posts. O'Connor LJ wrote:

> "[O]nce the nature of the representation is that the information is correct to the best of the defendant's knowledge and belief, what has to be investigated is whether he had a genuine belief that what he was saying was true."

[15–19]     The defendant had made his statement in good faith and so he could not be sued for misrepresentation.

### Sales Puffs

[15–20]     A mere sales puff cannot amount to a statement of fact—*simplex commendatio non obligat*. A sales puff is an exaggerated claim made for the product being sold. The rationale for this rule is similar to that of the exception to the rule on statements of opinion discussed above. Statements of opinion made by experts are actionable because the reasonable man expects them to be true and expects to be able to rely on them. Sales puffs are not actionable because no reasonable person believes them to be true. Thus, in *Smith v Lynn*[26] Curran J held that a statement that a house was "in excellent structural and decorative repair" was not a statement of fact, and so no action in misrepresentation arose when the house turned out to be infested with woodworm. Whether a statement is merely a puff will often be a question of detail. Thus, a description of land as "uncommonly rich"[27] was a mere sales puff whereas a more detailed description of a car as "[a]bsolutely mint. All the right bits... and does it go. Probably cost a fortune to build" was certain enough to be treated as a statement of fact. It should be noted that, while sales puffs fall outside the scope of misrepresentation, they are amply regulated by statute. Section 41 of the Consumer Protection Act

---

[24] [1927] AC 117; See similarly *Kyle Bay Ltd v Underwriters* [2006] EWHC 607.
[25] [1986] RTR 276.
[26] (1954) 85 ILTR 57.
[27] *Dimmock v Hallet* (1866) 2 Ch App 21.

2007 provides relief where a seller engages in misleading commercial practices. Section 42 defines a commercial practice as misleading if it would mislead the average consumer as to the nature of the product itself, inducing him to make a transactional decision he would not otherwise make. Section 52 further includes a "blacklist" of representations in respect of which especially severe penalties apply. In addition, sections 6 to 8 of the Consumer Information Act 1978 makes it an offence to make certain false or misleading statements about services being provided or about the price of goods or services being provided. The publication of false or misleading advertisements about goods, services or facilities is also prohibited.

## It Induces the Representee to Contract

It is not enough for the representee to demonstrate that a false statement of fact was made to him. He must also show both that the representor made the statement with the intention of inducing him to enter into the contract[28] and that he, in fact, relied on the misrepresentation by entering into the contract.[29]

[15–21]

### Materiality

There is some debate about whether it is possible to prove that the representee was induced to enter a contract by a trivial representation. A material representation is one that would have induced the reasonable person to enter the contract at issue.[30] *Smith v Chadwick*[31] sets out that material inducement is an essential element of misrepresentation. In *Gahan v Boland*[32] Murphy J held that a statement by the sellers of land that their property would not be affected by a motorway to be built in the area was a material one because:

[15–22]

> "I am satisfied that the existence of plans – albeit plans which have been in existence for some time and unlikely to be filled in the near future, if at all, - for the erection of a motorway through or even near property is a factor which would have a material influence on the mind of a hypothetical potential purchaser."

Some English cases have questioned whether proof of materiality is required in order to establish inducement, or whether materiality merely raises a rebuttable presumption of inducement. In *Museprime Properties Ltd v Adhill Properties Ltd*,[33] the Court held that if a statement was material, the Court would presume that the representee was induced by it to enter into the contract. It would then be open to the representor to prove that the representee was not so induced. On the other hand, if the statement was not material, the Court would presume that the representee was not induced by it. In this case, it would fall to the representee to prove that he was so induced. However, in *Pan Atlantic Co Ltd v Pinetop Insurance*,[34] the House of Lords

[15–23]

---

[28] *Peek v Gurney* (1873) LR 6 HL 377.
[29] *Gahan v Boland,* unreported, High Court, 21 January 1983.
[30] *Smith v Chadwick* (1884) 9 App Cas 187.
[31] (1882) 20 Ch D 27 *per* Jessel MR.
[32] Above, n 30.
[33] (1990) 36 EG 114.
[34] [1994] 3 All ER 581.

re-affirmed that the position adopted by Murphy J in *Gahan* is also the position at English law.

### Partial Inducement

[15–24] The representee's case will not be defeated simply because he had other reasons besides the misrepresentation for entering into the contract. Partial inducement is enough.[35] As Cranworth LJ observed in *Attwood v Small*[36]: "Who can say that the untrue statement may not have been precisely that which turned the scale in the mind of the party to whom it was addressed?" For example, in *Edginton v Fitzmaurice*[37] the misleading prospectus was one of the plaintiff's reasons for purchasing debentures in the defendant company. However, he had another reason for purchasing the debentures—he believed that he would get preferential creditor status if the company failed. Cotton LJ held that his case did not fail because he could only show partial inducement: "It is not necessary to show that the misstatement was the sole cause of [the plaintiff] acting as he did". It is important to note, nevertheless, that there will be no inducement where the misrepresentation did not represent a "real and substantial" reason for entering into the contract.[38]

### No Inducement

[15–25] There are three main situations in which the court will find that, even though a false statement was made to the representee, he was not induced to enter the contract by that statement but, rather, entered it for his own reasons.

[15–26] The first is that in which the representee never knew about the misrepresentation so that it could not possibly have affected his decision to enter the contract. *Re Northumberland and Durham District Banking Co ex p Bigge*[39] concerned false reports concerning a company in which the plaintiff had bought shares. Since he could not show that he had read any of these reports, he could not establish that they had induced him to enter into the contract for the sale of shares. *Horsfall v Thomas*[40] applies the same principle to a representation by conduct. In that case, the defendant had purchased a gun from the plaintiff. The breach of the gun was defective and the plaintiff had covered this defect with a plug of metal. The plaintiff had, therefore, misrepresented that the gun was fit to be fired. In fact, once fired, it exploded. The defendant had never examined the gun before purchase. Therefore, he never knew about the misrepresentation and could not claim that he was induced by it to buy the gun.

[15–27] Secondly, a representee will not be able to prove inducement where it is clear that, even though he knew of the representation, he did not allow it to affect his judgment. A pertinent case was *Smith v Chadwick*[41] in which a false representation was made in a prospectus for the sale of shares in a company that a particular

---

[35] *Floods v Shand Construction* [2000] BLR 81.
[36] (1838) 6 Cl & Fin 232.
[37] (1885) 8 App Cas 467.
[38] *JEB Fasteners v Marks, Bloom & Co* [1983] 1 All ER 583.
[39] (1858) 28 LJ Ch 50.
[40] (1862) 1 H&C 90.
[41] (1882) 20 Ch D 27 *per* Jessel MR.

eminent person would be on the board of directors. On cross-examination, the representee admitted that the representation had not affected him in the least. This is obviously an unusual case. More often, the court will find that the representee did not allow the representation to affect his judgment if he conducted his own investigations into the facts surrounding the agreement before contracting. In *Smith v Lynn*[42] the purchaser of a house based his action in misrepresentation on a false advertisement. However, before purchasing the house he had commissioned an expert to report on the condition of the property. He had relied on the judgment of an expert, not on the representation, and thus, he could not prove inducement. The same conclusion was reached in *Attwood v Small*[43] in which the purchaser of a mine engaged surveyors to investigate it before contracting. He was not allowed, therefore, to rely on the erroneous statements of the seller to raise an action in misrepresentation. Similarly, in *Intrum Justitia v Legal and Trade Financial Services Ltd*,[44] the vendor of shares in a company had assured the plaintiff purchaser that it had "no skeletons in the cupboard" and had fully and accurately disclosed all key financial factors. It transpired that one of the company's staff had embezzled funds from it. O'Sullivan J found that the purchaser could not prove inducement because it had relied on its own extensive due diligence process in deciding whether to buy the shares.

Finally, a court will find that no inducement was present where the representee [15–28] knew that the representation was false.[45] In *Grafton Court v Wadson*[46] the defendants had leased a unit in a shopping centre. The plaintiff developers had represented that the other tenants in the shopping centre would be upmarket. This turned out to be false; however, the defendants could not prove inducement. At the time they entered into the contract, the other units were occupied. Thus, the representees knew when they entered the contract that their fellow tenants fell below the standard promised. It falls to the representor to prove that the representee had unequivocal knowledge of the truth. Partial knowledge will not do.

Knowledge means actual knowledge, not constructive knowledge; it is [15–29] irrelevant that the representee should have known that the statement made to him was false. This was confirmed as part of Irish law in *Gahan v Boland*[47] in which Henchy J stated that only "actual and complete knowledge of the true situation" would debar an action in misrepresentation. Thus, an argument that the representee ought to have taken steps to verify the statements made to him will not succeed. In *Redgrave v Hurd*[48] Jessel MR said:

---

[42] (1954) 85 ILTR 157.
[43] (1838) 6 Cl & F 232.
[44] [2005] IEHC 190.
[45] *Colthurst v La Touche Colthurst*, above, n 2.
[46] Unreported, High Court, 17 February 1975.
[47] Above, n 30.
[48] (1881) 20 Ch D 1. See also *Nocton v Ashburton (Lord)* [1914] AC 932 *per* Lord Dunedin: "No one is entitled to make a statement which on the face of it conveys a false impression and then excuse himself on the ground that the person to whom he made it had available the means of correction".

"If a man is induced to enter into a contract by a false representation it is not a sufficient answer to him to say, 'If you had used due diligence you would have found out that the statement was untrue. You had the means afforded you of discovering its falsity, and did not choose to avail yourself of them.'"

**[15–30]**     In *Redgrave* the defendant entered into an agreement with the plaintiff under which he would become a partner in the plaintiff's solicitor's practice and buy the plaintiff's house. The plaintiff represented that the profits from the practice were £300 to £400 per year. He showed the defendant a bundle of papers which revealed that the profits were much less than that. However, the defendant did not examine them in any detail. The Court held that the misrepresentation stood: "nothing can be plainer ... the effect of a false representation is not got rid of on the ground that the person to whom it was made is guilty of negligence". Similarly, in *Phelps v White*[49] the plaintiff was told that timber would form part of a parcel of land transferred to him. When this proved untrue, it was of no avail to the defendant that he had provided documents to the plaintiff which would have shown the misrepresentation had he read them. By the same token, in *Gordon v Selico*,[50] Slade J held that it was no defence to an action for misrepresentation that the plaintiffs or their surveyor could have discovered flaws with the property purchased by conducting a closer inspection. It is important to remember that there is no general duty of disclosure in contract law. Once the representor chooses to make a statement, he casts off the protection of this principle and must bear the risk of his own inaccuracy. More recently, in *Strover v Harrington*,[51] Sir Nicolas Browne-Wilkinson V-C emphasised the imbalance in responsibility as between representor and representee.

"[I]f it is once shown that a misrepresentation has been made, it is no answer for the representor to say that the representee has been negligent and could have found out the true facts if he had acted otherwise. The representee is under no duty of care to the representor to check on the accuracy of the representation. The representor is bound by his representations, however careless the representee may have been."

**[15–31]**     The representor may try to get around the rule in *Redgrave* by expressly including a duty of verification in the contract. The difference between fraudulent, innocent and negligent misrepresentations will be discussed in the next section. For now, it is enough to note that such a duty of verification will work in respect of non-fraudulent misrepresentations only. Thus, in *Gordon v Selico*[52] Slade J observed that the rule "*caveat emptor* has no application where the purchaser has been induced to enter the contract of purchase by fraud". In *Pearson & Son v Lord Mayor of Dublin*,[53] the plaintiff agreed to do work for the defendant on the basis of plans provided by the defendant. It was a term of the contract that the plaintiff had to verify all representations made by the defendant for himself and not rely on their accuracy. Lord Loreburn LC stated that: "no one can escape liability for his own fraudulent

---

[49] (1880) 5 LR (Ir) 318.
[50] [1986] 1 EGLR 71.
[51] [1988] Ch 390.
[52] Above n 51.
[53] [1907] AC 351.

statements by inserting in a contract a clause that the other party shall not rely upon them". In *Dublin Port & Docks Board v Brittania Dredging Co Ltd*,[54] the Supreme Court held that a duty of verification was binding in respect of an innocent misrepresentation.

## III. The Causes of Action

The analysis is not complete once it has been established that a statement fulfils the elements of misrepresentation. The causes of action available for a misrepresentation depend on the nature of that misrepresentation. The three traditional categories of misrepresentation are fraudulent, negligent or innocent. A misrepresentation that is neither fraudulent nor negligent is innocent. There is also a limited type of statutory misrepresentation transcending these categories and created by s 45(1) of the Sale of Goods and Supply of Services Act 1980. Before considering the remedies then, one needs to explore the tests for each of these types of misrepresentation.

[15–32]

### Fraudulent Misrepresentation

It may come as a surprise to learn that the plaintiff sues for fraudulent misrepresentation in tort. The relevant tort is the tort of deceit. The test for fraudulent misrepresentation comes from *Derry v Peek*[55] and turns on the state of belief of the misrepresentor. Lord Herschell said in that case: "To prevent a false statement being made a fraud there must always be an honest belief in its truth". A misrepresentation is fraudulent where any one of three states of mind exists on the part of the misrepresentor. The first is where the misrepresentor knew that what he was saying was not true. For example, fraudulent misrepresentation was proven in *Fenton v Schofield*[56] where the vendor of land stated the river that ran over the plot of land he was selling yielded 400 salmon a year. He knew that this was a lie, and so the test in *Derry v Peek* was satisfied. The purchaser recovered damages in the tort of deceit. Similarly, in *Carbin v Somerville*[57] the vendor of a house had misrepresented to the purchaser that it was free from damp. In fact, the house was badly affected by damp. The Court held that the vendor must have known this as he had repeatedly taken steps to conceal the damp, i.e. re-papering the walls frequently and sealing them with black pitch paint. Accordingly, an action in deceit was established.

[15–33]

The second state of belief that will generate a claim of fraudulent misrepresentation is that where the misrepresentor makes a statement without belief in its truth. This may be illustrated by the facts of *Derry v Peek* itself. The directors of a company issued a prospectus that claimed they had the right to run steam-driven trams. The claimants, induced by this representation, purchased shares in the company. The directors honestly believed this—they knew that the consent of the Board of Trade was required, but they genuinely believed that this was a mere formality. In fact, the Board of Trade never granted its consent, and so the claimants sought damages in the tort of deceit. Lord Herschell found that there was no deceit here because the directors

[15–34]

---

[54] [1968] IR 136.
[55] (1889) 14 App Cas 337.
[56] (1966) 100 ILTR 69.
[57] [1933] IR 226.

genuinely believed their statement, that they had the right to run steam-driven trams, was true.

[15–35]     The third state of belief that will satisfy the test in *Derry v Peek* is recklessness—that the representor did not care whether what he was saying was true or false. Recklessness involves something more than negligence. Lord Herschell said in *Derry v Peek*: "I cannot assent to the doctrine that a false statement made through carelessness, and which ought to be known to be untrue, of itself renders the person who makes it liable to an action for deceit". The recklessness must be so severe as to justify treating it as the equivalent of a deliberate lie. It must be "such recklessness as to amount to a disregard for the truth". Thus, fraudulent misrepresentation will not be found where it can be established that the representor did care whether what he was saying was true and did honestly believe in the truth of his statement. In *Witter Ltd v TBP Industries*,[58] the vendor of a carpet manufacturing business had misrepresented the size of an expense in the company's accounts to a purchaser. The vendor had not sought a professional estimate of the size of the expense, making his representation instead on the basis of a rough estimate of his own. The purchaser argued that this was reckless. However, the Court found that the vendor honestly believed in the truth of his representation. The representation may have been negligent, but it was not fraudulent. In the Irish case of *Moran v Orchanda Ltd*,[59] McCracken J found that recklessness was present where the vendor of a licensed premises furnished the purchaser with false gross turnover figures for the premises. The misrepresentation was reckless and, therefore, fraudulent because the defendants had not kept any books or records. By providing the purchaser with a certificate of turnover in these circumstances, the vendors had "displayed a disregard for the accuracy of the certificate which ... amounted to recklessness on their part".

### Negligent Misrepresentation

[15–36]     There are two causes of action for negligent misrepresentation: one in tort, for negligent misstatement, and one in contract. The former originates in *Hedley Byrne v Heller*[60] and the latter in *Esso Petroleum v Mardon*.[61] It is important to understand the distinctions between the two. In many cases, it will be possible to plead both causes of action. In addition, while both causes of action turn on the representor's failure to exercise reasonable care as to the accuracy of the representation, the contract action is only available where a contract between the parties resulted from the misrepresentation and the tort action only where the representor owes the representee a duty of care.

[15–37]     A duty of care will only be imposed where there is sufficient "proximity" between the representor and the person affected by his statement—where there is a special relationship between them such that the law is justified in imposing a special

---

[58] [1996] 2 All ER 573.
[59] Unreported, High Court, 25 May 2000.
[60] [1964] AC 465.
[61] [1976] QB 801.

duty. The test for the existence of a duty of care was set out in *Stafford v Mahony*[62] by Doyle J:

> "[T]here must first of all be a person conveying the information or the representation being relied upon; secondly, that there must be a person to whom the information is being conveyed or to whom it might reasonably be expected that the information would be conveyed; thirdly that the person must act upon such information or representation to his detriment so as to show that he is entitled to damages."

It is important to notice how the duty of care can transcend the contractual relationship. For example, a valuer may prepare a report under a contract with a mortgagor, but he may be liable in negligent misstatement to the mortgagee,[63] and a solicitor's contract for the preparation of a will is with the testator, but he may be liable in negligence to the intended beneficiaries.[64] A duty of care may arise even where the representor and the injured party have never been in direct contact. In this regard, in *Caparo v Dickman*[65] Lord Oliver emphasised the requirement that the representor knows that his advice is required for a purpose and will be communicated to the plaintiff as an individual or as a member of an ascertainable class of people. This much can be gleaned from the key case of *Hedley Byrne & Co Ltd v Heller & Partners*.[66] The plaintiffs wanted to extend credit to Easipower. They, therefore, needed to check Easipower's credit, and so they asked their bank to enquire of Easipower's bankers. They relied on the reply they received, and they suffered substantial losses when the advice they received turned out not to be true. In this case, the advice had been passed through a middleman. Neither party knew the identity of the other. It was enough, however, to raise a duty of care that the defendant knew that the information would be passed to a customer of the enquiring bank and that the defendant knew the general purpose to which the information would be put. [15–38]

## Misrepresentation under s 45(1) of the Sale of Goods and Supply of Services Act 1980

This statutory cause of action only concerns contracts for the sale of goods, hire purchase agreements, agreements for the letting of goods to which s 38 of the Act applies and contracts for the supply of services. This section, the identical twin of 2(1) of the English Misrepresentation Act 1967, creates a new type of misrepresentation. [15–39]

Damages are recoverable under this section where two tests are fulfilled. First, the representee must make out the usual elements of misrepresentation. Second, the representor must fail to prove that he believed that his representation was true *and* that he had a reasonable ground for so believing. Note that the representor's defence is not one merely of honest belief but of reasonable and honest belief. So even if the representor can prove that he thought that his statement was true, but no reasonable [15–40]

---

[62] [1980] ILRM 53.
[63] *Smith v Eric S Bush* [1989] 2 All ER 514.
[64] *Ross v Caunters* [1979] 3 All ER 580.
[65] [1990] 2 AC 617.
[66] [1964] AC 465.

man would have thought it was true, he is liable under s 45(1). Note as well that the burden of proof has shifted. It is not for the representee to prove, as in the tort of negligent misstatement, that the representor's statement was unreasonable. Instead, the representor bears the burden of proving that his statement was reasonable. The equivalent statutory provision in England is often called "the fiction of fraud" because the statute is read as providing that, if the representor fulfils the test, he is liable as if the representation were fraudulent.

**[15–41]**    The burden of proving reasonable belief is a heavy one. In *Howard Marine & Dredging Co Ltd v Ogden & Sons Excavations Ltd*,[67] the defendants hired barges from the plaintiffs. The plaintiff's chairman represented that the barges had a particular capacity. In fact, this was not true. The defendants sued for misrepresentation under s 2(1) of the Misrepresentation Act 1967. The chairman had the task of proving that his belief, as to the capacity of the ship, was honest and reasonably held. He fell at the reasonableness hurdle. He had seen the ship's capacity in the original shipping documents and in Lloyd's Register—the "bible" of the shipping industry. He had relied on the figure in Lloyd's. The Court held that the belief as to the capacity of the ship was unreasonably held because the chairman could demonstrate no objective reason for preferring Lloyd's to the shipping documents. He was an expert in a position to verify the information contained in Lloyd's and he should have done so.

## IV. Remedies

### Rescission

**[15–42]**    Misrepresentation makes a contract voidable rather than automatically void. This means that the representee has the right to elect whether to rescind the contract or affirm it. The contract remains valid unless and until it is rescinded. A contract is rescinded when it is wiped out for all purposes. The contract is unpicked and both parties are put, as near as possible, in a position as if the contract had never existed. A contract is affirmed where the innocent party accepts the defects in its formation and decides to be bound by the contract as if nothing were ever wrong with it. Rescission may be distinguished from termination of a contract for breach because termination only ends a contract for the future (Chapter 24). In *Abram Steamship v Westville Shipping*[68] Lord Atkinson explained:

> "Where one party to a contract expresses by word or act in an unequivocal manner that by reason of fraud or essential error of a material kind inducing him to enter into the contract he has resolved to rescind it, and refuses to be bound by it, the expression of his election, if justified by the facts, terminates the contract, puts the parties *in statu quo ante* and restores things, as between them, to the position in which they stood before the contract was entered into."

**[15–43]**    Rescission is a self-help remedy. The party seeking rescission does not have to go to court to achieve it. All he needs to do is communicate his intention to rescind to

---

[67] [1978] QB 574.
[68] [1923] AC 773.

the representor in an unequivocal manner. But, unless and until he communicates his intention to rescind, he remains bound by the contract. Communication will be difficult in rogue cases where the representor has disappeared with his ill-gotten gains. For example, in *Car & Universal Finance v Caldwell*[69] the defendant had sold his car to a rogue for an invalid cheque. The cheque was a misrepresentation that the rogue had adequate funds in his bank account to meet it. The defendant was unable to contact the rogue when he discovered this misrepresentation. However, he provided adequate unequivocal notice of his intention to rescind by contacting the police and an automobile association.

Nevertheless, the courts' assistance will often be required to give effect to this intention as where the representor refuses to return goods or money to the representee. Rescission is an equitable remedy and, in principle, it is available for all three types of misrepresentation. However, the court retains discretion in granting this remedy and there are certain limitations on the representee's rights. These "bars" to rescission are applied less strictly where the misrepresentation is fraudulent. The bars to rescission are discussed in turn. [15–44]

## *Affirmation*

It has been noted that rescission is one prong of the representee's right of election: affirmation is the other prong. Once the choice to affirm or rescind is made, it is final. Therefore, the representee will not be entitled to rescind a contract where he has evidenced an intention to proceed with the contract. A dual knowledge limitation applies here. First, affirmation will not be held to have taken place where the representee was not yet aware of the misrepresentation. In *Lutton v Saville*[70] the seller of a defective tractor argued that the purchaser had affirmed the contract by retaining it. Carswell J held that there was no affirmation because the purchaser was not aware of the misrepresentation during the period he retained the tractor. Secondly, there will be no affirmation where the representee was not aware of his right to rescind. So, in *Peyman v Lanjani*[71] a representee was induced to buy the lease of a restaurant by misrepresentation. Although he had indicated an intention to continue with the contract, no affirmation had taken place because he was unaware of his right to rescind. [15–45]

Affirmation occurs where the representee has evidenced an intention to proceed with the contract. For example, a person who is induced to purchase shares by a misrepresentation might demonstrate the intention to affirm the contract of sale by selling the shares on or by retaining dividends.[72] This intention to affirm may be implied by the representee's conduct. Thus, in *Long v Lloyd*[73] the purchaser of a defective lorry lost his right to rescind the contract of purchase because he retained it for a time following the representor's second attempt to repair it. [15–46]

---

[69] [1965] 1 QB 525.
[70] [1986] NI 327.
[71] [1985] QB 428.
[72] *Re Hop & Malt Exchange and Warehouse Co ex p Briggs* (1866) LR 1 Eq 483.
[73] [1958] 1 WLR 753.

### *Laches*

**[15–47]** As is the case with all equitable remedies, the party seeking rescission must seek it promptly. The courts are concerned to promote certainty and finality in transactions — an aim that could not be achieved if a contract could be wiped out decades after its formation. The courts will be more forgiving of delay in cases of fraudulent than of non-fraudulent misrepresentation: if a party deliberately lies, he forfeits his right to certainty. In *O'Kelly v Glenny*[74] the plaintiff sold her interest in her deceased father's estate to her solicitor. The solicitor had fraudulently misrepresented her position. A delay of 10 years was not enough to destroy her right of rescission. By contrast, in *Leaf v International Galleries*[75] a delay of five years was too long in a case where the purchaser of a painting sought to rescind the contract of sale for innocent misrepresentation. Jenkins LJ opined that: "it behoves the purchaser either to verify, or as the case may be, to disprove the representation within a reasonable time, or else stand or fall by it". In the right circumstances, an intention to affirm the contract might be inferred from a particularly long delay.[76]

### *The Doctrine in Seddon v NorthEastern Salt*

**[15–48]** The doctrine in *Seddon v NorthEastern Salt*[77] states that the right to rescission is lost once the contract is executed, unless there has been equitable fraud. Thus, in *Lecky v Walter*,[78] the plaintiff sought to rescind a contract for the purchase of bonds because the vendor had innocently misrepresented that they were secured bonds. The Court held he was not entitled to rescission because the contract had been executed and the misrepresentation was not fraudulent. The doctrine in *Seddon v NorthEastern Salt* has been abolished in England by s 1(b) of the Misrepresentation Act 1967. It has also been restricted in Ireland by s 44(b) of the Sale of Goods and Supply of Services Act 1980. Thus, contracts for the sale of goods or supply of services, hire purchase agreements and contracts for the letting of goods to which s 38 of the Act applies may still be rescinded, notwithstanding that the contract has been executed and regardless of the type of misrepresentation.

### *Restitutio in Integrum Impossible*

**[15–49]** The aim of rescission is to restore both parties to the position they were in before entering into the contract — a concept summed up in the phrase *restitutio in integrum*. So, in *Northern Bank & Finance Co v Charlton*,[79] Griffin J set out that rescission will not be granted if "events, which have occurred since the contract and in which the representee has participated make it impossible to restore the parties substantially to their original position". To take a very simple example, if A was induced by B's misrepresentation to sell 10 bottles of beer to B, rescission will not be possible after the beer has been consumed.[80] The rationale here is the prevention of unjust enrichment. Rescission aims to deprive the misrepresentor of the benefit of the contract he has

---

[74] (1846) 9 Ir Eq R 25.
[75] [1950] 2 KB 86.
[76] *Clough v London and North Western Rly Co* (1871) LR 7 Exch 26.
[77] [1905] 1 Ch 326.
[78] [1914] 1 IR 378.
[79] [1979] IR 149.
[80] *Clarke v Dickson* (1858) EB & E 148 .

procured by his misrepresentation, not to punish him. Rescission of the contract would involve the return of the beer to A and the return of the purchase price to B. If B got his money back but did not have to return the beer, an injustice would be done. In *Spence v Crawford*[81] Lord Wright explained:

> "Though the defendant has been fraudulent, he must not be robbed, nor must the plaintiff be unjustly enriched, as he would be if he both got back what he had parted with and kept what he received in return. The purpose of relief is not punishment but compensation."

Rescission will still be granted where the events that make *restitutio in integrum* **[15–50]** impossible were not brought about by the participation of the representee. In *Carbin v Somerville*[82] the vendor of a house had misrepresented that the house was dry. In fact, it was badly affected by damp so that by the time the representee rescinded the contract, the house had deteriorated. This deterioration was irrelevant because the representee had not caused it. Fitzgibbon J noted of the representor: "He will get back his own defective house, which has deteriorated since he sold it through his own inherent vice, and has not been depreciated by any act of the plaintiff ..."

A second point is that the court may still grant rescission even where it is not **[15–51]** possible to bring the parties precisely back to their pre-contract position. In *Northern Bank & Finance Co v Charlton*,[83] O'Higgins CJ said that "it is the bounden duty of the court to do what is practically just—this being a case of fraud—even though the precise restoration of the parties to their previous position is now not possible". In *Clarke v Dickson*,[84] *restitutio in integrum* was impossible where the purchaser of a mine had exhausted all of its reserves. However, a different conclusion was reached in *Erlanger v New Sombrero Phosphate Co*.[85] In this case, the representee had purchased a phosphate mine from the representor, induced by false statements about the extent of recoverable deposits in the mine. By the time the representee sought rescission, he had extracted some phosphates from the mine. This did not defeat his right to rescind because the mine was in substantially, if not exactly, the same condition as when it was purchased. He was allowed to return the mine and compensate the representor for the phosphates extracted by giving him an account of profits. Sometimes the court will award an indemnity along with rescission to facilitate something closer to perfect *restitutio in integrum*. For example, in *Whittington v Seale-Hayne*[86] the claimant had been induced to enter into a lease for premises by the seller's misrepresentations that they were in a sanitary state. In fact, the premises were in such poor condition that the claimant's manager became ill and several of the poultry he was housing on the premises died. The claimant sought to rescind the contract. The contract was rescinded and he received an indemnity for the money he had spent as a *necessary* result of the contract—rent, rates and repair expenses. However, he could not recover for medical expenses and lost stock because, even though these losses were a consequence of

---

[81] [1939] 3 All ER 271.
[82] Above, n 58.
[83] [1979] IR 149.
[84] (1858) EB & E 215.
[85] (1878) 3 App Cas 1218.
[86] (1900) 82 LT 49.

entering into the contract, they were not losses he was obliged by the contract to undergo.

### The Intervening Rights of an Innocent Third Party

[15–52] Rescission may be refused where avoiding the contract would prejudice the rights of third parties. Suppose A sells his car to B, a rogue who fraudulently values the car at €1,000. B in turn sells the car to C. C has no idea that he is buying a car that has been swindled from its true owner. B then disappears with the proceeds of his enterprise. When A discovers the fraud, should he be permitted to rescind the contract? What about C's rights? In *Anderson v Ryan*,[87] Davis was the owner of a Mini car. He read an advertisement for a Sprite car and agreed with the person who had advertised the Sprite that they would swap cars with no money changing hands. Davis did not know that the advertiser did not own the car—he had fraudulently misrepresented that he had good title to it. Davis was dispossessed of the Sprite. Some time later, the Garda recovered the Mini and returned it to Davis. The problem was that in the meantime, the advertiser had sold the Mini to Anderson, who in turn had sold it on to Ryan. Could Davis rescind his contract with the advertiser and recover the Mini? The first important point to remember is that misrepresentation makes a contract voidable and not void. Davis, by the contract of sale for the Mini, had passed voidable title in the Mini to the advertiser. Does that mean the advertiser passed only voidable title to Anderson, which would dissolve the instant Davis decided to rescind? Section 23(1) of the Sale of Goods Act 1893 is designed to prevent the dissolution of chains of title by rescission. It provides that a seller of goods who possesses voidable title to those goods may pass on good title to the purchaser provided three conditions are fulfilled. First, the contract under which the seller obtained his voidable title must not yet have been rescinded. Secondly, the purchaser must have bought the goods in good faith. Thirdly, the purchaser must not have any notice of the defects in the seller's title. When the advertiser sold the Mini to Anderson, Davis had not rescinded the contract. Anderson purchased in good faith without notice of the misrepresentation. Accordingly, Anderson obtained good title to the Mini. He transferred that good title to Ryan by their contract of sale. Davis could not recover the car. Ryan's right to the car as a third party barred Davis from rescission.

### Damages in Lieu of Rescission

[15–53] Under s 45(2) of the Sale of Goods and Supply of Services Act 1980, where the misrepresentation is non-fraudulent,[88] the court has discretion to uphold the contract and award damages instead of rescinding it if the court is "of the opinion that it would be equitable to do so". There is no right to damages here. In *William Sindall v Cambridgeshire County Council*,[89] Hoffman LJ held, applying the equivalent English statutory provision,[90] that the Court should have regard to three matters in deciding whether to exercise this discretion: the nature of the misrepresentation; the loss to the misrepresentee if rescission is not granted; and the loss to the misrepresentor if

---

[87] [1967] IR 34. See also *White v Garden* (1851) 10 CB 919.
[88] Of course, if the misrepresentation is fraudulent, the representee already has an independent right to damages in the tort of deceit.
[89] [1994] 3 All ER 932.
[90] Misrepresentation Act 1967, s 2(2).

rescission is granted. In *Sindall* a builder had purchased playing fields from the council for 5 million. It was discovered after purchase that a sewer ran under the fields. By this time, the land had halved in value due to a general drop in property prices. The builder sought rescission. The Court applied the three-stage test and found that damages should be awarded in lieu of rescission. First, the misrepresentation was not fraudulent. Second, the builder would benefit unduly if rescission were granted in that he would be able to escape the consequences of having bought land at double its value. The loss he would avoid by rescission was completely out of proportion to the cost of re-routing the sewer-a mere €18,000. Third, if the contract were rescinded, the council would lose a very advantageous contract.

Does the fact that the right to rescission is lost because of one of the bars to rescission mean that the right to damages under s 45(2) is also lost? In *Thomas Witter v TBP Industries*[91] the purchaser of a business sought to rescind the contract under which he had purchased it because the seller had made several misrepresentations at the time of purchase. Jacob J held that the right to rescind was lost because innocent third party rights had intervened and *restitutio in integrum* was impossible. However, he held that it was still possible, in this instance, to award damages in lieu of rescission. This case seems to suggest that damages may be awarded even where rescission is impossible. However, the High Court decision in *Floods of Queensferry v Shand Construction*[92] and the first instance decision in *Zanzibar v BAE*[93] reached exactly the opposite conclusion. Most recently, however, in *Pankhania v Hackney Borough Council*[94] the judge returned to the *Thomas Witter* position, holding that the power to provide damages in lieu of rescission was not available in cases where the right to rescission had been lost by virtue of one of the bars. **[15–54]**

## Damages, Measures and Remoteness

So far, damages have been discussed only in general terms. It is necessary now to compare the rules by reference to which the damages are calculated under each cause of action. **[15–55]**

### *Negligent Misrepresentation and Negligent Misstatement*

In *Forshall v Walsh*[95] Shanley J confirmed that the measure or quantum of damages in respect of both negligent misrepresentation and negligent misstatement is the tort measure. It is important to understand the difference between the tort measure of damages and the contract measure. Where a contract has been breached, damages have the aim of putting the plaintiff in the position he would have been in had the contract been performed as agreed (25–32). If damages for fraudulent misrepresentation were calculated by this contract measure, they would be calculated as if the representation had been true and the contract had been performed on that basis. However, where, as in the tort of negligent misstatement, a tort has been committed, damages have the aim **[15–56]**

---

[91] [1996] 2 All ER 573. See also *UCB Corporate Services Ltd v Thomson* [2005] EWCA Civ 225.
[92] [2000] BLR 81.
[93] [2000] 1 WLR 2333.
[94] [2002] NPC 123.
[95] Unreported, High Court, 18 June 1997, confirmed in *Carey v Independent Newspapers* [2004] 3 IR 52.

of putting the victim in the position as if the tort had never happened. So damages in tort have the aim of putting the representee in the position as if the representation had never been made.[96] Damages are calculated by reference to the extent to which he is worse off as a result of entering into the contract on foot of the representation.

**[15–57]**     The rules as to remoteness (25–03) govern the types of loss for which damages may be recovered. The general rule in contract law is that a party breaching a contract will not be bound to pay for any consequences of his breach that were not reasonably foreseeable as likely to result from the breach. This test of foreseeability is traditionally considered to be stricter than the *Wagon Mound*[97] test of foreseeabilty in tort. Damages that are foreseeable as a matter of possibility are recoverable in tort, whereas damages may be recovered in contract only in respect of harms that are foreseeable as "not unlikely" or as a "serious possibility". In *Gran Gelato v Richcliff Group*[98] it was held that where the representee has also been at fault, the damages payable for negligent misstatement may be reduced in proportion to his contributory negligence.

### The Tort of Deceit

**[15–58]** The measure of damages in the tort of deceit is the same as that in negligent misstatement and negligent misrepresentation.[99] In *Smith New Court Securities v Scrimgeour Vickers*[100] Lord Steyn set out that: "[t]he legal measure is to compare the position of the plaintiff as it was before the fraudulent statement was made to him with his position as it became as a result of his reliance on the fraudulent statement".

**[15–59]**     However, the test for remoteness is a generous one. The test in *Re Polemis*[101] applies, which means that the representor is liable, not just for the losses reasonably foreseeable as arising from his misrepresentation, but for all of its direct consequences.[102] This more generous test reflects the courts' disapproval of fraud. In *Doyle v Olby*[103] the Court of Appeal observed that: "it does not lie in the mouth of the fraudulent person to say that [the damage] could not reasonably have been foreseen". It is important to understand the difference in effect between this test for remoteness and that applied where the misrepresentation is negligent. The difference is neatly illustrated by the case of *South Australia Asset Management Corp v York Montague Ltd*.[104] In this case, the plaintiffs had loaned money to property developers so that they could buy commercial property during a property boom. The plaintiffs loaned the money on the basis of the defendants' valuations, which subsequently proved to be negligent. The property market collapsed without warning and the plaintiffs suffered significant losses. The plaintiffs argued that they should be able to recover damages for

---

[96] *Smith New Court Securities v Scrimgeour Vickers* [1997] AC 254.
[97] [1961] AC 388.
[98] [1992] Ch 560.
[99] *Forshall v Walsh*, unreported, High Court, 18 June 1997.
[100] Above, n 97.
[101] [1921] 3 KB 560.
[102] *Northern Bank Finance v Charlton* [1979] IR 149.
[103] [1969] 2 QB 158.
[104] [1996] 3 All ER 365.

all of the losses that they had suffered as a result of entering into the contracts. They argued that if they had never entered the contracts at all, they would never have been affected by the market crash. Accordingly, they should be compensated for the direct consequences of the market crash. If the misrepresentation had been fraudulent, their argument would have succeeded. Because the misrepresentation was merely negligent, however, they were only entitled to recover for the losses that were a foreseeable consequence of the careless valuation. The consequences of the collapse of the market, therefore, fell outside the scope of recoverable loss.

The breadth of scope for recovery in the tort of deceit is limited somewhat by the representee's duty to mitigate his loss (25–50). The representee must take all reasonable steps to limit his loss as soon as he discovers the fraud. Thus, in *Downs v Chappell*,[105] the representee was induced to purchase a bookshop business on foot of a fraudulent misrepresentation. He purchased the business for £120,000. After he discovered the fraud, he was made an offer to buy the business for £76,000, which he unreasonably refused. Eventually, he sold the business for £60,000. Because of his failure to mitigate, he was not entitled to recover the full £60,000 he had lost as a consequence of the deal. He should have sold the business for £76,000 so that he would only have lost £44,000. Accordingly, he only recovered £44,000 in damages. **[15–60]**

### Damages under s 45(1)

*Royscot Trust v Rogerson*[106] established in respect of s 2(1) of the Misrepresentation Act 1967 that the applicable measure of damages here is the tort measure. However, the Court *obiter* also said that the applicable remoteness test was the same as that for fraud. English courts have expressed reservations about the principle in *Royscot* without overruling it.[107] While this generous test for remoteness is justifiable in cases of fraud, it is difficult to see that careless misrepresentations, which may satisfy the test under s 45(1) but which do not involve anything like the same degree of moral turpitude, should unlock the door to this sort of bounty. The ambit of s 45(1) is much narrower than that of s 2(1) of the 1967 Act. Nevertheless, it is worth noting that the courts' reluctance to treat a fool as a rogue has generated a reluctance to make a finding of misrepresentation in the first place.[108] **[15–61]**

Perhaps surprisingly, given this emphasis on equivalence to fraud in the area of damages, *Gran Gelato v Richcliff Group*[109] found that damages under s 2(1) can be reduced in proportion to the representee's contributory negligence. There is no equivalent rule in cases of fraudulent misrepresentation. Nevertheless, in *O'Donnell v Truck and Machinery Sales*[110] Moriarty J followed this judgment and found that contributory negligence on the part of the misrepresentee will not defeat his claim under s 45(1), but it may lead to a reduction in his damages. **[15–62]**

---

[105] [1997] 1 WLR 461.
[106] [1991] 2 QB 247; see also *Sharneyford Supplies Ltd v Barrington Black & Co* [1987] Ch 305.
[107] *Smith New Court Securities Ltd v Scrimgeour Vickers* [1997] AC 254.
[108] *Avon Insurance plc v Swire Fraser Ltd* [2000] 1 All ER (Comm) 573.
[109] Above, n 99.
[110] [1997] 1 ILRM 466.

### Damages in Lieu of Rescission

[15–63]  There is some debate as to how damages awarded in lieu of rescission ought to be calculated. It has been argued that the damages awarded should amount to the money's worth of actual rescission of the contract. However, this defeats the purpose of allowing the courts discretion to award damages in lieu. What would the point be in denying rescission because it would be too harsh on the representor only to have him pay out as much money to the representee as he would have lost had rescission been granted? In *William Sindall* Hoffmann LJ suggested that something akin to the contract test for damages should apply in respect of s 2(2) of the Misrepresentation Act 1967. He said that the section was concerned with "damage caused with the property not being what it was represented to be". This sounds very much like the contractual measure of damages, which aims to put the representee in the position as if the representation had been true.

### Abatement

[15–64]  A purchaser does not have to choose to rescind the contract. He may wish to have the contract specifically performed and receive a reduction on the purchase price, which takes into account the effect of the misrepresentation made to him. This may be the best solution where the subject matter of the contract is something unique, such as a plot of land, so that rescission would not be desirable. This deduction is called "abatement" of the purchase price. So, in *Connor v Potts*,[111] a contract was agreed for the sale of a plot of land, which turned out to be 67 acres less than it had been represented to be. The plaintiff was held to be entitled to specific performance of the contract for a purchase price reduced by the cost of the missing acres. Similarly, in *Moran v Orchanda Ltd*,[112] the agreed purchase price in respect of a licensed premises was abated where the vendors had fraudulently misrepresented the gross turnover.

---

[111] [1897] 1 IR 534.
[112] Above, n 61.

# CHAPTER 16
# Disclosure and Contracts of Insurance

*[S]uppose, for example, a time of dearth and famine at Rhodes, with provisions at fabulous prices; and suppose that an honest man has imported a large cargo of grain from Alexandria and that to his certain knowledge also several other importers have set sail from Alexandria, and that on the voyage he has sighted their vessels laden with grain and bound for Rhodes; is he to report the fact to the Rhodians or is he to keep his own counsel and sell his stock at the highest market price?*

Cicero, *De Officiis, Book III*

## I. Introduction

Consider Ciceros's question in the opening quotation. Cicero follows it with a dialogue    **[16–01]**
between Diogenes and his pupil Antipater. Diogenes argues that it is not wrong to
decline to reveal information to another, even if that information is to the other's
interest, while Antipater argues that the bonds of human fellowship compel the
merchant to disclose the information—to act in the interests of the community as a
whole. The common law takes Diogenes' side. The legal rule is that, generally speaking,
there is no liability for failure to disclose material facts. There is no duty to speak. In
*Smith v Hughes*,[1] Cockburn CJ laid down the principle as follows in the case of a man
who bought new oats believing that they were old oats:

> "[T]he seller neither said nor did anything to contribute to his deception. He
> has himself to blame. The question is not what a man of scrupulous morality or
> nice honour would do under the circumstances. The case put of the purchase of
> an estate, in which there is a mine under the surface, but the fact is unknown to
> the seller, is one in which a man of tender conscience or high honour would be

---

[1] (1871) LR 6 QB 597.

unwilling to take advantage of the ignorance of the seller; but there can be no doubt that the contract for the sale of the estate would be binding."

[16–02]     Keeton, writing in 1936, provides an interesting justification for this rule. He writes in the context of a commentary on the old US Supreme Court case of *Laidlaw v Organ*.[2] Hours before the general public knew, Organ had learned that the War of 1812 and the British blockade of New Orleans had been brought to an end by the Treaty of Ghent. He knew that the price of tobacco was likely to rise with the lifting of the blockade and so bought a large quantity of it at a low price without informing Laidlaw of the predicted increase in value. When the price went up 30 to 50 per cent, Laidlaw argued that the contract was void for fraud. However, Chief Justice Marshall found that Organ was not bound to communicate the extra information he had in his possession. In his commentary, Keeton argues that:

> "[T]he buyer in that case acted in the way in which buyers generally would be expected to act. If those facts were given to the normal person, as an abstract question, he would probably say that the buyer's conduct was unethical; on the other hand, if the same individual were given the opportunity that the buyer had in *Laidlaw v. Organ*, he would do precisely the same thing."[3]

[16–03]     Why does the law protect such selfish non-disclosure? First, the usual arguments against the enforcement of any duty of good faith in contract law are of application here. Selfishness is the driving engine of contract law. The paradigmatic contract transaction involves two autonomous, ruggedly individualistic parties, each bargaining in his own self-interest. Greed is good. As Collins has observed, there is no duty to bargain in good faith at common law, only a duty to negotiate with care.[4] Secondly, and from a law and economics perspective, Kronman has argued that an absolute duty of disclosure would be economically inefficient. If parties were obliged to make full disclosure of all relevant matters to one another at the pre-contractual stage, a major incentive to the acquisition of information would be removed.[5] The market seeks to encourage parties to invest in acquiring information; one way to do this is to allow parties to take advantage of their superior information in bargaining. In any case, why should the other party have the benefit of the knowledgeable party's research, resources and expertise? Of course this argument is weak where the non-disclosing party has expended little effort in acquiring his valuable information. Finally, a floodgates argument may be made against recognising a general duty of disclosure. In *Banque Financiére de la Cité v Westgate Insurance Co Ltd*,[6] Slade LJ observed that "in the case of commercial contracts broad concepts of honesty and fair dealing, however laudable, are an uncertain guide when determining the existence or otherwise of an obligation". How would the courts know where to draw the line in terms of disclosure?

---

[2] (1817) 15 US (2 Wheat) 178.

[3] Keeton, "Fraud – Concealment and Non-Disclosure" (1936) 15 Tex L Rev 32–33.

[4] Collins, *The Law of Contract* (LexisNexis, 2003), p 216–220.

[5] Kronman, "Mistake, Disclosure, Information and the Law of Contracts" (1978) 7 JLS 1.

[6] [1989] 2 All ER 952.

If the parties themselves agree to include a duty of disclosure in their contract, then the contract may be void if either party fails to adhere to that duty.[7] This exception is justified on the basis of the parties' individual bargain—the parties have agreed to cede their respective informational advantages. In other exceptional cases, the law will impose a duty of disclosure on contracting parties. Such duties apply, for example, to a creditor entering into a suretyship contract,[8] to a party who is in a fiduciary relationship with the other party to the contract[9] and to the vendor of leasehold property, which is subject to restrictive covenants.[10] A duty of disclosure is also contained in the misleading commercial practices provisions of the Consumer Protection Act 2007. Under s 45 of the Act, a trader is obliged to disclose to the purchaser any material information which the average consumer would need in order to make an informed decision on whether to enter into the transaction. The trader must disclose such information in a clear and unambiguous manner. However, space requires that this chapter is confined to the most important category of contracts to which a duty of disclosure applies; insurance contracts. Each of these categories has something in common: they are what Collins calls "relations of dependence".[11] One party has a substantial informational advantage over the other. The disadvantaged party has no reasonable means of remedying this disadvantage and so must rely on the other to tell him the truth. In the context of insurance contracts, "the Underwriter knows nothing and the man who comes to him to ask him to insure knows everything".[12] In addition, insurance contracts are particularly risky and, in the absence of a mechanism for acquiring enough information to assess that risk, players might be unwilling to enter into the insurance market and offer this very important service. The law redresses this unhealthy informational asymmetry by imposing a duty of disclosure to ensure that the truth is told to a reasonable extent. As Kronman has observed, "[i]nformation is the antidote to mistake".[13]

**[16–04]**

## II. The Duty of Utmost Good Faith and Insurance Contracts

Contracts *uberrimae fidei* are contracts of "utmost good faith". Insurance contracts, as contracts of utmost good faith, require an extremely high level of disclosure by the insured who makes a proposal for insurance to an insurance company. In *Joel v Law Union & Crown Insurance Co*,[14] Fletcher Moulton LJ commented that "[i]nsurers are thus in the highly favourable position that they are entitled not only to *bona fides* on the part of the applicant, but also to full disclosure of all knowledge possessed by the applicant that is material to the risk". According to Henchy J in the leading case of *Aro Road and Land Vehicles v Insurance Corporation of Ireland Ltd*,[15] the duty of disclosure

**[16–05]**

---

[7] *Geryani v O'Callaghan*, unreported, High Court, 25 January 1995.
[8] *Levett v Barclay's Bank plc* [1995] 2 All ER 615.
[9] A and B are in a fiduciary relationship if A necessarily reposes confidence in B as a result of which B gains influence over A. Examples of fiduciary contracts include contracts of partnership, family settlements and contracts of guarantee.
[10] *Power v Barrett* (1887) 19 LR (Ir) 450.
[11] Collins, *The Law of Contract* (LexisNexis, 2003), p 203.
[12] *Rozanes v Bowen* (1928) 32 Ll L Rep 98 *per* Scrutton LJ.
[13] Kronman, "Mistake, Disclosure, Information and the Law of Contracts" (1978) 7 J Leg St 1.
[14] [1908] 2 KB 863.
[15] [1986] IR 403.

in insurance contracts has two elements. First, the person filling in a proposal form is bound by a duty of utmost good faith—an extremely exacting duty of disclosure. He must answer any question on the form to the best of his knowledge. Secondly, if there is no proposal form, he must disclose all material matters within his knowledge. If the insured breaches this duty, the insurance company is entitled to avoid the contract of insurance and may repudiate liability if the insured comes to claim on his insurance policy.

## III. Knowledge and Disclosure

[16–06]     There are a number of important points to note at this stage regarding the insured's level of knowledge. The first point comes from examining the content of the duty set out by Henchy J in *Aro Road*. The insured is bound to answer and disclose to the best of his knowledge. He has no duty to disclose that which he did not know. The insured is required to be honest, not omniscient. In *Keating v New Ireland Assurance*,[16] Keating had entered a life assurance policy. Keating disclosed that he had undergone a medical examination for a digestive ailment. At that examination, in fact and unbeknownst to him, he had been diagnosed with angina. Later, Keating died as a result of the angina and the insurers tried to avoid the contract of insurance on the grounds of non-disclosure of a material fact. In his judgment, McCarthy J stated there was no obligation to disclose that of which you were not aware. The insurance company argued that constructive knowledge would suffice in place of actual knowledge. In other words, because Keating's doctor knew that he had angina, Keating himself ought to have known and, therefore, his non-disclosure of this fact was grounds for avoiding the insurance policy. However, McCarthy J stated that only actual knowledge would suffice, going on to say that "[i]f the proposer for life insurance has answered all the questions to the best of his ability and truthfully, his next-of-kin are not to be damnified because of his ignorance or obtuseness". However, McCarthy J acknowledged that there is a difference between genuine ignorance and wilful ignorance. In *Economides v Commercial Insurance*,[17] Brown LJ wrote:

> "Honesty of course requires ... that the assured does not wilfully shut his eyes to the truth. But that, sometimes called Nelsonian blindness – the deliberate putting of the telescope to the blind eye – is equivalent to knowledge."

[16–07]     That Nelsonian blindness is equivalent to knowledge is borne out by the case of *Curran v Norwich Union Life Insurance Co.*[18] The insured in this case had filled out a proposal form and in it declared that he was in good health. In fact, shortly before filling in the form, he had suffered what was diagnosed as a mild epileptic attack. He disagreed with his doctor and, accordingly, did not disclose it on the form. The court found that because the insured had good reason to believe, in line with medical advice, that he had suffered an epileptic attack, he was obliged to disclose this in his proposal form.

---

[16]  [1990] ILRM 110.

[17]  [1997] 3 WLR 1066.

[18]  Unreported, High Court, 30 October 1987.

A second important point is that the insurer will be presumed to already know **[16–08]** matters that are common knowledge so that the insured is not obliged to disclose these specifically. In *Brady v Irish National Insurance*,[19] an insurance company sought to avoid its contract with the owner of a boat on the basis that he had not disclosed that he would be using the boat's galley while the boat was laid up over the winter. O'Hanlon J held that it was a matter of common notoriety that boat owners use the galleys of their boats in this manner—the boat owner was not obliged to disclose it.

Thirdly, the test of failure to disclose is a strict one. The insurance company is **[16–09]** not obliged to prove that the insured was deliberately attempting to defraud them by non-disclosure. The law draws no distinction between innocent and fraudulent failure to disclose.

## IV. Materiality and the Reasonable Underwriter Test

It has been noted that only material matters must be disclosed. Materiality is not **[16–10]** linked in any way to the insured's ultimate reason for claiming on the insurance contract. Thus, in *Seaman v Fonereau*[20] the insured's failure to disclose that an insured ship was leaking rendered a contract of insurance on the ship voidable because the fact that the ship was leaking was a material matter. It did not matter that the insured party sought to claim on the insurance contract in respect of a matter unrelated to the leak. Similarly, in *Lambert v Co-operative Insurance Society Ltd*,[21] an insurance company was entitled to repudiate liability under an "All Risks" policy that covered some jewellery because the insured had not disclosed that her husband had been convicted of dishonesty offences.

The test for materiality is found in the judgment of Kenny J in *Chariot Inns v* **[16–11]** *Assicurazioni Generali.*[22] It is an objective test called the reasonable underwriter test:

> "What then is to be regarded as material to the risk against which the insurance is sought? It is not what the person seeking insurance regards as material nor is it what the insurance company regards as material. It is a matter or circumstance which would reasonably influence the judgment of a prudent insurer in deciding whether he would take the risk, and, if so, in determining the premium which he would demand. The standard by which materiality is to be determined is objective, not subjective."

Examples of matters that have been found to be material include the medical **[16–12]** history of a person taking out life assurance[23] and whether another company has refused to provide cover for the insured.[24] In order to determine what the reasonably prudent insurer would consider material in a particular situation, the court may call

---

[19] [1986] ILRM 669.

[20] (1743) 2 Stra 1183.

[21] [1975] 2 Lloyd's Rep 485.

[22] [1981] ILRM 173. The test here draws on that set out in s 18(2) of the Marine Insurance Act 1906.

[23] *Kelleher v Irish Life Assurance*, unreported, High Court, 16 December 1988.

[24] *Lockeyer & Woolf Ltd v Western Australia Insurance Co* [1936] 1 KB 408; *London Assurance v Mansel* (1879) 11 ChD 363.

experts in insurance matters to give evidence. *Chariot Inns* is a good example of the reasonable insurer test in operation. In that case, the insured had filled in an insurance proposal seeking insurance for licensed premises called Chariot Inns. A clause appeared in the form that asked the insured to disclose any claims made for loss over the previous five years. The insured had made a claim two years previously for a fire at another property on Leeson Street. They did not disclose this on the form; they considered that it was not necessary to do so because the fire had been at a different property to that being insured. When a fire occurred at the Chariot Inn, the insurance company repudiated liability. The insurance experts in court were unanimously of the opinion that the fire at Leeson Street was material to the risk that the insurance company was asked to insure. Accordingly, the Court found that this matter was one which would reasonably have affected the judgment of a prudent insurer in deciding whether to take the risk of insuring the Chariot Inn. The matter was material and ought to have been disclosed. Note that it is enough that the matter would have influenced the reasonable insurer's decision to accept the risk; it is not necessary to prove that it would have been decisive.

[16–13]     Because the reasonable underwriter test is not subjective, it does not matter that the actual underwriter in the case would not himself have thought a particular matter material. The contract may still be avoided. In the Australian case of *Mayne Nickless v Pegler*,[25] Samuels J explained as follows:

> "I do not think that it is generally open to examine what the insurer would in fact have done had he had the information not disclosed. The question is whether that information would have been relevant to the exercise of the insurer's option to accept or reject the insurance proposed."

[16–14]     This purely objective version of the reasonable underwriter test is subject to the criticism that it gives the underwriter the benefit of expert hindsight. This test does not catch the negligent or reckless underwriter. In *Zurich Central Accident and Liability Insurance Co Ltd v Morrison*,[26] Lord MacKinnon explained:

> "[I]t is not necessary further to prove that the mind of that actual insurer was so affected. In other words the insured could not rebut the claim to avoid the policy because of a material misrepresentation by a plea that the particular insurer concerned was so stupid, ignorant or reckless that he could not exercise the judgment of a prudent insurer and was in fact unaffected by anything the insured had misrepresented or concealed."

[16–15]     On this point, the modern English test for materiality is arguably preferable to the Irish. In *Pan Atlantic v Pine Top*,[27] a majority of the House of Lords added a subjective element to the existing reasonable underwriter test. An undisclosed fact will not be considered material unless a reasonably prudent underwriter would want to know the fact *and* the non-disclosure of that fact actually induced the insurer to enter

---

[25] [1974] 1 NSWLR 228.
[26] [1942] 1 All ER 529.
[27] [1994] 3 All ER 581.

into the contract of insurance. English courts are concerned with what the insurer would have done as well as with what he ought to have done.

There is a more general objection to the reasonable insurer test: why have the reasonable insurer test at all? Why not assess materiality by reference to the reasonable insured? McCarthy J asked this very question in *Aro Road* [28]: [16–16]

"Is it reasonable for an insurer to say: 'I expect disclosure of what I think is relevant or what I may think is relevant but which a reasonable proposer may not think of at all or, if he does, may not think is relevant?'"

The argument for imposing a duty of disclosure in insurance contracts rests on the presumption that the person completing the proposal form has an advantage over the insurer. The duty of disclosure and the penalty of voidability in the event of non-disclosure act as disincentives to the unscrupulous abuse of that advantage. However, although it has the aim of protecting insurers from fraud, the reasonable insurer test can also oppress parties who enter into contracts of insurance in good faith. It is important to remember that insurance companies enjoy far superior bargaining power to those who contract with them. Baron Richards was alive to this point in the old case of *Rose v Star Insurance Company* [29]: [16–17]

"It is most unjust to allow a company to disturb insurances after having taken the money of the party. The parties ensuring are frequently country gentlemen, ladies and other persons knowing nothing about the law. The papers are generally filled in the office of the company, and signed merely as a matter of form."

In theory, it is open to the insurer to consolidate its bargaining power by inflating the effect of the reasonable insurer test—for example, by using ambiguous or sparse proposal forms, which give the insured little guidance as to what matters will be considered material. Next we will consider how the Irish courts have restricted the effect of the reasonable insurer test, both by taking a liberal approach to the circumstances in which a lower duty of disclosure will be imposed on the insured and by limiting insurance companies' capacity to contract with the insured for a higher duty. [16–18]

## V. When the Reasonable Underwriter Test will not Apply

It is possible for the parties, if they choose, to contract out of the general requirement of utmost good faith disclosure. This idea was first introduced into Irish law in *Aro Road*.[30] In the Supreme Court, Henchy J found that the reasonably prudent underwriter test does not apply where the contract excludes the requirement of full disclosure. If an insurer chooses to exclude the disclosure requirement, then the principle of freedom of contract requires that that choice be upheld. Henchy J explained that the principle of utmost good faith [16–19]

---

[28] Above, n 15.
[29] (1850) 2 Ir Jur 206.
[30] Above, n 15.

"[l]ike most general legal rules ... is subject to exceptions. For instance, the contract itself may expressly or by necessary implication exclude the requirement of full disclosure. It is for the parties to make their own bargain – subject to any relevant statutory requirements – and if the insurer shows himself to be prepared to underwrite the risk without requiring full disclosure, he cannot later avoid the contract and repudiate liability on the ground of non-disclosure".

[16–20]     Henchy J contemplates that the insurer can waive the application of the reasonably prudent underwriter test by express provision in the contract. Aitken J in the English High Court accepted the same principle in *HIH Casualty v Chase Manhattan Bank* [31]:

"There are many cases where the courts have said that the insurer has 'waived' the duty of disclosure of the assured, usually by limiting the scope of the questions that it asks in a proposal form. It can also waive the duty by the nature of the insurance itself. If the scope of disclosure can be limited by these means then I think it can be accepted that it is conceptually possible to draft a clause in a contract of insurance whereby the parties agree that the *duty of disclosure* of the assured (or his agent) is excluded, or waived altogether."

[16–21]     However, the insurer may also be found to have waived the duty of utmost good faith by implication. Such a waiver may be inferred from the circumstances surrounding the conclusion of the contract or from the construction of the contractual document.

### The Circumstances of the Case

[16–22]     *Aro Road* was a case in which the plaintiff had agreed to sell and deliver goods to a company in Northern Ireland: there was no proposal form. When the carrier organised insurance for the goods, the underwriter only asked for the names and addresses of the consignor and the consignee and a description of the nature and value of the goods. The consignment was hijacked and lost. The insurance company repudiated liability on the basis that the plaintiff had not disclosed that its managing director had been convicted of a number of offences involving dishonesty several years earlier. Carroll J in the High Court applied the test in *Chariot Inns*. He found that the reasonable underwriter would have considered the managing director's previous convictions to be material, and, accordingly, the insurer was entitled to avoid the contract of insurance. However, Henchy J found that "over-the-counter" insurance contracts of the type concluded in this case implicitly waive the usual requirement of utmost good faith disclosure. This is because these types of contracts make full disclosure impractical and difficult, in particular because of the time factor. Thus, by adopting an over-the-counter method of sale, the insurer indicates to the insured that he is willing to provide cover even without disclosure to the usual standard. So, for example, when an air traveller buys insurance for his luggage at an airport just before boarding his plane, he cannot be expected to make full disclosure of all material circumstances. Henchy J wrote that in the instant case:

---

[31] [2001] 1 All ER 719.

"the informal, almost perfunctory, way in which CIE effected this insurance, their readiness to collect the premium and proceed to carry the goods to their destination as soon as they had ascertained the premium, showed a failure or unwillingness to give the insured company an opportunity to make full disclosure before the contract of insurance was concluded".

Accordingly, the standard of utmost good faith did not apply and the insurance policy could not be avoided. What standard applied instead? The judgment of McCarthy J indicates that in an over-the-counter situation, the insured is required to disclose only what *he* reasonably and genuinely considers material. Thus, the test that applies to this limited category of cases is not a "reasonable underwriter" test but a "reasonable insured" test. McCarthy J said further that the purchaser of insurance over the counter will not be penalised for a "failure of recollection". Thus, the managing director's long-forgotten convictions were immaterial. If the insurer who sells insurance in such circumstances wants to impose a higher standard on the insured, he must take time to ask the relevant questions. McCarthy J stated firmly: [16–23]

"If the judgement of an insurer is such as to require disclosure of what he thinks is relevant but which the reasonable assured, if he thought of it at all would not think relevant, then, in the absence of a question directed towards the disclosure of such a fact, the insurer, albeit prudent, cannot properly be held to be acting reasonably ... I do not know how the average citizen is to know what goes on in the insurer's mind, unless the insurer asks him by way of the questions in a proposal form or otherwise. I do not accept that he must seek out the proposed insurer and question him as to his reasonableness, his prudence, and what he considers material."

However, it is important to note that McCarthy J did not go so far as to give the insured free reign. While innocent non-disclosure will not avoid a contract concluded in these circumstances, fraudulent non-disclosure is still grounds for repudiating liability under an over-the-counter insurance policy. [16–24]

## Construction of the Contract

Sometimes a proposal form, by expressly asking certain questions, implies that disclosure of certain other matters is not required. Finlay CJ built on this idea in *Kelleher v Irish Life Assurance.*[32] He found that a court should hold that the insurer has waived the requirement that a certain, otherwise material, matter be disclosed "if a reasonable man reading the proposal form would conclude that the information over and above it which is in issue was not required". This test had already been proposed in the ancient case of *Carter v Boehm*[33]: [16–25]

"[I]f questions are asked on particular subjects and the answers to them are warranted, it may be inferred that the insurer has waived his right to information, either on the same matters, but outside the scope of the questions, or on matters kindred to the subject matter of the questions. Thus, if an insurer

---

[32] Unreported, High Court, 16 December 1988.
[33] (1766) 3 Burr 1905, ER.

251

asks, 'How many accidents have you had in the past three years?', it may well be implied that he does not want to know of accidents before that time, though these would still be material. If it were asked whether any of the proposer's parents, brothers or sisters had died of consumption or been afflicted with insanity, it might well be inferred that the insurer had waived similar information concerning more remote relatives, so that he could not avoid the contract for non-disclosure of an aunt's death of consumption or an uncle's insanity."

[16–26]     The facts in *Kelleher v Irish Life Assurance* were that the plaintiff had assured her husband's life under a special promotion. The offer of assurance consisted of two documents. One was the insurer's usual proposal form, asking general questions about the assured's health. A line was drawn through these questions indicating that these were not required to be answered. Instead the assured was asked to sign a declaration that he had not undergone medical treatment in the previous six months. The insurance company argued that, notwithstanding the second form, they were entitled to repudiate the contract because the fact that the assured had received treatment for cancer four years previously had not been disclosed. Finlay CJ found against the insurance company. He said that a reasonable man would assume that, provided he could truthfully answer that he had not had medical treatment within six months, he would be entitled to the insurance. The insurers had, therefore, limited the requirement of disclosure to this question and were not entitled to repudiate the contract for want of fuller disclosure.

## VI. Raising the Duty of Disclosure: "Basis of the Contract" Clauses

[16–27]     Often, insurance contracts will contain a clause called a "basis of the contract clause": a declaration warranting that the answers given in the proposal form are full and honest. A basis of contract clause makes the contract of insurance conditional on full and accurate disclosure. Disclosure under such circumstances must be absolutely accurate; even trivial inexactitude may be grounds for avoiding the contract. "Nothing tantamount will do or answer the purpose".[34] In *Keenan v Shield Insurance*,[35] Blayney J said that where an assured has signed a basis of contract clause, it is "not open to [him] to say that the obligation [to disclose] has been substantially complied with, or that the answer he made to a question was more or less accurate". In effect, a basis of contract clause imposes a higher standard of disclosure than utmost good faith. The standard becomes perfect accuracy, irrespective of its materiality and regardless of whether the insured has answered the questions in good faith and to the best of his knowledge. In *Keenan* itself, a contract for house and contents insurance was subject to a "basis of the contract" clause. The insured declared on the proposal form that he had made no previous claims. In fact, a claim for £53 had been made the previous year in respect of fire damage to a pump. Even though this was a trivial matter that would not have passed the reasonable and prudent underwriter test, the insurance company was entitled to avoid the contract. The insured had not met the higher standard of disclosure

---

[34] *Pawson v Watson* (1778) 2 Cowp 785.
[35] [1987] IR 113.

required of him; he had promised absolute disclosure and was obliged to make it. Similarly, in *Farrell v South East Lancashire Insurance Co Ltd*,[36] a basis of contract clause was grounds for avoiding a contract of insurance where a broker[37] mis-stated the value of a bus on the proposal form.

Again, the principle of freedom of contract applies here. If the insured party chooses to sign such a clause, he must abide by the consequences. However, the courts disapprove of basis of contract clauses as a practice. In *Zurich General Insurance v Morrison*,[38] Lord Greene MR described them as traps for the insured, while in *Anderson v Fitzgerald*[39] Lord St Leonards warned that the worst of these clauses are such that insurance contracts may not be worth the paper they are written on.[40] In keeping with the consumer welfarist attitude of the courts in these matters, it is crucial that if the insurer wishes to rely on a basis of contract clause that it makes the nature of the clause clear in plain and unequivocal language, such that a person of ordinary intelligence could understand without any difficulty. Lord St Leonards said as follows in *Anderson*[41]: [16–28]

> "A policy ought to be framed so that he who runs can read. It ought to be framed with such deliberate care that no form of expression by which, on the one hand, the party assured can be cut, or by which, on the other, the company can be cheated shall be found upon the face of it. Nothing ought to be wanting in it, the absence of which may lead to such results."

The threshold for the insurance company is a high one. In *Joel v Law Union*,[42] Fletcher Moulton J explained this requirement in terms of intention: [16–29]

> "[I]f there is the slightest doubt that the insurers have failed to make clear to the man on whom they have exercised their right of requiring full information that he is consenting thus to contract, we ought to refuse to regard the correctness of the answers given as being a condition of the policy. In other words, the insurers must prove by clear and express language the *animus contrahendi* on the part of the applicant."

McCarthy J imposed the same requirement in *Keating v New Ireland Assurance*[43] as follows: [16–30]

---

[36] [1933] IR 26.

[37] An insurance broker will be treated as the insured party's agent. Thus, though it was the broker who made the mistake here, the insured bore the loss. If a broker makes such a mistake through his own negligence then, naturally, the insured can recover the resulting loss by suing him for negligence and breach of contract.

[38] [1942] 1 All ER 529.

[39] (1853) 4 HL Cas 484.

[40] See also *Joel v Law Union* [1908] 2 KB 863 *per* Fletcher Moulton J: "I wish I could adequately warn the public against such practices on the part of the insurance offices".

[41] Above, n 39.

[42] [1908] 2 KB 863.

[43] Above, n 16.

"Insurers may stipulate for any warranty they please and if an assured undertakes that warranty, although it may be something not within his or her knowledge, he or she must abide the consequences. But when insurers intent that there is to be a warranty of that sort they must make it perfectly plain that such is their intention and they must use unequivocal language such as persons with ordinary intelligence may without any difficulty understand."

[16–31]     McCarthy J went on to say that where a basis of contract clause is not expressed in such unambiguous terms, it will be read *contra proferentem* —against the insurance company. Finlay CJ reaffirmed this proposition in *Brady v Irish National Insurance Co.* [44]

---

[44] [1986] IR 698. See also *Analog Devices v Zurich* [2005] IESC 12.

# CHAPTER 17
# Mistake

## I. Introduction

It often happens that a person, having made a contract, realises that it is not the contract he thought it was. He may protest that he has made a "mistake". As a matter of ordinary morality, it might be said that it is unduly harsh to hold such a man to his contract. On the other hand, it is clear that trifling errors should not be used as excuses by a person who wants to be released from a foolish bargain. Lord Baggally made this point in the old case of *Tamplin v James*[1] saying that:

> "[T]he Defendant cannot be allowed to evade the performance of [his contract] by the simple statement that he has made a mistake. Were such to be the law the performance of a contract could rarely be enforced upon an unwilling party who was also unscrupulous".

Contract law recognises a doctrine of mistake. However, it is a severely **[17–02]** restricted one. By limiting the categories of mistake which give rise to remedies at law

**[17–01]**

---

[1] (1880) 15 Ch D 215.

and at equity, the courts promote certainty. Parties can trust that their contracts will not lightly be set aside by the courts. In addition, by demonstrating to parties that they will generally have to bear responsibility for their mistakes, the courts incentivise the parties to provide for the consequences of any potential mistakes at the time of negotiation. The law of mistake is a wide and complex area, and so this chapter only deals with the essentials: when a contract can be avoided for mistake in law; when a contract can be set aside for mistake in equity; rectification of inaccurate contractual documents; the plea of *non est factum*; and the status of mistakes of law.

## II. The Categories of Mistake

[17–03]    There are two important categories of mistake: common mistake and "offer and acceptance" mistake.[2] The idea of common mistake (also called "shared" or "identical" mistake) contemplates that both parties make the same mistake. They do come to an agreement—their consent is real and present. However, the law nullifies that consent because it is based on a fundamental and shared misconception. An "offer and acceptance" mistake can occur where only one party is fundamentally mistaken ("unilateral mistakes"), or where both parties are fundamentally mistaken, but in different ways ("mutual" mistakes). The core idea here is that there is never a contract in the first place. The parties are not "singing from the same hymn sheet"—they are not *ad idem*. Thus, contracts are not, strictly speaking, void for unilateral or mutual mistake. It is simply that the mistake prevents an agreement from being formed at all. There is no talk of damages here: damages are not generally available for mistake. The contract is either declared void at law or rescinded at equity.

## III. Policies Underpinning Mistake

[17–04]    Two ideas are fundamental to our understanding of mistake. The first is the familiar idea of objective intent. In particular, mistake cases turn on how successful or careful each party has been in expressing his intent objectively so that his contract is shaped to his expectations. The second is the concept of risk. Parties to any contract run the risk that their information or judgement may fail them—that they may turn out to have been mistaken. Judges are reluctant to use the doctrine of mistake, preferring that contracting parties allocate the risk of error at the planning stage of the contract. When the doctrine of mistake is used, the cases are ultimately about deciding who should bear the consequences when errors come home to roost. So Wheeler and Shaw have called the law of mistake "the emergency toolkit of risk allocation in the law of contract".[3]

## IV. The No-Contract Scenario: When is a Contract Void *Ab Inito* for Mistake?

[17–05]    When a contract is void *ab initio*, that means that it is void from the beginning and for all purposes. When a court declares that a contract is void in this way, it is as if the contract never existed at all.

---

[2] McKendrick, *Contract Law* (6th ed., Palgrave, 2005), p 66.
[3] Wheeler & Shaw, *Contract Law: Cases, Materials and Commentary* (Clarendon, 1994), p 680.

## Common Mistake

Suppose A buys a rugby ball from B for €1,200. Both believe it to be a ball from the Munster victory over the All Blacks in October 1978. But it turns out to be an ordinary rugby ball of no significance. Does the contract for its sale still stand? The law is that a contract based on the parties' fundamental and shared mistake about the subject-matter of the contract is void. It is absolutely crucial to understand that in cases of common mistake, a contract is "voided" or prevented from arising, despite the objective presence of *consensus ad idem*.[4] Because the doctrine of common mistake allows a complete agreement to be set aside, it has significant implications for the idea of sanctity of contract. As Lord Atkin explained in *Bell v Lever Bros*[5]: **[17–06]**

> "[I]t is of paramount importance that contracts should be observed, and that if parties honestly comply with the essentials of the formation of contracts – i.e., agree in the same terms on the same subject-matter – they are bound."

As a result, the courts treat common mistake as the narrowest of escape hatches. In *O'Neill v Ryan*,[6] Costello J said that "the circumstances in which a shared common mistake will nullify a contract are extremely limited..." A contract can only be avoided for common mistake where the following three criteria are fulfilled[7]: **[17–07]**

1. The mistake is substantially shared by the parties—both parties are mistaken about the same thing.
2. The risk of mistake is not expressly or impliedly allocated to either party.
3. The mistake is fundamental in nature.

### *Allocation of Risk*

> "Logically, before one can turn to the rules as to mistake … one must first determine whether the contract itself, by express or implied condition precedent or otherwise provides who bears the risk of the relevant mistake. It is at this hurdle that many pleas of mistake will either fail or prove to be unnecessary. Only if the contract is silent on the point is there scope for invoking mistake."[8] **[17–08]**

Often the parties to a contract will expressly allocate the risk of common mistake as between themselves, for example by means of an exemption clause. Suppose A and B contract for the sale of A's violin. Both A and B believe that the violin is a Stradivarius. In fact, A has undertaken as part of his contract with B that the violin is a Stradivarius. However, both are mistaken. In fact, the violin is an imitation. Does the doctrine of mistake apply? The doctrine of mistake is irrelevant here because, by his express **[17–09]**

---

[4] *O'Neill v Ryan* [1992] 1 IR 166.
[5] [1932] AC 161.
[6] [1991] ILRM 672.
[7] See Collins, *The Law of Contract* (4th ed., LexisNexis Butterworths, 2003), p 126. See also *Great Peace Shipping v Tsavliris (International) Ltd.* [2002] EWCA Civ 1407.
[8] *Associated Japanese Bank (International) Ltd. v Credit du Nord SA* [1989] 1 WLR 255 *per* Steyn J.

warranty that the violin is a Stradivarius, A has assumed the risk that he may turn out to be mistaken.[9] Along the same lines, imagine that A, at the time of contracting, said to B, "I believe that the violin is a genuine Stradivarius, but I by no means guarantee it",[10] and B nevertheless entered into the contract to buy the violin. In this situation, the doctrine of mistake is also irrelevant. By entering into the contract despite A's warning, B assumes the risk associated with any mistake as to the genuineness of the violin. This rule was applied in *William Sindall v Cambridgeshire CC*.[11] In this case, a building company had agreed to purchase land from the county council. The land was sold expressly "subject to easements, liabilities and public rights affecting it". At the time, neither party knew that a foul sewer ran under the land. When this was discovered, the purchasers argued that the contract should be set aside for common mistake—both parties had mistakenly thought that there was no sewer under the land. However, because the purchasers had bought the land "subject to easements, liabilities and public rights affecting it", they had assumed the risk that there might be a sewer under the land. Therefore, the doctrine of common mistake did not apply.

[17–10]     In some cases, where the risk of common mistake has not been expressly assumed by either party, the court will imply an assumption of risk on the basis of fault. The Australian case of *McRae v Commonwealth Disposals Commissions*[12] is a case in point. The Commission in this case invited tenders for the salvage of a shipwrecked oil tanker, which they believed to be lying at a particular location. The plaintiffs' tender was successful, and they went to some trouble and expense in preparing for the salvage. As it turned out, the tanker had never existed. Thus, a common mistake existed sufficient to void the contract. However, the Court, rather than allow the contract to fall, found that the Commission had implicitly undertaken that a tanker such as that sought did exist. It seems clear that there is a strong connection between fault giving rise to a mistake and the imposition of responsibility for that mistake. The Court explained:

> "[T]he Commission cannot in this case rely on any mistake as avoiding the contract, because any mistake was induced by the serious fault of their own servants, who asserted the existence of a tanker recklessly and without any reasonable ground. There was a contract, and the Commission contracted that a tanker existed in the position specified. Since there was no such tanker, there has been a breach of contract, and the plaintiffs are entitled to damages for that breach."

### Fundamental Mistake

[17–11]     Only a fundamental common mistake will be sufficient to void a contract. This requirement is arguably the most important of the three because it explains precisely why common mistake can serve to void a contract despite the presence of *consensus ad*

---

[9] See *Smith v Zimbalist* 2 Cal App 2d 324, 38 P 2d 170 (1934); *Peco Arts Inc v Hazlitt Gallery Ltd.* [1983] 3 All ER 193; *Kalsep Lt v X-Flow BV, The Times*, 3 May 2001.

[10] See *Smith v Harrison* (1857) 26 LJ Ch 412 where the seller of land sold "my title *if any*" to the land.

[11] [1994] 1 WLR 1016.

[12] (1951) 84 CLR 377.

*idem*. The fact that a contract was concluded subject to a fundamental common mistake points to a serious defect in the parties' agreement. Consent is present in cases of common mistake, but it is not meaningful because the parties are labouring under a misapprehension as to the very "core" or "root" of the contract.

It appears from the cases that a mistake will be fundamental in one of two **[17–12]** situations. The first is where it renders performance of the contract impossible. The second is where it renders performance of the contract so different from the performance contemplated at the time of contracting that the court is justified in setting the contract aside.

## Makes Performance Impossible

What happens if parties enter into a contract for a subject matter which, unknown to **[17–13]** them, no longer exists? Cases in which this happens are known as *res extincta* cases. *Strickland v Turner*[13] concerned a contract of annuity relating to the life of a person who both parties, at the time of entering into the contract, mistakenly believed was alive. In fact, that person was already dead. The contract, therefore, was avoided for mistake as to the existence of the contract's subject-matter. It was impossible to perform the contract because it is impossible to insure the life of a dead man. Along the same lines is *Galloway v Galloway*.[14] The subject-matter of this contract was the parties' marriage. The contract was a separation agreement. Both parties, however, were mistaken in thinking that there was a marriage to separate. In fact, they were not married at all as the husband's first wife had been alive at the time of their purported marriage. Thus the separation agreement was void. It was impossible to separate the couple because they had never been married. The classic case, however, is *Couturier v Hastie*.[15] The contract here was for the sale of a cargo of corn which both parties believed was on its way from Salonica to England aboard ship. In fact, unknown to either party, before the contract was formed, the master of the ship had already sold the corn at Tunis because it had already begun to deteriorate. The subject-matter of the contract was not available for sale at the time the contract was made. Buyer and seller were mistaken to think it was available and, accordingly, the contract was avoided.[16] It was impossible to buy the corn because it had already been sold.

A similar category of cases deal with *res sua* —cases about mistakes as to title **[17–14]** where one party has agreed to transfer ownership of an item to another in the mistaken belief that he owns the item. *Cooper v Phibbs*[17] establishes that such a mistake will be

---

[13] (1852) 7 Ex 208. See also *Scott v Coulson* [1903] 2 Ch 249; *Pritchand and Merchants and Tradesmans Mutual Life Assurance* (1858) 3 CBNS 622.

[14] (1914) 30 TLR 531.

[15] (1856) 5 HL 673. See also *Associated Japanese Bank (International) Ltd. v Credit du Nord*, above, n 8.

[16] Section 6 of the Sale of Goods Act 1893 stipulates that a contract for the sale of goods will be void if the goods have perished at the time of the contract unless the seller is already aware that they have perished.

[17] (1867) LR 2 HL 149.

fundamental. That case concerned a contract for the sale of a fishery. The parties were under the mistaken belief that the purchaser did not already own the fishery. In fact, he was already the owner under a private Act of Parliament.[18] The contract was void because it was impossible for the purchaser to buy a fishery that he already owned.

### Makes Performance Essentially and Radically Different From That Bargained For

[17–15] A common mistake as to the fundamental character of the subject-matter of the contract will render it void. A distinction is traditionally drawn between mistakes as to identifying qualities of the subject-matter and mistakes as to other, less important qualities.[19] As was acknowledged by Lord Steyn in *Associated Japanese Bank v Credit du Nord*, and later by Lord Phillips in *Great Peace*, a mistake as to a quality of the subject-matter will only exceptionally be treated as fundamental. Outside the *res sua* and *res extincta* cases, the doctrine is rarely applied. Where the doctrine does apply, the thing actually delivered or received must be essentially and radically different in substance from the thing bargained. The classic explanation of the distinction between mistake as to quality and mistake as to identity is that set out by Lord Atkin in *Bell v Lever Bros*[20]:

> "Mistake as to the quality of the thing contracted for raises more difficult questions. In such a case a mistake will not affect assent unless it is the mistake of both parties, and is as to the existence of some quality which makes the thing without the quality essentially different from the thing it was believed to be."[21]

[17–16] Bell was chairman of a subsidiary of Lever Bros. The purported contract at issue here was a compensation agreement entered into because Lever Bros wanted to terminate Bell's contract of service. Under this golden handshake agreement, Bell agreed to accept £30,000 in exchange for his consent to the termination. At the time of the agreement, both Bell and Lever Bros were labouring under the mistake that the compensation agreement was necessary to terminate Bell's contract of service. Lever Bros subsequently discovered that they could have terminated the service contract without this compensation agreement and so sought to have the compensation agreement set aside for common mistake. The Court held, however, that the mistake here was not one as to an identifying quality of the compensation agreement. In the opinion of the Court, had Bell and Lever Bros been asked at the time of the

---

[18] Section 12 of the Sale of Goods Act 1893 implies a condition that the vendor of goods has good title to them. The innocent party has a right of repudiation or a right to damages in case of breach.

[19] Treitel, *An Outline of the Law of Contract* (6th ed, Oxford, 2004), p 124.

[20] Above, n 5. *Cf Sybron Corp v Rochem Ltd.* [1984] Ch 112.

[21] *ibid.* at 218. This view of mistake was adopted in *Western Potato v Durnan* [1985] ILRM 5.

compensation agreement what they were contracting about, they would have said "a compensation agreement". They would not have identified it as "a compensation agreement necessary to terminate Bell's contract of service". The mistake as to the necessity of the compensation agreement to terminate Bell's contract of service did not void the compensation agreement because that mistake did not go to the identity of the subject-matter of the compensation agreement. Lever Bros had received, in essence, what they bargained for.

The reasoning in *Bell v Lever Bros* is less than convincing. Remember that Lever Bros handed over £30,000, a fortune at the time, "by mistake". It is interesting to note that the minority in *Bell v Lever Bros* found that the mistake was "as fundamental to the bargain as any error one can imagine".[22] So what does "essentially different" mean? What is the difference between identity and quality? The ideas of essence and difference can be extremely subjective. Lord Atkin gave an example of non-fundamental mistake in *Bell v Lever Bros*[23], which vividly illustrates this point:

> "A buys a picture from B; both A and B believe it to be the work of an old master and a high price is paid. It turns out to be a modern copy. A has no remedy in the absence of representation or warranty."

What Lord Atkin is saying is that, fundamentally, the subject-matter of the contract between A and B is "a painting". This is a peculiar view. As Treitel observes:

> "[A] person who had just paid ten million pounds for what both parties believed to be an old master would surely say he had bought (for example) 'a Rembrandt'. It would be simply facetious for him to say that he had just bought 'a picture'."[24]

Treitel, therefore, argues that the better view is that such a mistake should be regarded as going to identity and, therefore, as fundamental.[25] However, *Leaf v International Galleries*[26] confirms the correctness of Lord Atkin's formulation. That case mirrored Lord Atkin's artwork hypothesis. The purchaser in *Leaf* bought a painting which he believed to be the work of the great artist Constable. The painting turned out not to be. The Court did not agree that this was a fundamental mistake. In the Court's view, the purchaser had obtained, in substance, exactly what he had

**[17–17]**

**[17–18]**

**[17–19]**

---

[22] *ibid.* at 208 *per* Warrington LJ.
[23] *ibid.* at 224.
[24] Treitel, *op. cit.*, p 125.
[25] It might be argued, however, that the later case of *Grist v Bailey* [1967] Ch 532 suggests a more liberal approach to the definition of fundamental mistake.
[26] [1950] 2 KB 86.

contracted to buy. As it stands, this test for fundamental mistake as to the identity of subject-matter is so narrow that it is difficult to imagine when it might be fulfilled.[27]

[17–20]     The identity/quality distinction as set out above is difficult as a matter of instinct. Indeed, Farnsworth has called such reasoning "specious and artificial" with a primary aim of concealing the exercise of judicial discretion.[28] An alternative explanation of this category of cases is available. It could be said that whether a mistake is fundamental depends on its effect on the performance of the contract—*on how the performance received differs from that intended and envisaged*. A simple example of this analysis in operation is the case of *Frederick E Rose Ltd. v William H Pim Junior & Co Ltd.*[29] The contract was for the sale of "feveroles". Both parties thought that "feveroles" were regular horsebeans. In fact, they were "feves", a less valuable type of horsebean. The Court did not find fundamental mistake here. The parties contracted for horsebeans, and horsebeans were what the plaintiff got, not something essentially different. There is a difference between horsebeans and feves, but not one so dramatic in its effect on the performance of the contract as to be fundamental.[30] The contract was not void. The *Great Peace Shipping* [31] case hammers this point home. A ship, the *Great Peace*, was hired to deviate from its route to come to the aid of another ship, the *Cape Providence*, which had gotten into difficulties. At the time of entering into the contract, both parties thought that the ships were only 35 miles apart. In fact, the distance between them was almost 410 miles. That was a material mistake, but was it fundamental? In the Court of Appeal's view, it was not. "The fact that the vessels were further apart than both parties had appreciated did not mean that it was impossible to perform the contractual adventure". The *Great Peace* could still have arrived in time to provide the same service contracted for in the manner contemplated by the parties. The mistake's effect on performance was minimal. Therefore, the mistake was not fundamental. *Great Peace* would appear to impose such stringent a test of fundamentality that the scope of this type of common mistake is very limited indeed. Lord Phillips described the doctrine of fundamental mistake as a rule by which "if it transpires that one or both of the parties have agreed to do something which is

---

[27] Certainly, the American doctrine is more flexible in its notion of fundamental mistake, as illustrated by the classic case of *Sherwood v Walker* 66 Mich 568, 33 NW 919 (1887). The case here concerned the sale of a cow called "Rose 2d of Aberlone", believed by both purchaser and seller to be sterile and sold by the pound for a total of $80. On the day when the purchaser came to collect Rose, the seller refused to part with her on the grounds that she was now in calf. As a breeder, Rose was worth at least $750. Both seller and plaintiff had been mistaken in thinking that she was barren. Was this mistake fundamental? Morse J argued that it was as follows:

> "It is true that she is now the identical animal that they thought her to be when the contract was made; there is no mistake as to the identity of the creature. Yet the mistake was not of the mere quality of the animal, but went to the very nature of the thing. A barren cow is substantially a different creature than a breeding one … [T]he mistake affected the character of the animal for all time, and for her present and ultimate use. She was not in fact the animal, or the kind of animal, the defendants intended to sell or the plaintiff to buy … The thing sold and bought had in fact no existence."

[28] Farnsworth, *Contracts* (2nd ed, Little, Brown and Co, 1990), p 692.

[29] [1953] 2 QB 450.

[30] See also *Harrison & Jones v Bunten & Lancaster* [1953] 1 QB 646.

[31] Above, n 7.

*impossible* to perform, no obligation arises out of that agreement". The Court of Appeal maintained this position in *Brennan v Bolt Burden*.[32]

An older case which demonstrates the importance of a substantial difference **[17–21]** between the bargain intended and the bargain received in establishing a case of common mistake is *Nicholson and Venn v Smith-Marriott*.[33] In that case, linen was sold by description as the authentic property of Charles I. Hallett J said that "a Georgian relic ... is an 'essentially different' thing from a Carolean relic"; what was purchased were "different things in substance from those which the plaintiffs sought to buy and believed they had bought". The Court relied in this decision on its finding that the description of the napkins was a term of the contract. The intent of the purchaser was to buy Carolean napkins. This went to the identity of the napkins and to the nature of the performance the purchaser bargained for. This observation points to a key method by which parties can protect themselves from common mistake—by being clear in their terms and undertakings.

This approach to *Bell v Lever Bros* was adopted recently in *Intrum Justitia BV v* **[17–22]** *Legal and Trade Financial Services Ltd*.[34] The plaintiff had agreed to purchase a subsidiary of the defendant. Neither party knew that one Colin Thorpe had been embezzling funds from the subsidiary company. The question for the Court was whether fundamental common mistake was therefore present. O'Sullivan J held that "the effect of the fraud [did] not mean that the subject matter of the share purchase agreement is essentially different from the one contracted for." O'Sullivan J in effect examined the difference between what the plaintiffs had intended to purchase and what they in fact purchased. He found that in purchasing the company, the plaintiff had specific objectives in mind, *inter alia*, the acquisition of the company's blue chip client base, its good employees and the disclosed revenue stream. None of these objectives had been substantially defeated by the revelations of embezzlement. Accordingly, no fundamental mistake was present within the meaning of *Bell v Lever Bros*.

## Offer and Acceptance Mistake

It has been noted that an "offer and acceptance" mistake (in which both parties are **[17–23]** mistaken but the parties do not share their mistake) prevents a contract from coming into existence in the first place.[35] In *Mespil v Capaldi*,[36] O'Hanlon J set out the nature of that category of mistake as follows:

"It is of the essence of an enforceable simple contract that there be a *consensus ad idem*, expressed in an offer and an acceptance. Such a consensus cannot be said to exist unless there is a correspondence between the offer and the acceptance. If the offer made is accepted by the other person in a fundamentally different sense from that in which it was tendered by the offeror, and the circumstances are objectively such as to justify such an acceptance,

---

[32] [2005] QB 3.
[33] (1947) 177 LT 189.
[34] [2005] IEHC 190.
[35] *Ferguson v Merchant Banking* [1993] ILRM 136.
[36] [1986] ILRM 373.

there cannot be said to be the meeting of minds which is essential for an enforceable contract. In such circumstances the alleged contract is a nullity."

[17–24]     The courts here are hard on the party prejudiced by his mistake. In order to negate consent, the mistake must meet three stringent criteria. First, it must have induced the contract (17–25). Secondly, it must be operative (17–26). Finally, it must be fundamental (17–39). If a mistake does not meet each of these three criteria, the affected contract cannot be avoided. The prejudiced party will have no relief at law and only limited relief at equity.

### Mistakes Inducing the Contract

[17–25]     The mistake must be one without which the mistaken party would not have entered into the contract. If, at the time of entering into the contract, the party was conscious of the possibility that he might be mistaken, he cannot subsequently rely on that mistake to invalidate the contract. O' Sullivan J raised this very point in *Intrum Justitia BV v Legal and Trade Financial Services Ltd.*[37]

### Operative Mistakes

[17–26]     It has already been said that an objective test governs all questions of intention at contract law. The cases on "offer and acceptance" mistake tap into the debate on the utility of the objective test. Some commentators argue that they form a limited category of cases where a mistake will be "operative", or, in other words, where the court will take account of a party's *subjective* mistake.[38] These cases can be explained perfectly well on a contextual view of the objective test. This debate will be explored through analysis of the three broad classes of operative mistake set out below. For now, however, the concept of "operative mistake" will suffice as shorthand for the idea of a mistake that prevents *consensus ad idem* in the objective sense.

### Mutual Mistake: Perfect Ambiguity

[17–27]     A mutual mistake occurs where the parties are at cross purposes. The mistake must be fundamental if the contract is to be avoided. Objectively, the plaintiff intends X while the defendant intends Y. A intends to sell pearls to B while B intends to buy melons from A. The classic case of *Raffles v Wichelhaus*[39] concerned a contract for the sale of cotton to arrive on the ship *Peerless* from Bombay. The plaintiff was referring to a ship called *Peerless*, sailing from Bombay in December. Alas, the defendant "meant and intended" another ship, also called *Peerless*, and also sailing from Bombay, but in October. The Court found that there was no agreement. There was a mutual mistake; the plaintiff intended to buy the cotton from one ship and the defendant intended to buy the cotton from another. There was no sensible basis for choosing between the conflicting intentions and, accordingly, no *consensus ad idem* could be found. This case is easily explained on the objective test. Oliver Wendell Holmes, in his *The Common Law*, did so as follows:

"The law has nothing to do with the actual state of the parties' minds. In contract, as elsewhere, it must go by externals and judge parties by their

---

[37] Above, n 33.

[38] McKendrick, *Contract Law: Text, Cases and Materials* (OUP, 2003), p 25.

[39] (1864) 2 H & C 906. See Simpson, "Contracts for Cotton to Arrive: the Case of the Two Ships *Peerless*" (1989) 11 *Cardozo Law Review* 287.

conduct. If there had been but one "Peerless", and the defendant had said "Peerless" by mistake, meaning "Peri", he would have been bound. The true ground of the decision was not that each party meant a different thing from the other ... but that each said a different thing. The plaintiff offered one thing, the defendant expressed his assent to another."[40]

*Megaw v Molloy*[41] is an old Irish case along the same lines. The plaintiff hired a broker to sell his maize for him. He intended the broker to sell some maize that had been imported on the ship, *Emma Pleasant*. The maize was sold by sample. However, on the morning of the sale, a mix-up occurred so that the sample of maize labelled as coming from the *Emma Pleasant* in fact came from another ship, the *Jessie Parker*. The defendant bought maize from the broker based on his inspection of this sample. Objectively, the defendant intended to buy maize from the cargo he had sampled—the cargo of the *Jessie Parker*. Objectively, the plaintiff intended to sell maize from the cargo he had named—the cargo of the *Emma Pleasant*. The parties were at cross purposes. They did not have any contract because of mutual mistake.

[17–28]

## Unilateral Mistake

*Raffels v Wichelhaus* is a "mutual" mistake case. The next category of "offer and acceptance" mistake is "unilateral". Only one party is mistaken. Ordinarily, a unilateral mistake will have no effect. To understand why this is, look at *Centrovincial Estates plc v Merchant Investors Assurance Co Ltd.*[42] In this case a landlord mistakenly offered to renew his tenant's lease at £65,000. Unknown to the tenant, the landlord had really meant to renew at £126,000 annually. This transaction must be viewed objectively, ignoring the landlord's innermost intent. On outward appearances there was *consensus ad idem*. The landlord appeared to offer at £65,000, and the tenant accepted at that rate. There was no objective indicator of the landlord's mistake and so that mistake was not operative. Similarly, the mistake in *Stapleton v Prudential Insurance*[43] was not operative. The plaintiff had entered into an insurance contract under the genuine misapprehension that she would receive £25 at the end of 11 years. Sullivan P held that, because her mistake was not objectively apparent to the insurance company at the time of entering into the contract, the contract could not be set aside. A unilateral mistake will only bite where it would be unjust to allow the non-mistaken party to take advantage of it as where he was aware of the mistake, or where the mistake was induced by his negligence.

[17–29]

## Where Mistake Known to the Other Party

If one party to a contract knowingly takes advantage of the other's mistake in order to "snap up" a bargain which the mistaken party would not want any part in, the law may avoid that contract. *Gill v McDowell*[44] clarifies the parameters of this rule. In *Gill*, the plaintiff had bought a hermaphrodite animal mistakenly believing it to be a heifer. Gibson J set out the law as follows:

[17–30]

---

[40] Holmes, *The Common Law* (1881) 242.
[41] (1878) 2 LR Ir 530.
[42] [1983] Com LR 158. See also *Wood v Scarth* (1855) 2 K & J 33.
[43] (1928) 62 ILTR 56. See also *Jameson v National Benefit Trust Co* (1902) 2 NIJR 19.
[44] [1903] 2 IR 463.

"Where the seller knows that the buyer is under a mistake as to the subject matter contracted to be sold there is no enforceable contract. The plaintiff bought what he thought the defendant was professing to sell as a heifer. If the plaintiff had expressed his meaning in words, and the defendant said nothing, or if the defendant had expressly sold the beast as a heifer, unquestionably there would have been no valid sale. Where nothing is said on either side, if the vendor knows that the purchaser intends a different contract from what he himself contemplates, he cannot by silence impose on the purchaser a contract which he knows the latter never intended to make ... The vendor cannot force on the purchaser an article which he knows the latter never proposed to buy."

[17–31]     Of course, where a party has no reason to suspect that the other party is mistaken, where the mistake is purely subjective, the contract cannot later be avoided. Russell LJ gave an eloquent defence of this rule in *Riverlate Properties v Paul*[45]:

"If a man may be said to have been fortunate in obtaining a property at a bargain price, or in terms that make it a good bargain, because the party unknown to him has made a miscalculation or other mistake, some high-minded men might consider it appropriate that he should agree to a fresh bargain to cure the miscalculation or mistake, abandoning his good fortune. But if equity were to enforce the views of those high-minded men, we have no doubt that it would ... be venturing upon the field of moral philosophy in which it would soon be in difficulties."

[17–32]     There are also pragmatic reasons for enforcing this principle. In *Mespil Ltd. v Capaldi,*[46] the Supreme Court noted that:

"[b]usiness relations would be thrown into undesirable uncertainty if a party to an agreement, who at the time gave no indication that he did not understand what he was doing, could later renounce the agreement on subjective considerations. If he freely and competently entered into the agreement, he will not normally escape being bound by it by saying that he misunderstood the effect".

[17–33]     The key case here is *Hartog v Colin & Shields,*[47] where the seller offered to sell 3,000 Argentine hare skins at a certain price "per pound". The buyer purported to accept this offer. However, the seller had made a mistake in making his offer. He should have priced the skins "per piece". The effect of his mistake was that he had offered to sell the skins at one-third of their value since there were three skins to the pound. Accordingly, the seller refused to deliver the skins and the buyer sued for damages. The Court held that there was no contract since the buyer "must have realised, and did in fact know, that a mistake had occurred". There are two ways of explaining *Hartog v Colin & Shields*. First, it could be said that where the buyer actually knows that the seller has made a mistake as to terms, he cannot take advantage of that mistake to "snatch" a bargain. However, it is difficult to understand

---

[45] [1975] Ch 133, 140.

[46] Above, n 35.

[47] [1939] All ER 566.

why *Hartog v Colin & Shields* is explained in terms of the subjective intent of the non-mistaken party when it can be adequately explained in terms of the objective intent of the mistaken party. Simply put, one can arrive at the same result in *Hartog* using the reasonable man test. The seller's subjective intent aside, in the *Hartog* case, the buyer "could not reasonably have supposed" that the seller had intended to sell the skins at a price per pound. No reasonable trader operating in the skins business in *Hartog*'s time would have thought that the offer at issue was genuine. Objectively viewed, the seller's intent was not to offer the skins at that price and so any purported acceptance of that offer is without effect.

To similar effect is *Cundy v Lindsay*.[48] Lindsay produced handkerchiefs. [17–34] Blenkarn was a fraudster who wrote to order handkerchiefs from Lindsay, signing his name to look like that of Blenkiron & Co, a reputable firm of whom Lindsay were aware. Lindsay supplied the handkerchiefs to "Blenkiron & Co" at the address Blenkarn had given, believing that they were contracting with Blenkiron & Co. The Court found that there was no contract between Lindsay and Blenkarn since Lindsay had mistakenly believed that he was dealing with someone else. Lord Cairns asked:

> "[H]ow is it possible to imagine that ... any contract could have arisen between the respondent Lindsay and Blenkarn, the dishonest man? Of him they knew nothing, and of him they never thought. With him they never intended to deal. Their minds never, even for an instant of time, rested upon him, and as between him and them there was no consensus of mind which could lead to any agreement."

The Court in this case takes a different approach to *Hartog*, explaining its [17–35] decision in terms of the mistaken party's subjective intent. It could be explained in the vein of *Hartog* by saying that Blenkarn should not be allowed to abuse a mistake of which he was subjectively aware. But, again, an objective explanation is available. The reasonable buyer looking at how Lindsay conducted themselves would have concluded that they did not intend to deal with Blenkarn and that they were mistaken in doing so. Of particular importance in this regard was the use of the name "Blenkiron & Co" in the correspondence between the two. Objectively viewed, Lindsay's intent was not to sell to Blenkarn, and so any purported acceptance of that "offer" cannot stand.

An example of an Irish case which applies this principle is *Lucy v Laurel* [17–36] *Construction*.[49] Laurel agreed to sell a house to Lucy on the basis of written plans. The plans mistakenly said that the site would be 170 feet long. In fact, Laurel intended the plot to be 120 feet long. Mr Lucy was not told this. Accordingly, Laurel's mistake was inoperative. The contract stood as originally agreed. Another interesting modern case is that of *Chwee King Keong v Digilandmall.com*.[50] The defendants had mistakenly advertised printers valued at $3,854 for $66 on their website. The plaintiffs ordered 1,606 of these printers via the website. Objectively, they knew very well that the defendants had made a mistake in the advertisement. Accordingly, the contract was void for unilateral mistake.

---

[48] (1878) 3 App Cas 459.
[49] Unreported, High Court, 18 December, 1970.
[50] [2005] 1 SLR 502.

*Where Mistake Negligently Induced by the Other Party*

**[17–37]**    The contract in *Scriven Bros v Hindley & Co*[51] concerned two lots at an auction, both part of the cargo of the same ship and both bearing the same shipping marks. The buyers inspected one lot, which consisted of hemp. They mistakenly presumed that the other lot was also hemp since it bore the same shipping mark. In fact, the other lot was tow. This was unusual since the custom of the trade was that different substances would never have the same shipping marks. The buyers bid for both lots and both were knocked down to them. The Court found that the buyers had been mistaken so as to negative any *consensus* between them and the seller. It is interesting to note that Lawrence J explains the Court's decision on the basis of fault:

> "[A] contract cannot arise when the person seeking to enforce it had by his own negligence, or by that of those for whom he is responsible, caused or contributed to cause, the mistake."

**[17–38]**    The question, as always, is one of responsibility in relation to potential risk. It should not be forgotten that the mistaken party's duty to safeguard himself from risk is as strong as the other party's duty not to induce mistake. The famous case of *Smith v Hughes*[52] is very clear on this point. The contract at issue was for the sale of oats. The buyer wanted to buy old oats. He did not mention this to the seller who offered to sell him oats by sample. The buyer, mistakenly believing these to be old oats, agreed to buy the whole stock. In fact, they were new oats. The Court found that an agreement was in place despite this mistake. Cockburn CJ reasoned in part as follows:

> "[T]he rule *caveat emptor* applies ... Here the defendant agreed to buy a specific parcel of oats. The oats were what they were sold as ... The buyer persuaded himself that they were old oats, when they were not so; but the seller neither did nor said anything to contribute to his deception. He has himself to blame."

**Fundamental Mistakes**

**[17–39]**    Only a fundamental "offer and acceptance" mistake, whether mutual or unilateral, will prove the absence of *consensus ad idem*. In *Smith v Hughes* the question was whether the mistake about oats or the difference between new and old oats could be termed "fundamental". Cockburn CJ's approach is clear and worth quoting at length:

> "If he gets the article he contracted to buy, and that article corresponds with what it was sold as, he gets all he is entitled to and he is bound by the contract ... [A]n argument ... was pressed upon us ... that the defendant in the present case intended to buy old oats, and the plaintiff to sell new, so the two minds were not *ad idem*; and that consequently there was no contract ... Both parties were agreed as to the sale and purchase of this particular parcel of oats. The defendant believed the oats to be old, and was thus induced to buy them, but he omitted to make their age a condition of the contract. All that can

---

[51] [1913] 3 KB 564.
[52] (1871) LR 6 QB 597.

be said is, the two minds were not *ad idem* as to the age of the oats; they certainly were *ad idem* as to the sale and purchase of them."

The point is this: the contract here was fundamentally about the sale of oats. [17–40] The buyer contracted for oats. The seller contracted for oats. The age of the oats was a mere collateral point, not a fundamental one and, accordingly, the mistake as to whether the oats were "old" or "new" could not have any effect on the contract. If a party wishes to guard against a potential mistake, which is less than fundamental, it is his responsibility to ensure that he provides for that mistake in the terms of his contract.

## Fundamentality and Unilateral Mistake as to Identity

The problem of mistaken identity is a difficult one. The case law here often deals with [17–41] rogues such as Blenkarn in *Cundy v Lindsay*, discussed above. These cases are marked by the usual concern to preserve the sanctity of contract, and so the prospects of raising a successful argument on mistake of identity are minimal. Mistake as to identity will very rarely be considered a fundamental mistake. In order to succeed in avoiding the contract the mistaken party must show that:

1.   The other party's identity mattered to the contract.
2.   The mistake was one of identity and not of attribute.

Other considerations include fault on the part of the mistaken party and the [17–42] interests of any innocent third parties.

### The Other Party's Identity Must Have Mattered to the Contract

The party seeking to void the contract must show that the identity of the other party [17–43] mattered—that it went to the root of the contract. In *Citibank NA v Brown Shipley & Co Ltd.*,[53] Waller J summarised this position as follows:

"The no contract situation, as opposed to the voidable contract, only arises if it is fundamental to the contract that one party to the contract should be who he says he is."

Identity will only matter in this way in very particular circumstances. In *Ingram* [17–44] *v Little*,[54] Pearce J distinguishes a case of fundamental mistaken identity from a non-fundamental one:

"If a man orally commissions a portrait from some unknown artist who had passed himself off, whether by disguise or merely by verbal cosmetics, as a famous painter, the impostor could not accept the offer ... The mistaken identity on such facts is clear and the nature of the contract makes it obvious that the identity was of vital importance to the offeror. At the other end of the scale, if a shopkeeper sells goods in a normal cash transaction to a man who misrepresents himself as being some well-known figure, the transaction will

---

[53]   [1991] 2 All ER 690.
[54]   [1961] 1 QB 31.

normally be valid. For the shopkeeper was ready to sell goods for cash to the world at large and the particular identity of the purchaser in such a contract was not of sufficient importance to override the physical presence identified by sight and hearing."

[17–45]     *Boulton v Jones*[55] is one of those rare cases where the identity of one party was found to be fundamental to the contract. The defendant in this case ordered goods from Brocklehurst's shop. He ordered the goods from Brocklehurst rather than from someone else because he had a set-off against him. Unknown to the defendant, Brocklehurst no longer ran his shop. He had, on the very day of the order, sold his shop to the plaintiff. So the defendant was mistaken in thinking that he was dealing with Brocklehurst. The Court found that this mistake was fundamental because the identity of the plaintiff was vital to the contract on account of the right of set-off.[56] This case can be distinguished from *Lewis v Averay*,[57] a case that concerned the sale of a car by the plaintiff to a man falsely claiming to be the actor, Richard Greene. Megaw LJ found that the plaintiff had not been concerned to sell his car to any particular person. It did not matter to him whether the purchaser of his car was Richard Greene or someone else. Accordingly, his mistake could not operate to void the contract for the sale of the car.

[17–46]     Mistaken identity cases are, broadly speaking, of two types. There are cases, such as *Boulton v Jones* and *Cundy v Lindsay*, where the mistaken party intends to deal with some real person other than the rogue. Then there are those cases where the rogue assumes an alias, merely giving himself another name rather than assuming the identity of some other actual person. The mistaken party is more likely to succeed in proving fundamental mistake in the former category of case than in the latter. In *King's Northan Metal Co Ltd. v Edridge, Merrett & Co*,[58] a man named Wallis ordered goods on credit from the mistaken party under the guise of a bogus business called "Hallam & Co". The order was written on impressive headed note-paper, and Wallis suggested that the business was reputable and thriving. The Court found that there was no fundamental mistake as to identity here since the mistaken sellers intended to deal with the writer of letter, whoever he might in fact be. In *Cundy*, by contrast, the mistaken party intended to deal with some other real entity whom he knew to exist. The Court of Appeal heard that the mistaken party could have succeeded in this case had they been able to prove that there was a separate entity called Hallam & Co with whom they intended to deal, and another called Wallis with whom they did not intend to deal. Again, the distinction between these categories of case is questionable as a matter of logic.[59] In both types of case, objectively viewed, the mistaken party does not intend to deal with the person who actually appropriates his goods. This is yet another moveable dividing line to be manipulated by the courts according to the dictates of risk.

---

[55] (1857) 27 LJ Ex 117.
[56] See also *Hardman v Booth* (1863) 1 H&C 803.
[57] [1972] 1 QB 198.
[58] (1897) 14 TLR 98.
[59] Poole, *Textbook on Contract Law* (7th ed., OUP, 2004), p 90.

An argument of mistaken identity is more easily defeated where the contract is exclusively in writing. As the Court observed in *Shogun Finance v Hudson*,[60] Lord Phillips stated that:

[17–47]

> "[t]he process of construction will lead inexorably to the conclusion that the person with whom the other party intended to contract was the person thus described".[61]

### The Mistake Must Be Of Identity Not Attribute

Only a very serious mistake as to identity will be considered fundamental. The familiar identity/quality distinction applies here. So it is said that a contract will not be affected because a party is mistaken as to some minor attribute of the person with whom he is dealing. Thus, for example, A may enter into a contract with B on the mistaken belief that A is rich or credit-worthy,[62] but such a mistake is of no consequence. Lord Denning in *Lewis v Averay*[63] noted, with his usual common sense, that the distinction between identifying and other attributes is "a distinction without difference". Again, the usual argument applies. This distinction is tremendously flexible and may be manipulated by the courts to allow the risk of mistake to be apportioned appropriately as between the parties.[64]

[17–48]

### Innocent Third Parties and the Voidability Alternative

Two other inter-related factors form a crucial obstacle to the recognition of mistake as to identity: the availability in these cases of an alternative remedy for misrepresentation and the rights of innocent third parties who frequently become embroiled in these cases. Mistake as to identity will almost always be one-sided since it is difficult to imagine circumstances in which a party might be mistaken as to his own identity. Usually, these cases double as cases of fraud where a rogue party misrepresents his identity to another (see Chapter 15). In such circumstances, the contract is voidable for fraudulent misrepresentation. An alternative remedy is open to the prejudiced party.

[17–49]

The courts have found it preferable to decide mistaken identity cases as misrepresentation cases instead, particularly where the rights of an innocent third party, to whom goods have been passed by the fraudster, are at stake. Suppose A sells his car to B, a rogue who fraudulently says that he is a sales representative for a local garage. B in turn sells the car to C. C has no idea that he is buying a car which has been swindled from its true owner. B then disappears with the proceeds of his enterprise.

[17–50]

Suppose, first, that one decides this case on the basis of unilateral mistake as to identity. One sees immediately that A entered into his contract with B while under a unilateral mistake as to B's identity. A's contract for the sale of the car with B is therefore void; A never really had a contract with B because *consensus ad idem* was lacking. This means that A's title in the car never passes to B. B sells the car on to C,

[17–51]

---

[60] [2001] EWCA Civ 1001.
[61] *ibid.*
[62] *King's Norton Metal Co Ltd. v Etridge, Merrett &Co Ltd.*, above, n 57.
[63] Above, n 56.
[64] See Poole, *op. cit.*, p 89.

but he cannot give C title in the car: *nemo dat quod non habet*.[65] Therefore, when A discovers his mistake, he can recover the car from C. C is left with nothing; he paid for a car which B was not entitled to sell.

[17–52]     Imagine, on the other hand, that we decide this case on the basis of misrepresentation. Misrepresentation does not void a contract. A contract is merely *voidable* for misrepresentation. In *Car and Universal Finance v Caldwell*,[66] Sellers LJ confirmed that, even though a contract is tainted by misrepresentation, it will subsist until the injured party makes a final and irrevocable decision to end the contract. So A sells the car to B. He does not yet know that B has misrepresented his identity. Title in the car passes to B. B sells the car to C. Assuming C buys in good faith and pays for the car, C obtains title to the car. If A discovers the misrepresentation after C buys the car, he likely cannot recover it. His only remedy will be in damages, which he must seek from B.

[17–53]
        One can see that the misrepresentation route is not a terribly attractive one from the mistaken party's point of view. It is a personal remedy. In three-party scenarios, when the court chooses voidability whether in misrepresentation or in mistake, the innocently mistaken party suffers. However, the courts can justify this approach where the mistaken party was in a position to protect himself from his mistake but failed to do so. In *Ingram v Little*,[67] Lord Denning argued that:

> "[i]t is wrong that an innocent purchaser (who knew nothing of what passed between the seller and the rogue) should have his title depend on such refinements. After all, he has acted with complete circumspection and entire good faith; whereas it was the seller who let the rogue have the goods and thus enabled him to commit the fraud".

[17–54]  *Fault and the Mistaken Party*

It is more difficult to prove mistake as to identity in contracts *inter praesentes* than in contracts made at arms length. The presumption that the mistaken party intended to deal with the individual in front of him is exceptionally difficult to rebut. The House of Lords in *Shogun Finance v Hudson* confirmed that the face-to-face principle is still important to the law of mistake.[68] A risk-based theory explains this idea very well. We know already that the doctrine of mistake abhors carelessness. Ordinarily, a party to a contract will have been able to ascertain and confirm the identity of the other party with minimal difficulty. Therefore, the courts require parties to take up their responsibility to protect themselves from mistake by exercising all reasonable care in their identification of the parties. As Lord Devlin observed in *Ingram v Little*[69]:

---

[65] You cannot give what you do not have. See ss. 12(1) and 21(1) of the Sale of Goods Act 1893.
[66] [1965] 1 QB 525.
[67] Above, n 54. *Re Ambrose's Estate* [1913] IR 506 suggests that a similar fault-based approach might be followed in Ireland.
[68] Above, n 60.
[69] Above, n 54.

"... if the fault or imprudence of either party has caused or contributed to the loss, it should be borne by that party in the whole or in the greater part".[70]

*Ingram v Little* demonstrates quite forcefully the flexibility with which the doctrine of mistake will be manipulated to calibrate the balance of risk in a particular case. In that case, two elderly spinster sisters sold their car to a fraudster claiming to be a Mr Hutchinson. He wanted to pay by cheque. The sisters only accepted his cheque having checked the name and address he had supplied against that provided in the telephone directory. The cheque bounced and the sisters tried to recover their car from the car dealer to whom the fraudster had sold it. The Court treated their argument of mistake favourably and voided the contract, allowing them to recover the vehicle. The generosity of the Court's decision is thrown into sharp relief when contrasting it with that in *Lewis v Averay*. As you will recall, this case also concerned the sale of a car to a fraudster purporting to be somebody else. The seller in *Lewis v Averay* was a student. He believed the fraudster was Richard Greene because the fraudster showed him an identity card from Pinewood Studios bearing that name together with the fraudster's photograph. This evidence of identity was surely as strong as that sought by the sisters in *Ingram*.[71] The fraudster sold the car on to a third party, this time an impecunious student rather than a car dealership. The Court would not void that contract for mistake. The distinction between these cases bears on the usual theme. It would appear to be based on the position of the third party to bear the consequences of the risk of mistake more than the degree of fault of the mistaken party.[72]

[17–55]

The tide may be turning in third party cases. *Ingram* was overruled by the House of Lords in *Shogun Finance v Hudson*.[73] A fraudster entered into a hire-purchase agreement with a finance company, signing the draft finance agreement with a false name. This mistaken identity avoided the contract. This was despite the fact that the car had been sold on to a third party, and despite the fact that, as Collins notes,[74] the hire purchase company was in a better position than the innocent buyer to ascertain the identity of the seller. Lord Nicholls in particular observed that, as between two innocent parties, it is wrong to always presume that the third party will be more deserving of aid than the mistaken party.

[17–56]

## V. The Voidable Contract Scenario: When is a Contract Liable to be Set Aside at Equity for Mistake?

If a contract is not void for mistake at law, the mistaken party may still seek relief at equity. The equitable remedy of rescission (15-42) has been covered in the discussion on

[17–57]

---

[70] It should be noted that the Law Reform Committee rejected this as a *test* for mistake in its *Twelfth Report on the Transfer of Title to Chattels* (Cmnd 2958, 1966).

[71] See also *Phillips v Brooks Ltd.* [1919] 2 KB 243. A jeweller supplied a fraudster claiming to be Sir George Bullough, and giving an address at St James's Square, with a ring on credit. Before supplying the ring, he verified that Sir George Bullough's address was that supplied by the fraudster. Yet this was not enough to ground a successful defence of mistake.

[72] The US courts adopt the same approach in relation to common mistakes. See *Wood v Boynton* 64 Wis 265, 25 NW 42 (1885); *Kolwalke v Milwaukee Elec. Ry. & Light Co*, 103 Wis 472, 79 NW 762 (1899).

[73] Above, n 59.

[74] Collins, *The Law of Contract* (4th ed., LexisNexis Butterworths, 2003), p 143.

misrepresentation. If a contract is not void for mistake, it may still be voidable at the discretion of the court.

### Common Mistake

[17–58]     A party seeking to have a contract set aside at law for common mistake must demonstrate that that mistake is "fundamental" in the sense discussed above. As we have seen, the idea of fundamental mistake is rigidly circumscribed. Equity may provide relief in respect of some limited categories of common mistake. First, the mistake must be something between fundamental[75] and trivial.[76] In the case of *Huddersfield Banking Co Ltd. v Henry Lister & Co Ltd.*,[77] Lindley LJ referred to "material mistake". In *William Sindall v Cambridgeshire CC*,[78] the type of mistake required was described as "wider than the kind of 'serious and radical' mistake" necessary to bring relief at common law. In addition, the mistake need not be linked to the subject matter of the contract in the way typical in the common law cases. So equity will give relief for a much wider category of mistake than the common law will.

[17–59]     The second point has to do with the express provisions of the contract. Lord Steyn said in *Associated Japanese Bank v Crédit du Nord SA*[79] that the Court will not hear a plea of common mistake if the contract has already made provision for that contingency.

[17–60]     Finally, *William Sindall v Cambridgeshire CC*[80] demonstrates that a court of equity will not set a contract aside in order to allow a party to escape the consequences of a bad bargain. Remember that the purchasers wanted to get out of the contract because they had discovered a sewer under the property they had purchased. The sewer could not be moved. A successful plea of common mistake would have allowed them to walk away from the contract. In addition, the property market had just collapsed and so, by successfully pleading common mistake, the purchasers could have escaped an ill-judged contract. The courts will be reluctant to allow a party to abuse a plea of common mistake in this way. In *Amalgamated Investments and Property Co*,[81] Sir John Pennycuick observed: "The purchaser of property takes, subject to the risk of future events, and it is for him to evaluate those risks in considering whether to buy and at what price."

[17–61]     The development on the law of equitable relief for common mistake is controversial. The old law under *Cooper v Phibbs*[82] was that equity regarded contracts tainted by fundamental common mistakes as null and void, but did not provide any

---

[75] *Solle v Butcher* [1950] 1 KB 671.

[76] *Debenham v Sawbridge* [1901] 2 Ch 98; *William Sindall plc v Cambridgeshire County Council*, above, n 11.

[77] [1895] 2 Ch 273.

[78] [1994] 3 All ER 932.

[79] [1988] 3 All ER 902.

[80] Above, n 78.

[81] *Amalgamated Investment and Property v Walker and Sons Ltd.*, [1976] 3 All ER 509, above, n 3. See also *Fitzsimons v O'Hanlon* [1999] 2 ILRM 551.

[82] Above, n 17.

separate relief for non-fundamental common mistake. However, in *Solle v Butcher*[83] Lord Denning held that equity will provide relief in cases of non-fundamental common mistake. This approach was followed in *Grist v Bailey*[84] and *Magee v Pennine Insurance Co.*[85] However, in England and Wales, rescission is not available at equity for common mistake any longer. The Court of Appeal has since held in *The Great Peace*[86] that this power of rescission is no longer available. In *Solle* Lord Denning had lauded the flexibility of rescission as a remedy—while the common law remedy of declaring a contract void is a blunt tool, the courts can use rescission to work a more sophisticated justice as between the parties. In particular, when a court sets a contract aside for mistake, it may attach such conditions to its order as are necessary to work justice as between the parties. However, in *Great Peace*, the Court rejected *Solle* as an illegitimate expansion of the remedies available for common mistake. *Solle* demonstrates an unorthodox approach to precedent. The same criticism may be made of this Denning invention as of promissory estoppel: *Solle* is an ill-supported creation that was not effectively reined in by later decisions. While *Bell* had set a firm test of "fundamental" mistake as the threshold for relief, *Solle* cast the gates wide open. In *William Sindell*, Evans LJ suggested that the categories of common mistake, for which relief is given at equity, might be "unlimited". Treitel has criticised this approach forcefully[87]:

> "Equity's more liberal treatment of mistake to some extent sacrifices the requirements of certainty emphasised by the common law. One cannot in this field have certainty and justice at the same time; and the present state of … [the] law presents a somewhat incongruous appearance, with common law striving for certainty while equity tries to promote justice."

The Court of Appeal agreed. In order to promote the key value of certainty in this area of law, it was deemed necessary to wipe the slate clean of the doubt that arose from *Solle*. These points notwithstanding, the Irish courts have not yet changed their position. In *O'Neill v Ryan*,[88] and more recently in *Intrum Justitia BV v Legal and Trade Financial Services Ltd.*,[89] *Solle* was cited with approval.

[17–62]

## Unilateral Mistake

A unilateral mistake may give rise to a right of rescission where it would be unconscionable for the other party to take advantage of it. The first requirement here is that the mistake must be one as to the subject matter or terms of the contract. Thus, rescission was not available in *Clarion Ltd. v National Provident Institution*.[90] Clarion and NPI had reached an agreement about an investment management scheme. However, NPI had entered the agreement under a mistaken belief about the

[17–63]

---

[83] Above, n 75.
[84] [1967] Ch 532.
[85] [1969] 2 QB 507.
[86] Above, n 7.
[87] Treitel, *The Law of Contract* (10th ed., Sweet & Maxwell, 1999), p 286.
[88] Above, n 6.
[89] Above, n 33.
[90] [2000] 2 All ER 265.

commercial effect of the contract; they had not realised that under the agreement, investments could be switched using a pricing system which benefited Clarion. Rimer J held that rescission was not available because:

> "I do not regard NPI's mistake as being a mistake either as to the terms of the contract asserted by Clarion or as to its subject matter. There was no mistake as to either of these things. If there had been then I would accept that NPI would have an arguable case for being released from its contract."

[17–64]     The second requirement is that an element of unconscionability must be present in the non-mistaken party's conduct. This requirement is in line with the status of rescission as an equitable remedy and might involve fraud, misrepresentation, inducement or acquiescence. In *Torrance v Bolton*,[91] the requisite unconscionabilty was found where the seller of property orally explained a mistake in the written advertisement of that property. The purchaser was deaf.

## VI. Rectification: What Can be Done if the Document which Records the Contract is Not an Accurate Record?

[17–65]     In some circumstances, where a contract is expressed in writing and where a written contractual document does not accurately set out the terms of a contract, the court can order it to be rectified. In *Crane v Hegeman-Harris Co Inc*,[92] Simonds J observed that:

> "If one finds that, in regard to a particular point, the parties were in agreement up to the moment when they executed their formal instrument, and the formal instrument does not conform with that common agreement, then this court has jurisdiction to rectify ..."

[17–66]     Rectification means that the document will be rewritten to reflect the parties' true agreement. "The essence of rectification is to bring the document which was expressed and intended to be in pursuance of a prior agreement into harmony with the prior agreement."[93] The court may also order the contract to be specifically performed as set out in the amended document.

[17–67]     Remember that contractual agreements cannot be rectified. When rectification is ordered, the document is rewritten to reflect the parties' true contract, but the contract itself does not change. Rectification applies to cases of mistake in the document, not to cases of mistake in the contract. So the parties cannot approach the court to reshape their agreement so as to get rid of their common, mutual or unilateral mistake. Thus, Peter Gibson LJ observed in *Swainland Builders Ltd. v Freehold Properties Ltd.*[94] that

> "The remedy of rectification is available only for the putting right of a mistake in the terms of a document which purports to record a previous transaction. It

---

[91] (1872) LR 8 Ch App 118.
[92] [1971] 1 WLR 1390.
[93] *Lovell and Christmas Ltd. v Wall* (1911) 104 LT 85.
[94] [2002] EWCA 560.

is not an appropriate remedy where the mistake relates to the transaction itself rather than the document which purports to record it."

This principle becomes clearer by contrasting the following two cases. In **[17–68]** *Craddock Bros v Hunt*,[95] C and H were successful bidders for two plots of land at auction. However, the written contracts of sale did not describe the lands purchased properly so that part of the land purchased by C was conveyed to H. Neither C nor H was mistaken as to any aspect of his contract. The sole problem was with the inaccuracy on the contract document. Therefore, rectification was available to remedy the defects in the contractual documents.

Another important point to understand is that rectification is an equitable **[17–69]** remedy. Therefore, the courts enjoy a wide discretion in relation to its operation and will take account of the usual equitable factors such as affirmation (15–45), lapse of time (15–47), *restitutio in integrum* (15–49) and the rights of third parties (15–52). Rectification will not be granted where it will work an injury.[96]

Rectification will only be ordered where it can be shown that the written **[17–70]** agreement does not reflect the parties' true prior common intention. In *Irish Life Assurance v Dublin Land Securities Ltd.*,[97] the Supreme Court held that the court will not rewrite a contractual document in the absence of convincing evidence. The burden of proof is not as high as beyond reasonable doubt but where, as in *Irish Life Assurance*, the only evidence of the parties' intention besides the written document is a collection of vague oral statements, the court will not order rectification. The evidence involved will often be oral and this generates problems of certainty justifying a cautious judicial approach to the question of evidence. In *The Olympic Pride*,[98] Mustill J explained:

> "The Court requires the mistake to be proved with a high degree of conviction before granting relief. There are sound policy reasons for this. The Court is reluctant to allow a party of full capacity who has signed a document with opportunity of full inspection to say afterwards that it is not what he meant. Otherwise, certainty and ready enforceability would be hindered by constant attempts to colour the issue by reference to pre-contractual negotiations. Those considerations apply with particular force in the field of commerce where certainty is important."

Rectification provides an important exception to the parol evidence rule **[17–71]** (13–12): oral evidence is admissible to contradict or vary a written agreement.[99] The courts' view is that the potential harm done in terms of uncertainty is offset by the potential injustice of allowing one party to take unscrupulous advantage of an error in transcription.

---

[95] [1923] 2 Ch 136.
[96] *McAlpine v Swift* (1810) 1 Ball & B 285.
[97] [1989] IR 253.
[98] [1980] 2 Lloyd's Rep 67.
[99] *Nolan v Graves and Hamilton* [1946] IR 377.

**[17–72]**     In order to demonstrate common intention, the parties need not demonstrate the existence of a legally binding oral contract. The old Irish approach in *Lucy v Laurel Construction*[100] was that rectification was only available where a legally binding oral contract was in existence. However, in *Joscelyne v Nissen*[101] the Court of Appeal held that it was sufficient that the parties had outwardly expressed a common intention, whether that amounted to a concluded oral agreement or not. This approach was approved by the Supreme Court in *Irish Life Assurance v Dublin Land Securities*.[102] The Supreme Court adopted the position set out by Lord Lowry in *Rooney & McParland v Carlin*.[103] The court must have regard to three things: First, the parties must have reached a concluded, though not necessarily legally binding, oral agreement. Second, and by contrast, it will be easier to demonstrate common intention where a legally binding oral agreement has been concluded. Third, there must be some outward expression of the parties' common intention which has been communicated between the parties.

### Rectification for Common Mistake

**[17–73]**     The first situation to consider is that where the parties reached an oral agreement, the terms of which were incorrectly recorded in the contractual document. Both parties share the mistaken belief that the document accurately records the transaction.

### Rectification for Unilateral Mistake

**[17–74]**     The second situation in which rectification is available is that in which only one party is aware of the mistake in the document, knows that the other party is not aware of it and signs the document anyway without alerting the other party to the mistake. An example of this type of case is *Nolan v Graves & Hamilton*.[104] Mrs Nolan agreed to buy a row of houses for £5,550. In recording the transaction, the auctioneer mistakenly recorded the price as £4,550. Mrs Nolan was not allowed to buy at the lower price. The written contract was rectified to reflect the true price agreed. Similarly, in *Nolan v Nolan*[105] a separation agreement was incorrectly recorded so that income tax advantages were recorded as going to the wife when they should have gone to the husband. The wife had recognised the mistake. She was not entitled to enforce the agreement as written and the written agreement was rectified.

**[17–75]**     Generally, the mistaken party will have to demonstrate some element of unconscionabilty on the part of the non-mistaken party before rectification will be granted. This requirement mirrors the common law treatment of unilateral mistake of fact. In *Commission for New Towns v Cooper*,[106] Stuart Smith LJ wrote:

> "Rectification is not ordinarily appropriate [in the case of unilateral mistake]. This follows from the ordinary rule that it is the objective intention of the

---

[100]  Unreported, High Court, 18 December 1970.
[101]  [1970] QB 86.
[102]  Above, n 99.
[103]  [1981] NI 138.
[104]  Above, n 99.
[105]  (1965) 92 LTR 94.
[106]  [1995] 2 All ER 929.

parties which determines the construction of the contract and not the subjective intention of one of them. Also, it would generally be inequitable to compel the other party to execute a contract, which he had no intention of making, simply to accord with the mistaken interpretation of the other party ... But the court will intervene if there are additional circumstances that render unconscionable reliance on the document by the party who has intended that it should have effect according to its terms."

Unconscionability does not necessarily imply sharp practice. In *Thomas Bates v Wyndham*,[107] Buckley J said that unconscionabilty depended more on the general equity of the position. In *Commission for New Towns v Cooper*,[108] Stuart Smith LJ stated *obiter* that unconscionability could be established where three conditions were satisfied: A intended B to be mistaken with regard to the construction of the agreement; A conducted himself to divert B's attention from discovering the mistake; and B actually made the mistake A intended.[109]

[17–76]

## VII. *Non Est Factum:* What Can be Done If a Party Signs a Document But is Under a Unilateral Mistake As to the Nature of the Document Signed?

It has been established that a person is bound by the terms of any contractual document which they have signed, regardless of whether they have read it (14–09). However, in certain limited circumstances where "the mind of the signer did not accompany the signature",[110] the law will void written contracts for mistake. This is a radical remedy. The contract is not merely voidable but is entirely void. The mistake is a fundamental unilateral mistake as to the nature of the document being signed—one which generates an entire absence of consent on the part of the signer.[111] The doctrine of *non est factum* has its origin in old cases of illiterate adults, such as William Chicken in the infamous *Thoroughgood's Case*,[112] who had executed deeds which had been read to them incorrectly. A plea of "it is not my deed" served to void the instruments. The modern doctrine is a little wider. In *Foster v Mackinnon*,[113] Byles J wrote:

[17–77]

"[I]f a blind man, or a man who cannot read, or who for some reason (not implying negligence) forbears to read, but has a written contract falsely read over to him, the reader misreading it to such a degree that the written contract is of a nature altogether different from the contract pretended to be read from the paper which the blind or illiterate man afterwards signs; then, at least if there be no negligence, the signature so obtained is of no force."

---

[107] [1981] 1 All ER 1077.

[108] Above, n 106.

[109] See also *Templiss Properties v Dean Hyams* [1999] EGCS 60; *Hurst Stores & Interiors v ML Europe Property* [2004] All ER 13.

[110] *Foster v Mackinnon* (1869) LR 4 CP 704.

[111] *Bank of Ireland v McManamy* [1916] 2 IR 161.

[112] *Thoroughgood's Case* (1584) 2 Co Rep 9a.

[113] Above, n 110.

**[17–78]**     Perhaps the most famous example of the doctrine in operation is *Lewis v Clay*.[114] The plaintiff pretended to the defendant that he needed him to witness some deeds. He had placed blotting paper with holes cut into it over the "deeds", allegedly to keep their contents private. The defendant signed. The "deeds" turned out to be promissory notes, obliging the defendant to pay the plaintiff £11,000. Of course, in these circumstances, the defendant's plea of *non est factum* was easily supported. An Irish case applying this rule is *Siebel v Kent*.[115] The plaintiffs were Germans who did not speak English. They signed a contractual document which purported to incorporate certain conditions attached to a contract for the sale of property. These conditions were not read to them and their attention was not drawn to them. Finlay J held that the plaintiffs were not bound because they did not understand that they were signing a contract in its final form.

**[17–79]**     As with all avenues for mistake-based relief, this is a narrow one. The courts do not want to undermine the authority associated with signed documents. This cautious approach is exemplified by the key English case of *Saunders v Anglia Building Society*.[116] In that case, Lord Reid emphasised that the doctrine must be treated gingerly in order "not to shake the confidence of those who habitually and rightly rely on signatures when there is no obvious reason to doubt their validity". The case concerned an elderly widow who signed a document which she believed had the effect of gifting her house to her nephew. She did not read the document because her glasses were broken. She wanted to help her nephew to raise funds for his business. In fact, the document dealt with the sale of the house to a man called Lee, through whom her nephew was planning to raise the money. The House of Lords held that the widow could not pray the doctrine of *non est factum* in aid. They first said that any person who has "no real understanding" of the document he is signing, "whether ... from defective education, illness or innate incapacity",[117] can rely upon the doctrine.

**[17–80]**     It seems clear, however, that it is only in the most unusual circumstances that the average person will be able to break free of the general rule that one is governed by one's signature. The doctrine is not a safety net for the careless or reckless.[118] Despite her various weaknesses, even an elderly woman of limited education should have checked that she was signing over her home to the right person. Lord Wilberforce said:

> "The law ought ... to give relief if satisfied that consent was truly lacking but will require of signers even in this class that they act responsibly and carefully according to their circumstances in putting their signature to legal documents."[119]

---

[114] (1897) 67 LJ QB 224.

[115] Unreported, High Court, 1 June 1976.

[116] [1971] AC 1004.

[117] *ibid.*

[118] See also *Norwich & Peterborough Building Society v Steed* [1998] Ch 116; *Avon Finance Co Ltd. v Bridger* [1985] 2 All ER 281.

[119] Above, n 117 at 1027. Accepted in *Bank of Ireland v McCabe and McCabe*, unreported, High Court, 30 March 1993.

The same principle was applied by Flood J in *Bank of Ireland v McCabe*,[120] **[17–81]**
where he said:

> "Even in circumstances where it is clearly established that the person relying on
> the doctrine did not understand the particular purport of the particular
> document, such person must establish that they took such precautions as they
> reasonably could to have the document explained to them and to acquire
> knowledge of the import of the document."

Where the vulnerable party makes reasonable efforts to discover the import of **[17–82]**
the document and is met with misrepresentation, evasion or negligent explanation, he
may be able to bring a successful claim in *non est factum*. In *Lloyd's v Waterhouse*,[121]
the illiterate defendant had signed a bank guarantee to enable his son to buy a farm.
He asked several questions about the document but the bank was negligent in
responding to them and misled him as to the document's effect. Accordingly, the
defendant's *non est factum* claim succeeded.

Secondly, *Saunders v Anglia Building Society*[122] establishes that this doctrine is **[17–83]**
also circumscribed by the idea of fundamental mistake. The House there held that the
difference between what the signer believed he was signing and the actual document
had to be "radical" or "essential" or "fundamental" or "substantial". The widowed
aunt in *Saunders* believed that she was signing a document which would help her
nephew to raise money for his business. The document she actually signed was not so
far removed from that purpose.[123] In *Bank of Ireland v McManamy*,[124] signing a bank
guarantee under the mistaken impression that it was an application for a load of
manure constituted a sufficiently radical mistake. The same was true of the mistake in
*Ted Castle McCormack & Co Ltd. v McCrystal*,[125] in which the plaintiff thought that
he was signing a solus agreement when in fact he was signing a guarantee.

A successful plea of *non est factum* does not require proof of wrongdoing by the **[17–84]**
other party to the contract. Lord Wilberforce in *Saunders* observes that "it is the lack
of consent that matters, not the means by which this result was brought about". A
successful plea of *non est factum* might be raised where the signer is not mislead by the
other party at all but by some third party. Unlike other areas of contract law that aim
to protect the vulnerable, this doctrine does not require that the other party knew or
should have known about the mistake. To some extent, therefore, this doctrine takes
the protective function of the law too far. It should be abolished and its functions
subsumed into the areas of undue influence and misrepresentation.

---

[120] *ibid.*
[121] [1991] Fam Law 23.
[122] Above, n 116.
[123] Since *Saunders*, the doctrine has been but sparingly used. See *Avon Finance Co Ltd. v Bridger*
[1985] 2 All ER 281; But see also *Lloyd's Bank plc v Waterhouse*, above, n 121.
[124] [1916] 2 IR 161.
[125] Unreported, High Court, 15 March 1999.

## VIII. What If a Party Pays Money Under a Mistake of Law?

[17–85]   Suppose A enters into a contract with B. A is under a misapprehension about the effect of a statute which has a bearing on his entitlements under the contract. When he discovers the true legal position, A seeks to have the contract set aside. Can he do so?

### Common Law

[17–86]   The old common law rule was that no relief was available for a mistake of law. The maxim *ignorantia juris neminen excusat*, or "ignorance of the law is no excuse", applied. So in *O'Loghlen v O'Callaghan*,[126] both parties to a contract were mistaken as to the applicability of a certain statute to their contract. The parties thought that the statute governed their contract. In fact, it did not, with the result that the plaintiff was entitled to an extra £100. The Court held that he was not entitled to this £100 because the mistake involved was a mistake of law. However, in *Kiriri Cotton v Dewani*,[127] Lord Denning created a limited restitutionary exception to this rule. It appears that money paid under a mistake of law is recoverable where, in addition to the mistake of law, there is "something in the defendant's conduct which shows that, of the two of them, he is the one primarily responsible for the mistake". This exception has been approved by the High Court and the Supreme Court respectively in *Dolan v Nelligan*[128] and in *Rogers v Louth County Council*.[129] In *Rogers*, the plaintiff had overpaid money to the defendant council in redeeming an annuity under the Housing Act 1966. The money was paid under a mistake of law, and the question for the Supreme Court was, therefore, whether the plaintiff or the defendant was primarily responsible for the mistake. Griffin J held that the defendant was primarily responsible for two reasons. The first was that this was not a voluntary payment. It was imposed on the plaintiff under conditions stipulated by the defendant. Secondly, the plaintiff was not fully informed of the facts so that she had no means of discovering her mistake. Therefore, she was entitled to recover the money overpaid. Similarly, in *Lord Mayor of Dublin v The Provost of Trinity College Dublin*,[130] Hamilton J held that excess monies paid to the college under a mistake of law were recoverable where the college was primarily responsible for the mistake.

[17–87]   Case law in England has abolished the distinction between mistakes of law and mistakes of fact. This process began with *Avon CC v Howlett*,[131] in which Slade LJ characterised a mistake as to an employee's contract of employment as a mistake of fact rather than one of law. In *Kleinwort Benson Ltd. v Lincoln City Council*,[132] the House of Lords excised the fact/law distinction from the law of mistake. Their Lordships held that there is a general right in English law to recover money paid under any mistake whether of fact or of law. Lord Goff justified this reform on the basis that application of the rule that ignorance of the law is no excuse produced unjust enrichment. It followed that judges were tempted, as Slade LJ had been, to avoid

---

[126] (1874) IR 8 CL 116.
[127] [1960] AC 192.
[128] [1967] IR 247.
[129] [1981] ILRM 143.
[130] [1986] ILRM 283.
[131] [1983] 1 WLR 605.
[132] [1998] 3 WLR 1095.

injustice by treating mistakes of law as mistakes of fact. This approach made the law uncertain and unpredictable to the point where abolition of the rule was justified. No Irish court has yet made a final decision on the retention of the distinction between mistakes of law and mistakes of fact.

## Equity

Equity draws a distinction between mistakes of private law (contracts, wills and so on) and mistakes of general law (the ordinary law of the country, such as legislation). Equity will set a contract aside where there is a common mistake as to private law. In *Cooper v Phibbs*,[133] Lord Westbury held that: [17–88]

> "Private right of ownership is a matter of fact; it may be the result also of a matter of law; but if parties contract under a mutual mistake and misapprehension as to their respective rights, the result is that the agreement is liable to be set aside as having proceeded upon a common mistake".

---

[133] Above, n 17.

# CHAPTER 18
# Duress, Undue Influence and Unconscionable Bargain

## I. Introduction

It is a key ideal of contract law that parties bargaining within the market do so on equal **[18–01]** terms. However, the reality of the market is that inequality of bargaining power is the rule rather than the exception. This chapter is concerned with the use and abuse of bargaining power. The ethos of contract law is strongly individualistic. On the traditional view, the ideal contract stems from a bargaining process in which both parties strive against one another, each in pursuit of his own self-interest, each seeking the agreement which will be most advantageous to him. Classical contract law did not impose duties of co-operation or fairness on either party. Over time, of course, the law has developed some limited rules of play for the bargaining process. In *Royal Bank of Scotland v Etridge*[1] Lord Nicholls in the House of Lords listed three types of unacceptable bargaining conduct. The first, "overt improper conduct", includes the legal doctrine of duress (18–03). The second, "abuse of influence", touches on the equitable notion of undue influence (18–35). The final type, "exploitation of vulnerable persons", encompasses the equitable doctrine of unconscionable bargain (18–85).

This chapter discusses those three doctrines. It focuses on two issues: the **[18–02]** defective consent of the weaker party to a contract and the illegitimate conduct of the

---

[1] [2002] 2 AC 773.

stronger party. These are the twin pillars of the courts' intervention in the contracting process. Over the years, attempts have been made to introduce a third pillar: substantive unfairness. It has been argued that the courts should be able to intervene in contract purely because the terms are foolish or oppressive. The traditional position is that such intervention is impermissible. The parties are expected to see to their own best interests. However, especially where the equitable doctrines are used, the courts emphasise procedural concerns as a back door route to the granting of relief from improvident contracts. For example, the doctrine of undue influence is grounded in consent-based justifications (18–35). However, a relationship of undue influence may be inferred from the improvidence of the transaction (18–51). In addition, the presumption of undue influence, where it arises, is based on "manifest disadvantage" to one party or on the fact that the transaction "calls for explanation" (18–53). The doctrine of unconscionability, formally at least, has its roots in illegitimate bargaining tactics (18–91). That said, the improvidence of a transaction is, in practice and especially in Ireland, the key factor which determines whether the contract stands or falls (18–95). Finally, consideration will be given to the developments at common law (18–100) that would allow contracts to be struck out almost entirely on the basis of unfairness. Before we turn to these common law rules, note should be made of the prohibition of "aggressive commercial practices" in section 49 of the Consumer Protection Act 2007. These practices include any coercion, harassment and undue influence which would be likely to significantly impair the average consumer's freedom of choice or conduct in relation to the trader's product, and cause the average consumer to make a transactional decision that the average consumer would not otherwise make. In determining whether a commercial practice fits this test, the court will take account of a number of factors. These include the timing, location, nature or persistence of the commercial practice the use of threatening or abusive language or behaviour by the trader and the exploitation of a consumer's misfortune or circumstance.

## II. Duress

*Michael Corleone: Well, when Johnny was first starting out, he was signed to this contract with a big-band leader. And as his career got better and better he wanted to get out of it. Now, Johnny is my father's godson. My father went to see the bandleader, with a contract for $10,000 to let Johnny go, but the bandleader said no. So the next day, my father went to see the bandleader again, only this time with Luca Brasi. Within an hour, the bandleader signed the release, with a certified check of $1,000.*

*Kay Adams: How did he do that?*

*Michael: My father made him an offer he couldn't refuse.*

From *The Godfather* (1972)

[18–03]  Furmston describes duress as "the pressure of the big stick or the bottom line".[2] More properly, duress is the term given to an excuse for non-performance of a contract. Where a party can demonstrate that he was induced to enter a contract, or to

---

[2] Furmston (ed), *The Law of Contract* (1999) para 4.128.

vary its terms involuntarily by the exercise of illegitimate pressure, he will be given an option to set that contract aside. There are two major reasons why the court will allow a contract to be set aside for duress.[3] Both are concerned with procedural justice: issues of fairness surrounding the making of the contract. In theory, a contract may be completely fair in substance, but the court will still allow it to fall because of the injustice surrounding its inception. In practice, the courts will use procedural doctrine to police the parties' bargain, setting aside contracts which are unjust in substance. The first justification for the doctrine of duress is that the courts feel that there is a limit to the tools that a person is rightfully entitled to use to obtain the contract of his choice. The deliberate exertion of some types of pressure over another is improper. In *Barton v Armstrong*[4] Lords Wilberforce and Simon explained:

> "Out of the various means by which consent may be obtained – advice, persuasion, influence, inducement, representation, commercial pressure – the law has selected some which it will not accept as a reason for voluntary action."

The second justification for the doctrine of duress is based in the idea of contractual consent. Consent is the fundamental element of any contractual agreement. For instance, the doctrine of misrepresentation is premised on the idea that this consent must be adequately informed (see para 15–02). In addition, consent must be sufficiently voluntary. Its quality must not have been diminished by the application of illegitimate pressure.　　　　　　　　　　　　　　　　　　　**[18–04]**

At one time, the courts took the view that duress destroyed its victim's consent to the contract completely so that he could not be regarded as having chosen to enter into the contract at all. For example, in *Occidental World-Wide Investment Corp v Skibs A/S Avanti*[5] the Court held that it "must in every case at least be satisfied that the consent of the other party was overborne by compulsion so as to deprive him of any *animus contrahendi*". Holmes J went further in *Fairbanks v Snow*.[6] He said that duress involved "such bodily compulsion as turns the ostensible party into a mere machine". This position was known as the "overborne will" theory. However, the courts have more recently developed a fresh understanding of the effect of duress on consent. Atiyah explained this new theory in an influential article.[7] He says that a party who enters a contract under duress *does* choose to enter the contract. He makes a very real choice: he can either enter into the contract or take the risk that the party making the threat will carry it out. For example, if A tells B he must sign a contract or A will shoot him in the head, B has a very clear choice to make—that between signature and death. In some ways, the pressure may be said to focus his mind, so that this is one of the most "real" choices he has ever made. So, in cases of duress, as the House of Lords has established in the criminal context, "the will is deflected, not destroyed."[8] The party affected by duress exercises a choice between alternatives. These alternatives may not be desirable. It may not be reasonable to choose one above the other. However, when the affected party　　　　　　　　**[18–05]**

---

[3]　See Dalton, "An Essay in the Deconstruction of Contract Doctrine" (1985) 94 Yale LJ 997.
[4]　[1976] AC 104.
[5]　[1976] 1 Lloyd's LR 293.
[6]　145 Mass 153, 13 NE 596, 598.
[7]　Atiyah, "Economic Duress and the Overborne Will" (1982) LQR 197.
[8]　*DPP v Lynch* [1975] AC 614.

makes his choice, he fully intends it. Therefore, in *The Universe Sentinel*[9] Lord Scarman, following this theory, noted that "[t]he classic case of duress is ... not the lack of will to submit [to the contract] but the victim's intentional submission arising from the realization that there is no other practical choice open to him". In the same case, Lord Diplock stated that in cases of duress "one party's apparent consent was induced by pressure exercised upon him by that other party which the law does not regard as legitimate". So duress does not cut consent out of the equation. Rather, it taints it such that the agreement which results is not considered real but only apparent.

### The Effect of Duress

[18–06] What happens to a contract if it is shown that one party entered it under duress? *Barton v Armstrong*[10] suggested that duress renders a contract void *ab inito*. However, we can only accept this view if we accept the old "will overborne" theory of the effect of duress on the affected party's consent. The courts' current view is that a contract is voidable, not void, where its inception is marred by duress. The rule that a contract is only voidable for duress reflects the real effect of duress on the victim's will. A choice made under duress is still a choice, albeit an imperfect one. The law respects this choice as an expression of contractual autonomy but will not bind the victim to it if he demonstrates a clear intention to cast it aside. A contract made under duress is voidable: the innocent party has the right to affirm if he wishes once he has escaped the influence of the original source of duress. However, he must make his choice to affirm or avoid the contract as soon as is reasonably practicable. Affirmation occurs if, once the duress is no longer operative and with full knowledge of his right to avoid the contract, the innocent party voluntarily chooses to treat it as subsisting or does not take any steps to set it aside. Undue delay, therefore, may affirm the contract. Mance J notes in *Huyton SA v Peter Cremer GmbH & Co*[11]:

> "[R]elief may not be appropriate, if an innocent party decides, as a matter of choice, not to pursue an alternative remedy which any and possibly some other reasonable person in his circumstances would have pursued. Relief may perhaps also be refused, if he has made no protest and conducted himself in a way which showed that, for better or for worse, he was prepared to accept and live with the consequences, however unwelcome."

[18–07] *The Atlantic Baron*[12] demonstrates the application of the principle that a contract must be avoided for duress within a reasonable time after the effect of the duress wears off or not at all. In this case, Hyundai Construction Co had threatened North Ocean Shipping with breach of a ship-building contract unless North Ocean Shipping would pay an increase of 10 per cent on the agreed contract price. North Ocean Shipping paid the increase. Macotta J found in principle that this extra payment had been made under duress. However, North Ocean Shipping were held unable to recover this extra sum because they were held to have affirmed the agreement to pay it. They had delayed in reclaiming the extra sum after the ship had been delivered. At this

---

[9] [1983] AC 336.
[10] Above, n 4.
[11] [1999] 1 Lloyd's Rep 620.
[12] [1979] 1 QB 705.

point Hyundai's threat could no longer be carried out: they were no longer under the influence of the initial duress. They should have acted with due haste to avoid the contract. It is important to remember that the duty to choose between affirmation and avoidance will not arise until the duress ceases to have effect. Thus, in *The Universe Sentinel*[13] Lord Scarman wrote that: "[t]he victim's silence will not assist the bully, if the lack of any practicable choice but to submit is proved".

## Types of Duress

### Duress to the Person

The courts have long been willing to recognise violence or threats of violence to the weaker party as an excuse for avoiding a contract. *Barton v Armstrong*[14] is the *locus classicus* here. Barton was managing director of Landmark Corporation Ltd and Armstrong was the chairman. Together, they were controlling shareholders in the company. Relations between the two were acrimonious. Matters came to a head when Barton eventually managed to have Armstrong ousted as chairman. Negotiations began with regard to buying out Armstrong's interest in the company. Armstrong had previously loaned $400,000 to the company and it was agreed that this loan would be repaid immediately. Unfortunately, Barton could not secure funds with which to do so. Instead, Barton executed a deed under which he agreed, amongst other things, to repay the loan, to buy Armstrong's shares for $180,000 and to make a further payment to Armstrong of $140,000. Before executing the deed, Barton had been placed under considerable pressure by Armstrong, who had made threats, including threats of murder against Barton and his family. Barton was in genuine fear that Armstrong was planning to have him killed and had hired a man, Vojinovic, to carry out the deed. On 10 January 1967, before an order was made for the winding up of Landmark, Barton brought a suit in equity against Armstrong, arguing that the deed was void for duress. The Court agreed that duress was present.

**[18–08]**

*Barton v Armstrong* illustrates that threats made against a party will vitiate his consent. Similarly, a contract made at gunpoint is voidable for duress,[15] as is one made where one party is the other's abductee.[16] Words are enough to generate this defence. This point is put eloquently in the US case of *Brown v Pierce*:

**[18–09]**

> "Actual violence is not necessary to constitute duress ... because consent is the very essence of a contract, and, if there be compulsion, there is no actual consent, and moral compulsion, such as that produced by threats to take life or inflict great bodily harm ... is everywhere regarded as sufficient, in law, to destroy free agency, without which there can be no contract."[17]

The case also suggests that threats directed against a third party, such as a family member, may be sufficient. This is borne out by *Byle v Byle*,[18] where a conveyance was

**[18–10]**

---

[13] Above, n 9.
[14] Above, n 4.
[15] *Colp v Hunker* (1911) 1 WWR 314.
[16] *Lessee of Blackwood v Gregg* (1831) Hayes 277.
[17] *Brown v Pierce*, 7 Wall 205, 19 L Ed 134.
[18] (1990) 65 DLR (4th) 61.

set aside on foot of threats of violence to one party's son. Neither need the threats involve violence at all; in *Rourke v Mealy*[19] Palles CB suggested that a claim of duress may lie where a person is threatened with criminal prosecution of a near relative.[20]

### Duress to Goods

[18–11]    Kerr J in *The Siboen and the Sibotre*[21] cited a threat to burn down another's house or to slash his painting as an example of duress to goods. For a long time the courts were reluctant to recognise any threat to the integrity of the weaker party's property as grounds for avoiding a contract.[22] In *Skate v Beale*[23] Denman CJ drew the following distinction between duress to the person and such threats as those:

> "The former is a constraining force, which not only takes away the free agency, but may leave no room for appeal to the law for a remedy: a man therefore, is not bound by the agreement which he enters into under such circumstances: but the fear that goods may be taken or injured does not deprive anyone of his free agency who possesses that ordinary degree of firmness which the law requires all to exert."

[18–12]    The Victorian virtue of the stiff upper lip thus prevented the growth of any substantial doctrine of duress to goods. The old doctrine of *pacta sunt servanda* also had its role to play. The courts were concerned that too flexible a doctrine of duress might enable parties to slip the bonds of contracts forged under reasonable but substantial commercial pressure. Denman CJ wrote in *Skate*:

> "It is of great importance that parties should be holden to those remedies for injuries which the law prescribes, rather than allowed to enter into agreements, with a view to prevent them, intending at the time not to keep their contracts."

[18–13]    However, by 1915 the law had become more tolerant of a little strategic weakness, as the judgment in *Maskell v Horner*[24] demonstrates. The plaintiff was a trader in the

---

[19] (1879) 13 ILTR 52.

[20] In general, proper use of the legal process will not amount to duress. However, abuse of legal proceedings in order to exert pressure on another to contract will usually be considered duress. See *Unwin v Leper* (1840) 1 Man & G 746 (approved by Lord Denman CJ in *Goodall v Lowndes* (1844) 6 QB 464 AT 467) where duress was found when the plaintiff paid money on the strength of a threat to sue him.

[21] [1976] 1 Lloyd's Rep 293 at 335.

[22] See *Blackstone's Commentaries* (1897) at p 131: "fear of battery ... is no duress; neither is the fear of having one's house burned, or one's good taken away or destroyed; because in these cases, should the threat be performed, a man may have satisfaction by recovering equivalent damages: but no suitable atonement can be made for the loss of life, or limb".

[23] (1841) 11 Ad & E 983.

[24] [1915] 3 KB 106. See *Lloyd's Bank v Bundy* [1975] QB 326 *per* Denning LJ: "A typical case is when a man is in a strong bargaining position by being in possession of the goods of another by virtue of a legal right, such as by way of pawn or pledge or taken in distress. The owner is in a weak position because he is in urgent need of the goods. The stronger demands of the weaker more than is justly due and he pays it in order to get the goods. Such a transaction is voidable. He can recover the excess".

Spitalfields Market. The defendant owner of the market demanded tolls for trading. He threatened that, if these were not paid, he would seize the goods. The plaintiff paid the money. Lord Reading CJ held that he was entitled to recover the money for duress:

> "If a person pays money, which he is not bound to pay, under compulsion of urgent and pressing necessity or of seizure, actual or threatened, of his goods he can recover it as money had and received ... The payment is made for the purpose of averting a threatened evil and is made not with the intention of giving up a right but under immediate necessity and with the intention of preserving the right to dispute the legality of the demand."

In later years, the courts lowered their expectation of contractual courage even further. Lord Goff set out in *The Evia Luck* [25] that the distinction between physical duress and duress to goods drawn by Lord Denman in *Skate v Beale* no longer held. Thus, in an appropriate case, duress to goods is a valid basis for a claim to have a contract set aside. So, in *Royal Boskalis Westminster NV v Mountain* [26] it was held that the Iraqi government's threat to detain a party's dredges unless he agreed to terms for their release amounted to duress to goods. **[18–14]**

## Economic Duress

Although Lord Chancellor Northington observed in 1761 that "necessitous men are not, truly speaking, free men, but, to answer a present exigency, will submit to any terms that the crafty may impose upon them", [27] the doctrine of economic duress is a newly formed one. Money paid under economic compulsion has been recoverable at common law since the old case of *Astley v Reynolds*. [28] The idea that a contract could be set aside for duress was, however, a controversial one. In *The Siboen and the Sibotre* [29] Kerr J opened the door to the development of a doctrine of economic duress when he held that duress was not restricted to threats of violence and duress to goods. In the Australian case of *Stott v Mettitt*, [30] Finlaison JA undermined the distinction between economic duress and the hitherto recognised forms of duress. He emphasised the equivalence between economic duress and the older doctrine of duress to the person: **[18–15]**

> "The term 'economic duress' is no more than a recognition that in our modern life the individual is subject to societal pressure which can be every bit as effective, if improperly used, as those flowing from threats of physical abuse. It is an expansion in kind but not class of practices that the law already recognises as unacceptable."

*D & C Builders v Rees* [31] demonstrates the operation of the doctrine of economic duress. The plaintiffs were owed about £480 by the defendants. The **[18–16]**

---

[25] [1992] 2 AC 152.
[26] [1997] LRLR 523.
[27] *Vernon v Bethell* 2 Eden 110.
[28] (1731) 2 Str 915.
[29] Above, n 21.
[30] (1988) 48 DLR (4th) 288.
[31] [1966] 2 QB 617.

defendants knew that the plaintiffs were in a desperate financial position. Exploiting this knowledge, they told the plaintiffs that they could only pay £300. The plaintiffs accepted the £300 in complete satisfaction of the debt. The plaintiffs could still recover the remaining £180 under the doctrine in *Pinnel's Case* (8–32). However, Lord Denning found that the plaintiffs had another string to their bow. The agreement to accept £300 in full and final satisfaction of the debt had been procured by economic duress. Accordingly, the plaintiffs were not bound by it. A clearer example of the doctrine in play is *The Atlantic Baron*.[32] The case concerned the legitimacy of vendor's demand of a 10 per cent increase in payment on the original contract price for the construction of a tanker. This demand was made on pain of breach of the contract. Any breach would have serious consequences for the purchaser, who needed the ship in order to fulfil a lucrative contract with a third party. The vendor refused to refer the matter to arbitration so there was no other option open to the purchaser. The Court found that, in the circumstances, the demand of a price increase amounted to economic duress. A more recent case is *Carillon Construction Ltd v Felix (UK) Ltd*.[33] Carillon entered into a contract to construct an office building in London. He engaged Felix as a contractor to design, manufacture and supply cladding for the building. During construction, Felix told Carillon that future deliveries would be dependent on Carillon's agreement of Felix's account. In other words, Felix would breach his contract unless the final account was agreed. Taking an injunction against Felix would be a time-consuming process. There were no other sub-contractors available. Carillon had no choice but to agree the account. Under these circumstances, the Court found that economic duress was present.

[18–17]      The development of the doctrine of economic duress is linked to the liberalisation of consideration. For example, the courts now recognise that the performance of a pre-existing contractual duty can be good consideration for a promise of extra money. The doctrine of economic duress performs the task of regulating the fairness of these increasing pacts. *Williams v Roffey Bros*[34] is a case in point. One of Glidewell LJ's six principles (para 8–25) is that the promise to pay extra money for the same work shall not have been procured by economic duress.

### Elements of a Duress Claim

[18–18]      Under *The Universe Sentinel*,[35] a successful duress claim has two elements. First, one party must have wielded some improper pressure against the other. Secondly, that pressure must have caused the victim to enter into the contract at issue. The "improper pressure" element reflects the wrongdoing justification for the law of duress. The "causation" element reflects the consent-based justification. Even though the elements of the claim of duress seem simple enough, the law of duress has been described as "bedevilled by conceptual confusion."[36] Three asides will suffice for now. The first is that the interdependence of the elements of the duress claim should not be underestimated. McKendrick argues that in controversial cases the courts "may prefer

---

[32] Above, n 12.
[33] [2001] BLR 1.
[34] [1990] 1 All ER 512.
[35] Above, n 9.
[36] McKendrick, *Contract Law*, (6th ed, Palgrave, 2005) p 357.

to apply a sliding scale according to which the causal threshold diminishes as the degree of illegitimacy increases".[37] The second is that neither element is enough on its own to establish duress. For example, suppose A threatens to kill B's daughter if B does not sell his car to C. The first element of the duress claim is satisfied because this threat constitutes improper pressure. However, if B does not take the threat seriously and sells the car to C for entirely unrelated reasons, there is no duress because causation will not be proven. The third point, established in *Alec Lobb (Garages) Ltd v Total Oil*,[38] is that pressure from third parties or outside pressure of circumstances is never sufficient to prove duress. The threat must come from the other party to the contract.

### Exertion of Illegitimate Pressure: Lawful and Unlawful Act Duress

It is not enough to ground an action for duress that the weaker party was under some pressure when he decided to enter the contract. That pressure must also be illegitimate.[39] Illegitimate pressure must be distinguished from what Dyson J called "the rough and tumble of normal bargaining".[40] Lord Hoffmann in *R v Attorney-General for England and Wales*[41] set out a double-barrelled test of legitimacy:

    [18–19]

> "The legitimacy of the pressure must be examined from two aspects: first, the nature of the pressure and secondly, the nature of the demand which the pressure is applied to support."

The first element of Lord Hoffmann's test is that the nature of the pressure applied must be somehow wrongful. In the Australian case of *Crescendo Management Pty Ltd v Westpac Banking Corpn*[42] McHugh JA stated that: "[p]ressure will be illegitimate if it consists of unlawful threats or amounts to unconscionable conduct".

    [18–20]

There is little debate about whether an unlawful threat should be considered illegitimate pressure: a threat to break the law cannot be countenanced as a bargaining tool. So a threat to commit murder or assault if another person will not enter into a contract will satisfy the first element of Lord Hoffmann's test. A threat to breach a contract may also fall under this heading.[43]

    [18–21]

---

[37] McKendrick, *Contract Law: Text, Cases and Materials*, (2nd ed, Oxford University Press, 2005) p 749.

[38] [1985] 1 WLR 173.

[39] Smith, "Contracting Under Pressure" [1997] CLJ 343, has suggested that this distinction between legitimate and illegitimate pressure is ill-conceived. After all, a person's consent to enter into a contract can be deflected as easily by legitimate as by illegitimate means. He argues for the distinction to be abandoned so that a party would be able to avoid a contract on account of pressure *simpliciter*.

[40] *DSDN Subsea Ltd v Petroleum Geo-Servicesper* [2000] BLR 530.

[41] [2003] UKPC 22.

[42] (1988) 19 NSWLR 40.

[43] *South Wales Miners' Federation v Glamorgan Coal Co Ltd* [1905] AC 239: "any party to a contract can break it if he chooses; but in point of law he is not entitled to break it". See however the suggestion in *DSDN Subsea Ltd v Petroleum Geo-Services* [2000] BLR 530 that a threat to breach a contract will not amount to illegitimate pressure where it can be described as "reasonable behaviour by a contractor acting *bona fide* in a very difficult situation".

**[18–22]**     Should conduct which is legal but unconscionable be treated as duress? On the one hand, the law on duress exists to preserve fairness and eliminate wrongdoing in the formation of contracts. The avoidance of contracts which were formed against a background of threats of illegality is entirely consistent with this aim. The expansion of the law of duress to encompass pressure which, though not illegal is nevertheless unfair, sends the courts into more dangerous territory. The courts do not impose obligations of good faith in the bargaining process. Will they regulate other types of distasteful behaviour? Professor Birks explained the dilemma[44]:

> "Can lawful pressures also count? This is a difficult question because, if the answer is that they can, the only viable basis for discriminating between acceptable and unacceptable pressures is not positive law but social morality. In other words, the judges must say what pressures [though otherwise lawful] are improper as contrary to the prevailing standards. That makes the judges, not the law or the legislature, the arbiters of social evaluation. On the other hand, if the answer is that lawful pressures are always exempt, those who devise outrageous but technically lawful means of compulsion must always escape restitution until the legislature declares the abuse unlawful."

**[18–23]**     Initially, the courts were unwilling to accept that a threat to do something which was not in itself unlawful could amount to illegitimate pressure for the purposes of the law of duress. However, the law now appears to be that a threat of lawful action will amount to illegitimate pressure *if* it is applied to support an illegitimate demand. In cases of lawful act duress, the second element of Lord Hoffmann's test *R v Attorney-General for England and Wales*[45] is to the fore. The importance of the demand is borne out by the early recognition of threats of blackmail as illegitimate pressure establishing duress. The threat involved in blackmail is not unlawful. As Lord Haines noted in *Thorne v Motor Trade Association*[46]:

> "The ordinary blackmailer normally threatens to do what he has a perfect right to do – namely, communicate some compromising conduct to a person whose knowledge is likely to affect the person threatened ...".

**[18–24]**     However, the nature of the demand involved in blackmail is suspect. Lord Atkin went on to say that "[w]hat he has to justify is not the threat, but the demand of money". Lord Atkin's principle was expanded to encompass threats other than blackmail in a number of later cases. For example, in *The Universe Sentinel*[47] the English courts accepted that a threat of lawful action may amount to illegitimate pressure if coupled with a demand for payment. In that case, a trade union "blacked" a vessel at Milford Harbour. This was not an unlawful action but it amounted to illegitimate pressure because the trade union demanded money to cease the action.

---

[44] Birks, *An Introduction to the Law of Resitution* (1989) p 177.
[45] Above, n 41.
[46] [1937] AC 797.
[47] Above, n 9.

That said, the impulse to restrict the growth of lawful acts of duress remains strong. In *CTN Cash and Carry Ltd v Gallaher*[48] Lord Steyn explained that a move to extend the doctrine would be:

> "... a radical one with far-reaching implications. It would introduce a substantial and undesirable element of uncertainty in the commercial bargaining process. Moreover, it will often enable bona fide settled accounts to be reopened when parties to commercial dealings fall out. The aim of our commercial law ought to be to encourage fair dealing between parties. But it is a mistake for the law to set its sights too highly when the critical enquiry is not whether the conduct is lawful but whether it is morally or socially acceptable."

[18–25]

### Inducing Victim to Enter the Contract

In addition to demonstrating the presence of illegitimate pressure, the party seeking to avoid the contract for duress must prove a causal link between the illegitimate pressure and his decision to enter into the contract. In New Zealand, Young J has said that is not necessary that "the party affected must have been psychologically crippled by reason of the pressure".[49] *Barton v Armstrong* establishes a very low threshold for inducement, similar to that used in misrepresentation (see para 15–21). The Court there stated that Barton was entitled to relief if Armstrong's threats were *a* reason for Barton's execution of the impugned deed. This was so even though it was established that Barton might well have executed the deed even if Armstrong had never threatened him. *Barton v Armstrong* indicates that the test for inducement here is not a "but for" test.

[18–26]

It is also irrelevant that the contract itself was to the advantage of the party now seeking to set it aside. Oliver Wendell Holmes once observed that "[i]t is always for the interest of a party under duress to choose the lesser of two evils. But the fact that a choice was made according to interest does not exclude duress."[50] As long as the illegitimate pressure was *one* reason for entering into the contract, the contract may be avoided, even though that pressure was not "the reason, the predominant reason, or the clinching reason". Smith criticises the courts' position on inducement on the grounds that "a party cannot disclaim responsibility for a decision that he would have made anyway, just because there exists an additional, potential excusing, reason for making the decision".[51]

[18–27]

### Inducement and Economic Duress

It would appear that a more stringent test of inducement applies in cases of economic duress than in cases of duress to the person. In *The Evia Luck*[52] Lord Goff stated that "economic pressure may be sufficient to amount to duress ... provided at least that the economic pressure ... has constituted a *significant* cause inducing the plaintiff to enter

[18–28]

---

[48] [1994] 4 All ER 714.
[49] *Haines v Carter* [2001] 2 NZLR 167.
[50] *Union Pacific R Co v Public Service Comm'n*, 248 US 67, 70.
[51] Smith, "Contracting Under Pressure: A Theory of Duress" [1997] CLJ 343.
[52] Above, n 25.

into the relevant contract". In *Huyton SA v Cremer GmbH & Co*[53] Mance J stated that the test of causation for economic duress was a "but for" test:

> "The illegitimate pressure must have ... actually caused the making of the agreement, in the sense that it would not otherwise have been made either at all, or at least, in the terms in which it was made. In that sense, the pressure must have been decisive or clinching."

**[18–29]**   The stronger causation requirement for economic duress is justified because economic duress is more acceptable than duress to the person or duress to goods. The courts recognise that parties may legitimately wish to renegotiate the contract terms. In this sort of circumstance, it is perfectly reasonable for one party to inform the other that he will require more money if he is to perform. For example, a change in circumstances short of frustration (see Chapter 22) may occur such that one party will be unable to perform the contract as agreed. In these situations, where the performance originally agreed is not viable, one party may benefit by agreeing to pay more money so that the contract may be carried out. Remember that there will be situations where the remedies available at court cannot adequately compensate for the consequences of a breached contract. From a law and economics perspective, as Birks has observed, the renegotiation of a contract which may follow a demand of extra money is more efficient than a breach. Such renegotiation may "minimize the waste and inconvenience between parties already embarked on a project, and ... bring projects safely to a conclusion without interruptions and unnecessary ill-will".[54]

**[18–30]**   How does the Court decide whether the level of causation involved in economic duress is proved? Birks has said that any attempt to prove this more demanding causation requirement is a wild goose chase; an "inscrutable inquiry into the metaphysics of the will".[55] In *Pao On v Lau Yiu Long*[56] Lord Scarman set out four material factors that the Court will take into account in answering this question. All of these factors are subject to the criticism that it is difficult to see how they relate to the presence or absence of inducement. The first factor is whether the oppressed party protested at the time of entering into the contract. The fact that the victim did not protest is supposed to suggest that he was not acting under duress. However, there are situations in which failure to protest indicates the presence of duress, as where the victim does not protest so as not to further aggravate the perpetrator.

**[18–31]**   The second factor is whether, at the time of entering into the contract, the victim had an alternative course of action open to him, such as seeking another legal remedy. Some cases have treated this as an independent element in an economic duress claim which must be proven in addition to illegitimate pressure and inducement. In *B and S Contracts and Design Ltd v Victor Green Publications*[57] Kerr LJ held that:

---

[53] Above, n 11.

[54] Birks, "The Travails of Duress" [1990] LMCLQ 342, 346.

[55] Birks, *An Introduction to the Law of Restitution* (Clarendon Press, 1991) p 183.

[56] [1979] 3 WLR 435.

[57] [1994] ICR 419.

"[A] threat to break a contract unless money is paid by the other party can, but by no means always will, constitute duress. It appears from the authorities that it will only constitute duress if the consequences of a refusal would be serious and immediate so that there is no reasonable alternative open such as legal redress."

This extra requirement is subject not only to the criticism that it breeds inconsistency between economic duress and other forms of duress but that it is of dubious morality. Should a party who has subjected another to illegitimate pressure be able to dictate his victim's actions by insisting that he snatch at whatever alternative action is open to him?   [18–32]

The third factor relevant to the issue of inducement in economic duress is whether the oppressed party obtained independent legal advice before entering into the contract. The trouble with this factor is that, while legal advice may enable the victim to assess his situation, it does not necessarily reduce the pressure on him.   [18–33]

Finally, under Lord Scarman's test, the Court considers whether the oppressed party took steps to avoid the contract soon after it was formed. The idea is that a party who has been pressured to enter into a contract will try to escape it. As with the first factor, there is no necessary link between this and the presence of inducement.   [18–34]

## III. Undue Influence

Like duress, undue influence is a defence to non-performance of a contract which has its roots in the law's concern for procedural fairness. A person who has entered into a contract because of the undue influence of another is entitled to set that transaction aside. This is because there are grounds, whether actual or probable, for believing that he has been improperly influenced by the other party to enter into the contract and that consequently the contract cannot fairly be treated as an exercise of his free will.[58] In *Royal Bank of Scotland v Etridge*[59] Lord Nicholls explained that the role of the Court is to:   [18–35]

"...ensure that the influence of one person over another is not abused. In everyday life people constantly seek to ... persuade those with whom they are dealing to enter into transactions whether great or small. The law has set limits to the means properly employable for this purpose ... If the intention was produced by an unacceptable means, the law will not permit the transaction to stand. The means used is regarded as an exercise of improper or 'undue' influence and hence unacceptable, whenever the consent thus procured ought not fairly to be treated as an expression of the person's free will."

In the key case of *Barclay's Bank v O'Brien*[60] Lord Browne-Wilkinson stated that there are two primary categories of undue influence: "Class 1" or "actual" undue influence and "Class 2" or "presumed" undue influence. Actual undue influence was   [18–36]

---

[58] *Royal Bank of Scotland v Etridge* [2002] UKHL 44.
[59] *ibid.*
[60] [1993] 4 All ER 417.

proved where the complainant could prove that the other party had positively exercised undue influence which induced him to enter the contract. Presumed undue influence did not involve any positive proof of undue influence. Instead, the undue influence was presumed from the complainant's proof of two things. The first was that a "relationship of trust and confidence" existed between the parties. A "relationship of trust and confidence" could be shown in one of two ways. Under "Class 2A" undue influence certain specific types of relationship were *automatically* treated as "relationships of trust and confidence". Under "Class 2B" undue influence the complainant had to *prove* that the relationship between the parties was in fact one of trust and confidence. The second *O'Brien* requirement was that the transaction was to the complainant's "manifest disadvantage". If both of these requirements were fulfilled, a presumption of undue influence arose. It then fell to the party seeking to enforce the transaction to rebut the presumption by showing that the complainant consented to the transaction. Proof of independent legal advice was the most usual way of rebutting the transaction. This structure is mirrored in Irish law.

[18–37]     The law of undue influence was restated and simplified by the House of Lords in *Royal Bank of Scotland v Etridge*.[61] The *Etridge* restatement has yet to be considered by an Irish court. In this case, their lordships stressed that Lord Browne-Wilkinson's categories of undue influence were misleading. There are no types of undue influence, merely different ways of proving it. Secondly, the House downplayed the 2A/2B distinction. As the law stands post-*Etridge*, there are two ways of establishing undue influence. Actual undue influence involves positive abuse of one's impact on another. Presumed undue influence involves failure to protect him from that impact. The distinction is something like that between fraudulent and innocent misrepresentation.

[18–38]     Actual undue influence rests on the *actions* of the dominant party. It may be something less than lawful act duress (18–22). It involves overt acts of persuasion against the complainant's interests. Actual undue influence may involve "excessive pressure, emotional blackmail or bullying".

[18–39]     Presumed undue influence rests on the parties' *relationship*. In these cases, no "specific acts of overt persuasion" need to be proven. Lord Nicholls said that two elements must be established. The first is "proof that the complainant placed trust and confidence in the other party in relation to the management of the complainant's financial affairs". The relationship between the parties must be such that, even without any persuasion, the weaker party is disposed to agree a course of action proposed by the other. The second element necessary to raise the presumption is "a transaction which calls for explanation". Lord Nicholls says that "proof of these two factors is prima facie evidence that the defendant abused the influence he acquired in the parties' relationship. He preferred his own interests. He did not behave fairly to the other". The transaction will therefore be set aside for undue influence unless the dominant party can demonstrate evidence to counter the inference raised from the parties' relationship and the character of the transaction.

---

[61] *Royal Bank of Scotland v Etridge*, above, n 58.

## Actual Undue Influence

Actual undue influence cases which involve the direct application of pressure by one party to another are rare. One example would be *Bank of Scotland v Bennett*[62] in which a wife had guaranteed her husband's business debts by a mortgage on the family home. The guarantee was set aside because the husband had actually unduly influenced the wife to sign it by using wounding and insulting language, accusing her of disloyalty. Similarly, in *Langton v Langton*[63] an ill man's transfer of his home to his son and daughter-in-law was set aside for actual undue influence because he had entered into the transaction after they had threatened to stop caring for him. The man was dependent on them for his care and, because he had been to prison, had a deep fear of institutionalisation. Actual undue influence was also established in the Irish case of *O'Flanagan v Ray-Ger Ltd*.[64] Pope and O'Flanagan were joint shareholders of a company. O'Flanagan was an impressionable man and, to Pope's knowledge, was close to death from cancer. Pope "had a strong and forceful personality and ... exercised considerable influence amounting to domination" of O'Flanagan. Pope brought O'Flanagan to a pub where the men agreed that, on either's death, the survivor would take full control of the business, regardless of the claims of the deceased's estate. The transaction was obviously improvident, particularly when one notes that O'Flanagan knew he was unlikely to survive Pope and knew that in effect he was giving his business to Pope instead of to his own wife and eight children.

[18-40]

Where there is no direct evidence of actual undue influence, it may be inferred from the circumstances. In *Re Craig*[65] the Court found actual undue influence where an elderly man had given some three quarters of his wealth to his younger female companion in the course of six years. Although there was no direct evidence that she had subjected him to pressure, the Court found actual undue influence because there was evidence of such pressure on other occasions, and because the man was utterly dependent on the woman.

[18-41]

It is important to note that even a good bargain can be set aside for actual undue influence. There is no "manifest disadvantage" or similar requirement. In *CIBC Mortgages v Pitt*[66] it was held that:

[18-42]

"[A]ctual undue influence is a species of fraud ... A man guilty of fraud is no more entitled to argue that the transaction was beneficial to the person defrauded than is a man who has procured the transaction by misrepresentation ... [it] must be set aside in equity as a matter of justice.

## Presumed Undue Influence

Under *Etridge*, undue influence will be presumed where the parties are in a "relationship of trust and confidence" and their transaction "calls for explanation".

[18-43]

---

[62] *Times Law Reports*, 4 August 2004.

[63] 7 De G M & G 30.

[64] (1963–1993) Irish Co. Law Reports 289.

[65] [1971] Ch 95.

[66] [1994] 1 AC 200.

### Relationships Which Are Always Presumed to be Relationships of Trust and Confidence

[18–44] The complainant must generally prove that his relationship with the other party was one of trust and confidence. However, there are certain limited circumstances in which the parties' relationship will be automatically presumed to be one of trust and confidence. These are the old *O'Brien* Class 2A cases. Note that what is presumed here is the nature of the parties' relationship *not* the presence of undue influence. The presumption of undue influence is raised later when both the nature of the relationship and that of the transaction have been shown. In *R (Proctor) v Hutton*[67] it was said that the types of relationship which are automatically treated as relationships of trust and confidence "have much in common with the doctrine of *res ipsa loquitor* in relation to negligence". The thing speaks for itself. Examples would be the relationship between parent and child,[68] guardian and ward,[69] religious advisor and follower,[70] trustee and beneficiary[71] or solicitor and client.[72] The courts presume a relationship of trust and confidence in these cases because certain types of relationship have an inherent power dynamic which gives one party an easily exploited capacity to exert influence over the other. In *Barclay's Bank v O'Brien*[73] the House of Lords found that the relationship between husband and wife was not a presumed relationship of trust and confidence.[74] This was because the idea that a wife is automatically subservient to her husband is anathema to prevailing concepts of the equality of the sexes. The House was also concerned that an automatic presumption of undue influence would taint transactions where the matrimonial home was used as security for loans. If banks were wary of accepting such security, an important asset would be rendered economically sterile. There is a strong public interest in avoiding such an outcome. The House in *Barclay's* did recognise that the sexual and emotional ties between husband and wife are such that the relationship is ripe for exploitation. However, the law remains that if a wife seeks to avoid a transaction made for her husband's benefit on grounds of undue influence she must show actual undue influence or prove that her relationship with her husband was such that he was the dominant and she the weaker party. It seemed for a

---

[67] [1978] NI 139.

[68] *McMackin v Hibernian Bank* [1905] IR 296; *Wallace v Wallace* (1842) 2 Dr & Wr 452; *Croker v Croker* (1870) 4 ILTR 181. The relationship of child and parent, on the other hand, will not attract the presumption: *Carroll v Carroll* [2000] 1 ILRM 210.

[69] *Mulhallen v Marum* (1843) 3 Dr & War 452.

[70] *White v Meade* (1840) 2 Ir Eq R 420. There must be a close relationship between the religious adviser and follower. The relationship between priest and parishioner will attract this presumption but the relationship between a person church member and a priest who is not his parish priest, confessor or religious advisor will not: *Murphy v O'Neill* [1936] NI 16; *Kirwan v Cullen* (1854) 2 Ir Ch Rep 322.

[71] *Murphy v O'Shea* (1845) Ir Eq R 329.

[72] *Lawless v Mansfield* (1841) Dr & War 557.

[73] Above, n 60. See *Northern Bank Co Ltd v Carpenter* [1931] IR 268; *Bank of Nova Scotia v Hogan*, [1996] 3 IR 239.

[74] See *Howe v Bishop* [1909] 2 KB 390; *Bank of Montreal v Stuart* [1911] AC 120.

time that a relationship of trust and confidence was easier to prove in the matrimonial than in other contexts. Lord Brown-Wilkinson wrote in *O'Brien* that:

> "... the sexual and emotional ties between the parties provide a ready weapon for undue influence; a wife's true wishes can easily be overborne because of her fear of destroying or damaging the wider relationship between her and her husband if she opposes his wishes ... I accept that the risk of undue influence affecting a voluntary disposition by a wife in favour of a husband is greater than in the ordinary run of cases where no sexual or emotional ties affect the free exercise of the individual's will."

Cretney[75] criticised even this special provision for wives in *O'Brien*, regarding this concession as unwarranted in an era where marriage is considered, legally and socially. as a relationship of equals. He says:

**[18–45]**

> "A rule which will require banks to treat married women, regardless of the particular facts, in a manner appropriate to children not yet emancipated from their father's control ... seems totally inappropriate at this stage in the evolution of family structures."

To similar effect is the Supreme Court judgment of Murphy J in *Bank of Nova Scotia v Hogan*[76]:

**[18–46]**

> "Notwithstanding that the relationship of husband and wife has been held not to raise a presumption of undue influence, some special status does appear to have been accorded to wives in a variety of decided cases ... The consequence appears to be that whilst the matrimonial relationship as such does not give rise to a presumption of undue influence it may be possible to identify circumstances in a particular case which would more readily raise that presumption in favour of a wife than any outside party. I confess that I do not find the conclusions of the House of Lords in this regard satisfying either as a matter of legal logic or fully acceptable as an analysis of the rights or capabilities of women generally and married women in particular."

### Proving a Relationship of Trust and Confidence

In cases such as that of husband and wife, where the court does not presume a relationship of trust and confidence, it will be necessary to show that the relationship between the parties in fact has that character. It is difficult to pin down the essence of what is required here. In *Royal Bank of Scotland v Etridge*[77] it was said that:

**[18–47]**

> "The relationship between two individuals may be such that, without more, one of them is disposed to agree a course of action proposed by the other. Typically,

---

[75] Cretney, "The Little Woman and the Big Bad Bank" (1992) 108 LQR 534.

[76] [1997] 1 ILRM 407.

[77] Above, n 1. See also *George Smith v William Kay* (1859) 7 HLC 750 *per* Lord Kingsdown: "The principle applied to every case where influence is acquired and abused, where confidence is reposed and betrayed".

this occurs when one person places trust in another to look after his affairs and interests, and the latter betrays this trust by preferring his own interests. He abuses the influence he has acquired ... Even this test is not comprehensive. The principle is not confined to cases of abuse of trust and confidence. It also includes, for instance, cases where a vulnerable person has been exploited. Indeed, there is no single touchstone for determining whether the principle is applicable. Several expressions have been used in an endeavour to encapsulate the essence: trust and confidence, reliance, dependence or vulnerability on the one hand and ascendancy, domination or control on the other. None of these descriptions is perfect. None is all embracing. Each has its proper place."[78]

[18–48]    In *Lloyd's Bank v Bundy*[79] it was held that the type of relationship required will:

"... tend to arise where someone relies on the guidance or advice of another, where the other is aware of that reliance and where the person upon whom reliance is placed obtains, or may well obtain a benefit from the transaction or has some other interest in it being concluded."

[18–49]    The first element of the relationship therefore will be trust: the weaker party expects that the stronger will look after his best interests in the transaction and depends on him to do so. In *Inche Noriah v Shaik Allie Bin Omar*[80] the relationship between an aunt and her nephew was held to be one of trust and confidence because she was aged and illiterate and depended on him to run her financial affairs. She had made a gift of land to him. It fell to the nephew to rebut the presumption of undue influence if he wanted the transaction to stand. Along similar lines is the Irish case of *McGonigle v Black*.[81] Mr McGonigle was a lonely alcoholic who lived by himself in some squalor in a mobile home on his large farm. He had been unable to cope since the death of his aunt. He was close to his married nephew who lived nearby. He and his nephew were in frequent contact and Mr McGonigle visited the nephew's home often. The case concerned a number of transactions whereby he transferred portions of his land to his nephew at significant undervalue. In the end, Mr McGonigle transferred all of his land to his nephew. The Court was satisfied that the nephew was the dominant partner in his relationship with his uncle. A relationship of trust and confidence was established. The required type of relationship will be especially easy to show where the weaker party depends solely on the stronger and does not seek advice or assistance elsewhere.

[18–50]    Reliance does not necessarily connote submission, although the requisite relationship will be easier to prove where one party is substantially weaker than the other, as where he is ill or frail or inexperienced. Thus, in *Gregg v Kidd*[82] the required relationship was established between George Gregg and his sister Mrs Hannah Kidd. George had made a settlement of his land in favour of Hannah's family. George was helpless by virtue of a very serious stroke and was entirely dependent on Hannah and her family for his care. The facts of the case showed that George was extremely

---

[78] *Royal Bank of Scotland v Etridge (No.2)*, above, n 1.
[79] [1975] QB 326.
[80] [1929] AC 127.
[81] Unreported, High Court, 14 November 1988.
[82] [1956] IR 183.

apprehensive about what might happen to him if Hannah refused to care for him any longer. His condition made him susceptible to undue influence. This conclusion is cemented by the fact that Mrs Kidd was "a woman of forceful and determined character". A relationship of trust and confidence may exist where the parties are otherwise equal, provided that the complainant generally reposes trust in the other where his financial affairs are concerned. Secondly, the stronger party must be aware of the other's reliance on him. These twin elements of trust and awareness generate an obligation on the part of the stronger party to deal fairly with the weaker. These elements were established in *Lloyd's Bank v Bundy*.[83] In this case, an elderly farmer, "Old Herbert Bundy", had mortgaged his farm up to the hilt at gross undervalue in order to help his son Michael. It was implicit in the nature of the transaction that the client was relying on the bank to advise and guide him.

A relationship of trust and confidence can be inferred, where appropriate, from the unfairness of the transaction. In *Crédit Lyonnais Bank Nederland NV v Burch*[84] a junior employee agreed to secure her employer's business debts by giving a personal guarantee and an unlimited charge on her small flat. On its own, the relationship between the employee and the employer was not one of trust and confidence, although there was potential for it to be so. The employee had worked for the employer for ten years and had occasionally visited his family and looked after his children. However, the Court was prepared to infer a relationship of trust and confidence as follows:

[18–51]

> "[T]he mere fact that a transaction is improvident or manifestly disadvanta-geous to one party is not sufficient by itself to give rise to a presumption that it has been obtained by the exercise of undue influence; but were it is obtained by a party between whom and the complainant there is a relationship like that of an employer and a junior employee which is easily capable of developing into a relationship of trust and confidence, the nature of the transaction may be sufficient to justify the inference that such a development has taken place; and where the transaction is so extravagantly improvident that it is virtually inexplicable on any other basis, the inference will be readily drawn."

In exceptional circumstances, therefore, the improvidence of the transaction can close the gap between a merely dubious relationship and one which may solidly be categorised as a relationship of trust and confidence, but only where that transaction is "virtually inexplicable on any other basis". Where the transaction can be explained on some basis unconnected with the nature of the parties' relationship, it will not be possible to satisfy this first element of the *Etridge* test. For example, in *Re Brocklehurst's Estate*[85] an attempt to infer a relationship of trust and confidence from the improvidence of an elderly man's transfer of a 99-year lease of shooting rights over his estate to a garage-owner failed. Even though the transaction was improvident, it could be explained on the basis that the man wanted to reduce the value of the estate before it was inherited by his hated nephew.

[18–52]

---

[83] Above, n 79.
[84] [1997] 1 All ER 144.
[85] [1978] Ch 14.

### A Transaction Calling for Explanation

[18–53] Once a relationship of trust and confidence has been established, whether it arises automatically or is proven, the complainant must demonstrate that the transaction is one which calls for explanation. It is not enough, in other words, to show a relationship of trust and confidence between the parties. There must also be some evidence that this relationship has been exploited. Under the *O'Brien* test, this requirement was known as "manifest disadvantage". There is some debate about its status in law. A manifest disadvantage requirement is arguably out of place in the context of undue influence since actual undue influence and even duress itself allow clearly beneficial contracts to be struck down. In addition, in *Allcard v Skinner*[86] Lindley LJ emphasised that the Court would not set a transaction aside for undue influence on the "ground of folly, imprudence or want of foreseight". Yet, in *National Westminster Bank v Morgan*[87] it was held that the presumption of undue influence should only be raised where the transaction was to the manifest disadvantage of the weaker party. Thus, it would not be possible to prove undue influence where the weaker party benefited from the impugned transaction. However, this extra element was consigned to the status of a mere evidential aid in *CIBC Mortgages v Pitt*.[88] Furthermore, the definition of "manifest" in *Barclay's Bank v Coleman*[89] significantly diminished the impact of any requirement of manifest disadvantage. Nourse LJ said: "There must be a disadvantage and it must be clear and obvious. But that does not mean that it must be large or even medium-sized. Provided it is clear and obvious and more than de minimis the disadvantage may be small".

[18–54] The Irish courts have not as yet imposed any manifest disadvantage requirement, as evidenced by the judgment of Budd J in *Gregg v Kidd*.[90] However, the improvidence of the bargain is a factor to be taken into account when the dominant party comes to rebut the presumption of undue influence. In *Provincial Bank v McKeever*[91] Black J said that "the less improvident the bargain, the less strong the presumption". Where the transaction is grossly improvident, it may be nearly impossible to rebut the presumption.[92]

[18–55] Now, *Royal Bank of Scotland v Etridge*[93] is often cited as authority for the death of the manifest disadvantage requirement in English law. However, in that case, Lord Nicholls merely suggested that the label of manifest disadvantage should be discarded because it gives rise to ambiguity. Their lordships made this criticism in the context of transactions between husband and wife, where the question of disadvantage is a difficult one to resolve because the parties finances will tend to be bound up with one another. However, their lordships emphasised that the law of undue influence required something more than a mere relationship, albeit that "something more" was

---

[86] (1887) 36 Ch D 145.
[87] [1985] AC 686.
[88] [1993] 2 All ER 433.
[89] [2001] QB 1.
[90] Above, n 82.
[91] [1941] 1 IR 471.
[92] See similarly *Re Brocklehurst's Estate*, above, n 85.
[93] [2001] 3 WLR 1021.

not adequately expressed by the concept of manifest disadvantage. That much was clear from the judgment of Lindley LJ in *Allcard v Skinner*:

> "It would be absurd for the law to presume that every gift by a child to a parent, or every transaction between a client and his solicitor or between a patient and his doctor was brought about by undue influence unless the contrary is affirmatively proved. Such a presumption would be too far-reaching ... The law would be rightly open to ridicule, for transactions such as these are unexceptionable ...".

The House of Lords therefore rephrased the second ground for the presumption of undue influence in line with *Allcard v Skinner*. Lindley LJ had held that in order to prove undue influence something must be "amiss". There must be "something which calls for explanation". The House in *Etridge* imposed the same requirement. **[18–56]**

In order to satisfy this requirement, the transaction must be clearly and obviously disadvantageous to the party seeking to avoid it. The requirement was fulfilled in *Cheese v Thomas*[94] where an elderly man paid everything he had for the mere right to live until his death in a house which his nephew had purchased. Similarly, in *Hammond v Osmond*[95] a frail, elderly man's transfer of 92 per cent of his liquid assets to a neighbour was a transaction which "called for explanation". **[18–57]**

### Rebutting the Presumption

Once the presumption of undue influence has been established, the transaction will fall unless the dominant party rebuts it on the balance of probabilities. The presumption has two functions. First, it is an evidential device. Jones LJ in *Proctor v Hutton*[96] explained that "the presumption enables a party to achieve justice by bridging a gap in the evidence, where there is a gap, because the evidence is difficult or impossible to come by". The presumption is also a device for the ascription of responsibility. If the parties to a contract are in a recognised category of relationship the dominant party, if he wishes his contract to be upheld, must show that he has been assiduous not to take advantage of his position. **[18–58]**

In order to rebut the presumption, the dominant party must show that the transaction was the spontaneous act of the weaker party and that he acted in circumstances which allowed him to exercise his will freely and independently. The presumption of undue influence was not rebutted in *White v Meade*.[97] In this case, a young lady transferred £1,100 and a substantial parcel of land to a religious order. She had lodged with the order as a possible precursor to joining it. The presumption of undue influence was not rebutted here because it could not be shown that the young lady had freely consented to the transaction. The transaction had been completed in an atmosphere in which members of the order were actively encouraging her to join them and she had been prevented from consulting with her brother. The contract was set aside **[18–59]**

---

[94] [1994] 1 WLR 129.
[95] *ibid.*
[96] Above, n 67.
[97] (1840) 2 Ir Eq 420.

for undue influence. In *Allcard v Skinner*[98] Allcard was a former member of the enclosed Protestant sisterhood of St Mary of the Cross. Skinner was the order's lady superior. Allcard donated property to the sisterhood. The presumption of undue infleunce was not rebutted because, in the words of Cotton LJ, it was not shown that "at the time she executed the transfer she was [not] under such influences as to prevent the gift being considered as that of one free to determine what should be done with her property ...".

[18–60]    In *Inche Noriah v Shaik Allie Bin Omar*[99] Lord Hailsham said that the most obvious, but by no means the only way, to rebut the presumption is to establish that:

> "[T]he gift was made after the nature and effect of the transaction had been fully explained to the donor by some independent and qualified person so completely to satisfy the court that the donor was acting independently of any influence from the donee and with full appreciation of what he was doing."

[18–61]    The idea is that independent advice will emancipate the will of the weaker party. Thus, in *Hammond v Osborn*[100] the presumption was not rebutted because the elderly man had not received any independent advice. He clearly did not have a full appreciation of the transaction. While he knew that he had made a substantial gift, its full size was not explained to him.

[18–62]    It is clear that the quality of advice received is as important as its provision. The Court in *Inche Noriah v Shaik Allie Bin Omar*[101] said that "[p]roof of outside advice does not, of itself, necessarily show that the subsequent completion of the transaction was free from the exercise of undue influence." The Court elaborated by saying that the advice "must be given with a knowledge of all the relevant circumstances and must be such as a competent and honest advisor would give if acting solely in the interests of the donor". This statement was adopted by Budd J as representative of Irish law in *Gregg v Kidd*.[102] The requirement has two elements. First, the advisor must be informed of all material aspects of the transaction. So in *Gregg v Kidd*[103] independent advice was held inadequate to rebut the presumption of undue influence because the adviser was not aware of the donor's mental deficiencies. Similarly, in *McGonigle v Black*[104] the presumption of undue influence was not rebutted despite the presence of independent legal advice because the solicitor was not aware that land transfer amounted to whole of Mr McGonigle's property. Secondly, the advisor must be truly independent. In *McMackin v Hibernian Bank*[105] Barton J stated that "independent advice must be a reality, not a sham; it must be a shield for the [weaker party] not a mere cloak to cover up the transaction". *Carroll v Carroll*[106] states that a solicitor who had acted for both parties in the matter, but acts primarily for the dominant party, is

---

[98] *Allcard v Skinner* (1887) 36 Ch D 145 *per* Lindley LJ.
[99] Above, n 80.
[100] [2002] EWCA Civ 885.
[101] Above, n 80.
[102] Above, n 82.
[103] *ibid.*
[104] Above, n 81.
[105] [1905] IR 296.
[106] [1999] 4 IR 243, [2000] 1 ILRM 210.

not independent for the purposes of rebutting the presumption. However, under *Bank of Nova Scotia v Hogan*[107] it will not be an obstacle to rebutting the presumption that the adviser has acted for the dominant party on a previous occasion. In the event that a solicitor is advised by both parties, he is obliged to instruct the weaker party to seek advice from another solicitor. The instruction is enough. Under *McCrystal v McKane*,[108] it is immaterial that the weaker party does not actually seek advice elsewhere. However, the question is different where the weaker party refuses to take any advice at all. In *Bank of Montreal v Stuart*[109] the Court found that a wife's refusal to take any independent advice showed "how deeprooted and how lasting the influence of her husband was".

The object of the advice is to make the weaker party aware of the consequences **[18–63]** of the transaction. It will not be enough simply to explain the document being signed: the party signing must be aware of the effect of his signature. The more vulnerable the weaker party, the more stringent the duty of the adviser. For example, in *Noonan v O'Connell*[110] an elderly farmer transferred property to a nephew on whom he was totally dependent. Lynch J held that, in these circumstances, "extra care" should be taken to "protect the plaintiff by fully informed and totally independent advice". As a final point, *Gregg v Kidd*[111] sets out that it is not necessary in all cases that the person to whom the advice is given actually takes it. It is enough that the advice sufficed to inform him fully of the nature and import of the transaction.

Because the purpose of the provision of independent advice is to bring the **[18–64]** import of the transaction home to the weaker party, the presumption of undue influence may be rebutted in the absence of independent legal advice where it is clear that the weaker party was fully aware of the nature and effects of the transaction. For example, in *McCormack v Bennett*[112] Finlay P held that the presumption of undue influence was rebutted even absent independent legal advice because the weaker party to the transaction was financially very astute. In *Provincial Bank v McKeever*[113] Black J held:

"[A] main object of such advice is to ensure that the party knows what he is doing. If the transaction is of so plain a character that it may fairly be believed that he did know what he was doing, that object is achieved without advice. Even the best independent advice, if not fully understood, might not achieve it."

## The Duty to Seek Relief Promptly

The party claiming undue influence will be denied a remedy if it can be shown that he **[18–65]** affirmed the contract. He therefore has a duty to reject the contract as soon as is reasonably practicable after escaping from the undue influence. This duty will be applied more strictly in cases of presumptive rather than actual undue influence. So, in

---

[107] [1996] 3 IR 239.
[108] [1986] NI 123.
[109] Above, n 74.
[110] Unreported, High Court, 10 April 1987.
[111] Above, n 82.
[112] Unreported, High Court, 2 June 1973.
[113] Above, 91.

*Allcard v Skinner*,[114] the plaintiff delayed six years before seeking the recovery of the property she had transferred to her sisterhood. Therefore, the transaction could not be set aside.

### Non-Commercial Guarantees: Imputed Undue Influence

[18–66] What happens if a person enters into a contract under undue influence, exerted not by the other party to the contract but by a third party? This scenario is common in banking, as when, for example, a wife enters into an agreement with a bank whereby she agrees to guarantee her husband's debts. If the husband has unduly influenced his wife to enter the contract with the bank (whether actually or presumptively), where does the bank stand?[115] In *Royal Bank of Scotland v Etridge*[116] Stuart-Smith LJ said that the courts are concerned to balance certainty in an important financial transaction with the need to protect vulnerable parties from the potentially serious consequences when a guarantee is enforced:

> "[T]he structure of the underlying [guarantee] transaction is so commonplace and the efficient funding of small businesses is so dependent on its validity, that the parties, and in particular the lending institutions, must be entitled to proceed in accordance with a settled practice which is effective to secure the validity of the transaction while at the same time affording the wife the protection of proper legal advice."

[18–67] The key case here is *Barclay's Bank v O'Brien*.[117] Bridget O'Brien signed a guarantee for an overdraft for her husband's business. It was secured on the family home, which they jointly owned. Nicholas O'Brien told his wife that the amount of the guarantee was £60,000. In fact it was £135,000. The business got into difficulties and Barclay's sought to enforce the loan. Bridget argued that the transaction should be set aside for undue influence and misrepresentation. The House further held that Barclay's could not enforce their contract of guarantee with the wife unless they could show that they had taken reasonable steps to minimise the risk that her decision to take on the loan was tainted by wrongdoing.

### *Wrong-doing*

[18–68] The *O'Brien* doctrine is a protective device. In certain circumstances, it allows the Court to hold a bank responsible for wrongdoing, such as undue influence or misrepresentation, perpetrated by someone unconnected with the bank, but which has affected a client's decision to take a loan from them. In *O'Brien*, Nicholas O'Brien procured his wife's consent to the loan by illicit means. Yet her loan contract was not with him. He was a third party to the contract and so, at first glance, his actions were not grounds for setting the contract aside. Their lordships, therefore, had to find a means of holding Barclay's, as the other party to the contract, responsible for the consequences of his wrong. They did so in two steps. First, they held that the bank was fixed with notice that Bridget O'Brien's consent to the guarantee was potentially

---

[114] (1887) 36 Ch D 145.
[115] See Mee, "Undue Influence and Bank Guarantees" [2002] 37 *Irish Jurist* 292.
[116] Above, n 1.
[117] Above, n 60.

flawed. They held that a bank will be fixed with such notice if two factors are present. The first is that the guarantor and the person receiving the benefit of the guarantee share some sexual or emotional link. Marriage, co-habitation,[118] parenthood[119] or even non-domestic relations may suffice. The second is that the transaction is objectively to the guarantor's financial disadvantage. Disadvantage will be proven, as in *O'Brien*, where a wife goes guarantor for her husband's personal or business debts.[120] On the other hand, as in *Ulster Bank v Fitzgerald*,[121] no disadvantage will be shown where a business loan is being made for joint purposes; for example, where spouses run a family business together on an equal footing.[122] In addition, ordinary transactions, of some benefit to the wife, such as a re-mortgage for a holiday home, will not fall under suspicion.[123]

### Bank Put on Inquiry

Once these two elements of relationship and disadvantage are established, the transaction is tainted with suspicion and the bank is put on inquiry. The bank then has a duty to satisfy itself that the wife understands the nature and effect of the transaction. The bank will be regarded as having fulfilled this duty if it takes "reasonable steps to satisfy itself that the wife has had brought home to her, in a meaningful way, the practical implications of the proposed transactions". These include the extent of the liability she is guaranteeing, the consequences for her should her husband default on his loan, and the importance of acquiring competent legal advice from an independent adviser before entering into the contract. It is not yet certain that the Irish courts[124] have wholly adopted the *O'Brien* principles on notice. In *Bank of Nova Scotia v Hogan*[125] Murphy J, *obiter*, speaking for the Supreme Court described the principles as "both relevant and helpful". However, it appeared that he would apply more stringent requirements to husband-wife guarantees. It was not apparent that he was prepared to fix a creditor with constructive notice of undue influence simply on the basis that the debtor and guarantor were married and that the transaction was not on its face to the financial advantage of the wife.

[18-69]

### Reasonable Steps

In these cases, the courts are alive to the possibility of imposing a disproportionate burden on the bank. In *Royal Bank of Scotland v Etridge*[126] Lord Nicholls in the

[18-70]

---

[118] Unmarried same-sex and opposite-sex co-habitants fall within this category: *Massey v Midland* [1995] 1 All ER 929.

[119] *ibid.*

[120] *Royal Bank of Scotland v Etridge*, above, n 58.

[121] [2001] IEHC 159.

[122] *Britannia Building Society v Pugh* [1997] 2 FLR 7.

[123] *CIBC Mortgages v Pitt*, above, n 88.

[124] See O'Callaghan, "Protection from Unfair Suretyships in Ireland" in Colombi Ciacchi (ed) *Protection of Non-Professional Sureties in Europe: Formal and Substantive Disparity* (Nomos, 2007).

[125] Above, n 76.

[126] Above, n 1.

House of Lords held that the bank cannot be expected to discover whether or not undue influence is present in every constructive notice case:

> "To require such an intrusive, inconclusive and expensive exercise in every case would be an altogether disproportionate response to the need to protect those cases, presumably a small minority, where a wife is being wronged ... The furthest a bank can be expected to go is to take reasonable steps to satisfy itself that the wife has had brought home to her, in a meaningful way, the practical implications of the proposed transaction. This does not wholly eliminate the risk of undue influence or misrepresentation. But it does mean that a wife enters into a transaction with her eyes open so far as the basic elements of the transaction are concerned."

**[18–71]**     In *Barclay's Bank v O'Brien*, Lord Browne-Wilkinson set out the reasonable steps which a creditor was obliged to take to avoid being fixed with constructive notice of the husband's undue influence as follows:

> "[U]nless there are special exceptional circumstances, a creditor will have taken such reasonable steps to avoid being fixed with constructive notice if the creditor warns the surety (at a meeting not attended by the principal debtor) of the amount of her potential liability and of the risks involved and advises the surety to take independent legal advice."

**[18–72]**     Lord Browne-Wilkinson did not require the wife to actually receive independent legal advice. He merely set out that a representative of the bank should attend a private meeting with the wife in which he warned the surety of the risks involved and advised her to obtain independent legal advice. In exceptional cases where the "creditor has knowledge of further facts which render the presence of undue influence not only possible but probable", Lord Browne-Wilkinson put the bank's duty no lower than *insisting* that the surety obtain independent legal advice. *Crédit Lyonnais v Burch*[127] (18–91) was one such exceptional case Nourse LJ held that the transaction in that case "[could not] possibly stand". It was an exceptional case and therefore it was not sufficient for the bank simply to advise the surety to obtain independent legal advice without ensuring that she has obtained it. Millett LJ in that case even went so far as to say that a mere insistence on independent advice may not always be sufficient to relieve a bank of its responsibilities in a case of this kind. Millett LJ set out his position as follows:

> "I should not be taken to accept that it would necessarily have made any difference even if the respondent had entered into the transaction after taking independent legal advice. Such advice is neither always necessary nor always sufficient. It is not a panacea. The result does not depend mechanically on the presence or absence of legal advice."

**[18–73]**     Millet LJ took the view that in some such exceptional circumstances independent legal advice would be irrelevant because the transaction was so

---

[127] [1997] 1 FLR 11.

improvident: "no competent solicitor could advise [Ms Burch] to enter into a guarantee in the terms she did."

There is, as yet, no clear guidance from the Irish cases on the steps which a bank   [18–74]
must take to ensure that *O'Brien*-type transactions will be upheld. In *Bank of Ireland v Smyth*[128] Blayney J referred favourably to the *O'Brien* standards. In *Bank of Nova Scotia v Hogan* Murphy J noted that: "[t]he availability of appropriate independent legal advice to Mrs Hogan would afford the bank a defence on a claim by her in respect of an equity to set aside the transaction if such an equity had existed." These dicta do not make clear whether an exhortion to obtain independent legal advice is essential. *Ulster Bank v Fitzgerald*[129] is often cited as authority for the proposition that it is not. O'Donovan J in that case considered that the fact that the bank's guarantee form contained a note at the top, headed by the word IMPORTANT, strongly recommending that anyone signing the guarantee should strongly consider seeking independent legal advice. He said that this notice went "above and beyond the call of duty". However, this statement has been roundly criticised.[130] In practice, it appears that lenders in this jurisdiction adopt a belt and braces approach, requiring sureties to obtain independent legal advice and to provide a solicitor's certificate that the advice has been obtained.[131] This strategy attempts to pass responsibility for the wife's protection on to solicitors. In any case, since 1 August 2006, Chapter 4(3) of the *Consumer Protection Code* requires all financial providers to display the following message on a guarantee: "Warning: As a guarantor of this loan, you will have to pay off the loan, the interest and all associated charges if the borrower does not. Before you sign this guarantee you should get independent legal advice".

Stuart-Smith LJ acknowledged in *Etridge*[132] that a "personal interview with the   [18–75]
wife is likely to expose the bank to far greater risks than those from which it wishes to be protected." In the Court of Appeal in *Etridge* he set out a number principles established in the case law which elaborate on the reasonable steps which the bank must follow in order to avoid the imputation of undue influence to it.

First, where a wife approaches the bank through her solicitor, the bank is not   [18–76]
ordinarily put on notice at all. This is the case even if the solicitor is also acting for her husband. This means that once the wife has legal representation, the bank need inquire no further. The bank must, however, provide the solicitor with any information reasonably required by the solicitor to advise the wife. This would include the necessary financial information.

Secondly, where the wife does not approach the bank through a solicitor, it is   [18–77]
enough for the bank to show that she was urged to take independent legal advice. Under *Etridge*, bank should protect itself still further by obtaining confirmation by the solicitor that he gave the requisite advice and that the wife appears to understand the

---

[128] [1996] 1 ILRM 241.
[129] Above, n 121.
[130] Clarke, *Contract Law in Ireland* (Roundhall, 2004) p 353; Mee "Undue Influence and Bank Guarantees" (2002) 37 *Irish Jurist* 292.
[131] Donnelly, "Undue Influence and Misrepresentation: What is a Bank to Do?" (1999) CLP 167.
[132] Above, n 58.

situation. A mere certificate from the solicitor to the effect that he has explained the transaction will suffice.

[18–78]     Thirdly, when advising a wife, a solicitor is acting exclusively as her solicitor. This is the case even if the solicitor is also acting for the husband or indeed for the bank itself. This means *inter alia* that even where the bank retains a solicitor to advise the wife, it is not fixed with imputed notice of what its solicitor learns in the course of advising the wife.[133]

[18–79]     Fourthly, the bank takes no responsibility for the advice given by the solicitor. A bank is not required to question the solicitor's independence or to question the sufficiency of the advice which he gives to the wife.[134] In *Bank of Baroda v Rayarel*[135] LJ stated that:

> "If a prospective surety deals with a bank through a solicitor, the bank is entitled to assume that the solicitor has given her appropriate advice. If there is a possibility of a conflict of interest between the surety and the other parties whom the solicitor is also advising, the bank is entitled to assume that the solicitor will have told her that she was entitled to take independent advice. The bank's legal department is not obliged to commit the professional discourtesy of communicating directly with the solicitor's client in tendering such advice itself. Nor is it obliged to inform the solicitor of his professional duties."

[18–80]     Even if the solicitor is also used by the bank itself, the bank is entitled to trust the solicitor to decide for himself whether a conflict of interest disables him from advising properly.[136]

[18–81]     Under *Etridge* the solicitor's duty is to satisfy himself that his client understands the nature and effect of the transaction and is willing to enter into it. He must explain the transaction to the wife, not merely formally but in a meaningful way, discussing her financial affairs and emphasising, in particular, the risks involved in the transaction. He should emphasise to her that she has a choice whether to enter into the transaction and ask her whether she wishes him to renegotiate the transaction on better terms. The solicitor does not have any obligation to veto the transaction where it is not in the wife's best interests, though he should advise her to that effect. The wife is entitled to make a bad bargain if she pleases. Lord Nicholls said that: "at the end of the day the decision on whether to proceed is the decision of the client, not the solicitor. A wife is not to be precluded from entering into a financially unwise transaction if, for her own reasons, she wishes to do so." The House of Lords did, however, suggest that he could indirectly prevent the transaction (by declining to act) if it is "glaringly obvious that the wife is being grievously wronged".

[18–82]     The *Etridge* approach to the provision of legal advice, therefore, restores certainty to the area of non-commercial guarantees by restricting the situations in

---

[133] *Midland Bank v Serter and Anor* [1995] 1 FLR 1034.
[134] See *Banco Exterior v Mann* [1995] 1 All ER 936; *Bank of Baroda v Shah* [1988] 3 All ER 24.
[135] [1995] 2 FLR 376.
[136] *Barclays Bank v Thompson* [1997] 1 FLR 156.

which such important transactions can be set aside. However, the decision does little to address the problem which the *O'Brien* doctrine was developed to tackle: the empowerment of vulnerable guarantors in situations where they are emotionally dependant on debtors. Lord Hobhouse in *Etridge* observed that the solicitor's advice required under *Etridge* is frequently a:

> "... formality or merely served to reinforce the husband's wishes and undermine any scope for the wife to exercise her independent judgment whether to comply ... The law has, in order to accommodate the commercial lenders, adopted a fiction which nullifies the equitable principles and deprives vulnerable members of the public of the protection which equity gave them."

The House of Lords in *Etridge* did, however, contemplate that, in two types of wholly exceptional case, the bank might be under a heightened duty to take extra steps: [18–83]

> "If the bank is in possession of material information which is not available to the solicitor, or if the transaction is one into which no competent solicitor could properly advise the wife to enter, the availability of legal advice is insufficient to avoid the bank being fixed with constructive notice."

In the "material information" scenario, the bank might be obliged to inform the wife's solicitor of its suspicions. It might also be bound to insist that the wife be advised by a solicitor who is wholly independent both of the bank and of her husband. The "no competent solicitor" scenario is more difficult. There may, as Millet LJ suggested pre-*Etridge*, even be some situations where independent legal advice cannot aid the bank. In such circumstances of heightened suspicion, the bank might be said to accept the guarantee at its own risk. Donnelly argues that this position is consistent with the existing Irish position on unconscionable bargain, under which the courts are willing to overlook the presence of independent advice where the bargain is grossly improvident.[137] [18–84]

## IV. Unconscionable Bargain

If a contract has been procured by threats or pressure, it can be set aside for duress or for actual undue influence. If the relationship between the parties has been exploited, it can be avoided for presumed undue influence. Can the contract be set aside where neither pressure nor relationship is present? The courts have an equitable jurisdiction to set aside unconscionable bargains. This power arises "from the circumstances of the parties contracting – weakness on one side, usury on the other, or extortion or advantage taken of that weakness ... It means an unconscientious use of the power arising out of these circumstances and conditions"[138] It is generally agreed that this doctrine has its foundation in a concern for procedural justice. [18–85]

Lord Templeman in *Boustaney v Piggott*[139] identified four essential and overlapping ingredients to the doctrine of unconscionable bargain. The first is that [18–86]

---

[137] Donnelly, "Undue Influence and Misrepresentation: What is a Bank to Do?" (1999) CLP 167.
[138] *Chesterfield v Janssen* Ves Sen Supp 297.
[139] (1995) 69 P & CR 298.

the party seeking to set the transaction aside must have been under a bargaining impairment which placed him at a serious disadvantage as against the other party. The second is that the enforcing party must have exploited this disadvantage. The third is that the resulting transaction is manifestly improvident for the party seeking to set it aside. The fourth is that the complaining party lacked adequate advice.

### Unconscionable Bargain and Substantive Justice

[18–87] The old cases emphasised the first *Boustaney* requirement; the circumstances of the weaker party and their effect on his ability to consent to the contract. For example, poor men were felt to lack full competence to contract.[140] The current justification remains procedural, but the focus now is on the second requirement: the exploitative behaviour of the party seeking to enforce the contract. The courts have denied that the main concern of the doctrine is with the third factor; the substantive justice of the transaction. In *Boustaney v Piggott*[141] Lord Templeman wrote that:

> "Unequal bargaining power or objectively unreasonable terms provide no basis for equitable interference in the absence of unconscientious or extortionate abuse of power ... equity will not provide relief unless the beneficiary is guilty of unconscionable conduct ... namely that unconscientious advantage has been taken of his disabling condition or circumstances."

[18–88] However, it is clear that the third factor is of crucial importance to the doctrine of unconscionable bargain. First, no relief is forthcoming where the transaction is not manifestly improvident. In addition, evidence of the third factor will allow the courts to infer the presence of the other three. Unimpaired parties tend to enter into beneficial transactions. Therefore, if the transaction is grossly unjust, the Court may infer that the disadvantaged party was labouring under an impairment which must have been clear to the other party. A grossly improvident transaction will also tend to suggest the absence of adequate advice. The four *Boustaney v Piggott* requirements will now be examined in turn.

### Bargaining Impairment

[18–89] In *Grealish v Murphy*[142] Gavan Duffy J noted that "[e]quity comes to the rescue when the parties to a contract have not met on equal terms". In *Blomley v Ryan*[143] it was suggested that the type of impairment contemplated would encompass "poverty or

---

[140] *Evans v Llewellin* J Cox 333; *Haygarth v Wearing* Law Rep 12 Eq 320. The effects of poverty on bargaining power are explained in Schwartz "A Re-examination of Nonsubstantive Unconscionability" (1977) 63 Va L Rev 1053. First, poverty may restrict a party's ability to buy a fair contract. For example, contracts that are subject to wide-ranging exclusion clauses are often cheaper than those that offer the weaker party substantial protection in the event of breach. Secondly, there may be a relationship between poverty and commercial know-how so that the poor have inferior bargaining skills and are less well able to understand contracts. Thirdly, the poor may have inferior access to information upon which to make their bargaining decisions.

[141] (1995) 69 P & CR 298.

[142] [1946] IR 35.

[143] (1956) 99 CLR 362.

need of any kind, sickness, age, sex, infirmity of mind or body, drunkenness, illiteracy, lack of education, lack of assistance or explanation where assistance or explanation is necessary". In *Carroll v Carroll*[144] Denham J held that an impairment was present where a frail elderly man transferred a pub to his son in circumstances where he had not received adequate legal advice. Similarly, impairment was present in *Grealish v Murphy*,[145] in which Gavan Duffy J memorably described the impaired party, Peter Grealish, as follows:

> "[He] is by way of being a farmer; he is a bachelor in his sixties; he is a man of a generous turn, but obstinate; he can hardly read and he signs as a marksman; he is affected with a worse than Boetian headpiece and a very poor memory; a long life has not taught him sense ... [N]eglected by his relatives and almost bereft of friends; he was loaded with possessions, far above his modest wants and beyond his modest capacity for management."

In the colourful English case of *Earl of Aylesford v Morris*[146] the Earl of Aylesford was held to be under a bargaining impairment. While still a young man, he borrowed from a money-lender at 60 per cent interest in order to repay his considerable debts. Lord Selbourne explained that the earl was at a disadvantage as against the moneylender because he was subject to "the follies and vices of unprotected youth, inexperience and moral imbecility". The judgment continues in dramatic tones:                    **[18–90]**

> "[H]e comes in the dark, and in fetters, without either the will or the power to take care of himself, and with nobody else to take care of him ... the effect of all the circumstances ... is to deliver over the prodigal helpless into the hands of those taking advantage of his weakness."

## Exploitation

The exploitative conduct of the party seeking to uphold the transaction is an essential element of the doctrine of unconscionable bargain. Millett LJ stated in *Credit Lyonnais Bank Nederland LV v Burch*[147] that it must be shown:                    **[18–91]**

> "... not only that the terms of the transaction were harsh or oppressive, but that one of the parties to it has imposed the objectionable terms in a morally reprehensible manner ... there must be some impropriety, both in the conduct of the stronger party and in terms of the transaction itself ...".

This is clear from *Portman Building Society v Dunsaugh*[148] in which the defendant was an elderly, illiterate man living on a low income. He agreed to mortgage his home to enable his son to buy a supermarket. The business failed and the mortgagee sought to take possession of the house. The transaction was not set aside:                    **[18–92]**

---

[144] Above, n 106.
[145] Above, n 142.
[146] Law Rep 8 Ch 484.
[147] Above, n 84.
[148] [2002] 2 All ER 221.

"True it is that it was a financially unwise venture because, absent good profit from the business, there was never likely to be the income to service the borrowing and the father's home was at risk. But there was nothing, absolutely nothing, which comes close to morally reprehensible conduct or propriety. No unconscientious advantage has been taken of the father's illiteracy, his lack of business acumen or his paternal generosity. True it may be that the son gained all the advantage and the father took all the risk, but this cannot be stigmatised as impropriety. There was no exploitation of father by son such as would prick the conscience and tell the son that in all honour it was morally wrong and reprehensible."

[18–93]  The first point to make here is that a party cannot be held to have taken advantage of circumstances of which he had neither actual nor constructive knowledge. Thus, in *O'Connor v Hart*[149] the senile dementia of one party was irrelevant to the validity of a contract because the other party was not aware of it and had no reason to suspect it. The issue of constructive knowledge of a party's disadvantage is especially important in the context of banking. For example, in *Commercial Bank of Australia v Amadio*[150] two elderly Italians who had emigrated to Australia guaranteed their son's business debts. The couple had no business experience, the transaction had not been properly explained to them and their grasp of English was poor. Circumstances of disadvantage were clearly present. Even though the bank did not have actual knowledge of the couple's disadvantage it was enough to fix them with knowledge of that disadvantage that they were "aware of the possibility that the situation [of special disadvantage] may exist, or [were] aware of facts that would raise the possibility in the mind of any reasonable person". The same principle was applied in *Morrisson v West Coast Finance*[151] in which a bank was fixed with constructive knowledge of a mortgagor's disadvantage. The mortgagor was an elderly lady who had taken out the mortgage to allow two strangers to pay of their debts to the same bank. In such circumstances, the bank reasonably ought to have known of her disadvantage.

[18–94]  Secondly, active victimisation of the disadvantaged party is not required. Mere acceptance of an offer from a party who is operating at a special disadvantage may establish grounds for unconscionabilty. Lord Selbourne stated in *Earl of Aylesford v Morriss*[152] that the proscribed conduct is that which "falls below the standards demanded by equity ... it is victimisation which can consist either of the active extortion of a benefit or the passive acceptance of a benefit in unconscionable circumstances". Arguably, this idea of passive exploitation is out of kilter with the classical contract law. Leff argues the point thus[153]:

"It seems to me that the real question underlying and masked by 'the unconscionability problem' is this: ought one to be allowed by the law to reap material gain from some advantage for which one is not responsible, that is, which one did not, commendably *or* evilly, cause? To put it another way,

---

[149] [1985] 1 NZLR 159.
[150] (1983) 151 CLR 447.
[151] (1965) 55 DLR (2d) 710.
[152] (1872–73) LR 8 Ch App 484.
[153] Leff, "Thomist Unconscionability" (1979) 4 Can Bus LJ 424.

should a person be allowed to arrogate to himself the fruits of being just smarter, or just stronger or just luckier than someone else with whom he is doing a deal?"

## Improvident Transaction

The next requirement is that the transaction is improvident. Often it will be possible to show that the transaction is objectively unfair, as, for example, where the subject-matter is sold at significant undervalue. The cases are full of examples of transactions which would be considered improvident by all but the most unreasonable observer. In *Fry v Lane*[154] £170 paid for consoles worth £475 was struck down as unconscionable. In *Rooney v Conway*[155] the sale of a farm for a quarter of its market value was unconscionable. A contract was struck down in *Slator v Nolan*[156] by which a young, reckless, bankrupt man sold his inheritance at significant undervalue to his brother-in-law, an experienced businessman with some legal knowledge. In *Rae v Joyce*[157] the requisite improvidence was shown where a pregnant woman on low income mortgaged a property at 60 per cent interest with a very astute money-lender. [18–95]

It appears from some of the cases that subjective improvidence will be enough to set the contract aside. Subjective improvidence does not turn on price or value. It refers to those situations where the transaction is not one which a rational self-interested person would not be expected to make. The impaired party in such transactions receives no direct benefit from the transaction but bears a heavy risk of loss. In transactions of this type, the Court will ask whether the bargain is explicable on the basis of the relationship between the parties. If it can not, it will be treated as improvident. An example comes from the famous case of *Grealish v Murphy*[158] in which the vulnerable Peter Grealish had invited Thomas Murphy to come and work his land for him. In exchange, he assigned his farm absolutely to Murphy subject to a life interest for himself.[159] The transaction was held to be an improvident one. First, the transaction afforded little benefit to Grealish, although it placed him at great risk. Gavan Duffy J described it as "shocking". This was an assignment by deed. Unlike a will, it was irrevocable, no matter what might happen in the future. "Murphy might have taken to drink or gone to the devil or married a shrew who would make Peter's life a torture." He might have predeceased Peter, in which case the land would have gone to his heirs, leaving Peter with nothing. Secondly, the transaction was inexplicable on the [18–96]

---

[154] (1888) 40 Ch D 312.
[155] Unreported, NI Chancery Div, 8 March 1992.
[156] (1876) IR 11 Eq 367.
[157] (1892) 2 LR (Ir) 500.
[158] Above, n 142.
[159] One must have some sympathy for Murphy, for whom "the golden prospect ... that he would be a rich man after a few years of not too arduous labour" must have faded somewhat in the face of the hostility which met him when he moved onto Peter's farm; "after his arrival, a quite unforeseen and particularly unpleasant series of attacks came from one of Peter's sisters, a bedlam, living some three miles away, who would descend in wrath upon Carnmore at intervals, giving tongue to loud maledictions at the grabber of her brother's land. Murphy ... actually went in fear of his life from some of the local roughs, a number of whom had stoned his car, and he found the onslaughts of the termagant almost equally hard to endure". Eventually, police protection was required for Murphy "on the dark nights, while he remained at Carnmore."

basis of the relationship between the parties. The transaction placed Peter "for the remainder of his life very much at the mercy of a rather impecunious young man, who had no ties of blood and was still unproved as a friend." A similar case is *Crédit Lyonnais v Burch*[160] in which an employee guaranteed her employer's significant debts by mortgaging her home to the bank. The transaction involved tremendous risk and no direct benefit. It was inexplicable on the basis of the parties' relationship. Accordingly, it was improvident. By contrast, in *Portman Building Society v Dunsagh*,[161] parents' guarantees to support loans to their children were not held as improvident. Even though these transactions are risky and do not benefit the parents directly, they are explicable on the basis of the parent-child relationship.

### Lack of Adequate Advice

[18–97] The fourth requirement under this doctrine is that the disadvantaged party should have had adequate and independent advice about the transaction. In *Fry v Lane*[162] the defendant, Lane had induced the Fry brothers to sell property to him. Kay J in this passage sets out his reasons for setting the bargain aside:

> "The price [paid for the land was] considerably below the real value. Both Fry and his brother George were poor, ignorant men to whom the temptation of the immediate possession of £100 would be very great. Neither of them in the transaction on the sale of his share was ... 'on equal terms with the purchaser'. Neither had independent advice. The solicitor who acted for both parties in each transaction ... had not been more than a year and a half on the roll ... I think in each transaction he must have been considering the purchaser's interest too much properly to guard that of the vendors ... I regret that I must come to the conclusion that, though there was a semblance of bargaining by the solicitor in each case, he did not properly protect the vendors, but gave a great advantage to the purchasers."

[18–98] By contrast, in *Kelly v Morrisroe*[163] the advanced aged of one of the parties cast an onus on the other party to show that he had not taken advantage of his stronger bargaining position. He discharged that onus by showing that she had been advised by her former employer, who he trusted and who was present with her when the final documents were signed.

[18–99] Similar issues arise here as arose in the undue influence cases, particularly in relation to the special impairment of the disadvantaged party. In *Grealish v Murphy*[164] Peter had received independent advice from an experienced solicitor. However, the solicitor was not fully aware of Peter's limited mental capacity. He had therefore treated Peter as he would a normal client, and accordingly had neither given him the complete explanation of the transaction that a man of his capacity required, nor

---

[160] *Times Law Reports*, 1 July 1996.
[161] Above, n 148.
[162] (1888) 40 Ch D 312.
[163] (1919) 53 ILTR 145.
[164] Above, n 142.

explored with him the need to take measures to protect himself and his own future. Thus the legal advice provided here was not enough to save the transaction.

## V. A General Doctrine of Unfairness?

In *Lloyd's Bank v Bundy*[165] Lord Denning attempted to establish a doctrine of "inequality of bargaining power". He stated that the courts would give relief where four ingredients were present. The first three focus on the party seeking relief. The first was that he had not had independent advice. Secondly, his bargaining power had been impaired by his own needs or desires, by his ignorance or by his infirmity. Thirdly, he must have been subjected to some undue influence or improper pressure. This pressure could be exerted by the other party to the contract or by someone else for that party's benefit. The final factor is that the consideration supporting the contract must have been inadequate. There was no requirement of actual wrongdoing by the stronger party. Lord Denning said that: "[t]he one who stipulates for an unfair advantage may be bound solely by his own self-interest unconscious of the distress he is bringing to the other". Furthermore, this new doctrine had nothing to do with the weaker party's consent to the transaction. Lord Denning's aim was to save weak people from the consequences of bad bargains entered into with their superiors in the market. Lord Denning's doctrine was wide-ranging and uncertain, and its potential to undermine bargains was immense. Small wonder then that it was rejected in *National Westminster Bank v Morgan*[166] and again in *Boustany v Piggott*.[167] However, there is some very slight support for a similar doctrine in Irish law in the High Court judgment in *Carroll v Carroll*[168] and in that in *Gregg v Kidd*.[169]

[18–100]

---

[165] Above, n 79.
[166] [1985] AC 686.
[167] (1995) 16 P and CR 298.
[168] Above, n 106.
[169] Above, n 82.

# CHAPTER 19
# Illegal Contracts

*"[N]o court of justice can in its nature be made the handmaid of iniquity"*[1]

## I. Introduction

A contract which falls foul of the doctrine of illegality will not be enforced. This is not because of the manner of its formation but because of "the kind of activity or action that is required by, or closely linked to" the contract.[2] The contract is struck down, in essence, for reasons of public policy which happen to be crystallised into principles of common law or statute. So we say that illegality can operate as a substantive limitation on the enforceability of contracts.[3]    **[19–01]**

How can refusing to enforce a contract on grounds of illegality be justified? The first justification is that illegal contracts go beyond the proper scope of contractual autonomy. Suppose A and B contract to kill C, who is a brilliant lawyer and a father of ten. A liberal theorist such as John Stuart Mill would have justified interference in this    **[19–02]**

---

[1] *Bank of the United States v Owens* 27 US (2 Pet) 527 (1829); *Stone v Freeman* 298 NY 268, 82 NE 2d 571 (1948) ("no court shall be required to serve as a paymaster of the proceeds of crime, or referee between two thieves").

[2] *ibid.*

[3] Smith, *Contract Theory*, (Oxford University Press, 2003) 245.

contract on the basis of what is called a "harm principle": respect for the parties' autonomy means that the courts should not generally interfere in a contract but may do so where it harms another. Law and economics theorists offer a similar perspective: where a contract results in negative "externalities", ie where a contract makes third parties worse off, the proper role of contract in maximising the overall wealth of society is defeated and the contract should not be enforced. Therefore, illegal contracts ought to be deterred. The courts have expressly referred to this object of deterrence. For example, in *Taylor v Bhail*,[4] Millet J described a judgment against a builder who had agreed to help a customer to defraud his insurance company by providing a false estimate as "a clear message ... to the commercial community".[5] However, the efficacy of the doctrine of illegality as a deterrent is to be doubted, besides which, deterrence is generally considered a goal of criminal rather than civil law.[6]

[19-03]      The courts also employ what Smith calls the "dignity of the courts"[7] justification. Havinghurst observes that:

> "[P]rotection of the good name of the judicial institution must provide the principal reason for the denial of a remedy to one who has trafficked in the forbidden."[8]

[19-04]      The courts' view is that as in AP Herbert's memorable phrase, "the dirty dog gets no dinner here". Corbin thought this justification humbug, writing that:

> "[I]t is not the part of either wisdom or justice for the representatives of the state to assume a 'holier than thou' attitude and to refuse a remedy in pious fear that the 'judicial ermine' might otherwise be soiled."[9]

[19-05]      The courts have also relied on the "wrong-doing" justification. This is a manifestation of the principle that a man shall not be allowed to profit from his wrongdoing. So in *Boresford v Royal Insurance Company Ltd*,[10] Lord Atkin noted that "the Courts will not recognise a benefit accruing to a criminal from his crime". Smith explains this justification in political terms.[11] The services available under contract law are a scare resource and, as a matter of political policy, the State chooses to deny that resource to wrong-doers. A similar justification was adopted by Lord Mansfield in the old case of *Holman v Johnson*[12]:

> "No court will lend its aid to a man who founds his cause of action upon an immoral or illegal act. If from the plaintiff's own stating or otherwise, the cause

---

[4] [1996] CLC 377.
[5] *ibid.*
[6] Havinghurst, "Book Review", (1952) 61 Yale LJ 1138.
[7] Smith, *op. cit.*, 246–268.
[8] Havinghurst, *op. cit.*. The US case of *Coppell v Hall* confirms that contracts are voidable for public policy "not for the sake of the defendant, but of the law itself" (1868) 74 U (7 Wall) 542.
[9] Corbin, *Contracts* (1964) § 1534.
[10] [1938] AC 386, 599.
[11] Smith, *op. cit.*, 264–265.
[12] (1775) 1 Cowp 741.

of action appears to arise *ex turpi causa*, or the transgression of a positive law of this country, there the courts say he has no right to be assisted."

There are, however, significant disadvantages associated with an unqualified **[19–06]** application of the illegality doctrine. First, any intervention into the parties' bargain on the basis of the substance of the contract conflicts with the principle of sanctity of contract and the general rule that bargains should be upheld. Secondly, and on a related point, any interference with a bargain should be in proportion to the harm sought to be avoided. However, the law of illegality has often been criticised as lacking the necessary nuance to deal appropriately with cases of varying opprobrium. In *Tinsley v Mulligan*,[13] Lord Goff described the illegality rules as "indiscriminate in their effect, and capable therefore of producing injustice." It will be demonstrated that a party who has been involved in a trivial or technical breach of the law may find that he forfeits property which has passed under the contract, that his contract falls and that no remedy is available to him. Lord Bingham in *Saunders v Edwards*[14] appeared aware of this dilemma and expressed the courts' difficulty thus:

"Where issues of illegality are raised, the courts have to steer a middle course between two unacceptable positions. On the one hand, it is unacceptable that any court of law should aid or lend its authority to a party seeking to pursue or enforce an object or agreement which the law prohibits. On the other hand, it is unacceptable that the court should, on the first indication of unlawfulness affecting any aspect of a transaction, draw up its skirts and refuse all assistance to the plaintiff, no matter how serious his loss or how dispropor-tionate."

In view of the disadvantages of a rigid illegality doctrine, the courts adopt a **[19–07]** flexible approach in these cases. First, where the contract is illegal under statute (19–08) the courts will use the canons of statutory interpretation to bring it outside the scope of illegality. Secondly, some categories of illegality, such as the category of "contracts tending to promote immorality" (19–19) depend explicitly on malleable and increasingly liberal notions of public policy for their meaning. There is even scope for leniency where the contract is proved illegal. For instance, a party can enforce a contract that is illegal in its performance rather than in its formation if he has not himself participated in the illegality (19–44). Even if a contract is unenforceable there are situations in which a party will be able to recover any property that has passed under the contract (19–46). Options for severing the illegal part of the contact and enforcing the remainder also appear to be expanding (19–62)

## II. Contracts Illegal Under Statute

The cases on statutory illegality are of two types. The first type, express illegality, **[19–08]** concerns the situation where an act is prohibited by statute and the parties enter into a contract to do that act. If an act is illegal under statute, then a contract to do that act will also be illegal and will therefore be unenforceable. For example, the Family Home Protection Act 1976 in s 3(1) prohibits a spouse from conveying an interest in the

---

[13] [1993] 3 All ER 65.
[14] [1987] 2 All ER 651.

family home without the prior written consent of the other spouse. Therefore, a contract to convey the family home in this manner is void as illegal. In employment law, contracts bargaining away holiday pay entitlements,[15] minimum notice periods,[16] redundancy payments or compensation for unfair dismissal will be unenforceable as illegal. The Gaming and Lotteries Acts 1956–1986 expressly provide that every contract by way of gaming or wagering is void (the purpose here is to stem the potentially crippling number of gambling contracts that would come to court had the courts the power to enforce them)[17]

[19–09]     The second type of case is one in which a contract is illegal under statute by implication. In this situation an act is prohibited by statute. The parties have formed a contract that touches on the prohibited act but is not a contract to deliberately *do* the prohibited act. It is a contract that is merely collateral to the commission of the illegal act. In *St John Shipping v Joseph Rank*,[18] Devlin J gave the following example which touches on this distinction:

> "For example, a person is forbidden by statute from using an unlicensed vehicle on the highway. If one asks oneself whether there is in such an enactment an implied prohibition of all contracts for the use of unlicensed vehicles, the answer may well be that there is, and that contracts of hire would be unenforceable. But if one asks oneself whether there is an implied prohibition of contracts for the carriage of goods by unlicensed vehicles or for the repairing of unlicensed vehicles or for the garaging of unlicensed vehicles, the answer may well be different. The answer might be that collateral contracts of this sort are not within the ambit of the statute."

[19–10]     In deciding whether a collateral contract is statutorily illegal by implication, the court will adopt a purposive interpretation of the statute at issue. It will ask, in other words, whether the object or intention of the legislature in setting down a particular section was to prohibit the type of contract at issue. The usual canons of statutory interpretation will apply here. In *Gavin Low Ltd v Field*,[19] the plaintiffs had sold a cow which was unfit for human consumption. The statute prohibited the exposure for sale, or deposit for the purposes of sale or preparation for sale of such animals. The question was whether a contract for their sale was illegal under statute. The Court found that it was not. The purpose of the statute was the protection of public health by making it illegal to expose a diseased animal for sale. The dissenting judges reasoned that since the legislature had prohibited all of the steps preliminary to completing a contract for the sale of an unfit animal it was unlikely that it did not intend to prohibit the contract itself: "Prohibition of the bud is then prohibition of the blossom."[20] In *Hortensius Ltd v Bishops*,[21] trustees of a bank invested funds in a manner which breached a statute. The Court, however, found that the contract was not illegal. The

---

[15] Holidays (Employees) Act 1973.

[16] Minimum Notice and Terms of Employment Act 1973, s 5(3).

[17] See further Clark, *Contract Law in Ireland* (5th ed., Thomson Round Hall, 2004) 389–394.

[18] [1957] 1 QB 267.

[19] [1942] IR 86.

[20] *ibid.*

[21] [1989] ILRM 294.

purpose of the statute was to prohibit trustees from entering into these types of contract, not to make such contracts illegal outright. Similarly, in *Smith v Mawhood*,[22] the purpose of a statute which prohibited the sale of tobacco without a license was held to be to raise revenue for the State and not to ban the sale of tobacco outright. Thus, a contract for the sale of tobacco was legal and enforceable albeit it was concluded without a license.

*St John Shipping v Joseph Rank*[23] is a good case study in the judicial approach to statutory illegality. Devlin J in that case stated that the Court will ask two questions. The first is whether the object of the statute is to void contracts at all. The second is whether the object of the statute is to void contracts of the type before the Court. *St John Shipping* itself turned on the Merchant Shipping (Safety and Load Line Conventions) Act 1932, s 44 of which provided that a ship "shall not be so loaded as to submerge" the appropriate load line. The illegal act here was loading the ship so that it was inappropriately submerged. A contract for the loading of the ship which necessarily had this effect would be illegal under the statute. The ship owner in this case, in contravention of the statute, committed this illegal act by overloading his ship. However, the contract at issue was not a loading contract but a contract for the carriage of goods: a contract collateral to the commission of the illegal act. This was one reason why Devlin J felt that the contract was not illegal under the statute. He was bolstered in this conclusion by the observation that the statute already exacted a criminal penalty for overloading. Similar reasoning was adopted in *Archbolds (Freightage) Ltd v S Spangletts Ltd*[24]: **[19–11]**

> "The purpose of this statute is sufficiently served by the penalties prescribed for the offender; the avoidance of the contract would cause grave inconvenience and injury to members of the public without furthering the object of the statute."

This is an important point which turns on the issue of proportion. If a statute already punishes an illegal act by levying a given penalty, and if the legislature has limited itself to the imposition of that penalty, it seems excessive to add to the wrongdoer's punishment by destroying his contract—an action which may have far more serious financial consequences than any criminal penalty. For example, in *Shaw v Groom*[25] a landlord failed to provide his tenant with a rent book in contravention of landlord and tenant legislation. The question for the Court was whether the lease itself was illegal under this legislation. The Court found that it was not. The purpose of the legislation was to penalise the landlord for non-provision of a rent book. That purpose was adequately achieved by the specific penalties set out in the legislation. Ruling the contract illegal, thereby allowing the tenant to escape his contractual obligation to pay rent, would be entirely out of proportion to this aim. **[19–12]**

Finally, Devlin J supported his conclusion in *St John Shipping* by laying down the conservative principle that where the legislature has not expressly stated that a type **[19–13]**

---

[22]  (1845) 14 M & W 452.
[23]  [1957] 1 QB 267.
[24]  [1961] 2 QB 374.
[25]  [1970] 2 WLR 299.

of contract collateral to the main offence is illegal, the Court should be reluctant to imply an intention to that effect. Devlin J wrote:

"I think a court ought to be very slow to hold that a statute intends to interfere with the rights and remedies given by the ordinary law of contract. Caution in this respect is, I think, especially necessary in these times when so much of commercial life is governed by regulations of one sort or another, which may easily be broken without wicked intent."

[19–14]    It is not true to say that a collateral contract will never be illegal under statute. However, Devlin J would not make such a finding of illegality except in limited circumstances. The contract must be one directly resulting from the illegal act and not merely one related to the illegal act.

## III. Contracts Illegal at Common Law

[19–15]    Common law illegality is based explicitly on principles of public policy. A court can declare that a contract that it considers contrary to public policy is illegal and unenforceable. This breed of illegality is subject to the criticism that the courts are usurping the function of the legislature by voiding contracts according to their own scruples. Thus, the courts must be alert to avoid abuse of this powerful doctrine and to keep their discretion within reasonable bounds.[26]

### Contracts to Commit a Crime or a Tort

[19–16]    An agreement is illegal if its direct or indirect object is the commission of a crime or a tort. Thus, a contract to commit an assault on a third party[27] or a contract to publish what is known to be libellous material[28] would be illegal. The maxim that governs this category of case is: *ex turpi causa non oritur actio* —no legal action may arise from circumstances of wrongdoing. A contract that has its basis in the circumstances of a crime or a tort is therefore unenforceable. So in the famous Highwayman's case,[29] an agreement between highway robbers to share the proceeds of their robberies was held unenforceable because it had its origins in a crime. In *Clay v Yates*,[30] a contract to publish a libel was held illegal because it was grounded in a tort. In *Gray v Hibernian Insurance*,[31] Barrington J held that the burden of proving the elements of the crime or tort falls on the party alleging that it has been committed.

[19–17]    This category of illegal contracts is of particular relevance to contracts of insurance and indemnity. The general rule is that the court will not uphold a contract of indemnity which has the effect of indemnifying a person against the consequences of unlawful conduct. In *Beresford v Royal Insurance Co,*[32] the relatives of a deceased man were denied the right to claim on a life assurance policy because he had committed

---

[26] See e.g. *Printing and Numerical Registering Co v Sampson* (1875) LR 19 Eq 462 *per* Jessel MR.
[27] *Allan v Rescous* (1676) 2 Lev 174.
[28] *Apthorp v Neville* (1907) 23 TLR 575.
[29] *Everet v Williams* (1893) 9 LQR 197.
[30] (1856) 1 H & C 73.
[31] Unreported, High Court, 27 May 1993.
[32] [1938] 2 All E 602.

suicide. At the time, suicide was a criminal act. Lord Atkin in part explained the courts' unwillingness to enforce such contracts in terms of deterrence:

"I think that the principle is that a man is not to be allowed to have recourse in a court of justice to claim a benefit from his crime, whether under a contract or under a gift. No doubt the rule pays regard to the fact that to hold otherwise would in some cases offer an inducement to crime, but, apart from these considerations, the absolute rule is that the courts will not recognise the benefit accruing to a criminal on his crime."

What will happen if the party seeking to rely on the contract has been acquitted of the crime alleged? In the controversial case of *Gray v Barr*[33] the plaintiff sued the defendant for negligently causing the death of her husband. The defendant sought to rely on an insurance policy covering liability for injury caused by home accidents. The defendant had made an unlawful and violent attack on the plaintiff's husband with a loaded gun but had been acquitted at trial of both his murder and his manslaughter. Lord Denning MR held that, despite the criminal acquittal, the defendant had committed a violent attack on the plaintiff's husband. The defendant should not be allowed to rely on his insurance policy to avoid the consequences of his wrongdoing. The Irish courts appear to take a different approach. In *Gray v Hibernian*,[34] Barron J considered the case of an insurance company that was refusing to honour a policy of insurance. The person relying on the insurance policy was a publican's widow. The publican had been acquitted of arson. At trial, two alleged accomplices testified that he had commissioned them to set fire to a pub in order to bring about an insurance claim. Later in the Circuit Court, during malicious damages proceedings, the same accomplices gave similar testimony and the Court ruled that they were probably telling the truth. The question for Barron J was whether this finding that the accomplices' testimony was credible was enough to outweigh the publican's acquittal of arson and justify a finding that the widow could not rely on the insurance policy because such reliance would reward criminal wrongdoing. Barron J held that in order to succeed the insurance company would have to provide more than mere allegations of wrongdoing. To sustain a claim of illegality in the circumstances of this case, they would have to make out a specific crime. The standard of proof required was heavier than the balance of probabilities. **[19–18]**

## Contracts Involving Immorality

A contract designed to encourage unlawful gambling is illegal. In *Devine v Scott and Johnston*[35] a lease of premises to a man who intended to carry out an unlawful bookmaking business was struck down as illegal. It was important that the landlord here had knowledge of the bookmaker's activity. **[19–19]**

A contract that tends to encourage or reward illicit sexual behaviour may also be unenforceable as illegal. A famous case here is *Pearce v Brooks*,[36] which involved a **[19–20]**

---

[33] [1971] 2 QB 554.

[34] Above, n 31.

[35] (1931) 66 ILTR 107.

[36] (1866) LR 1 Ex 213.

contract for the lease of an ornate brougham to a prostitute who planned to use it in attracting clients. The contract was struck down as illegal because of its immoral purpose. Notions of sexual immorality will change with the passage of time. An American judge has written:

> "That which is against public morals and public decency shall be subject to the condemnation of the courts in all generations. Righteousness is the same today as it was yesterday."[37]

[19–21]    However, courts on this side of the Atlantic have taken a more pragmatic view. Sable J once famously remarked:

> "Are the actions of people to-day to be judged in the light of the standards of the last century? As counsel for the plaintiff said, cases discussing what was then by community standards sexual immorality appear to have been decided in the days when for the sake of decency the legs of the table wore drapes ...".[38]

[19–22]    That changing morality has shaped this category of cases is clear from a comparison of two English cases. In *Upfill v Wright*[39] a contract to let a flat to people who were using it for adultery was judged illegal as contrary to public policy. Some 60 years later, however, in *Heglibiston Establishment v Heyman & Others*,[40] a contract of the same nature was held enforceable. More recently, in *Armhouse Lee Ltd v Chappell*[41] the Court of Appeal rejected an argument that the defendants, who ran a sex line service, were not obliged to pay for advertisements they had placed with the plaintiffs. The Court held that there was no general moral code that justified the Court in striking down the bargain here. It seems safe to say that this head of illegality has lost its teeth in recent years. Contracts are likely to be upheld except where the sexual misconduct involved has the status of a criminal offence.

### Contracts Injurious to Good Government

[19–23]    Contracts tending to weaken or interfere with good government are illegal under the common law. Contracts encouraging corruption are an important category under this heading. So, in *Lord Mayor, Alderman and Burgesses of Dublin v Hayes*[42] an agreement to pay money in exchange for an appointment to public office was struck down as illegal. Similarly, an agreement to use one's influence as a public representative to procure a government contract would be illegal. In *Wilkinson v Osbourne*,[43] Isaacs J said:

> "It would be disastrous to the community to permit this to be recognised as a legitimate subject of traffic; it would encourage those who are appointed to be

---

[37] *Crichfield v Bermudez Paving Co.* (1898) 174 Ill 466, 51 NE 552.
[38] *Andrews v Parker* [1973] Qd R 93 *per* Sable J.
[39] [1911] 1 KB 506.
[40] [1977] 36 P & CR 351.
[41] *The Times*, 7 August 1996 *cf. Hughes v Clewley* [1996] 1 Lloyd's Rep 35.
[42] (1876) 10 IRCL 226.
[43] (1915) 21 CLR 89.

sentinels of the public welfare to become ... the 'sappers and miners' of the Constitution."

## Contracts Prejudicial to the Administration of Justice

### *Compromise of Criminal Proceedings*

While compromise agreements to end private and civil proceedings are permissible, any agreement to end criminal proceedings or proceedings which have a bearing on the public at large is illegal. So, in *Keir v Leeman*[44] an attempt to compromise a criminal action arising from a riot was struck down as illegal. In *Nolan v Shiels*[45] an agreement to pay £50 in exchange for a promise to abandon a criminal prosecution was unenforceable. Similarly, in *Brady v Flood*[46] an agreement under which the defendant was paid to get criminal charges of conspiracy dropped was unenforceable for illegality. An exception arises where, as in cases of assault, the criminal proceedings can also be the subject of a civil action. The point on criminal proceedings is clear: an agreement to end a criminal prosecution cannot be sustained once prosecution has commenced. The same rule applies to proceedings that have an important public dimension. For example, in *Parsons v Kirk*[47] a petitioner had questioned the election of a Member of Parliament, alleging that voters had been bribed. His agreement to withdraw the petition was void because this was a matter of great public interest that should not be made subject to a private agreement.

[19–24]

The situation is different if the prosecution has yet to commence. Clark argues that the court will uphold an agreement not to prosecute, provided that there is no weighty public interest at stake which would justify striking it down.[48] In *Re Boyd*,[49] Sullivan LC held that "a threat of prosecution will not invalidate a security thereupon given, if there was no agreement to abandon the prosecution ultimately". In *Rourke v Mealy*,[50] the plaintiff held a negotiable instrument that he suspected had been forged by relatives of the defendant. He had not brought any case on the instrument. Instead he notified the defendant, who agreed to make himself personally liable on the instrument in exchange for the plaintiff's agreement not to charge any of his relatives with the forgery. This agreement was allowed to stand. It was not an agreement to end proceedings. It was an agreement not to bring them at all.

[19–25]

### *Maintenance*

The courts have traditionally taken a dim view of contracts that encourage speculative litigation by improperly assisting a litigant to bring a case. The old maxim applies: *Culpa est se immiscere rei ad se non pertinenti*; guilty is he who meddles in affairs that do not concern him. Thus, contracts of maintenance (19–27) and champertous contracts (19–29) are void and cannot be sued on. The courts are unlikely to stay

[19–26]

---

[44] (1846) 9 QB 371.
[45] (1926) 60 I.L.T.R. 143. See also *Brady v Flood* (1841) 6 Circ Cases 309.
[46] (1841) 6 Circuit Cases 309.
[47] (1853) 6 Ir Jur 168.
[48] Clark, *op. cit.,* p.371.
[49] (1885) 15 LR (Ir) 521.
[50] (1879) 13 ILTR 52.

proceedings in a main action on the grounds that it is tainted by such an illegal contract, preferring to award damages instead.[51] A stay may be granted where a link can be established between the presence of maintenance or champerty and a likely abuse of process.[52] The presence of maintenance will not justify a court in striking out the main action before a full hearing.[53]

[19–27]     A person commits the crime of maintenance when he lends improper assistance to a litigant. In *Re Trepca Mines*,[54] Lord Denning MR defined maintenance as "[i]mproperly stirring up litigation and strife by giving aid to one party to bring or defend a claim without just cause or excuse". In *Uppington v Bullen*,[55] a solicitor was running an action for a client, the cost of which was £300. He took a conveyance of land from a client for £400. £100 was paid in cash and the balance was to cover the cost of the action. The conveyance was set aside as unlawful maintenance.

[19–28]     A difficulty would arise if all contracts of maintenance were void for illegality. Increasingly, impecunious plaintiffs depend on organisations and benefactors to fund their actions.[56] If this were impossible, access to justice would be denied in a great many cases. In *O'Keeffe v Scales*,[57] Lynch J observed that the law on maintenance must accommodate the constitutional right of access to the courts to litigate reasonably stateable cases. The courts have established charitable motive as a defence to a proceeding for maintenance. In *Hill v Archbold*,[58] there was no maintenance where a trade union in good faith facilitated two of its members in bringing a defamation action against a third party in order to vindicate their good names. This was not a case of the improprer stirring up of litigation and strife. In addition, a claim of maintenance will not succeed where the alleged maintainer has an interest in the suit that exists "independently of the agreement which gives him a share in the proceeds of the suit".[59] In *Stocznia Gdanska v Latvian Shipping Co*,[60] a shipbuilding yard had built six vessels for a Liberian company. Payment was to be made in instalments. By a separate contract, the brokers were entitled to a commission of 4 to 5 per cent on each instalment. Most of the instalments went unpaid and the shipbuilding yard sued to recover them. The litigation was funded by an agent of the broker. Toulson J observed that the brokers, as funders of the action, had a legitimate interest in the action itself. This was because payment of the instalments would trigger the brokers' entitlement to their commission. They had an independent commercial and moral interest in the litigation. *Martell v Consett Iron*[61] establishes that the court will take a more liberal view of this independent interest where the litigation maintained concerns a matter of

---

[51] *O'Keeffe v Scales* [1998] 1 ILRM 393.
[52] *Stocznia Gdanska v Latvian Shipping Co* [1999] 3 All ER 822.
[53] Above, n 51.
[54] [1963] Ch 199.
[55] (1842) 2 Dr & War 184.
[56] See *Hill v Archbold* [1967] 3 All ER 110 *per* Lord Denning.
[57] Above, n 51.
[58] [1967] 3 All ER 110.
[59] *Fraser v Buckle* [1994] 1 IR 1.
[60] Above, n 52.
[61] [1955] 1 All ER 481.

wider interest, such as the pollution of a river, than if it concerns a person matter such as defamation.

## *Champerty*

Champerty is a breed of maintenance. It occurs where a man maintains a lawsuit to    **[19–29]**
which he is not a party and in exchange, receives a portion of any damages awarded if
the cases is successful. In *Giles v Thompson*,[62] Lord Mustill explained why
champertous agreements would not be upheld:

> "My Lords, the crimes of maintenance and champerty are so old that they can
> no longer be trace, but their importance in medieval times is quite clear. The
> mechanisms of justice lacked the internal strength to resist the oppression of
> private individuals through suits fomented and sustained by unscrupulous men
> of power. Champerty was particularly vicious, since the purchase of a share in
> litigation presented an obvious temptation to the suborning of justices and
> witnesses and the exploitation of worthless claims which the defendant lacked
> the resources and influence to withstand."

In *Littledale v Thompson*,[63] Whaley was a party to a dispute concerning a    **[19–30]**
clerical living. Thompson agreed to pay Whaley's legal fees if Whaley would convey the
clerical living to him in the event that he was successful. The agreement was
champertous. In *McElroy v Flynn*,[64] a contract to share in an inheritance in exchange
for providing information which would help with the intestacy case was illegal as
champertous. A similar case is *Fraser v Buckle*.[65] The plaintiffs were professional next-
of-kin agents, who had informed Buckle and the other defendants that they could be
heirs to an estate in New Jersey. The plaintiffs and the defendants entered into
contracts whereby the defendants agreed to give the plaintiffs a third of any money
they might inherit in exchange for the plaintiffs' assistance with their claim. The
Supreme Court refused to uphold the contracts because they were champertous.

An important issue arising under this heading is that of contingency fee    **[19–31]**
arrangements. These are arrangements in which the fee a lawyer will be paid depends
on the outcome of the case. Under these arrangements, the lawyer effectively purchases
a share in the litigation. In *Awwad v Geraghty*,[66] Schiemann LJ noted that the debate in
this area moves between:

> "... a historically widespread perception that if the lawyer has too much at
> stake in the success of the litigation then he may yield to the temptation to
> prolong litigation which could have settled or a temptation to act improperly in
> order to secure success, and, on the other side, a conviction that it aids access to

---

[62] [1994] 1 AC 142, 153. See also *Re Trepca Mines* [1963] Ch 199 *per* Lord Denning MR: "The reason why the common law condemns champerty is because of the abuses to which it may give rise. The common law fears that the champertous maintainer might be tempted, for his own personal gain, to inflame the damages, to suppress evidence, or even to suborn witnesses".
[63] (1878) 2 LR (Ir) 43.
[64] [1991] ILRM 294.
[65] [1996] 2 ILRM 34.
[66] [2000] 1 All ER 608.

justice if clients can litigate without fear of having to pay both sides' costs if they lose."

**[19–32]**     In *Fraser v Buckle*,[67] O'Flaherty J observed that "[t]he contingent fee is regarded as the cornerstone of the 'people's law' ... 'the key to the courthouse door for the poor and the middle class". However, in Ireland, contingency fee arrangements fall foul of s 11 of the Attorneys' and Solicitors' Act 1870 which prohibits any agreement between the solicitor and client in relation to proceedings where payment depends on the success of the action.

## Contracts to Defraud the Revenue

**[19–33]**  In *Starling Securities v Woods*,[68] a contract for the sale of land was not enforced where the consideration had been misstated in order to defraud the Revenue Commissioners. This category has taken on substantial significance in Ireland in the context of employment contracts. The line of authority here begins with *Tomlinson v Dick Evans 'U' Drive*.[69] The employee in this case had received a pay rise of £15 per week. Both he and his employer knew that this £15 was taken from the petty cash in order to avoid the payment of income tax. When the employee brought unfair dismissal proceedings, her action was dismissed as founded on an illegal contract. Bristow J emphasised the courts' strict approach to employee culpability here:

> "It is clear that both [employer and employee] knew exactly what they were doing and that both were in it up to the neck ... No doubt there are cases in which a junior employee goes along with an employer's tax fraud knowing it to be dishonest, in circumstances where more blame attaches to the employer than to him. But even in such cases the evil lies in the dishonesty in which the employee knowingly participated, and the law leaves the balancing of the respective degrees of blame to the discretion of the revenue in deciding who is to be subject to penalties or prosecuted, and the criminal court who has to decide upon what sentence to inflict. There is, for good reason, no relaxation in the rule that the dishonest party to the swindle cannot recover on the contract."

**[19–34]**     *Tomlinson* has been followed in this jurisdiction. In *Lewis v Squash Ireland Ltd*,[70] Lewis was employed as the managing director of Squash Ireland. He was paid £14,000 as a salary, together with £2,000 described as "expenses" in order to minimise Lewis's PAYE obligations to the Revenue. Lewis sued the company for compensation under the Unfair Dismissals Act 1977. The Employment Appeals Tribunal (EAT) found that both Lewis and his employer knew that his salary was being misstated to the Revenue. The EAT held that courts "should not lend themselves to the enforcement of contracts either illegal on their face or which the intended performance of obligations thereunder was illegal to the knowledge of the party seeking to enforce the contract". In *Hayden and Sean Quinn Properties Ltd*,[71] the defendant employee

---

[67] [1994] 1 IR 1.
[68] Unreported, High Court, 24 May 1977.
[69] [1978] ICR 638.
[70] [1983] ILRM 363.
[71] Unreported, High Court, 6 December 1993.

was denied a remedy for wrongful dismissal because he had accepted an expenses "top up" in addition to his official salary. The law in this area has been amended. Under the new s 8(11) of the Unfair Dismissal Act 1977 an employee is entitled to a remedy for unfair dismissal notwithstanding that his contract of employment is tainted by an agreement to defraud the Revenue. However, where such a case comes before the EAT, the Tribunal is bound to notify the Revenue Commissioners or the Minister for Social Welfare of the matter. Outside the realm of unfair dismissal, it appears that the old rules will continue to apply.

### Contracts to Trade with Enemies of the State

A contract between a national and an enemy alien is illegal as contrary to public policy. **[19–35]** In *Ross v Shaw*,[72] the plaintiff purchased yarn from a mill in Belgium. World War I intervened and Belgium was occupied by Germany. Belgium became part of enemy territory. When the plaintiff brought an action for non-delivery, the defendant was able to rely on illegality as an excuse for non-performance.

### Contracts that Breach Foreign Law

The courts will not enforce a contract if it is illegal according to the law of the place **[19–36]** where it is to be performed. In *Stanhope v Hospitals Trust Ltd*,[73] the plaintiff was in Natal. Sweepstakes were illegal in Natal. The plaintiff posted Irish sweepstake tickets to the Dublin office where the draw was to take place. The plaintiff was entitled to sue on this contract. It was illegal in the country of its formation, Natal. However, it was not illegal in the country of its performance, Ireland.

## IV. The Effects of Illegality

A distinction can be drawn between contracts that are illegal as formed and those that **[19–37]** are illegal as performed. Take the example of a contract between a hitman and a jilted wife for the murder of her adulterous spouse. The object of that contract is the commission of a crime. The contract is illegal on its face.[74] By contrast, consider a contract for the delivery of an ordinary batch of sausages from a sausage factory to a butcher. There is nothing illegal in the object of the contract. Suppose, however, that as he drives from factory to butcher, the factory's delivery man breaks the speed limit. The contract then becomes illegal because its performance is tainted by illegality.[75]

### Illegal as Formed

Contracts which are illegal as formed are void *ab initio*.[76] The court will treat such a **[19–38]** contract as if it had never made and neither party will take a remedy under it. The

---

[72] [1917] 2 IR 367.
[73] (1936) Ir Jur Rep 25.
[74] See *Ashton v Turner* [1981] QB 137; *Pits v Hung* [1991] 1 QB 24.
[75] *St John Shipping Corpn v Joseph Rank Ltd* [1957] 1 QB 267, 281.
[76] The old US cases on slavery are of historical interest here. *Willis v Bruce & Warfield*, 47 Ky (8 B Mon) 548, 550–551 (1848) (holding that a contract for freedom with one's slave is unenforceable); *Mary v Morris*, 27 La 135 (1834) (holding that a bequest of liberty to slaves was in contravention of the law of Georgia prohibiting manumission by will and as such the contracts were null and void).

maxim *ex turpi causa non oritur actio* applies. In *Gray v Cathcart*,[77] a lease of unsanitary premises was illegal as formed. The landlord could not recover any back rent under this contract. Johnson J explained:

> "Everyone commits a misdemeanour who does any act forbidden by statute; accordingly when these parties entered into an agreement to occupy a house which had been condemned it was a contract to do that which the statute says that you could not do. It was a contract to do an illegal thing, and, though the parties might go through the form, yet such a contract is not binding and cannot be sued upon."

[19–39]     So, in *Murphy & Co v Crean*,[78] a contract contained a provision which, in contravention of Irish licensing law, obliged the defendant to transfer a liquor license to any person in another public house nominated by the plaintiff brewers. This illegal provision rendered the whole contract unenforceable. This approach was affirmed by the Supreme Court in *Mackin & McDonald v Greacen & Co*.[79] It will be seen that where a contract is illegal only in its performance, the courts may enforce a contract where the party seeking enforcement was innocent of any intention to perform illegally. Such an exception cannot apply to contracts that are illegal as formed because the nature of such contracts is that both parties have expressly and deliberately agreed to do something which is illegal.

[19–40]     The courts' refusal to intervene in such contracts can work to the benefit of an unscrupulous party. Remember that a party can plead illegality as a defence—as an excuse for non-performance of his obligations under the contract. In effect, he can use his wrongdoing to escape his contractual obligations. Lord Dunedin in *Sinclair v Brougham*[80] once said that this defence "seems only worthy of the Pharisee who shook himself free of his natural obligation by saying Corban". However, this outcome is consistent with the courts' traditional approach to illegal contracts as stated by Lord Mansfield in *Holman v Johnson*[81]:

> "The objection that a contract is immoral or illegal as between plaintiff and defendant, sounds at times very ill in the mouth of the defendant. It is not for his sake, however, that the objection is ever allowed; but it is found in general principles of policy, which the defendant has the advantage of, contrary to the real justice, as between him and the plantiff, by accident if I may say so. The principle of public policy is *ex dolo malo non oritur actio*."

### Illegal as Performed

[19–41]     A contract that is perfectly innocent in origin may be infected with illegality if the parties, in order to perform the contract, do an act prohibited by law. A good example

---

[77] (1899) 33 ILTR 35.
[78] [1915] 1 IR 111.
[79] [1983] IR 61.
[80] [1914] AC 398.
[81] (1775) 1 Cowp 741.

of this type of case is *Marles v Philip Trant & Sons Ltd*.[82] The defendants sold wheat to the plaintiffs. There was nothing wrong with the contract as formed. However, in contravention of statute, the defendants did not deliver an invoice with the wheat. The contract, therefore, was illegal as performed. In the Irish case of *Namlooze Venootschap De Faam v The Dorset Manufacturing Co Ltd*,[83] the contract was for the sale of goods. There was nothing wrong with the contract *per se*. However, the contract fell foul of the rules as to illegality because its performance, in particular payment for the goods, involved an illegality. Payment was to be in guilders or in Sterling and the Irish law at the time was that it was illegal to export foreign exchange and to make payments to persons outside of the State without ministerial permission. The defendant had not obtained the correct permission and so the contract was illegal as performed. Dixon J refused to enforce the contract thus:

> "Whatever the terms of the court's order, the legal effect of it would be to put the plaintiffs in a position to secure the payment of the amount in question and it would thus, even if indirectly, compel the plaintiffs to do an act prohibited by the law for the time being in force."

This reasoning was adopted by the Supreme Court in *Fibretex v Beleir Ltd*.[84]

If both parties intended an otherwise legal contract to be performed illegally, then that contract is unenforceable and no damages will be awarded for its breach. In *Ashmore v Dawson*,[85] the plaintiffs owned some heavy equipment that was to be transported by lorry. The defendants were hauliers who agreed to transport the machinery. This contract was obviously legal in its formation. However, the contract was illegal as performed. The defendants intended to use a lorry that did not meet statutory requirements as to capacity. The plaintiffs' transport manager was present and so he was held to know that the statutory requirements were not being fulfilled. Joint illegal intent was present and so the contract was unenforceable. **[19–42]**

Suppose, however, that only one party had this illegal intent. If a contract is performed illegally but one party does not know of or participate in the illegality, that innocent party has the full range of remedies open to him. In *Whitecross Potatoes v Coyle*,[86] Coyle, a farmer in Meath, agreed to sell potatoes to the plaintiffs, a UK company that ran a chain of fish and chip shops. The parties suspected that the UK and Irish Governments were about to impose export and import restrictions on potatoes. They agreed that, if this occurred, a higher price would be payable in respect of the potatoes. Coyle intended to perform the contract illegally by smuggling potatoes into Northern Ireland, using the higher price to cover transport costs. However, the plaintiffs understood that, in the event that restrictions were imposed, Coyle would buy potatoes in Northern Ireland and supply them to the plaintiffs. This was perfectly legal. In this case there was no joint intent to perform the contract illegally. Accordingly, the plaintiffs were entitled to sue on the contract. **[19–43]**

---

[82] [1954] 1 QB 29.
[83] [1949] IR 203. See also *Fibretex v Beleir Ltd* (1958) 89 ILTR 141.
[84] (1958) 89 ILTR 141.
[85] [1973] 1 WLR 828.
[86] [1978] ILRM 31.

**[19–44]**      A similar case is *Archbolds (Freightage) Ltd v Spanglett Ltd*.[87] The defendant vehicle owners were not licensed to carry any goods but their own. They agreed to carry the plaintiffs' whiskey. The plaintiffs did not know that the defendants did not have the necessary license. The whiskey was stolen and the plaintiffs sued for damages. The question for the Court was whether they could rely on this contract which had been performed illegally. Because only the defendant intended to perform the contract in an illegal manner, the plaintiff was entitled to rely on it and sue for damages. Note that the courts do not weigh up the parties' guilt in determining whether the contract was performed illegally. They simply ask whether the party seeking to enforce the contract is guilty or innocent of the illegality with which the contract is tainted.

## V. Recovery of Property Passed Under An Illegal Contract

**[19–45]**      Sometimes a party, instead of bringing an action to enforce the contract, accepts that it has fallen and brings an action to recover the property which has passed under it. The general rule, from the old case of *Holman v Johnson*,[88] is that when a contract is voided for illegality the loss lies where it falls. This rule is a reflection of the courts' reluctance to become involved with any contract that is tainted by illegality. Wilmot CJ expressed this idea eloquently in the old case of *Collins v Blanton*[89]:

> "[No] polluted hand shall touch the pure fountains of justice. Whoever is a party to an unlawful contract, if he hath once paid the money stipulated to be paid shall not have the help of a court to fetch it back again."

**[19–46]**      The application of this principle means that if property has already passed under the contract, it remains with the receiver. The maxim which expresses the rule is *in pari delicto, potior est conditio possidentis*: where the parties are equally at fault in respect of the illegality, the party in possession is stronger. Often the court's denial of its intervention to the parties means that one will be unjustly enriched. This can be difficult to justify, particularly in cases where the illegality is minor, or where one party is more culpable in respect of the illegality than the other. In *St John Shipping v Joseph Rank*,[90] Devlin J focused on the inequities which can be wrought by the doctrine of illegality and set out the arguments for a more liberal approach to recovery:

> "Persons who deliberately set out to break the law cannot expect to be aided in a court of justice, but it is a different matter when the law is unwittingly broken. To nullify a bargain in such circumstances frequently means that in a case – perhaps of such triviality that no authority would have felt it worthwhile to prosecute – a seller, because he cannot enforce his civil rights, may forfeit a sum vastly in excess of any penalty that a criminal court would impose, and the sum forfeited will not go into the public purse but into the pockets of someone who is lucky enough to pick up the windfall or astute enough to have contrived to get it. It is questionable how far this contributes to public morality … Lord Wright said: 'Nor must it be forgotten that the rule by which contracts not

---

[87] [1961] 2 QB 374.
[88] (1775) 1 Cowp 341.
[89] [1767] 2 Wilson 341.
[90] [1957] 1 QB 267.

expressly forbidden by statute or declared to be void are in proper cases nullified for disobedience to a statute is a rule of public policy only, and public policy understood in a wider sense may at times be better served by refusing to nullify a bargain save on serious and sufficient grounds'. It may be questionable also as to whether public policy is well served by driving from the seat of judgment everyone who has been guilty of a minor transgression. Commercial men who have unwittingly offended against one of a multiplicity of regulations may nevertheless feel that they have not thereby forfeited all right to justice, and they may go elsewhere for it if the courts of law will not give it to them."

The tension between the courts' desire to aid deserving parties and the principle of not becoming involved in illegal contracts has bred a number of exceptions. [19–47]

## Parties Non In Pari Delicto

First, as you might expect, where the parties are *non in pari delicto* or not equally at fault, the *ex turpis* rule does not apply. If the receiver is the guiltier of two parties in respect of the illegality the court may intervene to restore the property transferred to the other party. There are a number of factors to which the court may have regard in determining whether the parties are *in pari delicto*. The first is the parties' knowledge. In *Oom v Bruce*,[91] the plaintiffs insured goods with the defendants. The goods were to be transported to Russia. The day before the contract was concluded, it was rendered illegal by the outbreak of hostilities between Russia and Great Britain. The plaintiffs did not know about this illegality. Accordingly, the parties were *non in pari delicto* as regards the illegality and the plaintiffs recovered the premiums they had paid under the contract. Secondly, in *Sumner v Sumner*,[92] Megaw J held that one party to an illegal contract may have a remedy where he enters into that contract because of the other's fraud, duress or undue influence. Thus, in *Hughes v Liverpool Victoria Friendly Society*,[93] the plaintiff was entitled to recover premiums that she had paid on illegal life insurance policies. This was because she had entered into the contracts of insurance on foot of misrepresentations by the defendants' agents that if she paid the premiums "everything would be alright". Banks LJ wrote: [19–48]

> "Given fraud ... an innocent plaintiff is entitled to say that he is not in pari delicto with the defendants whose agents by a false and fraudulent representation induced him to believe that the transaction was an innocent one and enforceable in law."

As regards duress, *Howard v Shirlster*[94] sets out that duress will excuse a party who has performed his contract in an illegal manner. The plaintiff contracted with the defendants to remove a plane from Nigeria for a fee of $25,000. The plaintiff had good reason to believe his life was in danger and so, contrary to Nigerian law, he did not [19–49]

---

[91] (1810) 12 East 225.
[92] (1935) 69 ILTR 101.
[93] [1916] 2 KB 482.
[94] [1990] 3 All ER 366.

obtain proper permission from air traffic control before he departed. Thus, he had performed the contract illegally. The defendants argued that this illegality justified them in not paying the plaintiff. However, the Court found that the illegality was negated by the duress and so the contract was enforceable. As Lord Ellenborough remarked in *Smith v Cuff*,[95] "[i]t can never be predicated as *par delictum* where one holds the rod and the other bows to it".

**[19–50]** Where the illegality is statutory illegality, one party will be held less guilty than the other if he is a member of the class which the statute broken was expressly or impliedly intended to protect. In *Browning v Morris*[96] Lord Mansfield wrote:

> "Where contracts or transactions are prohibited by positive statutes, for the sake of protecting one set of men from another set of men; the one, from their situation and condition being liable to be oppressed and imposed upon by the other; there the parties are not *in pari delicto*, and in furtherance of these statutes, the person injured after the transaction is finished and completed, may bring his action and defeat the contract."

**[19–51]** *Kiriri Cotton v Dewani*[97] concerned the payment of a premium by the plaintiff sub-lessee. The payment was illegal under the Ugandan Rent Restriction Ordinance. However, the sub-lessee was a tenant and the purpose of the ordinance was to protect a class of people: tenants exploited by landlords. Therefore, whenever an illegal contract was present, the landlord had to take primary responsibility for it. In other words, where a contract between a landlord and tenant fell foul of this statute, landlord and tent could never be *in pari delicto*. Lord Denning said:

> "[I]f as between the two of them the duty of observing the law is placed on the shoulders of the one rather than the other – it being imposed on him specially for the protection of the other – then they are not *in pari delicto* and the money can be recovered back."

**[19–52]** The Irish law appears to go further. Under the Supreme Court decision in *Martin v Galbraith*,[98] where the object of a statute is to protect not merely a class of persons but the public at large, there is no right to sue on a contract that falls foul of that statute unless the legislature has expressly provided for such a right.

**[19–53]** Finally, the parties will not be *in pari delicto* where only one party is to benefit from the illegal act. In *Euro-Diam v Bathurst*,[99] the plaintiff diamond merchants shipped $223,000 worth of diamonds to a client in Germany. However, they invoiced the client for $131,411 in order to aid the client in avoiding German customs duty. The plaintiffs did not benefit from this illegal action: it benefited the client alone. When some of the diamonds were stolen, the plaintiffs claimed under an insurance policy, valuing the diamonds at $142,174. Kerr LJ held that they were entitled to rely on the

[95] (1817) 6 M & S 160.
[96] (1778) 2 Cowp 790.
[97] [1960] AC 192.
[98] [1942] IR 37.
[99] [1988] 2 All ER 23.

insurance policy despite the illegality involved in the understated invoice. In the first place, the plaintiffs had understated the invoice for the client's purposes, not for their own gain. In the second place, the valuation provided to the insurance company was correct according to the plaintiffs' register. Kerr LJ said "[O]n the question of public policy and the relative culpability of the parties the scales would be heavily weighted against [the client]. They alone made a tangible profit out of the transaction".

The English courts have expanded the *non in pari delicto* principle so that **[19-54]** payment may be recovered for work done under an illegal contract on a *quantum meruit* basis. For instance, in *Mohamed v Alaga* [100] a translator made an illegal fee-sharing agreement with the defendant solicitors' firm. He would introduce Somali refugees to the defendants. The defendants would represent them. He would help in preparing and presenting the applications. In return, he would take one half of any fees received by the solicitors on legal aid. The translator did not know that this sort of agreement was illegal. By contrast, the solicitors' firm would be expected to be well aware of the rules. Accordingly, the parties were *non in pari delicto*. The translator could not enforce the contract so as to be paid the share of the solicitors' fees he had originally bargained for, but he was entitled to recover payment for his translation work.

## Independent Cause of Action

Property transferred under an illegal contract may also be recovered if the plaintiff can **[19-55]** assert title to the property without needing to rely on the illegal contract. This exception has its origins in *Bowmakers Ltd v Barnet Instruments Ltd*. [101] The plaintiffs in this case bought machine tools in contravention of the Defence Regulations. They then delivered the tools to the defendants under three illegal hire purchase agreements. The defendants breached these hire purchase agreements by selling some of the tools to third parties and refusing to return the rest. The plaintiffs sought to recover possession of the tools. They were able to do so because they could base their claim on their own legal title to the tools; they did not have to rely on the illegal contract for their claim. Du Parcq J held:

> "In our opinion, a man's right to possess his own chattels will, as a general rule be enforced against one who, without any claim of right, is detaining them, or has converted them to his own use, even though it may appear either from the pleadings, or in the course of the trial, that the chattels in question came into the defendant's possession by reasons of an illegal contract between himself and the plaintiff, provided that the plaintiff does not seek, and is not forced, either to found his claim on the illegal contract or to plead its illegality in order to support his claim."

A case along the same lines is *Amar Singh v Kulubya*. [102] The African plaintiff **[19-56]** was the registered owner of "Mailo" land. A Ugandan statutory ordinance prohibited the lease of this land by an African to a non-African. In contravention of this

---

[100] [2000] 1 WLR 815.
[101] [1945] KB 65.
[102] [1964] AC 142.

ordinance, the plaintiff leased the land to the defendant, an Indian. The agreement was void for illegality. Seven years into the lease, the plaintiff sued to recover the land. He succeeded because his claim to possession was based on his registered ownership of the land and not on the illegal contract.

[19–57]     *Tinsley v Mulligan*[103] is another such case but this time the right of ownership was equitable rather than legal. A lesbian couple had provided money for the purchase of a house. The women contracted that ownership of the house would be shared. However, they put the house in Tinsley's sole name, so that Mulligan could continue to claim social welfare unlawfully. The women's contract was therefore illegal. Mulligan therefore had no right to ownership of the house arising under the contract. Nevertheless, the House of Lords concluded that an independent cause of action was available to Mulligan in the form of a resulting trust. A resulting trust arose in her favour because she had contributed to the purchase price of the house and because there was a common understanding between her and Tinsley that they owned the house equally.

### Repentance

[19–58]     If a contract is illegal as formed, but has not been performed yet so that it is still executory, a party may recover property transferred under that contract by withdrawing from it in good time and seeking the aid of the court in regaining his property. This doctrine is sometimes called the *locus poenitentiae*, a phrase which means "time for repentance". The first point is that repentance must take place before too substantial a part of the agreement has been performed. In *Tribe v Tribe*,[104] Millet LJ said that in order to recover his property, a party "must have withdrawn from the transaction while his dishonesty still lay in intention only. The law draws the line once the intention has been wholly or partly carried into effect". In *Kearley v Thompson*,[105] Fry LJ gave the following vivid example: "Suppose a payment of 100l by A to B on a contract that the latter shall murder C and D. He has murdered C but not D. Can the money be recovered back? In my opinion it cannot be". In *Kearley*[106] the defendant solicitors, in return for the plaintiffs' payment of their costs, had promised not to appear at the public examination of a bankrupt and not to oppose his discharge. This contract was clearly illegal in its formation: performance necessarily required illegality. The solicitors stayed away from the public examination as promised. The plaintiffs then sued for the return of the money which they had paid to the defendants. However, they were unable to recover the money for repentance because they had repented too late: the contract had already been performed in substance. By contrast, repentance was permitted in the case of *Taylor v Bowers*.[107] The plaintiff had made a fictitious assignment of his goods to another person in order to avoid seizure of these goods by his creditor. The plaintiff had removed the goods. However, he had done nothing more to give effect to his illegal purpose before he repented the contract. Accordingly, the

---

[103] [1993] 3 All ER 65.
[104] [1995] 4 All ER 236.
[105] (1890) 24 QBD 742.
[106] *ibid.*
[107] (1876) 1 QBD 291.

court allowed him to recover the goods. In the leading case of *Tribe v Tribe*,[108] a father transferred assets to his son as part of a bogus sale in order to put the assets out of the reach of his creditors. The contract was obviously illegal in its formation. When the creditors did not sue as he had expected, the father asked the son to return these assets. The Court of Appeal held that because the purpose of defrauding the creditors had not yet been achieved, because the contract had not been fully performed, the father was entitled to repent the contract and be reimbursed.

The second requirement is that the repentance must have been both voluntary and genuine. This requirement comes from *Bigos v Bousted*,[109] where it was held that repentance would not be permitted where performance of the contract is impossible anyway. However, the need for an element of genuineness has not survived *Tribe v Tribe*.[110] Millet LJ in that case observed that it is enough that the withdrawal from the contract is voluntary. He wrote:

[19–59]

> "I would hold that genuine repentance is not required. Justice is not a reward for merit; restitution should not be confined to the penitent. I would also hold that withdrawal from an illegal transaction when it has ceased to be needed is sufficient."

Finally, in *Tappenden v Randall*,[111] Heath J suggested that recovery of property passed under an illegal contract would only be possible on grounds of repentance where the contract is not "of a nature too grossly immoral for the court to enter into any discussion of it". However, this is an old case and its relevance to the modern law is dubious.

[19–60]

## VI. Severance

Severance is the mechanism by which a court will attempt to save an illegal contract by cutting out the illegal part and enforcing the remainder. When restraint of trade is considered in Chapter 21 it will be seen that the courts adopt a relaxed attitude to severance in that area. Not so where the contract is illegal under common law. For example, in *Devine v Scott and Johnston*[112] the plaintiff had let premises to the defendant for the purposes of running his illegal bookmaking business. In fact, only part of the premises was used in bookmaking and so the plaintiff asked the Court to sever the illegal part of the transaction so that he could recover rent in respect of the parts of the business which were not used for the bookmaking. Thompson J refused to do so. In addition, *Murphy & Co v Crean*[113] establishes that an illegal covenant in a contract will taint the entire contract so that it is unenforceable. However, the old Irish cases of *Carolan v Brabazon*[114] and *Furnivall v O'Neill*[115] are authority for the

[19–61]

---

[108] Above, n 104.
[109] [1951] 1 All ER 92.
[110] Above, n 104.
[111] (1801) 2 B & P 467.
[112] (1931) 66 ILTR 107.
[113] [1915] 1 IR 111.
[114] (1846) 9 Ir Eq R 224.
[115] [1902] 2 IR 422.

proposition that severance is possible where the illegal element of the contract is incidental or peripheral to the contract's main purpose. In *Carolan*, Sugden LC wrote:

> "If parties chose to enter into a contract which is legal to a certain extent, and stipulate for something beside, which is to rest on an understanding which is not malum in se, but merely prohibited, I am not prepared to say that in such a case I should not decree a specific performance so far as the contract is legally capable of execution."

[19–62]    The case of *Carney v Herbert*[116] suggests that severance may be available where the contract is tainted by statutory illegality. The Privy Council in that case established that severance is available where two requirements are fulfilled. First, the illegal promise must be a collateral or incidental provision of the contract. This is likely to be the case where the statutory provision is technical and merely regulatory in nature. Secondly, there must not be any compelling social, moral or economic imperative which would be undermined by enforcing the rest of the transaction. The judgment in *Ailion v Spiekermann*[117] ties into this latter requirement. The Court in this case considered a contract to sell a lease for a premium which was illegal under statute. Templeman LJ held that the obligation to pay the illegal premium could be severed from the rest of the contract so that the vendor could simply assign the lease to the purchaser without the payment of the premium. This was possible because "the severance [was] in accordance with the enforcement of the principles which induced Parliament to outlaw the elements which are illegal ... the Rent Act is designed to protect persons in the position of the purchasers."

[19–63]    Where a party seeks to sever the illegal portion of a contract, his chances will be slimmer if he is to blame for the illegality. In *Ailion Spiekermann*,[118] Templeman LJ in granting severance noted to the purchasers that: "They could not insist on the elimination from the draft contract of the illegal premium without losing the flat. They had no choice if they needed somewhere to live. They committed no offence." By contrast, in *Lewis v Squash Ireland*,[119] the EAT refused to sever an illegal expenses agreement from the rest of the claimant's salary because he had incorporated the illegal agreement into his contract knowingly and without excuse.

## VII. Reform

[19–64]    For a time, it seemed that the English courts were about to embark on a project of judicial law reform of the principles concerning recovery of property passed under illegal contracts. The Court of Appeal, notably in the case of *Euro-Diam v Bathurst*,[120] fostered for a while what was known as the "public conscience" test. This test was a liberal one that provided the courts with a wide discretion to provide a claimant with a remedy in reliance on an illegal contract. Under the test, the court should only refuse to grant a remedy if "it would be an affront to the public conscience ... because the

---

[116] [1985] AC 301.
[117] [1976] Ch 158.
[118] *ibid.*
[119] [1983] ILRM 363.
[120] [1990] 1 QB 1.

court would thereby appear to assist or encourage the claimant in his illegal conduct or to encourage others in similar acts". However, that test was squarely rejected by the House of Lords in *Tinsley v Mulligan*, with Lord Goff in particular dismissing it as tantamount to a blanket discretion to grant or refuse relief and Lord Browne-Wilkinson expressing concern that contracts should not be destroyed on the basis of "such an imponderable factor".

In 1999, the English Law Commission published its Consultation Paper No. 154, "Illegal Transactions: The Effect of Illegality on Contracts and Trusts". To some extent, the Commission argues for a resurrection of the "public conscience" rule. The main provisional proposal in the Consultation Paper is that the current scheme of rules governing illegal contracts should be replaced by a structured discretion to enforce the transaction, to recognise the transfer or creation of property rights under it or to allow the recovery of benefits conferred under it. In exercising this discretion, the court should have regard to: (i) the seriousness of the illegality involved; (ii) the knowledge and intention of the party seeking relief; (iii) the deterrent effect, if any, of refusing such relief; (iv) the compatibility of refusal of that relief with the purpose of the statutory or common law rule breached; and (v) whether the refusal of relief would be proportionate to the illegality involved. The discretion would not apply in cases of express statutory illegality. The Commission has suggested that the approach under this new scheme would be a liberal one: a remedy would only be refused for illegality where there was a clear and justifiable reason for doing so. These rather vague proposals can hardly be said to remedy the uncertainty that dogs this area of law. However, the Commission argues that the structured discretion would facilitate the courts in giving open and explicit reasons for decisions on illegal contracts.

**[19–65]**

# CHAPTER 20
# Contract and Public Policy

## I. Introduction

This chapter deals with contracts that are void for public policy. As we saw in Chapter 19, public policy plays a role in the context of illegal contracts. There is no particular justification for the traditional distinction between illegal contracts and contracts that are void for public policy. It is perhaps possible to say that the former is a more serious version of the latter. This distinction is clear from the law of severance: it is easier to sever a provision from a contract that is merely void for reasons of public policy than it is to sever an illegal provision. In *Goodison v Goodison*,[1] Somervell LJ explained the distinction in these terms:

**[20–01]**

> "[T]here are two kinds of illegality of differing effect. The first is where the illegality is criminal, or contra bonos mores, and in those cases . . . such a provision, if an ingredient in a contract, will invalidate the whole, although there may be many provisions in it. There is a second kind of illegality which has no such taint; the other terms in the contract stand if the illegal portion can be severed."

Somervell LJ's "second kind of illegality" is what we would call "voidness for public policy". We have said in the previous chapter that it is increasingly rare for a contract to be struck down as illegal for policy reasons allayed to morality. The aim of this chapter, is nevertheless, to examine the proper scope of public policy as a reason for voiding a contract. We will examine first, a very traditional and non-controversial area in which public policy plays an important role: agreements to oust the jurisdiction of the Courts (20–03). The next two issues turn on the commodification of private life: the encroachment of contract law into areas which are often considered to be outside the proper scope of the market. The first is the use of public policy in contract law and the policy surrounding contracts touching on marriage (20–05). Finally, we will look at whether contracts governing reproduction should be void for public policy (20–16).

**[20–02]**

---

[1] [1954] 2 QB 118.

## II. Agreements to Oust the Jurisdiction of the Courts

[20–03]   In *Lee v Showman's Guild of Great Britain*,[2] Lord Denning MR said:

> "If parties should seek, by agreement, to take the law out of the hands of the courts and put it into the hands of a private tribunal, without any recourse at all to the courts in cases of error of law, then the agreement to that extent is contrary to public policy and void."

[20–04]   The best example of an agreement to oust the jurisdiction of the courts is a contract that seeks to allocate what should be a judicial decision exclusively to a private body or arbitrator. Such agreements are contrary to public policy and therefore void. The courts are the sole arbiters of law. Therefore, while it is permissible for a contract to give a private tribunal or an arbiter sole competence on issues of fact, it is not permissible to deny a person whose case comes before a private tribunal his right of appeal by providing that he shall not have any recourse to the courts. It is possible for the parties to provide that any dispute must be submitted to arbitration before the commencement of legal proceedings but the clause must not prevent ultimate recourse to the courts. The key decision here is that of the House of Lords in *Scott v Avery*[3] which laid down that it is lawful for the parties to contract that no action shall be brought upon until arbitrators have decided, and that effect must be given to such a contract. Where a contract contains an arbitration clause of this nature, the High Court has a power under s 5 of the Arbitration Act 1980 to force the parties to adhere to it by staying court proceedings where the clause has not been observed. As against that, the fundamental position of the courts is reaffirmed by the decision of O'Hanlon J in *Winterhur Swiss Insurance Co v ICI*[4] to the effect that, in certain circumstances, the court has a discretion to refuse a stay if it feels that a court hearing would be a more appropriate method of resolving the parties' dispute.

## III. Agreements Undermining the Sanctity of Marriage'

[20–05]   The two most important types of contract which cause difficulty under this heading are co-habitation agreements and pre-nuptial agreements.

### Co-habitation Agreements

[20–06]   Co-habitation is an increasingly common feature of Irish society, whether as an alternative to marriage or as an important prelude to getting married. Couples may choose to co-habit rather than to marry for a variety of reasons. In particular, they may make this choice to avoid the law governing maintenance and the division of property on the ending of a marriage. The trouble is that, by foregoing marriage, such couples also forego the certainty and legal protection which marriage brings. Solicitors, therefore, often advise couples to enter into a formal co-habitation agreement before embarking on a shared life together. *Ennis v Butterly*[5] was a case that considered the enforceability of co-habitation agreements. This case concerned a co-habiting couple

---

[2] [1952] 2 QB 329.
[3] (1856) 5 HL Cases 811.
[4] [1990] ILRM 159.
[5] [1996] IR 426.

each of whom was already married to another person. In 1993, the defendant orally promised the plaintiff that he would divorce his wife if divorce legislation were ever introduced in Ireland. He bought her an "engagement ring". The plaintiff understood that this meant that she would be "loved, honoured and cherished by the defendant as his wife, that he would be loyal and faithful to her, and that she would be emotionally and financially secure for life". When the relationship broke down, the plaintiff sought to enforce the co-habitation agreement as a contract. Kelly J refused to enforce the contract as contrary to public policy. He said that to allow "an express co-habitation contract (such as is pleaded here) to be enforced would give it a similar status in law as a marital contract". This was impermissible consistent with the constitutional protection afforded to marriage and, thus, the contract was contrary to public policy as it was one "the consideration for which is wifely services rendered on the part of a mistress".

In 2006 the Law Reform Commission in its "Report on the Rights and Duties of Co-habitants"[6] argued that *Ennis v Butterly*,[7] while precluding co-habitation agreements which attempt to replicate or replace marriage, does not prevent the enforcement of agreements which deal solely with the couple's finances and property. The Commission has recommended that such agreements, where they are fair, should be encouraged and enforced, in particular because private ordering of a couple's financial affairs tends to reduce potential litigation. The Commission has argued that, if they are to be enforced, such contracts ought to be written, signed and witnessed. Each party should have received separate and independent legal advice. The Commission points out that the usual tools of contract law will apply, for example, where the agreement is concluded under duress or where the agreement is unconscionable (Chapter 18) [20–07]

## Pre-nuptial Agreements

In *Jude the Obscure*, Thomas Hardy called marriage a permanent contract based on a temporary feeling. A pre-nuptial agreement is an agreement made before marriage which sets out how the couple's assets are to be divided between them in the event that the marriage breaks down. An engaged couple may sign a pre-nuptial agreement if they wish. However, the current law appears to be that the courts are not obliged to give effect to a pre-nuptial agreement[8] in the event that the couple later divorce or separate. Such agreements might be considered void as contrary to public policy: by facilitating a couple in explicitly agreeing how their property is to be divided in the event that their marriage breaks down, the law might be said to be undermining the notion of marriage as a lifelong union. This view was expressed in *Re Hope Johnstone*[9] by Kekewich J, who wrote that it "is forbidden to provide for the possible dissolution of the marriage contract, which the policy of the law is to preserve intact and inviolate." [20–08]

---

[6] LRC-82 2006.

[7] Above, n 6.

[8] See, however, the limited exception in relation to renunciation of the legal right share under s. 113 Succession Act 1965. See de Londras, *Principles of Irish Property Law*, (Clarus, 2007) Ch 16.

[9] [1904] 1 Ch. 470

[20–09]     However, it may be argued that the courts should recalibrate their understanding of the nature of the institution of marriage given the settled acceptance of divorce and judicial separation in Irish law. Arguably, the rhetoric of choice and autonomy has taken the upper hand in the modern discourse surrounding marriage: the enforcement of pre-nuptial agreements is one aspect of this.

[20–10]     There is one key obstacle to the recognition of pre-nuptial agreements. Marriage enjoys special protection under Art 41.3.1° of the Constitution. The State is obliged to protect it "as far as practicable" from "unjust attack". A key question then is whether the enforcement of pre-nuptial agreements would constitute an "unjust attack" on the institution of marriage. In *Zappone and Gilligan v Revenue Commissioners*,[10] Dunne J held that while the concept of marriage ought to be defined in the light of 1937 practice and understanding, matters corollary to marriage should be interpreted according to contemporary mores. April 2007 saw the publication of the Report of the Study Group on Pre-nuptial Agreements.[11] The Study Group argues that pre-nuptial agreements do not deal with the concept of marriage. They are not a material aspect of the formation of marriage; their purpose is to regulate the course and termination of a marriage. They are therefore a "corollary matter" and, as such, their enforceability ought to be determined, in light of the special constitutional protection of marriage, by reference to contemporary understanding.

[20–11]     Modern views concerning marriage would appear to support the enforcement of pre-nuptial agreements, especially considering the current trend in family legislation towards encouraging the private and autonomous settlement of marital disputes. For example, s 20(3) of the Family Law (Divorce) Act 1996 recognises the enforceability of separation agreements, and ss 6 and 7 of that Act require solicitors to discuss the possibility of parties to a legal separation entering into mediation prior to commencing legal proceedings. In addition, the Study Group notes the role that pre-nuptial agreements may play in actually promoting and facilitating marriage. For example, a divorced person may be reluctant to re-marry if she fears that the inheritance of the children of her previous marriage will be affected by her new marriage. A pre-nuptial agreement provides a means of solving that problem.

[20–12]     There are also, however, public policy arguments to be made against the enforcement of pre-nuptial agreements as binding contracts. Historically, the wife's inferior bargaining power within the relationship almost inevitably meant that she would emerge from the enforcement of any pre-nuptial agreement in a poor economic position. The opponents of pre-nuptial agreements argue that they are used to bypass the usual rules applicable to the division of wealth on marriage and rob the wife of her legal and moral entitlement. Thus, in an American case of a particularly unjust pre-nuptial agreement, the Court remarked:

> "The antenuptial contract was a wicked device to evade the laws applicable to marriage relations, property rights, and divorces, and is clearly against public

---

[10]  Unreported, High Court, 14 December 2006.

[11]  "Report of the Study Group on Pre-Nuptial Agreements" (Department of Justice, Equality and Law Reform, 2007).

policy and decency. It was nothing more, in effect, than an attempt on the part of the [husband] ... to legalize prostitution, under the name of marriage ...".[12]

In addition, the period before marriage is an emotionally charged time when the weaker party in an unequal relationship may be in an especially poor position to capitalise on his or her limited bargaining power. However, it is possible, by means of imposing certain formalities as pre-conditions to the enforceability of pre-nuptial agreements, to regulate their formation in such a way as to protect the weaker party's interests. So the Study Group recommends that any pre-nuptial agreement should be made in writing, signed and witnessed. Both parties should have received separate legal advice as to the effect and meaning of the agreement. In order to avoid rushed agreements, the Group recommends that the agreement should have been made not less than 28 days before the marriage takes place and each party should have made full disclosure of his or her financial affairs. The agreement would have to comply with general contractual principles; in particular, the doctrines of duress, undue influence and unconscionable bargain apply to pre-nuptial agreements. [20–13]

Most importantly, the existing Irish regime on the division of wealth on the termination of a marriage is such that a husband cannot rely on it to avoid his legal duty to make fair provision for his wife and dependants, and *vice versa*. The most important issue in relation to the enforceability of pre-nuptial agreements in Irish law relates to the content of the agreement sought to be enforced. Some jurisdictions simply require that the procedural elements of the pre-nuptial agreement be in order. If they are, the court will enforce the agreement and will not make any financial orders of its own. No Irish court would ever engage in such a process of rubber-stamping. In Ireland, before granting a divorce or judicial separation, a court must ensure that "proper provision" has or will be made for the spouses and any dependent members of the family.[13] The Study Group has recommended that the existing family law legislation should be amended to require a court to have regard to and scrutinise any pre-nuptial agreement between parties to divorce or judicial separation proceedings.[14] This recommendation would put pre-nuptial agreements in the same position as separation agreements. In other words, the court would have to take account of the pre-nuptial agreement in making financial orders upon divorce or judicial separation. However, the ultimate and over-riding question for the court would remain whether "proper provision" had been made for the spouses and their dependants. What constitutes "proper provision" always depends on the context of the case. The judge takes account of such factors as the financial resources and needs of the spouses and their dependants, their present and future financial obligations, their ages, their earning capacity and so on. In addition, former spouses are often entitled, not to just enough money to provide for the basic needs, but to extra financial provision: "the fruits of the marriage".[15] In "big money" cases, a non-earning spouse might expect to leave the [20–14]

---

[12] *In re Duncan's Estate*, 285 P 757, 757 (Colo 1930).

[13] See s 16(2) Family Law Act 1995 and s 20(2) Family Law (Divorce) Act 1996; Art 41.3.2° Bunreacht na h Éireann.

[14] The Study Group recommended that express statutory provision be made for pre-nuptial agreements by introducing a new s 16(2)A of the Family Law Act 1995 and a new s 20(3)A of the Family Law (Divorce) Act 1996.

[15] See *DT v CT* [2003] ILRM 321.

marriage with much more wealth than is necessary to live comfortably. Judges enjoy a very high degree of discretion in this regard. Thus, a pre-nuptial agreement would not be finally binding on a judge and he would not afford it any great weight where it seemed inappropriate for him to do so.[16] In the right circumstances, he would be perfectly entitled to make orders for financial relief that had not been agreed by the couple in their pre-nuptial agreement.[17]

[20–15]   A second important point is that "proper provision" is assessed at the date of the divorce hearing,[18] whereas pre-nuptial agreements are made before marriage. Baroness Hale has observed that "[w]hat seems fair and sensible at the outset of a relationship may seem much less fair and sensible when it ends".[19] If a significant or unforeseen change in the circumstances or wealth of the parties occurs between engagement and divorce, it is likely that the pre-nuptial agreement will have little influence on the judge.[20] A final point is that Ireland does not operate a "clean break" system of divorce. This means that several years after financial orders have been made in a divorce case, a party can re-apply to the court to have those orders re-assessed, and, if necessary, varied.[21] The upshot of all of this is that the main aim of a pre-nuptial agreement; making certain and final provision for the division of assets upon the termination of a marriage, is difficult to achieve at Irish law. The couple are very much at the mercy of the court. If their pre-nuptial agreement coincides with the court's view of proper provision, so be it. However, the agreement is of itself of little value.

## IV. Contracts and Reproduction

[20–16]   The application of contracts to the area of reproduction is a controversial idea. Should surrogacy agreements, under which one woman is paid to carry a foetus to term for another be enforced in courts of law? How would one breach such a contract? Would the surrogate, for example, be bound to pay damages to the commissioning couple in the event of miscarriage? Should a man be able to sell his sperm or a woman her eggs? If a man and woman create embryos together and later split up, should the woman be able to insist on using those embryos to produce a child, even if the man no longer wishes to be a father? Contracting about reproduction obviously involves complex moral and legal issues which we can only touch on briefly and in the most general terms.

[20–17]   A recent judgment of the High Court, suggests that the Irish courts will not invoke public policy arguments against contracts about reproductive issues. The judgment is largely about the status of embryos outside the womb in relation to the constitutional protection of the unborn. Initially, however, the court accepted that

---

[16] This is evidently the position in England and Wales: *S v S* [1997] WLR 1200; *N v N* [1997] 1 FLR 900; *G v G* [2000] 2 FLR 18; *M v M* [2002] 1 FLR 654; *K v K* [2003] FLR 120.

[17] As things stand, under s 14(1)(c) of the Family Law (Divorce) Act 1996 and s 9 of the Family Law Act 1995, the courts have the express power to make orders for financial relief which diverge from the provision made in any pre-nuptial agreement.

[18] Above, n 12 at 18.

[19] *Miller v Miller, McFarlane v McFarlane* [2006] 2 WLR 1283.

[20] *MP v AP*, unreported, High Court, 2 March 2005.

[21] See *JC v MC*, Unreported, High Court, 22 January 2007.

contract issues were of relevance to the dispute. In *MR v TR*[22] McGovern J in the High Court applied traditional principles of contract law to a dispute between separated spouses. They had undergone IVF treatment at a fertility clinic. Consent forms were signed by the couple in respect of treatment involving egg removal, embryo freezing, embryo transfer and the husband's consent. Six viable embryos were created. Three of these were immediately transferred into the plaintiff's uterus and three were frozen. Some time later, the couple's marriage broke down. The issue then arose as to what should happen to the remaining three frozen embryos. The mother wished them to be implanted in her uterus so that she could carry them to term if possible. The father did not wish this to happen. There was no document furnished to the plaintiff and the first defendant by the clinic setting out what was to happen to any frozen embryos, either in the event that the plaintiff became pregnant from the first implantation or in the event of their circumstances changing such as on the death of either party or a separation or a divorce. McGovern J ruled that the first issue to be decided in the case was the issue of private law: whether there was an agreement, expressed or implied, between the plaintiff and the first defendant as to what should happen to the frozen embryos.

He found that there was no evidence that the first defendant gave his express **[20-18]** consent to the transfer of the three frozen embryos into the plaintiff's uterus. He then applied the law on terms implied in fact (13-28) and found that could not be said that it was the presumed intention of the parties that the three frozen embryos would be implanted in the plaintiff's uterus in the circumstances which arose, namely, following the success of the first implantation procedure and the legal separation of the plaintiff and the first defendant. Finally, he applied the law on terms implied in law (13-52) and held that, having regard to the evidence and to the consent forms signed by the plaintiff and the first defendant, a term requiring that the frozen embryos should be implanted in the uterus of the plaintiff did not derive from the nature of the agreement itself. The matter of fact approach taken by McGovern J may be contrasted with that taken in the US, where issues of public policy around contracts for the disposition of embryos have exercised a number of courts.[23]

So what are the policy considerations in favour of the enforcement of **[20-19]** agreements about the disposition of embryos? The first issue is that, as yet, the Oireachtas has not passed any legislation to govern the complex area of assisted reproduction. The most obvious advantage associated with enforceable dispositional contracts is rooted in certainty. Such contracts may help to clarify the state of play as between partners and as between the couple and their fertility clinic.[24] The recognition of such contracts may in addition perform a cautionary function, encouraging couples to think about and discuss the possible contingencies and to plan for them. An enforceable contract might also provide couples with a certain security in their future decision-making. Clinics, in particular, would seem to be on firmer ground where they can rely on a settled agreement in counselling and advising clients and in disposing of

---

[22] [2006] IEHC 221.

[23] Enright, "Dispositional Contracts and Frozen Pre-Embryos: Right for Women?" (2006) 12 (1) *Medico-Legal Journal of Ireland* 31.

[24] Robertson, "Meaning What You Sign," (1998) 28(4) *Hastings Center Report*, 22–23.

the embryos if necessary. For the courts, as *MR v TR* indicates to some extent, the enforcement of dispositional contracts is an attractive dispute resolution option. They can resolve complex moral disputes in terms of contract principle and bright-line rules, thereby obviating the need for difficult value judgments. Arguably, no greater justice, and no greater vindication of the parties' autonomy, is achieved when the courts shift their focus from the concrete situation of the couple before them and decide these cases on the basis of nebulous conceptions such as "the right to be a mother" or "the right not to be a father".[25]

[20–20]     It is worthwhile, also, to look beyond more traditional policy arguments to feminist theory for an analysis of the use of contract to govern reproductive issues.[26] In many ways, contract law is an inherently male construct.[27] The contract paradigm is market rather than relationship-based, involving a preference for arms-length transaction, which might be seen as at odds with the proper substance of motherhood. It prefers abstraction to concrete thought, logic to intuition, and objectivity to subjectivity. The contractual paradigm imagines:

> "separate, atomistic, competing individuals establishing a [contract] to pursue their own interests and to protect them from others' interference with their rights to do so"[28]

Ostensibly, women privilege connectedness, co-operation and interdependence over contract's "egotism tempered by reason".[29]

[20–21]     In addition, it is said that we should exclude reproductive issues from the contractual realm because it too private[30] and precious an affair for contract. Recall Lord Atkin's observations on the domestic sphere in our discussion of intention to create legal relations (7–06). However, feminists argue that the distinction drawn at contract law between the private and the public ultimately does women an injustice. By excluding reproductive issues from the contractual realm, we fail women and, ultimately, exacerbate discrimination. Fineman has written that:

> "human activities in which women might be considered to have either a 'natural' monopoly or to possess more on the 'supply' than 'demand' side of the equation have been written out of contract."[31]

---

[25] Enright, "Justice, Convention and Anecdote: *Evans* and the Right to Become A Mother" (2006) 9 (4) *Irish Journal of Family Law* 11.

[26] See Bruhl, "Motherhood and Contract: Always Crashing in the Same Car" (2001) 9 Buff Women's LJ 191.

[27] See Dalton, "An Essay in the Deconstruction of Contract Doctrine" (1985) 94 Yale LJ 997.

[28] McClain, "'Atomistic Man' Revisited: Liberalism, Connection and Feminist Jurisprudence" (1992) 65 S Cal L Rev 1171, 1173.

[29] West, "Love, Rage and Legal Theory", (1989) 1 Yale J L & Feminism, 101,109.

[30] Much of feminist thought has been about demonstrating that the private is the public. See Fineman, "Contract and Care" (2001) 76 Chi-Kent L Rev 1403.

[31] Fineman, "Contract, Marriage and Background Rules", in *Analyzing Law: New Essays in Legal Theory* (Brian Bix ed.,) (Clarendon Press, Oxford, 1998) at p 183.

If contracts of this type are enforced, it is important to ensure that the conditions for full, free and informed consent are present at the bargaining stage of the dispositional process. A particular problem which bears discussion in some detail is set in the psychological and emotional context of fertility treatment. Studies suggest that infertile couples undergoing treatment tend to perceive information about their treatment selectively, consent to treatment whatever the odds and risks,[32] encounter difficulty processing medical information (particularly where it is of a nature likely to cause anxiety) and find it difficult to evaluate and act on the information provided in a controlled and rational manner. Stress, anger, depression, and low self-esteem affect a substantial number of couples undergoing fertility treatment. Couples seeking parenthood are also unlikely to direct their minds to the possibility of later difficulties which might compel the enforcement of the dispositional contract, such as divorce, separation or death.[33] One partner, aware of the other's desire for a child and caught up in the pressure of circumstances, may feel unable to voice his true wishes and concerns. Also problematic is the power imbalance as between clinic and couple in the "contracting" process and the resulting risk of procedural defects. In the absence of regulation, dispositional agreements will often be drafted by the fertility clinic. They will often be presented to the parties on what may be perceived as a non-negotiable basis. Because they will be drafted in advance they will frequently contain a limited range of dispositional choices and, ordinarily, there will be no option for couples to customise the range of those choices. Furthermore, there is always the danger that signature will take place in the absence of any legal advice. It is especially important, therefore, that each partner in the couple is counselled individually so that they can seriously contemplate the possibility of unpleasant future contingencies, free from the other's influence. It is also essential that they be given adequate time to consult with one another and with a legal advisor in the absence of clinic staff, ideally over a prolonged period away from the clinic environment.

---

[32] Daniluk, "Helping Patients Cope with Infertility", (1997) 40 Clinical Obstetrics & Gynecology 663 , 665. Houmard & Seifer, "Infertility Treatment and Informed Consent: Current Practices of Reproductive Endocrinologists", (1999) 93 Clinical Obstetrics & Gynecology 252 at p. 256.

[33] See generally Eisenberg, "The Limits of Cognition and the Limits of Contract", (1995) 47 Stan L Rev 211.

# CHAPTER 21
# Contracts in Restraint of Trade

## I. Introduction

Suppose that a skilled engineer is about to leave employment with a cutting-edge technology firm to seek a better job elsewhere. In his contract of employment there is a covenant which says that that he will not work with any rival firm in Ireland for a period of 10 years. Or suppose that a chain of cafés buy a local concern and, as part of the contract of sale, the vendors agree not to set up a new café within 10 miles of the one they have just sold. These sorts of covenant may fall foul of the rules on restraint of trade.[1] An agreement or condition[2] in restraint of trade is one which limits a person's freedom to trade or carry out a business or profession in the future.[3] Common examples occur in connection with sale-of-business contracts, post-employment covenants (such as the engineer's example above), exclusive service agreements (in which a party agrees to provide his service to the other party only) and exclusive dealing agreements (in which a party agrees to take his supply of a particular good from the other party only).[4] All restraints of trade are prima facie void. That does not mean that a covenant or condition in restraint of trade will never be enforced: remember that all contracts, to some extent, restrain the parties' freedom for the future. It simply means that there is a presumption of non-enforcement. The old case of *Nordenfeldt* establishes that if a restraint can be justified as reasonable in the interests of both the parties and the public, the contract embodying that restraint will be enforced.[5] The party seeking

[21–01]

---

[1] For a useful recent article see Kimber, "Restrictive covenants in employment law" (2006) 3(3) IELJ 85.

[2] There is some debate at Irish law as to whether the doctrine of restraint of trade only applies to express covenants and conditions in restraint of trade or may also apply to covenants that, although not express restraints of trade, have that effect. In *Kerry Co-operative Creameries v An Bord Bainne* [1991] ILRM 581, McCarthy J found that there was no requirement of an express restraint of trade. By contrast, O'Flaherty J. held that there must be an express condition or covenant.

[3] *Petrofina (Great Britain) Ltd v Martin* [1966] Ch 146.

[4] The doctrine has also been applied to sporting regulations in such sports as horse racing (*Nagle v Feilden* [1966] 2 QB 633 at 646); football (*Johnston v Cliftonville Football & Athletic Club* [1984] N I 9; *Eatham v Newcastle United Football Club* [1964] Ch 413); boxing (*Watson v Prager* [1991] 3 All ER 486); and cricket (*Greig v Insole* [1978] 1 WLR 302).

[5] *Nordenfelt v Maxim Nordenfelt & Co* [1894] AC 535.

to enforce the covenant will usually be granted an injunction compelling the restrained party to adhere to the covenant. If the restraint cannot be justified, it is void and the restrained party is free to ignore it and carry on his business as he pleases.

[21–02]     Before exploring the law on restraint of trade in detail, it is worth examining the policy considerations at play here. There are two major and conflicting policy strands to consider: freedom of contract and freedom of trade,[6] or "the right to bargain and the right to work".[7] First, the idea of contractual freedom mandates that a party should be able to contract for anything, even to the extent of restricting his own freedom to work. Equally, the technology firm and the purchaser of the café mentioned in the examples above should be free to use contract law to protect their valuable interests. Indeed, sales of businesses and employment contracts would likely be badly affected if such protection were not available. Lord Macnaghten in *Nordenfeldt* relates the effects of the old Elizabethan ban on all forms of restraint of trade: "Traders could hardly venture to sell their shops out of their own hands, the purchaser of the business was at the mercy of the seller, every apprentice was a possible rival." In *Leather Cloth Co v Lorsont*,[8] James V-C explained the competing public policy considerations at play in this area of law in terms of individual freedom:

> The principle is this: Public policy requires that every man shall be at liberty to work for himself, and shall not be at liberty to deprive himself or the state of his labour, skill, or talent, by any contract that he enters into. On the other hand, public policy requires that when a man has by skill or by any other means obtained something which he wants to sell, he should be at liberty to sell it in the most advantageous way in the market; and in order to enable him to sell it advantageously in the market it is necessary that he should be able to preclude himself from entering into competition with the purchaser. In such a case the same public policy that enables him to do that does not restrain him from alienating that which he wants to alienate, and therefore enables him to enter into any stipulation however restrictive it is, provided that restriction in the judgment of the Court is not unreasonable, having regard to the subject matter of the contract.

[21–03]     Despite the necessity for a *laissez faire* approach to some aspects of contracting, the courts have historically felt that some intervention is necessary to secure the public good. It has already been noted that a restraint of trade must be justified in terms of the public interest. Pearce LJ explains in *Esso Petroleum Co Ltd. v Harper's Garage (Stourport) Ltd.*[9]:

> "The rule relating to restraint of trade is bound to be a compromise, as are all the rules imposed for freedom's sake. The law fetters traders by a particular

---

[6] See *Herbert Morris v Saxleby* [1916] 1 AC 688 *per* Atkinson LJ: "Two principles or views of public policy come into conflict in cases such as these, namely freedom of trade and freedom of contract."
[7] *Mason v Provident Clothing and Supply Co Ltd* [1913] AC 724.
[8] (1869) LR 9 Eq 345.
[9] [1968] AC 269.

inability to limit their freedom of trade so that it may protect the general freedom of trade and the good of the community."

An unfettered capacity to contract in restraint of trade might limit competition. It might also limit freedom of movement of workers and general freedom of labour. The courts will also intervene paternalistically to prevent unfair or unconscionable use of the doctrine against the party burdened by the restraint.

[21–04]

Perhaps more controversially, the courts will intervene to prevent a party from going too far in restraining his own freedom to trade and earn a living.[10] In particular, he must not be permitted to deprive the state of his experience, skill and labour. It is this aspect of the doctrine of restraint of trade which makes it so contentious. It is even more so when noting that the courts have no general power to void a contract for want of reasonableness. The courts must walk a very fine line here.

[21–05]

## II. The Law in Detail

It is worth examining in more detail the law on restraint of trade. The first thing to note is that not all covenants or conditions that limit a party's freedom to work or trade will be covered by the doctrine of restraint of trade. The next section, therefore, looks at some of the more common areas of law which fall outside the scope of the doctrine. Once it has been established that a covenant or condition is covered by the doctrine, it is clear that there is an initial presumption that it is void. So, the issue for the court is whether it will be allowed to stand. The next two sections of the chapter follow the dual test adapted from *Nordenfeldt* and set out in the leading House of Lords judgment in *Esso Petroleum Co Ltd v Harpers Garage*.[11] First, is the restraint reasonable as between the parties? Second, is the restraint in the public interest?[12]

[21–06]

### Does the Doctrine Apply? The Exceptions

It has been noted that not all restraints of trade will fall to be examined under the test in *Esso Petroleum*. The first important set of exceptions falls under what is known as the "trading society" test. This is derived from *Esso* itself where Lord Wilberforce explained that the doctrine will not apply to certain restraints because they have

[21–07]

---

[10] See *Langan v Cork Operative Bakers TU* [1938] Ir Jur Rep 65. Note also Lord Denning's observation in *Nagle v Feilden* [1966] 2 QB 633 at 646 that "[a] man's right to work at his trade or profession is just as important to him, perhaps more important than, his rights of property".
[11] [1968] AC 269.
[12] This test adapts that set out by Lord Macnagten in *Nordenfelt*:

"The public have an interest in every person's carrying on his trade freely: so has the individual. All interferences with individual liberty of action in trading, and all restraints of trade of themselves, if there is nothing more, are contrary to public policy, and therefore void. That is the general rule. But there are exceptions: restraints of trade and interference with individual liberty of action may be justified by the special circumstances of a particular case. It is a sufficient justification, and indeed it is the only justification, if the restriction is reasonable – reasonable, that is, in reference to the interests of the parties concerned and reasonable in reference to the interests of the public, so framed and so guarded as to afford adequate protection to the party in whose favour it is imposed, while at the same time it is in no way injurious to the public."

"passed into the accepted and normal currency of commercial or contractual or conveyancing relations". This test strongly reflects the courts' traditional policy of deference to the market. These restraints need not be tested because:

> "That such contracts have [passed into currency] may be taken to show with at least strong *prima facie* force that, moulded under the pressures of negotiation, competition and public opinion, they have assumed a form which satisfies the test of public policy as understood by the courts at the time, or regarding the matter from the point of view of the trade, that the trade in question has assumed such a form that for its health or expansion it requires a degree of regulation".[13]

[21–08]  For example, restrictive covenants in which the purchaser of land agrees that he will not use the land for a particular purpose may have the effect of preventing the purchaser from carrying out a particular trade or business. However, because they have passed into common usage, these covenants are enforceable in principle. So in *Sibra Building Co v Ladgroves Stones Ltd.*,[14] a buyer of land argued that a covenant in the contract of sale that prevented him from erecting a pub on the land was void under the doctrine of restraint of trade. The Supreme Court upheld the determination of Keane J that the doctrine did not apply. The same principle applies to restrictive provisions in leases. Lord Reid elaborated on the exclusion of restrictive covenants from the scope of the doctrine on restraint of trade in *Esso Petroleum*:

> "It is true that it would be an innovation to hold that ordinary negative covenants preventing the use of a particular site for trading of all kinds or of a particular kind are within the scope of the doctrine of restraint of trade. I do not think that they are. Restraint of trade appears to me to imply that a man contracts to give up some freedom which otherwise he would have had. A person buying or leasing land had no previous right to be there at all, let alone to trade there, and when he takes possession of that land subject to a negative restrictive covenant he gives up no right or freedom which he previously had."

[21–09]  Similarly, so-called "exclusive dealing" or "vertical" agreements are outside the scope of the doctrine of restraint of trade, provided that they are commonplace. Again, "commonplace" is key. So in *Continental Oil v Moynihan*,[15] a "solus" agreement whereby a garage owner agreed to take oil from the plaintiff alone did not fall within the scope of the doctrine because such agreements were common practice in the industry. On the other hand, *Esso Petroleum* was a case where a solus agreement between a petrol company and a garage came within the scope of the doctrine. At the time, the arrangement was a novel one which had not yet passed into common usage, and so the doctrine of restraint of trade applied. Treitel also argues that even very ordinary exclusive dealing agreements may come within the scope of the doctrine where there is a great disparity of bargaining power as between the parties, and the contract is to the disadvantage of the weaker party.[16] Remember that where a type of

---

[13] Above, n 11 at 332–333 *per* Lord Pearce.
[14] [1998] 2 IR 589.
[15] (1977) 111 ILTR 5.
[16] Treitel, *An Outline of the Law of Contract* (6th ed., OUP, 2004), p 204.

exclusive dealing agreement is common within an industry, the issues which have already been discussed in respect of standard form contracts (see para 14–03) will likely arise, generating a need for judicial scrutiny.

The second important exception refers to employment contracts. It has already [21–10] been noted that restraints of trade refer to limitations on future freedom to trade. So covenants that restrict an employee once he has terminated his employment come within the scope of the doctrine, but covenants that restrict an employee during the period of his employment do not. In *McArdle v Wilson*,[17] the Court of Exchequer found a covenant that restricted a firm's employees' rights to terminate their employment, enforceable because it was operative during the period of their employment. Similarly, in *Schiesser International v Gallagher*,[18] a covenant that required an employee to repay training expenses on termination of employment did not fall foul of the doctrine on restraint of trade because it did not refer to the period after he had left work.

## Is the Restraint Reasonable as Between the Parties?

Once it has been shown that the restraint does not come within one of the ex- [21–11] ceptions discussed, the next issue is whether the restraint is reasonable as between the parties. The onus of showing that the restraint is reasonable rests on the party alleging that it is so. This proportionality requirement is a controversial one. In *Allied Dunbar v Weisinger*,[19] Millet J called it a "dangerous doctrine since it calls upon the courts to perform a balancing exercise which is not in reality capable of being carried out and which is best left to the parties to resolve by the process of negotiation".

## *Legitimate Interest*

The question boils down to whether the restraint is reasonably necessary to protect [21–12] some legitimate interest of the favoured party, having regard to the interests of the affected party. The restraint must not exceed what is necessary to protect that interest.[20] A key point here is that the favoured party may not restrain the other simply for the sake of it. He must show that he is protecting some interest of his own. So in *Vancouver Malt and Sake Brewing Company v Vancouver Breweries Ltd*,[21] a clause that prohibited the assignor of a license from brewing beer for 15 years was un-enforceable because the assignee did not brew beer. The cases give many examples of legitimate interests. The buyer of a business has a legitimate proprietary interest in the goodwill of its reputation.[22] That is why he is entitled to take reasonable steps to restrain the seller from devaluing that goodwill by setting up a new business in competition with the one he has just sold. It is important to note that the purchaser of a business is only entitled

---

[17] (1876) 10 ILTR 87.

[18] (1971) 106 ILTR 22.

[19] [1988] IRLR 60.

[20] See *Lennon v Doran*, unreported, High Court, 20 February 2001; *Leeds Rugby Ltd v Harris* [2005] EWHC 159.

[21] [1936] AC 181.

[22] *Nordenfelt v Maxim Nordenfelt & Co*, above, n 5. See also *Vancouver Malt and Sake Brewing Co Ltd. v Vancouver Breweries Ltd.*, *ibid*.

to a covenant that will protect the business which he has just bought. He may not use the covenant to protect his other business interests.[23]

[21–13]     An employer seeking to enforce a post-employment covenant with a former employee might have a legitimate interest in intellectual property[24] or trade secrets[25] with which his employee has become familiar during his employment. The employer has a proprietary interest in those things; he owns them and he is therefore entitled to impose a covenant on the employee preventing him from exploiting such knowledge in his future employment. So in *Forster & Sons Ltd. v Sugett*,[26] a restraint was upheld which prohibited the former works manager of a glass bottle factory from working in the glass-making industry in the United Kingdom for five years after ceasing employment at the factory. This restraint was justified because the former manager had learned confidential aspects of manufacturing bottles, including the correct mixture of gas and air in the furnaces. It is very important to be aware that an employer is not entitled to use an express covenant in order to restrain an employee from exploiting confidential information not amounting to a trade secret. That much is clear from the Court of Appeal decision in *Faccenda Chicken v Fowler.*[27] The Court held that employers do not have a legitimate interest in confidential information, such as pricing policies, delivery routes and customer lists, because they are not considered "trade secrets".[28]

[21–14]     An employer also has a legitimate interest in protecting his trade connections. He is, therefore, entitled to restrain his former employees from soliciting his customers and enticing them away from him. There is an important limitation to this freedom. These restraints will only be upheld in respect of an employee who could be reasonably expected to have influence over his employer's customers. In the recent case of *Murgitroyd v Purdy*,[29] Clarke J makes the point succinctly:

"Covenants against competition by former employees are never reasonable as such. They may be upheld only where the employee might obtain such personal knowledge of, and influence over, the customers of his employer as would enable him, if competition were allowed, to take advantage of his employer's trade connections ..."

[21–15]     Usually a restraint will be justified in this type of case where the employee is the main point of contact for certain customers. So these types of restraint have been

---

[23] *British Reinforced Concrete v Schieff* [1921] 2 Ch 563.

[24] *Fletcher Aluminium Ltd. v O'Sullivan* [2001] 2 NZLR 731.

[25] *Commercial Plastics Ltd. v Vincent* [1965] 1 QB 623.

[26] (1918) 35 TLR 87.

[27] [1985] ICR 589.

[28] However, the exploitation of such information will often be caught by the implied term in all contracts of employment that the employee will serve his employer faithfully. See e.g. *AF Associates v Ralston* [1973] NI 229, where employees deliberately took files from their employers on resignation, aiming to use them to start up a competing business. However, this implied term will only be breached by deliberate conduct. An employee who simply remembers certain confidential information and exploits it will not be in breach of contract.

[29] Unreported, High Court, 1 June 2005.

upheld in respect of a solicitor[30] and the manager of a brewery,[31] but not in respect of a bookmaker's assistant who had no personal contact with customers.[32]

The employer does not have any legitimate interest in his employee's "personal skill or knowledge", even if that skill and knowledge were acquired on the job. The employer only has a legitimate interest in those skills as long as he pays for them. Once the employee terminates his employment, he may use his own general skills as he pleases.[33]    **[21–16]**

## Reasonableness

The law recognises that the restraining party is entitled to take proportionate steps to safeguard his valuable interest. The question of what protection is proportionate in any given case is down to a balancing exercise. In *Esso*, Lord Wilberforce observed that the doctrine of restraint of trade is "one to be applied to factual situations with a broad and flexible rub of reason". However, it is possible to identify a number of factors on which the courts focus in their application of the reasonableness test.    **[21–17]**

First, the court, in applying the reasonableness test, deals in the *realities of the case* before it and not in generalities. A good illustration of this point is *McEllistrem v Ballymacelligott Co-Op.*[34] In that case, farmers who were members of the co-operative in Co. Kerry were in an exclusive dealing agreement with the co-operative. They were restricted from selling milk to any other local buyer within a radius of 10 miles. Now, a 10-mile radius is, at first blush, a small area, and Counsel argued that the restraint was reasonable because the farmers were free to sell their milk anywhere else in Ireland. On the contrary, Lord Birkenhead LC, holding that the restriction was an impermissible restraint of trade, stressed the importance of context to the notion of reasonableness:    **[21–18]**

> "[I]n a sparsely inhabited agricultural neighbourhood, with scanty means of communication, a prohibition of trade in every township within a radius of ten miles, might have precisely the same effect upon the business of a small trader as if the preclusion extended to the remotest region of Donegal."

Secondly, the *extent* of the restraint in terms of time, subject matter and area is important to the question of reasonableness. In *Silverstone Records v Mountfield*,[35] the members of the Stone Roses entered into a recording agreement, which extended to "the world and its solar system". Would an agreement of this kind survive an application of the test in *Esso Petroleum*? Even the very early case law on restraint of trade touched on this principle. For a time, a distinction was made between    **[21–19]**

---

[30] *Mulligan v Corr* [1925] IR 169.

[31] *White, Tomkins and Courage v Wilson* (1907) 23 TLR 469.

[32] *SW Strange Ltd. v Mann* [1965] 1 All ER 1069.

[33] See *Herbert Morris v Saxelby* [1916] 1 AC 688.

[34] [1919] AC 548. See similarly *European Paint Importers v O'Callaghan*, unreported, High Court, 10 August 2005.

[35] [1993] EMLR 229.

general restraints of trade, which were forbidden, and partial restraints, which were permissible.[36] Blanket restraints are, generally speaking, a bad idea. Nevertheless, there is no definitive rule here. A restriction which lasts a long time and stretches over a vast area may be considered reasonable where a particularly strong interest is at stake. Take the classic case of *Nordenfelt* in which the defendant owned a patent for manufacturing machine guns. He sold his business and the contract of sale was subject to two clauses, which prevented the defendant from making guns or engaging in any activity that would rival the business he had just sold. The clauses were worldwide in application and were to last for 25 years. The restraint might seem excessive at first glance. However, the Court focussed on the nature of the business at issue. It noted that the market in machine guns was a global one and involved only a small number of manufacturers. Therefore, the restraint was entirely reasonable. Similarly, in *Murgitroyd v Purdy*,[37] Clarke J found that a covenant which restrained a patent attorney from carrying out any business in competition with his former employers in the Republic of Ireland for 12 months was reasonable. This was because the market was a nation-wide market and involved only 10 attorneys. By contrast, an employer with two branches in large rural towns could not expect a post-employment covenant stretching across most of Connacht to stand. *Mulligan v Corr*[38] is the case in point. A man was taken on by a solicitor as his managing clerk. As part of his contract of employment, he agreed that he would not, himself, practise as a solicitor within a radius of 30 miles from the towns of Ballina and Charlestown or within 20 miles of Ballaghadereen. The solicitor had an office in Ballina and a branch office in Charlestown. The clerk had built up significant knowledge of the solicitor's clients and business. Although he had not been qualified for long, his contacts were such that he could potentially set up a practice in successful competition with his former employer. Of course, the solicitor was entitled to protect himself against such competition within reason. However, the area the restrictive covenant covered was too large. It included almost the whole of Mayo, more than half of Sligo and significant portions of Roscommon, Galway and Leitrim. The Court found that this went well beyond the limited area the solicitor reasonably required for his protection.

[21–20]      *Esso Petroleum* demonstrates the application of these principles to the duration of the contract. In that case a garage owner entered into an agreement with Esso that he would sell only their petrol in his garage. The agreement was to last for 21 years. The Court held that this was an unreasonable restraint of trade, *inter alia*, because Esso could not demonstrate that they took any particular benefit from this extended period of restraint which could not be achieved by a shorter period. Again, the nature of the business is important. In *Esso*, the instability and uncertainty involved in the petrol industry mitigated against the enforcement of a 21-year covenant. A long-term restraint might be reasonable in a business that moves slowly, as for example a high-technology business dependent on long periods of research. Such a restraint would be unacceptable in a fast-moving industry such as the music industry.

---

[36] See *Mitchel v Reynolds* (1711) 1 P Wims 181.

[37] Unreported, High Court, 1 June 2005.

[38] [1925] IR 170.

Thirdly, a distinction is drawn between contracts of employment and contracts [21–21]
for the sale of a business. Costello J in *John Orr Ltd v John Orr*[39] set out that greater
freedom to contract in restraint of trade is allowable in a covenant between the buyer
and seller of a business than is allowable in a covenant between an employer and an
employee. The 25-year worldwide restriction in *Nordenfeldt* was acceptable in a sale-of-
business contract but would not have been allowed were Nordenfeldt merely a former
employee of the firm. This distinction boils down to the relationship between
bargaining power and the principle that a properly negotiated contract is a binding
one. The seller and purchaser of a business are presumed to be dealing on roughly
equal terms, while an employer and an employee are assumed not to be on a level
footing.[40] However, even where post-employment covenants are concerned, markedly
able employees may be bound to quite draconian agreements. In *Bridge v Deacons*,[41] a
covenant was upheld which prohibited a partner in a Hong Kong solicitors firm from
dealing with any client of his former firm for a period of five years after he had ceased
employment with them. The Court upheld the agreement even though the firm had 10
branches. This particular partner had had no dealings with 90 per cent of the firm's
clients, and the covenant greatly restricted his capacity to work within Hong Kong as a
lawyer at all. Even outside of contracts of employment, inequality of bargaining power
will be a strong motivating factor in voiding a contract for unreasonable restraint of
trade, especially where the contract has been negotiated in the absence of legal advice.[42]

Finally, the court will examine the benefit which the restrained party takes from [21–22]
the restrictive contract. In sale-of-business contracts, this will often mean that the court
directs itself to the consideration given in exchange for the goodwill. In the New
Zealand case of *Helsby v Oliver*,[43] the Court noted that the greater the consideration
paid for the goodwill, the more likely the Court would be to uphold a restraint
designed to protect it. Somewhat similar issues arise in post-employment covenants. If
a restraint is substantively unfair and that lack of fairness is combined with inequality
of bargaining power, the courts are likely to void the restraint as unreasonable. There is
an obvious relationship between this factor and issues around equality of bargaining
power. Lord Reid set out the connections in *Esso Petroleum*:

> "Where two experienced traders are bargaining on equal terms and one has
> agreed to a restraint for reasons that seem good to him the court is in grave
> danger of stultifying itself if it says that it knows the trader's interest better than
> he does himself. But there may well be cases where, although the party to be
> restrained has deliberately accepted the main terms of the contract, he has been
> at a disadvantage as regards other terms, for example where a set of conditions
> has been incorporated which has not been the subject of negotiation – there the
> court may have greater freedom to hold them unreasonable."

---

[39] [1987] ILRM 702.
[40] See *Schroeder Music Publishing v Macaulay* [1974] 1 WLR 1308.
[41] [1984] AC 705.
[42] *Panayiotou v Sony, The Times*, 30 June 1994.
[43] [1999] 1 NZLR 77.

**[21–23]**     A clear example is *Schroeder Music Publishing v Macaulay*.[44] In that case, a young, unknown songwriter made an exclusive service agreement with a publisher. The songwriter could not publish with any other music publisher. The publisher was not obliged to publish his work[45] and was bound only to pay him nominal amounts. This lack of benefit to the songwriter was a key reason for voiding the restraining covenant. By contrast, a very significant benefit may justify an otherwise harsh restraining covenant. *Alec Lobb (Garages) Ltd. v Total Oil GB*[46] was a similar scenario to *Esso*. A garage was tied to a 21-year agreement with an oil company. The agreement was for the sale and leaseback of the garage. The arrangement was justified despite its long duration because, *inter alia*, the arrangement was a rescue operation designed to benefit the garage and the consideration for the lease equated with market value.

### Is the Restraint Reasonable in the Public Interest?

**[21–24]**     This final part of the test requires the court to look beyond the parties to the wider impact of the restraint at issue and restraints of its kind. For example, in *Fitch v Dewes*[47] a solicitor covenanted that on termination of his employment, he would not practise law within seven miles of Tamworth. The House of Lords, having held this restraint to be reasonable as between the parties, held that it was also reasonable in the public interest because "otherwise solicitors carrying on their business without a partner would be extremely chary of admitting competent young men to their office and to the confidential knowledge to be derived by frequenting those offices". Similarly, in *Kerry Co-Op v Bord Bainne*,[48] McCarthy J noted that the rules of a co-operative were not void as an unreasonable restraint of trade because they were reasonable *inter partes*, and because they served the national interest by promoting the expansion of Bord Bainne. *Herbert Morris Ltd v Saxleby*[49] and *Esso* itself suggest that the party alleging that the restraint of trade is contrary to the public interest bears the burden of proving as much.

**[21–25]**     In *Bord Bainne* and *Fitch*, public and private interests were congruent. What should happen where they conflict? The role of the public interest in restraint of trade cases is debateable at Irish law. In both England and Ireland, the effect of the public interest dimension of restraint of trade was minimised in a number of decisions. This, understandably, is because the parties' interests in freedom of trade and freedom of contract are often taken to be synonymous with the public interest. However, these interests are not always congruent: "a dual test in the doctrine recognises that the assertion of a private right can create a public wrong".[50] Therefore, the test in *Esso*, which is the core of the doctrine of restraint of trade in England, is firmly a dual one. Indeed, Lord Pearce in his judgment makes clear that the public interest is the key issue

---

[44] [1974] 1 WLR 1308.

[45] See *Societa Esplosivi Industriali SpA v Ordnance Technologies (UK) Ltd.* [2004] EWHC 48 (setting out that the lack of reciprocal obligation may justify the non-enforcement of a covenant in restraint of trade).

[46] [1985] 1 WLR 173.

[47] [1921] 2 AC 158.

[48] [1991] ILRM 851.

[49] [1916] AC 688.

[50] *Tank Lining Corp v Dunlop Industrial Ltd.* (1982) 140 DLR (3d) 659 at 671.

in any restraint of trade case: "there is one broad question: Is it in the interests of the community that this restraint should be held to be reasonable and enforceable?" In England, under *Esso* the position appears to be that even if a restraint is reasonable as between the parties, it may still be void as unreasonable in the public interest. Arguably, the role of the public interest in Irish law is even stronger than in England. The authority for this is the Supreme Court judgment in *Macken v O'Reilly*.[51] Here the show-jumper, Eddie Macken, challenged the rules of the Equestrian Federation as an unreasonable restraint of trade. The rules set out that Irish show-jumpers could only ride Irish-bred horses in competition. The High Court found that these rules constituted an unreasonable restraint of trade because Macken was prevented from riding the best horses available. Under the traditional reading of *Esso*, the rules should have fallen because they were unreasonable as between the parties. However, the Supreme Court upheld the rules as reasonable in the public interest. The Court referred to the effect that a change of rules, and the consequent loss of income, would have on the Irish horse breeding industry. Crucially, the Court held that this public interest "ought to have been considered as a balance to the harm or inconvenience caused to the plaintiff". This is a highly unorthodox reading of the law on restraint of trade. It seems to suggest a balancing test rather than the two-step test accepted under *Esso*. Certainly, O'Higgins CJ in setting out the test for reasonableness in restraint of trade refers again to balance in a manner which suggests the primacy of public over private interests:

> "Whether [the restraint] can be justified ... involves a careful examination of all the circumstances, the need for restraint, the object sought to be attained, the interests sought to be protected and the general interest of the public. What is done or sought to be done must be established as being reasonable and necessary and on balance to serve the public interest."

## III. Severance—A "Blue Pencil" Rule

A final question is whether a restraint of trade covenant, which is too wide in some respects, must fall in its entirety or whether the offending parts can be, as it were, cut away or severed, leaving the rest of the covenant to stand. The courts have held that this is possible; they may strike out the bad parts with a metaphorical "blue pencil" and retain the reasonable parts. In *John Orr Ltd and Vescom BV v John Orr*,[52] Costello J noted:     [21–26]

> "The courts may in some circumstances enforce a covenant in restraint of trade even though taken as a whole the covenant exceeds what is reasonable, by the severance of the void parts from the valid parts."

*Goldsall v Goldman*[53] shows the tool of severance in operation. The plaintiffs     [21–27]
were dealers in costume jewellery. They and the defendant, a competitor, agreed that the defendant would not compete with them in any capacity for two years. The agreement purportedly covered "the county of London, England, Scotland, Ireland,

---

[51] [1979] ILRM 79.
[52] [1987] ILRM 702 at 704.
[53] [1915] 1 Ch 292.

Wales, or any part of the United Kingdom of Great Britain and Ireland and the Isle of Man, or France, the United States of America, Russia or Spain, or within 25 miles of Potsdammerstrasse, Berlin, or St Stefans Kirche, Vienna". The Court of Appeal found that the covenant was unreasonable in its geographical scope. It severed all of the words after "and France" in the offending clause. The remainder of the clause stood. Severance was also employed in *Skerry's College v Moles*.[54] There the Court examined a contract in restraint of trade which forbade a teacher to work within seven miles of Cork, Dublin or Belfast for three years. The Court found that the restrictions as to Cork and Dublin were unreasonable, and so these were severed. However, the restriction as to Belfast was held to be reasonable, and so it remained enforceable.

[21–28]    The power to sever is a limited one and may not be exercised in such a way as to redraft the contract or to change its nature. The courts will mend no man's bargain. This means, first, that the "blue pencil" is only to be used for deleting words and not for adding or changing them. Secondly, it means that even if words can be deleted from the condition or covenant, leaving a perfectly workable restraint, the amended restraint will not be enforced if it is entirely different in nature from that originally agreed.[55] Finally, if, after the offending words have been deleted, the clause is incomprehensible, it must fall.[56] If severance is impossible the whole restraint falls. Yet, the courts guard their powers of severance jealously,[57] especially where post-employment restraints are concerned. Lord Moulton spoke eloquently to this effect in *Mason v Provident Clothing and Supply Company Ltd*[58]:

> "It would in my opinion be *pessimi exempli* if, when an employer had exacted a covenant deliberately framed in unreasonably wide terms, the Court were to come to his assistance, and, by applying their ingenuity and knowledge of the law, carve out of this void covenant the maximum of what he might validly have required. It must be remembered that the real sanction at the back of these covenants is the terror and expense of litigation, in which the servant is usually at a great disadvantage, in view of the longer purse of his master. [T]he hardship imposed by the exaction of unreasonable covenants by employers would be greatly increased if they could continue the practice with the expectation that, having exposed the servant to the anxiety and expense of litigation, the Court would in the end enable them to obtain everything which they could have obtained by acting reasonably ... [T]hey must take the consequences."

---

[54] (1907) 42 ILTR 46.

[55] In *Mulligan v Corr* [1925] IR 170, Fitzgibbon J said as much: "If, by eliminating the part which appears to be void, we can leave a valid and effective contract remaining, such a course is lawful, though the court cannot make a new covenant or mould one which is already complete in itself so as to create a different restriction which would be reasonable in the opinion of the court."

[56] But see *T Lucas & Co Ltd v Mitchell* [1974] Ch 129.

[57] But see *ECI European Chemical Industries v Bell* [1981] ILRM 345.

[58] [1913] AC 724.

# CHAPTER 22
## Frustration

## I. Introduction

Imagine that A and B have a contract for the hire of B's boat. On the day before A had **[22–01]** planned to use the boat, it sinks in a freak storm. What happens to the contract between A and B? Has B, for example, breached the contract because he was unable to deliver the boat A hired? Such cases are governed by the doctrine of frustration. If A sues B on foot of their contract, B can use the doctrine of frustration in his defence as an excuse for his non-performance. When a contract has been frustrated, it means that something has happened since the formation of the contract which is "altogether outside the control of the parties"[1] and which fundamentally undermines the possibility of performing the contract as originally agreed.[2] A plea of frustration will help B in the example above because it automatically discharges a contract.[3] This means that the contract comes to an end the moment the frustrating event occurs. There is no breach of contract, and accordingly, neither party will receive damages.

In many ways frustration is comparable with common mistake. Common **[22–02]** mistake often concerns cases where impossibility was present at the time the contract was made, whereas frustration is often, if not exclusively, concerned with impossibility which did not materialise until after the contract had been formed.

---

[1] *J Lauritzen AS v Wijsmuller BV (The Super Servant Two)* [1989] 1 Lloyd's Rep 148 *per* Hobhouse J.

[2] *Zuphen v Kelly Technical Services* [2000] IEHC 117. Gilmore says that the doctrine of frustration covers those situations where the real world has failed to correspond with the imaginary world hypothesised by the contract. Gilmore, *The Death of Contract*, (Columbus 1995), p 90.

[3] *Hirji Mulji v Cheong Yue SS Co* [1926] AC 497.

Compare, for example, the "coronation cases" of *Krell v Henry*[4] and *Griffith v Brymer*.[5] Both cases involved contracts for the hire of rooms from which to watch the coronation procession of Edward VII. After the contract in *Krell* had been formed, the coronation procession was cancelled. The contract was frustrated. In *Griffith*, unknown to either party, the procession had already been cancelled at the time the parties entered into their contract, thus, the contract was void for common mistake.

## II. The Development of the Doctrine

[22–03] Before exploring the elements of frustration, the history of this doctrine is worth examining in some detail. The old law was that supervening events were no excuse for non-performance. If we accept that, in essence, one enters into a contract to gain some control over the future,[6] it seems clear that a change of circumstances should be a poor excuse to set a contract aside. In short, contracts are to be performed, not avoided. Lord Sumner spoke to this effect in *Larrinaga v Société-Americaine*[7]:

> "[C]ontracts are made for the purpose of fixing the incidence of ...risks in advance, and their occurrence only makes it more necessary to uphold the contract and not to make them the ground for discharging it."

[22–04] In the old law these ideas found expression in the rule as to absolute contracts. The classic case is *Paradine v Jane*.[8] The contract was for the lease of a farm. After the contract was formed, armed Royalist soldiers fighting in the English Civil War occupied the farm and ejected the tenant. The Court directed that:

> "when the party by his own contract creates a duty or charge upon himself, he is bound to make it good, if he may, notwithstanding accident by inevitable necessity, because he might have provided against it by his contract...for the law would not protect him beyond his own agreement. And therefore if the lessee covenant to repair a house, though it be burnt by lightning, or thrown down by enemies, yet he ought to repair it."[9]

---

[4] [1903] 2 KB 740.

[5] (1903) 47 Sol Jo 493.

[6] Kastley, Post and Hom, *Contracting Law* (2nd ed, Carolina Academic Press, 2000), p 812.

[7] (1923) 92 LJKB 464.

[8] (1647) Aleyn 26. For an alternative view of *Paradine*, see Kelly, "Paradine v Jane: A Doctrine of Absolute Contractual Liability?" (2004) 12 ISLR at www.islr.ie .

[9] (1647) Aleyn 26 at 27. In later years, the Minnesota Supreme Court adopted the same position in *Stees v Leonard*, 20 Minn. 494 at 503 (1874): "If a man bind himself, by a positive, express contract, to do an act in itself possible, he must perform his engagement, unless prevented by the act of God, the law, or other party to the contract. No hardship, no unforeseen hindrance, no difficulty short of absolute impossibility, will excuse him from doing what he has expressly agreed to do. This doctrine may sometimes seem to bear heavily upon contractors; but, in such cases, the hard-ship is attributable, not to the law, but to the contractor himself, who has improvidently assumed an absolute, when he might have undertaken only a qualified liability". See also *Budgett and Co v Binnington and Co* [1891] 1 QB 35.

The effect was that the tenant was obliged either to perform the contract or pay damages for its breach, no matter how difficult the performance turned out to be—a deal was a deal. If the tenant had wished to avoid the rule as to absolute contracts, he should have so provided in his contract. Some relief came with the case of *Taylor v Caldwell*,[10] which gave explicit recognition to the doctrine of frustration: **[22–05]**

> "The principle seems to us to be that, in contracts in which the performance depends on the continued existence of a given person or thing, a condition is implied that the impossibility of the performance arising from the perishing of the person or thing shall excuse the performance. In none of these cases is the promise in words other than positive, nor is there any express stipulation that the destruction of the person or thing shall excuse the performance; but that excuse is by law implied, because from the nature of the contract it is apparent that the parties contracted on the basis of the continued existence of the particular person or chattel."[11]

*Taylor v Caldwell* relies on the law of implied terms (Chapter 13) to explain frustration. It claims to give effect to the presumed intention of the parties. This analysis was followed for many years, including in the Irish case of *Cummings v Stewart (No 2)*.[12] However, this theory of frustration eventually met with judicial scepticism,[13] most famously, in *James Scott & Sons Ltd v R and N Del Sel*[14] where Lord Sands set out the following scenario: **[22–06]**

> "A tiger has escaped from a travelling menagerie. The milkgirl fails to deliver the milk. Possibly the milkman may be exonerated from any breach of contract but, even so, it would seem hardly reasonable to base that exoneration on the ground that 'tiger days excepted' must be held as if written into the main contract."

The crux of Lord Sands' observation is that it is illogical to apply the doctrine of implied terms to something that the parties could not have foreseen and, thus, could not possibly have intended at the time of contracting.[15] In any case, how can one know that it is appropriate to imply a term that the contract should come to an end in the event that particular circumstances occur? Lord Wright observes in *Denny, Mott & Dickinson Ltd v Fraser*[16] that the parties are more inclined to have intended to **[22–07]**

---

[10] 3 Best & S 826.

[11] (1863) 3 B& S 826 *per* Blackburn J.

[12] [1913] 1 IR 95. See also *FA Tamplin Steamship Co v Anglo-Mexican Petroleum Product Co Ltd*, 404 *per* Loreburn LJ.

[13] But see *Port Line Ltd v Ben Line Steamers Ltd* [1958] 2 QB 156 *per* Diplock J.

[14] 1922 SC 592.

[15] Similarly *Davis Contractors Ltd v Fareham UDC* [1956] AC 696 *per* Radcliffe LJ.

[16] [1944] AC 265.

introduce modifications to the contract, allowing it to stand. The implied term theory is based on a fiction and, ultimately, it was rejected by Lord Denning in *The Eugenia.*[17]

[22–08]     The modern basis for frustration[18] is no longer one of implied terms. It is described in the judgment of Lord Radcliffe in *Davis Contractors v Fareham UDC*[19]:

> "Frustration occurs whenever without default of either party a contractual obligation has become incapable of being performed because the circumstances in which performance is called for would render it a thing radically different from that which was undertaken by the contract. *Non haec in foedera veni. It was not this that I promised to do.*"[20]

[22–09]     A restatement of Lord Radcliffe's rule is found in *National Carriers v Panalpina Ltd*[21] where Lord Simon set out the test for frustration as follows:

> "Frustration of a contract takes place when there supervenes an event (without default of either party and for which the contract makes no sufficient provision) which significantly changes the nature (not merely the expense or onerousness) of the outstanding contractual rights and/or obligations from which the parties could reasonably have contemplated at the time of its execution that it would be unjust to hold them to the literal sense of its stipulations in the new circumstances."

[22–10]     Broadly speaking, the approach of the modern law is to ask whether, as a matter of justice, the Court should depart from the rule as to absolute contracts. In *The Super Servant Two*,[22] Bingham LJ stated that:

> "The object of the doctrine was to give effect to the demands of justice, to achieve a just and reasonable result, to do what is reasonable and fair as an

---

[17] *Ocean Tramp Tankers Corp v V/O Sovfracht (The Eugenia)* [1964] 1 All ER 161. "It was originally said that the doctrine of frustration was based on an implied term. In short, that the parties, if they had foreseen the new situation, would have said to one another: 'If that happens, of course, it is all over between us.' But the theory of an implied term has been discarded by everyone, or nearly everyone, for the simple reason that it does not represent the truth. The parties would not have said: 'It is all over between us.' They would have differed about what was to happen. Each would have sought to insert reservations or qualifications of one kind or another."

[18] As many as five theories explaining frustration are recognised. See *National Carriers v Panaplina* [1981] AC 675 *per* Hailsham LJ.

[19] [1956] AC 696.

[20] Emphasis added. Another evocative justification of the doctrine was given in *Tamplin SS Co v Anglo-Mexican Petroleum Co* [1916] 2 AC 397 at 406 where the Court found that frustration discharges a contract on the basis that "the foundation of what the parties are deemed to have had in contemplation has disappeared and the contract itself has vanished without foundation."

[21] [1981] AC 675.

[22] *J Lauitzen A/S v Wijsmuller BV "The Super Servant Two"* [1990] 1 Lloyd's Rep 1.

expedient to escape from injustice where such would result from enforcement of a contract in its literal terms after a significant change of circumstances.[23]

There are some criticisms to be made of the new regime. The old implied term theory had the advantage that it at least paid lip service to the idea of the intent of the parties. Lord Sumner suggested that by implying a term, the law "is only doing what the parties really (though subconsciously) meant to do themselves".[24] While the construction of the parties' contract is important to the doctrine of frustration,[25] it is accepted that the doctrine owes more to considerations of fairness.

[22–11]

While the development of the doctrine of frustration represents a thaw in policy, the Courts remain keen that the doctrine should not be "invoked to relieve contracting parties of the normal consequences of imprudent bargains".[26] The Courts do not have any power of absolution.[27] Indeed, Lord Bingham's dictum above continues: "Since the effect of frustration is to kill the contract and discharge the parties from further liability under it, the doctrine is not to be lightly invoked."[28]

[22–12]

It is rare for frustration to be pleaded successfully. This is largely because, as the dicta already quoted demonstrate, parties are expected and encouraged to have the good sense to provide in their contract for "the ups and downs that the future may bring". The Courts, after all, recognise a wide variety of contractual clauses designed to provide for unexpected changes in circumstances.[29] That said, one must also recognise the difficulties involved in attempting to contract for every contingency:

[22–13]

> "Any contract reflects an infinite series of assumptions made by the contracting parties about the nature of the real world...Only an infinitesimal fraction of these assumptions ever comes to the conscious attention of the parties; as with an iceberg, the great bulk of the contractual consent lies beneath the surface. This self-evident proposition remains true even if the contractual agreement is memorialized by a carefully drawn writing, even if the writing is drafted by the most gun-shy of lawyers. For every contingency that can be identified and dealt with, a hundred others will escape detection. And, as any experienced contract draftsman knows, specificity soon becomes a self-defeating game."[30]

---

[23] *J Lauitzen A/S v Wijsmuller BV "The Super Servant Two"* [1990] 1 Lloyd's Rep 1. See *Notcutt v Universal Equipment Co (London) Ltd* [1986]1 WLR 641, which rejects injustice as the sole test of frustration.

[24] *Hirji Muljii v Cheong Yue Steamship Co* [1926] AC 497.

[25] *Denny, Mott and Dickinson v James Fraser & Co Ltd* [1944] AC 265 *per* Wright LJ.

[26] *The Nema* [1982] AC 724 *per* Roskill LJ.

[27] See Lord Loreburn in *Tamplin* [1916] 2 AC 397.

[28] *J Lauitzen A/S v Wijsmuller BV "The Super Servant Two"* [1990] 1 Lloyd's Rep 1.

[29] On hardship clauses, intervener clauses and *force majeure* clauses, see McKendrick, *Contract Law* (6th ed, Palgrave McMillan, 2005), pp 310–311.

[30] Kessler, Gilmore and Kronman, *Contracts: Cases and Materials* (3rd ed, Little, Brown and Co, 1986), p 861.

## III. Categories of Frustrating Event

[22–14]  The categories of frustration are never closed. It has been held that "ultimately the frustration of an adventure depends on the facts of each case".[31] As previously noted, the event must be one which radically alters the obligations owed by the parties to the contract such that the parties would be justified in saying: "It is not this that I promised to do". An event which makes performance of the contract absolutely impossible will do, but the categories of frustrating events may be wider than that. Performance may be delayed by the unavailability of some essential thing and this may operate to frustrate the contract. Supervening events may render performance of the contract impracticable though not impossible. This may amount to frustration. Finally, a contract may be frustrated even though performance is both practicable and possible because the supervening event undermines the whole purpose of performance.

### Impossibility

[22–15]  A contract will be frustrated where it is impossible to perform it. Impossibility will arise where something essential to the performance of the contract has been destroyed, where one of the parties to the contract is unable to perform by reason of his death or incapacity, or where a change in the law renders any further performance of the contract illegal.

### *Destruction of Something Essential to the Performance of the Contract*

[22–16]  In the old case of *Williams v Lloyd,* it was recognised that a bailee's duty to return a horse was discharged where the horse died through no fault of the bailee because "that is become impossible by the act of God".[32] The main case on impossibility is *Taylor v Caldwell.*[33] The defendants had granted the plaintiffs a licence to use the "Surrey Gardens and Music Hall" for four grand concerts with day and night fetes. Unfortunately, subsequent to the formation of the contract, the hall was destroyed in a fire. The question for the Court was whether the defendants were in breach of contract for failure to supply the plaintiffs with the hall as agreed. The Court held that the contract was discharged for frustration because it was impossible to perform the contract as agreed since the subject-matter was no longer available.

[22–17]      It is not necessary that the essential item is entirely obliterated, merely that it is so fundamentally changed that it is impossible to use it in the performance of the contract as agreed. In *Asfar v Blundell*[34] a cargo of dates was exposed to water and sewage. While the dates were later sold for £2,400, the cargo-owner's contract was discharged for frustration because the dates had become "for business purposes something else".[35] To similar effect is the more modern case of *Gramerco SA v JCM/ Fair Warning (Agency) Ltd*[36] where a contract to promote a Guns n' Roses concert was frustrated when the stadium at which they were to play, although not destroyed, was declared unsafe, and no suitable alternative venue could be found.

---

[31] *Bank Line Ltd v Arthur Capel and Co* [1919] AC 435.
[32] *Williams v Lloyd,* W Jones 179, 82 Eng Rep 95.
[33] (1863) 3 B & S 826.
[34] [1896] 1 QB 125.
[35] *ibid.*
[36] [1995] 1 WLR1226.

## Death or Incapacity

Sometimes the performance of a contract is personal in that it depends upon the personal skill of one of the parties. Examples include a contract to paint a picture or to write a book. Where the party who has contracted to exercise that skill dies, the contract is frustrated and dies with him.[37] Of course, the contract will not be frustrated by the death of the other party. It is almost never impossible to pay money.    [22–18]

Similar issues arise where a party is incapacitated by illness or injury. Crompton J makes this point memorably in *Hall v Wright*[38] where he says that:    [22–19]

"Where a contract depends upon personal skill, and the act of God renders it impossible, as, for instance, in the case of a painter employed to paint a picture who is struck blind, it may be that the performance must be excused."[39]

Thus, in *Robinson v Davison,*[40] an eminent piano player's contract to perform a concert was frustrated when she contracted a dangerous illness, which made it impossible for her to play the concert at all.    [22–20]

Obviously, whether the contract is frustrated will depend on the degree of seriousness of the incapacity. It would be too much if contracts of employment were discharged for frustration every time an employee was ill with flu.[41] So, in *Marshall v Harland and Wolff Ltd*,[42] the Court notes that the test for frustration of a contract of employment turns on whether the employee's incapacity was:    [22–21]

"of such a nature, or [appeared] likely to continue for such a period, that further performance of his obligations in the future would either be impossible or would be a thing radically different from that undertaken by him and accepted."

Factors which have to be taken into account in assessing whether incapacity was serious enough to frustrate a contract of employment include the terms of the contract and its provision for sick pay and the duration of employment prior to incapacity. Another crucial factor is the nature of the employment. Where the employee has a key post, the employment contract is more likely to be frustrated    [22–22]

---

[37] *Kean v Hart* (1869) IR 3 CL 388; *Hyde v Dean of Windsor* Cro. Eliz. 552. See 2 Wms. Exors. 1560 (5th ed.) "[I]f an author undertakes to compose a work, and dies before completing it, his executors are discharged from this contract; for the undertaking is merely personal in its nature, and by the intervention of the contractor's death, has become impossible to be performed." See also *Stubbs v Holywell Railway Co* (1867) LR 2 Ex 311.

[38] EB & E 746.

[39] *ibid*.

[40] (1871) LR 6 Ex 269. See also the US case of *Parker v Arthur Murray Inc* 295 NE 2d 487 where a person who had booked a course of dance lessons affected his capacity to receive performance so significantly that the contract between him and the dance instructor was frustrated.

[41] See *Notcutt v Universal Equipment Co (London) Ltd* [1986] WLR 641 for an especially harsh operation of the doctrine.

[42] [1972] 1 WLR 899. For more detail on the application of frustration to contracts of employment see Kelly, "Frustrating the rights out of you – the Doctrine of Frustration and Employment Contracts" (2004) 4 UCD Law Review 1.

by his incapacity.[43] The employee's chances of recovery are also important, and Kelly suggests that where an employee who has been disabled would be in a position to return to work with reasonable adjustments, the contract is more likely to survive.[44]

### Supervening Illegality

[22–23] A contract will be frustrated where a change in the law makes any further performance of the contract illegal. The Courts acknowledge that "[t]here cannot be default in not doing what the law forbids to be done".[45] Where performance of the contract already falls foul of the law in force at the time of contracting, there is no frustration. Such contracts are governed by the law on illegal contracts. The contract in *Fibrosa Spolka Akcyjna v Fairbairn Lawson Combe Barbour Ltd*[46] was for the manufacture of machines and their delivery to Lithuania via the port of Gdynia in Poland. After the contract had been formed, but before the machines could be delivered, Gdynia was occupied by Germany. Under the law presiding in England at the time, it was illegal to trade with or assist the enemy in a time of war. Once Poland was occupied, delivering the machines to Poland came within the definition of trading with the enemy, performance of the contract was illegal and, accordingly, the contract was frustrated.[47] A contract might also be frustrated where an Act of Parliament passed during the term of the contract renders it invalid. So, in *Ó Cruadhlaoich v Minister for Finance,*[48] a contract was discharged by frustration when a judicial position created by the first Dáil was revoked by a Free State statute.

### Temporary Unavailability of Some Essential Thing

[22–24] Contractual performance may be frustrated where something essential to the performance is unavailable for a time. These cases are distinguished from the *Taylor v Caldwell* scenario in that the essential "something" still exists and would be suitable for use in performing the contract if it were available. It simply cannot be used as intended at the time when it is needed. The delay is the frustrating factor.

### The Period of Unavailability

[22–25] In many cases the unavailability of the essential thing will merely interrupt performance rather than prevent it altogether. Where time is of the essence, or where a contract can only be performed on a particular day or days and the unavailability coincides with that period, the unavailability will frustrate the contract.[49] Here, the contract is frustrated because, once the assigned time for performance has passed, the performance is no longer of any use to the receiving party. There is a difference, however, between those cases where the delay lasts so long that no performance is possible and those where some performance remains possible. Remember how reluctant the Courts are to hold that

---

[43] *James v Greytree Trust* EAT/699/95.
[44] Kelly, "Frustration and employment contracts" (2004) 11(11) CLP 286.
[45] *Denny, Mott and Dickinson v Fraser* [1944] AC 265 *per* MacMillan LJ.
[46] [1943] AC 32.
[47] See similarly, *Ross v Shaw* [1917] 2 IR 367.
[48] (1934) 68 ILTR 174.
[49] *Robinson v Davison* (1871) LR 6 Exch 269.

frustration has killed a contract. Take, for example, the case of *Tamplin SS Co Ltd v Anglo-Mexican Petroleum Co.*[50] This case concerned a five-year charter, which was due to expire in December 1917. The ship was requisitioned in February 1915. Holding that the charter was not frustrated, the Court noted that "there may be many months during which the ship will be available before the five years have expired".[51] This case can be contrasted with *The Nema*,[52] which involved a charter party for six or seven trips. After the first trip, a long strike occurred at the end of which only one or two further voyages were possible. The strike was held to frustrate the contract. The point, then, is that the greater the proportion of the period available for performance that is eliminated by the delay, the more likely that delay is to frustrate the contract.

In other cases the contract may be frustrated "by reason of such a long interruption or delay that the performance is really in effect that of a different contract".[53] In other words, performing the contract in full after the delay would be significantly more burdensome for one party than it would have been had the contract been performed on time. One such case is *Bank Line Ltd v Arthur Capel & Co.*[54] In that case, a ship was chartered for 12 months. It was intended that the ship would be used during the period April 1915 to April 1916. The ship was requisitioned and the owners did not retrieve her until September 1915. It was then proposed that the contract period would run in full from September 1915. The Court found that the delay involved here was frustratory because freight rates had risen so much during the period of delay that performance for the 12 months of September 1915 to September 1916 was "as a matter of business a totally different thing"[55] from that originally contracted for.

[22–26]

## Unavailability of the Means of Performance

Where the parties have together agreed an exclusive means of performance, the contract will be frustrated if this becomes unavailable. So in *Nicholl & Knight v Ashton Etridge & Co*,[56] the unavailability of a ship, the *Orlando*, named in the contract between the parties, was held to frustrate that contract. Similarly, in *Howell v Coupland*,[57] a contract of sale for 200 tons of potatoes was frustrated when the crop on an expressly agreed portion of land failed.[58] The seller, therefore, was not liable to supply the quantity of potatoes agreed. Where no such specific provision is made, the unavailability of the means of performance is a matter for the performing party. In *Blackburn Bobbin C Lt v TW Allen & Sons Ltd*,[59] the contract was for the supply of Finnish timber. The seller's source of supply was cut off due to the outbreak of war. Nevertheless, the contract was not frustrated because the parties had not made any shared decision as to the source of supply. If a party wishes to guard against the risk of

[22–27]

---

[50] [1916] 2 AC 397.

[51] *ibid*. See also *Nordman v Rayner and Sturgess* (1916) 33 TLR 87.

[52] [1982] AC 724.

[53] *Tatem Ltd v Gamboa* [1939] 1 KB 132.

[54] [1919] AC 435.

[55] *ibid.*

[56] [1901]2 KB 126.

[57] (1876)1 QBD 258.

[58] The position is more difficult where there has been no express agreement. See *Re Badische Co* [1921] 2 Ch 331.

[59] *Blackburn Bobbin Co Ltd v TW Allen & Sons Ltd* [1918] 2 KB 467.

frustrating events, he should make the means of performance a term of the contract. If he does not do so, the contract will likely not be frustrated and he will be bound to find an alternative means of performance.[60]

### Impracticability

[22–28] Performance is said to be impracticable where, although the contract can still be performed, the performance would be much more burdensome than originally contemplated. It is important to realise that the degree of material or financial hardship suffered by a party as, a result of events which occur subsequent to the formation of the contract, is irrelevant to the question of whether frustration will be found.[61] Lord Roskill has said in *The Nema*[62] that the doctrine is "not lightly to be invoked to relieve contracting parties of the normal consequences of imprudent commercial bargains".[63] Changed circumstances may make a contract more inconvenient or onerous to perform than originally anticipated, but much more will be required if the contract is to be discharged. That much is clear from the dictum of Lord Simon in *British Movietonenews*[64] that:

> "The parties to an executory contract are often faced, in the course of carrying it out, with a turn of events which they did not at all anticipate—a wholly abnormal rise or fall in prices, a sudden depreciation of currency, an unexpected obstacle to the execution, or the like. Yet this does not in itself affect the bargain which they have made."[65]

[22–29] *Davis Contractors Ltd v Fareham UDC*[66] is an important case here. It concerned a contract to build 78 houses which were badly affected by shortages and rationing after the Second World War. Supply of some materials was delayed and some materials were simply not available. As a result, the cost to the builders of performing the contract was £18,000 more than estimated, and the contract took 14 months longer to complete than originally contemplated. However, the Court held that the contract was not frustrated. Lord Radcliffe explained that:

---

[60] *Howell v Coupland* (1876) 1 QBD 258.

[61] See *Davis Contractors Ltd v Fareham UDC* [1956] AC 696.

[62] [1982] AC 724. Toulson J observes at first instance in *Great Peace* [0]that "it cannot properly be the function of the law to relieve a party from … a bargain if it turns out to have been not merely bad, but very bad."

[63] [1982] AC 724.

[64] [1952] AC 166.

[65] [1952] AC 166. See also *Tennants (Lancashire) LS v CS Wilson & Co Ltd* [1917] AC 495 at 510: "The argument that a man can be excused from performance of his contract when it becomes 'commercially' impossible seems to me a dangerous contention which ought not to be admitted unless the parties have plainly contracted to that effect"; *Revell v Hussey* (1813) 2 Ball & B 280 *per* Manners LC: "Suppose a case that very frequently occurs of a colliery, where the company has contracted to supply iron works at a price agreed on; surely it can be no ground to rescind it that subsequent conditions have occurred to render it very prejudicial; that the coals may have greatly increased; that the expenses of working the mine may have considerably increased."

[66] [1956] AC 696.

"it is not hardship or inconvenience or material loss itself which calls the principle of frustration into play. There must be as well as such a change in the significance of the obligation that the thing undertaken would, if performed, be a different thing from the contracted for."[67]

The thing performed in this case was not a different thing from that contracted for. Seventy-eight houses were contracted for and seventy-eight were built. Accordingly, there was no frustration. This principle has been accepted as part of Irish law by Murphy J in *Zuphen v Kelly*.[68] In *Zuphen,* South African copper jointers were hired by the defendant recruitment agency on 12-month contracts to work for Eircom. Eircom withdrew work from the defendants and the defendants, therefore, claimed that their contract with the plaintiffs was frustrated. Murphy J found that the hardship and inconvenience caused to Eircom by this withdrawal of work was insufficient to bring the contract to an end. Another important case along these lines is the House of Lords judgment in the shipping case of *Tsakiroglou and Co Ltd v Noblee Thorl GmbH*.[69] The contract was for the sale of groundnuts, which were to be shipped from Sudan to Hamburg. Both parties expected that shipment would be via the Suez Canal. This turned out not to be possible as the canal was closed. The question was whether the unavailability of this method of performance frustrated the contract. It would have taken the ship two and a half times as long to travel an alternative route (via the Cape of Good Hope), and the cost of carriage would have been doubled. Nevertheless, the Court felt that the difference between the two methods of performance was not sufficiently fundamental to frustrate the contract. Suppose, however, that the contract provided that time was of the essence—for example, because the groundnuts would deteriorate over time. Or suppose it provided for a particular route or delivery date which could not be achieved owing to the Suez crisis. In any of those events, the contract would have been frustrated because the delayed performance which occurred would have been radically different from that contemplated under the contract. The thing performed would not have been the thing contracted for. Along the same lines is *The Eugenia*,[70] a case which concerned a voyage from Genoa via the Black Sea to India. In this case too, sailing via the Suez Canal was impossible. The case was argued on the basis that the ship could have sailed round the Cape of Good Hope—a journey of 138 days instead of the 108 days via the Suez Canal. Lord Denning did not accept that this difference was significant enough to amount to frustration. The Courts' strict approach here seems less so when recalling that the parties in *The Eugenia* might have specified in their contract that the trip was to be via the canal. Had they done so, their contract would have been frustrated for impossibility.

**[22–30]**

## Purpose of Performance Undermined

Sometimes a frustrating event will render performance of a contract possible but pointless. We say that the purpose of the contract has been frustrated. This category has its origins in what are known as the coronation cases. The coronation of Edward VII was to take place in Westminster Abbey on Thursday, 26 June 1902. It was the first

**[22–31]**

---

[67] [1956] AC 696 at 729.
[68] [2000] ELR 277.
[69] [1962] AC 93.
[70] *Ocean Tramp Tankers Corp v V/O Sovfracht (The Eugenia)* [1964] 1 All ER 161.

British coronation in 60 years. On that day, the coronation party was to process from Buckingham Palace to the Abbey. The next day, another parade was to take place throughout the whole city of London. Rooms were hired out, grandstands were erected, seats sold along the parade route and boats were chartered to bring people to see the naval review. However, Edward VII fell ill with appendicitis some days before the coronation ceremony and the coronation celebrations were postponed until the autumn. Two of the most important frustration cases sprang from this set of events:

[22–32]     The first is *Krell v Henry*.[71] In that case, Henry saw an advertisement in the window of Krell's flat, 56A Pall Mall, for the hiring out of windows from which the coronation process could be viewed. He arranged with Krell's agent that he would hire the flat for the daytimes of 26 and 27 of June for £75. Twenty-five pounds was paid in advance. When the coronation processions did not take place as anticipated, Henry refused to pay the balance owed. The Court, in this case, held that the contract was frustrated.

[22–33]     *Krell v Henry* is often contrasted with *Herne Bay Steamboat Co v Hutton*.[72] The defendant in *Herne Bay* hired *The Cynthia* to take a group of friends from Herne Bay in Kent to see the naval review and regatta at Spithead. He paid a £50 deposit. A further £200 was due on the day of the voyage. Unfortunately, as a result of the king's illness, the naval review was cancelled on the morning that *The Cynthia* was due to sail. The Court found that this contract was not frustrated.

[22–34]     It is worth examining the distinction between the cases at some length. In *Krell v Henry*, the Court considered the purpose of the contract, explaining that "the coronation procession was the foundation of this contract, and ... the object of the contract was frustrated by the non-happening of the coronation and its procession on the days proclaimed".[73] The Court in *Herne Bay,* however, found that the contract for the hire of the boat had more than one purpose. The object of *this* contract was to bring the parties on a cruise along the south coast of England, including two days at sea and a tour of the fleet. All of this could still be done, despite the non-happening of the naval review. The official naval review was only one part of the contract. In sum, the fact that one part of the contract could not be performed did not mean that the whole enterprise was frustrated.

[22–35]     This category of case can also be explained from another angle. It could be said that a contract is frustrated under this heading where the contract is "wholly devoid of purpose for both of the parties".[74] This explanation is consistent with the judgment of Lord Vaughan Williams in *Krell v Henry*[75] where he said that "the taking place of those processions on the days proclaimed along the proclaimed route, which passed 56A Pall Mall, was regarded by both contracting parties as the foundation of the contract". In the course of argument in *Krell v Henry*, counsel had asked whether a contract with a cabman to take someone to Epsom on Derby Day at an appropriately

---

[71] [1903] 2 KB 740.
[72] [1903] 2 KB 683.
[73] [1903] 2 KB 751.
[74] Poole, *Textbook on Contract Law* (7th ed, OUP, 2004), p 282.
[75] [1903] 2 KB 740.

inflated price would be frustrated by the cancellation of the races. Lord Vaughan Williams distinguished this hypothetical from the facts in *Krell v Henry* as follows:

"I do not think that in the cab case the happening of the race would be the foundation of the contract. No doubt the purpose of the engager would be to go to see the Derby, and the price would be proportionately high; but the cab had no special qualifications for the purpose which led to the selection of the cab for this particular occasion. Any other cab would have done as well... Whereas in the case of the coronation, there is not merely the purpose of the hirer to see the coronation procession, but it is the coronation procession and the relative position of the rooms which is the basis of the contract as much for the lessor as the hirer."

The view of the coronation procession from 56A Pall Mall was the foundation [22–36] of the contract for both parties. The contract here was not a mere contract for the hire of a room; no other room would have done the plaintiff quite as well. There was no point to the contract if not for the proximity of the room to the procession. Crucially, the defendant shared the plaintiff's purpose. The defendant had advertised that he was selling a view of the procession, not simply letting a room. To the same effect, he was only letting the room during the day, when the procession would be passing, and not during the night. The contract in *Herne*, however, is much more like that the hypothetical hire of the cab. First, there was nothing special about *The Cynthia*. Any other passenger boat could have brought the defendant's party to the review. Second, while the plaintiff had a particular object in hiring *The Cynthia*, there was nothing in the facts to show that this object was shared by the defendant. The defendant was not hiring his boat out especially for the purposes of the naval review.

## IV. Provision Made in the Contract

Once the Court has determined that the event which has befallen the parties is one with [22–37] the potential to frustrate the contract, it must look at whether the parties have already provided for it in their own contract.[76] As set down in *Joseph Constantine Steamship Line Ltd v Imperial Smelting Corporation Ltd*,[77] there is no frustration where "full and complete" express provision has been made in the contract for every event which occurs. So, in *Mulligan v Browne*,[78] a doctor's contract of employment with a hospital was expressed to be conditional on the availability of funds at the hospital. Therefore, when the hospital suffered a funding crisis, it did not frustrate the contract because it had been foreseen. It is worth noting, however, that even very broad language might not succeed in covering an especially grave frustrating event. Rix J recognised this in *The Safeer*[79] where he said that while it is, in theory, possible to cover a risk by expression provision of the contract, the contract may "nevertheless be frustrated where the risk materialises in some overwhelming form". For example, in *Metropolitan Water Board v*

---

[76] In *Ocean Tramp Tankers Corp v VIO Sovfracht* [1964] 1 All ER 161, Lord Denning refers to the supposed requirement of the doctrine of frustration that the frustratory event be "unforeseen". He says that this is not an essential feature of the doctrine. What is important is whether the parties have provided for the event in their contract.

[77] [1942] AC 154.

[78] Unreported, Supreme Court, 23 November 1977.

[79] [1994] 1 Lloyd's Rep 637.

*Dick, Kerr and Co*,[80] a contract for the construction of a reservoir provided that in the case of delay "whatsoever and howsoever occasioned", the contractors were obliged to apply to the engineer for an extension in time. After the formation of the contract, the Government required the contractors to stop work and sell their plant so that they were no longer able to build the reservoir. The Court found that, although this supervening event did delay the construction of the reservoir, the contract's delay clause was only intended to cover temporary delays rather than fundamental changes of the type which had occurred. The contract was frustrated in spite of the express contractual provision. To similar effect is *Jackson v Union Marine Insurance Co Ltd.*[81] This case involved the charter of a ship, which was to proceed from Liverpool to Newport with all possible speed, "dangers and accidents of navigation accepted". The ship sailed 2 January. One day out of port, the ship ran aground and was still under repair the following August. While the contract had provided for dangers and accidents of the broad type which occurred, the contract did not cover this particular frustrating event. It was not intended to cover an accident with such extensive consequences. The Courts are so strict in cases where express provision has been made for the frustrating event because the parties ought to be bound to their bargain in line with the principle of freedom of contract. By making a certain provision in his contract, one party may have taken on the risk of certain changes in circumstances. He has taken on the burden of being the insurer for the other, and he is not entitled to be released from that burden when the realisation of what he has really undertaken dawns.

### V. Self-Induced Frustration

[22–38]   A defendant cannot claim frustration where the frustrating event was brought about by his own conduct or that of those for whom he is responsible. The "frustrating event must take place without blame or fault on the part of the party seeking to rely on it".[82] So, for example, imagine that the fire in *Taylor v Caldwell* had been caused by the defendants' negligence. There would have been no frustration in that event because the frustratory event would have been attributable to the defendants. Lord Russell of Kilowen memorably remarked in *Joseph Constantine Steamship Line Ltd v Imperial Smelting Corp Ltd*[83] that the varieties of fault range from "the criminality of the scuttler who opens the sea-cocks and sinks his ship, to the thoughtlessness of the prima donna who sits in a draught and loses her voice".[84] In *Herman v The Owners of SS Vicia*,[85] a ship was unable to dock in Britain as required under the contract at issue. Ordinarily, the contract would have been frustrated. However, the reason that the ship could not dock was that its owner had negligently failed to obtain the requisite documentation. The frustration was self-induced and, therefore, inconsequential. *The Super Servant Two*[86] is

---

[80] [1918] AC 119.

[81] (1874) LR 10 CP 125. See also *Pacific Phosphate Co Ltd v Empire Transport Co Ltd* (1920) 36 TLR 750.

[82] *J Lauitzen A/S v Wijsmuller BV "The Super Servant Two"* [1990] 1 Lloyd's Rep 1.

[83] [1942] AC 154 at 179.

[84] See *FC Shepherd v Jerrom* [1987] QB 301 on whether a contract of employment can be frustrated if the employee is imprisoned for a crime which he has committed.

[85] [1942] IR 304.

[86] *J Lauritzen AS v Wijsmuller BV (The Super Servant Two)* [1989] 1 Lloyd's Rep 148 *per* Hobhouse J.

a classic English case here. The defendants had agreed to transport the plaintiff's oil rig on one of two named barges: *Super Servant One* and *Super Servant Two*. The defendants allocated this task to *Super Servant Two*. The ship sank, and, as the *Super Servant One* was by now indisposed, the defendants claimed that the contract was frustrated. However, Bingham LJ held that effective frustration has to arise from an "outside event" rather than from an act of the defendant. The frustrating event here was the defendant's choice to allocate the contract to the boat which sank, not the sinking of the boat. McKendrick criticises this on the basis that the decision to allocate *Super Servant One* to another customer's contract was not a "real" choice.[87] The decision in *The Super Servant Two* seems to leave the supplier to a "Hobson's Choice". However, the earlier case of *Maritime National Fish Ltd v Ocean Trawlers Ltd*[88] is to the same effect. The defendants had five fishing boats, one of which, the *St Cuthbert*, was chartered by the plaintiff. They applied for licenses for each of the five boats, but only three were granted. The defendants applied the licenses to three of the boats, but not to that chartered by the plaintiff. They then claimed that the charter of that boat was frustrated by the Minister of Fisheries' failure to license the boat. The Court found that the frustration was self-induced. It was not beyond the defendants' control but was caused by their choice not to apply the licence to the boat chartered by the plaintiff.

## VI. Effects of Frustration

Frustration freezes a contract. The contract ends at the date of frustration "forthwith, without more and automatically"[89] without either party having elected to end it. The parties are absolved of all further obligations. The contract is over only for the future. It is not void *ab initio* — all obligations which fall to be performed at the time of the frustrating event will still stand. The coronation case of *Chandler v Webster*[90] sets out the rule:

[22–39]

> "[I]t remains a perfectly good contract up to that point, and everything previously done in pursuance of it must be treated as rightly done, but the parties are both discharged from further performance of it. If the effect were that the contract were wiped out altogether, no doubt the result would be that money paid under it would have to be repaid as on a failure of consideration. But that is not the effect of the doctrine; it only releases the parties from further performance of the contract."

This principle is illustrated by facts of *Chandler v Webster*.[91] The contract here was for the rental of 7 Pall Mall for £141. The entire sum was to be paid immediately. Only £100 was paid up front and the remainder was still due to be paid at the time the coronation procession was cancelled. The duty to pay that remaining £41 was not absolved by the frustrating event. The duty to pay existed before the procession was cancelled, and so it still stood in spite of the frustration of the contract. *Chandler v Webster* can be contrasted with *Appleby v Myers*.[92] This case was about a contract for

[22–40]

---

[87] McKendrick, *Contract Law*, (6th ed, Palgrave McMillan, 2005), p 318.

[88] [1935] AC 524.

[89] *Hirjii Mulii v Cheong Yue Steamship Co* [1926] AC 497 *per* Sumner LJ.

[90] [1904] 1 KB 493.

[91] [1904] 1 KB 493.

[92] (1867) LR 2 CP 651.

the installation of a machine. A fire destroyed the building in which the machine was being installed, thereby frustrating the contract. Although the installation was partly complete, the installers could not recover any payment for their services. This was because, under the contract, the obligation to pay fell due after the frustrating event. Therefore, the obligation to pay was absolved by frustration. A more famous example of the harsh operation of this aspect of the doctrine of frustration is *Cutter v Powell.*[93] Cutter was second mate on a ship sailing from Liverpool to Jamaica. The contract of employment was entire. It stated that his wages would not be paid until he arrived back in Liverpool. Accordingly, when the contract was frustrated by Cutter's death midway through the voyage, the future obligation to pay his wages was extinguished.

[22–41]    There is no compelling justification for the rule in *Chandler v Webster.*[94] As the Court explained in that case:

> "The rule adopted by the Courts in such cases is I think to some extent an arbitrary one, the reason for its adoption being that it is really impossible in such cases to work out with any certainty what the rights of the parties in the event which has happened should be. Time has elapsed, and the position of the parties may have been more or less altered, and it is impossible to adjust or ascertain the rights of the parties with exactitude. That being so, the law treats everything that has already been done in pursuance of the contract as validly done, but relieves the parties of further responsibility under it."

[22–42]    This explanation of the rule was severely criticised in the Scottish case of *Cantiare San Rocco v Clyde Shipbuilding and Engineering Co*[95] as follows:

> "Thus the rule, admitted to be arbitrary, is adopted because of the difficulty, nay the apparent impossibility, of reaching a solution of perfection. Therefore, leave things alone: *potior est conditio possidentis*. The maxim works well enough among tricksters, gamblers and thieves, let it be applied to circumstances of supervenient mishap arising from causes outside the volition of parties: under this application innocent loss may and must be endured by one party, and unearned aggrandisment may and must be secured at his expense to the other party".[96]

[22–43]    In England, it has been set out in the *Fibrosa*[97] case that a party who receives no part of what he has bargained for as a result of a frustrating development is entitled to recover any money he paid to the other party, prior to the occurrence of the frustrating event. As noted in *Fibrosa*, the machines contracted for were never delivered as the contract was frustrated by the occupation of Poland. Accordingly, the purchasers were entitled to have the purchase money that they had already paid to the manufacturers repaid in full. The English law on the effects of frustration is now largely contained in an Act: The Law Reform (Frustrated Contracts) Act 1943.

---

[93] (1795) 6 TR 320.
[94] [1904] 1 KB 493.
[95] [1924] AC 226.
[96] [1924] AC 226 *per* Shaw LJ.
[97] [1943] AC 32.

# CHAPTER 23

# Agreement, Performance and Breach

## I. Introduction

Discharge of a contract is the process by which the primary obligations to perform arising under a valid contract come to an end. A contract may be discharged by frustration (Chapter 22), by agreement, by performance or by breach. A discharged contract ought to be distinguished from a contract which is void or voidable. Where a court finds that a contract is void, as for mistake (Chapter 17), the contract is without effect from the very beginning. No performance obligations arise under such a contract. If one party attempts to enforce the contract, the other may plead as a defence that it is void. By contrast, where a contract is discharged, the court recognises that it was valid and binding for a time but is now at an end. If a contract is voidable, as for misrepresentation (Chapter 15), the innocent party has the right to decide whether the contract remains in being or whether it is to be rescinded and set aside. If a voidable contract is rescinded, it becomes like a void contract. The contract is treated as if it never existed and any purported rights arising under that contract, past and future, must die. Where a contract is discharged, on the other hand, only future obligations to perform will come to an end. **[23–01]**

## II. Discharge by Agreement

Discharge by agreement will be discussed only briefly here.[1] Just as the contract was made by agreement so it can be ended by agreement. Discharge by agreement occurs when the parties together make a new agreement to end the original contract. Such discharge may occur where the parties mutually abandon their remaining performance obligations. However, it is wiser to provide for a specific agreement. The agreement may need to be memorialised in accordance with s 2 of the Statute of **[23–02]**

---

[1] See generally, McDermott, *Contract Law* (LexisNexis, 2000) 1058–1069; Clark, *Contract Law in Ireland* (5th ed, Thomson Round Hall, 2004) 501–506.

Frauds (Chapter 11) As seen in Chapter 8, a fresh agreement will require to be supported by fresh consideration. Discharge by mutual agreement is often called discharge through "accord and satisfaction": as well as the accord or agreement, satisfaction must be present in the shape of consideration. It will not be difficult to find fresh consideration where the contract is executory; where both parties still have obligations left to perform. This discharge, called a bilateral discharge, is binding because the giving up of rights on each side will amount to consideration. However, in a unilateral discharge, where only one party has obligations left to perform, the agreement to discharge the contract will not be binding unless it is supported by some consideration.

## III. Breach

[23–03]   A breach of contract consists in any failure to fully perform a contractual obligation without lawful excuse. Breach of contract triggers the non-breaching party's right to the remedies of specific performance, termination (Chapter 24) and damages (Chapter 25). Liability for breach of contract is not absolute: for instance, the law excuses failure to perform where the contract has been frustrated. However, the default position is that liability for breach of contract is strict rather than fault-based. Lord Edmund-Davies in *Rainieri v Miles*[2] said that: "it is, in general, immaterial why the defendant failed to fulfil his obligations, and certainly no defence to plead that he has done his best". It could be argued that fault-based liability is more just. However, the logical counter-argument is based in freedom of contract: the parties are generally free to limit or qualify their liability by means of exemption clauses, (Chapter 14) or obligations to use "best endeavours" or "reasonable endeavours". There are limited instances where it is not possible to contract out of strict liability, as is the case with some of the terms implied by consumer legislation (13-62). The mandatory imposition of strict liability here is justified by the need to protect the consumer.

[23–04]        In order to determine whether breach has occurred, the court will need to interpret the express and implied terms of the contract (see Chapter 13) to determine the scope of the performance obligations assumed under it. After all, a "defendant is not liable in damages for not doing that which he is not bound to do".[3] Breach may consist of defective performance. In *Chanter v Hopkins*[4] Lord Abinger noted that: "if a man offers to buy peas of another, and he sends him beans, he does not perform the contract". The same point is made by Dodd J in *Fogarty v Dickinson*[5]: "[i]f a man orders a golf cloth cap, the order is not fulfilled by sending him a stylish silk hat". Refusal to perform is also breach, as when a builder contacts the person employing him to build a house to say that he has changed his mind and will not be carrying out the work as agreed. Finally, a party breaches a contract where he makes his performance impossible. An example might be a singer who has contracted to play a particular club on Thursday 15 May and then contracts to play a different club at the same time on the same day. The singer is incapable of fulfilling both sets of contractual obligations. One contract must be breached.

---

[2] [1981] AC 1050.
[3] *Abrahams v Herbert Reiach Ltd* [1922] 1 KB 477 *per* Scrutton LJ.
[4] (1838) 4 M & W 399.
[5] (1913) 47 ILTR 281.

## IV. Where Performance Ends and Breach Begins

The traditional rule is that a contract is breached unless every element of performance [23–05]
is completed entirely and exactly as provided for in the contract. So in *Coughlan v
Moloney*,[6] a contract to build a house was breached even though the house was partly
built. Anything but a *de minimis* deviation from the performance agreed is a breach of
contract. In *Re Moore & Co. v Landauer*[7] the parties had agreed in their contract that
tins of fruit to be supplied to the purchaser would be packed 30 to a box. However,
some of the tins were packed 24 to a box. The contract was breached. Perhaps the most
famous example of the harsh operation of this rule is *Cutter v Powell*.[8] A sailor was
promised 30 guineas to act as the second mate on the slave ship *Governor Parry* sailing
from Jamaica to Liverpool. The sailor died before the voyage was completed. His wife
sued for a portion of his wages in proportion to the part of the journey he had
completed before his death. However, Lord Kenyon CJ invoked the so-called "rule as
to entire contracts" to deny her any recovery. Under the rule as to entire contracts the
obligation to pay does not kick in until the contract is performed in full.

### Divisible Obligations

The rule as to entire contracts may seem harsh. In *Coughlan v Moloney*,[9] it was [23–06]
observed that the rule was "always apt to work hardship". It has the underlying
rationale of holding men to the bargains which they have freely chosen.[10] Little wonder
then that the courts, in seeking to circumvent the rule, focus on interpreting the
obligations which the parties chose. In *Cutter*, the court was justified in treating the
sailor's contract as entire. The sailor had been paid four times the going rate "as a form
of insurance" that he would complete the contract. This satisfied the Court that the
parties intended that only complete performance would result in payment. This
approach is evident in other cases. The plaintiff in the Irish case of *Callan v Marum*[11]
sued the defendant for repair work that he had carried out at the defendant's house.
The defendant countered that the plaintiff had not executed the work as provided for
under their contract. The contract was entire and indivisible. Significantly, it provided
that a specific lump sum was to be paid on completion of the building. It is generally
accepted that "the law is that where there is a contract to do work for a lump sum, until
the work is completed, the price of it cannot be recovered."[12] Accordingly, the Court
found that the defendant was not bound to pay for half or a quarter of the work done.
The parties themselves had agreed to a contract which was entire, and it was not for the
court to remake that bargain. Whenever the parties expressly or impliedly stipulate for

---

[6] (1905) 39 ILTR 153.
[7] [1921] 2 KB 519.
[8] (1795) 6 TR 320.
[9] (1905) 35 ILTR 153.
[10] See also *Munro v Butt* (1858) E & B 735, 754 *per* Lord Campbell CJ.
[11] (1871) 5 IRCL 315. See also *Basten v Butter* 7 East 479.
[12] *Sumpter v Hedges* [1898] 1 QB 673, 674.

an entire contract, the court will not interfere.[13] The classic examples of indivisible contracts were given by Jessel MR in *Re Hall & Baker*[14]:

> "If a man engages to carry a box of cigars from London to Birmingham, it is an entire contract, and he cannot throw the cigars out of the carriage half-way there and ask for half the money; or if a shoemaker agrees to make a pair of shoes, he cannot offer you one shoe and ask you to pay half the price."

[23–07]    In other cases, the court will be able to interpret a contract so that it is "severable": divisible into several discrete obligations instead of one monolithic obligation.[15] Each "sub-obligation" can give rise to a corresponding obligation to pay a proportionate part of the contract price. For example, suppose A contracts to redecorate B's kitchen. There is a total contract price of €7,000. €3,000 is to cover the manufacture of new furnishings, €2,000 is for tiling and €1,000 is for painting. Suppose A makes the furnishings but does not complete the tiling or the painting. The court may divide the main contract into three contracts: furnishing, tiling and painting. A is entitled to be paid for his performance of the furnishings contract but not for the other two. This technique will normally only apply when the parties have themselves agreed the dividing lines of the contract. *Cutter v Powell* might be contrasted with another ship case. In *Taylor v Laird*[16] the plaintiff was employed as the commander of a steamer on an exploration and trading voyage up the Niger. The contract expressly said that he was hired at a rate of £50 a month. The Court held that, unlike the contract in *Cutter*, this contract was not entire because, by its express words, performance under the contract was divided up month by month. The court may be able to divide a contract even in the absence of express provision. An important example was that in *Brown v Wood*.[17] In that case the plaintiff had agreed to manufacture cloth from the defendant's yarn. The plaintiff paid money to the defendant as security for the yarn. He was to deliver the cloth in consignments and was to be paid manufacturing expenses and profit on delivery of the last consignment of cloth. The plaintiff did not manufacture all of the cloth. The defendant argued that he was not entitled to any money because the contract was entire. The Court disagreed and divided the contract into parts so that the plaintiff was able to recover payment for the cloth he had manufactured together with a proportionate sum of the security paid on the yarn. Generally speaking, where the contract is a substantial one, the parties will take the time to expressly divide the payment obligations within a contract and link them to performance obligations. The courts should be slow to step in where the parties have not divided the contract for themselves, as the right to withhold payment may be one of the few powers by which the paying party can compel the other's performance. One situation where a more interventionist approach is justified is where

---

[13]  *Nash & Co. v Hartland* (1840) 2 Ir LR 190.

[14]  (1878) 9 Ch D 538.

[15]  Where an employee terminates (but not where he breaches) a contract of employment, ss 2 and 5 of the Apportionment Act 1870 provide that salaries and pensions shall be considered as accruing from day to day. However, these sections do not apply to lump sum contracts.

[16]  (1856) 1 H & N 266.

[17]  (1864) 6 Ir Jur 221.

trade custom provides that a type of contract is divisible. For example, shipwrights are generally held to be entitled to payment in instalments.[18]

### The Doctrine of Substantial Performance

Even if the court is unable to divide the contract into its constituent parts, it has an exception to the rule as to entire contracts at its disposal. The courts are concerned to mitigate the harshness of the traditional rule using the doctrine of substantial performance. In *Dakin v Lee*[19] Cozens-Hardy MR said:    **[23–08]**

> "[I]t has been argued before us that, in a contract ... to do work for a lump sum, the defect in some of the items of the specification, or the failure to do every item in the specification, puts an end to the whole contract and prevents the builders from making a claim upon it: and therefore, where there is no ground for presuming any fresh contract, he cannot obtain any payment. The matter has been treated in the agreement as though the omission to do every item perfectly was an abandonment of the contract. That seems to me, with great respect, to be absolutely and entirely wrong...Take a contract for a lump sum to decorate a house: the contract provides that there shall be three coats of oil paint, but in one of the rooms only two coats of paint are put on, can anybody seriously say that, under these circumstances, the building owner could go and occupy the house and take the benefit of all the decorations which had been done in the other rooms without paying a penny for all the work done by the builder just because two coats of paint had been put on in one room where there ought to have been three?"

The courts take a pragmatic approach designed to reduce "opportunistic claims". So long as there has been substantial performance, the performing party is entitled to some payment. He will receive a sum amounting to the total payment due under the contract less a deduction proportionate to the value of the defects in his performance. This rule has an early incarnation in the case of *Boone v Eyre*.[20] However, the best known case on this exception is *Hoenig v Isaacs*.[21] The parties had agreed a fee of £750 for the completion of redecoration work on the defendant's house. The plaintiff left a bookcase unfinished. The court found that substantial performance had taken place and so allowed the plaintiff to recover his payment, less £55, the cost of completing the bookcase. As an aside, it should be borne in mind that if the performing party remedies the defects that are brought to his attention, he can claim the whole sum due under the contract.    **[23–09]**

Remember that what is required is not merely part performance but *substantial* performance. A party who has not substantially performed the contract is not entitled to any payment, proportionate or otherwise. Take, for instance, *Bolton v Mahadeva*,[22] in which the plaintiff had agreed to install a heating system in the defendant's house at    **[23–10]**

---

[18] *Roberts v Havelock* (1832) 3 B & Ad 404.
[19] [1916] KB 566.
[20] (1779) 1 Hy Bl 273n.
[21] [1952] 2 All ER 176.
[22] [1972] 2 All ER 1322.

a cost of £560. The work was carried out with some defects, the cost of remedying which was set at £174. Lord Justice Cairns found that, in determining whether substantial performance had been carried out in this instance, the Court should take into account both the nature of the defects and the proportion between the cost of rectifying them and the overall contract price. Both factors must be applied. In *Bolton* there was no substantial performance even though the contract was two thirds performed because of the nature of the defect. The heating system was so badly installed that it could not fulfil its primary purpose and so no obligation to pay arose in contract. A similar conclusion was reached in *Kincora Builders v Cronin*.[23] The plaintiff builders had contracted to build a house for the defendant. They refused to insulate the roof. The Court found that, even though the cost of installing the insulation was very small compared to the whole contract price, the nature of the defect was such that the plaintiffs had no claim in substantial performance. So, what sort of performance will count as "substantial"? Romer LJ in *Hoenig* gives a useful example:

> "In certain cases it is right that the rigid rule for which the defendant contends should be applied, for example, if a man tells a contractor to build a ten foot wall for him in his garden and agrees to pay £x for it, it would not be right that he should be held liable for any part of the contract price if the contractor builds the wall two feet and then renounces further performance of the contract, or builds the wall of a totally different material from that which was ordered, or builds it at the wrong end of the garden. The work contracted for has not been done and the corresponding obligation to pay consequently never arises. But when a man fully performs his contract in the sense that he supplies all that he agreed to supply but what he supplies is subject to defects of so minor a character that he can be said to have substantially performed his promise it is, in my judgment, far more equitable to apply the [doctrine of substantial performance] than to deprive him wholly of his contractual rights and relegate him to such remedy (if any) as he may have on a *quantum meruit*."

[23–11]        Let us examine the policy considerations at play here in more detail. In the New York case of *Jacob & Youngs Inc. v George Edward Kent*[24] the great Cardozo J probed the doctrine of substantial performance. In this case, the builder of a mansion did not perform the building contract exactly as specified. Instead of using all pipe of Reading manufacture in the plumbing as specified by the contract, he used some pipe made by a different factory. There was no difference in value, price or quality in the types of pipe used. The only difference in appearance was in the manufacturer's name stamped on the pipes. Cardozo J found for the builder, striking the balance as follows:

> "The simple and the uniform will call for different remedies from the multifarious and the intricate. The margin of departure within the range of normal expectation upon a sale of common chattels will vary from the margin to be expected upon a contract for the construction of a mansion or a 'skyscraper' … Those who think more of symmetry and logic in the

---

[23] Unreported, High Court, 5 March 1973.
[24] 230 NY 239, 129 NE 889 (1921).

development of legal rules than of practical adaptation to the attainment of a just result will be troubled by a classification where the lines of division are so wavering and blurred. Something, doubtless, may be said on the score of consistency and certainty in favour of a stricter standard. The courts have balanced such considerations against those of equity and fairness, and found the latter to be the weightier ... Where the line is to be drawn between the important and the trivial cannot be settled by a formula...The same omission may take on one aspect or another according to its setting. Substitution of equivalents may not have the same significance in fields of art on the one side and in those of mere utility on the other. Nowhere will change be tolerated, however, if it is so dominant or pervasive as in any real or substantial measure to frustrate the purpose of the contract ... There is no general license to install whatever, in the builder's judgment, may be regarded as "just as good" ... The question is one to be answered, if there is doubt, by the triers of the facts ... We must weigh the purpose to be served, the desire to be gratified, the excuse for deviation from the letter, the cruelty of enforced adherence ... The rule that gives remedy in cases of substantial performance with compensation for defects of trivial or inappreciable importance has been developed by the courts as an instrument of justice."

While Cardozo J bases his argument on justice for the party who has part [23–12] performed, there is a contrasting argument to be made from freedom of contract. Why should the courts make exceptions for minor breaches? Why should the mansion owner not be allowed to insist on Reading pipes, if that was what he wanted and if that was what the builder agreed to provide? What of the observation of Ashurst J in *Cutter v Powell* that "wherever there is an express contract the parties must be guided by it; and one party cannot relinquish or abide by it as may suit his advantage"? In *Smith v Brady*[25] the Court emphasised the link between the intention of the parties and the acceptable boundaries of performance:

"I suppose it will be conceded that every one has a right to build his house, his cottage, or his store after such a model and such a style as shall best accord with his notions of utility or be most agreeable to his fancy. The specifications of the contract became the law between the parties until voluntarily changed ... [The builder] can demand payment only upon and according to the terms of his contract, and if the conditions upon which payment is due have not been performed, then the right to demand it does not exist. To hold a different doctrine would be simply to make another contract, and would be giving to parties an encouragement to violate their engagements, which the just policy of the law does not permit."

The ruling in *Bruner v Hines*[26] attempts to resolve these competing positions: [23–13]

"The doctrine of substantial performance is a necessary inroad on the pure concept of freedom of contracts. The doctrine recognizes countervailing

---

[25]  17 NY 173.

[26]  295 Ala 111, 324 So 2d 265 (1975).

interests of private individuals and society, and, to some extent, it sacrifices the preciseness of the individual's contractual expectations to society's need for facilitating economic exchange."

### The Rule in *Sumpter v Hedges*

[23–14] It seems natural that if the injured party is willing to accept incomplete performance, he should be bound to pay for it. So it is possible for the performing party to claim payment for his partial performance on a *quantum meruit* basis, provided that the other party has voluntarily adopted the part performance.[27] In *Sumpter v Hedges*[28] Collins LJ set out that:

> "There are cases in which, though the plaintiff has abandoned the performance of a contract, it is possible for him to raise the inference of a new contract to pay for the work done on a *quantum meruit* from the defendant's having taken the benefit of the work done. It is only where the circumstances are such as to give that option that there is any evidence on which to ground the inference of a new contract."

[23–15] The key word here is "option": the injured party cannot have substandard performance forced on him but must genuinely have chosen to accept it. In this case, Sumpter had contracted to build two houses on Hedges's land for £565. Sumpter did part of the work to the value of £333. Hedges then completed the work on the buildings himself using materials which Sumpter had left behind on the site. Sumpter argued that by completing the buildings, Hedges had adopted the incomplete performance so that he had to pay Sumpter £333 for it. The Court found, however, that the necessary option was lacking. Hedges did not have any real choice in the matter: either he could finish the buildings himself or he would have to leave the unfinished buildings as a nuisance on his land. Therefore, his act in completing the building was not one of adoption. Similarly, the doctrine in *Sumpter v Hedges* could not have applied in *Bolton v Mahadeva* because the plumbing was now part of the defendant's property and could not be undone. The same principles applied in the Irish case of *Coughlan v Moloney*.[29] The plaintiff agreed to build a house for the defendant by Christmas 1902. There was no provision for periodic payments. The work was not completed. The defendants engaged another builder to finish the work. The builder sued for the work completed. The Court held that there was no implied agreement here to pay for the part performance. The employer had no real choice whether to accept or reject the work. The rule as to entire contracts applied.

### Prevention of Performance

[23–16] Where one party is deliberately preventing the other from completing his performance, the party attempting to perform can recover for such performance as he has been able to complete. So, in *Planché v Colburn*[30] the plaintiff agreed to write one of a series of books. Before he had finished, the publisher decided to discontinue publication of the

---

[27] A similar rule applies to sale of goods contracts under s 30(1) of the Sale of Goods Act 1893.
[28] [1898] 1 QB 673.
[29] (1905) 39 ILTR 153.
[30] (1831) 8 Bing 14.

series. Because the publisher had prevented the writer from keeping his end of the bargain, the writer was paid half the total payment due to him under the contract, as a reward for the work he had been able to complete. In *Arterial Drainage v Rathangan River Drainage Board*,[31] the plaintiffs were prevented from fully performing their obligations under a drainage contract with the defendants, because the defendants had failed to make land and plans available to the drainage contractors. The plaintiffs were entitled to sue for the value of the work they had completed.

### Tender of Performance

Tender of performance means attempted performance. Where the obligation is to pay a sum of money, tender will not discharge the debtor's obligation to pay.[32] Where the performance is non-monetary, and A cannot perform without B's concurrence and A is ready and willing to perform, but B rejects his performance, A will be discharged from all obligations under the contract. In *Startup v McDonald*[33] the plaintiff attempted to deliver 10 tons of linseed oil to the agreed purchaser. The purchaser refused to accept delivery, arguing that the delivery had taken place at an unreasonable time (8.30 pm). The judgment of Rolfe B in *Startup* sets out that in order for a tender to be valid, the person refusing the tender must have had adequate opportunity to examine the thing tendered, to ensure that it was really what it purported to be.

[23–17]

---

[31] (1880) 6 LR (Ir) 513.
[32] See further, McDermott, *Contract Law* (LexisNexis, 2000) 1049–1050.
[33] (1843) 6 Man & G 593.

# CHAPTER 24
# Termination of Contract

## I. An Outline of Termination: The Right of Election

It is often wrongly assumed that a contract will automatically come to an end when it is   **[24–01]**
breached. In fact, this is not the case. Termination of contract is a separate remedy that
the injured party may exercise at his discretion in certain limited circumstances. While
damages are available for any breach of contract, the remedy of termination is only
available when an especially serious breach of contract occurs. The types of breach that
will suffice will be examined in detail later. First comes an examination of the remedy
of termination itself. The right to terminate the contract is often called the right of
election. In *The Simona*,[1] Lord Ackner explained that where one party breaches:

> ". . . this will not automatically bring the contract to an end. The innocent
> party has an option. He may either accept the [breach] as determining the
> contract and sue for damages, or he may ignore or reject the attempt to
> determine the contract and affirm its continued existence."

So the innocent party is generally not obliged to terminate the contract. He   **[24–02]**
may instead choose to affirm it.

Termination is also known as accepting the breach. If the innocent party   **[24–03]**
terminates, the contract comes to an end there and then. Neither party is obliged to
perform any remaining obligations under the contract.[2] The terminating party can
reject any later attempt at performance by the other party. He can also claim damages
immediately to compensate him for any breach that occurred before the contract was
terminated and for the loss of opportunity to receive performance of the remaining
obligations under the contract.[3] This is because termination only ends the performance,

---

[1] [1988] 2 Lloyd's Rep 199.
[2] *Lombard North Central plc v Butterworth* [1987] QB 527.
[3] *ibid.*

or primary obligations under the contract. It does not end the secondary obligation of the guilty party to pay damages.

**[24–04]**        On the other hand, the innocent party may choose to reject the breach by affirming the contract. The contract then continues for the benefit of both parties and both the innocent and the breaching party must continue to perform their own primary obligations under the contract. An affirming party loses his right to damages in respect of the breach which has occurred.[4] Now he plays a waiting game. If the breaching party persists in his breach, or if the date for performance comes and he breaches again, the innocent party may claim damages. So, in *Howard v Pickford Tool Co.*[5] Lord Justice Asquith said that the rejected breach is "writ in water". The affirming party may also be granted, immediately, an order for specific performance that will compel the breaching party to carry out his contractual obligations when performance falls due.[6]

**[24–05]**        Now that the nature of affirmation and termination has been examined, it is necessary to make a few points about the choice to affirm or terminate. First, termination is, for a number of reasons, one of the most powerful remedies available in contract law. The most important of these is that termination is a self-help remedy. It does not depend on expensive litigation for its effect. Jacob Brehrens once noted the disutility of lawsuits thus: "[T]he rogue has a very ready answer. He says, 'Bring an action.' I have myself dared to bring actions, and my solicitor has said, 'It is not worth your while or expense; submit to it'."[7] Harris[8] explains how termination avoids this problem:

> "Termination is a unilateral act which does not require any prior approval from the court. If the defendant disputes whether the plaintiff was entitled to terminate, he must bring proceedings and allow the plaintiff the favoured defence position in the litigation. Termination is a potent form of self-help by which the plaintiff can avoid having to begin an action with its costs and uncertainties. He can also act quickly, and may be able to avoid the risk of the defendant's insolvency. If the plaintiff is entitled to terminate, there is no judicial power to control his choice, whether under the court's discretion or by a test of reasonableness: the sole issue is whether the plaintiff was legally entitled to terminate. The plaintiff is under no obligation to give the defendant any reasons for his decision to terminate."

**[24–06]**        Secondly, the choice to affirm or terminate is an important one: once it is made it becomes irrevocable. A party "cannot reprobate having already approbated".[9] So, the innocent party who has affirmed his contract cannot later change his mind and

---

[4] *Avery v Bowden* (1856) 6 E & B 953.

[5] [1951] 1 KB 417, 421.

[6] *Hasham v Zanab* [1960] AC 316.

[7] Jacob Brehrens, cited in Ferguson, "The adjudication of commercial disputes and the legal system in modern England" (1980) 7 Brit J Law and Society 141.

[8] Harris, "Incentives to Perform, or Break Contracts" (1992) CLP 29.

[9] *Safehaven Investments v Springbok Ltd* (1995) 71 P & CR 59.

terminate it: he must wait for a fresh breach[10] or prove continuing breach[11] before his right of election arises again. It is because affirmation is such a serious step that the courts will allow the innocent party a reasonable amount of time after breach to make up his mind whether to affirm or terminate. In *Yukong Line Ltd of Korea v Rendsburg Investments Corpn of Liberia*,[12] Moor-Bick J stated that: "the law does not require an injured party to snatch at a repudiation". Of course, if the innocent party takes too long, he runs the risk that his failure to explicitly terminate the contract will be treated as affirmation.[13]

Thirdly, the innocent party's choice must be communicated to the breaching party in some unequivocal manner so that the breaching party is left in no doubt as to whether his breach has been accepted or rejected.[14] The reason for the high threshold here is to allow the parties some room to negotiate their response to a threatened breach without binding themselves to end or maintain the contract. In *Yukong Line v Rendsburg Investments*,[15] the plaintiff charterparties telegrammed the breaching defendants expressing their upset at the breach, "strongly requesting" them to honour their contractual obligations and threatening to hold them responsible in damages if they did not do so. There was no affirmation here. Moore-Bick J was concerned to permit parties to negotiate with one another in the event if breach. This sort of negotiation could not take place if it was not permissible for one party to exhort to other to perform without running the risk of waiving the breach. **[24–07]**

The injured party's decision to affirm may be communicated by words or by action, as when the injured party does some act which is consistent only with an intention to keep the contract alive. Silence may also communicate intention where that silence "speaks" in the context of the surrounding circumstances.[16] Inaction, such as the innocent party's cessation of performance of his own obligations under the contract, may also suffice. In *The Santa Clara*[17] Lord Steyn explained this principle as follows: **[24–08]**

> "I respectfully disagree [that a failure to perform a contractual obligation is necessarily and always equivocal]. Sometimes in the practical world of businessmen an omission to act may be as pregnant with meaning as a positive declaration ... [A] failure to perform may sometimes be given colour by special circumstances and may only be explicable to a reasonable person in the position of the repudiating party as an election to accept the repudiation."

Fourthly, it is important to be cognisant of the risks that come with the choice to affirm or terminate. If the innocent party chooses to affirm, he cancels out the breach, he keeps the contract alive and he maintains his own contractual obligations in **[24–09]**

---

10 *Bentsen v Taylor & Sons* [1893] 2 QB 274; *The Kanchenjunga* [1990] 1 Lloyd's Rep 391.
11 *Johnson v Agnew* [1980] AC 367.
12 [1996] 2 Lloyd's Rep 604.
13 *Stocznia Gdanska v Latvian Shipping* [2002] EWCA Civ 889.
14 *Vitol SA v Norelf Ltd* [1996] AC 800 *per* Lord Steyn.
15 Above, n 12.
16 *Stocznia Gdanska v Latvian Shipping*, above, n 13.
17 [1996] AC 800.

being. This means that he is obliged to perform his side of the contract: he is not afforded any period of time after affirmation in which to assess whether the breaching party is going to come up with the goods. The innocent party also runs the risk that the breaching party will not be so forgiving if he later breaches the contract himself. This is what happened in the *The Simona*.[18] On 2 July, the charter-party repudiated (24–31) the contract. This is one of the types of breach which gives rise to the right of election. The owners elected to affirm the contract. Subsequent to their affirmation, they themselves breached the contract. The charterparty's previous breach had been extinguished by the owners' affirmation so that the contract survived. The owners' breach was a new breach of contract and the owner was liable to the charter-party for it. The same position applies to frustration (Chapter 22). In *Avery v Bowden*,[19] a ship was bound to load cargo at Odessa within 45 days. The ship's master received notice that no cargo would be available in time. This was a repudiatory breach which gave him a right to elect to terminate or affirm the contract. He affirmed the contract. Before the date for performance, war broke out and a law was passed which made it illegal to load cargo at an enemy port. The contract was frustrated. The ship's master, by affirming the contract, had lost the ship's owner the right to claim damages for the initial breach and had accepted the risk of frustration on his behalf. Atiyah has expressed sympathy for the innocent party:

> "[T]he innocent party is often placed in difficulties. On the one hand, he wants to claim damages for this breach, as he thinks it may be; but on the other hand, in the immediate hurly-burly of commercial activity it is not always clear what is a breach and what is a justified demand. So in such a case [he] may be desperately trying to do two things at once. He is trying to keep the contract alive, and so must be ready to perform it if at the last minute the [other party] says he will perform after all; and at the same time [he is trying to make provision for what will happen if the breach remains]. The innocent party can easily slip up in this situation."

**[24–10]**     On the other hand, a new set of risks arises if the innocent party elects to terminate. The first is that he may have misjudged the situation. A misused right to terminate is a breach. For example, A may conclude that B has breached a condition and that A is therefore entitled to terminate the contract. B disagrees, and sues A. The court finds that B was in breach of a warranty.[20] A will be found liable for wrongful repudiation and B will himself be entitled to a remedy, including the remedy of termination.

**[24–11]**     There are also risks of a different kind to consider. Harris[21] has written that termination is the most powerful incentive to perform provided by the common law. He explains:

> "Fear of termination provides the defendant with a powerful incentive not to commit a serious breach because the loss which termination may impose on the

---

[18]   Above, n 1.

[19]   Above, n 4.

[20]   See *Hong Kong Fir Shipping* [1962] 2 QB 26.

[21]   Harris, above, n 8.

defendant can greatly exceed any damages recoverable by the plaintiff. So the defendant's fear of his own potential loss may give him a most powerful incentive not to break the contract ... If the defendant had incurred expenditure in performing (or preparing to perform) his side, he may lose all the benefit of that expenditure if it is not saleable to a third party. So by terminating, the plaintiff is empowered in some circumstances to impose a heavy loss on the defendant: it is the fear of this which provides the defendant with the strongest incentive to perform ... His fear of wasting his effort may be more powerful in encouraging performance than his fear of liability in damages. Fear of his own loss may exceed his fear of paying for the plaintiff's loss. But the remedy of termination brings *both* losses to bear on the defendant: he cannot recover his own loss to date, but the plaintiff can till sue him for damages for the plaintiff's loss in not getting the benefit of the defendant's complete performance."

Why then might the innocent party be unwilling to exercise his right to     [24–12]
termination? Why might he be unwilling to inflict that kind of loss on the breaching party? Scholarship on relational contracts[22] reminds us that while contract law couches the right of election in the language of autonomy and free will, parties in business more often experience the world of contract as one of mutual interdependence:

"[P]arties treat their contracts more like marriages than one night stands. Obligations grow out of commitment that they have made to one another, and the conventions that the trading community established for such commitments; they are not frozen at the initial moment of commitment, but change as circumstances change; the object of contracting is not primarily to allocate risks, but to signify a commitment to cooperate. In bad times parties are expected to lend one another support, rather than standing on their rights; each will treat the other's insistence on literal performance as wilful obstructionism; if unexpected contingencies occur resulting in severe losses, the parties are to search for ways of dividing the losses; and the sanction for egregiously bad behaviour is always, of course, refusal to deal again."[23]

---

[22] Macneil (1974) 60 *Virginia Law Review* 598, 595. Relational contracts "are of significant duration (for example, franchising). Close whole persons relations form an integral aspect of the relation (employment). The object of exchange typically includes both easily measured quantities (wages) and quantities not easily measured (the projection of personality by an airline stewardess). Many individuals with individual and collective poles of interest are involved in the relations (industrial relations). Further cooperative behaviour is anticipated (the players and management of the Oakland Raiders). The benefits and burdens of the relation are to be shared rather than divided and allocated (a law partnership). The bindingness of the relation is limited (again a law partnership in which in theory each member is free to quit almost at will). The entangling strings of friendship, reputation, interdependence, morality and altruistic desires are integral parts of the relation (a theatrical agent and his clients). Trouble is expected as a matter of course (a collective bargaining agreement.) Finally the participants ... view the relation as an ongoing integration of behaviour which will grow and vary with events in a largely unforeseeable future."

[23] Gordon, "Macaulay, Macneil and the Discovery of Solidarity and Power in Contract Law" (1985) Wisconsin Law Review 565, 569. See similarly, Beale and Dugdale, "Contracts Between Businessmen" (1975) 2 Brit J Law & Soc 45.

**[24–13]**     The point then, is that while termination is an effective remedy, it is not without its risks, and the decision to terminate is one which ought to be preceded by much careful thought and analysis. The risk associated with the exercise of the right of election is an incentive to co-operative renegotiation of the contract. Consideration will now be given to the two types of breach which give rise to the right to terminate: breach of an important term and repudiatory breach.

## II. Termination for Breach of a Term

**[24–14]**     The law categorises contractual terms in a hierarchy of conditions, innominate terms and warranties. A warranty is a basic contract term: a term of minor significance. A condition is an essential term of the contract: a term which is key to the contract's purpose. Breach of a warranty sounds in damages only. Breach of a condition gives the innocent party the right to choose whether to terminate or affirm the contract.

### Promissory Conditions not Contingent Conditions

**[24–15]**     It is worth wandering down a sidetrack for a moment to clarify the sense in which the word "condition" is used here. An important distinction must be drawn between "promissory conditions", breach of which gives rise to the right to terminate a contract, and "contingent conditions".[24] A promissory condition, as its name suggests, consists of a promise to bring a particular event about. A contingent condition is an event upon which the obligation to perform turns, but which neither party has promised to bring about. Contingent conditions can be either conditions precedent or conditions subsequent.[25] For example, suppose A promises B that he will pay him €10,000 upon the birth of his first child. The birth of the child is a condition precedent to A's contractual obligation to pay B: A need not pay B anything unless and until his first child is born. Neither A nor B promises that B will have a child. An example of a condition precedent comes from *Pym v Campbell*.[26] The plaintiffs had agreed to sell a share of the invention of a "crushing, washing and amalgamating machine" to the defendants. The sale was subject to engineers' approval. However, one of the engineers could not be found. The plaintiffs were not obliged to sell to the defendants because the engineers' approval was a condition precedent to the contract of sale coming into existence. Suppose A promises B that he will pay B €10,000 a year until his son, C, turns 18. C's coming of age is the condition subsequent to A's contractual obligation to pay B: A's contractual obligation to pay B comes to an end when C turns 18. Neither A nor B promises that C will make it to 18. Conditions subsequent are much less common than conditions precedent. They usually occur in situations like that in *Head v Tattersall*[27] where the purchaser of goods accepts delivery but wants to examine them to see if they comply with the description given of them.

---

[24] Some of the older cases use the terms interchangeably, *Bentsen v Taylor Sons & Co*, above, n 10.

[25] For more see Clark, *Contract Law in Ireland* (5th ed, Thomson Round Hall, 2004) pp 239–243.

[26] (1856) El and Bl 370 119 ER 903.

[27] (1871) LR 7 Exch 7.

## Automatic Right of Election on Breach of Condition

Now, breach of a promissory condition gives rise to a right of election, no matter how     **[24–16]**
trivial the consequences. Take, for example, *Re Moore & Co. v Landauer*.[28] This was a
case in which it was a condition of the contract of sale for 3,100 cases of canned fruit
that they be packed 30 tins to the case. When the cans arrived, some were packed at
more than 30 tins per case. Some cases were packed with fewer than 30 tins. So a
condition of the contract was breached and the buyer was entitled to terminate even
though he had suffered no loss. A similar case is *Arcos Ltd v EA Ronaasen & Son*,[29]
which concerned a contract for the sale of timber staves, a term of which was that the
staves would be half an inch thick. The staves, when delivered, were a mere one
sixteenth of an inch thicker than specified and were perfectly good for the purpose for
which they had been bought; the manufacture of barrels. However, the measurements
of the staves were held to be a condition of the contract and so the purchaser was
entitled to terminate the contract. Lord Atkin commented thus:

> "No doubt there may be microscopic deviations which business men and
> therefore lawyers will ignore ... It will be found that most of the cases that
> admit any deviation from the contract are cases where there has been an excess
> or deficiency in quantity which the Court has considered negligible. But apart
> from this consideration the right view is that the conditions of the contract
> must be strictly performed. If a condition is not performed the buyer has a right
> to reject."

Breach of a warranty, on the other hand, never gives rise to a right of     **[24–17]**
termination no matter how serious the consequences of the breach. This absolute
approach to the consequences of breach of condition can be criticised as unnecessarily
strict. It can also be criticised as out of step with the realities of breach. Breach of a
condition, might, as in *Arcos*, bring a contract to an end even though the consequences
of that breach were insignificant. On the other hand, breach of a warranty might occur
with grotesque consequences for the injured party but he would have to content himself
with damages. The justification given by Lord Atkin for the *Arcos* decision was that
"[i]f the seller wants a margin he must and in my experience does stipulate for it" in the
express terms of his contract. Lord Atkin would place responsibility for risk allocation
firmly on the parties.

## Condition or Warranty?

The law on classification of terms features an important tension between a desire to     **[24–18]**
adapt the law to reflect commercial practice and the demands of certainty. On the one
hand, there is a need for a proportionate response to the breach which actually occurs,
so that one party is not allowed to end the contract on the basis of minute breaches.
Conditions are dangerous beasts because they may act as a temptation to the innocent
party to have done with the contract for a minor breach rather than attempt to sustain
the bargain. A too-rigid interpretation of the classification rules allows termination

---

[28] [1921] 2 KB 519.
[29] [1933] AC 470.

*mala fides* and economic opportunism so that one party may "nit-pick" to end a contract which has become inconvenient or expensive to perform.[30] On the other hand, it is important that the parties should be able to identify conditions and non-conditions with certainty, so that they can make assured and informed decisions in the event of breach. In *Bunge Corporation v Tradax Export SA*[31] Lord Lowry warns of the dangers uncertainty in the law: "litigation would be rife and years might elapse before the results were known." Lord Roskill also states in that case that "[p]arties to commercial transactions should be entitled to know their rights at once ...". There is the view that "in legal matters, some degree of certainty is at least as valuable a part of justice as perfection".[32]

[24–19]     The best statement of the approach which the courts take in classifying terms is the set of four questions developed by the Court of Appeal in *The Hansa Nord*.[33]

### 1. Express Provision for a Right of Election

[24–20]     The first question for a judge looking at a particular term is whether the parties have expressly set out in their contract that breach of that term should give rise to a right of termination. This stage requires the court to submit to the intention of the parties: if a contract clearly says that breach of a term gives rise to a right of election, the courts will give effect to it as a condition. Blackburn J said in *Bettini v Gye*[34]: "Parties may think some matter, apparently of very little importance, essential; and if they sufficiently express an intention to make the literal fulfilment of such a thing a condition ... it will be one".

### 2. Implied Classification of the Term

[24–21]     If a term is not expressly worded so that its breach gives rise to a right to terminate the contract, the court will ask whether such an intention is necessarily implied by the words used in the contract. The contract may not provide expressly that breach of a given term gives rise to a right to terminate the contract or reject the goods. However, it may use other words; for example, the word "condition" itself, or a phrase such as "of the essence of the contract".[35] It is surprising that the use of the word "condition" does not belong in Step 1 of the *Hansa Nord* test, under express provision. Yet the courts have held that using the word "condition" can only *imply*, albeit very strongly, that the parties intended a right of election for breach of this term. The court must be satisfied, in particular, that the parties intended the word "condition" to be used in its technical sense, "as a code word for the phrase 'shall be entitled to repudiate the contract or reject the goods'."[36] The tone in the relevant cases is one of caution. In *Tarrabochia v Hickey*[37] Baron Bramwell said that, since the parties can always give effect to their

---

[30] However, Brownsword notes that the courts do not take express account of the reasons for termination: Brownsword, "Retrieving Reasons, Retrieving Rationality" (1992) 5 JCL 83.

[31] [1981] 1 WLR 711; See also *The Seaflower* [2001] 1 Lloyd's Rep 341.

[32] *Broome v Cassell* [1972] AC 1027.

[33] [1976] QB 44.

[34] (1875) 1 QB 183.

[35] *Lombard North Central plc v Butterworth*, above, n 2.

[36] *The Hansa Nord*, above, n 33.

[37] (1856) 1 H & N 183.

intention by clear words, "those who construe the instrument should be chary in doing for them that which they might, but have not done for themselves".

So, for example, in *Schuler AG v Wickman Machine Tool Sales*,[38] the otherwise sloppily drafted contract said that "it shall be a condition of this agreement that" Wickman would send its representatives to visit certain manufacturers once a week to solicit orders. The question for the court was whether, by using the word "condition", the parties had intended that even the slightest breach, even one missed visit, should give rise to a right of termination. The majority held that, in the context of the agreement, this was a wholly unreasonable conclusion, and accordingly, the term could not be treated as a condition. This decision echoes the older observation of Palles CB in *Fearnley v London Guarantee Insurance Co.*[39] that the courts should not give effect to the label "condition" where such an interpretation would be inconsistent with the rest of the contract.

[24–22]

Again, the court will always be cognisant of the consequences of labelling a term as a condition, especially because the rule on express provision allows the parties to treat as a condition a term which would not otherwise be important enough to merit that classification.[40] This right might be abused in an opportunistic fashion.[41] Lord Roskill gave a warning to this effect in *The Hansa Nord*[42]:

[24–23]

> "In my view, a court should not be over ready, unless required by statute or authority to do so, to construe a term in a contract as a "condition" any breach of which gives rise to a right to reject rather than as a term any breach of which sounds in damages ... In principle, contracts are made to be performed and not to be avoided according to the whims of market fluctuations and where there is free choice between two possible constructions I think the court should tend to prefer that construction which will ensure performance, and not encourage avoidance of contractual obligations."

The courts may be especially reluctant to find that the breached term is a condition where the actual consequences of the breach are minor. So, even though the courts claim to give effect to the intention of the parties, as in *Schuler*, that "intention" becomes a cipher for the perceived reasonableness of treating a term as a condition. It is important to ask whether this talk of reasonableness is compatible with respect for contractual autonomy, as embodied in the elusive intention of the parties. In *Schuler*, Lord Reid noted that:

[24–24]

> "The fact that a particular construction leads to a very unreasonable result must be a relevant consideration. The more unreasonable the result, the more

---

[38] [1974] AC 235.

[39] (1881) 6 LR (Ir) 219.

[40] *Lombard North Central plc v Butterworth*, above, n 2.

[41] In order to combat this problem, Brownsword has suggested that the courts ought to have regard to the innocent party's reasons for termination. See Brownsword, "Retrieving Reasons, Retrieving Rationality? A New Look at the Right to Withdraw for Breach of Contract" (1992) 5 *Journal of Contract Law* 83.

[42] Above, n 33.

unlikely it is that the parties can have intended it, and if they do intend it the more necessary it is that they shall make the intention abundantly clear."

### 3. Term Defined by Statute or Stare Decisis

[24–25]   As a third resort, if the courts cannot find an expressed or implied intention that breach of the term should give rise to a right to terminate the contract, they will turn to statute and precedent. As noted in the discussion of implied terms (13-62), the Sale of Goods Act 1893 implies certain conditions into all contracts for the sale of goods. The seller must have title to the goods (s 12), the goods must comply with their description (s 13), they must not be unmerchantable or unfit for purpose (s 14) and they must correspond with the sample provided if they are sold by sample (s 15). If a seller fails to comply with any one of these statutory obligations, the buyer is entitled to terminate the contract. In *Rubicon Computer Systems Ltd v United Paints Ltd*,[43] the supplier of a computer system placed a time-lock on it which rendered it useless. This was a breach of the implied statutory condition of quiet possession. The purchaser was therefore entitled to terminate the contract.

[24–26]   The courts are also, of course, bound by precedent, especially where that precedent reflects time-honoured custom within a trade. It is important that, when negotiating their contract, the parties will be able to trust in certain time-honoured categories. Thus, a term will often be classified as a condition simply because this has always been the usual way of things, regardless of the significance of that condition. In *The Mihalis Angelos*[44] Megaw LJ held that an "expected readiness to load" clause in a charter-party was a condition so that the innocent party was released from all of his remaining contractual obligations by its breach. He rationalised the decision as follows:

> "One of the essential elements of law is some measure of uniformity. One of the important elements of the law is predictability. At any rate in commercial law, there are obvious and substantial advantages in having, where possible, a firm and definite rule for a particular class of legal relationship: for example, as here, the legal categorisation of a particular, definable type of contractual clause in common use. It is surely much better, both for shipowners and charterers (and, incidentally, for their advisers) when a contractual obligation of this nature is under consideration, and still more when they are faced with the necessity for an urgent decision as to the effects of a suspected breach of it, to be able to say categorically: 'If a breach is proved, then the charterer can put an end to the contract' rather than that they should be left to ponder whether or not the courts would be likely, in the particular case, when the evidence has been heard, to decide that in the particular circumstances the breach was or was not such as 'to go to the root of the contract'. Where justice does not require greater flexibility, there is everything to be said for, and nothing against, a degree of rigidity in legal principle."

---

[43] [2000] 2 TCLR 453.

[44] [1971] 1 QB 164. See also *Union Eagle Ltd v Golden Achievement Ltd* [1997] AC 514; *The Seaflower* [2001] 1 Lloyd's Rep 341.

In *Bunge v Tradax Export SA*[45] the House of Lords laid down a general [24–27] presumption that stipulations as to time in mercantile and commercial contracts will be held to be conditions.

## 4. Breach Going to the Root of the Contract

The fourth question in *The Hansa Nord* is rarely applied. The courts tend to rely on the [24–28] first two questions in the majority of cases. The test here is whether the breach is fundamental; whether it goes so much to the root of the contract that the aggrieved party is deprived of that which he has contracted for. If the fundamental or core obligation under the contract can still be obtained in spite of the breach of this term, no right of termination arises and the injured party must be content with damages. A similar test was applied in *Laird Bros v Dublin Steampacket*.[46] The plaintiffs agreed to build a ship which was to be delivered on 1 August 1897. The ship was not delivered until September 1897. The defendants had not suffered any loss but they argued that the due date was a condition of the contract. Andrews J held that the due date was not a condition because it was "impossible to hold that this delay went to the root of the matter so as to render the performance of the contract by the plaintiffs a thing different in substance from that which the defendants contracted for".

## What is an Innominate Term?

Almost 30 years after *Arcos*, the English Court of Appeal put forward a more flexible [24–29] view of the issue of breach of terms giving rise to a right of termination. In *Hong Kong Fir Shipping Co. v Kawasaki Kisean Kaisha Ltd*,[47] the Court of Appeal developed the innominate term. An innominate term was defined by Lord Scarman in *Bunge Corporation v Tradax SA*[48] as "one, which upon the true construction of the contract the parties have not made a condition, and breach of which may be attended by trivial, minor or very grave consequences." Innominate terms are a new, less rigid, category of contract terms. They are also called intermediate terms because they lie somewhere between conditions and warranties. Breach of an innominate term will not always give rise to a right of termination; only a very serious breach of an innominate term will do this. In *Hong Kong Fir*[49] the key term was a seaworthiness clause in a charter-party. The ship was to be "in every way fitted for ordinary cargo service". This was an intermediate term because its nature as a term could only be assessed in the light of the actual breach; in some circumstances, breach of the term should be treated in the same way as a breach of condition while in others, it should be treated akin to a breach of warranty. Lord Upjohn explained:

> "Why is this apparently basic and underlying condition of seaworthiness not, in fact, treated as a condition? It is for the simple reason that the seaworthiness clause is breached by the slightest failure to be fitted 'in every way' for service. Thus, to take examples ... if a nail is missing from one of the timbers of a wooden vessel, or if proper medical supplies or two anchors are not on board at

---

[45] Above, n 31.
[46] (1900) 34 ILTR 97.
[47] Above, n 20.
[48] Above, n 31.
[49] Above, n 20.

the time of sailing, the owners are in breach of the seaworthiness stipulation. It is contrary to common sense to suppose that in such circumstances the parties contemplated that the charterer should at once be entitled to treat the contract as at an end for such trifling breaches ...".

[24–30]    So, innominate terms are identified by the broad range of ways in which they may be breached. An obligation to give a certain number of days' notice is an example of a term which can never be innominate, because, as Lord Wilberforce noted in *Bunge Corporation v Tradax SA*,[50] there is only one way in which it can be breached: by giving less than 15 days' notice. This decision was followed in relation to notice clauses in *The Naxos*[51] and in *The Seaflower*.[52] By contrast, in *The Gregos*,[53] a clause that provided that a vessel would be redelivered at the end of a timecharter was held to be an innominate term. This was because the clause could be breached by a significantly or trivially late delivery, each leading to consequences with varying degrees of severity.

### Right of Election for Fundamental Breach of an Innominate Term

[24–31]    The effect of the breach of an innominate term is not dependant on its classification.[54] Only a very serious or fundamental breach of an innominate term will ignite the right to terminate. Lord Upjohn said in *Hong Kong Fir* that the availability of the right to terminate for breach of an innominate term depends "entirely upon the nature of the breach and its foreseeable consequences." He would have required a breach which goes "so much to the root of that contract that it makes further commercial performance impossible, or in other words ... [renders] the contract frustrated". The test here appears to be the same as the fourth step in the *Hansa Nord* questions discussed earlier. Lord Diplock's judgment gives a more detailed indication of the gravity of breach required to unlock the right of election. It must be a breach which will:

> "... deprive the party who has further obligations to perform of substantially the whole benefit which it was the intention of the parties as expressed in the contract that he should obtain as the consideration for performing those undertakings."

[24–32]    This test was adopted into Irish law by Costello J in *Irish Telephone Rentals v Irish Civil Service Building Society Ltd.*[55] In *Bunge Corporation New York v Tradax Export SA*[56] Lord Scarman said that the issue for the court was "whether the breach that has arisen is such as the parties would have said, had they been asked at the time they made their contract: 'it goes without saying that, if that happens, the contract is at an end'". So a very serious breach indeed is required. Again, in *Bunge*

---

[50] Above, n 31.
[51] [1990] 3 All ER 641.
[52] [2001] 1 Lloyd's Rep 341.
[53] [1995] 1 Lloyd's Rep 1.
[54] *The Hermosa* [1982] 1 Lloyd's Rep 570.
[55] [1990] ILRM 880.
[56] Above, n 31.

*Corporation v Tradax SA*[57] Megaw LJ in the Court of Appeal criticised this test as too harsh saying:

> "How could this right of election be anything other than a legal fiction, a chimera, if the election can arise only in circumstances in which, as a result of the breach, an event has happened which will deprive the innocent party of substantially the whole benefit which it was intended that he should receive? ... [I]f the test be right, the former principle of English law that the innocent party has the right to elect is no longer anything but an empty shadow, for a right to elect to continue a contract, with the result that the innocent party will be bound to perform his own contractual obligations when he will, by definition, have lost substantially all his benefit under the contract does not appear to me to make sense."

McKendrick notes that the type of consequences required by Lord Diplock are analogous to the consequences of frustration. He suggests that, in assessing the seriousness of the breach, the court will look at the breach from the perspective both of the innocent and the breaching party. From the innocent party's perspective the important factors are the losses caused by the breach, the adequacy of damages to remedy those losses and the value of the performance he has already received compared with the overall value of full performance. Factors relevant to the breaching party include the cost to the guilty party of completing performance, his willingness to complete performance and the likelihood of his committing further breaches.[58]    [24–33]

## III. Repudiatory Breach

We have seen so far that the right of election arises where a term that has been classified as a condition is breached, or where a breach of an innominate term occurs which deprives the innocent party of substantially the whole of the benefit due to him under the contract. The right of election also arises where one of the parties repudiates the contract. A contract is repudiated where a party clearly indicates by word or conduct that he no longer intends to be bound by its terms. In *Freeth v Burr*[59] a repudiation was defined as "an intimation of an intention to abandon and altogether refuse performance of the contract [or of] an intention to no longer be bound by the contract". A party may repudiate the contract by his express words. For example, in *Athlone RDC v Campbell and Son (No 2)*,[60] repudiation occurred where one party wrote to the other and informed them that their services were no longer required. Repudiation may also be implicit in the breaching party's actions. A party may repudiate the contract by putting it out of his power to perform the contract by taking on other, conflicting obligations.[61] So, in *Hochster v De La Tour*[62] Lord Campbell said that "if a man contracts to sell and deliver specific goods on a future day, and before    [24–34]

---

[57] Above, n 31.
[58] McKendrick, *Contract Law: Text, Cases and Materials* (Oxford University Press, 2004) p 965.
[59] (1874) LR 9 CP 208.
[60] (1912) 47 ILTR 142.
[61] *Alfred C Toepfer International GmbH v Itex Itagrani Export SA* [1993] 1 Lloyd's Rep 360.
[62] (1853) 2 E & B 678. See similarly *Synge v Synge* [1894] 1 QB 466.

the day he sells and delivers them to another, he is immediately liable to an action at the suit of the person with whom he first contracted". This situation is analogous to that of self-induced frustration (22–38).[63] Implied repudiation will also occur if the breaching party behaves in a manner inconsistent with the continuance of the contract.[64]

[24–35]    Lord Wilberforce in *Woodar Investment Development Ltd v Wimpey Construction UK Ltd*[65] said that: "[r]epudiation is a drastic conclusion which should only be held to arise in clear cases of refusal, in a matter going to the root of the contract, to perform contractual obligations." Thus, the courts will require objective evidence of "an absolute refusal to perform the contract" on the part of the breaching party. So there will be no repudiation where the breaching party *bona fide*, if incorrectly, asserts a different interpretation of the contract, provided he remains willing to perform on the basis of that alternative construction. "A mere honest misapprehension, especially if open to correction, will not justify a charge of repudiation".[66] This point is made clearer by comparing two cases: *Federal Commerce and Navigation Co Ltd v Molena Alpha Inc*[67] and *Woodar Investments v Wimpey.*[68] In *Federal Commerce* a dispute arose between shipowners and time-charterers. The owners, acting on legal advice and in the full belief that they were entitled to do so, instructed the master not to issue freight pre-paid bills of lading. The charterers were not able to operate ships without the freight pre-paid bills of lading. The House of Lords held that this amounted to repudiation of the contract. In *Woodar* the plaintiffs claimed to exercise a right of termination included in their contract with the defendants for the sale of a plot of land. They misinterpreted this right of termination. In fact, they were not entitled to exercise it in the circumstances. However, the House of Lords held that there was no repudiation here. Why the difference in the cases? In both cases the breaching parties demonstrated an intention to default on the contract in a fundamental way. In both cases, the breaching party believed that he was in the right. However, in *Federal Commerce* the time for completion of the contract was so near, and the pressure placed on the charterers by the owners' actions was so great that, objectively, the charterers were entitled to conclude that the owners were absolutely refusing to perform. In *Woodar*, by contrast, the date for performance was a long way off. The reasonable man would have concluded from the plaintiffs' actions simply that they were asserting their own interpretation of the contract. They had not indicated an absolute refusal to perform. Accordingly, there was no repudiation. In *Vaswani v Italian Motors*[69] the Privy Council confirmed that it is permissible to assert a claim based on an erroneous but good faith interpretation of the contract. However, if the party goes beyond any position consistent with an intention to continue with the contract, he is in breach and the contract is repudiated, good faith or no. A similar result was reached in the Irish case

---

[63]  *Universal Cargo Carriers v Citati* [1957] 2 QB 801.

[64]  See *Larkin v Groeger and Eaton*, unreported, High Court, 26 April 1988.

[65]  [1980] 1 WLR 277.

[66]  *Ross Smyth & Son v Bailey, Son & Co* [1940] 3 All ER 60.

[67]  [1979] AC 757.

[68]  [1980] 1 All ER 571.

[69]  [1996] 1 WLR 270. No such leaway is available in cases of actual breach; *Bliss v South East Thames Regional Health Authority* [1987] ICR 700.

of *Continental Oil v Moynihan*.[70] The defendant and the plaintiff were parties to a solus agreement. In response to a decision of the Minister for Industry and Commerce, the plaintiffs proposed a number of price changes to the defendants. The defendants treated these proposals as a repudiation of the contract. However, Kenny J rejected this claim, holding that there was no evidence that the plaintiffs did not intend to be bound by the contract. This set of decisions aims to provide more scope for negotiation between the parties. It should be remembered, however, that it may be difficult for the non-breaching party to tell the difference between a good faith assertion based on genuine mistaken belief and an out-and-out repudiation of the contract. An assertion which would not otherwise amount to repudiation may be treated as such where it is made in bad faith.[71]

## Anticipatory Repudiation

Suppose A contracts to buy B's car. A promises to pay B €7,000 on 9 June 9 and a further €3,000 on delivery of the car. The car is to be delivered on 12 June. On 5 June, B phones A and says: "I have found a new buyer for the car. Sorry." Is A entitled to terminate the contract there and then? No breach has occurred yet; in fact, A cannot be sure that B will in fact fail to deliver the car but the courts may nevertheless give relief in the form of a pre-emptive right of election. In *Yukong Line v Rendsburg Investments*[72] Moore-Bick J explained the nature of so-called anticipatory breach: **[24–36]**

"A renunciation of the contract by one party, prior to the time for performance is not itself a breach but it gives the other party, the injured party, the right to treat it as a breach in anticipation and thus to treat the contract as discharged immediately. In other words, if a person says he will not perform, the law allows the other to take him at as his word and act accordingly."

Lord Blackburn explained the situation more simply in *Mersey Steel and Iron Co v Naylor Benzon & Co*[73]: **[24–37]**

"Where there is a contract to be performed in the future, if one of the parties has said to the other in effect 'if you go on and perform your side of the contract I will not perform mine', that in effect amounts to saying 'I will not perform the contract'. In that case the other party may say 'you have given me distinct notice that you will not perform the contract. I will not wait until you have broken it, but I will treat you as having put an end to the contract, and if necessary I will sue you for damages, but in all events I will not go on with the contract'."

The key case here is *Hochster v De La Tour*.[74] The case sets out that "it cannot be laid down as a universal rule that, where by agreement an act is to be done on a future day, no action can be brought for a breach of the agreement till the day for doing **[24–38]**

---

[70] (1977) 111 ILTR 5.
[71] *House of Spring Gardens v Point Blank Ltd* [1985] FSR 327.
[72] Above, n 12.
[73] (1884) 9 App Cas 434.
[74] (1853) 2 E & B 678.

the act has arrived." The plaintiff in that case had agreed to serve the defendant as a courier for three months beginning 1 June. On 11 May, the defendant wrote to the plaintiff to tell him that he had changed his mind and no longer wished to employ the plaintiff as a courier. Lord Crompton set out that the sending of this letter amounted to an anticipatory breach of the contract, which gave rise to the option to terminate (he calls it "rescinding") or affirm:

> "When a party announces his intention not to fulfill the contract, the other side may take him at his word and rescind the contract. The word 'rescind' implies that both parties have agreed that the contract shall be at and end as if it had never been. But I am inclined to think that the party may also say: 'Since you have announced that you will not go on with the contract, I will consent that it shall be at an end from this time; but I will hold you liable for the damage I have sustained; and I will proceed to make that damage as little as possible by making the best use I can of my liberty'."

[24–39]     Cockburn CJ takes the same position in *Frost v Knight*.[75] In that case, a man had contracted to marry the plaintiff as soon as his father died. While his father was still alive, he absolutely refused to marry her. Cockburn CJ set out the position as follows:

> "The promisee, if he please, may treat the notice of intention as inoperative, and wait the time when the contract is to be executed, and then hold the other party responsible for all the consequences of non-performance; but in that case he keeps the contract alive for the benefit of the other party as well as his own; he remains subject to all his own obligations and liabilities under it, and enables the other party not only to complete the contract, if so advised, notwithstanding his previous repudiation of it, but also to take advantage of any supervening circumstances which would justify him to decline to complete it. On the other hand, the promisee may, if he thinks proper, treat the repudiation of the other party as a wrongful putting an end to the contract, and may at once bring his action as on a breach of it; and in such action he will be entitled to such damages as would have arisen from the non-performance of the contract at the appointed time, subject, however, to the abatement in respect of any circumstances which may have afforded him the means of mitigating his loss."

[24–40]     The doctrine of anticipatory breach has its roots in common sense. In *Stocnizia Gdanska v Latvian Shipping Co*.[76] Thomas J noted that:

> "To require an innocent party, who has by pressing for performance of the contract affirmed it, to wait until there is actual breach by the party in breach before he can bring the contract to an end might well … have required the innocent party to engage in performance that is entirely pointless and wasteful."

---

[75] Law Rep 7 Ex 112.
[76] [2002] EWCA Civ 889.

The principle in *Hochster* was applied in Ireland in *Leeson v North British Oil and Candle Co.*[77] The defendants contracted to supply the plaintiff's nominees with up to 300 casks of paraffin over the winter. In January, the plaintiff was informed that it would not be possible to supply the paraffin for two months due to a strike. It was held that this statement amounted to an anticipatory breach. The plaintiff was entitled to terminate the contract immediately and claim damages for his loss.

**[24–41]**

## IV. An Absolute Right of Election?

Suppose A hires B to write the definitive practitioner's textbook on Irish contract law. The book is to be written over a period of three years. B is to be paid a fee of €10,000. A year after the written contract is signed, A contacts B and says that he no longer wants B to write the book. B ignores him and continues to write. Two years later he produces the manuscript and demands his €10,000. Is he entitled to affirm the contract, perform his part and demand the full contract price? Should he not instead be obliged to A's repudiation by terminating the contract and contenting himself with damages? Should a court acquiesce in his wasted effort and expenditure? The Scottish case of *White & Carter v McGregor*[78] is the root case in this area. The pursuers in that case insisted on their right to advertise the defendant's business on litter bins for three years. The defendants had repudiated the contract on the very day it was made. The House of Lords, by a margin of three to two, held that the pursuer was entitled to affirm and perform despite the defendants' repudiation. The House refused to find that the pursuers were obliged to terminate and seek damages. Lord Reid justified his decision on the basis that:

**[24–42]**

> "It might be, but it never has been, the law that a person is only entitled to enforce his contractual rights in a reasonable way, and that a court will not support an attempt to enforce them in an unreasonable way. One reason why this is not the law is, no doubt, because it was thought that it would create too much uncertainty to require the court to decide whether it is reasonable or equitable to allow a party to enforce his full rights under a contract."

The decision is controversial because the pursuers were allowed to waste their own money and that of the defendants on carrying out a service which was no longer wanted. However, it is important to remember that the decision in *White* is subject to two very important exceptions. These refer to situations where the courts, as a matter of equity, will cease to allow the innocent party to enforce his contract according to its strict terms. First, as was confirmed in *Hounslow Borough Council v Twickenham Garden Developments*,[79] the right to insist on performing one's own part of the bargain is defeated if performance requires the other party's co-operation, whether active or passive. In *Hounslow*, Megarry J said that the rule in *White* will not apply where any work is to be done on one party's property, since his active or passive co-operation will be required in order for the work to be carried out.

**[24–43]**

---

[77] (1874) 8 IRCL 309.

[78] [1962] AC 413.

[79] [1971] Ch 233. See also *Ministry of Sound (Ireland) v World Online Ltd* [2003] 2 All ER (Comm) 823.

[24–44]        The second exception will only apply in those cases where damages would be an adequate remedy and where affirmation would be unreasonable.[80] The right in *White* is defeated if the repudiating party can demonstrate that the party who wishes to continue with performance has no legitimate interest in doing so. He must justify his resort to affirmation and performance instead of termination. Lord Reid had himself said in *White* that:

> "It may well be that, if it can be shown that a person has no [substantial] legitimate interest, financial or otherwise, in performing the contract rather than claiming damages, he ought not to be allowed to saddle the other party with an additional burden with no benefit to himself. If a party has no interest to enforce a stipulation, he cannot in general enforce it: so it might be said that, if a party has no interest to insist on a particular remedy, he ought not to be allowed to insist on it."

[24–45]        In *The Dynamic*,[81] Simon J said that the repudiating party bears a heavy burden which is "not discharged merely by showing that the benefit to the [party insisting on performance] is small in comparison to the loss to the contract breaker." In the absence of such legitimate interest, he must accept the repudiation and be satisfied with damages. This exception was applied in *The Puerto Buitrago*.[82] A charterer repudiated a charter-party by returning the ship early and unrepaired. They did this so that they could avoid their repair obligations under the contract. The ship owner sought to affirm the contract so that he would not have to accept the ship. If the contract was allowed to subsist, the charter-party would have to spend £2 million repairing the ship. The value of the repaired ship was only £1 million. The Court of Appeal refused to allow the ship owner to affirm the contract because affirmation would be unreasonable, damages were an adequate remedy and the ship-owner had no legitimate interest in continuing the charter-party.[83]

[24–46]        Both of these limitations are imposed in the interests of fairness. A party cannot traditionally sue for specific performance of any contractual obligation where damages would be an adequate remedy. If the innocent party is entitled to perform his side of the bargain come what may, he is, in effect, forcing specific performance of the obligation to pay by the back door. Therefore, as Lord Denning observed in *The Puerto Buitrago*,[84] the right to insist on performing:

> "... has no application whatever in a case where the plaintiff ought, in all reason, to accept the repudiation and sue for damages – provided that damages would provide an adequate remedy for any loss suffered by him."

---

[80]  *The Dynamic* [2003] EWHC 1936 *per* Simon J.
[81]  *ibid.*
[82]  [1976] 1 Lloyd's Rep 250.
[83]  See also *The Alaskan Trader* [1984] 1 All ER 129.
[84]  Above, n 82.

# Chapter 25
# Damages

## I. Introduction

The law on damages aims to provide financial relief in the event of non-performance. **[25–01]**
Damages aim to work a brand of corrective justice by providing the innocent party as
far as possible with a substitute for the performance he bargained for.[1] Surprisingly, the
law of contract is based on the premise that a man is often as free to break a contract as
he is to make one. Oliver Wendell Holmes famously wrote in *The Common Law*:

> "The only universal consequence of a legally binding promise is that the law
> makes the promisor pay damages if the promised event does not come to pass.
> In every case it leave him free from interference until the time for fulfilment has
> gone by, and therefore free to break his contract if he chooses."

The law on damages has at its heart a concern to balance this liberty to breach **[25–02]**
with the reasonable expectation of the innocent party that contracts are made to be
performed. Sir Frederick Pollock once famously observed:

> "A man who bespeaks a coat of his tailor will scarcely be persuaded that he is
> only betting with the tailor that such a coat will not be made and delivered

---

[1] See Friedmann, "The performance interest in contract damages" (1995) 11 LQR 628.

within a certain time. What he wants and means to have is the coat, not an insurance against not having a coat."

## II. Is the Loss too Remote?

[25–03] The rules on remoteness set a limit to the loss for which damages are recoverable for breach of contract. All sorts of disastrous consequences might flow from a breach of contract but the law will only allow damages to be paid in respect of some of them. In *British Columbia & Vancouver Island Spar v Nettleship*[2] Willes J set out a hypothetical scenario to illustrate the injustice that would be done if there were no rules as to remoteness:

> "[W]here a man going to be married to an heiress, his horse having cast a shoe on the journey, employed a blacksmith to replace it, who did the work so unskilfully that the horse was lamed, and the rider not arriving in time, the lady married another and the blacksmith was liable for the loss of the marriage."

[25–04] Asquith J in *Victoria Laundry v Newman Industries*[3] explains the basis for the rules on remoteness:

> "It is well settled that the governing purpose of damages is to put the party whose rights have been violated in the same position, so far as money can do so, as if his rights had been observed ... This purpose, if relentlessly pursued, would provide him with a complete indemnity for all loss de facto resulting from a particular breach, however improbable, however unpredictable. This, in contract at least, is recognised as too harsh a rule."

[25–05] Collins suggests that the courts recognise that a rule that allowed the plaintiff to recover vast sums in damages for all the direct consequences of a breach of contract would have the effect of deterring parties from forming binding contracts at all.[4]

[25–06] Lord Hope said in *Jackson v RBS*[5] that the rules on remoteness are "very familiar to every student of contract law. Most would claim to be able to recite them by heart". Through the rules on remoteness, the law draws a line beyond which losses must lie where they fall. The line is drawn according to the extent of liability to which the breaching party may be presumed to have agreed at the date of contracting.[6] *Hadley v Baxendale*[7], once called "an essentially uninteresting case, decided in a not very good opinion by a judge otherwise unknown to fame"[8] is the *locus classicus* in this area. Baron Alderson set out the law in a famous judgment, which is worth analysing

---

[2] (1868) LR CP 499.
[3] [1949] 2 KB 528.
[4] Collins, *The Law of Contract* (4th ed, LexisNexis, 2003) p 400.
[5] [2005] UKHL 3.
[6] Dawson, "Reflections on Certain Aspects of the Law of Damages for Breach of Contract" (1995) 9 JCL 125; *Jackson v RBS* [2005] UKHL 3 *per* Lord Hope.
[7] 9 Ex 341.
[8] Gilmore, *The Death of Contract*, (Ohio State University Press, 1995) p 54.

stage by stage. The test has two limbs. The first is that the breaching party is always liable for the normal consequences of his breach:

> "Where two parties have made a contract which one of them has broken, the damages which the other party ought to receive in respect of such breach of contract should be such as may fairly and reasonably be considered either arising naturally i.e. according to the usual course of things, from such breach of contract itself ...".

The second limb deals with liability for unusual or abnormal loss. A breaching party is only liable for such loss if it is reasonably foreseeable, if it is: [25–07]

> "... such as may reasonably be supposed to have been in the contemplation of both parties, at the time they made the contract, as the probable result of the breach of it."

Baron Alderson says that the second limb will be satisfied where: [25–08]

> "... the special circumstances under which the contract was actually made were communicated by the plaintiffs to the defendants, and thus known to both parties ... [I]f these special circumstances were wholly unknown to the party breaking the contract, he, at the most, could only be supposed to have had in his contemplation the amount of injury which would arise generally ... from such a breach of contract."

The plaintiff in *Hadley v Baxendale* was the owner of a flour mill and the defendant was a common carrier. The defendant contracted with the plaintiff to transport a broken crank shaft from the mill to an engineer so that it could be used as a model for a new shaft. The defendant, in breach of contract, was late in delivering the shaft. As a result, the new shaft was late in being made and the plaintiffs did not receive it until five days after the date agreed. The plaintiff claimed damages for the loss of profit for the five days that the mill was shut. This loss certainly resulted from the late delivery of the shaft. The question for the Court, however, was whether this loss was too remote to be recovered. Baron Alderson applied the first limb of the test as follows. He found that the loss of profit was an abnormal loss because usually the absence of a shaft would not have stopped the work of the mill as the miller would have kept a spare shaft. Therefore, the loss had to be covered by the second limb or not at all. The lost profits would only be recoverable under the second limb if the plaintiff had specifically told the defendant that failure to deliver the shaft on time would put the mill out of operation, so that the risk of lost profits might reasonably be said to have been in his contemplation at the time of entering into the contract. The plaintiff had not done so; therefore, the defendant was not liable. [25–09]

In *Victoria Laundry v Newman Ltd*[9] the Court of Appeal applied the test in *Hadley v Baxendale* to the plight of the plaintiffs, who were launderers and dyers. They bought a larger boiler from the defendant engineering firm. The boiler was to be delivered on 5 June. The plaintiffs had told the defendants in more than one letter that [25–10]

---

[9] Above, n 3.

they were "most anxious" to put the boiler in use "in the shortest possible space of time". However, the boiler was not delivered until 8 November. As a result of the delay, the plaintiffs lost profit which they would have earned if they had been able to use the boiler between 5 June and 8 November to take on extra laundering business. Their loss here was quite considerable because there was a shortage of laundries at the time. In addition, they lost a number of very lucrative dying contracts which they would have been in a position to accept if they had had the boiler. Could they recover for either or both of these losses? Asquith LJ found that the loss of normal profits arising from the lost laundering contracts and the loss of normal profits arising from the lost dying contracts were recoverable under the first limb in *Hadley*. These were ordinary losses and "[e]veryone, as a reasonable person, is taken to know the 'ordinary course of things' and consequently what loss is liable to result from a breach of contract in the ordinary course". This knowledge is imputed to the contract breaker whether he actually possesses it or not. However, what the "reasonable person" here may be taken to know will also take account of such knowledge as he *ought* to have according to his position and to the general circumstances of the contract. Unlike the common carriers in *Hadley*, the defendants in this case had some special characteristics that justified certain assumptions about their knowledge. They were engineers, they knew that the plaintiffs were launderers and dyers and they knew that the new boiler was to be put to immediate use. Accordingly, the Court assumed that they must have foreseen the likely loss of normal profits as a result of the unavailability of the new boiler. They were held liable in damages for this loss.

[25–11]      The loss of the "highly lucrative" dying contracts fell under the second limb in *Hadley*. This was because these were abnormal losses arising from special circumstances. They were outside the scope of the laundry's usual business. The defendants could not be held liable for these unless they had actual knowledge of the special circumstances. Because they were entirely ignorant of the existence of these especially valuable dying contracts, they did not have to compensate the plaintiffs for their loss.

[25–12]      An important point remains to be made about the first limb of *Hadley* concerning the knowledge that will be imputed to the breaching party as a reasonable person. The rule is that each party "must be taken to understand the ordinary practices and exigencies of the other's business".[10] So, in *The Heron II*[11] a ship-owner was liable to sugar merchants for the loss of profit which they suffered when he delivered their cargo to Basrah too late to take advantage of a good price. He was liable under the first limb in *Hadley*. The ship-owner did not know that the merchants had intended to sell the cargo immediately on arrival at the going market rate. However, he knew that there was a sugar market at Basrah and that the owners of the cargo were sugar merchants. This was enough to impute to him the knowledge that if the cargo was delivered nine days late the merchants would suffer some financial loss. The application of this rule will very much depend on the circumstances of the individual case. In *Balfour Beatty Construction (Scotland) Ltd v Scottish Power plc*[12] Lord Jauncey said:

---

[10] *Monarch ss Co Ltd v Karlshamns Oljefabriker* [1949] AC 196 *per* Lord Wright. See also *Ardennes v Ardennes* [1951] 1 KB 55.

[11] [1969] 1 AC 350.

[12] 1994 SLT 807.

"It must always be a question of circumstances what one contracting party is presumed to know about the business activities of the other. No doubt the simpler the activity of the one, the more readily can it be inferred that the other would have reasonable knowledge thereof. However, when the activity of A involves complicated construction or manufacturing techniques, I can see no reason why B who supplies a commodity that A intends to use in the course of those techniques should be assumed, merely because of the order for the commodity, to be aware of the details of all the techniques undertaken by A and the effect thereupon of any failure of or deficiency in that commodity."

Turning to the second limb of *Hadley*, another important question is whether [25–13] it is enough that the breaching party came to his knowledge of the special circumstances by any means or whether it must have been specifically told to him by the innocent party. The breaching party as a "reasonable person" will be fixed with constructive knowledge of the ordinary course of things. However, it appears that only actual knowledge of special circumstances giving rise to abnormal loss will do. For instance, in *Diamond v Campell Jones*,[13] the defendant breached a contract to sell leasehold premises in Mayfair to the plaintiff. The plaintiff had intended to convert the premises into offices and maisonettes and claimed the profit that he would have made had he done so. The defendants did not know that the plaintiff had bought with this intention. The plaintiffs argued that the defendants should be fixed with constructive knowledge of this intention because everybody recognised that the house was ripe for conversion. Buckley J refused to find that such constructive knowledge was sufficient to bring the conversion profits within the second limb of the *Hadley* test. It is quite clear that the defendant is not liable for the abnormal consequences of his breach unless he is possessed of such actual knowledge as would enable the reasonable man to foresee those consequences. For example, in *Waller v The Great Western Railway*[14] the defendant, in breach of contract, failed to supply horse boxes for the transportation of the plaintiff's horses to Dublin. As a result, the horses had to be ridden to the sale. Unknown to the defendant, the horses' diet had been changed recently, which meant that they suffered on what would normally have been an undemanding journey. Their condition deteriorated substantially and they were sold at a lower price than they would otherwise have fetched. Fitzgibbon LJ held that in order to hold the defendants liable under the second limb in *Hadley v Baxendale*, he would have to be satisfied that they were aware of the unusually fragile state of the horses at the time of contracting.

A further issue is whether the plaintiff himself told the defendant of the special [25–14] circumstances or whether he came to it by some other means. In *British Columbia Saw Mill v Nettleship*[15] Willes J explained that:

"There must have been knowledge under such circumstances as would raise the presumption that he intended to make himself liable for the special

---

[13] [1961] Ch 22. See also *Pilkington v Wood* [1953] Ch 770.
[14] (1879) 4 LR (Ir) 326.
[15] (1868) LR 3 CP 499. See also *Horne v Midland Rly Co* (1873) LR 8 CP 131.

consequences and that the person contracting with him believed, and had reasonable grounds for believing, that he intended to undertake such liability."

[25–15]     McKendrick argues by reference to this dictum that the test is more likely to be satisfied where the information was communicated specifically in the context of pre-contractual negotiations than where the breaching party just happened upon it.[16] So, in *Kemp v Intasun Holidays*[17] the defendant holiday company was not held liable for aggravation to the plaintiff's asthma caused by its breach of contract. The plaintiff had mentioned this special circumstance to the agent, but only in a conversational way and not as part of the booking arrangement. This was not enough to bring the asthma-related harm within the test in *Hadley v Baxendale*.

[25–16]     It is clear that the test in *Hadley v Baxendale* is based on the parties' knowledge. The idea is that, if a party knows about a risk, he should plan for it appropriately, perhaps by taking out insurance or by charging a higher price. Indeed, when fully informed about the risk he is assuming, he may decide not to enter the contract after all. If he does not plan, he should be liable. Baron Alderson noted of the defendants in *Hadley* that: "had the special circumstances been known, the parties might have specially provided for the breach of contract by special terms as to damages". Posner in his *Economic Analysis of Law* observes:

> "[W]here a risk of loss is known to only one party to the contract, the other party is not liable for the loss if it occurs. This principle induces the party with knowledge of the risk either to take any appropriate precautions himself or, if he believes that the other party might be the more efficient loss avoider, to disclose the risk to that party and pay him to assume it. In this way, incentives are generated to deal with the risk in the most efficient fashion."

[25–17]     Take, for example, the case of *Balfour Beatty Construction v Scottish Power plc*.[18] The plaintiffs were the main construction company on the Edinburgh bypass. The defendants agreed to supply them with electricity. The supply of electricity failed while the plaintiffs were constructing an aqueduct. The construction of the aqueduct required a constant supply of electricity so that when the electricity cut out, the work that was done was rendered worthless and it had to be demolished. The House of Lords refused to award full damages to the plaintiffs in respect of these losses because the losses were too remote. The damage done did not fall under the first limb in *Hadley* because it was not the sort of damage that usually arises in the usual course of things from a power-cut at a construction site. It did not fall under the second limb because the defendants did not know about the need for a constant supply of electricity, nor was there any reason why they should be presumed to know about it. The effect of the rule in *Hadley* is to allocate the risk of this loss appropriately. Balfour Beatty had freely entered into a construction project which required a constant supply of electricity. They failed to inform Scottish Power of their exceptional requirements and failed to

---

[16] McKendrick, *Contract Law: Text, Cases and Materials* (2nd ed, Oxford University Press, 2005) 1082. See *Simpson v London and North Western Railway Co* (1876) QBD 274.
[17] [1987] 2 FTLR 234.
[18] Above, n 12.

negotiate express terms in the contract which would have secured those requirements. Accordingly, it was right that they should assume full responsibility for the risk.

## Tort and Contract

Lord Denning in *Parsons (Livestock) Ltd v Uttley Ingham & Co. Ltd*[19] set out the difference between "reasonably foreseeable" loss in contract and "reasonably foreseeable" loss in tort. In the case of a breach of contract, the court must consider whether the consequences of the breach were such that a reasonable man, at the time of entering into the contract, would contemplate them as being of a substantial degree of probability. In contract, the consequences must be "liable to result" or there must be a "real danger" or "serious possibility of them occurring".[20] In tort, by contrast, the question is whether a reasonable man, at the time of committing the tort, would foresee them as being of a much lower degree of probability. A tortfeasor might be liable for consequences which were "liable to happen in the most unusual case" or in a "very improbable case".[21] Lord Reid in *The Heron II*[22] justified the imposition of a far wider range of liability in tort than contract as follows:

[25–18]

> "The defendant will be liable [in tort] for any type of damage which is reasonably foreseeable as liable to happen even in the most unusual case, unless the risk is so small that a reasonable man would in the whole circumstances feel justified in neglecting it. And there is good reason for the difference. In contract, if one party wishes to protect himself against a risk which to the other party would appear unusual, he can direct the other party's attention to it before the contract is made, and I need not stop to consider in what circumstances the other party will then be held to have accepted responsibility in that event. But in tort there is no opportunity for the injured party to protect himself in that way, and the tortfeasor cannot reasonably complain if he has to pay for some very unusual but nevertheless foreseeable damage which results from his wrongdoing."

## Type and Extent of Damage

It is clear from the case law that the breaching party is liable for any *type* of harm which falls within the limbs in *Hadley v Baxendale*. The injured party need not prove that the *extent* of the harm which occurred was foreseeable. A case in point is *H. Parsons v Uttley Ingham*.[23] In that case, the plaintiffs, who were pig farmers, ordered a storage hopper for storing pig nuts. The defendants negligently installed the hopper with the result that the nuts decayed. Two hundred and fifty-four pigs died of an intestinal disease which they contracted from eating the nuts. The defendants argued that they were not liable for the loss of profit suffered by the plaintiffs as a result of the pigs' deaths because the deaths were too remote a consequence of their breach of contract; the extent of the loss was unprecedented and unforeseeable. The court held them liable nonetheless. The defendants ought reasonably to have foreseen that, if the

[25–19]

---

[19] [1978] QB 791.
[20] *C Czarnikow Ltd v Koufos* [1969] AC 350.
[21] *ibid.*
[22] Above, n 11.
[23] Above n 19.

pigs were fed the mouldy pignuts, the pigs would become ill. Illness was foreseeable. It did not matter that the extent of the illness which occurred could not have been anticipated. Lord Scarman said:

> "It does not matter, in my judgment, if they thought that the chance of physical injury, loss of profit, loss of market, or other loss as the case may be, was slight, or that the odds were against it, provided they contemplated as a serious possibility the type of consequence, not necessarily the specific consequence, that ensued upon breach."

[25–20]    This type/extent distinction is a difficult one from the perspective of certainty. Burrows[24] makes the point well:

> "One could argue, for example, that since illness and death of pigs were regarded as the same type of loss and merely differed in extent, the majority's approach is irreconcilable with *Victoria Laundry*; for one could argue that the type of loss in issue there was loss of profits, and that the exceptional profits were merely a greater extent of the same type of loss. Presumably, the majority's answer to this would be that its test allows the courts a discretion as to how to divide up the types of loss, and that *Victoria Laundry* is reconcilable by regarding the ordinary loss of profits as a different type of loss from the exceptional loss of profits. But such discretion and flexibility in the test is only achieved at the expense of certainty."

### III. Can the Plaintiff get Damages for Mental Distress?

[25–21]    Ordinarily, a contractual damage claim will turn on injury to an economic interest, on damage to property or on personal injury. The general rule is that damages are not available in contract law for mental distress. One policy-based reason for this rule would appear to be a fear of inappropriately large awards. This objection is grounded in the suspicion that because it is difficult to quantify something as nebulous as distress, awards of such damages are likely to be both inaccurate and on the high side. In *Hayes v James & Charles Dodd*[25] Staughton LJ wrote:

> "I consider that English courts should be wary of adopting ... 'the United States practice of huge awards.' Damages awarded for negligence or want of skill, whether against professional men or anyone else, must provide fair compensation, but no more than that."

[25–22]    In limited circumstances, however, damages are available to compensate for the mental distress consequent on breach of contract. I may be disappointed that my contract has been breached but that disappointment, with nothing more, will not entitle me to claim damages. The law in this area is stated in the judgment of Bingham J in *Watts v Morrow*[26]:

---

[24] Burrows, *Remedies for Torts and Breach of Contract* (3rd ed, Oxford University Press, 2004) p 90.
[25] [1990] 2 All ER 815.
[26] [1991] 1 WLR 1421, 1445.

"A contract-breaker is not in general liable for any distress, frustration, anxiety, displeasure, vexation, tension or aggravation which his breach of contract may cause to the innocent party. This rule is not, I think, founded on the assumption that such reactions are not foreseeable, which they surely are or may be, but on considerations of policy. But the rule is not absolute. Where the very object of the contract is to provide pleasure, relaxation, peace of mind or freedom from molestation, damages will be awarded if the fruit of the contract is not provided or if the contrary result is procured instead ... In cases not falling within this exceptional category, damages are in my view recoverable for physical inconvenience and discomfort caused by the breach and mental suffering directly related to that inconvenience and discomfort."

### Object is to Provide Pleasure, Relaxation, Peace of Mind or Freedom from Molestation

The availability of damages for mental distress under this heading turns on the purpose [25–23] of the contract at issue. It would be ridiculous if the law only provided financial compensation for breach of a contract the "very object" of which is non-financial. In *Farley v Skinner*[27] Lord Steyn explained the "very object" requirement, holding that "it is sufficient if a major or important object of the contract is to give pleasure, relaxation or peace of mind". A classic example of a case falling under this heading is *Jarvis v Swan Tours Ltd.*[28] The plaintiff had booked a Christmas skiing holiday package with the defendant. He only took one fortnight's holiday a year. The holiday was to involve house parties, tea, cakes, fondue, yodelling and other such treats. The plaintiff's contract with the defendant was breached because *inter alia* the house parties were either small or cancelled, the cakes were replaced with crisps and nut cakes and the yodeller did not live up to expectations. Lord Denning found that Mr Jarvis was entitled to compensation for his disappointment because the purpose of his contract was to provide pleasure. A similar case was *Diesen v Samson*[29], in which a bride was awarded damages for loss of enjoyment when her wedding photographer failed to turn up as arranged to take pictures of her wedding. In *Dinnegan and Dinnegan v Ryan*[30] damages for distress were awarded where a publican, in breach of contract, refused entry to his pub to the newlywed plaintiffs and their wedding guests. In *Johnson v Longleat Property*[31] McMahon J found that damages for loss of enjoyment are available where a builder provides a substandard house.

Damages for distress were also awarded in *Heywood v Wellers*[32] where the [25–24] plaintiff had employed solicitors to obtain an injunction to prevent a man from harassing her. The object of the contract was to provide relief from anxiety, and as this object had not been achieved, damages were available for the resulting

---

[27] [2001] UKHL 49.

[28] [1973] QB 233.

[29] 1971 SLT (Sh Ct) 49.

[30] [2002] 3 IR 178.

[31] Unreported, High Court, 19 May 1976. See also *Murphy v Quality Homes*, unreported, High Court, 22 June 1976.

[32] [1976] 1 All ER 30.

mental distress. To the same effect, in *Hamilton-Jones v David & Snape*[33] the plaintiff sued her solicitors for breach of contract. She had approached them after the breakdown of her marriage and instructed them to take steps to prevent her husband from abducting her children and taking them with him to his own country, Tunisia. The Court held that a primary aim of the contract was to provide her with peace of mind and damages were available for distress when this aim was not achieved.

[25–25]     Remember that the courts' focus in this category of cases is on the special non-commercial purpose of the contract. Where the contract is primarily commercial in nature, no damages will be awarded even where it is breached in a distressing manner. So in *Smyth v Huey & Co*,[34] damages for distress and inconvenience were not awarded in an ordinary conveyancing case. To the same effect, in *Johnson v Gore Wood and Co.*[35] damages were not recoverable for injury to a businessman's pride and dignity in respect of a conveyance of land to his business.

## Consumer Surplus

[25–26]     An important category of cases under this heading are the so-called "loss of amenity" or "consumer surplus" cases. The phrase refers to "occasions where the value of the promise to the promisee exceeds the financial enhancement of his position which full performance will secure".[36] The last category of cases was concerned with the objective purpose of the contract. Objectively, the purpose of a consumer surplus case is commercial. For example, if I hire a builder to construct a summer house in my garden I have certain objective commercial interests which must be secured. However, I also have a subjective purpose in embarking on this contract. I may always have longed for a summer house in which to sit and watch my garden grow. If the summer house is not properly built, I will be distressed and disappointed and this subjective interest, called the "consumer surplus", will be frustrated. In the words of Oliver J in *Radford v De Froberville*,[37] failure to award damages for injury to this special interest in the appropriate case would be "so strange and so monstrously unjust that Mr Bumble's animadiversion on the nature of law seems, by contrast, a reasoned understatement".

[25–27]     In *Ruxley v Forsyth*[38] Lord Mustill justified compensation for the consumer surplus in terms of *pacta sunt servanda*:

---

[33] [2004] 1 WLR 924.
[34] [1993] NI 236.
[35] [2002] 1 AC 1.
[36] *Ruxley Electronics v Forsyth* [1996] 1 AC 344 *per* Lord Mustill.
[37] [1977] 1 WLR 1262.
[38] [1996] 1 AC 344. See also *Alfred McAlpine Construction Ltd v Panatown Ltd* [2001] 1 AC 518; *Radford v De Froberville* [1977] 1 WLR 1262 *per* Oliver J: "*Pacta sunt servanda*. If he contracts for the supply of that which he thinks serves his interests – be they commercial, aesthetic or merely eccentric – then if that which is contracted for is not supplied by the other contracting party I do not see why, in principle, he should not be compensated by being provided with the cost of supplying it through someone else in a different way, subject to the *proviso* of course, that he is seeking compensation for a genuine loss and not merely using a technical breach to secure an uncovenanted profit."

"Having taken on the job the contractor is morally as well as legally obliged to give the employer what he stipulated to obtain, and this obligation ought not to be devalued ... [In cases] where the contract is designed to fulfil a purely commercial purpose, the loss will very often consist only of the monetary detriment brought about by the breach of contract. But these remedies are not exhaustive, for the law must cater for those occasions where the value of the promise to the promisee exceeds the financial enhancement of his position which full performance will secure. This excess, often referred to as the 'consumer surplus' ... is usually incapable of precise valuation in terms of money, exactly because it represents a personal, subjective and non-monetary gain. Nevertheless, where it exists the law should recognise it and compensate the promisee if misperformance takes it away. The lurid bathroom tiles or the grotesque folly ... may be so discordant with general taste that in purely economic terms the builder may be said to do the employer a favour by failing to install them. But this is too narrow and materialistic a view of the transaction. Neither the contractor nor the court has the right to substitute for the employer's individual expectation of performance a criterion derived from what ordinary people would regard as sensible ...".

The courts' award of damages for unfulfilled bargains for personal preferences also acts as an incentive to the performing party to fulfil the contract as agreed. In *Ruxley,* Lord Mustill rejected the notion that the "promisor can please himself whether or not to comply with the wishes of the promise, which, as embodied in the contract, formed part of the consideration for the price". However, the consumer surplus cases are vulnerable to the objection that they involve the court in awarding damages for purely subjective loss. Nevertheless, Lord Mustill argued in *Ruxley*: **[25–28]**

"The amount [of damages] may be small and since it cannot be quantified directly there may be room for difference of opinion about what it should be. But in several fields the judges are well accustomed to putting figures to intangibles, and I see no reason why the imprecision of the exercise should be a barrier, if that is what fairness demands."

## Distress Consequent on Physical Inconvenience

Damages are available for mental distress where that distress results from some physical inconvenience caused by the breach of contract. For example, in *Hobbs v London & South Western Rly*[39] the plaintiff sued a railway company when he and his family were deposited at the wrong station and had to walk several miles on a wet night. Damages were recoverable for the distress consequent on this physical inconvenience. Similarly, in *Leahy v Rawson*[40] damages were awarded for the physical inconvenience arising from a builder's failure to complete work to an extension as agreed. The plaintiff was compelled for a time to occupy her garage as a residence. In *Farley v Skinner*[41] Lord Clyde distinguished "inconvenience" from the "purely **[25–29]**

---

[39] (1875) LR 10.
[40] Unreported, High Court, 14 January 2003.
[41] Above (n 27).

sentimental". Lord Scott in *Farley* outlined the strict manner in which this distinction is applied:

> "[I]f the cause is no more than disappointment that the contractual obligation has been broken, damages are not recoverable even if the disappointment has led to a complete mental breakdown. But, if the cause of the inconvenience or discomfort is a sensory (sight, touch, hearing, smell etc) experience, damages can, subject to the remoteness rule, be recovered."

[25–30]  The plaintiff in *Farley* was entitled to recover for the mental distress he suffered when a house, which he had bought on foot of a surveyor's negligent assurance that it was not affected by aircraft noise, turned out to be under a stacking point for Gatwick Airport. He was permitted to recover for this distress as it was clearly linked to sensory discomfort. Damages for mental distress were successfully recovered by the plaintiff in *Perry v Sidney Phillips & Sons*.[42] He had purchased a house in reliance on a survey carried out by the defendant surveyors. The survey stated that the house was in good order. However, after moving in, Mr Perry discovered that the roof leaked and that the septic tank was inefficient and gave off an offensive smell. These defects caused him distress and worry. Damages were available to compensate Mr Perry for this mental distress because it was linked to the physical inconvenience he had suffered as a result of the breach. A similar case was *Watts v Morrow*.[43] The plaintiffs had purchased a weekend home based on a survey which said that the house had no major defects. The survey was inaccurate and the plaintiffs had to carry out significant repairs. They recovered damages for the distress consequence on this physical inconvenience.

### Loss of Reputation

[25–31]  *Addis v Gramaphone Ltd*[44] was once the leading case in this area. The plaintiff had been wrongfully dismissed from his post in India in humiliating circumstances. The House of Lords held that he was not entitled to damages for his injured feelings or for the financial loss he suffered because of his difficulty in finding new employment. However, in the recent case of *Malik v BCCI*[45] the House of Lords held that a plaintiff can recover both damages for loss of reputation and "stigma damages" for the financial loss flowing from it on the basis that his employer was in breach of an implied term not to conduct his business in a dishonest and corrupt way. This position has been confirmed in *Johnson v Unisys Ltd*.[46]

## IV. How Much Money Will the Plaintiff Get?

### The Expectation Measure

[25–32]  Fried has written that damages in contract reflect what the promise made under that contract is worth: "If I make a promise to you, I should do as I promise; and if I fail to keep that promise, it is fair that I should be made to hand over the equivalent of the

---

[42] [1982] 3 All ER 705.
[43] Above, n 26.
[44] [1909] AC 488.
[45] [1997] 3 All ER 1.
[46] [2001] 2 All ER 801.

promised performance".[47] Therefore, the normal measure of damages in contract law is the "expectation measure". In *Robinson v Harman*[48] Parke B said:

> "The rule of the common law is, that where a party sustains a loss by reason of a breach of contract, he is, so far as money can do it, to be placed in the same situation, with respect to damages, as if the contract had been performed."

So the expectation measure of damages amounts to the net value of what the injured party would have received if the contract had been performed as agreed. The most obvious expectation loss is the profit which the plaintiff stood to make on the contract. The expectation measure is usually calculated by reference to diminution in value; the difference between what A expected to get and what A got. A simple example from the case law is *Watts v Morrow*.[49] The plaintiffs purchased a house for £177,500 on foot of the defendant's survey, which stated that the house was sound, stable and in good condition with only minor defects. In fact, the roof, windows and floorboards required repair. The house was therefore worth only £162,500. The expectation measure of damages was the difference in value between the house the plaintiffs would have purchased if the survey had been performed competently and the value of the house they actually purchased: £15,000.

[25–33]

## Sale of Goods and Difference in Value

The test applied in calculating the expectation loss in sale of goods cases is called the "difference in value" test. Damages aim to put the aggrieved party in the position he would have been in had the contract been performed. Suppose A has contracted to sell a Steinway baby grand piano to B for €10,000. A breaches the contract by failing to deliver the piano. The aim of an award of damages here will be to put B in the position as if the contract had been performed by enabling him to buy a substitute Steinway baby grand piano immediately. Suppose, however, that between the date of contracting and the date of breach the price of Steinway baby grand pianos has risen to €12,000. If B is to be enabled to bring about the same end result as if the contract had been performed, he must be awarded the €2,000 which will enable him to purchase at the new price. Therefore, s 50(3) of the Sale of Goods Act 1893 provides that where there is an "available market" for the goods at issue then, *prima facie*, damages are to be calculated by reference to the difference between the contract price agreed between the parties and the market price for those goods at the time when the goods ought to have been accepted or delivered. Under this rule, B will be awarded his €2,000. His contract, if performed, would have reaped goods to the value of €12,000. The law brings him as close to this situation as possible by supplementing his unspent €10,000 with €2,000 in damages. Section 51(3) sets out that this same rule operates to compensate a seller where the market value of goods drops between the date of agreement and the date of breach. Imagine A had delivered the piano to B but B had refused to take delivery. By the date of his refusal, the price of such pianos had dropped to €7,000. A would be entitled to €3,000 in damages. His contract, if performed, would have reaped €10,000. The law brings him as close to this situation as possible by supplementing his €7,000

[25–34]

---

[47] Fried, *Contract as Promise* (Harvard University Press, 1981) p 17.
[48] (1848) 1 Ex 850.
[49] Above, n 26.

worth of goods with €3,000 in damages. The relevant market value is that obtaining at the date of breach and not at the date when the purchaser buys his replacement goods or the date at which the seller sells his goods to a new purchaser. The law operates on the basis that the aggrieved party will act immediately to secure the equivalent of performance of his contract. Any dips or rises in market value subsequent to breach are no concern of the court.[50] Let us stay with the same example. Imagine that, at the time A refused to accept the piano from B, the market value of that piano was €7,000. B receives €3,000 in damages to make up the difference between what he expected to make from the contract and what he was left with after the breach. Suppose now that B does not sell the piano until six months later, by which time the market value of these pianos is €15,000 so that he is able to make a substantial profit. This profit does not affect his entitlement to damages one jot. You will have observed that ss 50(3) and 51(3) only apply where there is an available market. Where there is no available market, damages are calculated by reference to general principles.

### The Cost of a Cure

[25–35]    It has been noted above that, generally speaking, the expectation measure of damages is calculated by awarding the injured party the difference between the value of the performance that he bargained for and the value of the performance he actually received. A second method of calculating the expectation measure of damages is called the "cost of a cure".[51] Under this formula, the injured party is awarded the amount that it would cost to have a third party remedy the breaching party's defective performance. Normally there will be no need to choose between these measures because they will yield exactly the same amount in damages. For example, if you contract to sell me a bushel of apples for €30 and you fail to deliver them the difference in value approach and the cost of a cure approach will produce the same amount in damages. The difference in value between what I contracted for (€30 worth of apples) and what I received (€0 worth of apples) is €30. The cost of a cure (purchasing €30 worth of apples as a substitute) is also €30.

[25–36]    However, there are scenarios where the measures diverge substantially. Suppose A hires B to build a gazebo at the foot of his garden so that he can host garden parties there in the summer. The gazebo will not increase the market value of his house. B does a very bad job of building the gazebo. How should A's damages be measured? He is entitled to a small amount for his non-financial loss: the purpose of the contract was to provide him with a pleasurable facility and this purpose has not been fulfilled. The diminution in value approach does not yield a great amount of money as the gazebo would not have increased the value of A's property to any appreciable extent. Any financial damages awarded would therefore be nominal. Is A entitled to the cost of a cure: the cost of engaging another tradesman to demolish the gazebo and rebuild it? The law recognises that awarding a small amount in damages in respect of the consumer surplus is often insufficient. Nevertheless, as Lord Mustill observed in *Ruxley Elecronics v Forsyth*,[52] "[t]here is no need to remedy the injustice of awarding

---

[50] *Jamal v Moolla* [1916] 1 AC 175.
[51] See *Kincora Builders v Cronin*, unreported, High Court, 5 March 1973.
[52] Above, n 38. See also *Watts v Morrow*, above, n 26.

too little by unjustly awarding far too much". The law is, therefore, that A is entitled to the cost of a cure, within reasonable limits.

In *Jacob & Youngs v Kent*[53] Cardozo J said that: "The owner is entitled to the money which will permit him to complete, unless the cost of completion is grossly and unfairly out of proportion to the good to be attained". *Ruxley Elecronics v Forsyth*[54] affirmed that principle as part of English law. In that case, Mr Forsyth contracted for a swimming pool which was to be seven feet six inches deep. In fact, the pool built for him was nine inches too shallow. Forsyth claimed £21,560. This was the cost of curing the defect: demolishing the pool and rebuilding it as specified. Mr Forsyth had only paid £17,797 originally. The difference in value between the work bargained for and the work received was assessed as nil. The loss of pleasure which he could take from the pool was valued at a mere £2,250. The Court denied Mr Forsyth the cost of a cure. Such an award would be reasonable on the basis that the expense of the work involved was out of proportion to the benefit sought to be achieved by demolishing and reconstructing the pool. A cost of a cure award would also inflict undue hardship on Ruxley to little end.

[25–37]

The plaintiff's intention is also linked to the reasonableness of awarding cost of a cure damages. The court will not award the cost of a cure where it appears that the plaintiff has no intention of using those damages to effect the cure. In *Tito v Waddell*[55] Sir Robert Megarry V-C wrote:

[25–38]

> "[I]f the plaintiff has suffered little or no monetary loss in the reduction of value of his land and he has no intention of applying any damages towards carrying out the work contracted for, or its equivalent, I cannot see why he should recover the cost of doing work which will never be done. It would be a mere pretence to say that this cost was a loss and so should be recoverable in damages."

This was another reason why the Court did not award such damages to Forsyth. Forsyth had no intention of rebuilding the pool. Lord Jauncey observed that "were [Forsyth] to receive the cost of building a new one and retaining an existing one he would have recovered no compensation for loss but a very substantial gratuitous benefit, something which damages are not intended to provide". Similarly, in *Birse Construction v Eastern Telegraph Co*[56] the plaintiff claimed the cost of a cure where the defendant had built a residential college for him. There were numerous defects in the building. By the time the case came to court, the defendant had decided to sell the property. He took no steps to remedy the defects and the purchase price of the college was not reduced to take account of them. Judge Humphrey Lloyd QC awarded nominal damages of £2. By selling the building at an undiminished price, the plaintiff had avoided any financial loss. It was unreasonable to award the cost of a cure where there was no intention to use that money to remedy the defects.

[25–39]

---

[53] 129 NE 889.
[54] Above, n 38. See also *Watts v Morrow*, above, n 26.
[55] [1977] Ch 106. See also *Birse Construction Ltd v Eastern Telegraph Co* [2004] EWHC 2512.
[56] [2004] EWHC 2512.

### Speculative Loss

**[25–40]**  Sometimes the court may be asked to calculate damages based on an event which may or may not happen and which may or may not have certain effects. In *Hickey & Co Ltd v Roches Stores*,[57] for example, the plaintiff was awarded damages for lost profits on the basis of business that it argued, but could not definitively prove, would be lost over the next two years. The general rule is that, if expectation losses are too difficult to assess, the plaintiff must be satisfied with claiming for his reliance loss instead. However, the court will not be handicapped by such difficulties of assessment and may often award expectation damages even where a precise sum is cumbersome to calculate. In *Chaplin v Hicks*[58] Fletcher-Moulton J observed that: "the fact that damages cannot be assessed with certainty does not relieve the wrongdoer of the necessity of paying damages for his breach of contract." The Irish attitude is similar. In *Callinan v VHI*[59] Blayney J in the Supreme Court set down that once the plaintiffs can establish the existence of loss, it is not necessary to conclusively prove its extent. The approach of the courts is encapsulated in the observation of Finlay P in *Grafton Court v Wadson Sales*[60] that the court should be "alert, energetic and if necessary ingenious to assess damages where it is satisfied that a significant injury has flowed from breach".[61]

**[25–41]**  The issue of speculative loss is most acute where the plaintiff claims damages for loss of an opportunity. A loss of a chance is recoverable in damages if the plaintiff can show both that the loss was quantifiable in monetary terms and that it was substantially likely that the chance would have come to fruition. It was stated in *Kitchen v RAF*[62] that "[i]f the plaintiff can satisfy the Court that she would have had some prospect of success, then it would be for the court to evaluate those prospects, taking into account the difficulties that remained". In *Davies v Taylor*[63] Lord Reid elaborated on this requirement of "some prospect of success":

> "The issues and the sole issue is whether that chance or probability was substantial. If it was then it must be evaluated. If it was a mere possibility it must be ignored. Many different words could be and have been used to indicate the dividing line. I can think of none better than substantial on the one hand, or speculative on the other."

**[25–42]**  These principles were applied in *Chaplin v Hicks*[64] in which plaintiff sued the defendant theatrical manager on the strength of a contract that, if she would attend for interview, he would select 12 out of 50 interviewees for employment. She was able to recover some damages, even though there was no guarantee that she would have been successful. The Court felt that the plaintiff's lost opportunity could be assessed in monetary terms. Fletcher-Moulton J said that: "[w]here by contract a man has the

---

[57] [1980] ILRM 107.

[58] [1911] 2 KB 786.

[59] Unreported, High Court, 22 April 1983.

[60] Unreported, High Court, 17 February 1975.

[61] For examples of the calculation of speculative damages see *O'Keefe v Ryanair Holdings* [2003] 1 ILRM 14; *Hawkins v Rogers* (1951) 85 ILTR 129.

[62] [1958] 2 All ER 241.

[63] [1974] AC 207.

[64] Above, n 59.

right to belong to a limited class of competitors, he is possessed of something of value". The plaintiff was also able to satisfy the Court that there was a substantial chance (a 12 in 50 chance) that her opportunity would have borne fruit.

## The Reliance Measure

An alternative measure of damages, called the "reliance" measure of damages, is also available to the plaintiff. This measure concerns "wasted expenditure": the extent to which the injured party is worse off as a result of relying on the contract. The reliance measure of damages was recovered in *Lloyd v Stanbury*.[65] The contract here was for the sale of land. In anticipation of his purchase, the purchaser went to great expense in moving his caravan onto the land and in getting his furniture there. He was permitted to recover this wasted expenditure when the contract was breached.

[25–43]

As a general rule, the plaintiff may claim both his reliance loss and his expectation loss. Usually, this will mean that the plaintiff can claim both the net profit he expected to make from the contract and the expenditure he wasted in reliance on the contract.[66] "Net profit" is used here because awarding a party damages in respect of both gross profit and wasted expenditure would amount to double recovery.[67] The right to claim for both types of loss is subject to two further important limitations, which will be discussed in turn.

[25–44]

### *Bad Bargain*

The plaintiff may not recover expenditure spent in reliance on a "bad bargain". In other words, the non-breaching party may not recover his reliance loss where the contract was bound to make a loss anyway. Remember that the basic principle in damages is to put the party in the position he would have been in if the contract had been performed. The idea in compensating for the reliance measure is to allow the non-breaching party to recover expenditure that is now wasted because the contract will not be performed. A party cannot, therefore, on breach of the contract, use a claim for wasted expenditure to recover money which would have been wasted even if the contract had been performed. For example, in *C&P Haulage v Middleton*[68] C&P Haulage leased premises from Middleton. C&P undertook extensive building works on the premises despite a clause in the lease which said that any fixtures put in by the defendant had to be left on the premises on termination of the license. Middleton terminated the lease six months early in breach of the contract. C&P claimed damages for reliance loss in respect of their expenditure on Middleton's premises. They were not awarded the damages because, as Fox LJ observed:

[25–45]

> "[W]hile it is true that the expenditure could in a sense be said to be wasted in consequence of the breach of contract, it was equally likely to be wasted if there had been no breach ... A high risk of waste was from the very first inherent in the nature of the contract itself, breach or no breach."

---

[65] [1971] 1 WLR 535.
[66] *Hydraulic Engineering Co v McHaffie Goslett & Co* (1878) 4 QBD 670.
[67] *Cullinane v British ' Rema' Manufacturing Co* [1954] 1 QB 292.
[68] [1983] 1 WLR 1461.

[25–46]     The losses flowed from C&P's poor judgment in installing fittings that they could not take away, not from the breach. In *Bowlay Logging Ltd v Domtar Ltd*[69] Berger J of the Supreme Court of British Columbia explained the rationale behind this rule:

> "The law of contract compensates a plaintiff for damages resulting from the defendant's breach; it does not compensate the plaintiff for damages resulting from his making a bad bargain. Where it can be seen that the plaintiff would have incurred a loss on the contract as a whole, the expenses he has incurred are losses flowing from entering into the contract, not losses flowing from the defendant's breach ... If the law of contract were to move from compensating for the consequences of breach to compensating for the consequences of entering into contracts, the law would run contrary to the normal expectations of the world of commerce. The burden of risk would be shifted from the plaintiff to the defendant. The defendant would become the insurer of the plaintiff's enterprise. Moreover, the amount of damages would increase not in relation to the gravity or consequences of the breach but in relation to the inefficiency with which the plaintiff carried out the contract. The greater his expenses owing to inefficiency, the greater the damages."

[25–47]     It falls to the breaching party to show that the bad bargain rule applies. Unless he proves otherwise, the court will presume that the innocent party would have made enough profit on the performed contract to recoup his expenditure. In *CCC Films v Impact Quadrant*[70] the claimants sought to recover $12,000 that they had spent in reliance on their film distribution contract with the defendants. The contract concerned films called "Devil's Orgy" and "Children Shouldn't Play With Dead Things". They were entitled to recover this expenditure because the defendants could not prove that the bargain was a bad one; perhaps surprisingly, they could not satisfy the Court that these films were guaranteed to fail miserably at the box office.

### Impossible to Calculate Expectation Loss

[25–48]     In the discussion of speculative losses (25–40) reference was made to the rule that a party cannot claim his expectation loss where that loss would be impossible to estimate. In *Anglia Television v Reed*,[71] Robert Reed, broke his contract with Anglia Television to be the leading man in their film. As a result the film could not be made. Anglia claimed for their wasted expenditure but could not claim for their expectation loss because they could not say what profit they would have made from the film even if Mr Reed had not broken his contract. Lord Denning MR said:

> "[A] plaintiff in such a case as this has an election: he can either claim for his loss of profits, or for his wasted expenditure. But he must elect between them. He cannot claim both. If he has not suffered any loss of profits – or if he cannot prove what his loss of profits would have been – he can claim in the

---

69  [1978] 4 WWR 105.
70  [1985] 1 QB 16.
71  [1971] 3 All ER 690.

alternative the expenditure which has been thrown away, that is, wasted by reason of the breach."

[25–49] In *McRae v Commonwealth Disposals Commission*[72] the Commission had invited tenders for the purchase of a sunken oil tanker, said to contain oil, which was said to be lying on Jourmand Reef. The plaintiffs made the winning bid of £285 and spent £3000 in preparing their salvage expedition. There was no ship at the reef. What measure of damages could they recover? The High Court of Australia held that the plaintiffs could not recover the expectation measure because it was impossible to estimate with any certainty the value the plaintiffs would have recovered if the tanker had been found. The expectation loss was merely speculative and so the plaintiffs were only entitled to recover the £3,285 they had spent in reliance on the contract. The Court drew a firm distinction between damages which are difficult to assess, of which the Court must attempt to give some account, and damages which are impossible to assess. In the Irish case of *Afton v Film Studios*[73] Pringle J refused to award damages for lost future profits because he was unable to find that it was probable that the venture would have made a net profit at all.

## V. Will the Damages be Reduced for Failure to Mitigate the Loss?

[25–50] A plaintiff must take all reasonable steps to minimise such loss as he has suffered by the breach of contract.[74] So it is often said that the plaintiff has a duty to mitigate his loss. He will not be allowed to recover damages for any loss attributable to his failure to mitigate. The notion of mitigation is best explained by reference to some examples from the case law. Take, for example, *Malone v Malone*.[75] The plaintiff had taken out a loan to buy a boarding house. The vendor, in breach of contract, failed to complete the sale. Additional interest on the loan accumulated and the plaintiff sought damages to compensate him for this. Costello J held that the plaintiff had not taken reasonable steps to mitigate his loss. He should have repaid the loan to the bank in order to avoid the interest. In *Bord Iascaigh Mhara v Scallan*[76] a hirer abandoned a fishing vessel in repudiation of its contract with the owner. The owners' duty to mitigate their loss required them to retake possession of the boat. They were not permitted to allow the vessel to deteriorate and then claim damages for that deterioration. In addition, if a new prospective hirer had appeared, the owners would have been obliged to contract with him if it was reasonable to do so. Similarly, *Cullen v Horgan*[77] sets out that if a contract for the sale of goods is breached by non-delivery, the purchaser must mitigate his loss by buying substitute goods as soon as is reasonably possible. Failure to mitigate was proven in *Brace v Calder*.[78] The defendants were Scotch whisky merchants and the plaintiff was employed to manage their office business for two years. Before the two years were up, the defendants dissolved their partnership, wrongfully terminating

---

[72] (1951) 84 CLR 377.
[73] Unreported, High Court, 12 July 1971.
[74] *British Westinghouse Electric and Manufacturing Co v Underground Electric Railways Co of London* [1912] AC 673.
[75] Unreported, High Court, 23 November 1979.
[76] Unreported, High Court, 8 May 1971.
[77] [1925] 2 IR 1.
[78] [1895] 2 QB 253.

the plaintiff's contract. Two of the partners stayed in the business and offered to employ the plaintiff on the same terms as the original agreement. The plaintiff refused. He claimed damages for his loss of earnings over the remainder of the two years. However, his damages were reduced to a nominal award for failure to mitigate. It would have been reasonable to accept the partners' offer to remain in employment. The position would have been different if the relationship between employer and employee was a poor one, as where the employee was dismissed in humiliating circumstances.[79] Failure to mitigate was also found in *Payzu Ltd v Saunders*.[80] The defendants repudiated a contract under which it was bound to supply cloth to the plaintiff on credit. The defendants later offered to supply the cloth to the plaintiff on new terms, with payment to be made on delivery of each batch of cloth. The plaintiffs refused to accept the new deal. They claimed damages to cover the purchase of new cloth from an alternative supplier at an increased market price. The Court held that the plaintiffs had failed to mitigate their loss. Scrutton LJ held that in most commercial contracts, it will be reasonable to expect the plaintiff to accept an offer from the party in default. The breaching party bears the burden of proving failure to mitigate.[81]

[25–51]     There are two aspects to the duty to mitigate. First, the plaintiff must not do anything which will unreasonably increase his loss.[82] Secondly, the plaintiff must take all reasonable steps to minimise and contain his loss.[83] In *Dunkirk Colliery Co v Lever*[84] James LJ set out the rationale behind the rule:

> "The person who has broken the contract is not to be exposed to additional cost by reason of the plaintiffs not doing what they ought to have done as reasonable men, and the plaintiffs not being under any obligation to have to do anything otherwise than in the ordinary course of things."

[25–52]     The key word here is "reasonable". The law will not make substantial demands of the plaintiff in this regard. Tomlinson J observed in *Britvic Soft Drinks Ltd v Messer UK Ltd*[85] that the courts adopt a "tender approach to those who have been placed in a predicament by a breach of contract". Thus, if the innocent party's attempts to mitigate actually increase his losses, he may claim that extra expense, provided he has always acted reasonably. So in *Hoffberger v Ascot International Bloodstock*[86] the defendant breached his contract with the plaintiff by refusing to accept delivery of a horse which he had contracted to buy. The plaintiff kept the horse while he looked for a new buyer. He was entitled to claim the expense of keeping the horse in damages, as it was reasonable for him to house and feed the horse while attempting to mitigate his loss by selling it elsewhere. In the striking case of *Harbutt's Plasticine v Wayne Tank and Pump Co*,[87] the plaintiff built a new factory to replace one which was destroyed by

---

[79] *Payzu v Saunders* [1919] 2 KB 581.
[80] *ibid.*
[81] *James Finlay & Co v NV Kwik Hoo Tong HM* [1928] 2 KB 604.
[82] *Banco de Portugal v Waterlow & Sons* [1932] AC 452.
[83] *Pilkington v Wood* [1953] Ch 770.
[84] (1878) 9 Ch D 20.
[85] [2002] 1 Lloyd's Rep 20.
[86] 120 SJ 130.
[87] [1970] 1 QB 447.

fire occasioned by the defendant's breach of contract. He was allowed to recover the cost of building this factory. The Court held that by building the factory, he had been able to begin trading again, thus reducing the amount of time in respect of which he was claiming lost profits. He had therefore taken reasonable steps to mitigate his loss. In *Banco de Portugal v Waterlow* [88] Lord MacMillan warned against the danger of assessing reasonableness from the point of view of the breaching party. He emphasised that:

> ". . . the measures which [the injured party] may be driven to adopt in order to extricate himself ought not to be weighed in nice scales at the instance of the party whose breach of contract has occasioned the difficulty. It is often easy after an emergency has passed to criticize the steps which have been taken to meet it, but such criticism does not come well from those who have themselves created the emergency. The law is satisfied if the party placed in a difficult situation by reason of the breach of duty owed to him has acted reasonably in the adoption of remedial measures, and he will not be held disentitled to recover the cost of such measures merely because the party in breach can suggest that other measures less burdensome to him might have been taken . . .".

## VI. Will the Damages be reduced for Contributory Negligence?

Contributory negligence refers to the situation where the injured party has contributed to his injury through his own negligence. The Australian case of *Astley v Austrust Ltd* [89] presents a strong argument against the reduction of damages by reference to contributory negligence:  **[25–53]**

> "In contract, the plaintiff gives consideration, often very substantial considera-tion, for the defendant's promise to take reasonable care. The terms of the contract allocate responsibility for the risks of the parties' enterprise including the risk that the damage suffered . . . may arise partly from the failure of that party to take reasonable care . . . Rarely do contracts apportion responsibility for damage on the basis of the respective fault of the parties . . . Absent some contractual stipulation to the contrary, there is no reason of justice or sound legal policy which should prevent the plaintiff in a case such as the present recovering for all the damage that is causally connected to the defendant's breach even if the plaintiff's conduct has contributed to the damage which he or she has suffered . . . If the defendant wishes to reduce its liability in a situation where the plaintiff's own conduct contributes to the damage suffered, it is open to the defendant to make a bargain with the plaintiff to achieve that end."

Certainly, the English position under *Forsikringsaktieselskapet Vest v Butcher* [90] is that damages for breach of contract will not be reduced for contributory negligence  **[25–54]**

---

[88] Above, n 83.
[89] (1999) 197 CLR 1.
[90] [1988] 2 All ER 43.

except where liability in contract and in negligence are the same. However, in Ireland, damages may be reduced for contributory negligence under s 2 of the Civil Liability Act 1961. So, in *Lyons v Thomas*[91] the purchaser of property was awarded damages for the deterioration in the property between the time of agreement and the time the sale was completed. However, these damages were reduced by 10 per cent because the purchaser had noticed the deterioration but had failed to draw the vendor's attention to it.

## VII. Will the Court Award Punitive Damages?

[25–55]    The traditional view is that there is no possibility of awarding extra damages to punish the breaching party for the manner of his breach. In *Kuddus v Chief Constable of Leicestershire Constabulary*[92] Lord Nicholls explained the purpose behind punitive damages:

> "Stated in its broadest form, the relevant principle is tolerably clear: the availability of exemplary damages should be co-extensive with its rationale. As already indicated, the underlying rationale lies in the sense of outrage which a defendant's conduct sometimes evokes, a sense not always assuaged fully by a compensatory award of damages, even when the damages are increased to reflect emotional distress."

[25–56]    An award of damages to punish the breaching party is impermissible because it would be inconsistent with the overall aim of awarding damages. In *Ruxley v Forsyth* Lord Bridge observed that:

> "[D]amages for breach of contract must reflect, as accurately as the circumstances allow, the loss which the claimant has sustained because he did not get what he bargained for. There is no question of punishing the contract breaker."

[25–57]    In addition, the awarding of punitive damages clashes with the idea of contractual freedom. It has been noted already that a man is as free to break contracts as he is to make them. He should be free to breach his contract and pay compensatory damages if he chooses. Punitive damages would limit this freedom. Imagine A agrees to supply B with 1,000 crowbars for €1,000. If A does not supply the crowbars, B will suffer €250 loss and A will be liable to pay him €250 in compensatory damages. Before A supplies the crowbars to B, C offers to buy them for €1,500. In this situation, A can breach his contract with B by supplying the crowbars to C. He will have to pay damages to B but he will still make a profit because he has made a good bargain with C. In this situation, A arguably demonstrates the virtues expected by classical contract law. He has bargained well, rationally and selfishly. Law and economics theorists would also praise A for having made the economically efficient decision here. Law and economics say that a transaction is a good one if it is "Pareto

---

[91] [1986] IR 666. See also *O'Flynn v Balkan Tours*, unreported, Supreme Court, 7 April 1997.
[92] [2001] UKHL 29.

efficient", i.e. if it generates a net increase in wealth and does not leave anybody worse off as a result. If the courts had the power to award punitive damages to discourage parties from breaching their contracts as soon as a better deal came along, this desirable behaviour would be discouraged.

However, Cunnington in a recent article[93] has made a powerful argument in favour of awarding punitive damages. First, he notes that opportunistic breaches of contract do not generate a net increase in wealth: "the breaching party merely gains at the expense of the nonbreaching party. Opportunistic behaviour does not create wealth; it simply redistributes wealth from one another. And this redistribution actually consumes wealth because, 'potential opportunists and victims expend resources perpetrating and protecting against opportunism'." Opportunism should therefore be deterred by the award of punitive damages. Secondly, the threat of punitive damages would be an incentive to parties to renegotiate their contractual obligations rather than breaching. This is desirable because the transaction costs associated with assessing damages through litigation are very high. **[25–58]**

In *Johnson v Unisys Ltd*[94] it was clearly stated that punitive damages were not available for breach of contract in England. However, where a cause of action arises in both tort and contract, it is possible to justify an award of punitive damages by concentrating on the tortious aspect of the case.[95] In this jurisdiction, in *Garvey v Ireland*,[96] punitive damages were awarded to a Garda Commissioner who had been arbitrarily and summarily dismissed from his post in a manner incompatible with the Constitution. However, this appears to be a limited exception to the general Irish position that exemplary damages are not available for breach of contract.[97] The Law Reform Commission in its report "Aggravated, Exemplary and Restitutionary Damages"[98] has justified this position on the basis that the purpose of punitive damages is deterrence and an award of punitive damages is only justified where the case has some public element. Contract law is a private law subject and the breach of a contract tends only to affect the parties to it. **[25–59]**

Canada, by contrast, has a relatively well-developed body of case law on punitive damages. The cases provide that punitive damages are available "if but only if"[99] the compensatory award is insufficient. This will be the case where the contract "has been breached in a high-handed, shocking and arrogant fashion so as to demand **[25–60]**

---

[93] Cunnington, "Should Punitive Damages be part of the judicial arsenal in contract cases?" (2006) 26 LS 369.
[94] Above, n 46.
[95] *Drane v Evangelou* [1978] 1 WLR 459.
[96] Unreported, High Court, 19 December 1979.
[97] See Clark, *Contract Law in Ireland* (5th ed., Thomson Round Hall, 2004) p 550.
[98] LRC 60-2000.
[99] *Whiten v Pilot Insurance Co* (2002) 209 DLR (4d) 257.

condemnation by the court as a deterrent".[100] In *Whiten v Pilot Insurance*[101] Mrs Whiten sued her insurance company for breach of contract. The Whitens' home had burned down one night in mid-January. The family had fled the house in their night clothes. The temperature was minus 18 degrees Celsius. Mr Whiten suffered severe frostbite from standing in the snow in his bare feet and was confined to a wheelchair thereafter. The local fire chief and the insurance company's investigators concluded that the fire was accidental. The insurance company paid the family $5,000 for living expenses and covered their rent. However, in breach of contract, the insurance company stopped making the payments after a couple of months. They claimed that the Whitens had burned down their home themselves. The company persisted with these allegations in a hostile and confrontational manner for two years. The Supreme Court of Canada awarded $1 million in punitive damages because the insurance company had outrageously exploited the relationship of reliance and vulnerability between insurer and insured. They had aggravated the Whitens' vulnerability and loss as a negotiating tactic. The award was necessary to deter insurance companies from such behaviour.

## VIII. The Enforceability of Penalty Clauses and Liquidated Damages Clauses

[25–61] Freedom of contract entails that the parties have a limited entitlement to plan their own remedies. Sometimes the parties when negotiating their contract will provide that a certain figure in damages will be payable automatically in the event of certain types of breach. The aim of so-called agreed damages clauses is two-fold. First, the parties want to decide the issue of damages themselves in advance, rather than trusting to the expensive, and sometimes irrational, deliberations of the courts. Secondly, parties can assess the risk of breach more accurately where it is quantified in advance. These clauses are of two types: liquidated damages clauses and penalty clauses. Liquidated damages clauses are objectively reasonable[102] pre-estimates of the loss that will be occasioned by a breach of contract. They are enforceable. An example would be the clause in *Toomey v Murphy*.[103] The defendant agreed to complete construction work by a given date. He agreed to pay £5 per day for each day that the construction was late in being completed. This was held to be a liquidated damages clause. Penalty clauses are objectively unreasonable pre-estimates of the loss. They are designed to incentivise performance (so they are often called payments *in terrorem*) and to penalise non-performance. They are exemption clauses in reverse: just as an unreasonable limitation clause will seek to limit damages payable in the event of breach to a disproportionately small sum, so an unreasonable penalty clause will seek to impose damages which are wildly out of proportion with the harm caused by the breach. As is the case with exclusion clauses, the courts view these as abuses of contractual power, akin to Shylock's demand of a pound of flesh as a penalty for breach of his contract. An

---

[100] *Brown v Waterloo Regional Board of Commrs of Police* (1983) 103 DLR (3d) 748; *Pilato v Hamilton Place Convention Centre* (1984) 45 OR (2d) 652; *Fidler v Sun Life Assurance Co of Canada* [2006] SCR 3.

[101] Above, n 99.

[102] The cases often talk about the concept of "genuine" pre-estimates. See *Alfred Mc Alpine Capital Projects Ltd v Tilebox Ltd* [2005] EWHC 281 *per* Jackson J.

[103] [1897] 2 IR 601.

example of a penalty clause is that in *Giraud UK v Smith*.[104] The defendant was a driver whose contract of employment required him to give four weeks' notice before leaving his employment with the plaintiff. The contract provided that he would lose a day's wages in respect of each day for which inadequate notice was given. This penalty was to be in addition to damages for any actual loss occasioned by the breach. Maurice Kay J found that the clause was not an objectively reasonable pre-estimate of damages and that it operated in an oppressive manner. It was struck down as a penalty clause. In *Jobson v Johnson*[105] Nicholls J said that a penalty clause in a contract is "a dead letter" or a *brutum fulmen*. You can sue on a penalty clause but if the actual loss occasioned by the breach is less than the amount provided for in the penalty clause you will only be able to recover the lower amount.[106] Clark suggests that it may also be that if the actual loss suffered is greater than the amount provided for in the penalty clause, recovery will be limited to that amount.[107]

Anthony Kronman and Richard Posner in their book *The Economics of Contract Law* argue that "economic analysis of penal clauses makes clear that a clause of this sort cannot simply be condemned as nothing more than a side bet between the parties which serves no useful purpose". They call the courts' strict approach to penalty clauses a "medicine which kills the patient":   **[25–62]**

> "[Penalty clauses] have two important economic uses, and might be widely employed if they were permitted. First … a penal clause may be useful to a buyer who has reason to believe that his normal money damages remedy will be inadequate and who wants to force his seller to buy his way out of the contract before breaching. Second, for a seller who has not yet developed a reputation for reliability, agreeing to a penal clause may be the cheapest way to persuade his buyers that he is willing and able to perform …".

Penalty clauses, therefore, have their uses, and the courts' jurisdiction in respect of penalty clauses is an important exception to the general principle of freedom of contract. Because of this, the courts now tend towards a position of non-interference. The burden of proving that a clause ought to be struck down as a penalty falls on the party arguing that it is not a genuine pre-estimate of the loss. Furthermore, in the interests of certainty, the courts assess the clause at the date of entering into the contract: classification of the clause does not depend on future, unknown events.   **[25–63]**

The parties may label a clause as a penalty clause or a liquidated damages clause but their labelling, though relevant, will not be conclusive.[108] In *Dunlop Pneumatic Tyre Co. Ltd v New Garage & Motor Co. Ltd*[109] Lord Dunedin said that the question whether a sum stipulated was a penalty clause or a liquidated damages clause was a matter of construction. He proposed four important principles of construction   **[25–64]**

---

[104] [2000] IRLR 763.

[105] [1989] 1 WLR 1026.

[106] *Schiesser v Gallagher* (1976) 106 ILTR 22.

[107] Clark, *Contract Law in Ireland* (5th ed., Thomson Round Hall, 2004) p 584.

[108] *Toomey v Murphy*, above, n 104; *Gerrard v O'Reilly* (1843) 2 Connor and Lawson 165; *Kemble v Farren* (1829) 6 Bing 141; *Cellulose Acetate Silk Co v Widnes Foundry* [1933] AC 20.

[109] [1915] AC 79.

which were adopted into Irish law in *Irish Telephone Rentals Ltd v Irish Civil Service Building*.[110]

[25–65]     First, a clause "will be held to be penalty if the sum stipulated for is extravagant and unconscionable in amount in comparison with the greatest loss that could conceivably be proved to have followed from the breach ...". In *Clydebank Engineering and Shipbuilding Co. v Don Jose Ramos Yzquierdo y Castaneda*[111] Lord Halsbury gave the example of a contract to build a house for £50 which contained a clause to the effect that, in the event of breach, one million pounds was payable as a penalty.

[25–66]     Observe that the comparison is between the amount of damages provided for by the clause and the anticipated loss, not the actual loss which occurs as a result of the breach. This is a very difficult criterion to satisfy. In *Philips Hong Kong v A-G of Hong Kong*[112] Lord Woolf advocated a non-interventionist approach:

> "Except possibly in the case of situations where one of the parties to the contract is able to dominate the other as to the choice of the terms of a contract, it will normally be insufficient to establish that a provision is objectionably penal to identify situations where the application of the provision could result in a larger sum being recovered from the injured party than his actual loss. Even in such situations so long as the sum payable in the event of non-compliance with the contract is not extravagant, having regard to the range of losses that it could reasonably be anticipated it would have to cover at the time the contract was made, it can still be a genuine pre-estimate of the loss that would be suffered and so a perfectly valid liquidated damage provision."

Later English cases have confirmed that a clause will not be treated as a penalty purely because the amount payable on breach is greater than the loss sustained, provided that the amount payable is not extravagant. In *Lordsvale v Bank of Zambia* [1996] QB 752[113] Coleman J said that the clause would not always be struck down "if it could in the circumstances be explained as commercially justifiable provided always that the dominant purpose was not to deter the other party from breach".

[25–67]     Secondly, a clause "will be held to be a penalty if the breach consists only in not paying a sum of money, and the sum stipulated is a sum greater than the sum which ought to have been paid ...". The point here is clear. The value of the breach has already been decided and so, objectively, the fixing of a larger sum cannot amount to a genuine pre-estimate of the damage. So Lawson J noted in *Wright v Tracey*[114] that a clause is a penalty clause which requires a person to pay £200 upon failure to pay £50 in rent. The obligation to pay £50 rent is breached "only in not paying a sum of money". The sum of £200 is "a sum greater than the sum which ought to have been paid ...". Clauses that require the breaching party to pay the original sum of money

---

[110] [1991] ILRM 880.

[111] [1905] AC 6. See also *Ford Motor Co v Armstrong* (1915) TLR 267.

[112] (1993) 1 BLR 41. Confirmed in *McAlpine Capital Projects v Tilebox Ltd* [2005] EWHC 281.

[113] See eg *Murray v Leisureplay* [2005] IRLR 946; *Euro London Appointments v Claessens International* [2006] 2 Lloyd's Rep 463.

[114] (1873) IR 7 CL 134.

due plus commercial interest are not penalty clauses.[115] Acceleration clauses are not generally penalty clauses either. Acceleration clauses are used in contracts where a sum of money is payable in instalments. They provide that if one payment is missed the whole sum becomes due immediately. The validity of these clauses has been confirmed in England in *Protector Loan Co v Grice*[116] and in Ireland in *National Telephone Co v Griffen*.[117] However, interest charged on an accelerated payment cannot be any greater than the interest that would have been payable if the borrower had simply elected to pay off the loan early.[118]

Thirdly, "there is a presumption (but no more) that a clause it is a penalty when a 'single lump sum is made payable by way of compensation, on the occurrence of one or more or all of several events, some of which may occasion serious and others but trifling damage'." For example, in *Jobson v Johnson*[119] the defendant had purchased shares in a football club. The contract price was £351,668. The defendant paid £40,000 up front, with the balance due in six half yearly instalments. The contract provided that if the defendant defaulted on any one of the payments, he would have to sell the shares back to the plaintiff for £40,000. This clause applied whether the defendant defaulted on his first or on his final payment. This clause applied to all of several events (each of six potential failures to pay was a separate event). Each event had varying consequences: if the defendant defaulted in his fifth payment he would have to sell back more shares for £40,000 than if he had defaulted on his first payment. Therefore, it was a penalty clause. A similar case is *Schiesser International v Gallagher*.[120] The defendant went to Germany to be trained as a textile cutter. He agreed that if he left the plaintiff's employment within three years of returning to Ireland he would pay them for his training and travel expenses. He would have had to repay the same sum whether he left their employment on the day he returned to Ireland or two years later even though the consequences for his employer would have been very different depending on the date of his departure. Therefore, the clause was a penalty clause. On the other hand, where the clause relates to just one event, it is liquidated damages. So in *Law v Redditch Local Board*[121] a construction contract provided that if sewage works were not completed by 30 April, the contract would pay £100 and £5 for every seven days during which the work remained unfinished. Similarly, a clause is not a penalty clause which relates to several events, the consequences of which are of broadly similar importance. In *Re An Arranging Debtor*[122] patentees installed equipment under a contract. The contract provided that £30 would be payable if any of three events occurred: if the hirers allowed others to use, repair or purchase the machinery. The clause therefore applied to several events. However, these events were of equal and not varying importance. Therefore, the clause was not a penalty clause.

[25–68]

---

[115] *O'Donnell & Co Ltd v Truck & Machinery Sales* [1998] 4 IR 191.
[116] (1880) 5 QBD 529.
[117] [1906] 2 IR 115.
[118] *UDT Ltd v Patterson* [1975] NI 142.
[119] Above, n 106.
[120] Above, n 107.
[121] [1892] 1 QB 127.
[122] (1961) 51 ILTR 68.

[25–69]     The final principle in *Dunlop* is that it:

> "... is no obstacle to the sum stipulated being a [liquidated damages clause], that the consequences of the breach are such as to make precise pre-estimation almost an impossibility. On the contrary, that is just the situation when it is probable that pre-estimated damage was the true bargain between the parties ...".

[25–70]     This principle was applied in *Dunlop* itself. Dunlop sold car tyres to dealers who sold them on in turn. The dealers had agreed not to sell the tyres to private customers at below Dunlop's list price. The contract stated that, in the event that this obligation was breached, the dealers were to pay Dunlop £5 as "liquidated damages". There was evidence that failure to maintain the price sold would cause damage to Dunlop on a broad scale because all of Dunlop's business was done through dealers and when one dealer sold at undervalue, it encouraged other dealers to buy their tyres elsewhere. However, it was not possible to prove with any precision what loss would result to Dunlop from one sale at undervalue. However, as Lord Dunedin's test sets out, the difficulty of estimating the loss did not mean that the £5 clause was a penalty clause.

# CHAPTER 26
# Capacity to Contract

## I. Introduction

Contractual capacity refers to the ability to enter into a contract. The discussion in this chapter is confined to personal capacity. It does not cover lack of capacity arising through the doctrine of *ultra vires* in relation to companies. Generally, personal contractual capacity is presumed at common law. However, exceptions are made for the mentally ill, for those contracting under the influence of drugs or alcohol, and for minors. These categories of person, excluded from the usual realm of contract, have been called *civiliter mortuus*: those who are "dead in the eyes of the law". In *Hall v Butterfield*[1] the New Hampshire State Supreme Court explained why these categories of person are excluded from contract:

[26–01]

> "[T]he right of infants, lunatics, persons *non compos mentis*, and drunkards ... is placed on the same ground. They are considered to be devoid of that freedom of will, combined with maturity of reason and judgment, essential to enable them to give the assent necessary to make a valid contract."

## II. Minors and Contractual Capacity

In Ireland, a person reaches majority upon his 18th birthday or upon marriage.[2] Until one of those two things happens, he lacks full contractual capacity. Minor incapacity has been recognised since 1292.[3] It is the only category where incapacity is conclusively presumed. This means that the minor does not have to make any effort to prove that he lacked contractual capacity. He need only demonstrate that he was a minor at the time of contracting. The test of incapacity is based purely on age; the individual minor

[26–02]

---

[1]  59 NH 354 (1879).
[2]  Age of Majority Act 1985, s 3.
[3]  YB 20 & 21 Edw I 318 (1292).

party's maturity and ability to understand the contract are irrelevant. In addition, it is irrelevant whether the other party realised or ought reasonably to have realised that he was dealing with a minor. In most circumstances, the law presumes that all minors, from children spending their first communion money to 17-year-old students of contract law must be protected from exploitation. This is done by limiting their power to enter into binding contracts. There are three important categories of contract where minors are concerned: contracts which are always binding on a minor; contracts which are binding on a minor unless repudiated on the attainment of majority; and contracts which are void under the Infants Relief Act 1874. It is now over 20 years since the Law Reform Commission issued its *Report on Minors' Contracts.*[4] The Commission made a number of proposals for the drafting of legislation on the contractual capacity of minors. However, these have never been implemented. A few of the most important recommendations will be discussed in this section.

### Contracts Always Binding on a Minor

[26-03]  Contracts for necessaries and beneficial contracts of service will bind a minor.[5] This exception to the general rule of incapacity is justified on the basis that these types of contract benefit the minor. The adult who enters into a contract of this type with a minor is not taking advantage of his vulnerability in order to do him some harm.[6]

### *Contracts for Necessaries*

[26-04]  Contracts for necessaries are contracts for goods which are binding on the minor. It should be noted from the outset that, under s 2 of the Sale of Goods Act 1893, the minor is only bound to pay a "reasonable" price for them. What sort of goods will count as necessaries? The concept is such a vague one that the Law Reform Commission's 1985 Report recommends its abolition as a separate category of contract. The Court in *Merrick*[7] observed that: "[j]ust what are necessaries has no exact definition ... It depends upon many things, including the particular circumstances of the minor, his actual need, and the use to which the purchased article is to be put". In *Chapple v Cooper*[8] Baron Alderson provided the following explanation of the concept:

> Now it seems clear that an infant can contract so as to bind himself in those cases where it is necessary for him to have the things for which he contracts; or where the contract is, at the time he makes it, plainly and unequivocally for his benefit. It is with the former class that we are concerned. Things necessary are those without which an individual cannot reasonably exist. In the first place, food, raiment, lodging, and the like. About these there is no doubt. Again, as the proper cultivation of the mind is as expedient as the support of the body, instruction in art or trade, or intellectual, moral and religious information may be a necessary also. Again, as man lives in society, the assistance and

---

[4]  (LRC 15-1985), pp 5-6. See Clark, *Contract Law in Ireland* (5th ed, Round Hall, 2004) pp 461-464.
[5]  *Roberts v Gray* [1913] 1 KB 520.
[6]  *Ryder v Wombwell* (1868) LR 4 Ex 32.
[7]  337 SW 2d 713 (Mo Ct App, 1960).
[8]  (1844) 13 M & W 252.

attendance of others may be a necessary to his well-being. Hence attendance may be the subject of an infant's contract."

What will constitute a "necessary" depends very much on the facts of the case. Section 2 of the Sale of Goods Act 1893 defined necessaries as "goods suitable to the condition in life of such infant or minor ... and to his actual requirements at the time of sale and delivery". There are two distinct elements to the statutory definition: the minor's condition in life and his actual requirements. [26–05]

The "condition in life" element of the test enables the court to draw the line between necessaries and luxuries such as hunting horses,[9] flying lessons[10] or jewelled cufflinks[11]. If a minor enters into a contract for luxury goods or services, he is not bound to pay for them. If he does pay for them, he may recover his payment. That said, in the right circumstances, goods which would otherwise be luxuries may be characterised as necessaries. In *Chapple v Cooper*[12] Baron Alderson wrote that: "[an infant's] clothes may be fine or course according to his rank; his education may vary according to the station he is to fill". Thus, in *Peters v Fleming*[13] a breast pin and watch chain were held to be necessaries for the son of a "gentleman of fortune and a Member of Parliament". A bicycle will be a necessary where an infant needs it to get to work,[14] a motorboat will be a necessary for a minor who lives in a remote lakeland area,[15] a horse may be a necessary to an ailing minor who needs one for exercise[16] and a gun will be a necessary for a minor who works as a gamekeeper.[17] Treitel has observed that, in the case of some of the older judgments at least, the notion of "necessaries" was manipulated, not for the benefit of the minor, but in order to protect suppliers who gave credit to the sons of wealthy families. In addition, in the days when juries played a role in determining issues of fact in contract law, a jury of 12 shopkeepers might stretch the definition of "necessaries" beyond its proper limits.[18] [26–06]

The second element of the test, "actual requirements", may operate so that a good which would normally be considered a necessary will be treated as a luxury where the minor has plenty of that type of good already. *Nash v Inman*[19] concerned the supply of 11 waistcoats to a minor. Clothing would normally be considered a necessary, but in this case the waistcoats were treated as a luxury because the minor had sufficient clothes already. Cozens-Hardy MR applied the following dictum of Lindley LJ in *Barnes v Toye*[20]: "If he has enough of articles, more cannot possibly be necessary to him". [26–07]

---

9 *Skrine v Gordon* (1875) IR 9 CL 479.
10 *Adamowski v Curtis-Wright Flying Service* 15 NE 2d 467 (Mass 1938).
11 Above, n 6.
12 Above, n 8.
13 (1840) 9 LJ Ex 81.
14 *Scarborough v Sturzaker* (1905) 1 Tas LR 117.
15 *Prokopetz v Richardsons Marina* (1979) 93 DLR (3d) 442.
16 *O'Neill v Reid* (1845) 7 Ir L Rep 434.
17 *Dickson v Buller* (1859) 9 ICLR.
18 Treitel, *The Law of Contract* (11th ed, Sweet & Maxwell, 2003) p 540.
19 [1908] 2 KB 1.
20 13 QBD 410.

**[26–08]**    Contracts for necessaries are upheld because they are assumed to be of benefit to the minor. It stands to reason, therefore, that nobody can rely on a contract for the supply of necessaries to a minor if the terms of the contract are harsh or onerous. For example, in *Fawcett v Smethurst*[21] it was held that a contract for the hire of a motor vehicle, albeit a contract for necessaries in the circumstances, would not be enforced if it was subject to an express term placing the responsibility for loss or damage on the infant hirer in all circumstances.

### Beneficial Contracts of Service

**[26–09]**  Lord Coke defined a beneficial contract of service as "a contract for [the minor's] good teaching or instruction whereby he may profit himself afterwards".[22] A beneficial contract of service is one which enables a minor to earn a living, to obtain training or to gain an education. An example would be a contract of apprenticeship. It is important to note that this exception to the general rule of minor incapacity is confined to contracts of service. There is no broader exception encompassing all contracts which are of benefit to the minor.

**[26–10]**    Where a contract of service is not beneficial to the minor, he is not bound to it. The court in *Clements v London & North Western Railway*[23] said that, in determining whether the contract is beneficial, the court looks at the "true construction of the contract as a whole".[24] These principles were applied in *Doyle v White City Stadium*.[25] In that case, a minor entered into a contract under which he agreed to box under the British Boxing Board of Control Rules. This was a contract of service because it enabled him to start to make his living. The question for the Court was whether it should be upheld as beneficial. Under the Rules, Doyle was required to forfeit his purse if he was disqualified. Arguably, this was to Doyle's disadvantage. However, the Court felt that the contract was a beneficial one over all because it generally benefited him by upholding the dignity of the sport and secured his benefit by ensuring that rules existed to encourage clean fighting. A similar result was reached in *Chaplin v Leslie Frewin*.[26] The minor son of Charlie Chaplin had contracted to give a firm of publishers the exclusive right to publish his memoirs: *I Couldn't Smoke the Grass on my Father's Lawn*. The minor argued that the book would affect his reputation. Lord Denning agreed, holding that the contract was not binding as it was not for the minor's benefit that "he should exploit his discreditable conduct for money". However, the majority of the Court held that the contract was binding. On the whole, the contract was to the minor's benefit because it enabled him to make a start as an author and "the mud may cling but the profit will be secured". By contrast, in *De Francesco v Barnum*,[27] a girl contracted with Signor De Francesco to be taught to dance. She was bound to him for seven years. He was not obliged to maintain her. He was not even bound to pay her, unless he obtained engagements for her, in which case he paid her very little. She could

---

[21] [1914] 84 LJKB 473.

[22] Quoted by Fry LJ in *De Francesco v Barnum* (1890) 45 Ch D 430.

[23] [1894] 2 QB 482.

[24] *Clements v North Western Railway Co* [1894] 2 QB 482 *per* Lord Esher.

[25] [1935] KB 110.

[26] [1966] Ch 71.

[27] Above, n 22.

not obtain engagements for herself, or marry without De Francesco's consent. The contract was not enforceable because its terms were unreasonable and not for the girl's benefit. In the recent case of *Proform Sports Management Ltd v Proactive Sports Management Ltd and another*,[28] the footballer Wayne Rooney entered into a representation agreement with Proform when he was 15 years of age. The Court held that this agreement did not constitute a beneficial contract of service and so Rooney was not bound by it. This was because Rooney took no benefit under the contract: the agreement did not involve any element of education or training and there was nothing in it which enabled him to start to earn his living as a professional footballer.

A contract is unlikely to be treated as a beneficial contract of service where it is **[26–11]** subject to a wide-ranging clause excluding the adult party from liability in tort or for breach of contract. In both *Keays v Great Southern Rly Co*[29] and *Brennan v GNR*[30] minors had bought tickets for rail travel. Each contract was subject to a broad clause to the effect that the railway company was not liable for the consequences of its negligence. Neither contract was a beneficial contract because the exemption clauses were so wide as to deprive the minors of any significant rights against the railway companies. These contracts were prejudicial rather than beneficial to the minors and so they could not be enforced against them. These cases can be contrasted with the older case of *Clements v London and North Western Railway*.[31] A minor was employed as a porter with the railway company. His employment contract required him to give up any potential claim for personal injury under the Employer's Liability Act 1880. However, alternative provision was made for him. He was entitled to take on insurance, the premiums for which were partly paid by the railway. The statutory provision was more generous in some respects, the insurance in others. The Court looked at the overall character of the contract and decided that, on the whole, it was for the minor employee's benefit and therefore enforceable.

## Contracts Binding Unless Minor Chooses to Repudiate it on Attaining Majority

There are a number of instances in which contracts are voidable at the option of the **[26–12]** minor: the minor party will be bound by the contract unless he repudiates it on attaining majority or within a reasonable time thereafter.[32] The relevant categories of contract are: contracts of insurance,[33] contracts to buy or lease land, contracts for marriage settlements,[34] contracts to buy shares in a company[35] and contracts to enter into a partnership.[36] These contracts are said to be ones which impose recurring obligations on the minor.

---

[28] [2006] EWHC 2812.
[29] [1941] IR 534.
[30] (1935) 68 ILTR 145. See also *Harnedy v National Greyhound Racing Co* [1944] IR 160.
[31] [1894] 2 QB 482.
[32] *Edwards v Carter* [1893] AC 360.
[33] *Stapleton v Prudential* (1928) 62 ILTR 56.
[34] Above, n 32.
[35] *Steinberg v Scala* [1923] 2 Ch 352.
[36] *Goode v Harrison* (1821) 5 B & Ald 157.

**[26–13]**    Such contracts are entirely valid unless or until repudiated. Only the minor bears the right of repudiation. The adult is bound by the contract unless the minor casts it off in good time. It is important that the minor acts promptly to repudiate the contract once he achieves majority. "If he chooses to be inactive, his opportunity passes away; if he chooses to be active the law comes to his assistance".[37] So, in *Edwards v Carter*,[38] a minor sought to repudiate a marriage settlement four-and-a-half years after coming of age. It was held that he was bound by the contract as the repudiation came too late. This case can be contrasted with *Paget v Paget*.[39] The plaintiff in this case, unknown to himself, was 20 years old at the time when he agreed with his father upon terms for the resettlement of family property. The age of majority at the time was 21. Ten years later, the plaintiff discovered that he had been a minor at the time of the settlement. He was held entitled to repudiate the contract as he had acted within a reasonable time after learning the true facts.

**[26–14]**    Repudiation releases the minor from any contractual obligations to perform in the future. What of contractual obligations which have already accrued? It was held in the Irish case of *Blake v Concannon*[40] that any contractual obligations incurred before the repudiation will still be binding on the minor. So, for example, if a minor has entered into a lease, he is liable for the rent arising under the lease unless he repudiates it. However, the opposite conclusion was reached in *North Western Railway v McMichael*,[41] in which Baron Parke held that the minor's repudiation of the contract had retrospective effect. Repudiation was, in this sense, analogous to rescission: it unpicked the contract entirely and put the parties in the position they would have been in had the contract never happened.

**[26–15]**    If the minor has already paid money under a contract of this type, he can recover it if there has been a total failure of consideration, i.e. if he has not received anything at all in return for that money, or rather, if the other party has not performed any of the contractual duties in respect of which the money was due.[42] A minor succeeded in doing this in *Corpe v Overton*.[43] The minor in this case had agreed to enter into a partnership with the defendant. He was to pay the defendant £1,000 when the partnership deed was executed. He paid £100 immediately as security. The minor repudiated the contract as soon as he came of age. No part of the partnership contract had been performed at this point. The minor was able to show total failure of consideration and so he was able to recover his £100. By contrast, in *Stapleton v Prudential*[44] the Court held that a minor was not entitled to recover premiums paid under a life insurance contract. Sullivan P noted that she had received what she had

---

[37] Above, n 32.

[38] *ibid.*

[39] (1882) 11 LR (Ir) 26.

[40] (1879) 4 Ir Rep CL 320.

[41] (1850) 5 Exch 114.

[42] Above, n 35.

[43] (1883) 10 Bing 252.

[44] (1928) 62 ILTR 56.

paid for because, if she had died in the years before repudiation, the insurance company would have been bound to pay out on the contract of insurance. Similarly, in *Steinberg v Scala*[45] a minor was allotted shares in a company. She repudiated the contract in good time. She was not liable for future calls (demands to pay money still due on the shares). However, she could not recover the money she had already paid because there had not been a total failure of consideration: she had received her shares in exchange for the money paid. In *Holmes v Blogg*[46] a minor paid money to a lessor as part of a lease for a premises. The day after he came of age he repudiated the lease and left the premises. He could not recover the money he had paid because he had received the thing for which he had made payment: the use of the premises. In this respect, the minor's entitlements to restitution are no stronger than those of an adult in the same position. While the law is unduly indulgent of minors in some areas, it is arguably too harsh here. Under the Law Reform Commission's 1985 proposals, the minor would be able to apply to the Court for restitutionary relief in a situation such as that in *Stapleton*, *Steinberg* or *Holmes*.

### Section 1 of the Infants Relief Act 1874

Section 1 of this Act states that three types of contract are absolutely void: contracts for the repayment of money lent or to be lent to a minor, contracts for goods supplied or to be supplied to a minor (excluding, of course, contracts for necessaries) and all accounts stated with minors.[47] The Law Reform Commission's 1985 Report recommended that no action should be possible upon a loan made to a minor, even where that loan was used to pay for necessaries.     [26–16]

### Section 2 of the Infants Relief Act 1874

Section 2 of the Act sets out two key principles. The first is that a promise made after a minor has attained majority, to pay a debt which he incurred while he was a minor, cannot be sued upon. This principle is reinforced by s 5 of the Betting and Loans (Infants) Act 1892. The Law Reform Commission's 1985 Report favoured the retention of this rule. The second element of s 2 is a catch-all principle. It covers those situations not specifically dealt with by the common law rules including those where a contract for the sale of goods is held not to be a contract for necessaries and where a contract of service is not beneficial on the whole. It states that a minor's contract which is (i) neither a binding contract for necessaries, (ii) nor a binding beneficial contract of service, (iii) nor a voidable contract of the types discussed in paragraph 26-12 can never be sued upon even if the minor ratified that contract when he attained majority. The Law Reform Commission in its Report took the view that minors, upon coming of age, should have the option of ratifying contracts made during their minority. The Commission recommended a validation procedure which would enable the parties to approve such a contract where appropriate having regard to the nature, subject-matter and terms of the contract, the reasonable likelihood of performance, the minor's requirements, his financial resources and the wishes of his guardians.     [26–17]

---

[45] Above, n 35.

[46] (1818) 8 Taunt 508.

[47] An account stated is a statement (such as a bill or a collections of invoices) between a creditor and a debtor that a particular amount is owed to the creditor as of a certain date.

## The Rationale Behind the Doctrine of Minor Incapacity

[26–18] We have said that doctrine of minor incapacity is geared towards protecting minors, who are presumed to be inherently vulnerable and ill-suited to dealing within the market. The doctrine was explained thus in the American case of *Halbman v Lemke*[48]:

> "The doctrine of contractual capacity or the 'infancy law doctrine' is one of the oldest and most venerable of our common law traditions ... It is generally recognized that its purpose is the protection of minors from foolishly squandering their wealth through improvident contracts with crafty adults."

[26–19] By the common law rules on infant contracts, the courts discourage adults from exploiting their vulnerability: "one deals with infants at one's peril".[49] Take for example the subjectivity of the test for necessaries: whether a contract for the sale of a good will be upheld depends entirely on the idiosyncrasies of the minor purchaser's situation. We must ask whether this approach takes due account of the interests of the adult party dealing with a minor. In *Wharton v Mackenzies*[50] Lord Denman CJ simply stated that: "it is the duty of tradesmen to make themselves acquainted with the circumstances of the party they are supplying". This is an onerous duty. How is the adult to judge whether his contract will be upheld or not? He may be discouraged from dealing with minors at all.

## Criticisms of the Rule

[26–20] This strict application of a chronological test of capacity is controversial. In *Hall v Butterfield*[51] Judge Stanley said that the test "may well abate the boast, so often and so rashly made, that the common law is the perfection of reason". Certainly, a bright line distinction is certain and easy to apply. However, a universal threshold for capacity fails to appreciate the differing maturity and sophistication of individual minors. So it has been said that: "[t]he magical age limit ... as an indication of contractual maturity no longer has a basis in fact or in public policy."[52] It is further submitted that today's minors are much better equipped to deal in the market than were the innocent infants of the golden age of contract law. There is a sense in which the courts are privileging precedent above social reality. Mehler speaks eloquently to this point[53]:

> "The minor has long remained a special charge of the law. But in our fast-moving and rapidly changing society, the ancient timeworn cloak of protection thrown over him has long since lost its real need or useful purpose. The technologically oriented and knowledgeably mature youth of our hectic age is not at all comparable to the minor of even five or six decades ago who needed the solicitous attention and protection the law so thoughtfully afforded him."

---

[48] *Halbman v Lemke* 298 NW 2d 562 (Wis 1980).
[49] *Pollock v Industrial Accident Comm'n* 54 P 2D 695 (Cal 1936).
[50] (1844) 5 QB 606.
[51] 59 NH 354 (1879).
[52] *Kiefer v Fred Howe Motors Inc* 158 NW 2d 288 (Wis 1968).
[53] Mehler "Infant Contractual Responsibilty: A Time for Reappraisal and Realistic Adjustment?" (1963) 11 Kan L Rev 361.

It might further be said that the law on minor incapacity emphasises the protection of minors to the detriment of the rights of innocent adults who deal unknowingly in good faith with minors. In many cases, a minor has an automatic right to reject a contract purely on the basis of his age, regardless of the fairness of the contract or the interests of the other party. A minor might reject a contract *mala fides* with perfect impunity.[54] So an earlier commentator asked:

[26–21]

> "'Infantile Paralysis' is a term well applicable to the state of the law governing an infant's responsibility for [her] contractual obligations. The rigid niceties involved are indeed perplexing. Infancy has ever been a safe base from which one might embark upon piratical expeditions against innocent adults and to the technical defenses of which [she] could return for security. Shall its sanctity be preserved when justice obviously requires a remedy for the victims?"[55]

There has been some suggestion, therefore, both here[56] and in Canada,[57] that the law on unconscionability would form a better basis for the law of minor incapacity. Thus, oppressive contracts with minors could be set aside, while fair ones would remain in force. The Law Reform Commission's 1985 Report proposed that the existing regime be replaced with a more nuanced one based on restitutionary principles: "which seeks to impose contractual responsibility on minors to the extent that it would be fair to do so, but no further". A contract between a minor and an adult would be enforceable against the latter but not *vice versa*. Instead the adult would be entitled to apply to the court for compensation based on restitutionary principles, rectifying the current position under which he is generally unable to recover property or receive compensation.

[26–22]

What of taking responsibility for one's actions? Critics have pointed to the contrast between minor liability in criminal law and in tort and the liability of minors in contract. In *Porter v Wilson*[58] the Court remarked: "a stranger must think it strange that a minor may be liable for his crimes and yet is not bound by his contracts". There is an important issue here in terms of the law's role in encouraging people to keep their promises: what Macneil has called the "social purpose of contract".[59] An American Court has argued that the doctrine of infant incapacity undermines this purpose by absolving the young of responsibility for their promises[60]:

[26–23]

> "[The doctrine] does not appear consistent with practice of proper moral influence upon young people, tend to encourage honesty or integrity, or lead

---

[54] Limited remedies are available if a minor induces another to contract by lying about his age. He is not liable in the tort of deceit; *R Leslie Ltd v Shiell* [1914] 3 KB 607. However, he may be compelled to return any goods of which he has obtained possession by fraud, provided he is still in possession of them; *Lempriére v Lange* (1879) 12 Ch D 675. He may also be held liable to account in equity for any money obtained by fraud; *Stocks v Wilson* [1913] 2 KB 235.

[55] Comment, "Liability of an Infant for Fraudulent Misrepresentation" (1921) 31 Yale LJ 201.

[56] *Aylward v Kearney* (1814) 2 Ball & B 463.

[57] *Toronto Marlboro Hockey Club v Tonelli* (1979) 96 DLR (3d) 135.

[58] 209 A 2d 730 (NH 1965).

[59] Macneil, "The Many Futures of Contracts" (1974) 47 S Cal L Rev 691.

[60] *Dodson by Dodson* 824 SW 2d 545 (Tenn 1992) 550.

them to a good and useful business future … Such a doctrine can only lead to the corruption of principles and encourage young people in habits of trickery and dishonesty."

[26–24]     Finally, the doctrine of minor incapacity does not make a great deal of economic sense. It undermines the thriving market in products designed to appeal to children and teenagers. It also handicaps ambitious and competent young people who wish to contribute to the economy. "The law will not suffer him to trade, which may be his undoing".[61] Granted, if a minor makes his living through a sport, art or profession the relevant contract will often be enforceable as a beneficial contract of service. If he makes his living by trading[62] the story is different because, for example, contracts for the sale of equipment needed for business purposes[63] or of stock in trade[64] will not be treated as contracts for necessaries. The distinction between these two types of contract is illogical and the restrictive concept of necessaries acts as a disincentive to vendors who would wish to trade with enterprising minors on an equal basis. In *Zouch v Parsons*,[65] a founding case on the doctrine of necessaries, Lord Mansfield acknowledged that the rules on capacity serve to exclude minors from the market:

"[M]iserable must the condition of minors be; excluded from the society of the world; deprived of necessaries, education, employment and many advantages, if they could do no binding acts. Great inconvenience must arise to others, if they were bound by no act."

[26–25]     Arguably, the existing exceptional categories of contract do not go far enough towards redressing these disadvantages.

## III. Mental Incapacity

[26–26]     Contracts for necessaries are binding on a mentally incapacitated person, provided that it was intended that the necessaries were to be paid for.[66] The mentally incapacitated person is liable only to pay a reasonable price for them under s 2 of the Sale of Goods Act. All other contracts are voidable at the option of the mentally incapacitated person provided he can fulfil a two-fold test. First, he must show that he was unable to understand and thus consent to the transaction. Secondly, he must show that the other party knew of his incapacity and lack of understanding. In *Imperial Loan Co v Stone*[67] Lord Esher MR wrote:

"When a person enters into a contract, and afterwards alleges that he was so insane at the time that he did not know what he was doing, and proves the

---

[61]  *Whywall v Campion* (1738) 2 Stra 1083.
[62]  *Cowern v Nield* [1912] 2 KB 419.
[63]  *Mercantile Union v Ball* [1937] 2 KB 498.
[64]  *Whittingham v Hill* (1619) Cro Jac 494.
[65]  (1765) 3 Burr 1794.
[66]  *Re Rhodes* (1889) 44 Ch D 94.
[67]  [1892] 1 QB 599.

allegation, the contract is binding on him in every respect ... as if he had been sane when he made it, unless he can prove further that the person with whom he contracted knew him to be so insane as not to be capable of understanding what he was about."

This knowledge requirement is not applied to minors. One justification for the [26–27] addition of this extra element to mental incapacity cases is that it draws a distinction between minors and those affected by mental impairment and so avoids infantilising the latter. In addition, if transactions with apparently sane persons were presumptively void, parties dealing with certain classes of people, in particular the elderly, might take undesirable steps to protect themselves, such as requiring such persons to submit to tests of mental capacity, or involving their families. Such steps would have the effect of undermining the autonomy of certain vulnerable categories of contractor. However, the knowledge requirement may be criticised on the basis that A's knowledge of B's infirmity has no direct bearing on B's actual capacity to consent to a contract.

There has been some debate as to whether the courts should be able to set [26–28] aside a contract where one party is of unsound mind even where the other party lacks knowledge of it. In the old Irish case of *Hassard v Smith*,[68] Chatterton V-C softened the knowledge requirement by setting out a constructive rather than an actual test for knowledge of incapacity:

"The knowledge of lunacy or incapacity ... must be understood to mean not merely actual knowledge, but that which must be presumed, from circumstances known to the other contracting party, sufficient to lead any reasonable person to conclude that, at the time the contract was made, the person with whom he was dealing was of unsound mind."

Chatterton V-C accepted that such knowledge might be inferred from the [26–29] substantive fairness of the contract. For example, in some circumstances, if one party offers to sell at a gross undervalue, the other may be taken to know that he is labouring under a defect of reason.

In *Archer v Coulter*[69] the Court took a different route, proposing two [26–30] alternative tests for voidability. First, a contract with a person of unsound mind could be set aside for incapacity if the other party knew of that impairment. Secondly, a contract with an incompetent could be set aside for incapacity if the contract was substantively unfair to him. However, the Privy Council rejected the second test in *Hart v O'Connor*,[70] re-emphasising the importance of the knowledge requirement. In that case, the sale at undervalue of trust property by a mentally disordered vendor was not overturned for incapacity because the purchaser did not know about the vendor's incapacity. Lord Brightman wrote that "equity will not relieve a party from a contract

---

[68] (1872) IR 6 Eq 429.
[69] [1980] 1 NZLR 386.
[70] [1985] 1 AC 1000.

on the ground that there is contractual imbalance not amounting to unconscionable dealing".

## IV. Intoxication

[26–31]   A contract concluded under the influence of intoxicants may be voidable. A party who was drunk at the time of entering into a contract can set that contract aside if he fulfils two requirements.[71] First, he must have been so drunk at the time of contracting that he was prevented from understanding the transaction. Secondly, the other party must have known of his incapacity. In *White v McCooey*[72] Gannon J stated that:

> "Two issues of fact fall to be determined namely whether and to what extent the defendant was so intoxicated as to be incapable as he alleged, and whether this was known to the plaintiff at the time, and on these issues the onus of proof lies on the defendant."

[26–32]   It is also important that the intoxicated party repudiates the contract as soon as he regains his sobriety. Delay or affirmation will be fatal to his claim. So in *Nagle v Baylor*[73] a vendor sought to avoid a conveyance which he claimed he had concluded when drunk. He was not allowed to do so because he had affirmed the contract by executing a number of other deeds.

[26–33]   Contracts for necessaries are binding on the intoxicated person, provided that it was intended that the necessaries were to be paid for.[74] He is liable only to pay a reasonable price for them under s 2 of the Sale of Goods Act.

[26–34]   The fact that one party was frequently drunk may cause the court to examine the substantive fairness of the contract with particular care, even if he was not so drunk as to be incapacitated when the contract was formed. In *McGonigle v Black*[75] Barr J took account of an elderly farmer's alcoholism in examining his gifts of land to his neighbour stating that:

> "... although frequent drunkenness does not constitute absolute incapacity, it does lead a court to examine with particular care any transaction which may have been influenced by over-indulgence in alcohol even though the person so affected may have been sober at the time when the particular contract was made."

---

[71] *Gore v Gibson* (1843) 13 M & W 623.
[72] Unreported, High Court, 24 June 1976.
[73] (1842) 3 Dr & War 60.
[74] *Re Rhodes* (1889) 44 Ch D 94.
[75] Unreported, High Court, 14 November 1988.

# INDEX

# Index